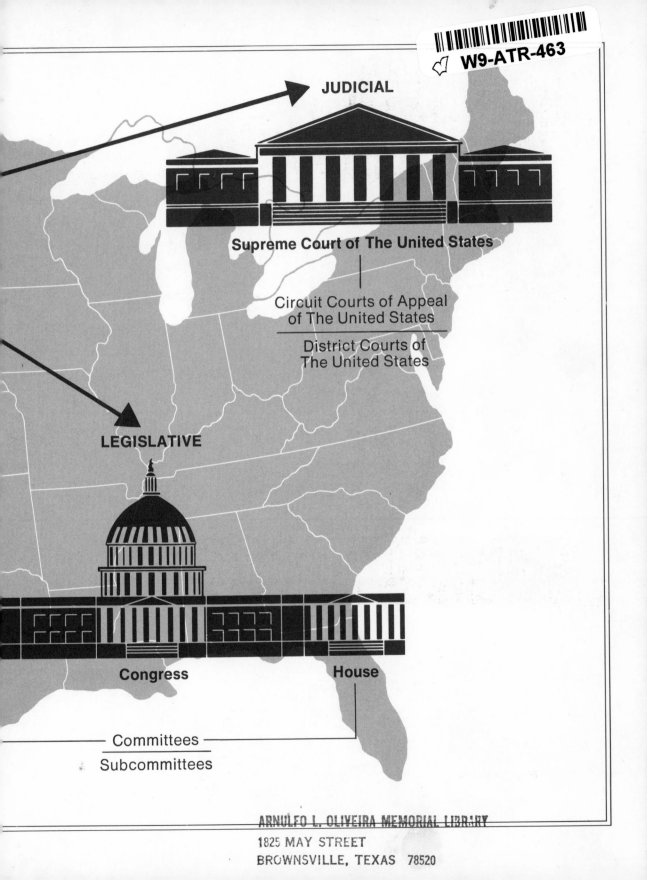

JUDICIAL

Supreme Court of The United States

Circuit Courts of Appeal
of The United States

District Courts of
The United States

LEGISLATIVE

Congress

House

Committees

Subcommittees

AN INTRODUCTION TO AMERICAN GOVERNMENT

AN INTRODUCTION TO AMERICAN GOVERNMENT

THIRD EDITION

KENNETH PREWITT

University of Chicago

SIDNEY VERBA

Harvard University

HARPER & ROW, PUBLISHERS
New York Hagerstown Philadelphia San Francisco London

Credits for Chapter Opening Photographs
Chapter 1, American Airlines; Chapter 2, Brown; Chapter 3. UPI; Chapter 4, Faller, Monkmeyer; Chapter 5, Brown; Chapter 6, Gross, Stock, Boston; Chapter 7, Adelman, Magnum; Chapter 8, UPI; Chapter 9, Herwig, Stock, Boston; Chapter 10, UPI; Chapter 11, Shelton, Monkmeyer; Chapter 12, Wide World; Chapter 13, Godfrey, Magnum; Chapter 14, Menzel, Stock, Boston; Chapter 15, Harrison, Stock, Boston; Chapter 16, Foldes, Monkmeyer; Chapter 17, Wide World; Chapter 18, Menzel, Stock, Boston; Chapter 19, Franken, Stock, Boston.

Other Photo Credits
Brown: 26, 30, 32, 80, 164, 396 (*top*), 468. Charles Gatewood: 519. Culver: 573. DPI: 539; Rona Beame, 426; Elinor Beckwith, 89 (*right*). Leo de Wys, Inc.: 260. Library of Congress: 476. Magnum: Eve Arnold, 204; Elliot Erwitt, 233; Roland Freeman, 411, 412 (*top*); Paul Fusco, 205; Mark Godfrey, 285, 391, 405; Charles Harbutt, 336; Eric Hartmann, 533; Richard Kalvar, 222, 283 (*bottom*); 327; Costa Manos, 318; Sepp Seitz, 514; Alex Webb, 358, 526. Monkmeyer: Irene Bayer, 247; Mimi Forsyth, 197, 540 (*top, right*); Hugh Rogers, 163, 540 (*middle*), 570; Sybil Shelton, 420, 540 (*bottom*); Zimbel, 540 (*top, right*). Stock, Boston: Jeff Albertson, 574; Ron Alexander, 503; Barbara Alper, 4 (*bottom*), 425; J. Berndt, 102; Daniel S. Brody, 167, 195 (*right*); Donald Dietz, p. 5; Owen Franken, 10, 51, 364; Arthur Grace, 60; Patricia Hollander Gross, 54, 175, 432; Elizabeth Hamlin, 483; Ellis Herwig, 65, 210, 241, 340; Bohdan Hrynewych, 430 (*bottom*); Norman Hurst, 173 (*top*); Mike Mazzaschi, 466; Peter Menzel, 286 (*bottom*), 585, 598, 612; Donald Patterson, 344; Jonathan Rawle, p. 9; Jim Ritscher, 286 (*top*); Peter Southwick, p. 7, 77, 126, 351; Peter Vandermark, 4 (*top*). 16; Cary Wolinsky, 13, 56. Taurus Photos: Eric Kroll, 89 (*left*). UPI: 14, 40, 42, 62, 81, 84, 86, 99, 100, 106, 113, 119, 123, 129, 131, 139, 140, 144, 157, 158, 173 (*bottom*), 190, 196, 203, 217, 221, 224, 226, 244, 246, 248, 249, 279, 281, 283 (*top*), 287, 302, 304, 305, 306, 307, 321, 339, 349, 355, 372, 383, 387, 394, 396 (*bottom*), 401, 403, 412 (*middle*), 430 (*top*), 437, 443, 448, 455, 472, 498, 501, 502, 544, 576, 577, 604, 609, 610, 621. Wide World: 8, 35, 53, 66, 90, 172, 194, 195 (*left*), 209, 225, 227, 230, 245, 256, 276, 277, 299, 311, 327 (*top, left and bottom*), 335, 345, 385, 412 (*bottom*), 465, 470, 480, 499, 512, 556, 567, 613, 616.

Sponsoring Editor: Dale Tharp
Project Editor: Lois Lombardo
Production Manager: Marion A. Palen
Photo Researcher: Myra Schachne
Compositor: Ruttle, Shaw & Wetherill, Inc.
Printer: The Murray Printing Company
Binder: Halliday Lithograph Corporation
Art Studio: Eric G. Hieber Associates Inc.

**AN INTRODUCTION
TO AMERICAN
GOVERNMENT
Third Edition**

Copyright © 1979 by Kenneth Prewitt and Sidney Verba

Library of Congress Cataloging in Publication Data

Prewitt, Kenneth.
    An introduction to American Government.

    Bibliography: p.
    Includes index.
    1.   United States—Politics and government—Handbooks, manuals, etc. I. Verba, Sidney, joint author. II. Title.
JK274.P76 1979   320.9'73   78-12041
ISBN 0-06-045279-X

Contents

V

16 Liberty and Order 491

17 White House, State House, and City Hall: Federalism in America 523

18 The Policy Process 561

19 Public Policies: Domestic and Foreign 589

Epilogue 623

Preface

The story is told of a British actor who was asked, as he applied for a visa to visit the United States, if he intended to engage in any activities aimed at overthrowing the American government. His reply was, "I wouldn't know where to begin!" This is a problem faced not only by someone who tries to overthrow the government, but also by someone who tries to understand it. The task of an American government textbook is to impose some order and intelligence on the bewildering number of political happenings and processes that, in one mix or another, add up to the way in which this country is governed. Though the task is straightforward, it is far from simple.

There are various ways to approach the introductory text. Most fall into five categories: macro-theory books, point-of-view books, current events books, factual encyclopedias, and research compendiums. Although each of these approaches has some merit, we have not adopted any single one of them as such. But it may help the reader to understand the approach we have adopted by contrasting it with the others.

Macro-theory books are organized around a general theoretical argument such as systems theory, input-output analysis, pluralism, elitism, or structural-functionalism. One difficulty of textbooks written in this tradition is that the authors often confuse writing about American government with writing about political science, and the result is confusion for the student as well.

It is our feeling that no one theory can do justice to the complexities of American politics. Too often, a fact that does not fit the theory is either made to fit or ignored entirely—a process which risks distorting political life. Understanding the theory becomes more important than understanding American government. Students can too easily develop a sense of "having the total picture" when it is more likely that they have only a vocabulary of abstract terms.

If we have not in this book adopted a particular theory, we have attempted to analyze various theories throughout the book. We have selected theoretical approaches that most appropriately guide the understanding of particular events or processes. For instance, we use behavioral theory in our discussion of belief systems and political participation; elite theory to help understand leadership recruitment; and pluralism to guide our discussion of group conflicts in American politics. The text is constantly analytical in that it attempts to probe the conditions and causes that give rise to various patterns.

Point-of-view books are similar in some ways to macro-theory books. They are organized around an overriding argument, but the argument is political. There is either a consistently negative stance taken toward American political institutions and policies, or there is consistent defense of these institutions and policies. The student is presented only one side of a story that is more likely to have two—or even six or twelve sides.

It seems more sensible to review both the weaknesses and strengths of the American political system and to understand that American leaders have often behaved creatively and honorably, as well as being incompetent and mean at times. We recognize that politics involves arguments and controversies. Our stance is a critical one, but in the strictest sense of the word: We try to be objective, to locate both strengths and weaknesses, and to stress alternative approaches to interpreting intellectual and political trends.

In fact, the theme of controversy is central to our conception of the book. At the end of many chapters, we raise a controversial issue and explore the alternative ways of looking at it. If at times the student is uncertain as to how to choose among the alternatives, he will have gotten our message. Uncertainty is an uncomfortable feeling with which to leave an introductory text, but it is healthier than a false sense of certainty.

One of the themes of controversy appearing throughout the book concerns the issue of inequality: How are the benefits of society allocated across different groups and social classes? How much inequality is necessary for our system of government and our type of economy to work? What is fair and just? Is there inequality because of natural differences in talent or because of elite rule or exploitation? How far should the government go in correcting inequalities in the private sector? These are the kinds of questions which make up a controversial issue, and students are given ample opportunity to look for their own solutions free from the authors' own points of view.

Current events textbooks place emphasis on being up to date and are often written by journalists or with the help of journalists. They deal with those things that are most likely to arouse the immediate attention of the student—a distinct advantage. But against this must be balanced a disadvantage: Dwelling on the latest headlines allows little time for understanding the deeper causes and conditions that bring those headlines about.

Of course, we do not ignore current topics. We have used recent debates about various policy issues (such as affirmative action and the United States' energy policy) to illustrate how institutions work and to describe the patterns of political interests in this country. There are times, as now, in the Vietnam and Watergate aftermath, when these underlying patterns are in rapid transition. Congress has recently gone through a number of fundamental changes, some of which have been directed at reasserting its powers in relation to the executive branch. These changes are reviewed in the text, as are the recent changes in the party system. What some have called "party decomposition" is best understood through a full account of how Carter won the Presidency, combined with an up-to-date treatment of the role of the media in national elections. In other words, our text uses current events not for their own sake but to chart the ongoing dynamics of American politics.

The *encyclopedia approach* was for a long time the dominant approach in introductory textbooks. The idea was to cram as many specific facts as possible between the covers, describe in detail every formal political institution, include a great deal of political history, name every member of the Cabinet, summarize dozens of Supreme Court cases, and so forth. Again, it is easy to see the advantages. All teachers want their students to know what is important about American government. But the encyclopedia-type textbook avoids deciding what is "important" by putting in as much as possible, while the nonencyclopedia makes those decisions.

In deciding what to include and what to exclude, we feel that we have developed the intellectual backbone of our book—a healthy process for authors and students alike. Special sections extend the basic factual material included throughout the book. We have also provided "nuts-and-bolts" sections in question-and-answer format which describe how key political institutions work (how a bill becomes a law, the workings of the federal budgetary process, the organization of political parties, and so forth).

A final category of textbooks is the *research compendium,* which focuses on the most recent findings in political science and the methodologies used in the research. Clearly, a good introductory textbook cannot overlook recent research, but it cannot restrict itself to this alone. Students should know the latest on voting behavior, for example, but they should also know the basis of such behavior as stated in *The Federalist Papers.* It is also important for the beginning student to have some general ideas about research methodology, but the introductory course should not endeavor to make a methodologist out of the student.

We have tried to base our book on the latest and most sophisticated research in political science but with the goal of revealing the political process to the students, not training them as researchers. We have provided special sections on the ways that political scientists study politics. One of these focuses on the study of political participation and public opinion; another on the use of documentary evidence in the study of political policies and political leaders.

To summarize, we have listed the five approaches to introductory textbooks in order to define the focus of this textbook. Though the book does not limit itself to any one of the approaches described, it is partly all of them. We have used theories, political viewpoints, current events, descriptive facts, and research findings to serve our purposes: to help the student recognize the difference between the significant and the superficial in political life, to show the broader interests that are related to specific policy disputes, to explain the interplay between the public and the private sectors, the individual and the institutional, and the political and the economic. But we have not lost sight of the central feature of this book—political analysis.

We start our text with an introductory chapter that provides answers to three basic questions: Why have a government? Why is there politics? Where do democratic principles fit in? We then turn to a series of chapters that provide the context of American politics. In Chapter 2 we review the Constitution as the basic "theory of government" for the United States, giving particular attention to the tension between the constitutional doctrine of limited government and the realities of today's large and powerful central government. In Chapter

3 we present an economic picture of American politics, stressing the current close-knit relationship between the privately owned economy and the public purposes of the state. In this chapter we also set up the paradox that receives full attention in Chapter 4, namely, a democratic doctrine, which promises equality of citizenship, and capitalistic doctrine, which rests upon economic inequality. After reviewing the issues and facts of egalitarianism in the United States, the chapter ends with a controversy on affirmative action.

The next four chapters move us closer to the actual political behavior of citizens in the United States. Chapter 5 discusses the political beliefs of American citizens and reviews such important issues as socialization, public opinion, racial differences in beliefs, and so forth. It is followed by a chapter on the basis of social conflict. Chapters 7 and 8 discuss political participation and political recruitment, returning to the connection between unequal economic resources and unequal political resources.

Next are three chapters that describe the major links between the government and the citizens: interest groups, political parties, and elections. Here we review central questions about the quality of democracy in the United States. Does the interest group system adequately represent the full range of citizen interests? Is there enough difference between the major political parties to provide meaningful choices for voters? Are the political parties in such a state of decay that they no longer function as effective organizations in our political life?

Chapters 12 through 17 put the major government institutions at the center of our attention, beginning with the chapter on the Congress. This chapter includes a review of recent reforms in Congress but places this review in the context of two larger questions: How well does Congress represent? How well does Congress legislate? The chapter on the Presidency distinguishes between the President as an individual and the Presidency as an institution that formulates and implements public policy. The chapter concludes with a section on Watergate and its consequences for the Presidency in the latter part of the twentieth century. Next we turn to a chapter added to the text for the first time: The American Bureaucracy. The bureaucracy is described in detail, and the complex issues of how "unelected" bureaucrats fit into democratic theory and politics are raised. We also analyze the growing importance of regulation through bureaucratic controls. Chapter 15 discusses the Supreme Court as

part of the general court system. Here we show how courts umpire conflicts among the different units within our government of separated powers, how courts resolve disputes among different social and economic interests in the society, and how they actually "make law," even at times in opposition to majority opinion. Chapter 16 continues the discussion of judicial processes, but concentrates on the rights of individual citizens against the powers of the state. We conclude our review of the institutions of government with a thorough discussion of federalism in Chapter 17, where the tension between centralization and decentralization of powers is the major theme.

Finally, there are two chapters on public policy. A chapter on the process of public policy-making shows the difference berween "incrementalism" and "planning" in the policy process. The final chapter presents several case studies of public policy that not only illustrate the policy process in action, but also provide an opportunity to see how the conditions of politics and the institutions of government come together to produce particular policies for the American society.

Putting a new edition of a text together is a major task that involves three sets of people: the publishing staff, the authors, and the people who are willing to criticize the text—in some cases providing such detailed commentary that it actually becomes part of the text. Karl Andresen of the University of Wisconsin-Eau Claire, Joseph Bessette of the University of Virginia, and William McAllister of the University of Chicago provided that type of commentary. In addition, we benefitted from the instructive criticisms of Richard F. Bensel, Texas A&M University, Choong-Shick Hong, Queensborough Community College, Nora Jenzen, East Los Angeles College, George T. Little, University of Vermont, Ralph H. Loewenthal, East Texas State University, Charles Longley, Bucknell University, Conrad L. McBride, University of Colorado, Boulder, Mary R. Mattingly, Texas A&I University, Kingsville, Gordon T. Randall, Chabot College, and Joel G. Verner, Illinois State University. The authors also wish to thank members of their own staffs who helped to prepare this edition, especially Linda Budd at the University of Chicago and Joan Hornig at Harvard University. Timothy Conlon gathered much material and contributed creatively to many chapters.

KENNETH PREWITT
SIDNEY VERBA

1

GOVERNMENT AND POLITICS IN A DEMOCRATIC AMERICA

Basic Questions, Preliminary Answers

Our introductory chapter alerts us to the basic questions of this book and provides an initial understanding of what the answers might be. Here are the four questions with which we are concerned:

Q. *Why have a government at all?*

A. Because in the absence of government it would be difficult (some say impossible) for people to have the security they need in order to go about their normal lives. In addition, government forces citizens to do things such as pay taxes, which then provide general goods such as public parks or postal service. In the absence of government coercion citizens might not contribute to the collective goals necessary to maintain the society.

Q. *If governments are necessary, why is there so much conflict about what they do?*

A. Not all citizens agree about the scope of government, about whether government should provide benefits such as medical care or regulate behaviors such as wearing seat belts. Moreover, there are different views in society about how the costs and benefits of government programs should be allocated. Should the cost of providing medical care for the aged be spread equally across the population, taxing the old as well as the young and the poor as well as the rich, or should the cost be assigned to the groups that can best afford the higher taxes? Out of these different views about the proper role of government, and about who pays and who benefits, comes political conflict.

Q. *Given the need for government in the United States and the unavoidable nature of politics, how do the principles of democracy fit in?*

A. Democratic *government* in the United States emphasizes the rights of individual citizens against the powers of government. The rights of citizens are protected partly because democratic *politics* in the United States emphasizes open political participation, the rights of citizens to criticize their government, regular elections in which leaders whose policies are unsatisfactory can be removed, and the equal right of all citizens to play a role in self-government.

Q. *Do we have a democratic government and democratic politics in the United States?*

A. This is a tough question. A lot of evidence and argument will be presented in this book that bear on this question, but we never give a straightforward yes or no answer. Although the United States has a 200-year-old constitution that provides for a democratic government, it also has a political agenda crowded with social problems and international challenges that seem to demand a government with vast powers of management and control. And while the Constitution promises citizenship equality, it also gives support to a free-enterprise economy that produces sharp inequalities of wealth and living conditions. At times these economic inequalities undermine the promise of political equality.

These questions are not the only ones that will interest us in this book. But much of what we want to learn about government and politics and democracy is hinted at in the issues introduced in this chapter.

Why Government?

We are so used to government that we rarely question why we have it. However, the answer to the question, Why government at all? is not obvious. Even though we may take government for granted, there is a good argument against it: Government makes us do things—pay taxes, drive at certain speeds, respect other people's property, serve on juries, pay our bills, and so on. What's more, we are not free to decide whether or not to obey. We must obey; if we don't, we are likely to be punished. Thus by forcing citizens to do things governments diminish individual choice and freedom. If we agree that choice and freedom are valuable and good, then the case against government is a strong one. If governments coerce, restrict, regulate, tax, and sometimes even imprison citizens, why do people put up with them?

MAINTAINING SOCIAL ORDER

One answer stresses the role of government in maintaining social order. Without government civilized life would be impossible. If people were allowed to live just as they pleased, society would be chaotic and full of conflict. We support government because it, in turn, provides law and order. It provides the social stability within which a citizen can raise a family, work at a job, get an education, enjoy leisure, and plan for the future.

In just about every area of life, government helps provide the orderly conditions necessary for even the most mundane activities. Take, for instance, economic activities. To work for a salary, to invest savings, to buy or produce a product depends on contracts—contracts between worker and manager, lender and borrower, or seller and buyer. Some guarantee is needed to make sure people don't back out on contracts—to make sure the car buyer doesn't drive off and quit making payments; the employer doesn't decide at the end of the month not to pay the workers; the bank doesn't close its doors and keep the savings deposits. One reason such contracts, which are necessary for economic exchange, are usually honored is that they are backed up by the authority of the government; that is, people fulfill their contracts because the government makes sure

An extensive, and expensive, military force protects American interests.

they do and may punish those who don't. Thus people comply with their obligations both out of fear for the consequences if they don't and out of respect for the government. In the area of social life and leisure activities, we depend on government to provide security for our lives and property. A man will be reluctant to buy an expensive hi-fi set if he thinks it will be stolen; parents will not want their children to go to school if there are no traffic laws to make street crossings safe; a woman will refuse an invitation to a party if to go across town at night is to risk assault.

PROVIDING NATIONAL SECURITY

It is commonly said that the United States has become a "national-security state." The government is expected to protect the national borders against the threat of foreign invasion and international outlaws. In a period of nuclear weaponry, international spy networks, worldwide business investments, multinational corporations, military treaties and trade agreements, international terrorism, and huge armies and navies deployed throughout the world, the task of providing "national security" becomes far broader than simply protecting national boundaries. For the past thirty years the United States has increasingly interpreted the need to maintain social order at home as also requiring the maintenance of international order.

This, then, is the classic justification for government. The legal processes, the police powers, and the national-security policies of the government establish the social order essential to civilized life. However, the government engages in many activities that cannot reasonably be considered as providing basic law and order: for example, repaving an interstate highway in Nevada; supporting a graduate student writing a dissertation on the tools used by prehistoric peoples in Central Africa; raising the tax on gasoline to conserve energy; publishing a booklet naming the trees and plants along a trail in the Smoky Mountains; sending a monthly check to a blind pensioner in New York.

Obviously we must look beyond the maintenance of social order to answer the question, Why government?

PROVIDING COLLECTIVE GOODS

Governments often make binding decisions when individuals have goals that cannot be achieved without government intervention. For example, all automobile drivers are interested in seeing that people drive on one side of the road or the other. It matters little which side is chosen as long as all drivers choose the same side. In such a case all benefit if they can turn over to the government the power to make a rule that each driver must drive on a particular side.

To understand why social goals may require binding decisions by government, we must understand the concept of *collective goods*. Governments often provide collective goods—benefits available to every individual whether or not he or she has worked toward the

Binding decisions by governments led to such collective goods as public parks.

attainment of that benefit. If the government opens a new park, it becomes available for my use whether or not I actively worked to create it. This helps explain why *binding* decisions are needed to create public facilities. If I benefit in any case, why should I voluntarily help create the park? I will benefit from it if *others* work to create it, so I will be wise to sit back and take advantage of their effort. On the other hand, even if I were to try to help create a public park it would probably do no good, because my effort — the money or labor I could contribute — would be relatively small unless I were a millionaire.

A park is quite different from a noncollective good such as a camper. I can get access to a camper only if I use my private resources. Therefore my efforts to buy a camper can be quite effective. If I put my resources into it and if I have enough resources, I can have the camper.

In short, for any *single* individual it makes a lot of sense to wait until others have created the collective good and then to take advantage of it. In that case, however, collective goods would never be created. Only a binding governmental decision that *makes* all people contribute to the park through tax revenues can lead to a beneficial collective gain for all citizens. No government has ever been supported through voluntary payments by citizens.

Here's another example. Air pollution caused by automobiles is a serious problem facing many communities. Reduction of air pollution would be a collective good in that all would benefit whether or not they did anything to help reduce it. Suppose a highly efficient pollution control device for cars is invented that costs $300. Every American would benefit from the reduction of pollution that would come from installing such a device on all cars. But can the installation and the beneficial social goal of pure air come from the voluntary activities of citizens? It is unlikely.

The situation from the point of view of the individual citizen deciding whether to spend his $300 is as follows: No citizen acting alone can have much impact on the overall pollution in his or her community. If Citizen A buys an antipollution device, the quality of the air in the city will not change very much if others do not. If Citizen A does not buy a pollution device but all the other citizens in the community do, he or she will benefit from the cleaner air and save $300.

Thus it is rational for individuals not to purchase such a device. They do not get clean air if they buy one and others do not, and they get almost pure air if others buy them and they do not. If every individual acts in the way that is most rational, a situation is created in which all lose. This is why all citizens gain if there is some way of *coercing everyone* to buy the device. And the most likely way to do this is a law requiring that all cars be equipped with the pollution control device. Only when individual choice is taken away can the overall social goal be achieved.

SUMMARY

We have discussed two different answers to the question, Why government? First, government provides the domestic order and the national security that make it possible for citizens to go about such normal activities as raising a family, going to school, earning a living, or enjoying leisure. Second, binding government decisions make it possible to convert individual goals into collective goods, thus satisfying the desires of the members of society.

Why Politics?

Government would be simple indeed if all government decisions were like the decision that people must drive on the right side of the road. For one thing, most drivers don't care whether they drive on the right or the left side, as long as everyone drives on the same side. Besides, this type of policy is costless. No one loses money because traffic laws require that everyone drive on the right. If government were simply a matter of using state authority to obtain goals that all citizens favor and from which all benefit equally, it would not be the complicated business it is.

DIFFERENT CITIZEN PREFERENCES

Government, however, is not always a matter of achieving goals that all citizens favor and that benefit all citizens equally. In fact government decisions are nearly always sources of conflict. The reasons are clear. It is not easy to agree on what collective goods government should provide or who should pay how much for them.

Not every group benefits equally from any collective good, and not every group pays equally or even pays in proportion to its use of that good. Thus government involves a competitive struggle in which individuals and groups seek to maximize the benefits they receive from government while minimizing their costs.

Consider, for example, public highways. Certainly they are a collective good in the sense that no single individual could afford to build one. They are also a collective good in the sense that they are not reserved for particular groups but are open to any adult who is willing to obey the traffic laws. Yet the politics of highway construction and location can become very intense indeed. Downtown merchants may want an expressway to come directly into the central city; apartment dwellers about to lose their homes to the bulldozers will fiercely oppose such a plan. Truckers and automobile manufacturers will be on the side of more and faster expressways; conservationists insist that cities would be more livable if resources went to mass transit and public parks instead. Another group, favoring lower taxes, doesn't want the expressway no matter where it is located and opposes public transit and parks as well. And still another group, perhaps the largest one, is indifferent to the whole issue.

Thus the first important point about politics and government is this: Individuals and groups have different preferences. A large, diverse nation like ours must include groups with different goals: labor and management, doctors and patients, whites and blacks, Catholics and Protestants, producers and consumers, landlords and tenants, and so on.

Doctors may want less government involvement in medical care; elderly citizens may want more complete care programs. Blacks may want the government to encourage integrated housing in suburbs; white suburbanites may want the government to stay out of this issue. Catholics may seek government aid for parochial schools; Protestants may oppose it.

The number of alternative preferences to be found in America is vast indeed. There are many issues, and on any issue we are likely to find some citizens on one side, some on the other side, and others who are indifferent. Different preferences by different groups lead of course to arguments over what collective goods the government should provide and who should pay the costs of these goods. It is these arguments that set in motion the struggle to control and influence government.

DIFFERENTIAL IMPACT LEADS TO DIFFERENT LEVELS OF INVOLVEMENT

If the political struggle begins with differential preferences, it is spurred by a second fundamental point about government and society: Government decisions have differential impact. Any given policy is likely to benefit one group a lot, benefit another a little, and leave another unaffected. It may even hurt some people. The

Citizens differ not only in their view but in the intensity with which they hold their views.

decision to build a highway next to my house benefits the highway builders a lot, benefits commuters a little, leaves most citizens unaffected, but may hurt me and a few of my neighbors substantially. The fact that government decisions have differential impact implies that on any particular issue we will find not only citizens with different preferences but citizens who hold those preferences with *different levels of intensity.*

The few citizens who have intense preferences—those who are most severely affected—will be concerned and active. Differential intensity leads to different levels of political involvement. With regard to any particular policy, some individuals and groups will be more active and will try harder to affect the outcome.

Government and Politics in the United States

We have been reviewing the meaning of government and politics without paying much attention to the United States. Yet this book is specifically about the United States. So it is time to consider how some of our definitions explain present-day government and politics in the United States. Of the several themes that recur throughout the book, perhaps none is more important than the simple observation that we are living through a period of government expansion. Moreover, this expansion of government is itself a source of serious political conflict.

It is true of course that at practically any time in the past 200 years one could have observed that the responsiblities and powers of government were expanding. But beginning in the 1930s this observation takes on special significance. It was then that the idea of the "social-welfare state" began to take shape. Then, in the period following World War II, the idea of the national-security state was joined with that of the social-welfare state. Both of these ideas will be discussed at length later in the book. For now, we simply note

In recent years, medical research has become defined as a collective good.

that, taken together, these two ideas have led to a tremendous increase in the *rate* of growth in government powers. Less and less is the government one of many institutions in society, sharing power with the business sector, the religious sector, the education sector. More and more the government, especially the federal government, is *the* dominant institution in America.

We can return to the idea of collective goods in order to see how government is expanding and why conflict over this expansion occurs.

COLLECTIVE GOODS AND THE GROWTH OF GOVERNMENT

If the idea of collective goods helps answer the question, Why govment? it also helps us understand why governments expand their powers. The more benefits in society become defined as collective goods, the greater the powers and responsibilities of government become.

As the United States enters the last part of the twentieth century, there is a marked tendency to define various social goals or benefits as collective goods. National defense, of course, has always been thought of as a collective good. It is difficult to exclude a citizen from the protection of a military security system; you can hardly let an enemy bomber fly across the country and bomb only the houses of noncontributors. Added to national defense are a number of things that were not considered collective goods only a few decades ago. One example is a clean environment, which has only in very recent years been considered a collective good and therefore a government responsibility. Another example is medical research. If cures for infectious diseases are found, every citizen will benefit, because every citizen will be inoculated in order to prevent an infectious disease from getting started. A public highway system is considered a collective good. So are public parks. So is a stable economy.

The tendency to define certain benefits as collective goods cannot but expand the powers of government. It is the justification for government intervention in the economic sector, in social and family life, in research and education. Creating a collective good such as national defense requires laws, programs, and agencies. Government powers expand, and government grows.

Collective Goods and Conflict It might seem that there would be no conflict over whether government should provide collective goods. Who would want to oppose national security or clean air and water or a highway system? But there *is* conflict. There is, in the first place, serious conflict over priorities. Should taxpayers' money be spent on building a faster fighter plane, cleaning polluted rivers, or improving the highway system? Mathematicians and economists have demonstrated that there are no rules for determining the

How far should the government go in deciding how citizens can use their private property?

socially preferred ordering for a series of collective goods. There is no way of knowing which collective good is better than another. Calling things collective goods does not eliminate conflict. It increases it. For now there is a struggle over the priorities.

There is a second source of conflict. It turns out that there are reasonable differences of opinion about what actually constitutes a collective good. Some economists believe that too many social benefits are being incorrectly defined as collective goods. They argue that the present trend toward collective goods is really the result of a government bureaucracy trying to expand its powers. And this trend is not producing the kind of society Americans want. The free-market system is more likely to produce such a society. For instance, when enough citizens prefer clean air to fast cars (or jobs in the factories that produce those cars), they will use their purchasing power to punish the polluters. The market will respond; cars that pollute will no longer be manufactured. The preferences of society will have been realized.

For government to try to take over the task of the marketplace only messes things up. It creates a bureaucracy, which then justifies itself by spending taxpayers' money and regulating the lives of individual citizens.

The people who stick to this view strongly oppose the trend toward defining various social goals as collective goods. They oppose the growth of government. They oppose an arrangement in which government and not the individual decides how best to spend the money an individual earns by his or her own labor.

In this book we discuss the continual growth of government powers and responsibilities, but we also review the conflict in society about how these powers are used and even about whether government should be taking on greater responsibilities.

PLANNING FOR SCARCITY

Yet another trend in American society is contributing to the growth of government. This is the trend toward increased planning—the attempt to anticipate and prepare for the future. Will there be enough doctors in the year 2000? If not, start spending more money on medical education now. Will there be enough wood pulp to satisfy our needs for paper in the year 2000? If not, support research that might discover alternative methods of making paper. Will there be too few open spaces for wildlife in the year 2000? If so, now is the time to stop the developments that destroy wilderness areas.

Whose task is it to anticipate and plan for the future? The simple answer is that it is everyone's task. But this won't work. So we turn the task over to an institution large enough, rich enough, and powerful enough to think about the future and to try to control events that are thought to affect the future. That institution is the government. Planning means a growth of government powers.

The planning task of government has taken on increased urgency in recent years because of a shift from abundance to scarcity. The period from the end of World War II (1945) until the early 1970s convinced many Americans that ours was a society of abundance. There was an enormous increase in educational opportunities, and literally hundreds of new colleges and universities were started. There was a substantial increase in the purchasing power of many Americans. And there were nice things to buy. American technology mass-produced such important labor-saving devices as automatic washing machines and dishwashers. It also produced entertainment through television and movies. Even work seemed to be easier. Shorter working hours and longer (paid) vacations became the custom. And there was an increase in the number of "high-status" jobs as professional and technical positions became available in government, in education, and in some of the newer industries. The result of all this was a growing and largely satisfied middle class.

Few Americans noticed that this abundance was based on fragile conditions. The "American way of life" was based in part on cheap labor, some provided in this country by the rural poor and the underpaid blacks; the remainder was provided by cheap labor abroad. The minerals needed by American industry were in part mined by cheap labor in South America and parts of Africa; the fresh fruit enjoyed by Americans was picked by migrant workers in California or local workers in Honduras.

Even less noticed by Americans was the importance of a constant supply of cheap energy, energy that filtered swimming pools and lit theater marquees, that heated university libraries in the winter and air-conditioned them in the summer, that drove motor boats and campers, that brought big-time sports into everyone's living room. The source of this cheap energy was cheap oil.

Oil is no longer as cheap. Neither is the labor that provided many of the services and products enjoyed by middle-class America in the 1950s and 1960s. It turns out that the world does not have an unending supply of resources and labor available to support the way of life many Americans have become used to.

Thus we enter a period in which abundance has become scarcity, or at least a period in which we can no longer assume a constantly increasing standard of living. For the past generation there was no doubt that their lives would be better than those of their parents. For the present generation this is very much in doubt.

There is now greater concern about how best to hold on to what we have. One result has been to place more emphasis on planning, on individual planning at the family level and on social planning at the government level. The energy crisis best illustrates this emphasis, but it is not the only illustration. The sharp increase in the cost of imported oil has led government into long-range planning for future energy needs and energy sources. There is momentum for a growing government.

Planning, Scarcity, and Conflict As the government extends its planning function, it does so in a way that contributes to deep social conflicts. A time of scarcity is a time when those who are already advantaged battle to hold on to what they have, to expand their wealth and security if possible, and to pass it along to their children. The less advantaged groups in society shout "foul." In a time of limited growth, fewer jobs, and sacrifices for the future, it does not seem fair to them that those who are already well off should continue to be so.

Government is in the middle of this conflict. It tries to distribute national wealth and yet plan for the future in the midst of conflicting, competing, and irreconcilable claims. Once again we find conditions that appear to lead to both greater government powers and greater political conflict.

THE DEMAND FOR EQUALITY

Also encouraging the growth of government are the programs and policies that are responsive to the demand for citizenship equality. Americans are proud that the nation was founded on the principles of equality: equal political rights, equal standing before the law, and equal opportunity to better one's social and economic condition. For the most part Americans have taken care to insist that equality refers not to equal conditions but only to equal opportunities and equal treatment. Every citizen does not deserve the same rewards. Every citizen should have a fair shot at the unequal rewards.

If equality of opportunity is the basic principle, we know that the practice has sometimes been flawed. The list of groups that have been denied equal treatment and equal opportunity is long: Irish, Italian, Eastern European immigrants; American Indians and Spanish-speaking Americans; blacks and women; the poor and the physically disabled.

Where do disadvantaged groups press their claims when they are treated unfairly? Increasingly in recent years the claims have been pressed on government. Not the church, not private business, not charity, but the government is looked upon as the effective agency for bringing about equal opportunities. Government has responded with programs and policies and laws; government has grown accordingly. Thus the more claims for equality that are pressed on government, the larger the government budget and bureaucracy needed to satisfy these claims.

Equality of Opportunity vs. Equality of Condition   During the past few years the pressures for equality have taken a new turn. The traditional emphasis on equality of opportunity is giving way to an emphasis on equality of condition. The principle of equal opportunity is that everyone should have a chance to compete for unequal rewards. There should be no arbitrary barriers—such as skin color or sex or social background—that unfairly penalize some groups and unfairly reward others. Equality of opportunity is denied if blacks cannot go to the same school as whites, if Catholics cannot have careers as scientists, if women cannot become corporate executives.

Equality of opportunity does not guarantee equality of outcome. Some will still succeed while others fail. Under the principle of equality of opportunity, the task of government is to clear the path so everyone can start the race at the same point and run the race according to the same rules. Equality of opportunity does not mean that everyone finishes the race in the same time.

Today the emphasis is shifting from equality of opportunity to equality of condition. This requires even greater state intervention. No longer is it enough that every child have the opportunity to go to school; every school should be equally good so that students are not penalized simply because of the school they attend. No longer is it enough to deny sex discrimination; affirmative-action programs should ensure that women have equal representation in medical schools or law firms or business offices.

Equality and Conflict   As government acts positively to protect equal opportunity and even to provide equal conditions, it clearly generates significant political conflict. In the first place, there are citizens who protest against the sheer growth of government. These citizens feel that government, however well-intentioned, is an awkward and costly instrument of social reform. Government tries to help disadvantaged groups but perhaps does as much damage as good. For instance, a government medical program seems like a good idea, especially if it ensures decent health care for people who are too poor

to pay the rising costs of hospitals and doctors. But then there is a new and costly government bureaucracy to contend with. And it is possible that the quality of medical service will decline if doctors and hospital administrators feel cramped by government regulations and paperwork.

The second source of disagreement with government action in the field of equality sees a tension between two principles: equality and freedom. Protecting the equality of one group can easily hamper the freedom of another. Busing children to schools might increase equality of educational opportunity; it might also decrease the freedom of parents to choose the kind of school they want for their children. Programs designed to provide equal rights for women are viewed by some people as destroying the traditional freedom of institutions to run their own affairs.

As government takes on more and more responsibilities for equality of opportunity and treatment, it also becomes the arena within which battles are fought over the principles and programs of equality. Some of the battles will be over the substance of the programs; others will be over the merits of greater government power.

Here we see a pattern that will repeat itself in many other areas of American social and political life in the coming decades. Problems are identified: inequality of opportunity, industrial pollution, unemployment, a fragile international monetary system, slippage in security arrangements. The government is looked upon as the source of programs and policies to deal with the problems. The government grows. It grows in the number of people it employs, in the share of the national income it needs, and in the volume of regulations and laws it passes. Because government becomes the central agency dealing with America's problems, it becomes the arena within which legitimate differences of viewpoint about those problems become expressed. Thus there is an increase in political conflict.

Democratic Principles

There is more to politics than conflict over the scope of government and over who is to pay and who is to benefit from government programs. Politics is also about principles, the basic laws and codes of political conduct that command the loyalty of citizens. In the United States the basic political principles are, of course, democratic principles.

Limited Government As we will see in Chapter 2, the United States was founded with explicit principles in mind. Because the founders feared political tyranny, they established a government based on the principle of limited government. Government was to be understood in terms of what it could not do as well as what it could do. To limit government and prevent tyranny, the founders divided the powers of government. They wanted no single group of leaders to centralize those powers. This division or fragmentation of powers was accomplished through (1) federalism—dividing powers between state and national governments; (2) separation of powers—establishing three independent branches of government; (3) checks and balances—the powers of the legislative branch being checked by the executive, those of the executive being checked by the judicial, and so forth, until every part of government was checked by every other part; and (4) a bill of rights—the basic political rights of citizens, such as freedom of speech and freedom to form political associations, would create a balance of power between the elected leaders and the citizens.

Individual Liberty   The idea of limited government and the system of divided powers were dedicated to an even more basic principle: individual liberty. Every citizen should be allowed to make his or her own way with an absolute minimum of interference by the government. The government was expected to clear the path for individual initiative and talent, and to provide the conditions of equal opportunity. But beyond this very limited concept of the task of government there was to be nothing that would infringe on individual liberty. A free-enterprise economy was part of the concept of limited government; it was to be an economy with, again, an absolute minimum of government interference or intervention.

Our book will have much to say about these democratic principles, but at this early point we emphasize two themes: principles versus practice and a limited government versus an activist state.

PRINCIPLES VS. PRACTICE

It is not easy to translate basic principles into political practices. We have already begun to see this in our discussion of equality. To protect equality of opportunity for some citizens may require government action that restricts freedom of choice for other citizens. A clear example of this is school busing programs. To ensure that every child has an equal chance to get a quality education, programs of forced integration across racial and neighborhood lines may be necessary. But this clearly takes away the freedom of parents to send their children to the school of their choice. Forced-integration programs also involve federal government intervention in matters that have traditionally been under local control. As we will see throughout the book, much of American politics is a trade-off between principles. There are few things that are more difficult than choosing between such equally attractive principles as equality of opportunity and freedom of choice.

A LIMITED GOVERNMENT VS. AN ACTIVIST STATE

We have briefly introduced the idea that the Constitution defined the government in terms of what it cannot do. The nation's founders greatly feared tyranny and greatly loved individual liberty. To avoid tyranny and to preserve liberty, they wanted to put wraps on government powers.

We have seen in this chapter, however, that we do not have a limited government. Instead, we have a large and expanding government. Today the government has become a vast bureaucratic agency concerned with coordination and management. The requirements of national security alone appear to demand a strong, centralized state. So do the assumptions of a social-welfare state. Providing such collective goods as a clean environment or a sound economy involves government regulation and intervention. Certainly government action seems to be called for if the demands for equality of opportunity and treatment are to be satisfied. And planning for the effective use of scarce resources, as we have seen, leads to government growth and state action.

We will have a better grasp of American politics if we add to the notion of limited government the somewhat contradictory idea of the *activist state.* Seeing government only in terms of what it does not do would blind us to the enormous number of things it is doing: regulating, coordinating, managing, intervening.

What, then, has happened to the democratic principles enshrined in the Constitution and repeated in our political ceremonies and political language for the past two centuries? It would be brash and wrong to say that these principles count for nothing. This book will make it clear that they continue to count in important ways. But it certainly is correct to conclude that there are tensions between the constitutional principle of limited government and the reality of an activist state.

The next chapter will outline in more detail the principles of constitutional democracy. We start with the Constitution because it is the basic law of the land, which is supposed to establish the framework for democratic politics and the principles of our government. Then we continue with a chapter on the economy of the United States. It may seem odd to start with something as ancient as a 200-year-old Constitution and then suddenly shift to a modern industrial economy. But these two chapters, taken together, develop one of the several major political tensions in American society: the principle of limited government versus the powers of an activist state.

From the chapter on the economy we move to a second and closely related tension. The Constitution and the democratic creed promise citizens equality. But a capitalist economy, as outlined in Chapter 3, promotes individual initiative and monetary rewards in a manner that leads to major inequalities of wealth and income. In Chapter 4, then, we concentrate on the apparent contradiction between political equality and economic inequality. And again we will be dealing with the role of an activist state. Now the focus is on how the state promotes equality, and especially on the shift from legal rights to social rights and from equal opportunity to equal conditions.

HOW WE FIND OUT ABOUT POLITICS: I

Few would argue with the statement that politics is important. The outcome of the struggle to control government affects us in many specific ways—the cleanness of the air we breathe and the water we drink, the standards (and costs) of the health care and education we receive, the security of the contracts we sign, the safety of the planes and trains we travel in, the honesty of advertisements we hear, and the quality of the merchandise we purchase. The ongoing and seemingly mundane activities of government add up to public policies that go far toward determining whether our own lives are healthy and happy or perhaps mediocre and disappointing.

Yes, politics counts. And it does so whether we like it or not, whether we pay attention or are indifferent, whether we understand or are puzzled. Politics counts because some of the largest issues of life are at stake: security and safety, justice and liberty, equality and happiness. The unending, often intense struggle to control the activities of government matters—very much indeed.

For this reason, if for no other, some effort to understand politics is worthwhile.

But understanding is not easy. Politics is puzzling. Issues are complicated and changeable and often seem to be affected by past history. The language of political debate is obscure at best, as if an effort were being made to disguise the "real" facts. Besides, political personalities come and go. The effort to "keep up with politics" can be very great. A busy undergraduate hardly has time to read a daily newspaper, let alone listen to and digest the amount of information necessary to even begin to understand current events. And even when you know what is going on, you may continue to be puzzled as to why it is happening.

In this book we wish to help the student understand why things happen as they do in American political life. We will concentrate on the struggle over government policies. Although we take it for granted that the government provides collective goods, we know also that these goods are not equally beneficial or equally costly to all citizens. We focus on who reaps the benefits and who pays the costs.

We will first look at several aspects of American society that affect the way the political struggle takes place. For one thing, the beliefs of citizens about politics affect how policies are chosen and carried out. Also important are the many conflicts and divisions among political groups. We will study the economic system as well, because economics and politics are very closely intertwined in our society.

Our attention will then turn to the actors in the political struggle. Chief among these are the pressure groups, the political parties, the voting public, and the political leaders. These actors play out the political game within a definite framework—a framework provided by the basic features of American government: constitutionalism, federalism, separation of powers, due process of law, majoritarian democracy. We will discuss these principles and the institutions that give them substance: the Supreme Court, Congress, the Presidency. We will constantly ask the question, How do these principles and institutions affect the democratic struggle over government policies? In the final chapters the policy-making process itself will interest us.

This is a lot to cover, considering that there are millions of facts about the politics, principles, institutions, and policies of American government. We will be very selective in the facts we give, and you as a student deserve an account of why we choose this set of facts and not another.

An understanding of politics rests on two kinds of knowledge: knowledge of facts and explanations of facts. We cannot study politics without some knowledge of the two parties, the role of pressure groups, the meaning of judicial review, the importance of federalism. It is useful also to have some detailed information about public policies and the way they have come to be.

But not all facts are equally important to an understanding of politics. The child who has memorized every state capital knows some political facts but does not understand much about politics. Even the adult who can name his or her representative in Congress and all the members of the President's Cabinet does not have very useful knowledge.

Such facts are of relatively little use for a variety of reasons. For one thing, they are temporary: Congress and the Cabinet change with each election. Moreover, names by themselves do not answer the more important questions one might have about the operation of the government. Why do the President and his Cabinet often favor one kind of legislation while Congress favors another? Why does Congress more often than the Cabinet consider the particular needs of local areas? Why can there be wide shifts in the portion of the vote going to the Democratic and Republican candidates for President (Johnson, a Democrat, won by a landslide in 1964; Nixon, a Republican, barely won in 1968 but then won by a landslide in 1972) with Congress remaining steadily in the hands of the Democrats? And why do the Democratic Congresses sometimes give as much support to Republican Presidents as to Democratic ones?

To answer questions like these we need more relevant facts than the names of the members of Congress. We need to know about the social backgrounds and careers of Cabinet members and members of Congress, for these facts help explain different views about policy. We need to know about party loyalties among voters and how these sometimes lead them to support a candidate from one party for President and a candidate from the other party for Congress, for this will help explain why a Republican can win the White House but face a Congress controlled by the Democrats. And we need to know about the organization of Congress and the party ties of its members, because this will help explain why a Democratic Congress may support a Republican President and vice versa.

Why are facts about the backgrounds and careers of members of Congress useful? Some facts can be linked to other facts to help us understand how they act in office. Most important, the information is useful in understanding congressional action on such topics as tax bills or foreign policy.

This gives some clues to the principles of selection we use in this book. We cannot describe all the facts of American politics and draw connections among all of them. Nor can we keep up with the latest events as reported in the daily press. Rather, we must choose what to discuss. Our principle is to choose our material in terms of what will give us the most generalizable knowledge.

Politics and Controversy

"Let's not talk about politics. It will ruin the evening." Why does political discussion often lead to argument, sometimes very bitter argument? Because people have different political values, and they often hold those values with passionate conviction. Neutrality about politics is difficult.

Those who write about politics — in the press, in magazines, in books — are usually committed to one political position or another. They are tempted to describe and explain politics from that viewpoint. Thus for any political issue we can usually find many interpretations, often completely opposed to one another. Nor is the study of politics an exact science in which the objective observer can always find one side clearly right and the other clearly wrong.

In this book we try to pay attention to the varying interpretations of American politics. We do not present one interpretation as gospel truth. Rather, we try to focus on some of the leading controversies in the interpretation of American politics. Understanding political controversies may well be the first step toward understanding politics.

2
THE CONSTITUTIONAL FRAMEWORK

What is a Constitution?

When a group of people decide to achieve some common goals by joining to form an organization, they often begin by writing a constitution. This is true of a group of students starting a club, a group of workers organizing a union, or a group of businesses forming a trade association.

A constitution normally accomplishes two things. It states the *principles* that the people bound by the constitution are thought to share, or at least are supposed to share. But people who write constitutions know that different interests will not always interpret the principles in the same manner. So constitutions, if they are to be effective, must state rules and procedures that tell us how to settle our disputes. *Procedures for dispute resolution* take their place alongside basic principles in any well-thought-out constitution.

The Constitution of the United States is frequently called the basic rule from which all other rules are derived. The Constitution establishes our institutions of government, vesting them with certain powers and setting limits to what they can do. The powers granted and the powers withheld are supposed to be in accord with the principles established by the Constitution. An act by the government or by an individual that violates these principles is said to be "unconstitutional," and unconstitutional acts are of course prohibited or punished if they occur. The criminal and civil codes that govern the citizens of the United States are designed to be "constitutional," that is, to be in accord with the principles established by the Constitution.

A Paradox In this chapter we tell the story of how the U.S. Constitution came into being and review the principles and the means of resolving disputes about those principles that are part of the Constitution. We immediately recognize a paradox. The basic principles of the Constitution include a government sharply limited in its powers, a heavy stress on individual freedom, and an emphasis on dividing and fragmenting the powers of government. These principles are not easily reconciled with many features of today's government, especially the political realities of an activist state, centralized, bureaucratic powers, and the merging of economic and political powers outlined in the next chapter. The tension between constitutional principles now nearly 200 years old and contemporary political practices is introduced in this chapter and examined throughout the book.

Understanding the Constitution

In the 1790s, farmers were free to grow whatever crops they wished; to pay their help any wages they agreed to; to prepare, transport, and market their products however they chose; and to set their own prices. Today, however, dozens of regulations affect how foodstuffs are grown, processed, and marketed. Which crops are planted, and in what amounts, are subject to government regulation; so also is the use of fertilizers and insecticides; so are farm wages and crop prices.

In 1790, if farmers were wealthy they sent their children to private schools or perhaps hired a tutor to educate them at home. If they became ill they depended on family or neighbors to care for the farm until they could go back to work. As they grew old and could no longer run the farm, they lived off their savings and the good will of their children. Today, by contrast, most farmers send their children to public schools, and they can rely on public health services and a state social-security system as protection against sickness and old age.

The growth of government regulation and services has greatly changed the relationship between citizen and state over the past two centuries. But no sooner do we recognize this than we come face to face with an interesting point: The same basic rule, meaning the Constitution, that governed American society in 1790 governs it today. In other words, the growth of the "service" and "regulated" state has taken place within a legal framework and set of political principles hammered out during a hot summer in Philadelphia nearly 200 years ago. What is this Constitution that could so long endure and accommodate itself to a society that has changed so much?

To understand the constitutional foundation of our government, we need to review a bit of American history. As we go back to the 1780s to study the politics that led to the Constitutional Convention and influenced the Constitution itself, we will see that our Constitution grew out of a period of turmoil. We will point out that although a constitution is supposed to "live for the ages," those who wrote it and those who argued for and against passing it were living in their own age. They had an eye on the immediate advantages and disadvantages of the new document as well as its future implications.

Then we will discuss the way our Constitution handles the fundamentals. To survive, a political community needs procedures for defending itself from external and internal enemies, a means for settling conflicts between its own members, methods of making and carrying out rules, and a basis for agreement on how to select the rule makers. It is also wise for it to have some way of limiting the uses of authority. It is often said that the way the U.S. Constitution handled these fundamentals accounts for its enduring so long.

Finally, we will examine how the Constitution has managed to adapt itself to the great political, economic, and social changes that have taken place since 1787.

The Founding

Between the early 1770s and the early 1790s, political events changed the eastern seaboard from 13 separate colonies under British rule into a nation of 13 states. Especially critical in this process were the events of the decade between the signing of the Declaration of Independence in 1776 and the writing of the Constitution in 1787. Following is a list of the major events of this period.

American Political History
1774   The First Continental Congress, formed extralegally. Fifty-six delegates from 12 colonies meet in Philadelphia to discuss problems common to all of the colonies.
1775   Military action between Britain and the colonies becomes stronger. The famous ride of Paul Revere; the British expedition against the Concord Minutemen; the Battle of Bunker Hill.
1776   Thomas Paine publishes "Common Sense," a radical call to break all ties with Great Britain. Signing of the Declaration of Independence.
1777   The Articles of Confederation are drafted. They link the 13 states in a loose "League of Friendship" and are finally adopted in 1781.
1782   The War for Independence comes to an end. Peace talks begin in Paris, and the treaty is ratified the following year.
1786   Shays' Rebellion in Massachusetts, an attack by debtors on their creditors.
1787   An assembly to draft a constitution meets in Philadelphia.
1788   Enough states ratify the new Constitution so it can be put into effect.
1789   George Washington is elected first President of the United States.
1791   Bill of Rights added to the Constitution.

ESTABLISHING A NATION: A TWO-STAGE PROCESS

The process of creating a new nation during the 1770s and 1780s involved two stages. During the first stage, the Declaration of Independence and the War for Independence, the existing ties with Great Britain were broken. A new government, a league of free and independent states, was set up under the Articles of Confederation. The Articles had a number of weaknesses, however, so there followed a second phase during which divisive forces threatened to disrupt the fragile confederation. In order to cope with these forces, a new government framework was drafted and adopted. The U.S. Constitution shifted the center of political power from a loose league of states to a strong federal union.

Those who have studied the process of nation building in other parts of the world will recognize this as an eighteenth-century version of a pattern that is common today. During the first stage colonial rulers are overthrown. Just as the American colonies gained their independence from Great Britain, so Kenya gained its independence from Great Britain, Indonesia from Holland, and Algeria from France. But simply gaining independence does not guarantee the establishment of a new nation. A second phase, in which centers of power struggle to maintain their authority against the forces that threaten to fragment and divide the new society, often follows. The civil wars in many new nations indicate how powerful such divisive forces can be.

THE WAR FOR INDEPENDENCE

During the War for Independence the inhabitants of the thirteen colonies were divided on the wisdom and justice of the war. To justify their positions the Tories and the Patriots appealed to different political principles. The Tories, opposed to the war, stressed that it was in the best interests of the colonies to remain loyal to the authority of Parliament and the legal system of the British Empire. The Patriots, on the other hand, maintained that by his tyrannous actions the King of Great Britain had forfeited any claim to the allegiance of the American people. Resting their arguments on a theory of natural rights, they proclaimed, in Jefferson's elegant phrases in the Declaration of Independence, that

> We hold these truths to be self-evident, that all men are created equal, that they are endowed by their Creator with certain unalienable Rights, that among these are Life, Liberty, and the pursuit of Happiness. That to secure these rights, Governments are instituted among Men, deriving their just powers from the consent of the governed. That whenever any Form of Government becomes destructive of these ends, it is the Right of the People to alter or to abolish it, and to institute new Government, laying its foundations on such principles and organizing its powers in such form, as to them shall seem most likely to effect their Safety and Happiness. Prudence, indeed, will dictate that Governments long established should not be changed for light and transient causes; and accordingly all experience hath shown, that mankind are more disposed to suffer, while evils are sufferable, than to right themselves by abolishing the forms to which they are accustomed. But when a long train of abuses and usurpations, pursuing invariably the same Object evinces a design to reduce them under absolute Despotism, it is their right, it is their duty, to throw off such Government, and to produce new Guards for their future security. Such has been the patient sufferance of these Colonies and such is now the necessity which constrains them to alter their former Systems of Government.

Other Patriots, like Thomas Paine in his influential pamphlet "Common Sense," emphasized that it was in the colonists' political and economic interest to break with Great Britain:

> I challenge the warmest advocate for reconciliation to show a single advantage that this continent can reap by being connected with Great Britain. I repeat the challenge; not a single advantage is derived. Our corn will fetch its price in any market in Europe, and our imported goods must be paid for, buy them where we will.
>
> But the injuries and disadvantages we sustain by that connection are without number, and our duty to mankind at large, as well as to ourselves, instruct us to renounce the alliance. . . .[1]

However important economic interest may have been in stimulating support for the Revolution, it is clear that many Americans were motivated by a belief in individual freedom, a belief that emphasized the right to rebel against a tyrannical government. Authority was illegitimate unless it was based on the consent of the people.

TOWARD A NEW GOVERNMENT

Throughout the Revolutionary period the small group of leaders who had served in the initial Continental Congress, written the Declaration of Independence, and financed and fought in the war began to think of themselves as a national political elite. Of course there was no real "nation"—only thirteen independent states, formerly separate colonies, loosely linked together by the Articles of Confederation. Nevertheless those who led the colonies during the war years were aware of their role in establishing a nation.

These national leaders recognized that, in spite of the revolutionary emphasis on individual liberties, stable, effective government demands obedience. Newly formed governments often have

[1] Nelson F. Adkins, ed., *Common Sense and Other Political Writings* (Indianapolis: Bobbs-Merrill, 1953), p. 22.

difficulty reasserting authority after a period of rebellion. During the 1780s the nation's founders took it as their job to make sure authority would be reasserted.

THE ARTICLES OF CONFEDERATION:
THEIR WEAKNESSES

The Articles of Confederation, framed in the spirit of the War for Independence, were ratified in 1781; they lasted less than a decade. The Articles were a compromise between complete state sovereignty and a strong central government. They reflected the beliefs that local self-rule could best preserve the liberties gained in the successful war and that some minimum level of coordination among the thirteen states would benefit all, especially in the areas of national defense, foreign affairs, and commerce.

What kind of government was provided for in the Articles of Confederation? Essentially, the Articles established a Congress consisting of delegates from the thirteen states. Like ambassadors, these delegates served entirely at the pleasure of their home states. Deadlock was almost inevitable. Regardless of its size or resources, each state had only one vote; nine votes—more than a two-thirds majority—were required to pass major legislation; the vote of only one state could veto an amendment to the Articles. The Articles did not establish a separate executive branch. This meant that Congress had to entrust the execution of its policies to various committees, ad hoc panels, and individuals, making for a disorderly and inefficient system of administration.

Furthermore, Congress had many limitations on its powers. First of all, it exercised no direct power over individuals. People held citizenship only in their respective states. Any congressional law— say, a law drafting men into the military—would not be binding on an individual unless his state chose to enforce it. Many regulations were never enforced by state authority. A comparison can be made with the United Nations. If the UN Assembly passes a resolution calling for trade sanctions against S. Africa, no manufacturer or shipper can be punished for trading there unless its own nation passes similar legislation. Alexander Hamilton was later to call this aspect of the confederation its "great and radical vice."[2]

In addition, Congress had no independent taxing power. It was limited to requesting contributions from the states. However, just as the UN cannot collect dues from any nation that refuses to pay, Congress could not enforce such requests. This system of voluntary compliance proved unsuccessful, and as a result the confederation verged on bankruptcy.

Finally, Congress could neither regulate commerce nor impose tariffs. This not only closed off an important source of potential revenue but also led to economic warfare among the states.

[2] *The Federalist Papers* (No. 15).

THE CRITICAL PERIOD

The Articles of Confederation were soon discredited by their failure to achieve the purposes of union. In the area of national defense the Revolution had conclusively demonstrated that the national government was poorly constructed for dealing with the exigencies of armed conflict. A strong, independent executive branch seemed to be required. In foreign affairs the United States spoke with thirteen voices as often as with one. Some states actually conducted formal negotiations with European powers, and all states retained the authority to set their own duties on imported goods, thus making it virtually impossible for Congress to enter into general commercial treaties with other nations. As a result Congress simply could not exercise the collective strength of the new nation in bargaining for commercial and military advantages. To many, however, the most serious defect of the confederation was its impact on domestic commerce. Because Congress was denied the power to regulate domestic commerce, this was left entirely to the thirteen separate states. But state-imposed tariffs often crippled small industries in a neighboring state and generally inhibited the free flow of goods among the colonies. The various restrictions on interstate trade slowed the growth of a vigorous, integrated national economy.

ECONOMIC GROUPS HURT
BY THE GOVERNMENT'S LACK OF POWERS

It is obvious, then, that the merchant and commercial interests, small though they may have been, were suffering under the Articles of Confederation. But these were not the only economic groups hurt by the weaknesses of the Articles. In addition, those who had lent money for the war effort would lose everything if the government went bankrupt. People like Hamilton were aware that if the government defaulted on its debts it would be hard to raise money in the future. And those who wished to open the vast areas west of the Appalachians to settlement and trade felt that their interests were hurt by the weakness of the Articles. The inability of the central government to protect settlers from Indians and to dislodge the British from their trading posts severely hurt land speculators.

In short, economic interests were severely hampered by the inability of the central government to maintain a standing army, to tax citizens in order to pay its debts, to regulate commerce among the states, to impose tariffs on foreign goods, and to protect economic investments.

THE CONFLICT BETWEEN DEBTORS AND CREDITORS

But some groups—particularly debtors—were not hurt, at least in the short run, by the weakness of the central government under the Articles. Many farmers who were in debt benefited from the cheap paper money being issued by state governments. Using their influence in state legislatures, they were able to pass laws delaying the collection of debts.

Debtors benefited not only from some of the economic conditions but also from the central government's lack of effective police power. Incidents of open rebellion against creditors, the most famous of which was led by Daniel Shays, were fairly common. Although the rebellion was put down by a mercenary army, the lesson of Shays' Rebellion was not lost on citizens who were concerned about protecting property. Many citizens felt that the central government was too weak.

THE CONSTITUTIONAL CONVENTION

By the mid-1780s there was widespread agreement that something had to be done. There was less agreement as to the specific reforms required. What resulted was the Constitution of 1787, formulated by a group of the new nation's most accomplished and respected political leaders. This time, however, national leadership stressed authority over liberty, emphasizing that liberty could be secured only by a strong and stable government.

Congress had requested the states to send representatives to Philadelphia "for the sole purpose of revising the Articles of Confederation." Without question, the 55 delegates who gathered in May 1787 did more than revise the Articles. As soon as they arrived they agreed to two principles. First, the meetings were to be held in strict secrecy, and second, the Articles were so inadequate that nothing would do but to create an entirely new Constitution. Knowing that not all the states would adopt the Constitution, they decided that it would go into effect when only nine states had ratified it. It is clear that they violated the authority under which they were gathered, but the country was ready for something new, and these were the people who provided the leadership.

Writing a constitution is a difficult business. Political leaders are often strong willed, and if they differ in their views of the social order, in their personal interests, and in the people they represent they are unlikely to write a document agreeable to all.

Yet during a single summer these 55 men succeeded in writing a constitution that is still perhaps the most effective such document ever written. The statesmanship of Washington, the tactical brilliance of Hamilton, the profound insights of Madison, and the practical wisdom of Franklin have become political folklore passed along from generation to generation of American citizens.

The delegates who gathered in Philadelphia were in fact a remarkable group. The document they wrote reflected their political experience as well as close study of political philosophy. As many as twenty of the delegates had had previous experience writing state constitutions, and in many respects the federal Constitution was an extension of basic rules that had proved their worth in the different states. Thirty of the delegates were serving in state legislatures at the time of the convention. Thus they knew well the weaknesses of some of the existing charters and were able to avoid certain mis-

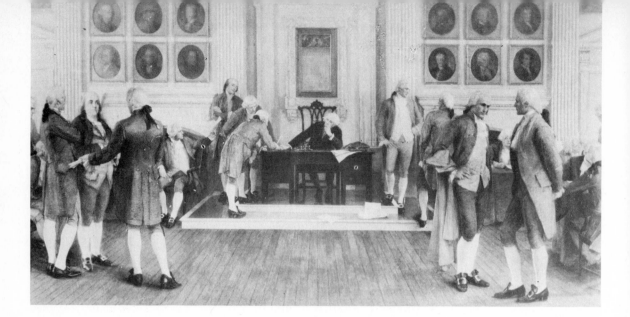

takes. More than three-fourths had been members of the national Congress established by the Articles of Confederation. Their disappointment with this institution played a large part in the Philadelphia convention.

If the founders could draw on personal experience, they could also draw on political theory. John Locke's *Two Treatises on Government*, James Harrington's *Commonwealth of Oceana*, both seventeenth-century writings, and Montesquieu's *Spirit of the Laws*, written forty years before the Philadelphia convention, were familiar to all educated people. In these writings were many of the basic ideas that found their way into the Constitution. More than half of the delegates were trained in law and had read some of the great commentaries on English common law, a system that remains the basis of our own legal system.

It was nevertheless a difficult document to draft. Any constitution must balance freedom and authority—the freedom of citizens from arbitrary or unjust government, yet the authority of government to settle disputes and manage the society. It is important to recognize that the politics in the convention hall (and outside it) was as instrumental in the balance between freedom and authority as the personal traits of the founders. Three political factors are relevant to understanding the considerable success of the Constitutional Convention: The founders agreed on certain basic issues; the convention skipped the hardest issue; and the delegates were willing to compromise when feelings ran high.

Agree on Basic Issues   Missing from the convention were conservatives who might have opposed the more liberal provisions of the Constitution. Also missing were several forceful democrats who might have refused to give so much authority to a central government. Patrick Henry, for instance, refused to attend and commented, "I smelt a rat." He was to be a vigorous opponent of adoption of the Constitution.

The men who dominated the convention reflected solid, conservative financial interests. Thus they had no difficulty in agreeing that the Articles of Confederation should be dropped and an entirely new document written. They shared a philosophy that included mistrust of human nature, belief in the sanctity of property, anxiety about the excesses of democracy, and confidence in their right to fashion a new government. But if they were conservative in these respects, they were also committed in varying degrees to the experiment of self-government.

Through a process of self-selection and self-elimination, the writing of the Constitution was left largely to men of influence with basically similar political philosophies. Others either chose to ignore the convention or were not sent as delegates. Perhaps for this reason the most difficult battles over the Constitution occurred not in Philadelphia but in the various state legislatures. For instance, the founders completely ignored the question of a bill of rights and were able to win ratification in several states only when the first ten amendments were promised.

Skip the Hardest Issue   The strongest political feelings of the time centered on the question, Should there be state sovereignty such as existed under the Articles, or should there be a unitary government in which sovereignty rests with the central power? *Federalism,* in which sovereignty is shared between the states and the central government, was a brilliant compromise and was probably the major reason the Constitution was finally adopted. Yet the Constitution simply avoided the hardest issue of all, that of whether member states had the right to secede. If the right to secede had been written into the Constitution, it is doubtful that the Union would have lasted more than a few decades. If the right to secede had been expressly prohibited, it is doubtful that there ever would have been a "united states." The founders simply passed this question along to a later generation, and it finally took a bitter civil war to settle it.

Compromise When There Is Strong Political Opposition   The Constitution was a compromise document on many counts. For instance, there is evidence that among the delegates in Philadelphia were many who recognized that slavery was basically inconsistent with a government proclaiming inalienable rights. A Virginia delegate, George Mason, attacked the slave trade as "infernal traffic" and warned that slavery "would bring the judgment of heaven on a country." Other delegates, however, said their states would not join the union if the Constitution made slavery illegal. The compromise, included in Article 1, prevented Congress from banning the slave trade until 1808. Congress did outlaw the slave trade, though not

The Constitution compromised
on the issue of slavery.

slavery itself, in that year. But southern states continued to import slaves until the beginning of the Civil War.

The most famous compromise was in the makeup of Congress. The question was whether the individual states would be represented in Congress in proportion to their population, giving an advantage to larger states, or on an equal basis, giving an advantage to smaller states. The latter arrangement prevailed under the Articles of Confederation and was considered unworkable by representatives from the populous states. They argued that the new government was to be the instrument of the people themselves, not of thirteen equal sovereign states. Thus it should be based on a broad foundation of popular representation. But delegates from small states like Maryland and New Jersey were strongly opposed to assigning seats in Congress on the basis of population. A few large states could easily outvote all the smaller states.

In what is known as the Connecticut Compromise, the Constitution established a Congress in a form that is familiar today. There would be a House of Representatives in which seats would be granted depending on the size of the state. And there would be a Senate, or upper house, in which each state, no matter how small, would have two seats. Because most important legislation must be passed by both the House and the Senate, this compromise allowed the smaller states to check the larger ones.

RATIFICATION: FEDERALISTS VS. ANTI-FEDERALISTS

The new Constitution was completed in September 1787 and presented to the nation for ratification. Special conventions for considering the Constitution were elected in each state; a positive vote by nine of these conventions was necessary to bring the new government into existence.

Those opposed to the Constitution, called the Anti-Federalists, maintained that the delegates at Philadelphia had gone too far. They conceded that reforms were needed. The national government should be strengthened by adding an independent, but limited, taxing power and the power to regulate domestic and foreign commerce. But this new government, with its unlimited taxing power, its power to raise and maintain large standing armies, its complete reorganization of Congress (denying the states equal suffrage in one branch), its establishment of an independent executive who would have command of the nation's armed forces, and its creation of an independent federal judiciary that could dictate to the state courts, would soon eclipse the state governments, the true home of democracy, and thereby threaten the very liberties that the Revolution had been fought to secure.

The Federalists, however, denied that the states had been effective in securing the rights set forth in the Declaration of Independence. They criticized the states for their democratic excesses, especially for the "multiplicity," "mutability," and "injustice" of state laws. Only a strong and effective union would truly secure the rights they had fought for. The national government must be made competent to accomplish its proper tasks, and at the same time must be structured so as to be safe. The Constitution of 1787, the Federalists maintained, would provide the competent and safe republican government America needed. Their argument prevailed, and in 1789 the new government went into effect.

SUMMARY

We have reviewed the events that led to the creation of the United States of America and to the writing of the U.S. Constitution. We have discussed the way many of the concerns that arose during the War for Independence shaped later political events and the kind of government that was created. We saw that the Articles of Confederation proved unworkable, having created a government that was too weak and decentralized to govern effectively. Then we saw that the delegates who gathered at the Constitutional Convention were anxious to create a strong and effective government without repeating the mistakes of the Articles.

How were they able to handle the difficult task of writing such a constitution? In part, because they shared a conservative philosophy, they agreed on the basic issues. Furthermore, they were willing to compromise on certain issues, such as the representation of large and small states. Finally, they simply skipped the hardest issue, that of sovereignty, by creating a federal system and not answering the question of whether the states had the right to secede.

Constitutional Principles

The constitution of a society will reflect the philosophical ideas that are acceptable to that society. And our Constitution does have a philosophical basis, one that was acceptable to many citizens in the 1790s and, we suspect, to many citizens today. Here is what John Adams had to say to his cousin Samuel Adams:

> Human appetites, passions, prejudices and self-love will never be conquered by benevolence and knowledge alone. . . . "The love of liberty," you say, "is interwoven in the soul of man." So it is (also) in that of a wolf; and I doubt whether it be much more rational, generous, or social in one than in the other. . . . We must not, then, depend alone upon the love of liberty in the soul of man for its preservation. Some political institutions must be prepared, to assist this love against its enemies.

In other words, Adams was saying that without institutional restraints people are not to be trusted. They would break their contracts. Their passions and ambitions would dominate their reason and self-restraint. Minorities, if they were in control, would tyrannize majorities and plunder in order to expand their own privileges. Majorities, if unrestrained, would destroy the rights of minorities, forcing them to conform to majority wishes.

What was behind the writing of the Constitution, and imbedded in it, was a pessimistic view of human nature but an optimistic view of social and civil institutions. A good political constitution, backed by the government, could protect liberties and guard the social order.

But if there must be authority, it too must be curbed. No single group—be it a minority within government, the government itself, or the majority outside the government—must be allowed final control. It is a tribute to the founders that they were consistent in applying these principles. They feared the unchecked ambitions of leaders just as they feared the excesses of the public. They were as careful to impose restraints on those in authority as they were to guarantee the authority needed to govern the community.

The checks on authority were expressed through three constitutional fundamentals: popular control over elected representatives, fragmentation and separation of government powers, and the idea of limited government.

A REPRESENTATIVE FORM OF GOVERNMENT

Distrustful as the founders were of the excesses of democracy, they were also strongly opposed to arbitrary rule. They were sympathetic to republican government, and in this they followed the seven-

teenth-century English political idealists who favored political representation and popular rule. Did not the Declaration of Independence speak of "the consent of the governed"? And did not Madison report that "a dependence on the people is, no doubt, the primary control on the government"?

Titles of Nobility Abolished   One of the first acts of the founders was to abolish hereditary titles of nobility and hereditary positions of power. This trend had started in the state legislatures, but to put it into the Constitution was to break sharply from a practice that was common in Europe and England. Time and again the founders stressed their belief in the principle that no arbitrary standard, especially birth, should give some people the right to rule and deny it to others. *The Federalist Papers* (No. 57) asserts:

> Who are to be the objects of popular choice? Every citizen whose merit may recommend him to the esteem and confidence of his country. No qualification of wealth, of birth, or religious faith, or of civil profession is permitted to fetter the judgment or disappoint the inclination of the people.

Open Access to Office   The founders did feel that the "best" people should rule. They believed that every society contained a wide variety of human types, and that only a few — the natural aristocracy — possessed the moral and intellectual qualities necessary for political leadership. The electoral process was designed to raise these individuals to the top of the political hierarchy, but no one could claim a *right* to rule based on personal qualities or social position. The people were completely free to choose their own leaders.

Regular Elections   "Consent of the governed" found its most concrete expression in regular elections. *The Federalist* explained the House of Representatives as follows:

> As it is essential to liberty that the government in general should have a common interest with the people, so it is particularly essential that the branch of it under consideration should have an immediate dependence on, and an intimate sympathy with, the people. Frequent elections are unquestionably the only policy by which this dependence and sympathy can be effectually secured.

The right of suffrage extended only so far, of course. Individual states were allowed to legislate their own voting regulations. Moreover, only members of the House of Representatives were directly elected by citizens. Senators, who were expected to be members of a more "aristocratic" house, were indirectly elected, being nominated and chosen by the state legislatures. (Indirect election of senators was changed to popular election in 1913, when the Seventeenth Amendment was ratified.) The President and Vice-President were even further removed from popular election; they were chosen by

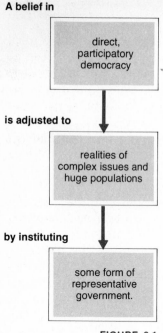

FIGURE 2.1
Conception of Representative
Government Today

an electoral college, which, in turn, was appointed by the state legislature. And judicial posts of course were filled by appointment.

Though limited, the right to vote was firmly stated in the Constitution. And elections were to become a major prop supporting the evolution of representative government. Periodic elections mean officeholding is probationary. Leaders serve limited terms, at the end of which they face the electorate (or other agencies) that granted them power in the first place. The purpose was to create in political leadership a "habitual recollection of their dependence on the people," as stated in *The Federalist* (No. 57). In a manner recalling the founders' belief, shared with Lord Acton, that "power tends to corrupt," this passage continues:

> Before the sentiments impressed on their minds by the mode of their elevation can be effaced by the exercise of power, they will be compelled to anticipate the moment when their power is to cease, when their exercise of it is to be reviewed, and when they must descend to the level from which they were raised; there forever to remain unless a faithful discharge of their trust shall have established their title to a renewal of it.

This passage contains much that is relevant to an understanding of representative government. Being elected to political office is to be "elevated," and being evicted from that office is to be "punished." Officeholders therefore use power in a manner "faithful" to the trust placed in them by the electorate.

Representative Government The Constitution established a government based on the consent of the governed. In reading back into history present-day conceptions of democracy, we very often misinterpret what happened in 1787 and either see the founders as more radical than they actually were or blame them for being too cautious. Neither of these views fits the facts.

Today we think of representative government as a compromise between the principles of "perfect" democracy, direct popular participation in making the laws that govern the people, and the realities of huge and complex nations. Because there is no way for the people to assemble, debate, and decide, we compromise our commitment to these principles and institute representative government, in which a select group of people meet and decide on the issues of the day but are always aware of the wishes of those who sent them. We can diagram the logic of this position as shown in Figure 2.1.

What the founders had in mind was something far different. Because they feared arbitrary rule, they believed that people with political power must somehow be checked in their use of that power. And because they felt some sympathy toward republican government, they saw a system of political representation as an appropriate check. Representative government was not a compromise with a deep commitment to democracy; it was a cautious move away from the prevailing practices of hereditary rule. Compare Figure 2.2 with Figure 2.1, and you will see that the initial conception of political representation was very different from how it is often thought of today.

The founders feared

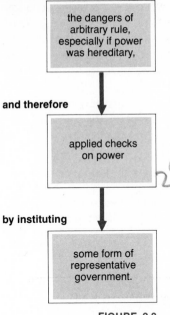

the dangers of
arbitrary rule,
especially if power
was hereditary,

and therefore

applied checks
on power

by instituting

some form of
representative
government.

**FIGURE 2.2
The Founders' Conception of
Representative Government**

The same point can be stressed from another angle. Whereas today we view representational processes as means by which the larger population can express itself on political issues, the founders saw the possibility of limiting the impact of the public. The representatives would be wiser and more cautious of the social order than the masses. As Madison put it, representative government would "refine and enlarge the public views by passing them through the medium of a chosen body of citizens."

FRAGMENTATION OF POWERS

In addition to external checks, whereby citizens could restrain the use of authority, the founders considered internal checks, whereby those in authority checked one another.

The Constitution can be viewed as a search for the means by which governments can rule and yet not rule unfairly. It is a search for the delicate balance between authority, or ability to rule, and liberty, or protection against unfair rule. We have seen that the writers of the Constitution wanted a strong national government, one strong enough to create a single nation out of thirteen separate states. Yet the founders worried that in setting up a national government they would be establishing a tool with too much power. One check on this power, periodic elections and limited tenure of office, has just been reviewed.

The founders were not satisfied. As it was put in *The Federalist* (No. 51), "a dependence on the people is, no doubt, the primary control on the government; but experience has taught mankind the necessity of auxiliary precautions." These extra precautions were to be found in the fragmentation of powers *within* government.

Federalism Some powers went to the national government; some were reserved to the individual states. This is fragmentation of powers across the layers of government. It was a great act of political engineering, for it served two seemingly contradictory ends. The first goal was to establish a strong, effective central government. Nothing short of this would guarantee social order, pay the public debt, provide a monetary system, and make it possible to develop the country's resources. Yet it was also necessary to preserve the independence of the state governments, for this would check the concentration of powers in the federal government. Out of the tension between these two goals grew the federal system. Federalism is reviewed in detail in Chapter 17.

Separation of Powers The writers of the Constitution were not content with federalism. They also divided powers across three different branches of government, giving different powers and resources to the legislative, executive, and judicial branches. This served as protection against political tyranny, defined in *The Federalist* (No. 47) as "the accumulation of all powers, legislative, executive, and judiciary, in the same hands." It was not enough to have popular control over government. It was not enough to have two layers of government. Beyond these controls was the need to further fragment the powers of government.

The separation of the federal government into legislative, executive, and judicial branches was, according to *The Federalist,* to accomplish three goals.

First, the powers of government were to be fragmented. Thus the federal form of government was complemented by the separation of powers. The argument is stated clearly in *The Federalist* (No. 51):

> In the compound Republic of America, the power surrendered by the people is first divided between two distinct governments (Federal government and the States), and then the portion allotted to each subdivided among distinct and separate departments. Hence, a double security rises to the rights of the people. The different governments will control each other, at the same time that each will be controlled by itself.

Second, through a system of checks and balances each branch of government could check the activities of the others. There are many examples. Congress legislates, but the President can veto a law of Congress. Then again, Congress can override the veto, though it takes a two-thirds vote. The President appoints judges, but they must be confirmed by the Senate. The judges are appointed for life, unless impeachment proceedings begun in Congress are successful. So it goes throughout the federal government, and every state government as well: a multitude of cross-checking restraints on authority. Table 2.1 shows how often some of these restraints have been used.

Third, the kinds of checks and balances just described mean that various units of government must cooperate with one another to reach common goals. A wider range of interests is thereby reflected in government policy. Moreover, each branch has its own outlook. The blending of these different perspectives should, in theory, result in better government. The system of separated functions also requires a greater effort at communication among various groups.

TABLE 2.1
The Use of Checks and Balances, 1789–1970

Between 1789 and 1970
There were 2255 Presidential vetoes of congressional acts.
Congress subsequently overruled 75 of those vetoes.
The Supreme Court ruled 85 congressional acts or parts of acts unconstitutional.
The Senate refused to confirm 27 nominees to the Supreme Court (out of a total of 138 nominees).
Congress impeached 9 federal judges; of these, 4 were convicted. The Senate rejected 8 Cabinet nominations.

Source: Senate Library, *Presidential Vetoes* (New York: Greenwood Press, 1968); *Congressional Quarterly;* and *Current American Government* (Washington, D.C.: *Congressional Quarterly,* Spring 1973), p. 106.

This is more likely to produce a true "national interest" than a government that is under the control of a single branch.

It cannot be said that each of these goals has always been achieved in American political history. The separation of powers has worked out differently than the founders thought it would. Yet the fragmentation of authority and the need for cooperation remain basic features of American government. And over the years the goals of the founders have been served remarkably well.

LIMITED GOVERNMENT

A third basic principle of the Constitution is limited government. The problem was to establish a government with enough authority to govern, but one that would not interfere with individual freedom and initiative. Friedrich Hayek's definition of liberty comes close to what the founders wanted to accomplish by insisting that the government was to be a limited government. Hayek writes that liberty is "that condition of man in which coercion of some by others is reduced as much as possible in society."[3] The coercion that worried the writers of the Constitution was government coercion, they attempted to guard against it in various ways.

The Bill of Rights   First, there are certain things government cannot and should not do. It cannot restrict the protections for the individual citizen stated in the first ten amendments, the Bill of Rights. The government was explicitly prevented from denying citizens the right to practice the religion of their choice, the right to say and write what they pleased, the right to assemble for political purposes, and the right to bear arms. Moreover, the government cannot take life, liberty, or property without due process of law, which includes the right to a speedy, public, and fair trial and to a trial by a jury of peers in certain cases.

The complications of applying such principles in concrete cases are discussed in Chapter 16, and throughout the book there are examples showing that the protections promised by the Bill of Rights have had a checkered political history. At this point, however, we are interested in constitutional *principles* rather than political realities. The principle of limited government holds that the rights of individuals are derived from a higher law than government (natural law) and should be protected by placing limits on government, as in the Bill of Rights.

"Government of Laws, Not of Men"   The second idea behind the principle of limited government is constitutionalism itself. By this is meant simply the familiar phrase "government of laws, not of men." There is a basic law against which all lesser laws should be measured. This law, the written Constitution in our case, is based

[3] Quoted in the *New York Times,* September 21, 1977.

The courts offer citizens the means to check arbitrary government.

on the consent of the governed. Any lesser laws passed in accordance with the Constitution, then, should have the same basis. Moreover, the basic law as well as the lesser laws regulate the operation of government and, thus, the governors. No one is "a law unto himself" or should "stand above the law," not even the President of the United States—as was so dramatically demonstrated by Richard Nixon's fall from power.

The Court System   The court system in the United States provides the means for testing the constitutional character of the government. A citizen who has been hurt by an act of the government can challenge that action in the courts. If the courts accept jurisdiction, the government must show that its action was based on an authorizing law. A police officer cannot simply arrest any citizen; the citizen must be charged with violating a specified statute, and the officer must be able to show the legal basis for the arrest. Welfare officials cannot simply issue checks to friends or refuse to pay those whose hair styles they dislike; in each instance they must be prepared to show in court that their decision was controlled by whether or not the applicant for welfare was in one of the welfare categories authorized by law. In principle, if not always in practice, courts offer the citizen the means to check arbitrary government power.

But the courts play an even more important role in American politics. Even if a government official can show that his or her act was in accordance with a local, state, or national law, that act can still be reversed if it can be shown in court that the *law itself* is contrary to the Constitution. The American system of government thus allows courts to limit what the popularly elected branches of government may authorize the government to do. Only a constitutional amendment—a cumbersome, time-consuming, politically awkward expedient—can reverse the United States Supreme Court's interpretation of the Constitution. (Of course the Court itself can always reverse its earlier decisions.)

Like the Bill of Rights, the idea of a "government of laws" has had a checkered history. Secrecy, duplicity, and lawlessness are not unknown in the highest government circles. The law can be bent, and often is, for those with power and money. Some examples appear in the chapter on the Supreme Court (Chapter 15) and throughout the book. But however misshapen by political pressures, the principle of constitutionalism remains a constant check on arbitrary government.

SUMMARY

We have covered two major topics: how the Constitution came to be written and the fundamental principles on which it rests. The material provides a partial answer to the question we asked at the beginning of the chapter: What is this Constitution that could so long endure and accommodate itself to a society that has changed so much over the past two centuries? One part of the answer is that the Constitution was and is a political document. And at least some of the political conflicts of the 1780s are still with us today, though in different forms. An example is the conflict between central power and local control. Thus a document that was sensitive to political realities remains workable because those realities remain important.

Another partial answer lies in the constitutional fundamentals. Popular control over elected representatives, fragmentation and separation of governmental powers, and limited government were attractive enough in 1787 so that the Constitution could be adopted. We can only guess that they remain attractive enough; despite major changes in society, so that the Constitution continues to be supported. Political history reveals only one major challenge to the U.S. Constitution in 200 years—the attempted secession of the Confederacy. The Civil War was fought to "defend and maintain the supremacy of the Constitution and to preserve the union," in the words of a congressional resolution of July 1861. Except for the Civil War, no significant political movement has tried to call into question the Constitution.

But these are partial answers. A further explanation rests in the adaptability of the Constitution and its constant reinterpretation to deal with new political realities and social conditions.

A Flexible Constitution

"The Constitution belongs to the living and not to the dead," Jefferson wrote. No document of a few thousand words written in 1789 could possibly anticipate and resolve the political-legal issues that would emerge as the nation developed and changed. Jefferson, speaking of the Constitution, said that "as new discoveries are

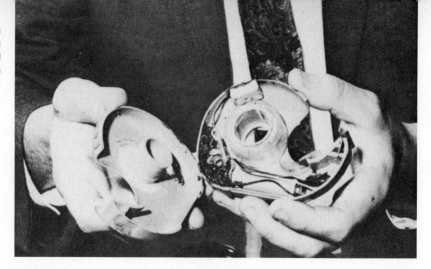

The language of the Fourth Amendment, prohibiting unreasonable searches, is used to challenge the use of hidden microphones.

made, new truths disclosed, and manners and opinions changed . . . institutions must advance also, and keep pace with the times."

The Constitution has kept pace with the times, or else it would long ago have been discarded. Three factors have contributed to its flexibility: constitutional generalities, constitutional silences, and a formal amendment process.

CONSTITUTIONAL GENERALITIES

The Constitution seems in places to have been purposely ambiguous. Maybe this was the best way the founders had of winning approval of the various factions. In any case this ambiguity has allowed later generations to interpret the Constitution as giving broad grants of authority to key institutions. We will see in Chapter 15 that the power of the Supreme Court to declare acts of Congress unconstitutional is not explicitly stated in the Constitution; nor is it denied. But the Supreme Court ruled that it did have the power of judicial review, a decision that greatly enlarges its political significance. The executive power of the President is not clearly spelled out in the Constitution either. The change from George Washington's staff of a half-dozen clerks to the huge federal bureaucracy of the 1980s has been justified by a simple constitutional phrase: The President "shall take care that the laws be faithfully executed."

New Meanings for Old Words   Using a general language allows new meanings to be given to old words. Consider the example of "unreasonable searches." The founders disliked the way colonial officers searched private homes at will, so in the Fourth Amendment they declared that "the right of the people to be secure in their persons, houses, papers, and effects, against unreasonable searches and seizures, shall not be violated." This expresses a clear principle in such general language that it can still be applied today, despite an entirely different technology of search and seizure. Today the right of government agents to use electronic surveillance techniques—

telescopic cameras, wiretaps, and hidden microphones—is challenged according to the principle and with the language of the Fourth Amendment as adopted in 1791. A new technology, yes, but an old argument that places individual rights above the government's right to know.

CONSTITUTIONAL SILENCES

One of the best examples of a constitutional silence permitting political flexibility is the matter of political parties. The political-party system is entirely extraconstitutional, yet who could imagine twentieth-century politics in the United States without political parties of some sort? All major elected officials, and most appointed ones, take office under the banner of a political party (Chapter 10). And political parties largely organize and manage the elections, including primaries and nominating conventions. All of this takes place outside the framework of the Constitution, and indeed largely outside of any type of federal law at all.

Thus it is that political institutions and the formal government adapt themselves to the requirements of twentieth-century politics, very often because the Constitution has nothing to say on the matter.

THE AMENDMENT PROCESS

The writers of the Constitution knew that very specific changes would become necessary as the conditions in society changed. So they provided for a formal amendment process. It is a two-step process: proposing an amendment and then ratifying it. It is complicated because there are two separate ways amendments may be proposed and two separate ways they may be ratified. The standard practice, however, has not been as complicated; the procedure is shown in Figure 2.3.[4]

The formal amendment process has been used infrequently (leaving out the Bill of Rights, only sixteen times), sometimes for minor changes in the mechanics of government. Most of the amendments, however, have been significant in adapting government to new social conditions. The famous "Civil War amendments" (the Thirteenth, Fourteenth, and Fifteenth) outlawed slavery; defined the privileges and immunities of national citizenship and set limits on state interference with equal protection and due process; and gave the right to vote to all men without regard to race, color, or prior servitude. Other amendments have broadened the democratic meaning of the Constitution, providing for direct election of

Amendments are proposed

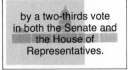

by a two-thirds vote in both the Senate and the House of Representatives.

Amendments are ratified

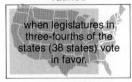

when legislatures in three-fourths of the states (38 states) vote in favor.

**FIGURE 2.3
Standard Practice for
Amending the Constitution**

[4] Amendments also may be proposed by a special national convention called by Congress at the request of two-thirds of the state legislatures. This has never happened. And amendments may be ratified by special conventions in three-fourths of the states. This procedure has been used once, when the Twenty-First Amendment, which repealed prohibition, was ratified by state conventions rather than state legislatures.

senators, women's suffrage, repeal of the poll tax, and a voting age of 18. One of the most important amendments, the Sixteenth, ratified in 1913, authorized the income tax.

The proposed Twenty-Seventh Amendment, the Equal Rights Amendment, is currently being debated in state legislatures. This amendment will require equal treatment of males and females (see the discussion in Chapter 3).

THE DYNAMICS OF CONSTITUTIONAL CHANGE

Saying that the Constitution is flexible is another way of saying that it does not provide ready-made answers for new political questions and social issues. We have identified aspects of the Constitution that give it flexibility, but we have not yet accounted for specific examples of major constitutional change.

No general formula can account for each major change and reshaping of the Constitution, but it would help to hold in mind the following: The genius of the Constitution is also its weakness. A document that gives powers to different political institutions is sooner or later going to be caught in a squeeze when the interests of those institutions are in conflict. The clashes leading to constitutional crises have been of four general sorts: (1) clashes between the federal and state governments, (2) clashes over the authority of a particular branch of government, (3) clashes over the separation-of-powers doctrine, and (4) clashes over the extension of citizenship rights.

Federalism   In Chapter 17 we will learn how easy it is for conflicts to occur over which level of government is responsible for and authorized to do what. The genius of the Constitution in splitting government powers between the national government and the independent states is also its weakness when different levels are in conflict. The Civil War was fought to establish the supremacy of the national government, a supremacy that was ratified by the adoption of the Thirteenth, Fourteenth, and Fifteenth Amendments. The war did not end disputes among the levels of government, and the principle of federalism is constantly being tested.

Scope of Authority   Many of the new social conditions that government has had to deal with over the past two centuries have been handled within the guidelines set by the Constitution. But some conditions have presented such new and complicated problems that traditional definitions of government authority have been of little use. The interpretation of the Constitution has shifted in response to these problems. As we will see in Chapter 15, sometimes the courts have resisted the process of constitutional adaptation. For example, the great economic depression of the 1930s seemed to require broad new government authority and programs. But the Supreme Court declared important new legislation unconstitutional, claiming that Congress and the Presidency were increasing their authority illegally. Heavy political pressure from the Roosevelt administration caused the Court to reverse itself. In other times the Court itself has stimulated constitutional adaptation. Thus citizenship rights and liberties were greatly enlarged in a series of decisions by the Warren Court (so called because the Chief Justice was Earl Warren) in the 1950s and 1960s.

Separation of Powers   We have noted that the writers of the Constitution feared a government in which all powers were centered in only one institution, and that they therefore devised one in which each branch would have the means and the incentive to keep the others in their proper place. This situation has led to many disputes and conflicts between the Presidency and Congress, between Congress and the courts, or between the courts and the Presidency. Most of these disputes have been settled without major constitutional revision, but we have recently gone through a separation-of-powers conflict with broad implications for constitutional government. This conflict, the Watergate affair and the resignation of Richard Nixon from the Presidency, will be reviewed in detail in the chapter on the Presidency (Chapter 13).

The Meaning of Citizenship   American history has put the Constitution to many severe tests, but probably none has been as severe as the problem of defining the principle and the practice of equal citizenship. In Chapter 4, and again in Chapters 15 and 16, we review the gradual transformation of the principle of equal citizenship. The elimination of barriers to citizenship rights has been a long and politically painful process. And now we are struggling as a society with an altogether new issue: Should the results of past discrimination and inequalities be corrected today through reverse discrimination and affirmative action?

HOW INSTITUTIONS WORK: I
the structure of the U.S. government

On what basis is the U.S. structured? The general structure of American government is based on the Constitution and on two principles in particular: federalism and separation of powers. In the federal system the powers and functions of government are divided between the national government and the states. Then, in accordance with the separation-of-powers principle, the authority given to the national government is divided among three separate branches: legislative, executive, and judicial. (See Figure 2.4.)

What are the institutions and agencies of government that make up each of the three branches?

Legislative

All power to make laws lies in a Congress composed of two houses, the Senate and the House of Representatives. Their authority and limitations are set forth in the Constitution. The Senate consists of 100 members (2 from each state) and the House of 435 members (with the number from each state determined by population). The Constitution does not say how Congress is to be organized internally, but both bodies have chosen a committee structure.

Executive

The executive power is in the President alone; no other executive body is called for in the Constitution. However, an enormous establishment has grown up around the President. Directly serving the President is the Executive Office, which consists of several operating units established either by the President or by law. The Executive Office serves the President's managerial needs and includes the White House Office, the Office of Management and Budget, and the National Security Council.

The executive branch also includes the twelve executive departments that together make up the Cabinet. As with the Executive Office, the Constitution makes no provision for a Cabinet. All of the executive departments have been created by acts of Congress, the most recent addition being the Department of Energy (1977).

In addition to the major departments, there is a group of independent government agencies of two general types: independent executive agencies and independent regulatory commissions. The former perform specialized tasks; the CIA, NASA, and the Veterans Administration are in this category. Also grouped with the executive agencies are the government corporations such as the U.S. Postal Service and the Tennessee Valley Authority. The independent regulatory commissions include such bodies as the Interstate Commerce Commission and the Federal Power Commission. Although they are formally part of the executive branch, they have been designed to be independent of the President.

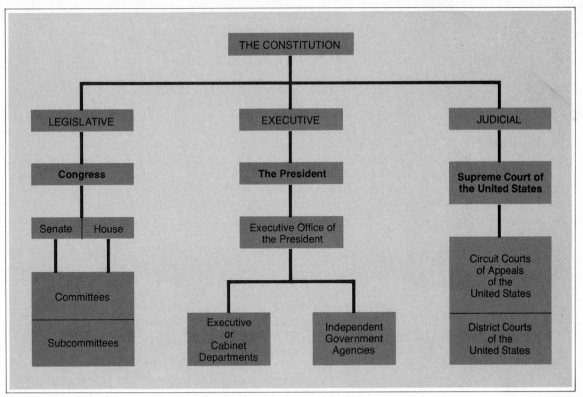

FIGURE 2.4   The Government of the United States

Judicial   The Constitution locates the judicial power in one Supreme Court and in lower courts established by Congress. Even the size of the Supreme Court is left open to congressional decision. Over the years Congress has created a structure of lower federal courts made up of the U.S. circuit courts of appeals and the U.S. district courts.

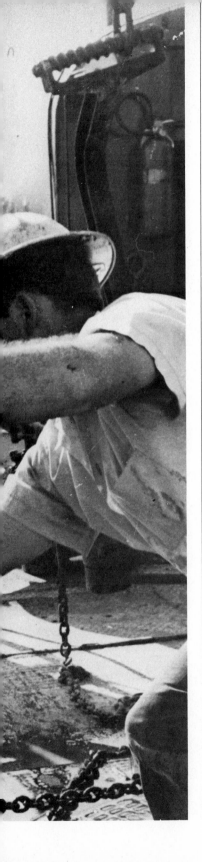

3

THE AMERICAN ECONOMY AND POLITICAL LIFE

Why have a chapter about economics in a book on American government?

A fair question. It would seem more appropriate to concentrate on political participation or the role of interest groups or the institutions of American government. We will, of course, get to these topics later, but we believe that a reasonable case can be made for an early and careful look at the economic context of political life. The argument has two parts.

First, and fairly obvious, the actual things that the government does are in large part economic. Consider a few recent headlines:

Federal Reserve Board Eases Interest Rates
Labor Department Acts to Head Off Coal Strike
White House Concerned About Sluggish Economy, Promises to Act
Federal Program for Unemployment Provides City Jobs
Government Investigates Soaring Prices

What do these headlines have in common? They all refer to an *economic* issue or problem: interest rates, strikes, recession, unemployment, inflation. They all refer as well to a *government* action or program.

Here are some more headlines; note what they have in common:

Parents of College Students Demand Tax Relief
Taxpayer Revolt Predicted If Social Security Taxes Increased
Bank Depositors Threaten Withdrawal Unless Government Increases Protection
Auto Workers Support Congressmen Who Promise Higher Tariffs on Foreign Cars
Defense Plant Employees Out of Work, Claim Unemployment

Again we see the connection between economics and politics. In these headlines a citizen's economic role leads to a political act.

We cannot explain American politics without understanding how the government affects the economy and the economy affects the government. We cannot explain individual political beliefs and actions without understanding the connection between government and the citizen as consumer, taxpayer, investor, and worker.

There is a second, less obvious answer to the question of why we have a chapter on economics. A book about American government is ultimately a book about power: how it is organized, who has access to it, for what purposes it is used. Already we have noted the growth of government power. And in reviewing the Constitution we began to see how these powers are organized, who uses them,

and to what purposes, giving particular attention to the likely tension between a "limited government" and an "activist state."

It would be naive to think that the growth of government power has gone unnoticed by the interests that are harmed or benefited by how that power is used. In particular, we expect that economic interests have been attentive to the growth of government power, an expectation that is easily confirmed. Indeed, it does not make too much sense to think of the power of wealth, of corporations, and of private property as necessarily distinct from the power of government. There are not two different sources of power in the United States, one economic and one political, struggling against each other. It is more realistic to think of these powers as gradually merging. In this chapter we outline the active partnership and shared goals of powerful government actors and powerful economic actors.

This, then, is the major reason that we start our book with a discussion of economics. There is no way to separate the substance of politics from economics. And there is no way to consider the powers of government without at the same time considering the nature of our capitalist economy. We do not record this feature of American politics in order to pass judgement on it. It is an aspect of American political life, just as the fact that there are 216 million Americans scattered across 50 separate states is an aspect of American political life. It would be difficult to study American politics without recognizing that our government and our economy are closely connected.

What Is Economics?

Economics is the study of how society chooses to use *scarce* resources—labor, minerals, land, water, capital, knowledge—to produce various goods and to distribute those goods, now and in the years ahead, among different groups and people in society.

This definition of economics poses interesting questions. For what purposes should scarce resources be used? Difficult decisions have to be made, such as whether limited oil supplies should be used to heat homes or to keep gasoline prices down or to maintain the military at full strength. How much should go to satisfying current needs and how much to investing in long-range goals? Again these are difficult decisions, such as whether to close down a factory in Gary, Indiana and throw some breadwinners out of work, or keep the factory operating even though it is contributing to the pollution of Lake Michigan. How should the goods in society be distributed among many competing groups? More difficult decisions: for example, providing free medical care for the elderly may mean reducing research on children's diseases.

Underlying all of these difficult questions is the most difficult question of all: Who in society will make the decisions about the use of scarce resources, the balance between present needs and long-term goals, and the distribution of goods among many groups? Should these decisions be made by the government?

There was a time in American history when it was out of the question to think of the government as an agency for making economic decisions. The American economy was based on the principles of free enterprise, which, roughly translated, meant that government should keep its hands out of economic affairs. An unregulated and unplanned free interplay among workers and owners, sellers and buyers, producers and consumers would be just the thing for a healthy, growing economy.

Things never quite worked out in practice the way they were supposed to in principle. As we will see, right from the start of American history the government was called upon to perform certain economic functions. The government's involvement in economic affairs has increased steadily since then. That involvement will be reviewed under three headings in this chapter: "A Supported Economy," "A Regulated Economy," and "A Managed Economy."

What has resulted from the government's economic activities is not, however, the destruction of the free-enterprise system. Many important features of the capitalist economy have been kept, though they have been changed by the role of the government. This we review in the section called "A Capitalist Economy."

What is difficult for the student to understand is the very complex relationship between a capitalist economy and a government that is involved in economic activities. For while the government exercises economic controls it does not in fact control the economy. This we try to make clear in the final section of the chapter.

A Supported Economy

Economic activities benefit from government supports in at least three ways. First, the government provides the legal framework needed in a free-enterprise economy. Second, it provides direct subsidies to many economic activities. Third, it is a major, sometimes *the* major, customer for producers in the economy.

THE LEGAL FRAMEWORK FOR A FREE-ENTERPRISE ECONOMY

When James Madison, the chief author of the U.S. Constitution, wrote in 1787 that the first goal of government is to protect the different and unequal ability of citizens to acquire property, he was echoing themes from Europe and England. In Europe democracy began as a reform movement led by a commercial middle class against the oppression of absolute rulers and hereditary nobilities. The privileges and special status enjoyed by the king and his noblemen blocked the commercial activities of a small but growing group of merchants, traders, and craftsmen.

These early "capitalists" knew that a free-enterprise economy de-

Tourists examine newly printed two-dollar bills, part of the government-provided monetary system which facilitates economic exchange in society.

pends on the right of individuals to enter into valid contracts and to have those contracts upheld by law; it depends on the right to sell one's products and labor in the free marketplace; and it depends on the right to use one's abilities to gain material goods. Free enterprise cannot survive when legal restrictions block the exchange of goods and labor and when social position is fixed at birth.

In the beginning the assault on class privilege was a reform movement that freed commerce and trade. In doing so it introduced democratic principles such as due process of law, equal status as citizens, protection from arbitrary arrests and unfair seizure of property, and at least limited voting. Stated differently, the U.S. Constitution reflects the victory of individual rights and limited government over class privileges and royal absolutism. Just as the European middle-class reformers expected, such a constitution would also make possible a free-enterprise economy.

Although capitalism as we know it did not take hold until after the Civil War, the legal framework and constitutional system necessary to a free-enterprise economy were fairly well established as early as 1800. Even then a police force protected private property; a court system dealt with violations of contracts; a monetary system provided the bills and coins used in economic transactions; and a system of common weights and measures, patents, and copyrights provided the necessary uniformity and protection for exchanges of goods and titles. These have been accepted government functions since 1789, and they continue today—on a larger scale—to provide the legal framework that allows a capitalist system of production and exchange to operate.

SUBSIDIES TO PRIVATE ENTERPRISE
Direct support of private enterprise through state powers and with public moneys is as old as the nation itself. Alexander Hamilton, the first Secretary of the Treasury, insisted that the new government set up a national bank. Credit would be increased this way, and according to Hamilton this would help "the operations of commerce among individuals. Industry is increased, commodities are multiplied, agriculture and manufacturers flourish; and herein consists the true wealth and prosperity of a state." As the most decisive member of President Washington's Cabinet, Hamilton got his way, and the government has been supporting private business ever since.

In 1974 a Joint Economic Committee of Congress defined a subsidy as "the provision of Federal economic assistance, at the expense of others in the economy, to the private sector producers or consumers of a particular good, service or factor of production."[1] Under this definition federal subsidies amount to more than $100 billion a year.

[1] Quoted in Philip Shabecoff, "U.S. Subsidizes Nearly Everything," *New York Times,* March 20, 1977.

There are four major categories of subsidies: cash payments, tax subsidies, credit subsidies, and benefit-in-kind subsidies.

Cash Payments Medical-school scholarships to encourage the training of more doctors illustrate this type of subsidy. So do government payments to help support artists, to move workers from welfare to jobs, or to build airports that become available to commercial airlines.

Tax Subsidies Actual cash is not transferred by this type of subsidy. Instead certain individuals or corporations pay a smaller tax than might normally be required. A famous example is the oil depletion allowance, which allows oil companies to deduct a certain amount from their taxes so that they can invest it in exploration for new oil sources. Another well-known example is the tax relief on mortgage interest paid by homeowners. Every homeowner who makes mortgage payments benefits from a tax subsidy. While the government does not actually spend anything on these subsidies, it does forgo revenues.

Credit Subsidies In this type of subsidy the government makes loans at lower interest rates than those charged by banks or other lending agencies. Student loans to finance a college education are credit subsidies. So are loans provided by the Small Business Administration to help people start up businesses.

Benefit-in-Kind Subsidies Food stamps and medicare are examples of this form of subsidy. A product or service, paid for by the government, is provided to individual citizens.

As one commentator has observed, federal subsidies are such an important part of economic life that "it is difficult to determine, even under close examination, where the public sector ends and the private sector begins."[2] Every person or business, from Lockheed Aircraft Corporation to the sick and the hungry, has been subsidized in one way or another.

THE GOVERNMENT AS CUSTOMER

The gross national product (GNP) is the dollar figure obtained by adding together all the consumption goods, services, and investments produced by the land, labor, and capital resources of a society. GNP is the yardstick that tells a society how well it is doing. When more goods are being produced (apples, tanks, medicines), more services are available (health care, police protection), and more investments are being made (new factories, skill training), the GNP of a society is increasing. When there is a slowdown in the production of goods, services, and investments, GNP drops.

The importance of government to the private economy can be seen in the percent of GNP accounted for by government expendi-

[2] *Ibid.*

tures. Figure 3.1 shows how large this has been in the past decade. The federal government alone accounts for more than one-fifth of GNP. A large part of the government's contribution to GNP figures is in the government payroll: salaries for the military, for teachers, for judges, for clerks in the State Department, for the FBI, for medical researchers. But government is also a consumer of goods produced by private industry: It buys food for school lunches, typewriters to type order forms to buy more typewriters, cars to drive people around on "government business," paper to publish the annual budget, military hardware to keep the armed forces equipped.

Since World War II the U.S. government has become the largest single customer for American industrial products and services. Were government purchases to stop, huge gaps would be left in the economy. This is especially true of the industries that supply the military. Many of the nation's largest and most powerful corporations hold direct contracts with the various defense-related agencies of the federal government, especially the Pentagon. Not only do these contracts involve huge amounts of money, but some of the largest defense contractors—notably General Dynamics and Lockheed Aircraft—depend on government contracts for almost all their business. Defense contractors include many of the nation's largest corporations; 65 of the 100 leading firms are heavily involved in the military market. Besides, direct defense contracts are only the tip

**FIGURE 3.1
Federal Outlays as a Percent
of GNP**

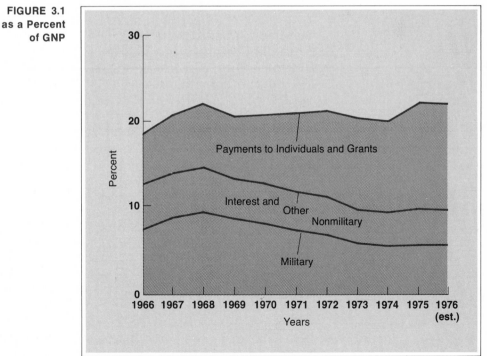

Source: U.S. Office of Management and Budget.

The government is the single largest customer for American industrial products and goods, especially for those industries which supply the military.

of the iceberg. The companies that provide the raw materials like aluminum and plastics and the manufactured parts like airplane tires and gaskets are equally dependent on the government's involvement in vast defense spending.

The best way to understand the magnitude of government as a customer is to know just how much government spends. In 1977 government expenditures at the local, state, and federal levels totaled approximately $715.7 billion. This figure does not make much sense until you realize that it amounts to an average of almost $10,000 for every household in the United States.

A Regulated Economy

Government economic regulation dates back to the latter part of the nineteenth century, when a nation of farmers and traders was slowly being transformed into one of factory workers and industrialists. It was in the post-Civil War era that the United States was crisscrossed with railroads. Canals and harbors were opened up for shipping. Natural resources—especially coal, lumber, and oil—were being put to industrial use. Factories were beginning to mass-produce everything from shoes to stoves. The telegraph and then telephones were spreading. Electricity was being introduced into homes, at least city homes. American exports were being shipped around the world.

The growth and transformation of the economy had some harmful effects. But the government took little notice of them. A free-enterprise system should benefit from government supports and protection but not be hampered by government regulation. Thus the government provided little help to those who were hurt by an unregulated capitalist economy—small businessmen forced out of the market by the ruthless practices of monopolies like Standard Oil, farmers gouged by the high prices charged by the railroads that shipped their crops, workers who toiled long hours in unsafe and unsanitary conditions for very little pay. As a matter of fact, not only were judges and politicians unsympathetic to the cause of industrial regulation; they often owed their jobs to industrial interests. "Capitalists, seeking land grants, tariffs, bounties, favorable currency policies, freedom from regulatory legislation, and economic reform, supplied campaign funds, fees, and bribes and plied politicians with investment opportunities."[3] Few politicians resisted the temptations: "One might search the whole list of Congress, Judiciary, and Executive during the twenty-five years 1870 to 1895," concluded Henry Adams, "and find little but damaged reputation."

CORRECTING THE FLAWS

It was not until the 1890s that discontented farmers, middle-class reform groups working with small-business interests, protesting consumers, and labor agitators began to call for government regulation of the economy. Although they had only limited success, they did establish a political climate in which the flaws of a capitalist system—child labor, economic insecurity, deceptive advertising, price fixing, shoddy merchandise, unsafe working conditions—could be seen and corrected through government regulation.

A second, and perhaps more significant, stimulus toward regulatory legislation came from the business community itself. An unregulated economy was difficult to manage. Some corporation chiefs recognized that the federal government could be very helpful in bringing order to the sometimes chaotic economic situation if the business community could define the limits of government intervention in the economy. Business was largely successful in doing this. Thus the early regulatory legislation meant not the "triumph of small business over the trusts," as has often been suggested, but the "victory of big business in achieving the rationalization of the economy that only the federal government could provide."[4]

Today government activities to regulate the economy are many and varied. There are regulations on the training necessary to be-

[3] Richard Hofstadter, *The American Political Tradition* (New York: Vintage, 1954), p. 170. The quotation from Henry Adams appears in this work as well, p. 107.
[4] Gabriel Kolko, *The Triumph of Conservatism* (New York: Quadrangle, 1967), p. 284.

come a licensed barber, the number of exits from an airplane or a movie theater or a day nursery, the wording of wills and contracts, the advertising claims made by a medicine or food or automobile manufacturer, the price of electricity and gas. Government regulations affect how a corporation sells stocks, whether it will be allowed to expand its operations, the way it advertises its products, and how often and in what way it must make a public accounting of its transactions.

"TRUST-BUSTING"

The romanticized version of early American capitalism stated that the force behind economic expansion was the small businessman. This was not the case. Starting in the nineteenth century and continuing today, industrial corporations, not small businessmen, have put together the capital and know-how necessary for opening canals and harbors, cutting timber, mining oil and coal, building railroads, inventing new production techniques, and experimenting with new products. The early "captains of industry" are remembered for the industrial empires they established: Rockefeller (oil), Carnegie (steel), Armour and Swift (meat-packing), Pillsbury (milling), Vanderbilt and Stanford (railroads), and Morgan (banking).

The new way of doing business sometimes gave rise to monopolies, as when a single firm (say, Standard Oil of New Jersey) could so monopolize an industrial sector (mining, refining, and distribution of oil) that it could set prices at will. No other firm would be big enough to provide serious competition.

These conditions were considered the very root of the economic evils so distressing to the late-nineteenth-century reformers. The reformers wanted to break up the enormous concentrations of economic power. "Trust-busting" became a popular political slogan; Supreme Court Justice Louis D. Brandeis, speaking of "industrial absolutism," warned of the danger to democracy when "there develops within the State a state so powerful that the ordinary social and industrial forces existing are insufficient to cope with it." Regulatory legislation was passed, such as the Sherman Antitrust Act of 1890, which prohibits monopolistic activities in restraint of trade, and the Federal Trade Commission Act of 1914, which prohibits unfair competition. Laws were also passed regulating working conditions and hours of work, especially for children and women.

FROM MONOPOLY TO OLIGOPOLY

Antitrust legislation has enabled the government to limit monopolistic power. Whenever a single corporation takes over a large share of the market for its products, the antitrust division of the Attorney General's Office begins to investigate. In recent years two giant corporations, IBM in the field of computers and electronics and ATT in the field of communication, have been the subjects of antitrust court action.

Government regulation of monopolies, however, has not eliminated concentration of economic power and resources. Much of the economy is under the control of what economists call *oligopolies*, in which only a few corporations control a particular part of the economy. A good example is automobile manufacturing, where three giant corporations — Ford Motor, General Motors, and Chrysler — jointly dominate the manufacture and sale of automobiles.

Economic concentration can occur even when there are many firms producing the same service or goods, as in the following examples:

- There are 67,000 separate corporations actively involved in the utilities and communication industry. Of these corporations, only 33 control half of all assets in electricity, natural gas, transportation, and communication.
- There are 13,511 commercial banks in the United States. The 50 largest, or 0.1 percent, contol about half of all banking assets.
- In 1970 the Securities and Exchange Commission listed 202,710 manufacturing corporations. But only 100 of them (0.05 percent) controlled more than half of all manufacturing assets in the nation. This concentration has been increasing steadily for the past two decades, as shown in the following table:

Percent of Manufacturing Assets Under Control of 100 Largest Corporations

1950	1955	1960	1965	1970
39.8%	44.3%	46.4%	46.5%	52.3%

Not all industrial sectors show equal amounts of oligopolistic control. For example, in retail clothing and food distribution the assets are more evenly divided. It is in the key sectors of the economy — transportation, iron and steel, oil, banking and finance, communication, industrial chemicals — that the concentration is greatest. Note that this concentration has not been reduced by government regulation. Regulation has made it difficult for a firm to gain monopolistic control but not for huge industrial corporations to pile up large amounts of economic resources.

REGULATION AND FREEDOM

The complex relationship between government regulation and individual freedom is one of the most difficult issues facing American society. It is an issue that we discuss at several points in this book. Some believe that government regulation is suffocating the individual freedom and the spirit of incentive traditionally associated with a free-enterprise economy. They point to the seventy-seven different federal agencies that regulate one aspect or another of private activity.

Others believe that we live in a dense society. A dense society is one in which every part of society is interdependent with, if not dependent on, every other part. Only by close regulation can a comfortable and civilized life be preserved as a society becomes more dense. If a northern Illinois factory is polluting the drinking water of

It requires massive concentrations of capital resources to maintain technological growth.

a southern Illinois town, then pollution regulation becomes necessary.

Elsewhere in the book you will have an opportunity to consider the pros and cons of regulation. Here we continue our overview of the economic context, but with the reminder that seemingly uninteresting economic matters, such as government regulation, are not far from the central issues of individual freedom and democracy.

A Managed Economy

Regulation should not be confused with management of the economy. Regulatory activities are piecemeal—they attempt to correct particular flaws in the economic system. The flaw might be deceptive advertising: The government steps in to protect the consumer from being misinformed about what he or she is buying. Or the flaw might be something as substantial as monopoly control: Here the government steps in to break up the monopoly. But regulation has never been intended to manage the economy. It was not until the Great Depression of the 1930s that the government turned its attention to management questions.

ESTABLISHING ECONOMIC POLICY

During the period of industrial growth between the Civil War and the Great Depression of the 1930s, it was believed that a capitalist economy was self-adjusting. Full employment and price stability could occur if workers freely traded their labor for pay, if supply and demand regulated production and prices, and if profits guided the rate of growth and investment.

Until the depression of the 1930s this view was challenged only by a few "radical" economists and business leaders who said that a "boom–bust" cycle, in which periods of economic growth are followed by periods of recession and unemployment, is built into an unmanaged capitalist system and, thus, that capitalism is by nature unstable.

ECONOMIC POLICY IN THE 1930s

During the Depression, as unemployment climbed, banks failed, and factories closed, the argument that the economy would straighten itself out began to be less persuasive. Government leaders began to pay attention to a new argument put forward by John Maynard Keynes. He stated that government intervention in the economy—adjusting taxes, increasing or decreasing government spending on public projects, controlling the supply of money and credit—could stop the boom–bust cycle.

These economic tools began to be used in the 1930s in what is generally called the New Deal of Franklin D. Roosevelt. Today government economic policy is a major force in the free-enterprise system. In accepting such policies the business and political leaders were in effect admitting that no citizen—worker, pensioner, investor, or owner—was secure during periods of depression. The government assumed responsibility for monitoring the business cycle and trying to maintain a relatively low level of unemployment while at the same time keeping prices from creeping up and destroying the value of the dollar.

The responsibility of the government for the health of the privately owned economic sector was firmly established by the Employment Act of 1946, which declared that "it is the continuing policy and responsibility of the federal government . . . to promote maximum employment, production, and purchasing power." The economy remains privately owned, but it is increasingly subject to public management.

Government policy has not been entirely successful in managing the economy. Americans still suffer through business cycles, though to date none has been as severe as that of the 1930s. The 1970s have seen particularly difficult times. Unemployment has been on the increase; by 1975 it had reached levels well above what is considered "safe" by government economists. At the same time, inflation has been a major problem for many Americans. The prices of food, services, and goods have been increasing more than 5–6 percent a year. This is a much greater increase than normal wage increases can match. The dollar is buying less and less.

There have been, then, louder demands for the government to "do something." Various things have been tried, even wage and price controls, but so far nothing has worked. The failure of the government to manage the economy is one thing, but the very fact that the government is trying to manage the economy is another.

FREE SOUP COFFEE & DOUGHNUTS FOR THE UNEMPLOYED

FREE SOUP

What was charity in the 1930s has become public responsibility today.

A story about the stock market crash in 1929 shows just how much has changed in recent decades. The economic crisis in 1929 was severe, the worst in American history. The stock market closed and banks failed. J. P. Morgan, the nation's leading banker, called a meeting of major bankers and financial figures. This group, meeting in New York, issued a statement saying that *they* would act to correct the economy. Newspapers reported the statements of the bankers as if the crisis was a problem for Wall Street to solve. Few thought of an *economic* crisis as something *government* should deal with.

Much has changed since 1929. Today when there are economic problems we naturally look to the White House and government leaders for action, not to Wall Street and the bankers. The responsibility for managing the economy has shifted to the government.

The federal government has tried to manage the economy with the tools introduced by President Roosevelt and his advisers in the 1930s: fiscal policy (primarily the powers of taxation and government spending) and monetary policy (primarily the powers to set interest rates for money loaned by the government and to affect the money supply). To aid the government in using these tools, a small group of economists serves as the President's Council of Economic Advisors.

A PLANNED ECONOMY?

One of the major political debates that was prevalent in the 1930s, and one that is still with us, concentrated on how much the economy should be planned by the government. On one side of the debate was the argument that planning was increasingly necessary. Production targets should be established for different industries. There should be long-range planning that would guide the prices of different raw materials and finished products, and long-range planning that would set wages. Those who favored planning felt that an unplanned economy tolerated much wasted effort, many misdirected projects, and a high risk of "boom-bust" economic cycles.

The other side of the debate argued that government planning would discourage business investment, destroy the initiative that an unplanned economy promoted, and result in so much government bureaucracy that economic freedom and, eventually, individual liberties would be threatened.

Although specific economic plans can be found throughout government and the corporate world, these plans are limited to particular products or policy areas. Ford Motor, for example, would have a detailed plan for the introduction of a new automobile; a plan to organize resources, materials, and labor; and a marketing strategy. This plan would try to control the future environment so as to ensure appropriate sales for the automobile. For instance, Ford could not afford to invest millions of dollars in designing, testing, and then mass-producing a car that failed to meet government safety standards or air pollution requirements. These standards and requirements would have to be known as much as five years in advance. If the government suddenly changed these standards, Ford could stand to lose millions of dollars. At this level, then, there is a great deal of both corporate and government planning.

In a more general sense, however, the federal government has not yet attempted to plan *the* economy, though as the problems of the 1970s persisted people started talking about a major economic planning agency. Such an agency would coordinate the many activities of government that affect the present and future state of the economy. Included along with taxation, the government budget, interest rates, and the money supply would be energy policy, a cost-of-living policy, and international trade policy. If such an agency is formed—and it would be much larger and more powerful than the present Council of Economic Advisors—then the partnership between government and the economy would require even closer cooperation. More than ever would it be true that every major economic issue is also a political one and every major political issue also an economic one.

Thus far we have learned that the government is actively supporting, regulating, and to an extent managing the economy. Later in the book we will see that the government provides economic welfare for individual citizens through such programs as social security, unemployment compensation, medicare, education, and aid to disabled people—adding up to increasingly growing government involvement in the economy. Is America, then, still a capitalist society?

A Capitalist Economy

What defines a society as capitalist involves a number of complex things. We can touch briefly on only three matters: private ownership, individual economic choices, and material incentives.

THE PRIVATELY OWNED ECONOMY

The United States was founded on the idea that the job of government is to protect life, liberty, and property. Individual citizens own property, and the government must ensure that a citizen can acquire, use, and dispose of his or her property according to personal choice. This idea is as central to our political life now as it was two centuries ago.

But if the principle of private property has remained firm, the kind of property that is privately owned has dramatically changed character. To the nation of farmers and small tradesmen that existed in 1780, land itself was the most valuable form of property. And though land remains valuable, many other forms of property have become increasingly important to our modern industrial nation. Especially valued are the natural resources and the productive processes that convert natural resources into consumer goods. Iron, the natural resource, becomes steel, and steel becomes automobiles, the consumer good.

Natural resources, productive processes, chemical patents, means of transporting goods, and related components of an industrial economy are privately owned in the United States. And the economy is run so as to return a profit to the owners. In this sense the economy is still very much a capitalist one. Private individuals and institutions, not the public or the state, own and reap the profits of the economy.

In this way the United States is unusual among industrial nations. Of course we expect that in socialist nations such as the Soviet Union or East Germany much of the economy is state owned. But it is easy to overlook the fact that there is much public ownership of economic enterprises even in Western democracies such as France or Great Britain. The United States is an exception, for there is very little government ownership and operation of natural resources, factories, transportation and communication systems, and basic social services.

Table 3.1 makes this very clear. Public ownership of major industries and services is compared for five Western nations: France, Britain, West Germany, Canada, and the United States. The amount of private ownership in the United States is striking. Note that this table presents data on *ownership*, not on government regulation or support. The airline industry is as closely regulated in the United

Natural resources, though often developed with government assistance, remain under private ownership in the United States.

States as it is in the other four nations. But each of the other nations has a major government-owned airline: Lufthansa in Germany, Air France in France, British Airways in Britain, and Air Canada in Canada. There is no publicly owned airline in the United States. Gas and electricity are wholly state owned in the three European democracies and 80 percent state owned in Canada. In the United States, the manufacture and distribution of gas are overwhelmingly in private hands, while the ownership of electricity is mixed; some firms are privately owned (Pacific Gas and Electric) and some publicly owned (Tennessee Valley Authority).

The resistance in America to public ownership of major businesses can be seen in the recent history of the railroads. Railroads, especially in the northeastern part of the nation, have been operating at a loss. Under a free-enterprise system a business that could not make a profit would simply close up shop. Yet if the product of that business is a socially valued product that is too expensive for private enterprise to maintain, closing down the business would be socially harmful. Certainly a transportation network that carries millions of passengers and millions of tons of freight is an important asset to society.

TABLE 3.1
Public Ownership of Various Industries and Services

	Roads	Postal Services	Electricity	Rail ways	Telephones	Airlines	Radio, Television	Gas	Coal	Oil	Steel	Banks
France	S	S	S	S	S	S/p	S	S	S	S	P	S/p
Great Britain	S	S	S	S	S	S/p	S/p	S	S	s	S	P
West Germany	S	S	S	S	S	S	S	S	s	P	P	P
Canada	S	S	S/p	S/p	s	S/p	S/p	P	P	P	P	P
United States	S	S	s	s	P	P	P	P	P	P	P	P

S   = predominantly state ownership.
s   = element of state ownership in predominantly private system.
S/p = state and private sectors both substantial.
P   = predominantly private sector.
Source: Based on Anthony King, "Ideas, Institutions and the Policies of Governments: A Comparative Analysis: Parts I and II," *British Journal of Political Science*, 3 (July 1973), 296.

Unlike most nations of the world, the United States has no State-owned airline.

In most countries a bankrupt but important transportation system would be taken over by the government. Or such a valuable national asset would have been state owned in the first place. People who have used the efficient rail services in Holland or Switzerland, indeed throughout Europe, have used state-owned and state-managed railroads.

The response in the United States has been different. A government agency, the U.S. Railway Association, was formed to restructure rail service in 17 northeastern and midwestern states. In early 1975 this agency announced a vast long-term plan, eventually to cost $7 billion. No public ownership is involved. Instead, there will be a private corporation, aided with large amounts of federal money, to take charge of the restructuring and to manage the new rail system.

INDIVIDUAL ECONOMIC CHOICE

The economy is regulated and managed by the government. And many resources and powers are concentrated in large corporations. Yet we live in a society in which many economic activities are a result of thousands and even millions of uncoordinated and unregulated individual choices. Consider New York City, the residence of eight million people and the work place for thousands more who pour into the city each day. How are these millions of people to be fed? Certainly they do not grow their own crops or fatten their own livestock. Rather, they depend on a daily supply of food coming into the city—a supply that comes from fifty states and dozens of nations: Wisconsin milk, Iowa beef, French cheeses, Brazilian coffee. Some of the food has been traveling for months.

What can be said about the process that puts food on the tables of New Yorkers? That there is an immense network of food production and processing, packaging and transportation, marketing and sales. That this network functions without direction or coordination by any central agency. It rests on millions of individual economic activities: growing, producing, exchanging, selling, transporting.

This example reminds us that much economic life occurs without the involvement of either government planning bureaus or corporate oligopolies. The example of feeding New Yorkers is only one of many that could be cited. Consider the thousands of American families that move each week. These moves reflect economic decisions as breadwinners seek new jobs, new neighborhoods, or new housing. No agency regulates or coordinates the population shifts that take place in America.

If an economy is capitalist when it allows citizens to choose what to buy, where to live, what jobs to seek, how much of their earnings to save and how much to spend, then the American economy is capitalist. We often take note of how much the government does to control economic activities. And we often see that the powers of corporations restrict the choices open to the individual citizen. We will discuss these controls and restraints in the next section, where we describe contemporary capitalism. But it would not do to leave out the many ways in which economic activities are based on individual choices.

A MATERIAL INCENTIVE SYSTEM

Democratic ideology rejects inequalities based on "natural" superiority or inferiority. In the words of the Declaration of the Rights of Man and Citizens, proclaimed in France in 1789, "Men are born and remain free and equal in rights." But democratic ideology does not reject inequality itself, as that radical declaration makes clear: "Social differences can only be based on general utility."

"Social differences based on general utility" can be translated into three propositions:[5]

1. Certain jobs are more important to society than others; some are so important that if they are poorly performed society itself suffers.
2. Certain jobs, often the socially important ones, require long and difficult training and are not easy to carry out.
3. People will work only if given suitable rewards.

It is the third proposition that is of interest: People work when they are rewarded. If they are not rewarded, they do not work, or at least they work less. The question arises: What are the rewards to be? A capitalist society stresses money as the reward, though of course the payment of different wages for different jobs is not true only of capitalism. It occurs in communist countries such as China or socialist countries such as Tanzania.

But capitalism declares differential wages for different jobs to be a basic principle. People's worth is measured by the income they can attract when they place their talents and skills on the market. If the shop foreman earns twice what the assembly line worker does, this is because the foreman's job requires more experience, skill, and responsibility. If the owner of the factory, in turn, earns several times what the foreman does, this is because the owner, after all, took the risk and established the business that now provides employment and income in the community. If line workers are good at production, their reward is in their paychecks, perhaps even in a promotion. If the foreman fails to manage the workers, his punishment is the suggestion that he seek a job elsewhere. If the owner makes an error in judgment, perhaps bankruptcy follows. If she is innovative, perhaps a fortune follows.

The deliberate use of unequal wages to attract talented individuals to key positions, and to motivate them to work hard, is a basic tenet of capitalism. The large majority of Americans endorse this principle. They believe that individual initiative and hard work should be rewarded and laziness and incompetence punished. As we will see in the next chapter, this leads to substantial gaps between the highest and the lowest incomes—though it is not always clear that income differences are related only to different levels of effort and different talents.

---

[5] What is often called the "functional theory of social stratification" is an elaboration on these propositions. The argument is developed in Kingsley Davis and Wilbert E. Moore, "Some Principles of Stratification," *American Sociological Review*, 10 (April 1945), 242–249.

Private ownership, unplanned and uncoordinated economic exchanges, and a material reward system are important features of economic life in the United States. They distinguish the American capitalist economy from, say, the economy of Russia or China. In Russia, greater emphasis is put on centralized authority to direct behavior in socially productive ways. In China, there is more emphasis on the techniques of education and propaganda to instill appropriate social values in the population. The United States relies more on the marketplace, the incentives, the temptations, and the coercive nature of economic reward.

Contemporary Capitalism

Two facts are now clear. First, the government is heavily into economic affairs. This is shown by the importance to society of the annual government budget, possibly the single most critical document produced by the government. (See Chapter 14.) It is shown in the structure of the government. The President's Cabinet includes Secretaries of Commerce, Agriculture, Labor, Treasury, Transportation; important executive agencies include the Federal Trade Commission, the Interstate Commerce Commission, the Securities and Exchange Commission; the most powerful committees in Congress are those that deal with taxation, budget review, and appropriations. (See Chapters 12 and 13.) Through its involvement in the economy, the government supports private enterprise, regulates economic activities, and attempts to manage general economic conditions.

The second fact, however, balances this picture of government involvement. Major features of capitalism remain. Private individuals own the mines, the trucks, the chemicals, the factories, the grocery stores, and the land of America. These private individuals are very often organized as corporations, and the amount of resources and wealth controlled by the larger corporations is great indeed. Because the economy is privately owned, it is run in order to make profits for the owners.

We now reach an important point in our discussion. We have on the one hand an interventionist government. We have on the other hand huge privately owned corporations that can be influenced, for better or worse, by the activities of the government. What is the outcome of this situation?

Most observers agree that the United States has evolved into a partnership between the state and the economy. Large economic units, including not only corporations such as General Motors or Sears Roebuck but also organized labor, have joined in a partnership with the government. It is not without strains and differences of opinion, but it is held together by some important shared goals.

Economist John Kenneth Galbraith, in *The New Industrial State,* spells out the chief goals of the state: "The state is strongly concerned with the stability of the economy. And with its expansion or growth. And with education. And with technical and scientific advance. And, most notably, with the national defense."[6] These national goals have their counterparts in the corporate sector: Stability is necessary to long-term planning; economic growth brings profits, promotions, and prestige; trained manpower, scientific research, and technical development are necessary to a modern industrial system; defense spending directly supports, through government contracts, a large part of the economy. There are, then, shared goals between the public and the private sectors, between government and corporation leaders.

CRITICS OF CONTEMPORARY CAPITALISM

Although most observers agree on the facts of the partnership between the economy and the government, not all feel comfortable with these facts. The critics note that the growth of concentrated economic and political power, and especially the joint operation of these powers, makes it more and more difficult for citizens to control their own lives.

Milton Friedman, a professor at the University of Chicago, is one such critic. Freedom, he writes, "is a rare and delicate plant." Great care is necessary to protect it. "Our minds tell us, and history confirms, that the great threat to freedom is the concentration of power." Friedman is especially concerned about concentration of power in the government. Although government is necessary to preserve freedom, it can also threaten freedom. The truly free person will ask, "How can we keep the government from becoming a Frankenstein that will destroy the very freedom we establish it to protect?"[7]

In this analysis it is the concentration of power in the government that is to be avoided. The government has grown huge because it is so involved in the economy. If it allowed the economy to take care of itself, the need for large government bureaucracies and budgets would be less. And there would be less risk that the government would restrict individual freedom.

Other critics give more attention to the dangers of concentrated economic power. This criticism takes note of the ease with which great wealth in the hands of a small group can be converted into political control. If there are great inequalities of control over economic resources, the argument goes, it is hard to see how the equal political influence promised by a democracy is possible.

Paul Baran and Paul Sweezy, noted Marxist economists, claim that "the incessant repetition that the political regime in the United States today is a democracy" is a falsehood "devoid of all descriptive or explanatory validity." In the United States, they continue, "the propertyless masses have never been in a position to determine the

[6] John Kenneth Galbraith, *The New Industrial State* (Boston: Houghton Mifflin, 1967), p. 304.
[7] Milton Friedman, *Capitalism and Freedom* (Chicago: University of Chicago Press, 1962), p. 2.

conditions of their lives or the policies of the nation's government."
A tiny group "resting on vast economic power and in full control of
society's political and cultural apparatus makes all the important
political decisions. Clearly to claim that such a society is democratic serves to conceal, not to reveal, the truth."[8]

Whether they express fear of government power or fear of corporate power, the critics share a concern that the political-economic
partnership in the United States is a threat to individual liberty and
democratic values, a fear that is somewhat confirmed in this book.
Friedman's concern over the erosion of individual liberty, for instance, seems to be well founded when we begin to review the
enormous government bureaucracy and the range of government
regulations that impinge on individual citizens. And the strong
language of Baran and Sweezy, who claim that the wealthy class of
owners and managers is not subjected to democratic controls, is
supported by evidence of how economic inequality affects political
participation (Chapter 7) and political recruitment (Chapter 8) and
by data on the strong role of interest groups (Chapter 9) and the
weaker role of parties (Chapter 10).

SUPPORTERS OF CONTEMPORARY CAPITALISM

Balanced against the critics are the voices of other observers who
believe the partnership between the government and the economy is
healthy. In this view a powerful government and a powerful corporate economy have joined forces to secure beneficial goals: a
steady growth in production based primarily on improved technology and efficiency; a steady increase in consumer goods, which
means higher standards of living; international stability and larger
world markets for American products; constant improvement of
public education to supply trained men and women. Those who
speak in favor of the American political economy take into account
the problems of poverty, unemployment, and inflation but believe
the best way to solve such problems is to strengthen rather than
weaken the partnership between a public government and a private
economy.

THE POLITICAL ECONOMY: CONTEXT FOR ANALYSIS

The critics as well as the supporters of contemporary capitalism
raise important points; these points will be considered from a
variety of viewpoints in later chapters. Indeed, the picture of the
American economy and government that emerges from this chapter
is in large part the context within which many aspects of politics
must be examined. In the next chapter, for example, we look more
closely at the tension between citizenship equalities, on the one
hand, and economic inequalities, on the other. In later chapters we

[8] Paul A. Baran and Paul M. Sweezy, *Monopoly Capital: An Essay on the American
Economic and Social Order* (London: Pelican, 1968), p. 327.

review how citizens' political participation and choice of leaders are affected by the distribution of wealth. The economy also sets the context within which many political conflicts take place. For example, interest groups compete to attract federal moneys to the causes they represent, as when a truckers' association wants more money spent on the federal highway program and a citizen action group wants that money spent on mass transportation. Because so many of the issues of American politics are derived from contemporary capitalism, the formulation of public policies in the legislative, executive, and judicial branches of government is closely linked with the political economy. As briefly noted earlier, the organization of the government reflects concern with the economy. There are huge government programs that fund research and train personnel; there are huge government bureaucracies that regulate economic activities; there is the taxing and spending power of government, which is used to influence prices, employment, and private investment.

As we turn to the actual working of the national, state, and local governments in the United States, we will be constantly reminded that there are political-economic conditions that loom large in the who, what, how, and why of American politics.

A general conclusion emerges from our discussion of the close partnership between government and business and between the state and the economy. Neither government nor business can exist independently of the other. We have seen that government provides the framework of laws that allows businesses to operate. It is also the government that provides the currency needed for economic exchanges, the police force that protects private property, and the courts that enforce economic contracts. Business could not operate without the active support and cooperation of government.

The reverse is true as well. Government could not govern without the active support and cooperation of business. Taxes that pay government salaries and fund government programs come from the private economy. It is the economy that produces the consumption goods so sought after and valued by the American citizen. It is the economy that produces the jobs for American citizens, without which there is political and social instability for government to contend with. The American "way of life" is also dependent upon imports from other nations, especially natural resources such as oil and minerals. Only a productive economy will have the goods that can be traded with other nations.

Our conclusion, then, is that the most important "business" of government may be to provide for a healthy capitalist economy. Both Democratic and Republican administrations understand this. Political careers are jeopardized when the state of the economy is poor. Voters tend to blame whichever political party is in power when jobs are scarce, when prices increase faster than wages, or when savings are eroded by inflation. Simply, when the economy fails, governments tend to fall. It is, therefore, in the interest of most politicians and government leaders to encourage economic growth and to be attentive to the requests of business. This strengthens the close partnership between the capitalist economy and the democratic state, but it also creates certain tensions in American life—one of which is the topic of the next chapter: A capitalist economy depends upon inequalities of wealth and income, whereas a democratic polity promises citizenship equality.

4
POLITICAL EQUALITY, SOCIAL INEQUALITY

Does "One Person, One Vote" Lead to "One Person, One Dollar"?

Not at all. The commitment to political equality suggested by the phrase "one person, one vote" does not translate into economic or social equality. America proclaims *political equality* as part of the democratic creed while preserving and even praising *economic inequality* as part of the capitalist creed. Charles A. Beard, in his famous book *The Economic Basis of Politics*, saw this as a major paradox:

> Modern equalitarian democracy, which reckons all heads as equal and alike, cuts sharply athwart the philosophy and practice of the past centuries. Nevertheless, the democratic device of universal suffrage does not destroy economic classes or economic inequalities. It ignores them. Herein lies the paradox, the most astounding political contradiction that the world has ever witnessed.[1]

This "astounding political contradiction" is what this chapter is about. First we look at the idea of democratic citizenship and how this idea has affected equality in the United States over the past 200 years. Then we turn to some facts and figures that demonstrate just how much economic inequality there is in the United States, despite the doctrine of citizenship equality. The next task is to review four major political strategies that are thought to create a more economically equal society: the progressive income tax, social-welfare programs, the War on Poverty, and affirmative-action programs. This review teaches us that economic inequalities are quite resistent to political challenges.

We conclude the chapter by returning to the "astounding political contradiction" of citizenship equality on the one hand and sharp economic inequalities on the other. With this contradiction firmly understood, though not yet explained, we will be prepared for the subsequent chapters, in which various pieces of the explanation will begin to fall into place.

Democracy and Equality

"We hold these truths to be self-evident," says the Declaration of Independence, "that all men are created equal." Those who signed

[1] Charles A. Beard, *The Economic Basis of Politics* (New York: Vintage, 1960), p. 69.

One person, one vote does not produce one person, one dollar.

this document knew, of course, that all people were not created equal; differences in ability, intelligence, ambition, and talent could hardly be denied. Yet they were not just spouting empty political slogans. The signers wanted to go on record against a political order in which members of society were *legally* unequal.

In this regard the nation's founders were being boldly innovative. They were deliberately breaking with traditions in which members of society are assigned to different legal classes. In those traditions certain privileges and rights would be allowed to one class of citizens but denied to others. For instance, to be allowed to participate in the exercise of public authority one had to belong to the nobility. The commoners or serfs were legally inferior. They were subordinate to the law that was fashioned by the nobility.

A term often used in discussions of first- and second-class citizenship is *aristocracy:* rule by the "best," which usually meant the wealthy and the privileged. The aristocratic justification of different classes of citizenship is well summarized in the following passage:

The lot of the poor, in all things which affect them collectively, should be regulated for them, not by them. They should not be required or encouraged to think for themselves, or give to their own reflection or forecast an influential voice in the determination of the destiny. It is the duty of the higher classes to think for them, and to take responsibility for their lot. . . . The rich should be [like parents] to the poor, guiding and restraining them like children.[2]

Democratic thought contrasts sharply with this point of view. It rejects the idea that people who are richer, more accomplished, more intelligent, or of nobler birth than others are somehow "better." The principle of citizenship elbows aside the ancient beliefs that formed the basis of monarchies, aristocracies, hereditary privileges, a class system, and racial prejudice. It is no accident that the principle of equal worth developed at the same time as radical religious movements. The idea that all people are equal in the eyes of God gave rise to the idea that all people are equal in the eyes of the state.

It is of course true that the principle of equal worth is not completely accepted, and probably never will be. Nevertheless it is deeply rooted in Western political systems. Justifications for special status or hereditary rights have been undermined, and this in itself is a major achievement. This does not mean that privileges and special rights no longer exist, but it does mean that they no longer have the open protection of the state.

The constitutional guarantees of citizenship are supposed to bring about the equality promised by the Declaration of Independence. The two major forms of citizenship protected by the Constitution are *legal citizenship* and *political citizenship.*

[2] John Stuart Mill, *Principles of Political Economy, II* (Boston: Little, Brown, 1848), pp. 319–320. Here Mill is summarizing the aristocratic viewpoint, not endorsing it.

Legal Citizenship

Early American political history was dominated by legal-constitutional issues. The problems to be solved included the definition of citizenship rights and the extension of these rights to the entire population. Legal citizenship, or what we today call civil rights, includes the basic freedoms of speech, worship, and assembly. It also includes economic rights, especially the right to acquire and dispose of property, the right to choose one's place and type of work, and the right to enter into valid contracts knowing that they will be upheld in courts of law.

The institutions that are central to legal citizenship are the courts. And here the basic citizenship principle is called *due process of law.* This refers to many things: A citizen is presumed innocent until proved guilty. A citizen has the right to be tried by a jury of fellow citizens. No one can be kept in jail unless there is reasonable evidence that he or she is guilty of a crime. Due process of law also includes the right to legal counsel, the protection against self-incrimination (no one can be forced to testify against himself or herself), the right to face and to question witnesses, and protection from unreasonable searches such as telephone taps.

In later chapters, in which we review the role of the courts and discuss basic freedoms in detail, we will see that the translation of citizenship principles into specific laws is an ongoing process.

Political Citizenship

The second major form of citizenship is political participation. Democratic theory states that government should be based on the consent of the people. Because all members of society are governed, they should all have an equal right to choose the governors. The principle of equal political citizenship is clearly stated in *The Federalist* (No. 57):

> *Who are to be the electors of the federal representatives?*
> Not the rich, more than the poor; not the learned, more than the ignorant; not the haughty heirs of distinguished names, more than the humble sons of obscurity and unpropitious fortune. The electors are to be the great body of the people of the United States.

Perhaps the authors of *The Federalist Papers* believed that the Constitution they had helped write guaranteed these equalities. However, they forgot two things: Many barriers were placed between the voter and the government, and the Constitution did not actually guarantee universal suffrage. Until the Seventeenth Amendment was passed in 1913, senators were chosen by state legislatures rather than by the voters. Of course, as prescribed by the Constitution, the President is not directly elected but is chosen by the Electoral College. Furthermore, Supreme Court justices are appointed rather than elected.

THE GROWTH OF VOTING RIGHTS

The Constitution did not really answer the question of who may vote and under what conditions. This has required no fewer than four amendments.

Initially the Constitution left voting laws to the states; if a person could not vote in a state election, he could not vote in a federal election. Generally states restricted the vote to white male property owners. And in some states as few as 10 percent of the white males could vote. During the Presidency of Andrew Jackson (1829–1837), most property standards were dropped, and universal (white) manhood suffrage became the rule. America was hailed as a model for the democratic world. It was fifty years before Britain reached the same level of voting rights.

Still, as Figure 4.1 shows, less than 40 percent of the adult population could vote at the time of the Civil War. Blacks of course were forbidden to vote in the South, and with few exceptions they were also unable to vote in the North. After the Civil War the Fifteenth Amendment established that "the right of citizens of the United States to vote shall not be denied or abridged by the United States or by any State on account of race, color, or previous condition of servitude." But in the South the reality of blacks voting faded with the end of Reconstruction. When white southerners got back in control of their state governments, they moved quickly to undermine the Fifteenth Amendment through such means as the poll tax (one had to pay to vote), phony literacy tests, and the all-white primary, as well as intimidation and violence.

FIGURE 4.1
Proportion of the Adult Population Eligible to Register to Vote, 1860–1970

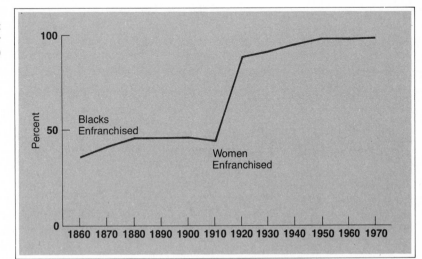

Source: Robert Lane, *Political Life* (New York: Free Press, 1959), p. 21; U.S. Department of Commerce, Bureau of the Census, *Statistical Abstract of the United States: 1969* (Washington, D.C., 1969), p. 369.

Throughout the late 1800s the electorate continued to grow as new states were added and large numbers of immigrants arrived. However, although some blacks could vote in some areas, and although women were gaining the right to vote a little at a time, in the early twentieth century most of the electorate was white and male.

The next major expansion of the electorate was the addition of women. In 1869 Wyoming became the first state to grant voting rights to women; it was followed by several other states, chiefly in the West. The drive for women's rights—the suffragette movement—was led by, among others Susan B. Anthony and Elizabeth Cady Stanton. Beginning in 1917 the suffragettes began marching in front of the White House, only to be arrested and jailed. Their cause triumphed in 1920 with the adoption of the Nineteenth Amendment, which states that the right to vote cannot be denied on account of sex.

Over the past decade federal action has been taken to remove barriers set up by certain states and localities. In 1964 the Twenty-Fourth Amendment banned the use of the poll tax in federal elections, and the Voting Rights Act of 1965 extended the ban to cover state elections. But the real significance of the Voting Act was to put federal authority behind the drive to enable southern blacks to vote: Federal examiners were given the power to register voters. The effect of this legislation was dramatic. Between 1964 and 1968 black registration in the eleven southern states increased by over 50 percent. (See Table 4.1.) In 1970 Congress extended and broadened the Voting Rights Act to suspend the use of literacy and character tests in all states and to establish uniform residency requirements (30 days) for voting in federal elections.

**TABLE 4.1
Estimated Percent of
Blacks Registered to Vote in
Southern States, 1940–1970**

Year	Percent Registered
1940	5%
1952	21
1960	28
1964	45
1968	62
1970	66

Source: Based on data reported in The American Negro Reference Book (Englewood Cliffs, N.J.: Prentice-Hall, 1966); Harry A. Polshi and Ernest Kaiser, eds., The Negro Almanac (New York: Bellwether, 1971).

The suffrage was extended again in 1971 with the Twenty-Sixth Amendment, which lowered the voting age to 18. About 10.5 million people were thus added to the electorate.

The history of citizenship rights starts with the principle that all citizens are to be treated equally. There is to be no such thing as first- and second-class citizenship, with one group having rights and privileges denied to the other. We have already begun to see that actual practice has often failed to live up to this principle. In particular, black Americans and other minorities, as well as women of all races, have found their legal and political rights to be less than those of white males.

SECOND-CLASS CITIZENSHIP: SLAVERY

The essence of slavery is the denial of citizenship. Slavery was protected by law in the United States until after the Civil War, and of course in the eighteenth century most American blacks were slaves. Slaves could not say what they wanted to, be with people they wanted to be with, sell their labor power to the highest bidder, or enter into binding contracts. American citizenship gave people the right to the product of their labor; slavery forbade this right. Despite the promises of the Declaration of Independence, the Constitution allowed a double standard. One class of people had rights and privileges that were denied to another class.

At first this double standard was not a racist doctrine. It separated free people and slaves, but it did not separate whites and blacks. And there were free blacks. Nearly 100,000 had escaped slavery; they had bought their freedom or been given it by their owners and lived in the North and West much like other citizens. They paid taxes, voted, and in a few cases held political office. But in 1857 this was changed by the infamous Dred Scott case, which held that blacks, free or slave, "had no rights which the white man was bound to respect."

Dual citizenship based on race continued long after the Civil War had officially ended slavery. The clear language of the Fourteenth Amendment, "all persons born or naturalized in the United States, and subject to the jurisdiction thereof, are citizens of the United States. . . . No state shall make or enforce any law which shall abridge the privileges or immunities of citizens," was modified by later court decisions and blocked by the "Jim Crow" society.

Jim Crow laws allowed nearly total segregation of blacks into separate and inferior institutions. As described by the Commission on Civil Rights (1963), Jim Crow was applied to "waiting rooms, theaters, boardinghouses, water fountains, ticket windows, streetcars, penitentiaries, county jails, convict camps, institutions for the blind and deaf, and hospitals for the insane." This is just a partial list. Jim Crow laws affected schools, businesses, clubs, churches, and the armed forces. Facilities reserved for blacks were always inferior, though equal prices had to be paid for the unequal services.

Dramatic increases in black voter participation followed federal voter registration in the South.

Racist ideologies received the backing of the Supreme Court. As Justice Brown remarked in *Plessy* v. *Ferguson* (1896), the case that established the "separate but equal doctrine," which remained in force until 1954: "If one race be inferior to another socially, the Constitution of the United States cannot put them upon the same plane." So much for the Fourteenth Amendment, and so much for the idea that citizenship placed everyone on an equal footing before the law.

In Chapter 15 and elsewhere we will review the court cases and political programs that have slowly been reversing the racist doctrines that established slavery in the first place and led to the Jim Crow society after the Civil War. Later in this chapter we begin a discussion of *affirmative action,* a political movement and a set of government programs. Affirmative action—or what some call "reverse discrimination"—is today being proposed as the major method of further reducing second-class citizenship for racial minorities and, increasingly, for women.

SECOND-CLASS CITIZENSHIP: WOMEN

"Equality of rights under the law shall not be denied or abridged by the United States or by any state on account of sex." These are the terms of the Equal Rights Amendment, which has been passed by Congress and by 35 of the 38 states that must ratify it before it becomes the Twenty-Seventh Amendment to the Constitution. Two hundred years after the Declaration of Independence, women are trying to gain the same rights in society as men.

Women have long been second-class citizens. Except in some state and local elections, women were not allowed to vote until 1920. Certain government jobs, especially in the military, have until recently been reserved for males. Many states have laws that discriminate against women in property ownership, in employment and salaries, and in the terms of marriage and divorce. Women find it hard to get loans because credit agencies see them as "bad risks."

In addition to legal and political discrimination, there are many informal barriers to full women's rights. Women are paid less than men, even for doing the same work. (See Figure 4.2.) And women have had a difficult time reaching high positions. There are very few women among the directors and officers of the largest corporations in America. There are 300,000 doctors in the United States; fewer than 10 percent are women. The number of women in political office is small: There is at present one woman in the Senate, only 18 (out of 435) women in the House of Representatives, and 2 women governors.

The Equal Rights Amendment attempts to eliminate the legal barriers that have prevented women from enjoying equal rights with men. It states that women are to be absolutely equal to men. For this reason some women's groups have opposed it because it provides "too much" equality. For instance, it makes women equally liable for child support when a couple gets a divorce, equally subject

FIGURE 4.2
Women Doing the Same Work
as Men Receive Less Pay

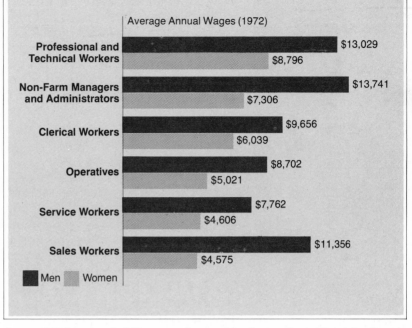

FIGURE 4.2
Women Doing the Same Work
as Men Receive Less Pay

Average Annual Wages (1972)

Professional and Technical Workers — $13,029 / $8,796
Non-Farm Managers and Administrators — $13,741 / $7,306
Clerical Workers — $9,656 / $6,039
Operatives — $8,702 / $5,021
Service Workers — $7,762 / $4,606
Sales Workers — $11,356 / $4,575

Men / Women

Source: U.S. Department of Commerce, Bureau of the Census, *Current Population Reports*, Series P-60, no. 90 (Washington, D.C., December 1973).

to the military draft (should it ever be reinstated), and no longer exempt from dangerous jobs such as mining.

The Equal Rights Amendment to the Constitution is but one of many legal and political challenges to second-class citizenship for women. In 1978 there were over 100 bills and resolutions in Congress that, if passed, would affect women's rights. For example, the Pregnancy Disability Act would prohibit sex discrimination on the basis of pregnancy. Employers would have to cover pregnant workers under standard health insurance programs and under temporary disability plans so that a woman who became pregnant would not risk losing her job. Related to questions of employment are dozens of other bills that would authorize more flexible work hours for working mothers with small children. There are also proposals for increasing and improving day care facilities.

Protection of rape victims is another issue that has come before legislators and judges. A provision of a bill currently in Congress would protect rape victims from being cross-examined on their sexual histories in federal courts. The Supreme Court has also dealt with complicated questions surrounding rape. For instance, in mid-1977 the Court ruled that it is unconstitutional to impose the death penalty as punishment for the rape of an adult woman. This ruling was interpreted as a victory by important women's-rights groups.

The reason for the death penalty for rape in the first place, these groups argued, was related to the idea that a wife was her husband's property and that rape was therefore a crime against a man's property. To strike down the death penalty was indirectly to affirm the legal independence of women.

One of the most hotly debated questions in the area of women's rights is that of abortion. Over the past decade restrictions against abortion have gradually been weakened, until today the legal barriers are practically nonexistent. But economic barriers persist. In the mid-1970s as many as 300,000 women a year were having abortions that were paid for out of medicaid funds (government-supported medical-care programs). Under pressure from the "right to life" groups, Congress and the Supreme Court considered this issue in 1977. The Court ruled that neither the Constitution nor current federal law requires states to use federal funds for elective abortions. Moreover, public hospitals are not required under the Constitution to provide or even permit elective abortions. In short, women can have abortions but may not pass the bill along to the taxpayer.

The attack on second-class citizenship for women is a broad one. It is far from finished. As we will see later in the chapter, there are certain affirmative-action programs that are designed to overcome disadvantages that women have experienced in the economy, in social life, and in legal rights.

SECOND-CLASS CITIZENSHIP: MINORS

In 1971 nine students were suspended from Columbus, Ohio high schools after a period of student unrest and racial demonstrations. The suspensions were for less than ten days, but they went onto the students' records. The action took place without any formal hearings. The suspended students challenged the procedures, claiming that they were deprived of liberty (though no proof of involvement in the demonstrations was provided) and of property (their legal right to an education) without due process of law. Thus, the students argued, the action by the school authorities violated the Fourteenth Amendment.

In 1975 the students' case came before the Supreme Court. In a split decision (five to four) the Court ruled in favor of the students.[3] Public school authorities cannot suspend students without following certain basic procedures: giving formal notice of the charges, explaining the evidence against the student, and allowing students to present their side of the story.

In other words, students had rights. And these rights could be supported in federal courts. The case has important implications for school systems around the country. It is estimated that as many as 10 percent of all students in urban schools are suspended at least once a year; in New York City alone there are 20,000 suspensions a year. Because these suspensions become part of a student's record,

[3] *Goss* v. *Lopez* 73-898 U.S. (1975).

no doubt having a negative effect on job and college applications, the majority of the Supreme Court justices felt that students should be allowed at least to present their case.

Note, however, that the Court did not grant full rights of due process. A suspended student cannot hire a lawyer, cross-examine witnesses, call his or her own witnesses, or have a jury trial. A suspension is not the same as a sentence for a crime, and it is understandable that the full range of rights given an accused criminal are not given a suspended student. The Court did leave open the possibility that more formal proceedings would be required when students were suspended for a long time or expelled from school.

The Supreme Court ruling has opened wider than ever the complex issue of the rights of minors. It is true that minors have always been "second-class" citizens in the sense that they do not vote, cannot run for office, cannot enter binding contracts without parental permission, and are politically and legally limited in lots of other ways. It is also true that minors receive special protection from the state. A minor convicted of a crime, even murder, is treated much less harshly than an adult convicted of the same crime.

Citizenship rights for minors is a new area of concern for constitutional lawyers and judges. It is too early to know the end result of what is sure to be a long and sometimes painful process. But it is clear that the momentum that has forced major changes in the citizenship rights of minority groups and women will change the way minors are treated in the legal and political processes of the nation.

We have reviewed two general themes in citizenship—equal legal rights and equal political rights. These were the rights with which the Constitution was primarily concerned. And normally it is thought that if these rights can truly be equally available to all members of society, then the promise of democracy will have been kept. But there is a third form of citizenship that occupies more political attention today than either of the others.

Social-Rights Citizenship: A New View of Equality

President Roosevelt's twelfth State of the Union Address, delivered in 1944, contained a surprising departure from earlier definitions of citizenship. His speech began on a familiar note: "The Republic," he said, "had its beginning and grew to its present strength, under the protection of certain unalienable political rights—among them the right of free speech, free press, free worship, trial by jury, freedom from unreasonable searches and seizures. They were our rights of life and liberty." As he continued, however, he spoke of America's failure to provide for its citizens and stated the principle behind a whole new area of citizens' rights. He said that the legal and

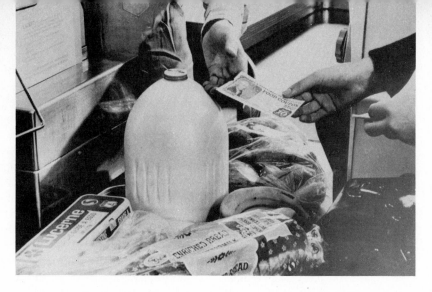

Social citizenship includes the right to an adequate diet, which food stamps help provide.

political rights set forth in the Constitution were not enough and that citizenship must include social well-being and security against economic injustices.

> As our Nation has grown strong in size and stature, however — as our industrial economy has expanded — these political rights proved inadequate to assure us equality in the pursuit of happiness. . . . We have come to a clear realization of the fact that true individual freedom cannot exist without economic security and independence.

Roosevelt also mentioned areas in which the rights of social citizenship should apply:

> We have accepted, so to speak, a second Bill of Rights under which a new basis of security and prosperity can be established for all — regardless of station, race, or creed.

Among these rights are

- The right to a useful and remunerative job in the industries or shops or farms or mines of the Nation.
- The right of every farmer to raise and sell his products at a return which will give him and his family a decent living.
- The right to earn enough to provide adequate food and clothing and recreation.
- The right of every businessman, large and small, to trade in an atmosphere of freedom from unfair competition and domination by monopolies at home or abroad.
- The right of every family to a decent home.
- The right to adequate medical care and the opportunity to achieve and enjoy good health.
- The right to adequate protection from the economic fears of old age, sickness, accident, and unemployment.
- The right to a good education.

When Roosevelt used the word *right,* he was describing a new concept of citizenship, a citizenship enlarged far beyond what was included under the original concept of due process of law. Roosevelt was also summarizing his understanding of what had been accomplished by the New Deal legislation passed during the economic depression of the 1930s. In a major address to the parliament of India in January of 1978, President Carter repeated the theme used by Roosevelt. "While civil and political liberties are good in themselves," said Carter, "to have sufficient food to live and to work, to be adequately sheltered and clothed, to live in a healthy environment and to be healed when sick, to learn and be taught — these rights too must be the concerns of our Government." There are three important things to understand about the concept of social citizenship and legislation that intends to establish it: (1) social citizenship and the social-welfare state, (2) social citizenship and the market system, and (3) social citizenship and economic inequality.

The Social-Welfare State   To hold out the promise of social citizenship is to actively involve the government in creating what is best known as the social-welfare state. This is a state in which the basic rights of the sort listed by President Roosevelt — a useful job, decent housing, an adequate diet, medical care, education, and economic security against the threats of sickness, unemployment, and old age — are brought about by direct government action. Social citizenship, then, is a major component of the activist state.

The past four decades have been a period of much direct government action of this sort, especially, but not only, at the federal level. And though Democratic administrations have been more active than Republican administrations, the latter have not dismantled the social-welfare state and in some instances have promoted new programs. The government programs that make up the social-welfare state include social security, unemployment insurance, urban renewal and housing, food stamps for the poor, medicare and medicaid, job training, and aid to mothers of dependent children. In addition, the earliest "welfare program," public education, has grown. These programs have given rise to great controversy, and even today many of the most hotly debated public issues are in the area of social-rights citizenship: federal support for education, the negative income tax, the minimum wage, a national health insurance program, public housing, and increasingly, consumer protection. What is interesting about these debates, however, is that even conservatives accept some form of welfare state. This is a major change from earlier conservative thought.

Social Citizenship and the Market System   A traditional market system is one in which supply and demand are in balance, with goods and services priced according to what "the market will bear" or according to what people are willing to pay. In a market system people with more resources are presumably able to buy a greater amount and a higher quality of goods and services than people with fewer resources. This is one of the reasons that people are willing to work hard in order to earn the income that can be translated into more and better things.

The idea of social citizenship does not destroy the traditional market system, but it certainly affects it. For some people, often a large number, social services are separated from the market price system. People who are strongly committed to the free-enterprise system don't like this. Medical care, housing, food, insurance, and even education have traditionally been priced in terms of what the market will bear. Who gets what quantity of these various social benefits depends on purchasing power. Those who can pay get better medical treatment, better housing, more nourishing food, more security against illness and old age, and better education. Those who are "worth less" get fewer of these benefits of society, or the quality of the benefits they receive is lower.

Social-rights citizenship separates social services from the price system by shifting them from the private to the public domain in the name of citizenship. A decent standard of living is said to be a right rather than a privilege to be paid for, or a gift. The activist state, rather than the market place, provides these rights.

Social Citizenship and Economic Inequality It might be thought that the notion that citizenship implies social as well as legal and political rights would substantially affect economic inequality. The poorer classes in society would use their equal political rights to work the social-welfare system in such a way that great disparities in wealth and income would be reduced. The "astounding political contradiction" with which we began this chapter would wither away, and America would become an egalitarian state in the economic as well as the legal-political sense.

But the contradiction has not withered away. As we will see in the next section, there is as much economic inequality today as there was fifty years ago, before the depression of the 1930s and the establishment of a social-welfare state. After looking at the pattern of inequality, we will review some specific programs in order to better understand why the idea of social citizenship can coexist with economic inequality.

Economic Inequality in the United States

In the previous chapter we learned that the doctrine of capitalism includes the principle of unequal rewards for different tasks. Under capitalism men and women sell their labor power to the highest bidder. The more valuable their labor power, the higher the wages they can command. Unequal economic rewards are viewed as fair: More talented and harder-working people should receive greater rewards than the less talented and the lazy. And unequal economic rewards are viewed as practical: Society needs an incentive system to ensure that the most important positions are filled by the people who are best able to perform well in them. Unequal economic re-

Capitalism stresses the need for economic incentives but does not answer the questions of distributive justice—how much inequality is necessary or fair?

wards, in the doctrine of capitalism, operate like a great big grading system. To the most deserving go the "A's," to the least deserving the "F's," and to those who are somewhere in between the "B's," the "C's," and the "D's."

DISTRIBUTIVE JUSTICE

Unfortunately, the doctrine of capitalism does not tell us *how much* inequality is fair or necessary. For example, Table 4.2 gives us an idea of some of the higher salaries paid in the United States. The chairman of General Motors earned nearly $1 million in 1977, an amount about equal to what 100 or so assembly line workers might earn. Is it fair that the chairman of a company earns 100 times as much as an employee? Maybe the chairman should earn only 50 times as much or 20 times as much; or maybe he should earn 200 or

**TABLE 4.2
Salaries and Bonuses of
Leading Executives, 1977**

Company	Name and Title	Remuneration
International Harvester	Archie R. McCardell, President	$1,076,666
Ford	Henry Ford 2d, Chairman	992,420
ITT	Harold S. Geneen, Chairman	986,054
General Motors	Thomas A. Murphy, Chairman	975,000
ABC	Leonard H. Goldenson, Chairman	750,000
Mobil	Rawleigh Warner, Jr., Chairman	724,610
ATT	John D. deButts, Chairman	721,763
IBM	Frank T. Cary, Chairman	669,845

Source: Based on data in U.S. News & World Report, June 12, 1978.

300 times as much. Whatever is "fair," is it necessary to pay people $1 million a year to get them to do a given job? Would it not be possible to find a talented person who would work for a half-million or even a quarter-million a year?

Trying to figure out the "how much" aspect of inequality is what we mean by *distributive justice.* Some amount of inequality is considered fair and necessary, but how much? In the next chapter, when we review the political and social beliefs of American citizens, we will learn that different groups in America have different views about the appropriate amount of inequality. Not surprisingly, people in high-paying positions think there should be a larger gap between the highest and the lowest salaries than people in less prestigious positions.

Here we will not sort out all the arguments about different amounts of inequality, but we will initially concentrate on just how much inequality there is in the distribution of wealth in America.

INCOME AND WEALTH

We start with a distinction between income and wealth. Income is the money that people receive from various sources. Most of the income people receive comes from wages and salaries. But people also have investments such as stocks and bonds, which produce yearly income in the form of dividends or capital gains. The rent received by owners of rental property is also income. Income is what people report on their income tax return each year, as in "How much did I make?"

Wealth is the value of the possessions and property that people own. A family's house, furniture, and automobile are part of its wealth. Included in wealth would be the market value of the stocks and bonds owned by the family. A farmer's wealth would include not only land but also livestock and farming equipment. The simplest way to think about wealth is to ask how much cash your family would have if all the things it owned were sold. If about income we ask, "How much did I make?" about wealth we ask, "What am I worth?"

How, then, is income and wealth distributed in the United States? Although there are many, sometimes contradictory, measures of income and wealth, a general picture is available to us if we think in terms of quintiles. A *quintile* is 20 percent of the population. If there were perfect equality in income or wealth, any 20 percent of the population would have 20 percent of the wealth, as in the left-hand side of Table 4.3. If there were great inequality, then most of the income or wealth would go to the top 20 percent (or quintile) and only a little of the income or wealth would be distributed to the rest of the population, as in the right-hand side of Table 4.3.

In Table 4.4 we show the actual distribution of income received by the poorest 20 percent and the wealthiest 20 percent of families in the United States. The figures cover a forty-year period, from 1929

TABLE 4.3
Hypothetical Distributions of Income, Contrasting Perfect Equality with a Pattern Showing Substantial Inequality

PERFECT EQUALITY		SUBSTANTIAL INEQUALITY	
Population Ranked by Quintile	Percent of Income Received	Population Ranked by Quintile	Percent of Income Received
Highest	20%	Highest	60%
Next highest	20	Next highest	20
Middle	20	Middle	10
Next lowest	20	Next lowest	7
Lowest	20	Lowest	3
	100%		100%

TABLE 4.4
Percentage Distribution of Family Personal Income by Quintiles, Selected Years, 1929 to 1970

Families Ranked from Highest to Lowest Income	1929	1941	1950	1960	1970
Highest fifth	54.4%	48.8%	42.6%	42.0%	41.6%
Next highest	19.3	22.3	23.5	23.6	23.5
Middle fifth	13.8	15.3	17.4	17.6	17.4
Next lowest	9.0	9.5	12.0	12.0	12.0
Lowest fifth	3.5	4.1	4.5	4.9	5.5
	100.0%	100.0%	100.0%	100.0%	100.0%

Source: U.S. Bureau of the Census, Current Population Reports, Series P-60, no. 80 (October 4, 1971), Table 14, p. 28, for 1950, 1960, 1970. For 1929 and 1941, Edward C. Budd, ed., "An Introduction to a Current Issue of Public Policy," in Inequality and Poverty (New York: Norton, 1967), pp. x–xix.

to 1970. While 1980 figures are of course not yet available, research that is now under way indicates that the change in this decade will be no greater than the change in the preceding decade. We can therefore take the 1970 figure, as a good approximation of what the 1980 figure will look like.

Three facts are striking: (1) The richest 20 percent of the families in the United States receive about eight to ten times as much income as the poorest 20 percent of the families; (2) from 1930 to 1950, a period that includes the New Deal legislation and World War II, there is a marked drop in the percentage of income received by the richest families (from 54 percent to 42 percent) and a slight increase in the amount of income received by the poorest families (from 3.5 percent to 4.5 percent); (3) for the past 20 to 30 years there has been almost no change.

Another way to think about income inequality is to ask what the average earnings are for families in the richest as against the poorest quintiles. In 1976 no family in the richest quintile earned less than $25,000, and no family in the poorest quintile earned more than $6,000. This fact can be stated graphically:

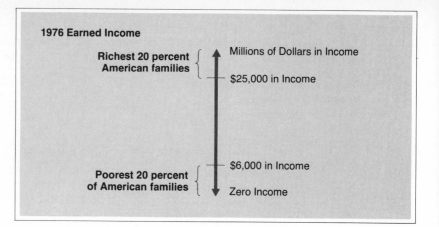

1976 Earned Income

Richest 20 percent
American families

Millions of Dollars in Income

$25,000 in Income

$6,000 in Income

Poorest 20 percent
of American families

Zero Income

Distribution of Wealth The distribution of wealth in the United States is much more unequal than the distribution of income. Wealth is an estimate of who has what, and though available measures are far from complete it is certain that a very large share of the personal wealth in the United States is owned by a very small percent of the population. Table 4.5 shows that since the founding of the United States the wealthiest *1 percent* of the population has owned between 20 and 30 percent of all privately owned wealth. In one study, carried out in 1962, it was estimated that the richest fifth of the families owned 77 percent of the wealth while the poorest fifth of the families owned less than 0.5 percent.[4]

Of course even this fact fails to take into account different forms of wealth. The most common forms of wealth are personal possessions: house, car, hi-fi set, appliances. Personal possessions of this sort produce pleasure for their owners, but such wealth is not influential. Influential wealth is wealth that produces more wealth in the form of income for its owners: rental property, stocks and bonds, patent rights, royalty rights. Close to 100 percent of this income-producing wealth is controlled by the richest 20 percent of the families. Indeed, most of this form of wealth is owned by a very small number of families. For instance, the top 1 percent of wealth owners in the United States control approximately one-quarter of all notes and mortgages, one-half of all bonds, and three-quarters of all corporate stocks.

Summary The facts and figures just presented record the magnitude of economic inequality in the United States. It is clear that sharp inequalities exist. And of course these income and wealth inequalities translate into different standards of living: Some citizens have big, comfortable houses, work at jobs they enjoy doing,

[4] Robert J. Lampman, *The Share of Top Wealth-Holders in National Wealth, 1922–1956* (Princeton, N.J.: Princeton University Press, 1962).

TABLE 4.5
Percents of Personal Wealth Held by the Top 1 Percent of the Population, Selected Years, 1910 to 1956

TOP 1 PERCENT OF FAMILIES[a]			TOP 1 PERCENT OF ADULTS[b]			
1810	1860	1900	1922	1939	1949	1956
21%	24%	31%	31.6%	30.6%	20.8%	26%

[a] *Sources:* Robert Gallman, *Six Papers on Size Distribution of Wealth and Income*, ed. L. Soltow (New York: National Bureau of Economic Research, 1969), 23:6.
[b] Robert Lampman, *Changes in the Share of Wealth Held by Top Wealth-Holders 1922–1956* (New York: National Bureau of Economic Research, 1960), Occasional Paper 71, p. 21.

can take vacations, can send their children to college, and can save enough to protect them against illness or unemployment. At the other end of the economic scale are people who live in crowded and poor-quality housing, do the dirty, dull jobs, worry more about feeding their children than about what college to send them to, are usually in debt, and always worry about sickness or unemployment.

Political Challenges to Economic Inequality

Despite the expansion of legal, political, and even social citizenship, there has not been a major redistribution of wealth in the United States. This fact confounds the fears of conservative political thinkers, who have long felt that equal political rights would eventually be translated into equal economic condition, a leveling of society.

When equal political rights were first proposed, many opposed the idea. They feared that those who lacked money would use their voting power to tax away the profits and savings of the talented and hardworking citizens. More correctly, they feared that the rights of property would be threatened by, as they put it, "too much democracy." In 1821 political leaders in New York were debating the merits of extending the vote to all white males. An active opponent was Chancellor James Kent, the highest official in the state. He felt that

> That extreme democratic principle, universal suffrage, has been productive of corruption, injustice, violence, and tyranny. . . . The apprehended danger from the experiment of universal suffrage applied to the whole legislative department, is no dream of the imagination. It is too mighty an excitement for the moral constitution of men to endure. The tendency of universal suffrage is to jeopardize the rights of property and the principles of liberty. There is a constant tendency in human society, and the history of every age proves it; there is a tendency in the poor to covet and to share the plunder of the rich—in the debtor to relax or

avoid the obligation of contracts—in the indolent and the profligate to cast the whole burthens of society upon the industrious and the virtuous. . . .[5]

Echoes of this sentiment can be heard today. In the spring of 1977, for instance, there was widespread discussion of universal voter registration, a program designed to increase the number of Americans who go to the polls. The supporters of this program viewed it as one more step toward universal suffrage and citizenship equality. But the opponents believed that the nonvoters include too many poor people who, with voting made more easy, would support political programs that would radically redistribute wealth in the United States. One of the most forceful statements appeared in a nationally published newspaper column by the political writer Patrick J. Buchanan:

> Universal registration . . . may be the method through which the nation's tax-consumers and nonproducers set about the systematic plunder of the tax-paying and producing majority. . . .
> [Members of the welfare class are] parasitic slugs who pay no taxes, who show such disinterest in the political process that they will not get off their duffs to register, have no business at the ballot box election day, casting a vote in ignorance and canceling out the ballot of some conscientious citizen.[6]

This argument has the same difficulties as it did when it was used by Chancellor Kent, in 1821: Universal suffrage has not brought about a radical redistribution of wealth. The next sections explain why.

THE PROGRESSIVE INCOME TAX

The principle of the progressive income tax is simple enough: The more money a person earns, the higher the portion he or she pays in taxes. The progressive income tax would be one of the easiest ways in which the poorer citizens might bring about a redistribution of wealth. The poorer citizens would vote for sharply graduated taxes, taking a very low percent from people like themselves but a very high percent from the richer classes. This would be the method by which political equality ("one person, one vote") would lead to economic equality ("One person, one dollar").

In practice nothing like this has happened. Table 4.6 presents relevant figures. The first column gives different income levels; the next shows what portion of income should be paid. The poorest family, for instance, would pay only 1.9 percent of its income in taxes, while the richest families, those making $1 million or more, would pay 60 percent. The table shows the average amount actually paid by different income levels and the average amount saved be-

[5] Quoted in Alpheus T. Mason, ed., *Free Government in the Making*, 2d ed. (New York: Oxford University Press, 1956), p. 399.
[6] Patrick J. Buchanan, "Reform Aids Welfare Class," a nationally syndicated column that appeared in the *Chicago Tribune*, March 3, 1977.

TABLE 4.6
Portion of Family Income
Paid in Income Taxes

Family Income	Payment Required by Tax Law	Average Paid After Deductions	Average Amount Saved via Loopholes
$ 2,500	1.9%	0.5%	$ 35
5,000	7.5	2.8	235
10,000	12.4	7.6	480
20,000	20.8	12.1	1,740
75,000	46.0	26.8	14,400
250,000	58.0	29.6	71,000
1,000,000	60.5	30.4	301,000

Source: Based on data from Philip M. Stern, The Rape of the Taxpayer (New York: Random House, 1974), p. 11.

cause of tax loopholes. It is clear that the progressive income tax is not as progressive as it is supposed to be. Why is this so?

The Sixteenth Amendment, which authorized the progressive income tax, allows Congress to tax income "from whatever sources derived," but tax legislation has played havoc with this principle. Dollars earned from some sources, though they are worth just as much in consumer goods, leisure, or the like, are not taxed at the same rate as dollars earned from other sources. The dollars that are most heavily taxed are earned in wages and salaries; those that are least heavily taxed are earned on various types of investments: long-term capital gains, real estate, stock options, oil, and state and local bonds. For example, a family of four earning an income of $10,000 would, under existing laws, pay the following federal income taxes:

- $905 if the income is all in the form of wages and salaries
- $98 if the income is all in the form of profits from selling stocks or land
- $0 if the income is all in the form of interest on state and local bonds

Thus the person who gains his or her income by working pays a greater share of it in taxes than the person who gains it without lifting a finger. Furthermore, since the income of the wealthy is derived primarily from nonwage sources, it is the wealthy, not the low- and middle-income wage earners, who benefit from these different rates of taxation.

Every year a lot of money is lost to the government through tax deductions and loopholes. Such uncollected taxes are a gift to those who are able to take advantage of such deductions, generally the wealthy. If this money could be collected, the official tax rates could be cut nearly in half, or perhaps needed social services such as mass transit or clean air and water could be provided. It is ironic that the annual budget of the antipoverty program is less than 3 percent of the loss from the "tax welfare" program, but what is even more ironic is the distribution of these tax handouts: The 6 million poorest families receive about $92 million while the wealthiest 3000 families receive $2.2 billion, or about 24 times as much.

The progressive income tax does flatten out the income distribution at the lower end of the scale. For example, the income tax brings the family with an income of $16,000 closer to the family with an income of $8,000. But its impact on the top of the income scale is much less. Before taxes the average income of the richest 20 percent in the country is about 10 times that of the poorest 20 percent; the effect of the income tax is to reduce this only to 9 times as much. In general, under present laws the progressive income tax is not nearly as progressive as is often thought; it does not greatly reduce the distance between the wealthy and the poor.

Other types of taxes are even less progressive. The sales tax, for instance, takes a much larger share of the income of the poor than of the rich. Say, for example, a family earns $5,000 and pays a 5 percent sales tax on the $4,000 it spends on consumer goods and basic necessities. This family would pay $200, or 4 percent of its total income, in sales taxes. A family that earns $25,000 and spends $8,000 on items bearing the 5 percent sales tax would spend $400, or 1.6 percent of its total income, in sales taxes. Thus the poorer family is being taxed at a higher rate.

Scholars who have tried to assess the total effect of all U.S. taxes — sales tax, income tax, property tax, payroll tax — have come to the conclusion that there is very little progressiveness. Practically everyone, rich and poor alike, pays approximately one-quarter to one-third of his or her income in taxes. And this actual rate has not changed much since the end of World War II. The extent of economic inequality in the United States has not been much affected by the various taxes that the government uses to pay for its programs. It follows that the concentration of income and wealth we observed in Tables 4.4 and 4.5 is about the same whether we use before-tax or after-tax figures.

Taxes should be looked at from another perspective as well. People who earn more money do make more of a contribution to government programs and public policies than people who earn less money. In 1976, for example, about half of the households in the United States earned less than $10,000 and the other half more than $10,000. Consistent with what we have already shown, the wealthier half of the nation earned most of the income (81 percent) that year and enjoyed most of the tax breaks (88 percent of all tax breaks). However, they also paid the income-tax tab in the United States. Ninety-four percent of all federal income taxes collected in 1976 came from families earning more than $10,000; only 6 percent, then, came from the half of the nation earning less than $10,000. While it is true that the wealthy enjoy the biggest tax breaks, they also contribute heavily to the overall tax burden of the society.

But, to return to the central point, the progressive income tax system does not sharply reduce income inequality. The gap between the rich and the poor persists.

THE PROGRAMS OF THE SOCIAL-WELFARE STATE

If the progressive income tax is not very progressive, has inequality been affected by the programs of the social-welfare state? Social security, unemployment compensation, public education, and medicare are the major social-service programs in America. A strong case can be made that these programs have made citizens more equal. But the relationship is a complicated one. First we must describe two different types of inequality: inequality of distance and inequality of scope.

Inequality of distance refers to the size of the gap between the richest and the poorest, or between any two points along the income distribution scale. In a society where the richest group earns 20 times as much as the poorest group, the inequality of distance is great. In a society where the richest group earns only 5 times as much as the poorest group, inequality of distance has been reduced. The kinds of social-service programs that provide a cushion for the sick, the old, and the unemployed do not greatly reduce the distance between rich and poor. The major social-service programs are simply government-managed insurance plans to which workers contribute during their working years. For instance, nine out of ten working people in America are now contributing to social security. Other social-service programs, such as medicare, help a citizen out in times of financial need, in this case older citizens who cannot afford high medical costs. But these programs do not "level" society in the sense of cutting heavily into the wealth of the rich and increasing that of the poor.

Does this mean that social-service programs are unrelated to equality in America? Not at all. But now we must speak of *inequality of scope.* This term refers to the number of ways in which the rich are better off than the poor.

Assume the following extreme case: *Every* social benefit is available only through the private sector and is priced so that its owners make the highest profit possible. Education, medical care, insurance, recreation, transportation, communication services, and even security against personal attack are available in unequal amounts and unequal quality. The wealthy, therefore, have greater access to these services than the poor. They even hire their own security force to protect their possessions. The less wealth you have, the less of any of these services you can get, until we get to the bottom of the scale, where none are available — there is no public education, no free medical care, no public parks, no social security, no transportation or communication systems except those used by the wealthy, not even a police force. Under such conditions inequalities of scope would be enormous. Every social value would be more available, and in a better form, to the wealthy than to the poor.

Now assume the opposite case: *No* social benefit is priced; all are equally available to every citizen. Public schools are excellent, and educational attainment is based on intelligence; health and insurance programs protect all citizens equally against illness, accident, and disability; there are many public parks, and entertainment is widely available; transportation is efficient, as are telephone and mail services; and the standing army and police force protect everyone's possessions. Under such conditions inequalities of scope are greatly narrowed. There are still rich and poor, and the rich can afford luxuries that are denied to the poor. But the rich cannot buy superior social services. The advantage of wealth is limited to certain areas of consumption.

The difficult question of whether basic social services should be available to all citizens equally or only to those who can afford to pay was recently posed to President Carter. At a news conference in July 1977 Carter had spoken against using federal funds to support abortions. A reporter asked:

> Q. Well then, how fair do you believe it is that women who can afford to get an abortion can go ahead and have one and women who cannot afford to are precluded from this?

And Carter replied:

> A. Well, as you know there are many things in life that are not fair, that wealthy people can afford and poor people can't. But I don't believe that the federal government should take action to try to make these opportunities exactly equal, particularly when there is a moral factor involved.

The question of what is fair is exactly the issue that was dealt with by President Carter. It is the issue of whether government programs should reduce the benefits of wealth by making available social services to the poor and the rich alike. Whereas the phrase "inequality of distance" describes *how much* better off the rich are, the phrase "inequality of scope" describes *how many ways* they are better off.

Welfare policies are egalitarian in the sense that they increase the number of services for which wealth is unnecessary. The point is made by Julius Nyerere, president of socialist Tanzania, when he urges that inequalities be reduced through "the provision of social services which are available to all, regardless of income; for a man who suddenly has new medical services available to him and his family, or a new house, or a new school or community center, has had an improvement in his standard of living, just as much as if he had more money in his pocket."

If citizenship reduces inequalities of scope, it has made a major contribution to equality. This has happened, though less than either supporters or critics of the social-service state admit. For one thing, the benefits of social programs are not always directed toward the poorer groups in society. Free higher education, for instance, has serviced the middle class and to a lesser extent the working class, and has not done much for really poor families. The impact of welfare programs has also been lessened by the method of paying for

them. For the most part the relevant taxes are spread across the population, meaning that the poorer groups pay for services designed to equalize their income in exact proportion to what they pay in taxes anyway. Their payments would have to be subtracted from any exact calculation of benefits.

The results of social-rights citizenship have been less egalitarian than some hoped and others feared; nevertheless if decent social services are provided by the government, either free or at minimal cost, then inequalities of scope are reduced. The rich can still support private universities and send their children to them, but excellent public universities reduce this advantage. Government programs therefore equalize somewhat the opportunities to compete for the benefits of quality education.

THE WAR ON POVERTY

The usual approaches to social services and public welfare were greatly extended in the mid-1960s. The antipoverty programs, with an annual budget of around $2 billion, introduced Head Start, Job Corps, VISTA, and various other such programs. We will not review the failures and successes of President Johnson's War on Poverty (greatly modified by President Nixon and now being revised by the Carter administration), but will simply ask how antipoverty programs affect inequality.

The War on Poverty did not improve living conditions for many urban poor, as Carter learned when he toured New York after the looting that followed the black-out in 1977.

The purpose of antipoverty policy is to raise the floor levels of society. The poor are those who are living below some socially acceptable standard. An affluent society should not have poor people in its midst. People should not be so poor that they cannot enjoy their political and economic rights. A successful antipoverty program moves every citizen above the tolerable level, which, in the words of the War on Poverty, eliminates poverty "by opening to everyone the opportunity for education and training, the opportunity to work, and the opportunity to live in decency and dignity."

The goal is to increase the portion of the population who compete in an economic system based on wage differentials and wealth earned from private property. This is no small accomplishment, but it should not be confused with egalitarianism. The only way the elimination of poverty can affect inequality is by reducing slightly the distance between the rich and the poor, not by making the rich less wealthy but by making the poor better off. The War on Poverty did not close the gap between rich and poor by very much.

A more recent idea is the negative income tax. What is proposed is a plan whereby families at a given income level, say $5000, would pay no taxes. Families earning less than this amount would receive an income supplement (the "negative income tax") that would bring them up to the level of $5000. Only families earning more than that amount would pay income tax. The negative income tax has been tried out in a few communities, but is not yet a national program. Even if it were enacted it would have had little overall effect on inequality. It would help the poorest families in America live a little more decently, but it would not reduce the distance between the wealthiest and the poorest classes except marginally.

AFFIRMATIVE ACTION

In the 1970s the United States experienced a new debate about citizenship. And like the debates that preceded it, this one is about equality. The catch phrase "affirmative action" is at the center of the debate. Should society take affirmative action to compensate for past inequalities and discriminations? Crudely stated, affirmative action is reverse discrimination. *It is intended to discriminate in behalf of those who have been discriminated against in the past.*

We can best understand the dynamics of affirmative action by concentrating on racial equality, though the logic of affirmative action is also applicable to sex discrimination or age discrimination or any other form of discrimination.

It is not a historical accident that the issue of affirmative action emerged in the 1970s. It followed a decade of very successful civil-rights activity. Many forms of racial discrimination have been eliminated. Blacks and other minorities are no longer systematically excluded from the rights of citizenship, such as voting or office-holding. And they are no longer legally excluded from jobs or housing or good schools or restaurants or baseball teams. An enormous social transformation has taken place in the past two decades.

But this social transformation has failed to accomplish two important things. It has not ended segregation, and it has not ended severe economic inequalities between black and white citizens. For example, in Chicago the public schools are 70 percent nonwhite; in Baltimore the figure is 75 percent; in Detroit, 81 percent; and in Washington, D.C., 96 percent. Persistent segregation is accompanied by persistent economic inequality. The 1970 census was taken at the end of a decade that gave a lot of attention to racial justice— more books were written, more meetings held, more marches organized, more legislation passed, more programs started, more commissions formed, more money spent on solving "the American dilemma" than in any other period of our history. At the end of that decade the median income of white families was $9,961 whereas for black families it was $6,067. And this was not due simply to the fact that whites have better jobs. Blacks are paid less than whites for similar jobs. The median income of white male "professional, managerial and kindred workers" in 1970 was $11,108. The median for the *same category* of blacks was $7,659. The situation is similar in all job categories; and there has been little change since 1970.

It is out of frustration with the persistence of segregation and inequality that the drive for affirmative action arises. We can trace the roots of this frustration by quickly summarizing the recent history of racial values in American society.[7]

1. *A "Colorblind" Government* The initial breakthrough in racial values occurs just after World War II and is best illustrated by the Supreme Court's decision in *Brown* v. *Board of Education* in 1954. This decision (discussed in detail in later chapters) ruled that segregated public schools were illegal. More broadly, the implication was that the government could take no action that discriminated against or treated separately people of different races. To correct for government discrimination was to end it.

---

[7] This summary draws heavily from Ben L. Martin, "The Parable of the Talents," *Harper's*, January 1978, pp. 22–24.

2. *A "Colorblind" Society* Gradually the society followed the lead of the government. Professional sports, television programs, colleges and universities, corporations, and dozens of other sectors of the society paid less and less attention to race. As we will see in the next chapter, public opinion also shifted. Fewer and fewer whites thought that blacks should be kept out of their neighborhoods or away from "white" colleges. The traditional commitment of Americans to equal treatment based on merit began to wash away racist attitudes.

3. *Private Action to Encourage Black Achievement* It did not take long for people to realize that ending discrimination would not necessarily promote the interests of the black population. Many private institutions, especially in the educational sector but also to some extent in business and the professions, began actively to seek out qualified blacks. Often special training programs or fellowship money was provided as a way to compensate for past educational disadvantages or family poverty. It was the logic of Head Start, in which groups that had been discriminated against in the past would now be given a chance to catch up and compete on an equal footing.

4. *Affirmative Action* Progress was slow. Ending discrimination did not correct for the lingering effects of past discrimination: inferior schools, urban ghetto living, poverty, broken homes. And initiatives in the private sector produced little more than tokenism.

It is at this point that the actions of government have begun to force society to abandon the principle of colorblindness. The civil-rights movement of the 1960s sought to make the law colorblind, to rid the law and society of a tradition of discrimination. The affirmative-action move of the 1970s seeks to again make the law take color into account. But now it is the "haves" who will be inconvenienced and even discriminated against, so that the "have-nots," especially blacks, Native Americans, Mexican-Americans, and Puerto Ricans, can have a better chance at the good schools and the good jobs that will produce economic equality with whites.

The language of affirmative action is that of "targets" or "goals" or "quotas." If the outcome of college admission procedures or employment and promotion practices is not proportional to the representation of racial minorities in the population, this is taken as evidence that discrimination lingers. Guidelines are then suggested for the college or the business, with the threat that federal moneys may be withdrawn or other penalties imposed if the target figure is not reached.

Implicit in affirmative-action programs is the shift from equality of opportunity to equality of condition. The success of a college admissions program is not measured by whether it gives everyone an equal chance at admission but whether it achieves a certain outcome. Given past discrimination, a colorblind admissions program will probably result in very few blacks being qualified for college entrance. Only if the college takes color into account and attempts to meet some quota is it likely to enroll a large number of blacks.

Difficult Political Choices Probably no set of political issues is more complex or difficult than those that are stirred up by affirmative action. The entire question of citizenship rights is in the process of being defined. The principle of affirmative action is that the effects of past discrimination can be overcome only by reverse discrimination.

Here are just a few of the political issues that have emerged under the banner of affirmative action:

Career Advancement Because of past discrimination black workers do not have the job seniority that white workers do. If career advancement is based on seniority, it will take decades before we begin to have black union leaders or police chiefs or school principals. But to advance blacks at a faster pace than whites seems unfair to the white workers who have worked hard to build up their own seniority.

Housing Because of residential segregation and years of poverty, few blacks can afford to live in the suburbs. But it is in the suburbs that one finds the most job opportunities and the best schools. Should low-income housing be built in white suburbs so that urban blacks can escape the vicious cycle of unemployment, poverty, and poor schools? But to force neighborhoods to accept low-income housing is to chip away at the freedom of communities to plan their own land use.

Busing Black children are concentrated in inferior, segregated schools in the centers of industrial cities. White children attend public schools in the suburbs, where their parents have fled in order to find good schools and better housing. Can black children ever be expected to compete equally with white children unless some program of forced integration is put into effect? But is it fair to bus white children out of their neighborhoods in order to create integrated schools and a more equitable distribution of educational resources?

Various programs to rid society of the effects of racial discrimination will be hotly debated in the near future. Affirmative action is a new and troublesome phase in the history of citizenship. It moves beyond equal protection of the law and even beyond equal opportunity to a new concept of citizen rights: the right to be treated unequally, though favorably, in compensation for previous unequal and unfavorable treatment.

Such treatment cannot avoid being called reverse discrimination. Groups that have struggled to succeed under the old rules—white union leaders, for example—will resent the change in the rules that would seem to penalize them just because they are white and male. The controversy at the end of this chapter provides an opportunity to discuss the complexities of affirmative action.

Conclusions

We have now established three things about equality in the United States. First, under the insistent pressure of citizenship rights substantial legal, political, and social equalities have been achieved.

Second, economic inequalities have been slightly lessened but certainly not eliminated by such government programs as the progressive income tax, social-welfare programs, the War on Poverty, and affirmative action. Third, there coexist in our society the democratic creed, which promises political equality, and the capitalist creed, which promises economic inequality. This "coexistence" is the "astounding political contradiction" with which we began this chapter.

To find this contradiction is not to conclude that politics makes no difference. Indeed, political action has brought about some remarkable changes in the meaning of citizenship. For instance, the phrase "equality of opportunity" has taken on renewed meaning as a result of the civil-rights movement of the 1960s and the women's movement of the 1970s. It is a phrase that will change even more as the issues of affirmative action work themselves out in society. Political action has also put a floor under poverty. It has established the concept of the "social minimum" below which no citizen should have to live. The old idea that each person should get only what he or she earns has been softened to take into account sickness, unemployment when no jobs are to be had, old age, and other personal and social conditions that make it difficult for an individual to earn much.

But contrary to the predictions of many people, political action has not radically redistributed wealth. Sharp differences in income and wealth will continue to provide different standards of living for different classes and groups in the society. Even as Americans have accepted the democratic creed of equality, they have also accepted the capitalist doctrine that certain inequalities are just and necessary. This is why the astounding political contradiction persists. Understanding the contradiction as outlined in this chapter will help us understand important features of American politics that we present in the following chapters.

controversy

The Supreme Court recently decided a critical affirmative-action case. The case is *Regents of California* v. *Bakke.* The issue is whether state universities may reserve a number of places for minority students and fill those places through special admissions programs. The Court's decision was mixed. It rejected the specific California program because it reserved a specific number of places for racial minorities, but it said schools could take race into account in considering applicants. Consider the issue that the Court faced:

Allan Bakke, a 37-year-old white engineer, applied to the University of California medical school on its campus in Davis, California. Bakke was refused admission but then learned that minority students with lower grade point averages and test scores had been admitted. The minority candidates had been assigned to a special admissions committee that had an allotted number of places to fill, and this committee used less demanding criteria than those that were used in the regular admission process. Bakke went to court, claiming that the quota system discriminated against him. The California Supreme Court eventually agreed with him in a ruling that declared preferential admissions unconstitutional — a denial to white applicants of the "equal protection of the laws" guaranteed by the Fourteenth Amendment. The case was appealed to the United States Supreme Court by the University of California.

It immediately gained national attention. The issue of reverse discrimination and quota programs was aggressively debated in the newspapers and on university campuses. A large number of organizations and universities filed "friend-of-the-court" briefs with the Supreme Court, statements that attempt to influence the Court's decision by providing legal and constitutional rationales for one side or the other. A listing of those who have filed such briefs appears in Table 4.7. While we cannot review the details of this case, the pro and con arguments outline the controversy over affirmative action.

One Side The University of California vigorously defended its special admissions program, arguing in its brief to the Supreme Court that "there is, literally, no substitute for the use of race as a factor in admissions, if professional schools are to admit more than an isolated few applicants from minority groups long subjected to hostile and pervasive discrimination." Various studies supported the University's assertion. The Association of American Medical Colleges said in its brief:

> Without special admissions programs it is not unrealistic to assume that minority enrollments could return to the distressingly low levels of the early 1960's. This would mean a drop from the present level of 8.2 percent enrollment of underrepresented minorities . . . to slightly over 2 percent.[8]

In the absence of special admissions programs, similar drops in minority enrollment would occur in law schools, according to the Association of American Law Schools. In its brief it cited a study by the Educational Testing Service that showed that without such programs the number of blacks admitted to American law schools in the previous year would have dropped by 60 percent and the number of Chicano students by 40 percent.

The argument for affirmative action proceeds not only from the type of facts just cited but also from considerations of justness and equity. Equal protection of the law is not enough to overcome centuries of racial and sexual discrimination and unequal treatment. To simply apply equal criteria at this stage in history is as if there were a race between two people, one of whom had been in training for ten years while the other had been in chains for ten years. If the chains were removed, both runners started at the same point on the track, and the rules of the race were applied to the runners equally, would we say that each runner had an equal chance to win? Affirmative action, supporters argue, is intended to help the chained runner get in condition so that the race will be fair.

The Other Side The arguments against affirmative action frequently start by pointing out how quota programs are unfair to blacks and other minorities. The assumption is made that "blacks will not succeed in rising more or less on their own merits, as other minorities have. Nothing could more surely

[8] Cited in *The Chronicle of Higher Education*, 15, no 3. (September 19, 1977), 4.

handicap able blacks further than the assumption that they have become doctors or lawyers not by individual merit but by a preference based on skin color."[9]

Moreover, affirmative-action programs turn innocent people into victims. Though his grade point average and test scores were good enough to enter medical school, Bakke was denied admission. Similar things happen whenever there are quotas or special selection procedures. Some qualified applicants cannot enter college or a professional school or a training program or find employment in "reserved" jobs. As Supreme Court Justice Brennan wrote in a previous case, "We cannot ignore the social reality than even a benign policy of assignment by race is viewed as unjust by many in our society, especially by those individuals who are adversely affected by a given classification."[10]

The case against affirmative action is also made on straightforward constitutional grounds. Two well-known professors of constitutional law state the issue forcefully:

> If the Constitution prohibits exclusion of blacks and other minorities on racial grounds, it cannot permit exclusion of whites on racial grounds. For it must be the exclusion on racial grounds which offends the Constitution, and not the particular skin color of the person excluded.[11]

These professors argue that if someone is denied admission to a medical or law school *because* he or she is white, this is racial discrimination and therefore is unconstitutional. "Discrimination on the basis of race is illegal, immoral, unconstitutional, inherently wrong and destructive of democratic society."

TABLE 4.7
Briefs in Bakke Case

In Support of Allan Bakke		In Support of the University of California
	International Conference of Police Associations	Young Americans for Freedom
American Federation of Teachers (A.F.L.-C.I.O.)	International Association of Chiefs of Police	**In Support of the University of California**
American Jewish Committee	Italian-American Foundation	
American Jewish Congress	Jewish Labor Committee	American Association of University Professors
American Subcontractors Association	Jewish Rights Council	American Bar Association
Anti-Defamation League of B'nai B'rith	Mid-America Legal Foundation	American Civil Liberties Union
Chamber of Commerce of the U.S.A.	National Advocates Society	American Civil Liberties Union of Northern California
Committee on Academic Nondiscrimination and Integrity	National Jewish Commission on Law and Public Affairs	American Civil Liberties Union of Southern California
Conference of Pennsylvania State Police Lodges of the Fraternal Order of Police	National Medical and Dental Association	American Coalition of Citizens with Disabilities
Council of Supervisors and Administrators of the City of New York	Order of the Sons of Italy in America	American Medical Student Association
Fraternal Order of Police	Pacific Legal Foundation	Americans for Democratic Action
Ralph J. Galliano (unsuccessful white applicant to U. of Florida law school)	Polish-American Affairs Council	American Federation of State, County, and Municipal Employees (A.F.L.-C.I.O.)
Hellenic Bar Association of Illinois	Polish-American Educators Association	American Indian Bar Association
Timothy J. Hoy (student at Oberlin, planning to apply to law school this year)	Polish American Congress	American Indian Law Students Association
	Queens Jewish Community Council	
	Ukranian Congress Committee of America (Chicago Division)	
	UNICO National	
	Rep. Henry A. Waxman, Democrat of California	

[9] Editorial, *Wall Street Journal*, September 15, 1977, p. 20.

[10] Quoted by Anthony Lewis, "Racial Quotas Will Come Again Before High Court," *New York Times*, March 13, 1977.

[11] Philip Kurland and Alexander M. Bickel, quoted in Nina Totenberg, "Discrimination to End Discrimination," *The New York Times Magazine*, April 14, 1974. © 1974 by the New York Times Company. Reprinted by permission.

American Indian Law Center

American Public Health Association

Asian-American Bar Association of the Greater Bay Area

Aspira of America (national organization of Puerto Rican educators and students)

Association of American Law Schools

Association of American Medical Colleges

Association of Mexican American Educators

Bar Association of San Francisco

Black Law Students Association at U. of California at Berkeley

Black Law Students Union of Yale U. Law School

Board of Governors of Rutgers, the State University of New Jersey

Children's Defense Fund

Cleveland State U. chapter of Black American Law Students Association

Columbia University

Council on Legal Education Opportunity

County of Santa Clara, Cal.

Fair Employment Practices Commission of the State of California

GI Forum

Harvard University

Howard University

Image

International Union of Electrical, Radio, and Machine Workers (A.F.L.-C.I.O.)

International Union, United Automobile, Aerospace, and Agricultural Implement Workers of America (U.A.W.)

Japanese American Citizens League

Jerome A. Lackner, director of California Dept. of Health

La Raza National Lawyers Association

Law School Admissions Council

Lawyers' Committee for Civil Rights Under Law

League of United Latin American Citizens

Legal Services Corp.

Los Angeles County Bar Association

Los Angeles Mecha Central

Mexican American Legal Defense and Educational Fund

Mexican-American Political Association

N.A.A.C.P. Legal Defense and Educational Fund

National Association for Equal Opportunity in Higher Education

National Association for the Advancement of Colored People

National Association of Equal Educational Opportunity

National Association of Minority Contractors

National Bar Association

National Council of Churches of Christ in the U.S.A.

National Council of La Raza

National Council of Negro Women

National Education Association

National Employment Law Project

National Fund for Minority Engineering Students

National Health Law Program

National Lawyers' Guild

National Legal Aid and Defender Association

National Medical Association

National Organization for Women

National Urban League

Native American Law Students of the U. of California at Davis

Native American Student Union of the U. of California at Davis

North Carolina Association of Black Lawyers

Puerto Rican Legal Defense and Education Fund

Rutgers Law School Alumni Association

Society of American Law Teachers

Stanford University

State of Washington and University of Washington

Student Bar Association of Rutgers School of Law—Newark

U.C.L.A. Black Law Students' Association

U.C.L.A. Black Law Alumni Association

Union of Women's Alliance to Gain Equality

Unitas

United Farm Workers of America (A.F.L.-C.I.O.)

United Mine Workers of America

University of Pennsylvania

U.S. National Student Association

John Vasconcellos (Democratic member of the California Assembly)

Marion J. Woods, director of California Dept. of Benefit Payments

Young Women's Christian Association

Others

Antioch School of Law—Urges that the case be sent back to lower court for re-hearing.

Equal Employment Advisory Council—Urges Court to set guidelines for determining to what extent race or sex-conscious employment decisions are constitutional.

Price M. Cobbs and Ephraim Kahn, representing 22 doctors and medical educators—Takes position that Court should not have agreed to hear case because of inadequate lower court record.

National Association of Affirmative Action Officers—Urges that case be sent back to lower court for re-hearing.

National Conference of Black Lawyers—Urges that the case be sent back to lower court for re-hearing, but if decision is made, should be for U. of California.

Source: Chronicle of Higher Education, 15, no. 3 (September 19, 1977), 4.

5

POLITICAL BELIEFS OF AMERICANS

To understand American politics we must understand the American people—their beliefs and feelings about politics and government, and how they act in politics. This point seems clear, but it is often ignored. Some observers think politics can be understood by studying the formal structures of government. If we asked them what the important features of the American political system are, they would reply with facts like the following: In the United States we have a presidential rather than a parliamentary system; we have a federal system with power divided between the national and the state governments; we have a Constitution with formal guarantees of liberty. These features of the formal structure of government are of course important. But in this chapter we deal with something more basic—the beliefs and feelings of the American people about the American political system.

There is a simple reason why knowing the formal structure of government is not enough unless one understands the beliefs of those who live under that structure: Those beliefs affect how the political structure works. This lesson has been learned the hard way by those who have tried to transfer political forms from one society to another. A classic example is the Weimar Republic in Germany, founded after World War I. This new republic replaced the empire of the Kaisers and had one of the most carefully worked-out democratic constitutions ever written. But the constitution never took root among the people—it was not respected; the democratic institutions it set up were challenged from both the left and the right. And after a short, stormy existence the new democracy fell to the totalitarian rule of the Nazis.

Similar results have been seen in many of the new nations in Africa and Asia. Their constitutions have been borrowed from countries with long histories of functioning democracy—Britain or the United States. These constitutions provide for the basic institutions of democracy: periodic elections, the right of political opposition, basic freedoms, and so forth. But in many cases the democratic governments have been replaced by military regimes or one-party states. The explanation given is that the institutions were "motivationally hollow"; the democratic forms were there, but the democratic beliefs were not. This experience of other nations has reinforced a widely held belief about American democracy: that it has its roots in the "hearts and minds" of the American people.

Calculation vs. Culture

We can explain a person's political behavior in two different ways: as a result of *rational calculation of interests* or as a result of *cultural commitment to values.* The citizen who chooses how to take part in political life on the basis of rational calculation of interests acts like a person in a marketplace: He or she calculates the benefits of a particular political act, compares them to the costs, and chooses to do that which maximizes benefit at the least cost. A person who acts on the basis of cultural commitment to values does not make such a calculation in choosing how to act: He or she is guided by basic beliefs or values, often learned in early childhood. These beliefs and values are unquestioned *habits of thought.*

An example of a rational calculation is the purchase of a major appliance by a careful shopper. The shopper compares the various brands in terms of cost and quality and chooses that which gives the most value for the least money. An example of cultural commitment is religion. Most people do not rationally choose their religion by calculating which religion gives the most benefit for the least cost. Rather, religious commitments are usually basic, unquestioned beliefs, in most cases inherited from one's family.

Or consider two ways in which an individual can decide how to vote. The voter can calculate which candidate is more likely to carry out policies that are in his or her interest and vote accordingly. If presidential candidate A will do more about unemployment than candidate B, the voter who is unemployed or worried about unemployment and votes on the basis of calculation will be inclined to vote for candidate A. Or a voter might vote on the basis of habitual commitment. Many voters have long-term, habitual identifications with one or the other of the major political parties. They have always been Democrats or Republicans. Often that partisan identification is a family tradition. When it comes to a choice between candidates A and B, such voters make no calculation as to the benefits to be gained from the victory of one candidate over the other. They vote for the candidate of the party with which they are habitually affiliated. (In Chapter 11 we will discuss more fully how voters decide how to vote.)

CULTURAL COMMITMENTS AND DEMOCRACY

The distinction between cost–benefit calculation and cultural commitments is fundamental to one theory of how democracy works. The theory is as follows: Democracy survives if citizens act culturally when it comes to basic democratic beliefs but make rational calculations when it comes to specific issues. According to this argument, citizens must agree — largely without questioning them — on some basic cultural and political beliefs. The two that are most important are belief that the government is *legitimate* (i.e., that it deserves the support and obedience of its citizens) and belief in the *rules of the democratic game* (i.e., key democratic procedures such as freedom of speech and free elections). If there is widespread agreement on the legitimacy of the government and on the rules of the democratic game, the nation can stand the strain of disagreement on more specific matters. For example, citizens may calculate which presidential candidate will act in their interest. Some may support one candidate; others the opposing candidate. Or citizens may calculate whether a stiff tax on gasoline in order to encourage energy conservation is in their interest. Some may favor such a tax while others oppose it. But citizens ought not to calculate whether to accept the outcome of a free election or whether to obey the law and pay the gasoline tax.

The point about the absence of cost–benefit calculations when it comes to the basics of democracy is terribly important. Democracy allows — indeed, fosters — the free expression of political preferences. Citizens can work to get the government to carry out the policies they prefer. They do this by supporting candidates in elections or by pressuring government officials. Since citizens have different preferences, some will support one candidate and others the opponent. Or some will want a particular policy while others will oppose it. The result is that there are participants who win and others who lose. Why should the losers accept a result that is not in their immediate interest? Why should those who prefer the Republican candidate accept the election of a Democrat? The answer is that the losers accept their loss because they have a deeper commitment to the rules of procedure by which elections are held. They believe in free elections even if they sometimes lose. Furthermore, if both winners and losers agree on the rules, the losers will have another chance to win. The winning party — because it too shares the democratic commitment — will not use its position in office to abolish elections.

Similarly, those who oppose a gasoline tax will nevertheless obey the law because they consider the government that passed the law to be legitimate. Legitimacy is an important concept in political science and deserves further discussion. When a citizen considers a government to be legitimate, he or she considers it to be worthy of obedience even if it does not act in his or her immediate interest. You obey the new tax law not because a cost–benefit calculation tells you that you will gain from it but because the law was passed by a legitimate government. It is easy to see why legitimacy is basic to democracy. Democracy depends on voluntary consent by citizens. If most citizens do not give such consent, the government is likely to rely more and more on force. Citizens, in turn, are likely to be attracted to political movements that are opposed to democracy.

What makes a government legitimate in the eyes of the people? For one thing, citizens may accord the government legitimacy simply out of long-term cultural habit. They may accept the government as proper because early in life they have developed a commitment to the symbols of American democracy and a basic sense of

Citizens accord the government legitimacy out of long-term habit.

trust and confidence in the government. As long as the government follows the proper procedures—as long as elections are carried out freely and fairly and laws are passed in the way authorized by the Constitution—it will be accepted as worthy of support over and above any calculation of interest.

Political Beliefs of Americans: The Evidence

The argument that certain basic beliefs are fundamental to democracy was developed a while ago. It was uncertain, however, whether the public actually held this set of beliefs. Fortunately, in recent years social scientists have developed such techniques as the in-depth sample survey of public attitudes. We can now look at data on the beliefs of the American people. As we will see, they do believe in the legitimacy of the government and in the rules of the democratic game. But such commitments are by no means unqualified.

We will look closely at these beliefs about democracy. They define what Americans mean by liberty and freedom. But there is another set of crucial values that affect politics in America—beliefs as to what kind of society we ought to have. Americans have some distinctive views about the nature of equality and the role of the state in relation to equality. These views affect what Americans want from the government. We will look at these views in this chapter as well.

	United States	Great Britain	Germany	Italy	Mexico
Percent who are proud of "nothing"	4%	10%	15%	27%	16%
Percent who are proud of the political institutions	85%	46%	7%	3%	30%

Source: Based on data from Gabriel Almond and Sidney Verba, *The Civic Culture: Political Attitudes and Democracy in Five Nations* (Princeton, N.J.: Princeton University Press, 1963). Copyright © 1963 by Princeton University Press. Reprinted by permission of Princeton University Press.

LEGITIMACY OF THE GOVERNMENT

Are Americans committed to the American political system? Do they give it their long-term trust and loyalty? One way in which such trust and loyalty are shown is through commitment to the *symbols* of American democracy. Over the years studies have found that Americans have, in general, a deep commitment to the symbols of the American political community. Reverence for the flag and the Constitution is taught in the schools and maintained throughout the life of the average American.

A major study of democratic attitudes in 1959 compared the political beliefs of Americans with those of citizens in four other countries. (See Table 5.1.) The researchers asked citizens what they were proud of about their countries. Two results are important. For one thing, few Americans—only 4 percent—replied that there was nothing they were proud of, a response that would have showed general hostility to the political community. (In the other four countries the portions who were proud of "nothing" ranged from 10 percent to 27 percent.) More interesting is what Americans were proud of. Compared with the citizens in other nations, Americans showed pride in political aspects of their society—the Constitution, political freedom, democracy. Eighty-five percent of those who were interviewed in the United States—twice the percentage in the next-highest country—mentioned political aspects of society.

American politics has changed a lot since 1959. But the basic attitude toward the political system does not seem to have changed as much as one might expect. In 1972 a sample of the American public was asked to choose between two statements: "I am proud of many things about our form of government" and "I can't find much about our form of government to be proud of." Eighty-six percent chose the first alternative. And in response to the question of whether there is a need for major change in our form of government, only 15 percent said that a "big change is needed."[1]

The public may still respect the American form of government, but it has become much more dissatisfied with the way the government has been run. Over the years researchers have asked citizens

[1] Jack Citrin, "The Political Relevance of Trust in Government," *American Political Science Review*, 68 (September 1974), 975.

FIGURE 5.1
The Growth of Distrust in the Government

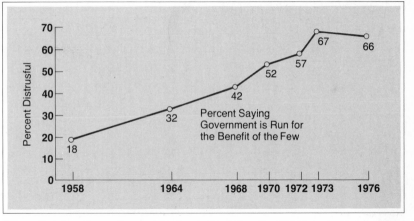

Source: Data from Survey Research Center studies, University of Michigan, Institute for Social Research and National Opinion Research Center study, University of Chicago.

questions about their trust and confidence in the government: Do they think the government is run for all the people or for a few special interests; do they trust the government to do what is right? In the past decade there has been a large increase in the portion of the public that responds in ways that show dissatisfaction. (See Figure 5.1.) In 1958, 18 percent of the public thought the government was run for the benefit of a few; by 1976 this figure had risen to 66 percent.[2]

Along with the decline in trust in the government has come a general decline in optimism about the future. One group of scholars has been studying the hopes and fears of Americans for a number of years. In 1959 and 1964 they found that Americans had a clear view of steady progress: The present was better than the past; the future would be better yet. But in the 1970s they found a striking change. The citizens viewed the second half of the 1960s as a time of decay, not progress. Things had gotten worse. They still believed America would recover lost ground and still hoped for future progress, but the view of continuous progress had been shattered.[3]

The decline in optimism and trust in political leaders had begun well before the Watergate scandal. Watergate increased public dissatisfaction, but the decline in confidence seems to have its roots in a belief that the government could not cope with the many serious problems it faced during the late 1960s and the 1970s—racial tension, Vietnam, law and order, pollution, and so on.

The long-term implications of this decline in trust in government are unclear. Some believe the decline is a temporary reaction to

[2] Data from University of Michigan Survey Research Center election studies. Data for 1973 from National Opinion Research Center study.
[3] William Watts and Lloyd A. Free, *The States of the Nation, 1974* (Washington, D.C.: Potomac Associates, 1974).

specific policies and personalities. Others argue that there is a deeper *alienation* in the land that could threaten democracy. Thus far the evidence shows that the public is dissatisfied with political leadership but has not yet lost confidence in the "form of government." They seem to be saying that "the system is all right; it is just working badly." But a long period of dissatisfaction with the way the system works might lead to a more general loss of legitimacy for the political process as a whole. As yet there is little evidence that this is happening. Indeed, under Presidents Ford and Carter there has been a recovery of confidence in the Presidency, though not to the level of confidence the public used to have. The firm support for the government once found among the American people is now somewhat weaker.

Citizens' Belief in Their Political Efficacy   Another citizen attitude closely related to belief in the legitimacy of the government is *political efficacy.* This is the belief of citizens that they have a voice in the government. Democratic government is supposed to be responsive to the people. If citizens do not believe they can influence the government, they are less likely to feel that it deserves support.

Do Americans have a sense of political efficacy? In general, yes; but as with trust in the government, the number who feel this way has declined recently. Most Americans believe the vote is effective for controlling government officials, and they believe government officials are basically responsive to the people. In short, they feel that they have some political influence. If we compare Americans to citizens of other nations, we find that they are more likely than most others to think they can have some effect on a local government regulation or a law of Congress they consider unfair or unjust. (See Table 5.2.) About three out of four Americans say they could do something about such a regulation. The percentages are generally smaller elsewhere.

American citizens, this suggests, do not feel helpless before the government. And, to some extent at least, believing that they are not helpless makes them less helpless. The same study shows that those who feel able to influence the government are likely to try.

TABLE 5.2
Can You Do Something
About a Regulation
You Consider Unfair?

	United States	Great Britain	Germany	Italy	Mexico
Percent saying yes in relation to local government	77%	78%	62%	51%	52%
Percent saying yes in relation to national government	75%	62%	38%	28%	38%

Source: Based on data from Gabriel Almond and Sidney Verba, *The Civic Culture: Political Attitudes and Democracy in Five Nations* (Princeton, N.J.: Princeton University Press, 1963). Copyright © 1963 by Princeton University Press. Reprinted by permission of Princeton University Press.

In addition, Americans believe that a person has an obligation as a citizen to try to influence the government. When asked what role the individual should play in the local community, a majority of Americans replied that they should take some *active* part—a higher portion than that found in the other countries studied.

The data reported here come from a 1959 study. How have things changed since then? We have no information from other nations to see if the relative position of the United States has changed. But we do have periodic measures of "citizen efficacy" during the 1950s and 1960s. And the best evidence shows that feelings of efficacy rose in the 1950s and fell in the 1960s and early 1970s. In 1952, 69 percent of a sample agreed that "people have some say about what the government does"; by 1960 the figure had risen to 72 percent. By 1973, at the height of the Watergate scandal, the portion agreeing with that statement had fallen to 49 percent. By 1976 it was up again to 56 percent.[4] Thus citizen efficacy, after a sharp decline, appears on the upswing again.

SUPPORT FOR THE DEMOCRATIC RULES OF THE GAME

Agreement on the "rules of the game" means agreement on the basic procedures of democracy such as regular elections and freedom of speech. We have seen why agreement on the rules of the democratic game is important. Let us spell out the argument further: Certain political elements are necessary if a democracy is to work: Opposing groups must be able to organize and to express their views; there must be public control over officials through periodic elections; government leaders must be willing to step down when the voters choose other leaders. These elements are written into the Constitution and formal laws. However, they survive only because the people of the United States are committed to them. The Constitution states that the winning presidential candidate will replace the former President. The change takes place, however, not only because it is in the Constitution but also because there is agreement that this is the way things should be. Supporters of both parties—even that of the loser—agree that it is right for the winner of a Presidential election to take office.

Those who argue that the survival of democracy depends on the commitment of the citizens to democratic procedures stress the importance of citizen support for freedom of speech. The Bill of Rights may provide formal guarantees of freedom of speech, but unless the public supports the right of freedom of speech the Bill of Rights will be meaningless. Democracy depends, they claim, on the willingness of the majority to tolerate unpopular political views.

If Americans agree on these basic rules, the argument goes, they will be able to disagree on other issues. Should there be federal

---

[4] Data from University of Michigan Survey Research Center studies.

control of the railroads? Should there be laws against abortion? Americans disagree on such matters, sometimes quite sharply. But as long as all tolerate the right of opponents to express themselves and as long as they accept the outcome of the dispute when it is settled according to the rules of the game, democracy survives.

Do Americans in fact agree with the rules of the democratic game? In part the answer is implied in the fact that the symbols they are committed to include the Constitution and the Bill of Rights. When they talk about the political institutions they are proud of, they mention the symbols of democracy.

The commitment of most Americans to the Constitution is crucial. That is where the basic procedural rules for American democracy are laid down. And it is the Constitution that most Americans believe gives the government its legitimacy. In 1974, for example, Gerald Ford became President. He had been appointed to the vice-presidency after the resignation of Spiro Agnew and succeeded to the White House after Nixon's resignation in August. He had never won a national election. Yet no one—Democrat or Republican—questioned the fact that he took office properly and was the legitimate President. During that time a French newspaper questioned the commitment of Americans to democracy. How could the American people, it asked, accept as the occupant of the nation's highest office someone who had not been elected by the people? The answer is that Ford's appointment to the Presidency was accepted as legitimate because it followed the procedures laid down in the Constitution, in particular the Twenty-Fifth Amendment.

Commitment to Democratic Procedure—How Consistent Is It? Several studies have shown that the American people generally agree with the principles of democratic government. (By "generally" we mean that usually more than nine out of ten agree.) They agree that the rights of minorities to freedom of speech should be protected, that all people should have the right to vote, that political leaders should be responsive to the people, and that democracy works best when there is strong competition between political parties.[5] For example, in the early 1970s the Harris poll found that 91 percent of the people agreed that "every citizen has the right to express any opinion he wants to" and only 5 percent disagreed.[6] In short, most Americans support the basic rules of the democratic game.

But other research on the political beliefs of Americans shows that commitment to the rules of democratic procedure seems to be greatest in the abstract; it seems less firm in particular cases. The

[5] James W. Prothro and Charles M. Grigg, "Fundamental Principles of Democracy: Bases of Agreement and Disagreement," *Journal of Politics,* 22 (Spring 1960), 276–294; Herbert McClosky, "Consensus and Ideology in American Politics," *American Political Science Review,* 58 (June 1964), 361–382.
[6] Louis Harris, *The Anguish of Change* (New York: Norton, 1973), p. 278.

same American population that agrees that freedom of speech in general is a good thing is less sure that certain groups should have this freedom. When one asks whether groups with unpopular views (e.g., communists or socialists) should be allowed to make speeches, the American people are not sure speech should be that free. Indeed, a large number of Americans are opposed to letting groups of this sort make speeches in their community, and large numbers would remove their books from the local library. For example, a study in the early 1970s found that only 58 percent would allow a communist to make a speech in their community and only 65 percent would allow an atheist to do so.[7] Similarly, the same study that found over nine out of ten Americans favoring freedom of speech in general found that two out of three favored outlawing "organizations that preach the violent overthrow of the government." One study, conducted in Tallahassee, Florida, found that there was broad agreement that minority groups should have the right to participate fully in politics. But among the same people 42 percent thought that a black should not be allowed to run for mayor of their city.[8]

In theory one should favor freedom of speech no matter how one feels about the speaker or the content of his or her speech—at least if the speaker does not directly preach violence or breaking the law. In 1971 the National Opinion Research Center studied this subject. It is clear from this study that citizens would allow free speech for things they favor but not for things they oppose. "Should a group of people be allowed to circulate an antipollution petition?" Ninety-three percent of the people said yes. "Should a group be allowed to circulate a petition calling for the legalization of marijuana?" Only a bare majority, 52 percent, said yes.

Similarly, people would allow freedom of speech for those they like but not for those they dislike. Ninety-five percent of the population said yes when asked if "a group of your neighbors" should be allowed to circulate petitions to ask the government to act on some issue—a clear commitment to democratic procedures. But only about 70 percent thought that "black militants" or "radical students" should be allowed to circulate a petition. (See Tables 5.3 and 5.4.)

The fact that citizens like freedom of speech in general does not mean that they support it where it really counts—when the speakers come from unpopular groups with unpopular views. The commitment to democratic rules is hardly meaningful if they are applied narrowly.

So the data present a puzzle. If democracy depends on commitment to the values of democracy, democracy would be weak indeed

[7] Kay Lehman Schlozman and Kristi Andersen, "Changes in the Level of Tolerance for Dissent, 1954–1974," unpublished paper based on National Opinion Research Center data.

[8] Prothro and Grigg, p. 294.

TABLE 5.3
Citizens Favor Free Speech More When They Approve of the Views of the Speakers

	Percent Saying Yes
Should a group be allowed to petition *to stop a factory from polluting the air?*	93%
Should a group be allowed to circulate a petition expressing *concern with crime* in their community?	95%
Should a group be allowed to circulate a petition calling for the *legalization of marijuana?*	52%
Should a group be allowed to circulate a petition calling on the government to make sure that *blacks can buy and rent homes in white neighborhoods?* (asked of whites only)	70%
Should a group be allowed to circulate a petition calling on the government to *prevent blacks from buying or renting in white neighborhoods?* (asked of blacks only)	51%

Source: National Opinion Research Center study, University of Chicago, 1971.

TABLE 5.4
Citizens Approve Free Speech When They Like the Group

	Percent Saying Yes
Should a *group of your neighbors* be allowed to circulate a petition?	95%
Should a *group of black militants* be allowed to circulate a petition?	69%
Should a *group of radical students* be allowed to circulate a petition?	71%

Source: National Opinion Research Center study, University of Chicago, 1971.

if the values are supported only in general terms but are not supported when it comes to specific applications. But fortunately we can go one step further. We have seen that citizens take a strong position in favor of democratic freedom when asked general questions and a more limited one when asked more concrete questions. But how in fact do they act? They act differently from what one might expect from some of their answers. In Tallahassee, Florida— where 42 percent of a sample said that a black should not be allowed to run for mayor—a black *had* campaigned for mayor a few months earlier. No one had tried to stop him. And in the communities where citizens said that various unpopular speakers should not be allowed to speak and that their books should be removed from the library, these opinions were not acted upon.

Thus the position of the American people on the rules of the democratic game is by no means clear. Americans support the rules in general. When you ask about specific cases, they are less supportive of democracy, but when you get even closer to reality and ask about what they do, you find that they do not act on these political views. One thing this tells us is that people are not consistent; their general values may not be consistent with the specific ways in which they apply their values, and their values and attitudes may not be consistent with their actions.

TABLE 5.5
Political Activists Are More Tolerant Than Ordinary Citizens of Unpopular Views

	Among a Cross-Section of Citizens	Among Political Activists
Percent saying they would allow an admitted communist to speak in public	58%	88%
Percent saying they would allow an atheist to speak in public	65%	95%

Source: Kay Lehman Schlozman and Kristi Andersen "Changes in the Level of Tolerance for Dissent, 1954–1974," unpublished paper based on National Opinion Research Center data.

One possible explanation of why the citizens of Tallahassee would report in large numbers that they thought a black should not be allowed to run for mayor and yet do nothing to stop him is that they were expressing negative feelings toward blacks when the question about a black running for mayor was asked, but that their actions were guided by the more general value of equal opportunity to run for office. And this may in part be true. But there is another explanation. Individuals express political views to researchers, but often these views are lightly held and are not acted upon. Studies suggest that much of what individuals say about public issues during an interview represents positions in which they believe, but not very strongly, or at least not strongly enough to act on them.

This is not true of all Americans. For some, politics is a very important activity. The people who are politically concerned and active form a minority of the population. They are more likely to have advanced education, and they are particularly committed to the democratic rules. Like the rest of the public, political activists agree with the general principles of democracy, but they also support those principles when they are applied to specific cases.

Thus the study that found Americans opposing freedom of speech for various unpopular groups also found that highly educated, active citizens were much more likely to support freedom of speech for such groups. (See Table 5.5.) Or, as another study found, almost one-third of all Americans thought that the majority has the right to deny freedom to minorities; a much smaller percentage — 7 percent — of the nation's political leaders (in this case delegates to the national conventions) took this undemocratic position.[9]

These data suggest that democratic values may be less firmly held among most of the American people than is generally believed, but that they may be stronger among those who are likely to have a greater voice in how things are in fact run — those who are active in politics and in organizations. Democracy may be based on democratic political commitments, but it may be a narrow base.

[9] Herbert McClosky, "Consensus and Ideology in American Politics," *American Political Science Review*, 58 (June 1964) 361–382.

Several additional points can be made—some discouraging, some encouraging for democracy. A discouraging point is that a large group in the population is not in favor of political freedom for unpopular groups and may therefore tolerate antidemocratic politics. This discouraging thought must be measured against two others. For one thing, the general commitment to the values of democracy— vague though it may be—counteracts the less democratic views. At least it provides a set of values one can appeal to. And further, all evidence shows that commitment to democratic values—in both the general and the concrete sense—is strongest among people with higher education. As the population becomes more and more educated—as will happen over time, since the college-educated population is growing—one can expect a large portion of the population to have political views that are consistently democratic.

Summary We have looked at some data on the beliefs of Americans and compared them to what we would expect of a democratic public. The data and the expectations were similar in some ways, different in others.

We expected that citizens would believe the government is legitimate and give it trust and support. In general, they do so, but they have recently expressed strikingly high levels of distrust for government officials. We expected that citizens would be committed to the democratic rules of the game. In general, they are, though the commitment is vaguer in specific cases. However, this lack of clear commitment to democratic values is offset by the fact that those who are least consistently committed are least active in politics.

In short, the system works, but not exactly as democratic theory might have us believe. There is a commitment to democratic values and to the political system, but it may not be as strong as is generally thought.

BELIEFS ABOUT EQUALITY

We have just considered the beliefs of Americans about liberty. The other great democratic ideal at the heart of American political beliefs is equality. The Declaration of Independence declared it to be "self-evident that all men are created equal." Most Americans would accept the abstract ideal of equality, but this does not stop them from arguing about what equality means and how much the government should intervene to create equality. One of the main themes of this book is that the issue of equality is a fundamental political controversy in the United States.

Foreign observers, such as the Frenchman Alexis de Tocqueville, who visited the United States in the early decades of the Republic, were struck by the extent of equality in the United States, both as an ideal in which people believed and as a reality. There were many reasons for the special place of equality as an American value. The Puritan religious tradition was one that stressed the equality of individuals before God. America had no feudal past as the nations of Europe did, and therefore it had not experienced the rigid class

Americans have a basic belief in individualism.

system of feudalism. Most Americans in the early nineteenth century were farmers who owned their own land—we did not have a large class of landless peasants. (Of course all this can be said only if one ignores the system of black slavery in the South. The American tradition of equality was for the white population only.) Lastly, American equality depended on a belief in social and geographic mobility. One could always start afresh on the frontier, where all people were equal.

During the nineteenth century the United States was transformed from an agrarian nation into an industrial one. No longer was it a nation of independent farmers; it had become a nation of industrial managers and workers. Millions of immigrants poured into the country, immigrants who did not share the Puritan heritage. And at the end of the century the frontier closed. It was no longer an outlet for those who were discontented with their station in life. Yet the commitment to equality remained after the conditions that had created the commitment disappeared. Lord Bryce, an Englishman who visited the United States at the end of the nineteenth century—sixty years after De Tocqueville and after the transformation of the United States into an industrial nation—still commented on the egalitarian attitude of Americans. One of the reasons that the belief in equality remained so strong was that the new population of industrial workers accepted the view that America was a land of opportunity where individuals could improve their lives by their own efforts. Historians debate whether in fact social mobility in the United States was greater than in Europe. But most agree that Americans believed, more than people in other nations, that mobility was possible.

Equality can have many meanings. To Americans it has almost always meant equality of opportunity, not equality of condition. Americans do not believe that everyone should have an equal income or an equal life style. Rather, they believe that everyone should have an equal chance to get ahead. Such a belief is a highly individualistic one: Each individual should be free to develop his or her talents to the utmost.

The commitment of Americans to the ideal of equality of opportunity is illustrated in a recent study of leaders in the United States. Leaders from all areas of American life were asked their views on equality. Some—such as black or feminist leaders—come from the segments of society that have been challenging the status quo in America; they have been demanding more equality. Others—such as business leaders—come from more conservative segments of society. The leaders were asked whether they believe in "equality of opportunity: giving each person an equal chance for a good education and to develop his or her ability" or "equality of results: giving each person a relatively equal income regardless of his or her ability." The top part of Table 5.6 shows the results. Equality of opportunity is indeed the dominant ideal for American leadership

TABLE 5.6
Agreement and Disagreement
on Equality

Type of Leader	AGREEMENT ON IDEALS	
	Prefer Equality of Opportunity	Prefer Equality of Condition
Business leaders	98%	1%
Labor leaders	86	4
Black leaders	86	7
Feminist leaders	84	7
Democratic leaders	84	8
Republican leaders	98	0

Type of Leader	DISAGREEMENT ON REALITY	
	Believe Poverty is the Fault of the Poor	Believe Poverty is Caused by the System
Business leaders	57%	9%
Labor leaders	15	56
Black leaders	5	86
Feminist leaders	9	76
Democratic leaders	5	68
Republican leaders	55	13

Percentages do not add up to 100 percent, because some had no opinion or took a middle position.
Source: Sidney Verba, Gary Orren, and Donald Ferree, "The Meaning of Equality: A Leadership Survey," unpublished manuscript, Center for International Affairs, Harvard University, 1977.

groups. It is not surprising to find business leaders believing in this form of equality. But more than four out of five of the leaders in each of the groups accepts this individualistic ideal.

As we saw in relation to beliefs about freedom of speech, agreement on abstract ideals does not imply agreement on more specific matters. The fact that most leadership groups agree on an abstract ideal of equality does not mean that it is a noncontroversial matter. These same leaders differ sharply on a number of more concrete issues. They disagree on the extent to which the American system actually provides equal opportunity for all people. The same study asked these leaders whether the main cause of poverty in America was that the American system did not "give all people an equal chance" or that the poor have "themselves to blame." As we can see from the second part of Table 5.6, the consensus that appears in relation to the philosophical ideal of equality disappears in relation to the question of the extent to which the United States lives up to that ideal. On this issue business leaders and leaders of the Republican party take a sharply different view from that of labor leaders, black and feminist leaders, and leaders of the Democratic party. These differences in perception are also reflected in differences in policy. The same study shows large differences among these groups in their views on how active a role the government should take in reducing inequality. For instance, only 14 percent of the sample of business leaders think the government should do more to reduce the income gap between rich and poor, while 82 percent of the black leaders feel this way.

These leaders differ on whether there should be more equality in America, but they agree that some inequality is acceptable. As we saw in Chapter 4, one of the major characteristics of the American economic system is that it provides for wide differences in rewards to those in different occupations. Do Americans think such differences are justified? The same set of leaders were asked what they believe people earn in various occupations and what they *ought* to earn. The various leadership groups agreed that the top executive of a major corporation probably earns about thirty times as much as an unskilled elevator operator. When asked whether that gap is proper, business leaders say, "Yes, a reward thirty times as great is about right." Leaders of labor unions, black leaders, and leaders of feminist organizations say, "No, such an income gap is too large." But they do not believe that the executive and the elevator operator ought to earn the same amount. They feel that the executive ought to earn about 11 to 15 times as much as the unskilled elevator operator. They would reduce the gap but still leave a substantial one.

In sum, there is a broad philosophical consensus in America on the ideal of equality. Equality means the right of each individual to do the best that he or she can. This consensus fades, however, when it comes to the question of the extent to which the American system in fact lives up to this ideal and the question of how active the government should be in trying to reduce inequality. The agreement on an abstract ideal does not prevent political controversy on the extent to which that ideal is matched by reality.

Where Do Political Attitudes Come From?

POLITICAL SOCIALIZATION

Basic beliefs are formed early in life. This is true for basic religious beliefs; we usually learn them in the family. It is true for basic political beliefs as well. *Political socialization* is the term given to the process by which young people learn basic political beliefs. This process takes place in the family and in the school.

As we have shown, a crucial political belief is that the political system is legitimate. Such basic beliefs begin to be formed quite early in life. In elementary school children learn to prefer the American flag over other flags. This symbolic attachment comes early; kindergarten children already show a preference for the stars and stripes. Only after symbolic attachment to the political system is formed do children begin to give some content to their beliefs. During the elementary school years children come to identify America with the rules of the democratic game—with "freedom" or

Practice in political participation starts in the school.

the "right to vote." At the same time, they learn what it means to be a "good citizen." They come to identify a good citizen with political responsibilities: voting, keeping informed, and the like.

The President plays an important role in the political socialization of children. Children first personalize the government; it is identified with the President. The President is, furthermore, first seen as an idealized figure. Young children think of him as similar to their fathers, as wise and supportive. Only later do they develop a more precise and realistic understanding of what the President actually does.

The sequence by which children learn about political life is important. They are first exposed to the symbols of government—the flag, the President, and so forth. This creates a solidly supportive attitude toward the political system long before there is much understanding of how that system works and what it produces in the way of policies. This support is the kind of cultural commitment that we discussed earlier: a belief in the legitimacy of the government over and above any calculation of whether it is acting in the individual's interest.

During the Watergate crisis children's idealized view of the Presidency was somewhat tarnished. Even young children ceased to have as high a view of the office. But it is too early to say whether the "Watergate generation"—that is, those who were in elementary school at the time—will have less positive and trusting a view of politics throughout life.

Children learn other political lessons early in life. In the home and at school children have their first exposure to authority—to parents and teachers. There is some evidence that they generalize from what they see in the home and school to politics. If children are given opportunities to participate in decisions within the family or in school, they are more likely as adults to believe that they are capable of participating in politics. One study shows that the child's

FIGURE 5.2
Average Scores on a Political
Efficacy Scale

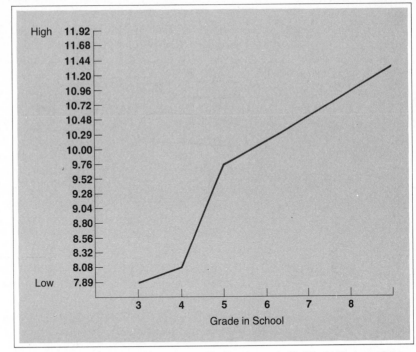

Source: Robert D. Hess and Judith V. Torney, *The Development of Political Attitudes in Children* (Chicago: Aldine, 1967), p. 69.

sense of political efficacy (the belief that one can influence the government) increases dramatically during the elementary school years. (See Figure 5.2.)

SOCIALIZATION AND LATER LIFE EXPERIENCES

The fact that children learn about politics early does not mean that learning stops then. Political beliefs are affected by experiences throughout life. As we have seen, the trust of adult Americans in the institutions of politics—particularly the Presidency—declined during the years of the Vietnam War and the Watergate scandal. Despite the habitual trust that we assume most Americans to have learned as children, their experience with politics led them to become much more cynical. Yet the early habitual trust continued to play a role. It is probably because of this reservoir of trust that the cynicism that emerged about those who were running the government did not lead to a more thoroughgoing rejection of the political system. Furthermore, as we have seen, there is some evidence for a recovery of confidence in government with the end of the Vietnam War and the end of Nixon's Presidency. This return to a more trusting view of the government is what one would expect from a citizenry that was taught early in life to have trust and confidence in political authorities.

There is another reason why political learning continues during adult life. As one child might learn general beliefs—faith in government, a sense of political efficacy, and so forth—that carry over to adult life. One cannot learn specific views on specific issues. For instance, one cannot learn as a child which candidate to support in an election or what position to take on an issue like energy conservation. The candidates and issues will have changed by the time one has become an adult. What one learned as a child about candidates or issues would be irrelevant.

OTHER SOURCES OF POLITICAL ATTITUDES

Where do attitudes on specific political issues come from? When individuals are faced by a political issue—a policy, controversy, or decision on how to vote—they are likely to seek guidance. How do they know that their opinions or choices are right? Citizens usually have no direct information about an issue: "What is really going on in China?" "Who is to blame for inflation?" When they cannot test their opinions against reality, they test them against the opinions of others. And the person that has an opinion on a subject, on which most others have a different opinion, is likely to change his or her opinion.

Who are these "others" that help shape opinions? They include peers, political authorities such as the President or the Supreme Court, the political party, and the mass media.

Peers Studies have shown that groups of individuals who are in contact with one another are likely to have similar opinions. This is particularly true of what are called *primary groups*—friends, families, neighbors, and others who come into face-to-face contact. In part the opinions of members of such groups are similar because they are in similar real circumstances—members of primary groups tend to have similar occupations, to live near one another, and so forth. Thus they may face similar political and social problems.

In addition, individuals will change their opinions to fit those that are dominant in the groups they belong to. This becomes a way of increasing one's acceptance by such groups, reduces tensions with friends and relatives, and gives the individual some sense that his or her view is right—others agree with his or her opinion.

Is this irrational behavior? Yes and no. It may be irrational in the sense that an individual's opinions—how to vote, what to do about inflation—are not based on the "real" political situation. In other words, they are not based on consideration of the issues or on the merits of a candidate. Rather, they are derived from social forces within the group—the desire to be socially accepted, for instance. On the other hand, under certain circumstances this may be a reasonable way to form a political opinion (given that one cannot afford the time and effort to find out all the information on an issue). The opinions of one's associates are perhaps as good a guide as any to political beliefs.

Individuals in close contact with one another usually—but not always—have similar political opinions.

Political Authorities Another place one can turn for guidance in political uncertainty are leading political authorities. The Supreme Court holds such authority for many Americans. If it has taken a position on an issue, many Americans feel that it must be the right one. Another such figure is the President. In one sense he may be less useful than the Supreme Court as a guide for public opinion, since he represents only one opinion and one political party, while the Supreme Court is a nonpartisan institution representing nine opinions. But the President is well covered by the news media, so that his views are widely known and usually respected. This is particularly true on issues that are "distant" from the average American, such as foreign policy.

During the Vietnam War, for instance, observers noticed an interesting fact. Over time popular support for the war declined. Polls showed a steady drop in the number of people who thought the President was doing a good job with Vietnam. But whenever the President did something dramatic—increasing the bombing or stopping the bombing, taking a new hard line or a softer line—the portion of the population who approved of his activities went up, only to fall again shortly. The increase in support for the President when he made a dramatic announcement was due largely to his importance in the public mind and the willingness of the people to be guided by him in matters that they do not understand.

The Watergate scandal and the resignation of President Nixon probably made citizens less likely to think of the President as an authority figure. But the President will probably continue to hold a dominant role as a source of political beliefs. No other figure gets as much attention from the public.

The Political Party For a long time party identification was a major source of political opinions. It was often transmitted from generation to generation. Children took on the partisan identification of their parents, and that identification served as a guide to later political behavior. The importance of party identification has faded in recent years, as we will see in Chapter 11. Nevertheless it remains an important guide on many issues. Issues are often complicated, and they change all the time. Furthermore, a candidate's position on an issue may be unclear. It is therefore understandable that many citizens use their party as a guide to political opinion. The party is a handy anchor for political beliefs in a rapidly changing world.

The Mass Media Citizens also learn about the political world through the mass media: television, newspapers, and magazines. By far the major source of information for the average American is television news. More Americans are exposed to the political world through the evening news than through any other medium.

The news media vary in how broad a segment of American society they reach. Television reaches into almost every home; the network evening news is watched by people from all walks of life. Newspapers are read widely, but the educated and politically involved citizens are more likely to read news about national and international affairs than those who are less well educated or less politically involved. Newspapers differ from television in a crucial way. It is easier to be selective in reading the news in a newspaper than in watching the news on television. The newspaper reader who has little political interest can easily skip to the sports page with hardly a glance at the political news. In contrast, the TV viewer must sit through the political news before the sports news comes on. For this reason television news reaches many people who were previously uninvolved in politics.

Certain key national newspapers play a special role. The *New York Times*, the *Washington Post*, and the *Wall Street Journal*, plus national news magazines such as *Time* and *Newsweek*, are followed closely by political leaders and others who are politically active. They have a political influence far beyond their circulation. In addition, magazines that express political opinions play an important role. Such magazines as the *New Republic* or the *National Review*, as well as specialized journals such as *The Public Interest* or *Foreign Affairs*, are read by a very select audience of involved and influential people.

The fact that the various media reach different audiences means that the bulk of the American public receives a much more limited and more homogeneous set of messages than citizens who are more politically concerned. Television news offers little variety and little depth. News magazines offer greater depth and a richer variety of views.

There is a continuing debate in America as to the extent of bias in the mass media. People from all parts of the political spectrum attack the media for slanting the news. The media are criticized both for being too conservative and for being too liberal. There is some truth to each complaint. Newspapers and television stations

Americans from all walks of life follow the news on TV.

are owned by businessmen, who tend to be more conservative than the public at large. The owners are more likely to be Republican. In any Presidential election, a high percentage of newspapers will endorse the Republican candidate.

On the other hand, many reporters are liberal in their views. This is particularly true for the national newspapers. The "eastern establishment" represented in these news media was a subject of sharp attacks by President Nixon, who felt that they were out to "get" him.

It is difficult to determine whether there is a systematic bias in the media. It is more likely that the media are by their nature likely to be in an adversary position in relation to the government in power. "The national media," Theodore H. White has observed, "have put themselves into the role of permanent critical opposition to any government which does not instantly clean up the unfinished business of our time."[10] Of course this means that no government can ever satisfy the press.

The media and the government have different institutional interests. "The media have an interest in exposure, criticism, highlighting and encouraging disagreement and disaffection within the executive branch." The media want to spur political debate. In contrast, national leaders, especially those in the executive branch, "have an interest in secrecy, hierarchy, discipline, and the suppression of criticism."[11] The federal bureaucracy wants to limit political debate.

Before he left the government in disgrace, Vice-President Spiro Agnew spoke forcefully against the role the national press had taken upon itself:

[10] Quoted in Samuel P. Huntington, "Postindustrial Politics: How Benign Will It Be?" *Comparative Politics,* January 1974, 184.
[11] Ibid.

This little group . . . of network commentators and self-appointed analysts . . . not only enjoy a right of instant rebuttal to every presidential address but, more importantly, wield a free hand in selecting, presenting, and interpreting the great issues in our nation . . . a tiny, enclosed fraternity of privileged men elected by no one.[12]

TV commentator David Brinkley responded to the Nixon administration's criticism of the press by pointing out that

. . . if, over the last generation, the politicians and the bureaucrats in Washington have made such a mess of things with the press keeping some kind of watch over them, what would they have done with nobody watching?[13]

In recent years investigative reporting has become a major media activity, stimulated no doubt by the success of Carl Bernstein and Bob Woodward in their investigation of the Watergate scandal for the *Washington Post*. Such reporting has as its goal the revelation of government corruption or inefficiency or bias. This reinforces the view among many government officials that the media are opposed to them.

The media, in turn, do not take on investigative reporting in order to push a particular political point of view. They do it because they feel it to be their job to expose the shortcomings of government. It is also good business. Bad news is more interesting than good news. In the competition to gain readers and viewers, the media often stress the negative. Indeed, one analyst of the media claims that a good deal of the decline in trust in government found in the American public (look again at Figure 5.1) results from its greater exposure to politics—particularly through the medium of the evening TV news.[14]

Currents and Crosscurrents

In this chapter we have been looking at the American public in rather broad terms, and one may get the impression that all Americans are the same. But that is not the message we wish to convey. Indeed, when we look more closely at American opinion, what seems at first glance like consensus—say, on democratic values—appears on closer study to represent a much greater variety of opinion. All (or at least most) Americans agree with the general principles of democracy, but when it comes to specific cases the portion supporting these principles falls to one-third, one-half, or two-thirds, depending on the groups we are talking about. And figures such as one-third or one-half taking a particular position indicate just the opposite of consensus. They indicate quite a bit of disagreement.

[12] Television address, November 13, 1969.
[13] *Parade,* January 14, 1973.
[14] Michael J. Robinson, "Television and American Politics: 1956–1976" *The Public Interest,* 43 (Summer 1977), 3–39.

SOCIAL BASES OF POLITICAL BELIEFS

So far we have not asked which groups disagree with which in American society. This is, of course, one of the main questions that may be asked about politics in any society: What groups of the population are opposed to one another, or, in other words, what are the social bases of political beliefs? In the United States there are many such bases—people who live in different regions, people with different occupations, people of different races, ages, religions, or ethnic origins may well have different political views. This theme is so important that we will devote the next chapter to it. The struggle among opposing groups—and the problem of which groups are important—goes to the heart of American politics. Here we want to glance at some of the different viewpoints of such groups in terms of the underlying set of American political values.

There are, as we have just suggested, many ways to divide up the American population: into northerners and southerners, men and women, young and old, rich and poor, black and white—that is, by region or sex or age or income or race—and many other ways as well. Each such division of the population would reveal some interesting differences in political viewpoint. But when it comes to some of the basic political beliefs that we have been discussing in this chapter—basic commitment to political freedoms, sense of ability to influence the government, basic trust in the government, and basic sense of obligation to participate in politics—many of these divisions of the population would reveal little difference in overall attitudes. Although there are some differences, inhabitants of different regions, the young and the old, men and women do not differ very much on these basic political principles.

The division of the population that makes the most difference in attitude on these matters is between the better educated on the one hand and the less well educated on the other. We have already seen that commitment to democratic values is strongest among political activists and leaders of organizations. This is probably because such commitment is most often found among people with more education, and such people are also likely to be the political activists and the organization leaders.

The model of the democratic citizen—a person who is committed to the values of democracy, with a strong sense of obligation to participate, and with well-thought-out and consistent political views—does not fit the American population very well, but it fits the educated part best. Americans, as we have seen, are much more likely than citizens of other countries to believe that a citizen should be active in his or her local community—an important part of the democratic model. But the portion who feel this obligation is different at different levels of education. Only one-third of the citizens who have a primary education feel such an obligation, in contrast with two-thirds of those with a college education. Or consider the sense of ability to influence the government. In 1972 citizens were asked whether they could do anything about an unjust or corrupt public official. Fifty-eight percent said yes. But among those with only a grade school education 35 percent said yes, while among the college educated 71 percent said yes.[15]

Black Americans and White Americans

Suppose we turn from the average white middle-class American to those who have generally been deprived of the full benefits of citizenship and of the full opportunity to participate in political life — the blacks, the Chicanos, the Appalachian poor. What are their political attitudes? One might expect less general belief in the "system," more demand for rapid change. Detailed data are hard to get for some deprived minority groups, but we know quite a bit about the political attitudes of blacks. And what we know confirms that they only partly share the outlooks of the average white American.

In some ways black and white Americans have similar political attitudes. When it comes to some general views about the American political system, we do not find as much difference as we might expect. Yet when asked about the workings of the government as it affects them, blacks respond much more negatively than whites.

Consider the kind of treatment citizens expect from officials of the government. A study of political attitudes found that Americans were much more likely to expect equal treatment in a government office than citizens in most other nations. Table 5.7 shows how different the attitude of the average American is from that of the citizen of, say, Italy or Mexico. The American has much more trust in government agencies. Indeed, the percentages expecting equal treatment are so different that the authors of this study suggest that citizens in the United States and in Mexico live in "different political worlds." The majority of Americans expect fair treatment; Mexicans are much less likely to have such expectations.

But it can also be said that the average black American lives in a different world from that experienced by the average white American. Consider the difference between the races with regard to expectations of equal treatment. Almost 90 percent of white Americans expect equal treatment from the government; a little less than half of the blacks have such expectations.

These differences between blacks and whites, first noted in 1959, have appeared again and again in more recent studies. Most dramatic are the differences between the races in attitudes toward the police. Urban blacks have less confidence in the honesty of the police, less favorable expectations of fair treatment by them, and less favorable experiences in dealing with them. Furthermore, blacks are less satisfied with public services in their neighborhoods;

[15] U.S. Senate Subcommittee on Intergovernmental Operations of the Committee on Governmental Operations, *Confidence and Concern; Citizens View Their Government,* December 3, 1973.

TABLE 5.7
Attitudes Regarding Equal Treatment in Government Offices in Five Nations

	United States	Great Britain	Germany	Italy	Mexico
Percent saying they expect equal treatment in a government office	83%	83%	65%	53%	42%

Source: Based on data from Gabriel Almond and Sidney Verba, *The Civic Culture: Political Attitudes and Democracy in Five Nations* (Princeton, N.J.: Princeton University Press, 1963). Copyright © 1963 by Princeton University Press. Reprinted by permission of Princeton University Press.

they complain more about high prices and the quality of the goods in neighborhood stores.

In sum, when it comes to their actual lives and their relations with the government, blacks differ sharply from whites in attitude. Furthermore, many of the distinctive characteristics of black attitudes appear early in life. Black schoolchildren are more likely to be skeptical about the government, less likely to see the President as a benign figure, and less likely to believe in the equality of all Americans.

Do the different outlooks of black and white Americans mean that the consensus one sees among "average" Americans covers up basic differences when one looks more closely at a minority group like the blacks? Since the issue of race relations is a major one in American politics today, it is useful to look fairly closely at some evidence before answering this question.

RACIAL HOSTILITY

Have blacks and whites become more hostile to each other over the years? Certainly someone comparing the newspapers of the early 1950s with those of the early 1970s would have to conclude that hostility had grown. Twenty years ago one read little about racial issues in the papers; today hardly a day goes by without some news of racial conflict. But this is merely to say that racial differences have come into the open. It does not mean that bitter race hatred has developed.

In 1971 the National Opinion Research Center asked people how they felt about various groups in America. Those who were interviewed were given a scale on which they could rate various groups in terms of how much they liked them. Figure 5.3 shows how white and black Americans differ in the ratings they give each other. Note that whites have a more favorable view of whites than they have of blacks, while blacks favor blacks more than whites. That is not unexpected. More important, both racial groups place the opposite group on the favorable side of the neutral point. On the average, blacks do not say they dislike whites, and whites do not say they dislike blacks.

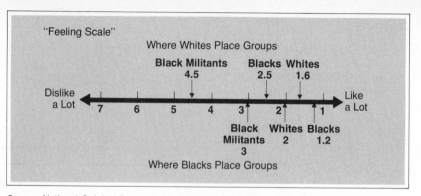

"Feeling Scale"

Where Whites Place Groups

Black Militants   Blacks   Whites
4.5   2.5   1.6

Dislike
a Lot   Like
        7   6   5   4   3   2   1   a Lot

Black   Whites   Blacks
Militants   2   1.2
3

Where Blacks Place Groups

Source: National Opinion Research Center study, University of Chicago, 1971.

The racial groups differ in their views toward black militants. Whites, on the average, say they dislike such militants and place them far down the scale. Blacks are not hostile to black militants. But even if blacks are more favorable toward black militants than whites are, they still rate them only neutrally. Indeed, the average black reports more favorable views of whites than of black militants. The data suggest a major difference in viewpoint, but not racial hatred.

In the years since the racial issue "exploded" in America, white attitudes toward blacks have undergone striking, but somewhat ambivalent, changes. In general, whites have become more favorable toward blacks, more responsive to their demands. In 1949 the National Opinion Research Center asked people whether "Negroes were as intelligent as whites." At that time only 42 percent of whites thought so. By 1956 the percentage had risen to 78 (where it has stabilized). In 1942 only 30 percent of white Americans said that white and black children should go to the same schools. By 1956 (shortly after the Supreme Court decision) the percentage had risen to 48; by 1968, to 60 percent. In 1972 the Harris poll found that 71 percent of white Americans favored desegregated schools. And the same is true of attitudes toward integration of housing. From 1942 to 1972 the percentage of whites who would not object to integration of housing had risen from 35 percent to over 70 percent. The era of more open racial conflict was also one in which white attitudes toward blacks improved a lot.

But there are several qualifications to this generalization. For one thing, as the data indicate, many whites still oppose integration. Furthermore, white support for the goals of blacks has been accompanied by a general and growing rejection of black tactics—at least of militant tactics. We have seen the negative attitudes of whites toward black militants. And whites have generally rejected direct action by black groups, even when it is peaceful and fully within the law. Thus the Harris poll found in 1968 that 80 percent of black Americans favored Martin Luther King's Poor People's March on Washington—a massive, peaceful rally at the Lincoln Memorial— whereas only 29 percent of whites did. Or consider the data in Table

**TABLE 5.8
Percentage of White
Americans Saying That
Integration Is Going Too Fast**

February 1964	30%
April 1965	34%
July 1966	46%
September 1966	52%
August 1967	44%
April 1968	39%
October 1968	54%
July 1969	44%
March 1970	48%
November 1972	52%

Source: Gallup poll data, cited in Jerome H. Skolnick, *The Politics of Protest,* Staff Report to the National Commission on the Causes and Prevention of Violence (New York: Ballantine, 1969). Copyright © 1969 by Jerome H. Skolnick. Reprinted by permission of SIMON & SCHUSTER, a Division of Gulf & Western Corporation. 1970 data from Gallup poll; 1972 data from Harris poll.

5.8 on the proper speed of integration: Whites seem to think things are beginning to go too fast. Thus as whites are starting to accept some of the goals of blacks they are also beginning to feel that things are moving too quickly, that blacks are pushing too hard with inappropriate tactics.

The picture is quite mixed: more favorable attitudes of whites toward blacks coupled with less favorable attitudes. One explanation of the ambivalence of whites may lie in the "rugged individualist" beliefs of Americans. Whites have come less and less to believe that blacks are racially inferior, but they remain firm in the belief that people should get ahead on their own steam and that in America anyone who wants to get ahead can do so if he or she tries hard enough. Thus they see lower levels of black education or income as a result of lack of effort. If blacks do not succeed, it is because they do not try hard enough. Such an attitude leads to reluctance to favor social programs aimed at improving the conditions of blacks.

The ambivalent nature of white attitudes toward blacks can be seen in Figure 5.4, which compares the attitudes of whites and blacks on racial issues. People were asked to choose between opposing positions on what to do about urban unrest and on the speed of progress for blacks. On the question of what to do about urban unrest, people could choose between using all necessary force to put down riots and solving the underlying problem of poverty. Blacks clearly favor the latter course, while the position of whites falls be-

**FIGURE 5.4
Differing Positions of Whites
and Blacks**

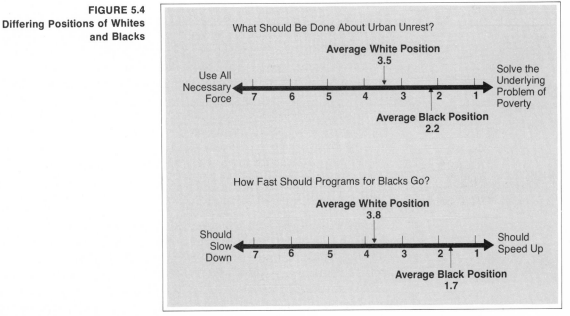

Source: National Opinion Research Center study, University of Chicago, 1971.

137

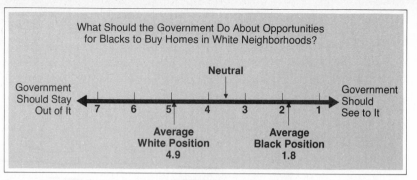

Source: National Opinion Research Center study, University of Chicago, 1971.

tween the two alternatives. A similar pattern is seen in relation to the proper speed of further progress for blacks. Blacks, as one might expect, want faster rather than slower progress. Some whites would prefer a slower pace. On these two issues one finds blacks firmly in favor of faster change. Whites, while not completely opposed, are certainly holding back compared with the blacks.

Some issues, however, lead to greater division between whites and blacks. Consider Figure 5.5, which shows how whites and blacks differ on what the government should do about segregated housing. Here is an issue that divides the population more sharply: Whites want the government to stay out of it; blacks want the government to see to it.

The data on political differences between blacks and whites suggest both the basis for continuing conflict and some hope for cooperative progress. The progress could be based on the commitment of the two groups to the democratic system, at least in a general sense. It could also be based on the absence of racial antagonism between blacks and whites and on greater acceptance by whites of black goals.

But the danger of continuing conflict lies in the greater differences between the races when one gets down to specifics. Blacks may trust the system in general, but they have less confidence in government officials. Whites may accept black goals but are more hesitant about specific aspects of those goals, are opposed to pressure from blacks to achieve those goals, and have begun to feel that things are moving too fast.

Radical Politics in America

Traditionally, the United States has been described as the wrong place for radical politics. This, the argument went, was not because radicals were suppressed. Rather, there were tendencies in American politics that took away many of the issues around which radical politics might be organized. And the two major political parties were good at "stealing the thunder" of such groups by taking up some of their positions.

Though blacks and whites have developed more favorable attitudes toward each other in recent years, some issues still produce racial antagonism.

The 1960s and early 1970s called into question the assumption that radicalism was out of place in America. We cannot discuss basic political values in America without asking why some black and Chicano and student radical groups have challenged the workings of the political system in recent years.

We are not interested here in groups that are radical on some issue, groups that want basic changes in our foreign policy or in the economic structure of our country. Rather, we are interested in those who have radical attitudes toward the democratic process itself, who think decisions should be made by some other rules. Such radicalism can come from either end of the political spectrum. Democratic procedures may be rejected by those who see them as blocking rapid social change—"Problems such as war, pollution, the cities, poverty, racism are too great to be dealt with through the 'system,'" they might argue. Or the rules of democracy may be rejected by those who see such rules as the cause of violence and decay in our society—"We have too much freedom of speech. We cannot tolerate the political views of those who would destroy the 'system.'"

In fact few groups take such a position. As we have seen, the commitment to the rules of democratic procedure (at least on the general level) is widespread—even among those who could be expected to be very dissatisfied with the operation of that system. The young are much more critical of political institutions in America than the population as a whole. A 1972 poll asked young

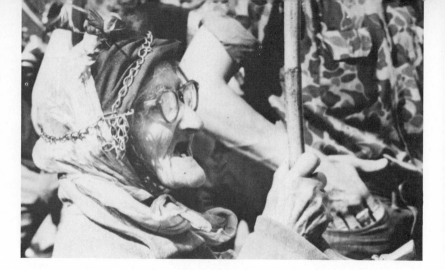

adults about American democracy. About six out of ten thought the country was democratic in name only and was run by special interests. But only 18 percent thought the system was inflexible and needed radical change. Sixty-two percent thought political parties needed major change; only 12 percent thought the Constitution did.[16]

Many of the more radical criticisms of American politics come not from those who would prefer other rules but from those who see the rules working poorly and would prefer to see more effective democracy in the United States. These would include those who want more real participation in the political process or greater power in the hands of local government.

Where one sees direct radical criticism of the rules—rejection of elections or free speech—it seems to come less from the belief that such rules are bad per se than from the belief that these rules have resulted in a poor performance on some issue.

SUMMARY

It may be useful to summarize what we have learned about the basic beliefs of Americans and how they affect politics.

It has long been believed that democracy is based on consensus on certain democratic values such as freedom of speech. In the United States we find consensus on general principles along with a tendency to limit these values in practice. This tendency is, however, partly offset by the fact that the citizens who are likely to be most politically involved and active—those who are better educated, the leaders of organizations—have a greater commitment to democratic values.

Perhaps the most striking thing about the basic political beliefs of Americans is the fact that there have been important changes in

[16] Daniel Yankelovich, *The New Morality: A Profile of American Youth in the 1970's* (New York: McGraw-Hill, 1973), p. 116.

the past decade. For one thing, Americans are no longer as optimistic about their nation as they once were. And this has happened at a time when politics has become more visible to the average citizen and when citizens seem to be developing more consistent sets of political attitudes.

These changes in political attitudes, coupled with powerful and divisive issues—race, the urban crisis, unemployment—can lead to a situation in which hostile groups of citizens are in conflict on a wide range of issues. The data on the political beliefs of blacks and whites suggest that this may be happening, but not as much as would seem to be the case if one considered only the views of the most militant members of each group.

This theme is so important in America today that we will devote a good deal of the next chapter to it.

Does Public Opinion Make a Difference?

We have looked at American attitudes toward government in general and toward some specific issues such as race. But a major question has not yet been answered: What difference, if any, does public opinion make? Does it shape government programs? Or do officials pay it lip service and largely ignore it?

When the public-opinion poll was originated in the 1930s, some thought it would be a great thing for democracy. Now the officials in Washington could get an accurate idea of the feelings of the American people on the important issues of the day. Policy could really follow the views of citizens. An accurate poll could tell what the American people thought of unemployment insurance, defense spending, or farm supports. At the same time, other observers expressed concern. Polls would cause trouble: The public was too ill informed, too fickle, too "irrational" to guide public policy. Good policy requires careful study and thought, something that is possible only if officials are protected from the day-to-day opinions of the majority.

Actually, the public-opinion poll has never been used to set government policy, as the optimists hoped and the pessimists feared.

Two somewhat contradictory points can be made about the impact of public opinion on government leaders. One is that most officials—especially elected ones—pay great attention to the public-opinion polls, to the mail, to all sorts of indicators of public opinion. Not only do politicians follow the Gallup and Harris polls; they also have special polls taken for them to find out public opinion on a particular issue. Furthermore (and this is important), political leaders believe that public opinion is important and should be followed—at least up to a point. On the other hand, policy is rarely made directly on the basis of public opinion.

Why is this the case?

PUBLIC OPINION DOES NOT ALWAYS BECOME PUBLIC POLICY

One might imagine that if the polls showed that the majority favored a particular position, that position would sooner or later become law. But this is clearly not the case. In 1972 the Harris poll asked a sample of Americans whether there should be a strict federal law requiring that hand guns be registered. Seventy percent said yes. Yet no such law has been passed. One might answer that such things take time; if the public continues to feel that way, a law is likely to be passed. But in one of the earliest public-opinion polls, conducted in 1940, the Gallup poll asked an almost identical question. At that time 79 percent favored the gun control law.

How can the public overwhelmingly favor a particular piece of legislation for over thirty years and yet have no response from Congress? The answer is simply that the large majority that favor gun control do not feel very strongly about it, while some members of the minority that oppose gun control do feel strongly on the matter and are active in support of their position.

The example of gun control teaches two important lessons. One has to do with the making of policy in America. It is that a small, intense minority is usually more effective than a large majority that is not as concerned with the problem. This fact is so central to American politics that it will be the theme of the next two chapters. The second lesson is that public-opinion polls can sometimes give misleading information on the preferences of the public. Most public-opinion polls give equal weight to the opinions of all who answer. "Do you favor gun control?" Four out of five say yes, one out of five says no. But if those who say yes do not care much while those who say no are committed to their position, it would be misleading to see the results as showing great support for the position of the majority. You have to consider *intensity of preferences* as well.

PUBLIC OPINION TENDS TO REACT TO, NOT GUIDE, CURRENT POLICY

The public official who is trying to choose a policy does worry about the public and usually tries to keep informed about its attitudes. But on most issues the public is ill informed and its policy preferences are unclear. We have seen evidence of this statement.

But officials also know that the public may react negatively if they do badly. Thus much of their concern is worry about public reaction. They do not learn from the public-opinion polls what policy to pursue. But they often learn what troubles they are likely to face at the next election if they do not deal with certain problems. The public will not tell the political leader how to deal with inflation, but it will let him or her know if it is concerned about high prices.

The history of public attitudes toward the Vietnam War illustrates this point. No war has ever aroused as much public concern and disapproval. From the time the war first became a leading public issue

—around 1964 or 1965—the portion of the American people who were satisfied with government policy went steadily downward. The low point was reached around the time of President Johnson's 1968 decision not to run for office again. And public unhappiness with the war certainly had something to do with that decision.

Yet public opinion was a far from adequate guide for specific policy. When pollsters asked citizens for their preferences on the war—Should we escalate to win, deescalate and get out, or keep up our present policy?—they typically found the public divided across all three positions. How can a President follow that lead? Furthermore, the public seemed to be pleased whenever the President did anything—increased our military commitment or decreased it—as long as something was done. The pleasure ended as soon as it became clear that the new move was not going to end the war. But the conclusion was obvious: The public was unhappy and wanted results. And political leaders had to pay attention to that unhappiness or they would lose in the next election, as the Democratic party learned in 1968. But what the public wanted done was less clear. The administrations involved—the Johnson and Nixon administrations—were under public pressure to do something, but they were not under pressure to do something specific.

LIMITS TO PUBLIC TOLERANCE

There is another way of looking at the role of public opinion in the policy process. This involves recognizing that public opinion sets certain limits to acceptable policy: Some things the public will not stand for. There is probably some truth to this. Public tolerance sets some outer boundaries to acceptable policies. But even here the role of public opinion is by no means clear. One reason is that one can never tell what those boundaries are from the answers to the questions asked in public-opinion polls. We do not know the limits to public tolerance in advance; we may have to test the public to find out.

An example will help make the point and teach us some important lessons about public opinion. For many years observers claimed that the American public set definite limits to foreign policy. The public, we were told, would not stand for recognition of China or allowing it to join the United Nations. Students of foreign policy often complained that this kept American political leaders from establishing better relations with China. And indeed public-opinion polls over the years showed that a large majority of the American public was against recognition of China.

But when President Nixon made his historic trip to China in 1972, the Harris poll found that 73 percent of the people approved. The notion that public opinion stood in the way of better relations with China was probably a myth. This shows the importance of leadership in setting public opinion. Government policy toward

Citizens follow the lead of authorities in foreign policy: Americans became more favorable to China after Nixon's visit.

China did not reflect public attitudes; rather, public attitudes reflected government policy. Change the policy and the attitudes change.

The case of China may exaggerate the changeability of public opinion and the real flexibility this gives to leaders. Such flexibility is probably greater in foreign affairs, about which most citizens do not have firmly fixed opinions. On issues closer to home the limits set by public opinion may be more rigid. Attitudes on racial matters are less easily manipulated, and the threat of electoral punishment by an unhappy public on such an issue may be more real to an elected official than the supposed threat of public disapproval of a new China policy. On such matters public attitudes may have a strong effect on leadership. Yet even in these areas, where public opinion seems firmer, one can never be sure how much it can be manipulated. As we have seen, public support for integrated schools showed a large increase after the Supreme Court declared segregated schools unconstitutional.

A NATION OF MANY PUBLICS

We can end our discussion of the impact of the public on government policy by making one major point: In most cases one cannot think of *the public* as a single entity. There are many publics: There are the citizens who are inactive in politics, and those who are active. There are those who are uninterested in political matters, and a smaller number who are interested. There are, above all, differences in what it is that interests citizens. Different citizens become interested in and active on different sets of problems. This is important in understanding how the attitudes of the public affect government policy. Political leaders are likely to be responsive to certain parts of the public, especially those that are active on a particular issue. Rather than asking about the impact of public opinion as a whole, we have to ask about the impact of the special publics involved. We turn to this topic in the next chapter.

HOW WE FIND OUT ABOUT POLITICS: II
public opinion and voting

Because politics is so complicated and political realities are sometimes hidden, political scientists worry a lot about their methods of study. Their concerns are realistic, for it is easy to get distorted information about politics. When you are given "information" about politics, you should always ask: *Where did that information come from? How was it gathered? What are its possible biases?*

Public Opinion: How Do We Find Out About It?

Throughout this book we present information about the attitudes and behavior of the American people. We look at their political beliefs, the ways they act politically, how they vote, and how they decide to vote the way they do. How do we find out about the American public?

We all think we know how the American public feels about things. In a sense we have a right to think so. For one thing, each of us is a member of the American public, and thus our own views are part of public opinion. For another, we talk to many other people who are also members of the public; we read newspapers, where we see reports of public attitudes or letters to the editor; and we watch television. But for several reasons such information—based on observation of the world around us—can often be wrong, sometimes seriously wrong.

First of all, we often look at our own views and assume that other people share them. This is not a safe assumption. People have widely differing views on political issues and react to political events in varied ways.

Sometimes we feel that we learn more about public opinion by talking to our friends, neighbors, or fellow workers. Such conversations are likely to give us distorted views of public opinion, since most of us meet only certain kinds of people.

An example is the college campus. During the late 1960s students on some campuses, noticing that there was a great deal of activity against the Vietnam War, began to think that everybody under 30 was against the war and to talk of a "generation gap" between their generation, which seemed to be solidly opposed to the war, and the older generation, which was in favor of the war. However, if one looked at the entire younger generation—students on all college and university campuses and those who did not go to college—one found a much wider range of opinions and a great deal of support for the war. Thus by talking only to people like themselves some students had gotten a distorted view of public opinion.

Even reading newspapers or watching television can give us a distorted view of public opinion. For example, it is difficult to know whether people who write letters to the editor—people who obviously have time, interest, and the ability to express themselves—are representative of the general public. Furthermore, the mass media have a well-known tendency to look for the dramatic. The expressions of public opinion that are likely to wind up on the evening news are a demonstration by a small minority or a speech by a well-known celebrity. This, too, is information about one part of the public. It is difficult to know whether this small part is representative of the larger public.

The Sample Survey: Its Strengths and Weaknesses

The sample survey, or public-opinion poll, was developed to get around the weaknesses of the commonsense approach to public opinion. Such surveys—the Gallup or Harris polls, surveys by scholarly organizations, and surveys done for political candidates—can be very accurate in estimating public opinion. Sample surveys must be used with care, however, if one is to arrive at an undistorted picture of Americans' views on a given subject.

To understand how sample surveys can give us more accurate information than our commonsense observations of public opinion, we must consider the sample used and the instrument, or questionnaire, applied to the sample, that is, who the pollster talks to and what questions he or she asks.

Sampling

The notion of sampling is basic to the survey. To know about public opinion it would be ideal to talk to all Americans. But obviously that is not feasible; it would be too costly and time-consuming. One can talk to only some Americans. The important point is that one should try to choose people who are representative of the public as a whole. That is, one takes a sample of the American population and tries to generalize to the population as a whole.

But what is a good sample? Imagine a government inspector who wants to find out whether the jam produced by a certain company meets government standards of purity. To find out if the jam is pure, the inspector must open a jar and test it. But she cannot open all the thousands of jars produced by this company; that would be too costly and would leave the company with no unopened jars to sell.

Thus the inspector decides to take a sample of the jars and check them — just as a public-opinion pollster takes a sample of citizens. *What kind of sample does she look for?*

1. *An Adequate Number*   The government inspector will probably not be satisfied by looking at one or two jars of jam. Any particular jar may be unlike all the others. She will want enough so that she is likely to find contamination if it exists.

2. *A Wide Geographic Spread*   If the company produces jam at a large number of factories, the inspector should not be satisfied by going to the factory nearest her own office, even though this would save time and effort. Since the various plants may differ in cleanliness, a careful inspector would select jars from all the jam factories owned by the company.

3. *A Wide Range of Types*   If the company makes all kinds of jam, the inspector would do well to sample the various kinds and not limit the inspection to strawberry jam. Again, the reason is simple: What the inspector finds out about the strawberry jam will not tell her about the raspberry jam.

4. *A Random Selection*   The inspector selects at random; she does not let anyone else select for her. The clever inspector will be careful to avoid any kind of bias in the particular jars she looks at. She will not sit in her office and allow company officials to bring her a few jars of each kind of

jam, for they might select jars from the cleanest part of the factory or from the newest, most sanitary equipment. Rather, she will go out into the factory and *randomly* choose which jars to test.

How does the public-opinion pollster deal with this kind of issue?

1. *An Adequate Number* A good survey researcher will not be satisfied by talking to one, two, or a few dozen citizens. Even if they are chosen at random, they will be too few to tell us much about the general population. There is too much chance that one will accidentally find people who are very different from the rest of the public. Most good public-opinion polls interview about 1500 people.

2. *A Wide Geographic Spread* It is important that the people interviewed come from a wide range of places, not just the pollster's home town. Survey organizations conduct interviews all over the country to get a good geographic spread.

3. *A Wide Range of Types* The most important thing about a sample is that it allows all types of citizens an equal chance to be interviewed. If the selection process is biased so that one type of person is eliminated, the resulting sample will not represent the population as a whole. In former years many surveys were taken of people who happened to pass by in public places such as railroad stations. It is not difficult to see why such surveys were often inaccurate. They omitted people who do not commute by railroad—homemakers, college students, elderly pensioners, automobile riders, and so on. Certain groups, such as working men, were overrepresented, and other groups were not represented at all.

4. *A Random Selection* The pollster selects; he does not let the respondent self-select. An important aspect of a good sample is that a pollster chooses—on the basis of statistics—who it is that he wants to interview. He does not wait for people to volunteer to be interviewed. This point is important, and it is this that makes the sample survey different from the ways of finding out public opinion that are used in everyday politics.

The member of Congress who judges public opinion on the basis of letters written to him or her is acting very differently from a professional pollster. The member of Congress is assuming that the opinions of those who *voluntarily* write to him or her are representative of the opinions of his or her constituents as a whole or of the public as a whole. As we have discussed, this is probably an incorrect assumption, for letter writers may differ in important ways from those who don't write.

The fact that the pollster talks to all kinds of people—those who do not volunteer their opinions as well as those who do—is the greatest strength as well as the greatest weakness of the public-opinion poll. The great strength of the poll is that it gets at the opinions of all citizens, whether or not they have chosen to volunteer their views. In this sense a good survey represents all citizens—the articulate few who volunteer their views as well as the "silent majority."

But this can be a source of weakness as well, because the pollster records the opinions of many citizens who basically have no opinion. Often a person has not thought about a particular problem until a public-opinion pollster appears to ask about it. Rather than admitting that he or she has no opinion or doesn't know anything about the issue, the uninterested or uninformed person will usually give an offhand answer. Such a response is highly changeable; if the pollster returned the following day, a different answer might be given. Every sample survey contains such answers by respondents who don't really know or care about the issue; this must be borne in mind when interpreting sample survey data.

The Questions Used

Sometimes two different polls will come up with what seem to be different or contradictory results. When this happens it is usually because the two polls have asked different questions. This, then, is another general principle of survey technique: The answers you get depend on the questions you ask.

Those who have worked professionally with sample surveys know how even small changes in the wording of questions can change the results. People respond to the symbols contained in questions. If you ask a question about "Russia," people will respond one way. If you ask a question about "Communist Russia," people will respond more negatively, simply because you have added the negative symbol of communism. Similarly, if you asked about "aid to families with dependent children" you would get a different set of answers than if you had asked about "welfare" or "government giveaway programs."

Thus polls are quite accurate in telling you how Americans responded to a particular question. But the wording of the question always has an effect on the response. Public-opinion polls provide very useful information about the American public, but the information is valuable only if it is used carefully.

6
THE
SOCIAL BASIS
OF CONFLICT

Politics in America—as everywhere—is about conflict and competition. The reason is obvious. The government allocates benefits to the citizens in the society. And the major decisions of the government involve the questions of who gets the benefits and who pays the costs. There would be conflict in America even if there were no differences of opinion on what kinds of policy the government should pursue, simply because the pie that the government is dividing is not infinite. Suppose everyone thought the most important thing for the government to do was to spend more on roads. Conflict over government policies would still arise, since choices have to be made as to what kind of road to build and where. Citizens in one part of the country would try to pressure the government to favor their area. Citizens in one town would prefer to have the new superhighway close enough to be convenient but not so close as to disrupt their community. They would prefer that it run through the neighboring town.

But of course not everyone wants roads. Some citizens think more should be spent on mass transportation and less on roads. Some think spending on transportation is not as important as spending on education or housing. And some think what is most important is cutting spending in order to cut taxes.

Thus conflict arises not only about who should benefit from a particular policy but also about which policy to pursue. And, to take it one step further, conflict also arises because a policy intended to benefit one group is seen by others as a policy that hurts them; a decision to place public housing projects in suburban communities may be favored by blacks and others who want integrated housing, but opposed by some suburban residents. Higher tariffs on imports of textiles from Japan may be favored by American textile manufacturers, but opposed by some clothing manufacturers who like to use the cheaper Japanese textiles or by consumer groups who prefer the lower-priced imports.

This chapter is about the groups who compete for benefits. Note that we talk about "groups" that compete, not about individuals. Political competition is usually among groups. Consider the following newspaper headlines:

Auto Workers' Convention Calls for Job Guarantees
Legislature Seat for Chicanos Demanded
Republicans Ask Court to Nullify Convention Seats
Pilots Call for Hijack Protection

Women's Group Challenges All-Male Court Nominations
Parents' Group Calls for Busing Boycott
Fishermen Protest Shortened Season
Conservationists Sue to Block Superhighway

In each case we see a group of citizens demanding something, challenging something, expressing some position. They become politically relevant because they are groups of citizens, not separate individuals. Groups like these are sometimes called *interest groups,* sometimes *pressure groups.* The members of these groups have interests in common. This forms the basis for their working together in politics. And they *pressure* the government to further those interests. Both terms are important — for not all groups of individuals have interests in common, and not all of those that have such interests put pressure on the government. Which brings us to the question, Which groups in America are politically relevent and why?

What Makes a Group Politically Relevant?

Anything a set of individuals have in common can be the basis of a group. In the headlines we see groups based on sex (women), occupation (auto workers), leisure preference (fishermen), political belief (Republicans), and ethnic background (Chicanos). But almost anything might form the basis of a group. What about citizens of Japanese descent, tea drinkers, red-haired citizens, hot rod racers, people who live in odd-numbered houses, people who are opposed to vivisection, sausage makers? Not all groups are equally politically relevant. Chicanos and blacks are relevant political groups. A few years ago women were not; now they are. Suburbanites may or may not be, depending on the particular suburb. Hot rodders usually are not but might be if they want a local town to set up a drag strip. But residents in odd-numbered houses are unlikely ever to be a politically relevant group.

Since politics is about competition among groups making claims on the government, it is important to ask why some social groups are politically relevant while others are not. Why are Chicanos politically relevant but tea drinkers not? Why women now, but not fifteen years ago? Three things make a group of people politically relevant: a common interest, awareness of that interest, and organization. In addition, groups are likely to be successful in achieving their political goals if they can get their members to give time, effort, and resources to the group.

COMMON INTERESTS

A group is likely to be politically relevant if the thing that defines the group — sex or race or occupation or type of house — is something that creates a common interest, particularly a common interest for which government policy is relevant, that is, an interest that can best be served by some action by the government. Blacks clearly have such common interests in housing policy, desegregation policy, voting rights, and so forth. Tea drinkers have a common interest in government tariff policy on tea. But residents of odd-numbered houses do not, and it is hard to believe they ever would.

However, not all common interests lead to the formation of politically relevant groups. Some interests are more important than others. Tea drinkers may have interests in common, but those interests are not important enough to get them to act. The change in the price of tea that might come from a change in tariff has too little impact on them to make any difference. On the other hand, it would be hard to imagine an American black being unaware of policies that affect blacks.

But though tea drinkers may not consider the price of tea important, tea importers do. The price of tea, as affected by tariff policy, has a large impact on the lives of those who earn their living from the import and sale of tea; it has a small impact on those for whom it is just one item in a shopping bag.

This illustrates a most important principle of American political life. Different groups of citizens are interested in different areas of government policy. Tea importers and tea drinkers may be interested in tea tariffs. Coffee drinkers probably could not care less. Chicanos—citizens of Mexican-American descent—will be interested in Spanish-language teaching in the schools. Citizens in states with no Spanish-speaking minority will be uninterested. Furthermore, even when several sets of citizens are interested in a particular area of government policy, the interest may be very strong for some but relatively mild for others. Chicanos will be interested in Spanish-language teaching in the public schools, and so will the non-Spanish-speaking residents of their communities. But for the former it is an important issue relevant to their culture, to the latter perhaps a less important issue having to do with the costs of schools. What this means is that on any policy some citizens may be very concerned; others will be only mildly involved; and many others will not care. This fact structures much of the political conflict that takes place in America.

Long-Term vs. Short-Term Interests Citizens are more likely to be deeply concerned about common group interests that are *long term* rather than *short term* in nature. There are some group identifications that we have all our lives; there are some that we move in and out of; and there are some in which there is a variation from individual to individual in terms of length of group membership. Our sexual, racial, and ethnic identifications are among those that we have all our lives. These create permanent interests and identifications. On the other hand, we are students or "youth" for a limited period. One reason that it is hard to organize student or youth movements with staying power is that one's membership in such a group is only temporary. Those who become active and involved in student political movements soon find that they have graduated.

Consider as an example the difference between black Americans and unemployed Americans. Blacks as a group have become an important political force in America. There are many reasons for this, one of which is the seriousness of their common interests. Furthermore, these common interests are long-term ones. Black Americans have that identification throughout their lives. The unemployed in America in recent years numbered over 7 million. The unemployed have an important common interest in getting jobs and in government policies that will produce jobs. But the interest is less long term in nature. Unemployment—except in rare cases—is not a lifelong identification. People move in and out of that status. This makes it harder for unemployment to form the basis of a political movement.

The comparison between black Americans and unemployed Americans illustrates another point about the group basis of political conflict. The two groups, of course, overlap. Many blacks are unemployed. But the issue is: Which identification is likely to become the basis of a politically relevant group? Does the black unemployed person identify in politics more as a black or as an unemployed person? Black identification is likely to be more salient, for the reason just mentioned—it is a long-term identification—as well as for other reasons that we will come to shortly.

In some cases membership in a group may be long or short term, depending on the individual. One can be a long- or short-term resident of a community, or one can have a particular occupation for a long or short time. Those who have long-term affiliations—who have lived in a community for a long time or have stuck to a particular job—are likely to consider the interests associated with that identification to be important.

Group Solutions vs. Individual Solutions   A number of individuals may have similar interests, but the satisfaction of those interests may not require any common action on their part. Insofar as individuals can solve their problems by individual effort, they are less likely to form a cohesive group even if other individuals have similar problems. Consider again the contrast between blacks and the unemployed. Each group faces problems that require a combination of individual effort and common activity. The unemployed could improve their condition either by individual effort to find jobs or by working in common to have the government intervene to reduce unemployment or increase unemployment benefits. Blacks can also deal with their problems as individuals or in concert with others. But while the main problem faced by an unemployed individual can be solved if he or she finds a job, many of the problems faced by blacks—job discrimination, inadequate schools—can be solved only by government intervention. Common action on the part of blacks will more effectively influence the government.

SELF-AWARENESS

It is not enough that a group of citizens have interests in common; they have to be aware of those interests. Interests become politically important when they are not merely objective but subjective as well. American blacks have such objective interests, and, further, they are aware of them. In many cases groups may have objective interests in common for a long time, but these interests become politically relevant only with group self-awareness. In recent years women's groups have been active in trying to equalize the pay received by men and women. The objective problem—lower pay for women when they do work equal to that of men—is not a recent one. Such unequal treatment was traditional. But it is only when people become *concerned* about such unequal treatment that they become politically relevant.

ORGANIZATION AND LEADERSHIP

Groups that are organized can pressure the government more effectively; groups that have leadership have spokesmen who can represent them to the government. And such leadership can get greater efforts and commitment from group members.

Self-awareness and leadership reinforce each other. One of the main tasks of a leader is to arouse the self-awareness of followers. When that happens, social movements are born. If not, there is leadership but no one to lead.

Common interests, self-awareness, organization—these make for relevant political groups. Blacks in America have all three. Many economic and professional groups such as unionized workers, farmers, and doctors have all three. In some cases one finds the first two but not the last. Until recently groups such as migratory farm workers have had common interests and some self-awareness but little organization. Groups with interests in common but little shared sense of group membership and little organization have been called *potential groups*. For a long time such a description might have fit consumers or city dwellers who suffered from polluted air. Potential groups become more active as they become aware of their common interests and form organizations dedicated to furthering those interests.

Organization of a group is easier if its members are often in contact with each other. If the members of a particular group live in the same neighborhood, attend the same churches, and work in the same place, they are more likely to form a cohesive and organized group. Again we can contrast blacks and unemployed people. Blacks can organize more easily because they tend to live in the same neighborhoods. The unemployed do not live in socially segregated ghettos.

Summary We can use our example of blacks and unemployed Americans to summarize some of the factors that make it likely for a group to become a politically relevant group. Note in Table 6.1 how many characteristics blacks have that foster the formation of

a politically relevant group, characteristics that the unemployed lack.

MOTIVATING GROUP MEMBERS

Why do citizens join in political activity with others who have similar interests? Why do they give time and effort to working with others to further such interests? At first the answer seems obvious. Citizens work together because they want to pressure the government to respond to their needs. Women work with other women to influence government policy in relation to sex discrimination; blacks join with other blacks to get the local government to improve neighborhood facilities; businessmen join with other businessmen to lobby for favorable economic laws.

Goals like these are the "policy goals" of political groups; they are what the group wants the government to do. Some have argued that it would not be "rational" for a citizen to become involved actively in a group in order to achieve such policy goals. To see why they make this argument, we can return to a point that we made at the beginning of this book about government in general. In the introductory chapter we talked about collective goods and why citizens might not voluntarily contribute to their achievement. A collective good is something that is available to each individual

| TABLE 6.1 | | |
| Why Blacks Are More Likely Than the Unemployed to Form a Politically Relevant Group | | |

Characteristics that Foster a Political Group	Blacks	Unemployed
Common interests?	Yes: jobs, schools, integration, and other issues	Yes: jobs and unemployment benefits
Intense interests?	Yes: Racial issues affect the vital interests of blacks	Yes: Jobs are crucial
Long-term interests?	Yes: One's racial identity sticks for life	No: For most people unemployment is temporary
Interests that need a common solution?	Yes: Many of the problems blacks face require government intervention	Not necessarily: Getting a job solves the problem, at least for the individual
Self-awareness?	Yes: Blacks identify as blacks	No: Being unemployed is not an important self-identity
Organization?	Yes: There are many black organizations	No: The unemployed are unorganized
Leadership?	Yes: many leaders	No
Geographic concentration?	Yes: Blacks live in black neighborhoods	No

One reward of group membership is a feeling of solidarity.

whether or not he or she has contributed to the creation of the good. If I can use the park that my city opens even if I did not contribute to its creation, why not sit back and let others work and pay for it? But if everyone felt that way no park would be created and all would lose.

In the introductory chapter we argued that binding decisions are often needed to achieve such collective goods; all benefit if citizens can be made to contribute to such benefits. Thus tax funds (which citizens must pay whether they want to or not) are used to build parks.

This is related to the question of why citizens join with others in political activity to achieve some group interest. Why should a woman work with other women to achieve equal-pay legislation? The effort of one more person would not have much effect on the outcome. So it should make little difference if she does nothing. Furthermore, she benefits from the regulation if it is passed, even if she did not work for it.

Why should a black join a community group working for better facilities in the neighborhood? His effort does not add that much. And he can use the facilities when they are provided even if he did not help get them.

As with collective goods that the government provides, the "logic" of the situation would result in no activity by women or blacks (or any other group that wanted something done). For each individual woman or black it would be "rational" to wait for the others to act and then get a "free ride." The result: No one would act and all would be worse off.

Furthermore, groups of citizens with common interests cannot make binding decisions and force their members to contribute to the policy goals of the group. The government can make citizens pay taxes to support the park, just as it can make them obey laws in other respects. But the women's movement cannot force other women to join, nor can a black community group force blacks to take part. People have to volunteer.

Why do people contribute time and effort to group causes despite the "logic" that says it would be irrational to do so? One answer is that people don't think in terms of logic. People work for the group's cause even if it might not be logical. But the groups that are successful in getting people to work for them usually offer something more than a chance to work for the group's policy goal. Successful groups offer their members other rewards. One such reward is the feeling of solidarity that comes from participating with others to achieve some goal. The feeling of solidarity—of belonging to a group—is, at least in part, the "payoff" for participation. Social movements like the women's movement or the black movement give participants a sense of belonging, and this plays a big role in keeping members committed and active.

There are other rewards for members of groups as well. Some political groups can provide economic benefits—one may make job contacts through the group. Or the group provides recreational opportunities. For some, activity in a political group is a way of meeting people.

We are not saying that members of political groups claim to be committed to the group's policy goals but really take part in order to make friends or get a sense of solidarity. Participants may be strongly committed to the policy goals of the group. But the other rewards that the group offers reinforce their activity. Political groups are likely to be more successful if they can offer these additional rewards.

Groups in America: Many and Varied

This ability to form groups of like-minded citizens is typical of American political life. In one study that compared Americans with citizens elsewhere, people were asked how they would go about trying to influence their local government. In the United States over half said they would try to get their friends and neighbors to join in with them. This way they could approach the government as a group. In other nations fewer citizens gave such a response. (See Table 6.2.)

In recent years there has been a growing tendency for groups of citizens who were previously politically irrelevant (because they were not aware of their common interests or were not organized) to become politically relevant. We have mentioned women as an example. Many other types of groups have recently become more politically involved. One reads of groups of consumers, commuters, homosexuals, welfare recipients, tenants, and so on. These groups have had interests in common for a long time, but they have recently added to those interests the self-awareness and organization that make them important politically. In this they are following in the footsteps of groups that have been organized for many years, such as factory workers, businessmen, and farmers.

Let us consider some of the different types of political groups in America.

TABLE 6.2
The Use of Informal Groups
to Influence the Government

	United States	Great Britain	Germany	Italy	Mexico
Percent saying they would form an informal group to protest an unjust law	56%	34%	13%	7%	26%

Source: Based on data from Gabriel A. Almond and Sidney Verba, *The Civic Culture: Political Attitudes and Democracy in Five Nations* (Princeton, N.J.: Princeton University Press, 1963). Copyright © 1963 by Princeton University Press. Reprinted by permission of Princeton University Press.

CLASS: THE ABSENT BASIS OF GROUP CONFLICT

We can begin our discussion of the politically relevant groups in America by looking at one group difference that has been less important as a basis for political conflict in America than it has been in other democracies. In most democracies class differences are the major basis of political conflict. The working class has been organized in opposition to the middle class. These nations usually have a strong socialist party that is supported by the working class and sees itself as opposing the "bourgeois" forces in society.

In the United States class has not been as important as a basis of political conflict. Socialism, as a movement of the working class, has never been successful in the United States. Few Americans consider themselves socialists. The largest vote the Socialist party ever received was in 1912, when 6 percent of the electorate voted for Eugene V. Debs for President.

This is not to say that there are no class differences in American political behavior. Factory workers are much more likely to vote Democratic than businessmen. Most of the latter support the Republican party. But each party receives support from people of all social classes. Class differences have not been the *dominant* basis of conflict here as they have elsewhere.

Why should social class be less important as a basis of political conflict in America than in many of the democracies of Europe? The categories of common interest, self-awareness, and organization will help us answer this question.

Class Interests   Members of the working class in America have interests in common: full-employment policies, laws that facilitate labor organization, and so forth. But these common interests have not been as intense as the common interests of workers elsewhere. One reason is the general affluence of American workers. There is much poverty in America, but a high portion of the American working class has a fairly decent standard of living. Furthermore, many workers believe that opportunities for social mobility exist. This reduces the extent to which workers see their interests as conflicting with those of management. The opportunities for mobility mean that workers can deal with their problems as individuals. There is less need for a common solution through a class movement.

Self-Awareness   In the previous chapter we described the commitment of Americans to an ideal of *individualistic equality*, a belief that all individuals have an equal chance to improve their station in life through their own efforts. This belief in the American dream of success has generally been accepted by workers in America. Insofar as they think of themselves as individuals, workers are less aware of their class identity. Most observers of the American working class have commented on the relative absence of class consciousness in America, that is, the absence of a belief that the interests of workers and managers are opposed and that workers should stick together to improve their lot.

Class consciousness has been weakened by a number of special characteristics of American history. The United States does not have a feudal past. We have never had the rigid social structure of Europe, where people were born into a particular social class, clearly distinct in its way of life from other classes, in which they were destined to remain for life. Class boundaries were always more fluid in America. (The exception is black Americans, and as we will see, race is more politically important than class.) Workers did not see the middle class as occupying an unassailable enemy territory; rather, they saw it as a group that they could aspire to join.

The class consciousness of American workers was weakened further by the existence of other identifications that divide the working class. American workers come from different ethnic backgrounds; they are both black and white. These characteristics have often been more important to them than their class identification.

Organization The most important organizations for class politics are political parties and unions. In Europe, socialist unions support the political activities of Socialist parties. In the United States, the political parties have not depended on one class for support. They have been multiclass parties. The fact that the American parties antedate the growth of the American working class is important. When America industrialized in the nineteenth century there already existed a political-party structure—particularly the Democratic party in the major industrial cities—that was anxious to obtain the support of the working class. There was no need for workers to form their own party; instead, they were welcomed into the existing parties—especially the Democratic party. This provided an organization for the American working class, but not one that was exclusively theirs. Workers were not isolated from other groups.

Furthermore, unions in America did not concentrate their efforts on political activity. Rather, under the leadership of Samuel Gompers, they focused on improving the economic condition of American workers—particularly skilled craft workers. Unions in America never fostered a sense of class consciousness among American workers.

ETHNICITY AND RACE
If we wish to describe the various groups on the American political scene, we must look beyond class to ethnic identity. When we talk of ethnics or ethnic politics, we tend to think of Irish Americans, Polish Americans, Jewish Americans, or perhaps black Americans. There is no generally agreed-upon definition of ethnicity, but what we're talking about is fairly clear. *Ethnicity* refers to the fundamental sense of identity that is based on national origin. This sense of identity is transmitted through the family. It is associated with where one lives or comes from. It forms the core of the answer an individual might give upon being asked, "What are you?"

How important is ethnic identity in America? America, the saying goes, is a melting pot. It is inhabited by people from Europe, Asia, and Africa who melted together, mixed, and formed the American poeple. This is essentially true. For one thing, these immigrants have by and large become American citizens. (This fact is not as obvious as it may sound. In some countries immigrants may live for generations without obtaining local citizenship — either because they prefer not to or because they are not allowed to.)

Furthermore, the stamp of "Americanization" was placed on all these immigrants in terms of language. The people who poured into the United States in the late nineteenth and early twentieth centuries wound up a generation later speaking a single language. The earlier language rarely survived. Again, this was not inevitable. In many lands two or more languages continue to be spoken and sooner or later form a basis of conflict. The dominance of English in America is in part a result of policy. Teachers and government officials believed that to be an American meant to speak English, and the schools enforced this in the training of immigrant children. (Former Justice Felix Frankfurter of the United States Supreme Court, who came from Austria, reports that he said something in German on one of his first days in school. The teacher slapped him and told the rest of the class not to speak to him unless he spoke English.) It is important to note that the immigrants themselves largely accepted the argument that to be an American meant to speak English.

Thus, say the history books, out of the immigrants from Europe and Asia and Africa the melting pot made one nation. Not quite. Some groups did not melt easily. Members of other races did not fit the melting-pot model. Blacks of course were denied citizenship and freedom until the Civil War. Even then they did not get the real benefits of citizenship. Similarly — though not as openly — immigrants from Asia were denied full citizenship. The only Americans who were not immigrants — the Native Americans — were also denied full citizenship. The melting pot never fully applied to non-Caucasians.

But neither did it apply fully to white immigrants. Long after the melting pot was supposed to have done its work, ethnic identity remains, ethnic organizations flourish, and ethnic interests come into conflict. And language is still an issue. We consider ourselves an English-speaking nation, but 12 million Americans speak Spanish. And in recent years they have been pressing to have their language accepted.

Ethnic patterns are found throughout American politics. Groups like Irish Catholics or Polish Catholics traditionally support the Democratic party, usually voting over 70 percent Democratic. Or they support candidates who are members of the same ethnic group. Sometimes ethnic politics takes the form of concern about the "old country" — Americans from Eastern Europe are concerned about political problems in that area of the world, Jewish Americans about developments in Israel.

Language is an issue in America. Twelve million Americans are Spanish speaking.

There are two reasons for ethnic politics, both having to do with the interests, direct and indirect, of the various ethnic groups. The direct interests involve the desire—despite the melting pot—to preserve ethnic identity. In earlier times this meant the desire to live near, depend on, or marry others with a similar background and language—for only in that way could one find security in a strange land. Nor have things changed very much. Americans who should have been assimilated long ago have been rediscovering the language, culture, history, and customs of the old country. The richness of American life that was almost lost through pressure for Americanization may still be preserved by the self-awareness of ethnic groups.

More important politically may be the indirect interests associated with ethnicity. The fact that many ethnic groups were immigrants is important here. The groups that today form the various ethnic communities tended to come as immigrants. And each group in turn found itself the most deprived. When the Irish came in the mid- and late nineteenth century, they found themselves in the poorest neighborhoods, with the worst jobs, and in communities controlled by established residents. Their struggle was with the older Yankee residents for better jobs and housing and political power. A generation later, when the Italian immigrants came, history repeated itself—with the Irish likely to be in a somewhat more stable economic position and in control of the local government.

American politics—particularly in the large cities—was for many years an ethnic politics. The waves of immigrants who came to

163

Urban machines sought votes from the new immigrants.

America in the late nineteenth and early twentieth centuries often settled in the cities. And because such immigrants came in groups, joining family members or seeking places where they would find familiar faces or a familiar language, large numbers from the same place of origin would concentrate in particular cities. These groups —the Irish, the Poles and Slavs, the East European Jews, the Italians—usually occupied the lowest economic levels. But their numbers and the ease with which they could become citizens gave them one basis of power: the vote.

The large urban political machines in New York, Boston, and Chicago were based on the ethnic vote. In return for the vote the machine offered the new immigrant help in getting a job, aid if there was trouble with the police, perhaps a Christmas basket—important comforts in a hostile new country. Members of these white ethnic groups, particularly Catholics and Jews, have usually become Democrats.

The white ethnics illustrate the three factors that make a set of citizens into a politically relevant group. They had common interests because they were newcomers in an unfamiliar country; they were aware of these common interests because they lived in ethnic neighborhoods; and they were organized by the political parties, which wanted their votes. The parties as a whole did not appeal to a single ethnic group, but particular local political clubs often had an ethnic base. These groups could get members to work on political matters by providing a sense of solidarity. The social services promised by the machine also encouraged political activity.

All this happened early in this century. For several decades observers have been predicting the end of ethnic politics. As the generations pass, the common set of interests that hold the ethnic groups together fade. They are no longer new residents holding the low-level jobs; their children move into the mainstream of the American economy. Many move out of the ethnic neighborhoods to the newer suburbs, into areas that are ethnically mixed. This reduces the level of common interest and the possibility of developing strong self-awareness. Finally, the urban machine has lost much of its power; the welfare services it provided have been taken over by federal social-security and other welfare programs. In short, the basis for ethnic politics seems to be fading.

But though ethnicity is not as powerful a political factor as it once was, it has remained strong. After a generation of attempts to bury the customs and identities of the Old World, many third-generation immigrant children are returning to a sense of ethnic self-awareness. Ethnic voting continues in many cities—the candidate with the right ethnic name can count on support from many people of similar backgrounds. And studies show that ethnicity plays a role in presidential elections. Ethnic associations and, in some cities like Chicago, ethnic neighborhoods remain.

In part this renewal of ethnic politics is a reaction to a challenge from other groups—particularly black Americans. Many of the American ethnic groups have "made it"—skilled work, a reasonably good income, a house and car, children in a good school. Challenged by what they see as a threat from expanding black neighborhoods, and by a group with what seems to be a firmer sense of identity — the black militants — white ethnics have begun to renew their ethnic ties.

Blacks As mentioned earlier, the melting pot never applied to blacks. Other groups might participate fully in America, but the racial barrier was harder to cross. Black Americans have been important in American politics from the beginning — but as the subjects of government policy, not as participants in politics. The history of America from the early nineteenth century through the Civil War was largely one of conflict about blacks. And since the Civil War politics has often centered on the issue of race.

Before the Civil War blacks were barred from political life. Even in states with slavery, free blacks were usually denied the vote. Studies have suggested that there is some similarity between the current position of black Americans as the newest immigrants to northern cities and the position of the earlier white immigrants. Such an analogy is useful, for it helps us see some general patterns underlying the experiences of various groups. But in relation to the position of blacks in America it would be unrealistic not to notice the vast differences between the position of the blacks and that of the Irish, Italian, or Eastern European immigrants to America. The major differences can be summed up in two words: slavery and race.

Consider the position of the white immigrants to the United States in the nineteenth century. They were poor and often uneducated. They were looked down upon and discriminated against. They were crowded into urban ghettos. But their situation was sharply different from that of blacks. The white immigrants entered a nation where the dominant principle was one of equality; where the aristocratic tradition of Europe in which one's position in life was determined at birth had been rejected. And they entered a society in which the laws supported this principle. By the 1840s almost all men could vote. But the principle of equality and the ability to vote were clearly limited to whites — in the North as well as in the South.

The Civil War and the constitutional changes that followed it — the Thirteenth, Fourteenth, and Fifteenth Amendments — tried to change this situation. The American black could not be denied citizenship, the vote, or the protection of the laws.

At least this is what the Constitution said. It had still to be fully applied in practice. As part of the process of reconciliation between North and South (northern whites and southern whites, that is), the meaning of these amendments was watered down. The right to vote was effectively taken away from blacks in the South. Segregated facilities were legally accepted. And in many ways the gains of blacks at the end of the Civil War were seriously reduced.

Political conflict, as we have pointed out, arises when groups have conflicting goals but are interdependent. If they have no conflicting goals, there is no conflict. If they are not interdependent, they can each go their own way and there is no need for conflict over what policy the government should pursue. The conflict between American blacks and American whites arises because of a combination of interdependence and conflicting goals. Where the conflict between goals is severe and there appears to be little chance of agreement, one solution is to reduce the interdependence — to separate. And throughout the history of the blacks in America this has been done. In the early days of the Republic many white leaders thought the solution to the issue of slavery would be to return blacks to Africa. And black leaders have often supported that position, for example, in the movement under Marcus Garvey in the 1920s for a return of blacks to Africa. This movement — though it was supported by part of the black population — never received support among the bulk of American blacks and has never been a realistic alternative. Its more recent forms — the various versions of black nationalism and separatism — call for separation within the United States: separate communities, separate schools and institutions, sometimes separate states or sections of the country.

The failure of these movements points up the fact that political conflict will continue. The black nationalist movements are significant not for their goal but for the increased sense of black identity that they foster. As pointed out earlier, one of the factors that makes a group of citizens politically important and effective is the sense of identity that binds them together. And this has been fostered to a large extent by the sense of deprivation of blacks in America.

American blacks have become a strong political force in recent years because they have developed self-awareness and organization. The third factor — common interests — is something they have had from the beginning. But common interests are not enough if the group is not aware of those interests. This self-awareness grew in the 1950s and 1960s.

The growth of black self-awareness has many sources. The role of the civil-rights movement of the 1950s and 1960s is important. So is the role of the mass media — especially television — in communicating the new movement to the black community. In earlier times a civil-rights demonstration in one part of the country might have little impact on other areas. But when a nation is linked together by the media, it is easier to create a community among people living in different regions, in cities and in rural areas.

The increased importance of blacks in American political life depends also on organization. Ths history of the recent black movement has been a history of organization as well: the NAACP, the Southern Christian Leadership Council, CORE, the Black Muslims, the Black Panthers, Operation Breadbasket. This list — and it could be much longer — shows how many and varied the bases of black political organizations are. Blacks are by no means organized into a

single group, nor are they all organized. But organizations of all sorts are making blacks a political force.

Other Minority Groups   Blacks are not the only racial or ethnic minority. We have seen how white ethnic politics has responded to what is seen as a black challenge. Other minority groups—Chicanos, Native Americans—have also moved into active politics. In each case their activity shows how interests or needs in common, self-awareness, and organization make a group politically relevant.

Chicanos, for instance, have long had common interests and needs. Speaking a language that was foreign in the United States, often given only the lowest-paying agricultural jobs, discriminated against in housing and schools, the Chicanos were not politically active until recent times. However—again perhaps in response to similar activities among black Americans, but also in response to such leaders as Cesar Chavez—they have moved into the center of political conflict.

They form an interesting contrast to another group—Americans of Japanese origin—many of whom, like the Chicanos, live on the West Coast. Japanese Americans also have a long history of common problems and discrimination. They were long barred from American citizenship and from owning land. And in World War II most Japanese Americans were put in concentration camps—called relocation centers—as dangerous aliens. In addition, Japanese Americans have a fairly strong sense of group identification.

But unlike Chicanos and blacks, Japanese Americans are not an active political force. One of the three factors is missing. There is a sense of identification and even some organization, but little common political interest. Japanese Americans face almost no housing or schooling discrimination and have moved into high-status jobs in most places. With few common political interests—that is, no set of policies that they want the government to pursue—they do not become a potent political force.

OTHER TYPES OF GROUPS

There are so many ways in which citizens group together that we could go on describing them endlessly. As we began to run out of relevant groups, new ones would be forming and old ones fading from political involvement. Let us, then, look at some of the other *types* of groups that one finds in America. We can then turn to the more interesting question of how they relate to one another.

Occupational Groups   Broad social distinctions like social class may not form the bases of politically relevant groups. But particular occupations may. Occupation is an important concern of most Americans. But occupational groups vary in political relevance in terms of common interests, self-awareness, and organization.

Not all occupational groups have common interests to the same extent. Small shopkeepers represent an important occupational group, but the members of the group do not necessarily have a "common fate": One shopkeeper may do well while another goes bankrupt. Of course sometimes they will have common problems. All shopkeepers may be hurt by inflation or a business downturn, but these problems will have an impact on them as members of the general economy, not as shopkeepers. Or the shopkeepers in a particular town may be hurt by the development of a shopping center outside the town. In this case they may form a politically relevant group on a local basis.

Compared with shopkeepers, such groups as teachers or auto workers are much more likely to have a common fate and a set of common interests. Teachers have common interests because their salaries and working conditions are all set by the governments for which they work; auto workers, because they depend on a single industry.

In addition, there is the question of how much these interests are affected by government policy. The more the government is active in relation to a particular occupation, the more the occupational group is likely to be politically involved. Doctors and lawyers show a contrast here. Government policies that affect the practice of medicine—from community and state hospitals to medicare to drug regulations—are much more extensive than those that affect the practice of law. And doctors as an organized occupational group have, through the American Medical Association (AMA), been most active in politics. This illustrates the point we made earlier about the different degrees of citizen concern about particular interests. All citizens have an interest in health care. But the medical profession—because it earns its living through health care, because it is organized and has leadership—has had a greater voice in such matters than the much larger number of ordinary citizens.

Note that we are dealing here with the extent to which various occupational groups become politically active *in relation to the interests of that occupation*. Lawyers are generally more active in politics than doctors; indeed, they are more active than members of most other professions. They are more likely than members of other professions to run for office or to take government appointments. But they do not do so as representatives of the interests of the legal profession.

This difference among occupational groups is related to a simple but important generalization about politics: Where the government is active, citizens are likely to be active as well. When new government programs touch the lives of particular groups, they are likely to become more politically involved.

Occupational groups also differ in self-awareness and organization. These two characteristics are of course linked. The better a group is organized, the more likely it is that its members will be aware of their common problems and the relevance of the government to them. Farmers have been an important political force because they have participated in a variety of farm organizations. Or rather, farmers who have organized have been a strong force; those who have not organized (poorer farmers, tenant farmers, and so on) have been weak politically. A most important distinction is between organized and unorganized labor. Workers who are not unionized are politically weak—both because they have no organization to speak for them and because they have no self-awareness. This was the case for many decades for such groups as teachers and migratory workers. Teachers remained unorganized because they believed unionization was not appropriate for a professional group; migratory workers remained unorganized because the conditions of their work made it difficult to form groups. In recent years, as both groups have become more unionized, they have become more active and effective.

Regional Groups The place where people live and work also forms a basis for common interests. Different regions, different states and cities, suburbs versus central cities—all these differences may have political importance. Regional politics has of course been important throughout U.S. history. The South is the most distinctive region in terms of culture, history, and political behavior. Its voters tended to vote in a distinctive way—traditionally for the Democratic party—long after the basis for that identification had faded. And its representatives in Congress formed a bloc—often voting with northern Republicans to form a strong conservative force. But the "solid South" has become less solid since Republicans began to make inroads during the Eisenhower years. Industrialization and population migration, as well as the political awakening of the southern black, have changed the social and political life of the region.

With the South one sees another example of the importance of common interests and common experiences with government policy. Southerners had the shared experience of the Civil War and Reconstruction. Even when they had become history, these experiences could be seen in the South's heightened self-awareness as a region.

Recently the major regional division in America has been between the "Sunbelt" and the "Snowbelt." The states of the South and Southwest, the Sunbelt, have been growing in population and in industry while the older states of the Northeast and upper Midwest have been declining. The political conflict has centered on government policies on energy (the Snowbelt being more concerned over the cost of fuel) and the allocation of government aid (each region arguing that it is being shortchanged by the formulas used by the federal government to allocate aid).

Regional politics in the United States is important because it is always well organized. By this we simply mean that elections in America have a regional structure. We elect representatives to Congress from particular districts or states. This point is so obvious that we may miss its importance. Why not elect representatives from occupational groups—all plumbers elect a certain number, all lawyers, all farmers? Or by race—the blacks elect theirs, the whites theirs, the Chicanos theirs? Why not indeed? Other countries have experimented with such alternatives, and one can make an argument for them. The argument for geographic representation is that citizens living in the same area have similar interests, but this is only partially true. In some ways we have interests in common with those who live in the same congressional district, but in some ways we may have more interests in common with citizens of similar occupation or religion or race living in other parts of the state or nation.

But whatever the basis of representation (and probably none is perfect), the fact is that the American system is organized on the basis of place of residence, and this is unlikely to change. This automatically makes geography important as a basis of citizen interests. As we shall see in Chapter 12, when we discuss the representativeness of Congress, this basis of representation has a major impact on how the government operates.

Recently conflict has arisen between citizens who have moved to suburbs to avoid the noise, crowding, and social tensions of the cities and those who remain in the central cities, for whom the noise, crowding, and social tensions are an unavoidable part of life. The latter claim that the problems of the central city could be solved if those in the suburbs would help—if their schools were open to central-city children, if their communities would construct low-cost housing. The suburban citizens often reply that these are the problems of the cities, and they are pleased to have left them behind. The fact that the central-city resident is often black and the suburban citizen white does not make the problem easier to solve.

Religious Groups In many nations religious conflict is severe. In America religious divisions have been politically relevant but have not been the source of severe conflict. Catholics have had a traditional identification with the Democratic party; Jewish groups have been active on American policy in the Middle East; fundamentalist Protestant groups have lobbied for blue laws and the like. When the first Catholic candidate (Al Smith) ran for the Presidency in 1928, he was bitterly opposed by many Protestant groups, which thought his election would represent a takeover by the Catholic Church. When the second Catholic candidate (John F. Kennedy) ran and won in 1960, he was also opposed for similar reasons. But his behavior in office could in no way be considered distinctively Catholic. It may be that the Kennedy experience will lead to a decline in the religious basis for political groups.

Perhaps the major reason for the lack of severe religious conflict in American politics is the constitutional ban on laws affecting religious belief. If our generalization is correct, groups become politically active when government policy affects them. The constitutional ban on legislation affecting religion may explain why religion has not been the explosive issue it might have been. On the other hand, the Constitution does not eliminate all religious-based issues. The exact meaning of the constitutional provision for separation of church and state has given rise to conflict in the past and continues to do so. Is it a violation of the Constitution if a city pays for school buses for children going to Catholic schools? Is it a violation if there is prayer in the schools? On such issues one finds religious groups active and concerned. Similarly, religion can affect a group's attitude on foreign policy—as is illustrated by the strong views of American Jews on relations with Israel.

Sex Is the male–female difference a basis for politically relevant grouping? A decade ago many observers would have answered no. Today it is clear that it is. Women are not a minority group; they actually amount to 51 percent of the population. But they share many of the problems faced by disadvantaged minorities. And the history of the women's movement parallels in many ways the history of the formation of other politically relevant groups.

Women had interests in common for a long time, but few people —women or men—were aware of them. The report of a presidential commission on the status of women, issued in 1963, listed a number of ways in which women were treated inequitably. A number of states had inequitable laws on such matters as child custody and property rights. The commission documented widespread job discrimination.

What has changed in the past decade is the level of consciousness of women regarding their common problems. Not that all women share the beliefs of more militant feminists. But many more women have come to be aware of their common interests. Furthermore, many have come to see these interests as requiring action on the part of the government. They have worked for the passage of laws banning discrimination on the basis of sex in employment, in obtaining credit and loans, and so forth. Much of the political activity of women's groups has focused on the Equal Rights Amendment to the Constitution, which would bar discrimination on the basis of sex. The amendment has yet to be ratified by a sufficient number of states.

The self-awareness of women has been fostered by the emergence of feminist leaders and feminist organizations. The National Organization of Women (NOW) was founded in 1966, and other women's organizations have followed. Critics of social movements like the women's movement often accuse these groups of inventing the problems about which they complain. "Women never knew they were discriminated against until the women's liberation types told them." But this is exactly what leadership must do if it is to succeed in creating a movement. It must create awareness of the problems faced by a group in order to make that group politically active. Furthermore, feminist leaders do not create grievances for women

any more than black leaders create grievances for blacks. What they usually do is make individuals aware of the fact that others have similar grievances and that collective action may help improve their situation.

Age At times age can become the basis for a politically relevant group. In the late 1960s the youth movement, youth culture, and the "generation gap" made age a basis for political action. More important may be the growth of old age as a politically relevant category. As medical care improves and as people retire earlier, the number of older citizens has become more important. These citizens clearly have interests in common: social-security payments, inflation, housing. As the government has taken on more of the problems of the elderly, the common interests of this group have increased. The medicare program, which provides medical care for older citizens, has been the focus of much concern.

The elderly have also become more organized. The National Association of Retired Persons has over 7 million members, and other groups such as the Gray Panthers have succeeded in organizing the elderly into an effective lobby.

Special-Concern Groups We have been describing groups of American citizens in terms of ethnic background, occupation, sex, age, place of residence. These things are likely to form the basis of lasting political groups, but they become politically relevant, we have argued, only if they are accompanied by an awareness of some common interest—a black political interest, a women's political interest.

But there are times when groups are based more directly on shared interests and less on basic social characteristics. As with social characteristics, the variety of specific interests is also vast. Groups form around common recreational interests (skiing, hunting, bird watching); around social concerns (mental health, pollu-

tion, government corruption); around intellectual or cultural interests (book clubs, literary groups, art groups).

As with the other groups, these special-concern groups become politically relevant when their interests are somehow affected by government action or inaction. For instance, recreational groups may begin as organizations with no particular interest in government policy; they may be simply groups of citizens with a common interest in skiing or hiking or bird watching. But as the pursuit of these nonpolitical interests becomes dependent on government programs—on the preservation of a wilderness area, for instance—these groups can become politically active.

Multiple Memberships

As we have seen, Americans have many different group identifications. To understand how these affect political life, we must look at the relationships among these identifications. There are two points to note:

1. There is a great variety of groups and potential groups in America. There is no set of dominant groups.
2. More important is the fact that the groups can overlap. Each citizen belongs to many groups at once. Citizens have an ethnic identity, an occupational status, a regional location, a religion, and so forth.

Which of these group affiliations will be important politically? The answer is that it varies. At some times and on some issues, one group affiliation will be important, at other times others will matter. The Catholic steelworker living in a suburb of Cleveland will sometimes act politically as a steelworker. He will support policies or candidates based on his view of the interests of steelworkers or on the advice of his union. At other times he may act as a Catholic, perhaps voting for a candidate who is of the same faith or considering an issue such as abortion law or aid for parochial schools from that point of view. Another time he may act as a suburbanite, perhaps opposing plans to tax suburban dwellers who work in the cities. In short, citizens have many potential political interests. At times they act in terms of one such interest; at other times they act in terms of others.

At least this is the case with most Americans. For some, one identification overrides all others: Black militants respond to all issues in terms of racial identity, militant members of women's groups in terms of sexual identity, and so forth. The results for political life are important. If a citizen has a variety of identifications, he or she is likely to hold none as strongly as the citizen who puts all his or her energy into one identification. The citizen with many identifications is more willing to compromise, less firm in action. The "single-identity" citizen is likely to be more militant, firmer, less compromising.

CROSSCUTTING VS. REINFORCING IDENTIFICATIONS

An important characteristic of group identifications in America is the extent to which they *crosscut* rather than *reinforce* one another.

Let us explain what we mean by these terms, since they help us understand how political conflict in America works itself out. Imagine a society in which people are divided by religion (into Catholics and Protestants), by occupation (into workers and managers), and by place of residence (into suburban and central-city residents). If these three divisions of society were reinforcing rather than crosscutting, one would find that all citizens who were similar on one characteristic would be similar on the other two. The society might be divided in this way:

| Catholic workers living in the central city | Protestant managers living in the suburbs |

And insofar as there were interests associated with these identifications, the society would be divided into two groups with conflicting interests. Catholics want aid to parochial schools; Protestants do not. Workers want controls over profits; managers want controls over wages. City dwellers want suburban residents to share in the cost of urban services; suburban residents do not want to. Thus the society would be divided into two groups with the following interests:

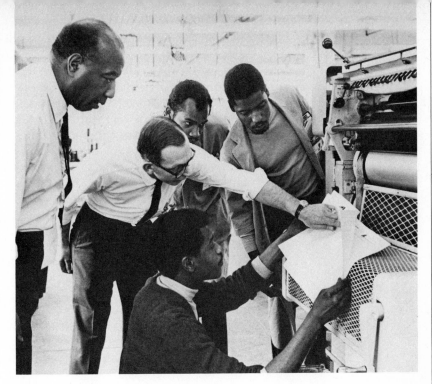

Conflict is less intense when individuals divided by one characteristic, such as race, are united by another, such as occupation.

One Group Would Be	The Other Group Would Be
a. in favor of aid to parochial schools.	a. opposed to aid to parochial schools.
b. in favor of control over profits.	b. opposed to controls over profits.
c. in favor of taxing the suburbs to pay for city services.	c. opposed to taxing the suburbs to pay for city services.

Such a situation is likely to be one of high political tension. The two groups have nothing in common. They are divided on every issue. If government power were in the hands of the Protestant managers who live in the suburbs, the city-dwelling Catholic workers would have little reason to believe that their interests would be protected—for the group in power would differ from them in every way.

But suppose the identifications were crosscutting, not reinforcing. In this case some workers would be Protestant and others Catholic; some would live in the suburbs and some in the city. The important point here is that citizens who were divided on one interest would be united on others. The Catholic worker would disagree with the Protestant worker on aid to parochial schools, but they would agree on controls over profits. If he lived in a suburb, he would share interests with Protestants who lived there, as well as with managers who lived there. And in his church he would meet (maybe not socialize with, but at least see) people from different economic backgrounds.

In general, American politics is characterized by crosscutting patterns of group identification. Catholic workers join with Protestant workers on some issues (economic ones) and with Catholic businessmen on others (e.g., parochial schools). These patterns have an important impact on American politics, since they affect the political coalitions that can be formed. People have often talked of forming a liberal (or radical) coalition in the United States, bringing together all who are interested in major changes in the social and economic systems. But such a coalition is very difficult to build, for any such group will contain people with very different views on some issues, much as they may agree on others.

Take a simple example: One of the major positions of a liberal or radical coalition is likely to be tax reforms that increase taxes on higher-income groups and eliminate many of the loopholes in tax laws that benefit such groups. Such a position would find agreement among many of the groups that would form the core of a liberal or radical coalition — blacks, white workers, middle-class liberal intellectuals. But these three groups would differ when it came to other issues. The blacks and the white workers might differ on matters of integration; both might differ from the middle-class intellectuals on matters of civil liberties. Such a coalition would obviously be hard to hold together.

Patterns of Division and Competition

We have described the politically relevant groups in American society at some length because it is around such groups that the political struggle takes place. These groups have different interests and therefore make different claims on the government. Each seeks policies that benefit it and, in so doing, often comes into conflict with other groups.

The wide range of groups in America, the variation in the intensity of citizen concern with one set of interests rather than another, and the fact that groups crisscross one another all suggest that no single pattern of division and competition is found in America. From issue to issue, from group to group, the ways in which parts of the society compete with each other may differ.

DIFFERENT PATTERNS OF POLITICAL BELIEF: IMPLICATIONS FOR CONFLICT

It will be useful to sketch a variety of patterns of competition or conflict among groups, along with some examples. The reader will understand a good deal about any particular issue or conflict in America if it can be fit into one of these patterns.

Scale of Political Positions   Political conflict begins with conflicting interests. One group of citizens prefers one policy (we can call it A); another prefers an alternative policy (call it B). In addition,

FIGURE 6.1
Scale of Political Positions

Strongly Favor A	Mildly Favor A	Indifferent Between A and B	Mildly Favor B	Strongly Favor B

some citizens feel strongly about the issue, others feel less strongly, and some are indifferent. Thus we can put various citizens and groups somewhere on the scale, as shown in Figure 6.1. A might stand for being for integrated housing, B for being opposed. Or A and B might stand for being for or against gun control, or for or against various welfare programs. Some citizens will support A or B strongly, some more mildly, and some not at all.

If we convert the scale of political positions into a graph, with the amount of space under the curved line indicating how many people hold that position, we can see a variety of patterns of competition. Consider Example 1. Here the largest group of Americans doesn't care about A or B, and those who do have a position hold that position rather mildly. Furthermore, the figure is quite symmetrical—the numbers of citizens on either side of the issue are about equal. Many issues take this form, and for obvious reasons they tend to be those on which there is little conflict, little excitement, and perhaps no government activity. It will make little difference what action the government takes, because there is little concern on either side. With a pattern like this, government officials are fairly free to do anything they want about the issue—if they want to do anything at all.

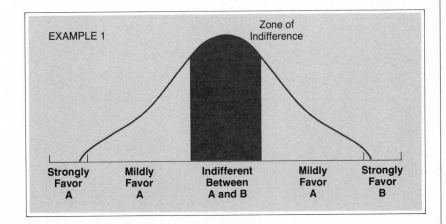

Example 2 shows a different pattern of interests or preferences. Like Example 1, it is a situation in which one would expect little conflict or competition, simply because all citizens seem to agree in their strong support for position A.

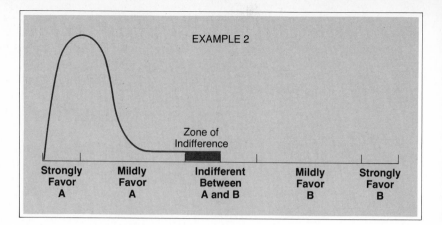

Examples of such a situation might be the attitudes of Americans toward the enemy in most wars before Vietnam. Most Americans were strongly antagonistic to the enemy. Such a pattern does not lead to internal conflict. It can be a strong political force, a resource used by government leaders if they want public support for an all-out war effort. Or it can greatly limit their freedom of action if, for instance, they want to pursue a more conciliatory policy toward the opposing group.

A pattern of interests of this type, however, can have dangerous results for democracy—woe to the few citizens in favor of policy B! Even those who don't care may be in trouble. Freedom of speech or rights of political association have been most severely limited when American opinion has been shaped as shown in Example 2. Thus in wartime we have often seen the suspension or diminution of the freedoms guaranteed in the First Amendment.

FIGURE 6.2
Attitudes Toward Medical Care

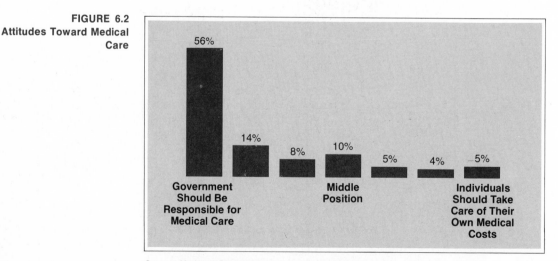

Source: National Opinion Research Center study, University of Chicago, 1973.

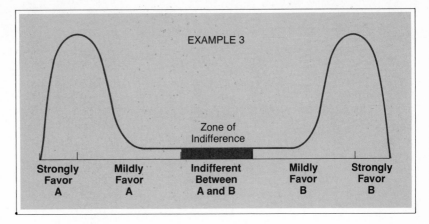

The same pattern arises when an issue in American politics is "settled." For instance, there used to be sharp controversy over the degree to which the government should pay for medical care. After the medicare plan was passed the issue became less controversial. Look at the data in Figure 6.2, which shows the responses people gave to a question asked in 1973. They were asked to place themselves on a scale showing whether they felt that the government had a responsibility to help people pay for medical care. Most agreed that the government had such a responsibility.

Example 3 is very different from the first two. It shows a major division—about half the citizens strongly prefer A and about half strongly prefer B. Very few are in between. It is obvious that a population divided in this way—especially if the choice between A and B is an important one—is deeply divided indeed. This may describe the United States just before the Civil War.

The point to be made, though, is that this pattern has been relatively rare (though a variation on this pattern, which we will discuss later, is becoming more common), simply because issues that are so sharply defined that they split the population down the middle have been infrequent in America. Consider two of the most important political controversies in recent decades: Vietnam and the racial issue.

At the height of the controversy over what to do about Vietnam, citizens were asked to place themselves on a scale showing their policy preferences. They could place themselves at an "extreme dove" position, which meant that they wanted to withdraw from Vietnam immediately no matter what; they could place themselves at an "extreme hawk" position, which meant that they wanted to use all force to win. Figure 6.3 shows where they placed themselves. Some citizens took strong positions at either end of the scale. But the largest group is found in the middle, and many others took mild positions on one side or the other.

FIGURE 6.3
Positions on the U.S. Role in
Vietnam

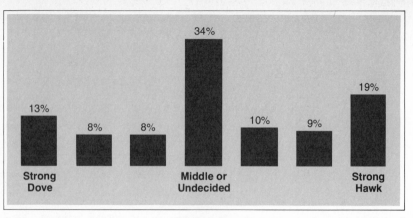

Source: Based on data from an unpublished study on Vietnam and urban crisis by Richard Brody, Benjamin Page, and Sidney Verba, 1968.

Or consider a similar scale of opinions on what to do about the "urban crisis." Citizens were asked to place themselves on a scale from favoring major reform to deal with the social and economic issues underlying urban unrest to favoring maximum "law and order" to stop urban unrest. (See Figure 6.4.)

As with the Vietnam issue, there were many Americans in middle positions. Thus on two of the most controversial issues of the day citizens were not divided into two opposing camps.

Indeed, the general position of Americans on a broad scale ranging from liberal to conservative is reflected in the results of a 1973 Gallup poll. (See Figure 6.5.)

Opinions tend to lie near the center. In fact the pattern of citizen preferences in America when looked at across a number of issues may often take this form. It can be seen in Example 4.

FIGURE 6.4
Positions on the Urban Crisis

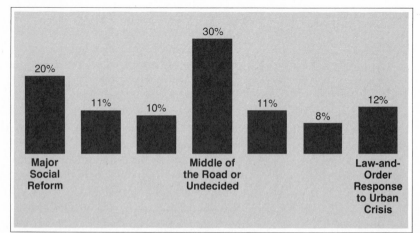

Source: Based on data from an unpublished study on Vietnam and urban crisis by Richard Brody, Benjamin Page, and Sidney Verba, 1968.

**FIGURE 6.5
Political Attitudes of
Americans**

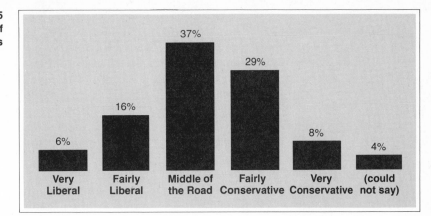

Source: National Opinion Research Center study, University of Chicago, 1973.

This situation represents a slight variation on Example 1. There is little intensity of political opinion, but what there is seems to favor position B. Many ordinary political issues take this form—a fairly large portion of the population mildly favors one alternative; another group, not quite as large, favors the other. And in between is a large group that doesn't care. Policy B stands a good chance of getting favorable action, though it is by no means certain. Those who hold position B may have no organization or leadership; or they may need to win the support of some of those who don't care, and because they feel mildly about the issue they may not try hard enough. In any case if they succeed it will cause little conflict because both groups are not strongly committed.

This pattern is a fairly good illustration of one major division of the American population: the division into Democrats and Republicans. Most Americans have one identification or the other; some

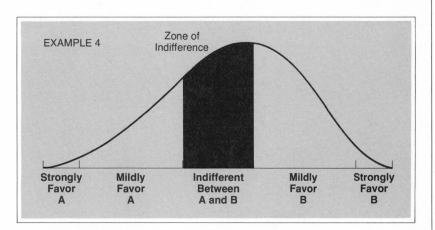

are independent. But few Americans hold their partisan identification so intensely that they would be fundamentally opposed to having members of the other party in leadership positions (or else all elections would be potential civil-war situations). Over the years more citizens have identified with the Democrats than with the Republicans. But this does not mean that there is a Democrat in the White House at each election. Since these identifications are not very strong, many citizens can be swayed from one side to the other. And as we will see in Chapter 11, election victory often depends on the pull of many forces besides those that identify a citizen with a party.

In general, the pattern of division in the United States has tended to resemble that shown in Example 4. This situation has often been praised by students of American politics because such a situation makes for stability. Granted, a society that resembles Example 3, with citizens far apart and hostile, is more likely to fly apart. But the pattern shown in Example 4 means stability in another sense of the word: Nothing changes. And it is just this tendency—when one considers the nation as a whole—that may lead to stagnation in government policy.

There are two other patterns that are relevant in America—one a traditional one that has applied to many issues, the other one that is becoming more apparent in recent years. Consider Example 5. Here is a small group of the population that is strongly in favor of a particular position, faced by the bulk of the population, which either does not care or is mildly on the other side. That such a pattern of preferences is common is suggested by the generalization presented earlier—different problems are of different degrees of concern to different groups of citizens. Drug manufacturers care intensely whether the government regulates the manufacture or sale of their product, since such regulations may cut into their profits. Citizens who do not use many drug products won't care. Citizens who use a lot would prefer such regulations but will care far less intensely than the manufacturers.

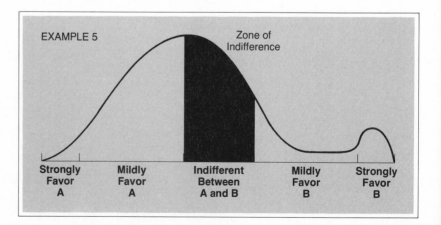

EXAMPLE 5   Zone of
                            Indifference

Strongly   Mildly   Indifferent   Mildly   Strongly
Favor   Favor   Between   Favor   Favor
A   A   A and B   B   B

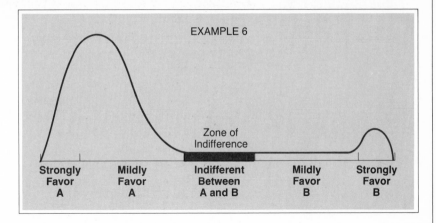

EXAMPLE 6

Zone of
Indifference

Strongly | **Mildly** | **Indifferent** | **Mildly** | **Strongly**
Favor | **Favor** | **Between** | **Favor** | **Favor**
A | **A** | **A and B** | **B** | **B**

The situation in Example 5 repeats itself in many areas. The special role of the medical profession in medical legislation fits this pattern; so does the special importance of hunters and sportsmen in gun control. As we have seen, about 70 percent of the American people favor gun control. The opposition is small, but it is intense. The pattern of Example 5 can produce pressure group politics, which we discuss later. The main characteristic is that the intense minority is, under such circumstances, likely to win the day. It is more likely to be vocal and to be organized. What it lacks in numbers it makes up for in intensity.

Let us look at one more example (Example 6). Here we see an intense minority faced by an opposing but also intense majority. Such a situation would exist if there were groups in society that were severely deprived but were cut off from the rest of the population by a set of reinforcing divisions. Consider the situation in many of America's metropolitan areas. In the decaying central city lives a population that is poor and black; surrounding it are the suburbs, rich and white. They are divided by race, economic condition, and place of residence. And therefore they have very few common interests. The central-city residents want social services and want the costs of those services shared by those outside the city; they want access to better schools; they want chances for housing outside of the cities. Residents of the suburbs differ on all these issues. Further, they have few social ties with city dwellers; they differ in all respects.

We illustrate this division of opinion in Figure 6.6. In 1973 citizens were asked how they felt about housing integration: Should the government see to it that blacks can buy houses in white neighborhoods if they want to, or should it stay out of it. The answers show that most Americans took positions at one or the other end of the scale — they either felt strongly that the government should see to it that blacks can buy houses in white neighborhoods or felt strongly

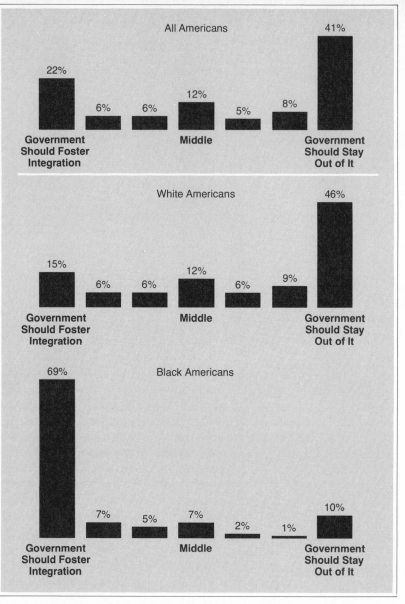

Source: National Opinion Research Center study, University of Chicago, 1973.

that the government should stay out of it. Those who felt that the government should stay out outnumber the others by two to one.

The degree to which this issue polarizes our society is seen more clearly if we look at white and black opinions separately. Look again at Figure 6.6. There are some whites who strongly favor housing integration, but the bulk of the white population is at the other end of the scale. They want the government to stay out of it. The bulk of the black population wants the government to foster integration. A pattern like that shown in Figure 6.6 leads to conflict. And that, of course, is the situation on this issue.

Conclusions

There are many patterns of division in America. On some issues there is wide agreement among almost all Americans; on others the public may form two hostile camps; and on still others an intense minority may face a less intense majority. We cannot predict the specific issues that will arise. But the patterns that we have described should be helpful in understanding the nature of new issues and the impact they are likely to have on the political process.

7
POLITICAL PARTICIPATION IN AMERICA

How do American citizens participate in the political life of their country? How active are they? In what ways do they participate? And which citizens participate?

How American democracy works depends largely on who participates and how. Through participation citizens tell the government what they want: what goals they want it to set and how they want it to allocate resources. If citizens do not participate, government officials are not likely to be aware of their needs and desires. If some citizens participate while others are passive, government officials are much more likely to pay attention to the needs and desires of the active citizens and ignore the inactive ones. Thus to understand the role of participation in American politics we have to consider *which* citizens are active.

Participation is important for another reason. Not only does it tell the government what citizens want; it has more direct benefits. The ability to participate in decisions that affect one's life is an important source of human dignity. Participation is thus an end in itself. In a democracy it is probably the best evidence of full membership in the society.

How Do Citizens Participate?

Participation refers to the ways in which citizens influence what the government does, and this can be accomplished in many ways.

VOTING

Through the vote citizens help choose their political leaders. The vote of any single individual is not a very powerful political tool. But elected officials are sensitive to the needs and desires of groups of voters.

cooperation

CAMPAIGN ACTIVITY

Each citizen is limited to one vote in an election. That vote is only one of thousands or millions and can play only a small role in the results. But citizens can increase their voting influence in one perfectly legal way—they can try to influence the vote of others. One of the most common forms of political activity takes place at the time of an election. Citizens ring doorbells, work at the polls, and talk to their friends and neighbors to try to affect their votes. Or they give money to a candidate or party. And if political leaders pay attention to voters, they may pay even more attention to the citizens who supply the work and money needed to conduct a campaign.

Communal Activity Elections are an important way in which citizens influence government officials. But elections have a big drawback—they are very blunt instruments of citizen control. Elections take place only at fixed intervals: every two, four, or six years, depending on the office. And the choice is between only two or maybe three or four candidates.

Citizens, on the other hand, have many and varied interests. In fact one can imagine each group as having a list of priorities that it would like to see the government act on. Sometimes these interests have to do with broad national policies—American Jews are concerned with Middle East policy, conservationists with nuclear testing, blacks with federal laws on segregation. Sometimes these are local interests—a group of neighbors wants to prevent the building of a road in that section of town, a group of parents wants to improve school facilities, a group of high school students wants the community to provide a recreation center.

These interests are indeed varied. An election could not possibly offer a choice in all of these areas. Citizens often find that the issues that concern them the most are not election issues, for both candidates take the same position (or none). Furthermore, the problems and interests that citizens want the government to deal with do not arise only at election time. Thus participation in election campaigns is not enough to tell government officials what citizens want.

Other means of participation are needed to fill in the gaps left by elections—some way in which specific sets of citizens can tell their more precise concerns to the government as they arise. We call this *communal activity,* meaning the activity of groups of citizens working together to try to influence the government. They may work through informal groups, as when neighbors join to protest to city hall about some issue. Or they may work through more formal organizations such as unions, PTAs, or civic associations. This kind of activity—which, as we will show, is very common in the United States—has two important features. First, citizens work together. This is important because the government is influenced more by a group than by a single individual. Second, citizens are active on the problems that concern them most—parents will work in the PTA, welfare recipients in a welfare mothers' group, and so forth.

Citizen-Initiated Contacts So far we have mentioned ways in which citizens participate along with others—as part of the voting population, in campaigns, or in cooperation with their fellow citizens. But some citizen activity is carried on alone, as when one writes to one's congressman or to a newspaper, or visits a govern-

ment office to make a complaint. We do not often think of this as political participation, for citizens may be dealing with very narrow and specific problems that concern only them. They may ask their district's member of Congress to help a relative get a discharge from the army, or they may complain about the condition of the sidewalk in front of their house. But this is another way in which citizens influence what the government does—and often in areas that are important to them.

Protests, Marches, Demonstrations   Citizens sometimes use more dramatic and direct means of showing their point of view. They may march to protest American foreign policy, busing for integration, or the lack of school busing. Such protests, sometimes called "demonstration democracy," have become more common in recent years. Some of these activities are ways of showing political preferences in a more dramatic way. Some are ways of directly affecting the workings of the government—blocking the entrance to a military induction center, preventing school buses from running. Such means of participation are used by citizens who feel that the "ordinary" means won't work or think the problem is so urgent that it cannot wait for the ordinary political processes.

How Active Are Americans?

One can hear quite contradictory things about political participation in America. Some say it is very active. Others say there is very little. This contradiction may come in part from what people expect. If one expects all citizens to be fully active in politics, the finding that only 10–20 percent of the population is active will be disappointing. If one expects citizens to be private, home-centered individuals, one might be surprised to find that *as many as* two out of ten Americans bother to take part in election campaigns.

The reader will have to judge for himself or herself whether participation in America is high or low. But we will give some standards for comparison. Table 7.1 reports the percentages of citizens who are active in various ways—voting, campaign activity, communal activity, and contacting the government.

A number of facts are illustrated by the data on participation rates. Only in presidential elections do we find a majority of the people active. The turnout in presidential elections is usually 60–65 percent of the voting-age population, though it fell to a low of 53 percent in 1976. In local elections a little less than half vote regularly. Note that voting is the easiest political act. It takes little time and, more important, little initiative. Thus it is not surprising to find the highest activity rates in voting. (Another important question about voting, to be considered in Chapter 11, is: How rationally do citizens vote?)

Campaign activity takes more time, initiative, and commitment to a particular candidate or party. And it is clear that this is not an activity for everyone. Less than one-third of all citizens say they try

TABLE 7.1
Activities Performed
by Citizens

Mode of Activity	Percent Active
A. Voting	
Voted in 1972 presidential election	55%
Voted in 1968 presidential election	62
Votes regularly in local elections	47
B. Taking Part in Campaign Activities	
Persuade others how to vote	28
Ever worked for a party	26
Attended political rallies	19
Contributed money in a political campaign	13
Member of a political club or organization	8
C. Cooperative Activities	
Worked through local group	30
Helped form local group	14
Active member of organization engaged in community activities	32
D. Contacting Officials	
Contacted local officials on some problem	20
Contacted extralocal officials on some problem	18
Wrote a letter to a public official	17
Wrote a letter to an editor	3

Source: All but the first three and last two items based on data from Sidney Verba and Norman H. Nie, *Participation in America: Political Democracy and Social Equality* (New York: Harper & Row, 1972); the last two items in D based on data from 1964 presidential election study, University of Michigan, Institute for Social Research, Survey Research Center.

to persuade others how to vote; only about one-quarter have done work for a political party, and other campaign activities are performed by even smaller portions of the population. Only 13 percent have given money to a campaign.

About one-third of the citizens participate in communal activity—working with some local group on a community problem. And a similar number have worked through formal organizations.

Finally, citizens often say "I'm going to write to my congressman!" about all sorts of problems. But only about one American in six has ever written to any public official. And only about one in five has ever contacted a local official or an official outside of his or her community on a problem.

What about more dramatic political activities—protest marches, demonstrations, and the like? It is hard to get accurate figures, but it is likely that few citizens have taken part in such activities. At the height of the Vietnam War protests in the late 1960s, one study found only eight citizens (out of 1500 interviewed) who had ever taken part in a demonstration about Vietnam—about 0.15 percent. Another study of a city in upstate New York found that only about 2–3 percent of the white citizens had ever been in a street demonstration, and only 4 percent said that they had gone to a protest meeting.

But one point should be made about such activity. Only a small percentage of all citizens may take part in demonstrations, but larger portions of particular groups may do so. Thus the same study that found that only 2–3 percent of whites had taken part in a street demonstration found that 11 percent of blacks had. And over half of the students who were in college during the Vietnam War reported taking part in antiwar demonstrations.

Is There Much or Little Participation?

How much political participation is there in the United States. The reader can look at the figures and judge. But we can provide some guidelines for judgment. In the first place, we should be careful how we read the data. Remember that, aside from voting, no more than one-third of the population is politically active—that's the portion that participates in local organizations—and the most usual campaign activity (convincing others how to vote) is reported by only 28 percent. But this does not mean that only one-third of the American public is involved in any activity besides voting. The citizens who are involved in activity in their community are not always the same as the ones who work in campaigns. Thus the 28 percent who have tried to convince others how to vote and the 30 percent who have worked in an informal group on some community matter only partially overlap.

TYPES OF PARTICIPANTS

We can divide the American public into six types of participants based on how active they are in politics and the kind of activity in which they participate.[1]

1. *Inactives* These citizens, who account for 22 percent of the population, never take part in campaigns, are involved in no communal activity, and never contact an official. They are not regular voters, though they may vote from time to time. In other words, about one-fourth of all Americans are not politically active.
2. *Voting Specialists* Some citizens are very regular about voting in elections; they almost always vote. But that is all they do. This group is similar in size to the inactives—about 21 percent of the population.
3. *Parochial Participants* These citizens contact government officials. In this sense they are active. But the reason they do this is some problem affecting them or their family. And this is all their political activity. They avoid all activity that is likely to affect more public issues. These "parochial" participants form 4 percent of the population.[2]
4. *Communal Activists* A fairly large part of the population is active in the life of its community, but only in nonpartisan activities—vol-

[1] Sidney Verba and Norman H. Nie, *Participation in America: Political Democracy and Social Equality* (New York: Harper & Row, 1972), chap. 4.
[2] Note that this figure is lower than the number of people who write to government officials, just as the figure for "voting specialists" is lower than the number of voters. We are talking about people who *only* vote or *only* write to their congressman.

TABLE 7.2
How Active Should the
Ordinary Person Be in
the Local Community?

Percent Who Say the Ordinary Man Should:	United States	Great Britain	Germany	Italy	Mexico
Be active in his community	51%	39%	22%	10%	26%
Only participate in more passive ways (be interested, etc.)	27	31	38	22	33
Only participate in church affairs	5	2	1		
Total who mention some outgoing activity	83%	72%	61%	32%	59%
Only be upright in personal life	1%	1%	11%	15%	2%
Do nothing in local community	3	6	7	11	2
Don't know	11			35	30
Other	2			7	7
Total percent	100%	100%	100%	100%	100%
Total number of cases	970	963	955	995	1007

Source: Gabriel Almond and Sidney Verba, *The Civic Culture: Political Attitudes and Democracy in Five Nations* (Princeton, N.J.: Princeton University Press, 1963). Copyright © 1963 by Princeton University Press. Reprinted by permission of Princeton University Press.

untary groups, school issues, and the like. These citizens join civic groups, work in charitable campaigns, and keep all kinds of community activities going. They form about 20 percent of the population.

5. *Campaign Activists* A group of similar size takes part fairly regularly in political campaigns but is not involved as much in the less partisan community activities. They form 15 percent of the population.

6. *Complete Activists* This is a small but important part of the population—11 percent. They are active in every way. They rarely miss an election, are active in nonpartisan community affairs, and ring doorbells and participate in other partisan activities at election time.[3]

PARTICIPATION IN THE UNITED STATES AND OTHER NATIONS

To see whether American participation is high or low it may be useful to compare it with participation in other nations. One point should be made first: Americans are more "participation oriented" than citizens elsewhere. They are more likely to believe that they can influence the government if they want to than citizens in other countries, and this makes them more likely to act. And perhaps more important, they are more likely to feel that the citizen has a *responsibility* to be active in the life of his or her community. In a study conducted in five democratic nations, people were asked what responsibility a citizen had to his or her community. In the United States, as Table 7.2 indicates, over half of those who answered said

[3] Seven percent of the sample studied was unclassifiable because of mixed patterns or missing information.

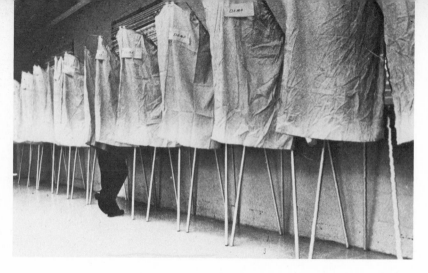

Voter apathy has been growing; these are a row of almost entirely empty voting booths in a Democratic primary election.

that a citizen should take an active part in the life of his or her community—many more than in any of the other countries. By an "active role" they meant participation in local government (willingness to run for office, to serve on boards, and to attend meetings) as well as activity of a nongovernmental nature (working for the local Red Cross or the PTA).

Voting   When it comes to actual participation, the pattern is mixed. Voting turnout is usually lower in the United States than in many of the European democracies. The turnout in U.S. presidential elections tends to be between 55 and 65 percent. In many European countries the turnout is 80–90 percent. This does not necessarily reflect a lower level of political interest and involvement in the United States than elsewhere. The usual explanation of such low voting rates was that election laws sometimes made voting difficult. Many areas had residency rules that prevented new residents from voting until some time had passed. Literacy tests also blocked some potential voters.

In recent years federal law has done away with literacy tests, lengthy residency requirements, and other legal impediments to voting. However, voting turnout has continued to decline. In 1960, 60.1 percent of the eligible voters went to the polls. In 1972 this figure had fallen to 55.4 percent, and in 1976 it fell further, to 53.3 percent. Political scientists are not sure why this decline has occurred and whether it is a permanent or a temporary decline. One explanation is that the decline in turnout reflects the changing composition of the electorate, in particular the enfranchisement of 18-year-olds in 1972. Turnout among younger members of the electorate has always been low, and turnout among the 18- to 20-year-olds has been especially low. In 1976 only about one-third of all citizens under 21 voted.

Another explanation of the decline in voting turnout is based on changing attitudes among American voters. As we will see in Chap-

Difficult registration laws used to keep turnout low. Laws have eased in recent years.

ter 11, there has been a decline in identification with the political parties. Citizens without partisan ties are less likely to vote. In addition, failure to vote is highest among citizens who feel politically powerless. A CBS survey in 1976 found that nonvoters were much more likely to say that one person's vote makes no difference or that it makes no difference which party or candidate wins an election. As we saw in Chapter 5, the sense of political efficacy has been declining recently. If it continues to decline, voting turnout will probably decline along with it.

Participation in political activities that take more time and effort may be more important. Data on this subject are harder to find, since they are not recorded officially the way voting turnout is, but some are available. Only a small minority of Americans have ever tried to influence a decision of their local government (28 percent say they have), and an even smaller number say they have tried to influence a decision of the national government (16 percent). But in both cases the percentages are substantially larger than those found in other nations. Political participation is more likely to be an important activity in the United States than in many other democracies.

In one way participation in the United States seems particularly well developed compared with other nations. This is in communal activity, in which citizens come together to work on some community problem or join in a group to pressure the government. Citizens in several countries were asked how they would go about influencing the government. In the United States, over half of those who thought they could have some influence felt that they could best do so by joining with others. In the other countries studied, citizens would be more likely to work alone or through some more formal organization like a political party. And the willingness to work with others—friends, neighbors, and others at work—is found in all social groups in the United States.

Data on the actual behavior of citizens show that in the United

A 10,000-signature petition against the Panama Canal treaties.

States there is much more community-oriented activity involving the cooperation of citizens: more groups of citizens formed to deal with some local problem and more active associations connected with the schools, recreational problems, and the like. (See Table 7.3.) In fact this type of behavior is not new in America. It was noted over 100 years ago by Alexis de Tocqueville, who commented on the zest for cooperative activity that he found in America compared with Europe.

And as noted, such activity is important because it can deal with the most immediate problems of citizens. In this way the individual citizen increases his or her own influence on the government—because many voices generally carry more weight with government officials than a few.

Equality of Political Access

Compared with citizens in other nations, citizens in the United States feel a fairly high level of responsibility to be active and are relatively active. But there is another standard by which we can measure political participation in the United States: How *equally* do citizens participate in America? Are all types of citizens equally active, or is participation mostly in the hands of a few? The answer is very important in understanding how participation works in America. Citizens *communicate* their needs and desires to government leaders through participation. They also use participation to pressure leaders to act on these needs and desires. Thus the citizen who does not participate may be ignored. The government will respond to the participant.

But the issue is not whether all citizens participate but whether the citizens who do are *representative* of the rest. As we have seen, not all citizens are active in politics; nor is it realistic to expect them to be. But if the activists have the same problems, needs, and

TABLE 7.3
Community Activity of Citizens

	United States	Austria	India	Japan	Netherlands
Percent who belong to an organization active in community affairs	32%	9%	7%	11%	15%
Percent who have worked with a local informal group to solve a community problem	30%	3%	18%	15%	16%

Source: Based on data from Sidney Verba, Norman Nie, and Jae-On Kim, *Participation and Political Equality: A Seven Nation Comparison* (New York: Cambridge University Press, 1978).

There is much community-oriented activity in America.

preferences as the nonactivists, they may speak for those who do not take part. On the other hand, if they are different from the rest of the population—come from selected social groups, have particular problems, want the government to do special things—then the fact that only a subgroup of the population participates means that the government will act on some of the needs and desires of the population and not on others.

WHO ARE THE PARTICIPANTS?

Citizens from all walks of life participate in American politics—no group is totally barred. But certain kinds of citizens participate much more than others.

Close studies come to the following conclusions about which citizens are likely to be active in politics:

1. *Education* If you have a college education, you are much more likely to be politically active than if you have less education.
2. *Income* People with higher incomes are likely to be active; the poor are much less likely.
3. *Race* Black Americans are, on average, somewhat less active than whites. But the difference is not very great for most types of activity.
4. *Sex* Men are somewhat more active than women, but the difference between the sexes is less in America than in most other nations.
5. *Age* Both young and old citizens tend to be somewhat less active than those in their middle years.

In sum, if you are highly educated and wealthy you are much more likely to be a political activist than if you are less well educated and poor. Being white, male, and middle-aged helps as well. But race, sex, and age are less important than education and income. The important point is that the differences in participation rates among these various groups do make a difference in what the government is told. Those who are inactive—the poor, the less well educated—have different problems than those who are more active. And inactive citizens have different ideas about what the govern-

FIGURE 7.1
Problems Facing Inactive and Active Citizens

Proportion Saying They Have Recently Been Faced with a Serious Problem of Employment, Paying for Medical Care, or Adequate Housing

Inactive Citizens	Most Active Citizens
38%	22%

Source: Based on data from Sidney Verba and Norman H. Nie, *Participation in America: Political Democracy and Social Inequality* (New York: Harper & Row, 1972), chap. 15.

ment should do. Suppose we compare the problems of the most active citizens with those faced by the least active. (See Figure 7.1.) We find that the inactive citizens are nearly twice as likely as the active ones to say that they have recently faced serious problems in paying for medical care, getting a job, or finding adequate housing.

In other words, if participation is how government officials find out about the problems of citizens, those leaders will not be aware of some of the more serious economic problems that citizens face. The ones who have these problems are inactive. Nor do the inactives let the government know how they think it should deal with social and economic problems. If they did, the government would see a different picture of citizen desires than it gets from the activists. Consider the data in Figure 7.2. Active citizens believe that the poor must solve their problems through their own effort. Those who are inactive are less likely to think this. They think the government should deal with such problems. But their views are not communicated. The government official who learns what the public wants by considering the preferences of the active citizens will find a majority who feel that the economic problems of the poor are their own responsibility and not an area for government action.

The fact that the activists differ from the inactives in their political preferences does not necessarily mean that political leaders will receive more conservative messages from political activists. Though the active citizens are more affluent and are therefore less likely to have income or job problems, on some issues they may be more liberal than the citizenry as a whole. We saw this to be the case when we considered attitudes toward freedom of speech (see Chapter 5). In addition, there has been a growing number of well-educated political activists with liberal views—mostly identified with the Democratic party. These activists take a more liberal position on economic, racial, and foreign-policy matters. The result of the increase in the number of liberal activists is that the activist population contains both more conservatives and more liberals than the citizenry as a whole. Inactive citizens are more likely to be in the middle of the road on issues or to have no opinion. Activists take sides.

Campaign Contributions This is an area of political activity in which wealth plays a special role. Political campaigns are expensive, and large contributors have been able to achieve special influence with candidates. Recent campaign finance legislation has attempted to change this by providing for public funding of presidential campaigns and by limiting individual contributions. As we will see in Chapter 11, this has had an effect, but it has not eliminated the special power of money in politics.

PARTICIPATION AND EQUALITY

The data show up a major problem of American politics: Those who need government intervention the most—the poor, the less educated, the victims of racial discrimination—are the ones who are

Proportion Saying the Poor Have the Primary Responsibility for Solving Their Economic Problems

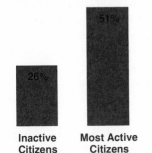

| Inactive Citizens | Most Active Citizens |

Source: Based on data from Sidney Verba and Norman H. Nie, *Participation in America: Political Democracy and Social Inequality* (New York: Harper & Row, 1972), chap. 15.

least active. Those who need government help the least—because they are already wealthier, better educated, less discriminated against—are the most active. Because of the inactivity of the poor and the greater activity of the rich, the government may underestimate citizens' need and desire for government intervention.

What causes this situation? Why do those who need help least participate most? The answer is that what makes them better off in social and economic terms makes them better able to participate.

Education and wealth provide the resources needed for participation. Wealth is the most obvious resource. Few citizens can give tens of thousands of dollars to political candidates. Those who can are likely to have greater political influence. Skills are another resource, and these come from education. The educated are more likely to "know the ropes" of politics: whom to see and what to say.

The wealthy and the better educated are more active in politics for another reason. Many studies have shown that the more educated citizens are more motivated to take part in politics. Political motivation is important. It is not enough to have the necessary resources; one must be willing to use them. Education creates a set of attitudes—a belief that one can be effective in politics, that one has a responsibility to be active—that leads citizens to participate. We pointed out earlier that half the citizens in America think the ordinary person should be active in the affairs of his or her community—a much larger figure than in other countries. But in Table 7.4 notice the way educational groups differ in that sense of responsibility. Among those with no high school education, only one-third think the ordinary person should be active in the community; among those with some college training, two-thirds think the ordinary person should be politically active.

Similarly, educated citizens are more likely than less educated ones to have a sense of *political efficacy,* to believe that they can influence the government. Table 7.5 shows this. These two beliefs— that one *has a responsibility to be active* and that one *can influence the government*—lead to political activity. Those who hold such views are likely to be active.

TABLE 7.4
Which Citizens Think the Ordinary Person Should Be Active in the Community?

	Among Those Without High School Education	Among Those with Some High School	Among Those with Some College
Percent saying the ordinary person should be active	35%	56%	66%

Source: Based on data from Gabriel Almond and Sidney Verba, *The Civic Culture: Political Attitudes and Democracy in Five Nations* (Princeton, N.J.: Princeton University Press, 1963). Copyright © 1963 by Princeton University Press. Reprinted by permission of Princeton University Press.

	Among Those Without High School Education	Among Those with Some High School	Among Those with Some College
Percent saying they could influence a decision of the local government	60%	82%	99%

Source: Based on data from Gabriel Almond and Sidney Verba, *The Civic Culture: Political Attitudes and Democracy in Five Nations* (Princeton, N.J.: Princeton University Press, 1963). Copyright © 1963 by Princeton University Press. Reprinted by permission of Princeton University Press.

The situation illustrates the paradox of political equality as an ideal (reflected in "one person, one vote") contrasting with sharp social and economic inequalities. The real inequalities in social and economic terms—the fact that some citizens have substantially more education or income than others—means that the political ideal of equality is not achieved. The wealthy and the better educated have greater resources and motivation for political activity. Though opportunities to be politically active may be legally equal for all, those who are already well off take more advantage of these opportunities.

EQUALIZING POLITICAL PARTICIPATION

Can political participation be made more equal so that citizens who are less well off in income or education are not the least effective participants? There are several ways to achieve greater political equality.

Put a Ceiling on Political Activity   One way is to limit individual political activity. The most obvious place to do this is at the polls. Each citizen, no matter how rich or well educated, is limited to one vote for each political office.

If voting were the only way citizens took part in politics, the rule of "one person, one vote" would make all citizens equal politically —at least they could easily be equal if they all voted. But as we have seen, there are many other forms of participation, and these are often more powerful than voting. Millionaires, like factory workers, have one vote, but their contributions to candidates give them a lot more voice than factory workers. Can one put a ceiling on campaign contributions?

In the wake of the Watergate episode Congress passed the Public Finance Bill of 1974. Under this law individuals can give no more than $1000 to a candidate in any federal election. (A person can give $1000 to a presidential candidate, $1000 to a Senate candidate, and so forth. The limit is $1000 in any single race.) This hardly makes campaign contributions as equal as the vote; very few citizens can give $1000. But it should reduce the great influence of those who traditionally gave campaign contributions well above $1000.

The 1974 law limiting campaign contributions also introduced public financing of campaigns. We will look at some of the ways this may affect political campaigns in a later chapter.

But limits on campaign contributions would not completely equalize political participation. There are many kinds of political activity that cannot easily be limited without severely limiting freedom of speech. Nor would anyone want to limit such activities, since the essence of democracy is that citizens be free to express their preferences to the government. But since such activities depend on motivation, and the better-educated citizens are more likely to be motivated toward political activity, it is the better educated and the wealthy who are most likely to participate.

Mobilizing the Disadvantaged Another way to equalize participation is to mobilize the disadvantaged. Rather than putting a ceiling on the activity of the wealthy, one *raises* the level of activity of the poor. The poor obviously have an interest in common—higher income. But they would need the other two ingredients we discussed in the previous chapter. The two things that are necessary to mobilize citizens so that their activity level will rise to that of the wealthy and better educated are (1) awareness of their disadvantaged position and (2) organization.

Awareness Observers of American politics—particularly those who compare it with politics in Europe—often comment on the absence in the United States of any strong sense of economic class. This is very noticeable among American workers. It is particularly striking because a sense of class can be found in many other industrialized democracies. American workers sometimes think of themselves as workers and make political decisions from that point of view. But sometimes they think in terms of other groups. They may think politically as Catholics, as suburbanites, as whites or blacks, and so forth. This separates them from other workers, from Protestants if they are Catholic, from blacks if they are white. A sense of membership in a *working class* is absent.

Organization What about organization? Two kinds of organization might help disadvantaged citizens participate more in politics: political parties and voluntary groups. They might help by providing channels for activity and by increasing a sense of group identity. In many countries political parties are organized along class lines—they are parties of the working class, parties of the farmers, parties of the middle class. Parties that are limited to a particular class tend to do a better job of recruiting the members of that class. Thus socialist or workers' parties tend to mobilize working-class citizens. But the parties in the United States have no clear class basis. Democrats are more likely to receive support from workers and Republicans from business. But both parties get support from all levels of

TABLE 7.6
Which Citizens Belong
to Organizations?

	Among Those Without High School Education	Among Those with Some High School	Among Those with Some College
Percent who are members of an organization	49%	67%	78%
Percent who are active in an organization	27%	43%	59%

Source: Based on data from Sidney Verba and Norman H. Nie, *Participation in America: Political Democracy and Social Equality* (New York: Harper & Row, 1972).

society. The result is that citizens of lower social status have no party organizations trying to bring them into politics.

The same can be said for voluntary groups. These organizations can help citizens become more active. We discuss how this happens in Chapter 9. But here we can note that members of these associations tend to be of higher social status. As Table 7.6 shows, citizens with more education are more active in organizations: Only about half the citizens who have not finished high school belong to a voluntary organization; over three-quarters of those with some college training do. And only about one-fourth of those without a high school degree are active in an organization, whereas over half of the college group is.

If organization is a way to make groups of citizens politically meaningful, then it is clear that this resource is also more available to upper-status citizens.

BLACK VS. WHITE: POLITICAL
MOBILIZATION OF A DISADVANTAGED GROUP

Among black Americans—at least in recent decades—one can observe the beginnings of a break in the participation cycle that leaves the disadvantaged even more disadvantaged. And the break has come, we believe, through organization and self-awareness. American blacks have a history of relatively effective organization—at least more effective than that of white Americans of similar social and economic status. There are many reasons for this, perhaps the most important being the fact of segregation and social separation. Forced to live apart from whites, blacks are better able to organize as a separate group. In addition, numerous black organizations— from the NAACP to more militant groups—have played an important role. Nor should one forget the role of the black churches. It is clear that blacks have developed an organizational base.

In addition, they have developed—as whites have not—a clear sense of identity. The slogans "Black Power" and "Black is Beautiful" are examples of this awareness. And their separation from the mainstream of white society makes this possible. The point is that the segregation of American society—which finds blacks living apart, going to school apart, holding certain kinds of jobs—produces

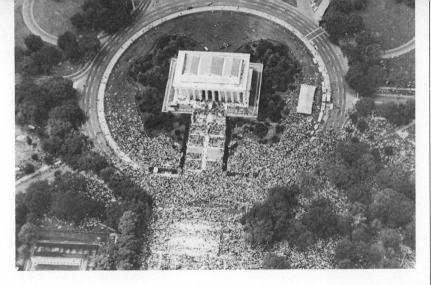

The civil rights march at the Lincoln Memorial.

more unity and less of the multiple identification that hampers self-awareness and organization among disadvantaged white citizens.

Studies show that through black self-awareness citizens who might not otherwise participate can be active in politics. Black Americans, on the average, participate in politics somewhat less than white Americans. This is what one would expect, given the fact that blacks generally have lower incomes and less education than whites. But if we consider blacks who have a sense of group identity (who, for instance, mention problems of race when asked what are the most important problems for themselves or the nation), we find that they are as active in politics as whites. In other words, the sense of black identity is a way to overcome the disadvantage in political activity resulting from lower educational and income levels.[4]

The situation can be seen more clearly if we look at the situation over time. A series of studies of American voting behavior has been made by the University of Michigan since 1952. This lets us trace the difference in black and white participation rates in political campaigns over a long period. These data are presented in Figure 7.3.

In 1952 — two years before the Supreme Court's historic school desegregation decision and three years before the first bus boycott led by Martin Luther King in Montgomery, Alabama — black Americans were much less active in political campaigns than the average white. In the 1960s the difference between black Americans and white Americans declined. The average level of black activity has remained a touch below that of whites, but the difference is much less than at the beginning of the awakening of black self-awareness.

The data on black–white differences do not mean that political problems for black citizens are over. Their participation rate is still below that of whites. And of course we have information only on how much activity they attempt, not on the all-important question

[4] Verba and Nie, chap. 10.

203

of how effective that activity is. Blacks may have increased their political activity, but they remain a minority group and their political activity is not always—perhaps not often—effective.

Most participation still comes from the white population and, within that population, from those who are richer and better educated. But because blacks have developed a group identity and are relatively well organized, their disadvantage in political activity compared to whites has been reduced. Compare 1952 with the years since 1962 in Figure 7.3.

Two more conclusions can be drawn from these data. Both have to do with the relationship between the more ordinary ways of participating—elections, community work, letters to one's congressman—and the more dramatic, more direct, and sometimes illegal kinds of political activity—protest demonstrations, marches, and the like.

One conclusion is clear from the data on black–white differences in campaign participation over the past two decades. Although direct political activity among blacks, and the origin of that activity in an increased sense of black identity, has attracted much attention, it is quite clear that along with this has come more ordinary political activity.

The second conclusion is that the increase in "demonstration democracy" may be explained in part by some of the differences in participation rates found among social groups in America. If indeed the ordinary ways of participating are so heavily in favor of the

FIGURE 7.3
Level of Campaign Activity Among Blacks and Whites

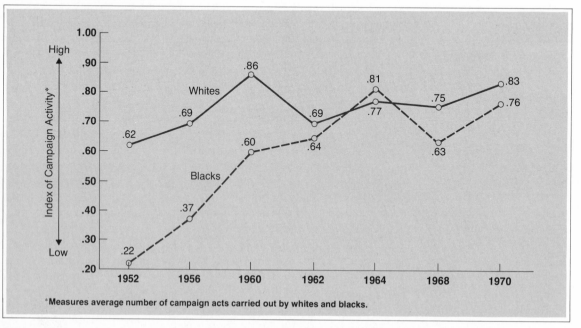

*Measures average number of campaign acts carried out by whites and blacks.

Source: Based on data from Sidney Verba and Norman H. Nie, *Participation in America: Political Democracy and Social Inequality* (New York: Harper & Row, 1972), chap. 14.

Women are as likely as men to be campaign workers; they are less likely to run for office.

"haves" rather than the "have-nots," citizens who are unhappy with the results might seek other, more direct means of political pressure.

POLITICAL ACTIVITY OF WOMEN

Women have generally been less active in politics than men. Traditionally, they were less likely to vote, to be active during election campaigns, or to run for office. Some of the reasons that poorer and less educated citizens are less politically active probably apply to women as well. We have seen that those with lower levels of education are more likely to feel that they have no responsibility to take part in politics, and that they have a weaker sense of their ability to influence politics. Studies of schoolchildren have shown that girls are usually raised to believe that politics is not for them. The result is that women felt less politically able and were therefore less active.

Though women are still less active than men, the difference between men and women in political activity is much less in the United States than in other democracies. Figure 7.4 shows the results of a comparative study of political participation in several democracies. Men and women were given scores on a political-participation scale based on how active they were. The difference between men and women was found to be much greater in the other nations than in the United States.

But there is an important qualification to be added before one concludes that there are few differences between men and women in political activity. Men and women are most similar in the United States when it comes to "low-level" political activities. Women are as likely as men to be ordinary campaign workers — to ring doorbells, send out letters, and make telephone calls soliciting votes. When it comes to "higher-level" activities, the male–female gap widens.

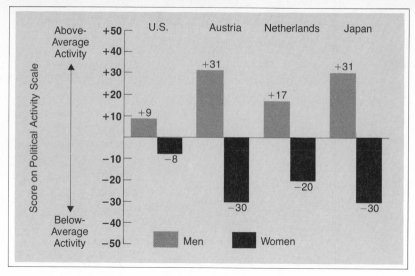

FIGURE 7.4
Political Activity Levels of Men and Women in the United States and in Other Democracies

Source: Adapted from Sidney Verba, Norman H. Nie, and Jae-on Kim, *Participation and Political Equality* (New York: Cambridge University Press, 1978), chap. 13.

Women are as likely to work in campaigns as men; they are less likely to direct campaigns. They are as likely as men to work *for* a candidate; they are less likely to *become* candidates themselves. (We will discuss the recruitment of women to political office in the next chapter.) As one moves up the ladder of politics one finds fewer and fewer women.[5]

The Politics of Protest: A Closer Look

So far we have given most of our attention to the "ordinary" means of participation: political campaigns and communal activity. But a full account of political activities in America has to pay close attention to direct political activity: political demonstrations, marches, and violence. These activities have become more important in recent years. Protests have focused on racial matters and the Vietnam War, but they have spread to other issues as well. Although there are no clear data on the subject, it seems likely that groups are more willing to disrupt (to seize a building, to march on an office) than in the past. Is this something new in America—a new political style that grew out of the tensions of the 1960s?

VIOLENCE, PROTESTS, AND THE RECORD
To begin with, we must make it clear that protest and violence are not the same thing. A study done for the National Commission on the Causes and Prevention of Violence found that only about one-third of the protests recorded in the press involved violence; most

[5] Kristi Andersen, "Working Women and Political Participation," *American Journal of Political Science,* XIX (August 1975), 439–454. Andersen also found that political activity was highest among working women.

were nonviolent. In fact the figure of one-third may be somewhat large, since the newspapers pay more attention to violent incidents.

Furthermore, violence is hard to define. "Violent language"—rude and insulting words—is often used in political confrontations, but is this violence? Also, as studies of clashes between police and demonstrators have shown, it is hard to tell "who started it" when confrontations become violent. As the report to the commission put it, "It is often difficult to determine who was 'responsible' for the violence. The reports of our study teams, however, clearly suggest that authorities bear a major responsibility. . . . Of the violent incidents [analyzed], in only half did the violence seem to be initiated by the demonstrators."[6]

Although the recent growth of political protest (and the violence that sometimes goes with it) is often thought of as a new development, this is not the case. U.S. history is filled with political violence and conflict. Not only was the nation born in violent protest against the British; less well known is the history of violent protests against the government by poor Appalachian farmers throughout the second half of the seventeenth century. Violence was used by the southern states in trying to secede from the Union and by the North in preventing it. It was used by WASPs (White Anglo-Saxon Protestants) against various immigrant groups in American cities in the nineteenth century. It was used by worker groups to protest economic conditions, and it was used by the authorities to put down those protests. None of the demonstrations against the Vietnam War matched the violence of the antidraft riots in New York during the Civil War, when draft offices were burned and many people were killed. Above all, there was violence in the South after the Civil War—violence against blacks (with the approval of the authorities) that successfully maintained the power of whites over blacks in that area.

WHAT ARE PROTESTS ABOUT?

In recent decades protest activity has focused on two issues: the Vietnam War and racial matters. The busing of schoolchildren to achieve integration is another major issue. But as the historical record makes clear, there have been protests on many issues. Such activities are often thought of as irrational, with no political goal. But this does not seem to be the case. Usually there is some political goal. That goal may not be clear in the mind of the demonstrator, but then neither is the goal of voting always clear in the mind of the voter.

There is also the so-called riff-raff theory: The demonstrators are those who are the least well integrated into society. Among blacks these would be the jobless, the young, and the most poverty

[6] Jerome H. Skolnick, *The Politics of Protest,* Staff Report to the National Commission on the Causes and Prevention of Violence (New York: Ballantine, 1969), pp 3–4.

stricken. But studies show that protests do not have such a narrow base. They find that many urban rioters are young and unemployed, but they are drawn from all parts of the community and have at least the passive support of the majority. Thus the makeup of the protest groups also shows that these are political activities.

The Motivation for Direct Action   Most protests have one thing in common: belief that the ordinary political channels are unresponsive or (perhaps the same thing) too slow. As the Chicago Riot Study Committee put it, "There is a conviction on the part of a clear majority of our Black citizens that political representation is entirely unsatisfactory and must be improved."[7]

Direct action, furthermore, is likely to take place under certain conditions: when a group lives apart from the rest of the society, has its own life style, and has (or believes it has) little in common with others. There are no ties to the rest of the society; the group feels that other channels are not open to it. If the ordinary political channels are closed, the buildup of tensions and frustrations may result in the use of more direct means.

Is Direct Action Appropriate?   Here of course is a big problem for those who try direct action. Some argue that such activities are never appropriate in a democracy, where there are other, more peaceful channels. Certainly the ordinary channels must be tried first. And even then the switch to direct action is inappropriate. If everyone who could not get his or her way used violence, society would become a war of all against all.

Others answer that in many cases all channels have been tried. Furthermore, the democratic channels are not available equally to all: Some groups are excluded and have no choice but direct activity. Finally, those who favor direct activity argue that some issues are so important—stopping a war or providing civil rights or preventing the busing of children away from a neighborhood school— that one must act firmly and directly.

It is not our job to decide who is right. Part of the debate is a factual one: Are channels open to all, and were all channels tried before direct action was undertaken? But these questions have no easy answer. And the legitimacy of stepping outside of the ordinary political channels, as well as the tougher question of the legitimacy of violence, are not factual questions but moral ones.

IS PROTEST EFFECTIVE?

Protests are political acts by citizens who want some response from the government. In this sense we can judge them by asking how effective they are.

This again is an area where it is hard to find clear answers. It is difficult to tell how much more effective protest is than the slower processes of ordinary participation. Many people—particularly

[7] Chicago Riot Study Committee Report (Chicago, 1969), p. 112.

Protests in America have been on many issues. Here police move in on a "Jobs for Youth" demonstration.

government leaders who would like to discourage such activity—claim that they pay no attention to them. President Nixon once made quite a point of watching a football game on TV while the White House was surrounded by Vietnam War protesters. Others—particularly the leaders of demonstrations—claim that they are the only effective political activity.

Probably the truth lies in between these positions. The most effective political activity is often the slowest and hardest—the doorbell ringing and patient talk that go with campaigning. Protest activities sometimes flash quickly and then fade, leaving no results. But the opposite often happens. An urban demonstration ending in violence, a big march on Washington by angry war protesters, attempts by citizens to block school integration—all such activities may cause government leaders to change their course sharply.

We can find examples showing clearly that direct action caused changes. The Riot Commission Report says:

> Northern violence ended Southern slavery, and Southern terrorism ended radical Reconstruction. The transformation of labor–management relations was achieved during a wave of bloody strikes, in the midst of a depression and widespread fear of revolution. And black people made their greatest political gains, both in Congress and in the cities, during the racial strife of the 1960's.[8]

Protests are particularly important as "signals." The dramatic nature of protests and their coverage by the media make them a powerful tool for signaling discontent to political leaders. And they may often attract participants as well. It is not accidental that the growth of black participation in the electoral process came when direct protests were becoming more common.

Yet there is another side to the coin. Direct action is generally

[8] Skolnick, p. 16.

Most demonstrations are peaceful. They signal the government about strong public feelings.

disapproved of by the majority of Americans—even when they approve of its goals. A great majority (75–85 percent) of the American people disapproved of student protests on the Vietnam War. Indeed, one study showed that this view was held even by citizens who thought the Vietnam War was a mistake.[9]

Public-opinion polls on racial matters make clear that there is a "white backlash" to black militant activities. The 1960s was an era of increasing acceptance by whites of the goals of blacks—better housing, integration, and the like—coupled with greater disapproval of militant activities. Furthermore, though protests represent powerful signals to political leaders, the signals are by no means clear. Riots in poor neighborhoods that involve property damage and looting will be signals to some that living conditions in urban slums need to be improved. They will call for better housing, better social services, more jobs. Others will see such riots as signaling the existence of a lawless element in urban slums. They will respond by calling for more rigorous law enforcement.

Does militant activity do more harm than good? It is hard to tell, partly because the results are mixed and hard to measure and partly because one's judgment on these issues depends on one's values. Some may believe that violence (or the risk of violence) is wrong in almost any case. Others may feel that it is necessary if social change is to happen. Out of such differences come "ordinary" politics as well as violent politics.

controversy

There has been a steady decline in voter turnout in recent presidential elections. Voting rates were always lower in the United States than in many other democracies, but they have rarely been as low as in recent years. Turnout in presidential elections used to be around 60 to 65 percent. In 1972 it was 55 percent; in 1976 it fell to 53 percent. This fall in turnout comes despite the fact that federal law has made it easier to vote by eliminating literacy tests, long residency requirements, and other impediments to voting. Also, the barriers to voting by blacks in the South have largely been removed. Yet turnout has fallen.

There is much to debate as to why this is the case and what ought to be done. Some feel that the laws are still restrictive. They advocate national registration laws that allow people to register by postcard. Others feel that the reason is citizen apathy. They advocate better educational programs. Some feel, on the other hand, that low voter turnout is not a real problem.

There are some who have advocated a law that makes voting compulsory, perhaps by levying a small fine on those who do not vote in a presidential election. Some other democracies have such laws, and almost everyone votes, unlike the situation here, where almost half of the electorate misses the opportunity to take part in presidential elections.

[9] Milton J. Rosenberg, Sidney Verba, and Philip E. Converse, *Vietnam and the Silent Majority* (New York: Harper & Row, 1970), pp. 44–45.

One Side   The election of the President is the most important democratic act performed by the American public. It is through such an election that the
public expresses its approval or disapproval of the government. Democracy is functioning badly if almost half of the public stays away from the
polls. Furthermore, those who stay away from the polls tend to be those
who are poorer and less well educated. It is especially worrisome if their
voice is missing. Lastly, voting is not only a right of a citizen; it is a basic
obligation. It is not too much to expect every American to take part by
casting a ballot. A law making it compulsory to vote would be a good
thing.

The Other Side   Our laws give all Americans the right to vote. If some do not take advantage of this right, it is their fault and not that of the government or anyone
else. It would be a mistake to compel such apathetic citizens to vote. For
one thing, they are likely to be less well informed about politics. They are
not likely to bring more wisdom and rationality into the electoral process.
It may be true that the nonvoters come from the poorer and less advantaged groups in the society, but if their voice is not heard they have only
themselves to blame. Lastly, while it would be good if more people wanted
to vote, it is not healthy for a democracy to compel them to do so. A law
making it compulsory to vote would be a bad thing.

8

LEADERSHIP RECRUITMENT AND POLITICAL POWER IN THE UNITED STATES

Political Power

For the student of politics no issue is more central, yet more elusive, than the issue of power. It is tempting to reduce the study of politics to the study of power: who has power, how it is organized, for what purposes it is applied, how concentrated it is. But this temptation should be resisted. Not all that is interesting about the political life of a society can be squeezed into the terminology of power; if it could, the terminology would have to become so broad and vague as to be useless.

But if there is more to politics than power, certainly it is also true that one cannot discuss politics without sooner or later dealing with power. We have already begun that discussion: in Chapter 3, for instance, where we reviewed the tensions between the powers of a privately owned economy and the powers of a government concerned with public action; or in Chapters 5 and 7, where the individual's powers were discussed under such headings as citizenship rights, patterns of political participation, and public opinion. Additional discussion will be found in Chapters 9, 10, and 11, where the powers of interest groups and political parties and electorates become part of our analysis. And of course the issues of legal and institutional powers are rooted in an understanding of the Constitution and in an analysis of the dominant institutions of American government: Congress, the Presidency, and the courts.

In this chapter we turn to another facet of power: Who has it and how is it obtained? More generally, this is the question of political recruitment — how some small number of citizens seek and gain the positions in American society through which power is exercised.

The Classic Definition of the State

Most people who try to define the "power of the state" start with the definition made famous by a German sociologist, Max Weber. The state is the institution in society that has a legitimate monopoly over force. Only the state is granted the right to hire and arm police, to build and fill prisons, to punish wrongdoers by taking away their property or their rights. Emphasis is placed not only on the idea of force or coercion but also on the idea of legitimacy. The use of force by the state is accepted as right and proper.

Other institutions in society might be powerful in their own sphere of activity: corporations in the economy, universities in education, the mass media in entertainment and news; medical associations and hospitals in health care. But these institutions cannot exercise physical control the way the state can. They cannot arrest or imprison.

The institution that comes closest to the state in this regard is the most private of all institutions in society: the family. The parent can punish the misbehaving child by taking away some valued thing ("Just for that, you can't watch TV tonight"), by imprisonment ("Go to your room and stay there until you can learn to behave yourself"), and by old-fashioned physical means ("Give me that hairbrush and bend over"). The only other institution that uses physical power in a systematic way is organized crime, which is in some respects a "private state" within the state. Organized crime regularly punishes members who misbehave, even imposing the death penalty at times.

BROADENING THE CONCEPT OF POWER

We would not want to restrict our definition of power simply to the exercise of physical force or control. Many institutions and individuals exercise power in ways that are unrelated to force. In modern societies, banks and insurance companies and other financial institutions have important powers in determining what kinds of capital investments are made in society. Educational institutions determine what kinds of people learn what skills, which, in turn, influences who is likely to get ahead in the society. Corporations, businesses, and farm owners help determine employment patterns in society and generally influence wage levels for the American worker and the price of goods for the American consumer. Medical and legal institutions influence what kinds of health and legal services are available to the population and at what cost. And of course the notion of government powers includes more than physical force and coercion. Throughout this book we review the many ways in which government regulations and laws shape and direct the lives of citizens. The many institutions that make up the government or the public sector are powerful for some of the same reasons that the institutions that make up the private sector are powerful. Both public and private institutions organize the efforts of large numbers of people; they have access to financial resources; they command the respect and often the obedience of significant parts of the population.

LEADERSHIP

As a working definition, we will consider the leaders of American society to be the men and women who own, manage, direct, or otherwise control the major public and private institutions. We are interested primarily in *national* leaders, people whose positions provide national visibility and influence that is felt on a national scale. Our definition stresses institutional positions. Leaders are

TABLE 8.1
Dominant and
Nondominant
Institutions

Social Sector	Dominant, Nationally Important Institutions	Nondominant, Less Important Institutions
Business	IBM	Brown Shoe Company
Government	Department of Agriculture	Oshkosh County Mosquito Control Agency
Newspapers	*New York Times*	Oak Creek *Herald*
Banks	Chase Manhattan Bank of New York	City National Bank of Kansas City
Professional associations	National Academy of Sciences	Southern Political Science Association
Military	The Pentagon	Utah National Guard
Civic organizations	Kennedy Center	Linda Hall Library

people who hold high positions in specific institutions: banks, public bureaucracies, corporations, newspapers, universities, law firms, Congress, labor unions, hospitals, churches, civic organizations, and so forth.

Institutions differ in importance; some are much more important to the society than others. They can be classified as *dominant* and *nondominant.* Table 8.1 presents examples of dominant and nondominant institutions in different social sectors.

A close look at various parts of American society shows that a fairly small number of institutions control a very large share of the total resources of society. Chapter 3 told how economic resources are concentrated in a few corporations, banks, and insurance companies. For instance, 0.1 percent of all manufacturing corporations control more than half of all manufacturing assets in the country. Although there are over 6000 foundations in the United States, the dozen largest ones control approximately 40 percent of all foundation assets. Although there are more than 2500 colleges and universities, about 20 of them receive well over half of all government contracts and control a very large share of college endowment money.

National leaders have important positions in the dominant institutions of American society. They are the officers and directors of IBM, the Secretary, assistant secretaries, and program directors in the Department of Agriculture, the publisher and editors of the *New York Times,* the officers and trustees of the Chase Manhattan Bank of New York, and so forth.

SIZE OF LEADERSHIP GROUP

The most striking fact about national leadership is how few people are directly involved in it.

In all assemblies and groups and organized bodies of men, from a nation down to a committee of a club, direction and decisions rest in the hands of a small percentage, less and less in proportion to the larger size of the body, till in a great population it becomes an infinitesimally small proportion of the whole number. This is and always has been true of all forms of government.[1]

This is easy to prove. There are 140 million adult citizens in the United States, yet how many of them are directly involved in making major decisions about the society? Although it is difficult to select a procedure that would provide an exact count, one study has attempted to do so. It reports that fewer than 4000 people

> . . . control half of the nation's industrial assets, half of all assets in communications, transportation and utilities, half of all banking assets, and two-thirds of all insurance assets; they control nearly 40 percent of all the assets of private foundations, half of all private university endowments; they control the most prestigious civic and cultural organizations; they occupy key federal government positions in the executive, legislative, and judicial branches; they occupy all of the top command positions in the Army, Navy, Air Force, and Marines.[2]

This estimate may be low because it leaves out leaders of important social movements such as civil-rights groups or consumer protest organizations; it also overlooks institutions with few financial resources but great prestige, such as scientific organizations. But even adding another 1000 or 2000 people does not change the fact that American society is led by a very small number of people.

Starting from this fact, we ask three questions about the selection of leaders in American society:

What people are chosen to be national leaders?
Do leaders tend to agree or disagree among themselves?
In what ways and how fast can the leadership group be changed?

Most of our discussion and examples will focus on political leaders, that is, on top elected and appointed officials in the government. Space does not permit full attention to corporate executives, university presidents, leading scientists, newspaper publishers, or military generals, but much of what we say here applies to these other leaders as well.

The most striking fact about national leadership is how few people are directly involved in it.

Choosing National Leaders

How do people move into and out of the top circles? Are particular groups given special advantages? What political viewpoints dominate within the governing group? What actions or mistakes typically result in the downfall of individual leaders or even in the fall of entire ruling groups? If, for instance, in Figure 8.1 the box on the bottom represents the entire adult population of the United States

[1] J. Bryce, *Modern Democracies* (New York: Macmillan, 1942), p. 542.
[2] Thomas R. Dye and John W. Pickering, "Governmental and Corporate Elites: Convergence and Differentiation," *Journal of Politics,* November 1974, p. 905.

FIGURE 8.1
**Which Citizens Will Achieve
Leadership Roles?**

and the dot on the top stands for the political leaders, which few citizens will succeed in reaching leadership positions?

For much of human history there was no question who would rule. People either were born into the ruling class or were not. Birth determined leadership, just as it determined who owned property and who did not. Of course hereditary rule did not prevent quarrels within the ruling group and palace revolutions. But it did prevent recruitment from the lower social orders. Political office and its privileges were matters of birthright.

The democratic revolution changed this. It separated birthright from officeholding. Authority could no longer be claimed because of family name. The powerful positions had somehow to be earned.

Sometimes it is thought that the democratic revolution was a challenge to leadership itself. Although this might have been intended by a few radicals, it was not a major part of the democratic revolution. The challenge was to inherited leadership. Our own Constitution recognized that a few would govern, while insisting that power and position were to be won through merit, performance, and talent.

STANDARDS FOR CHOOSING LEADERS

We can understand leadership choice in American politics by looking again at Figure 8.1. Think of the ancient Chinese box puzzle. In this puzzle different-sized boxes are designed so that the smallest box fits into the next-largest one, which, in turn, fits into the next-largest one, and so forth. The largest box contains all the others. To find the very smallest box you have to open all the boxes between it and the largest one.

Now imagine that the largest box represents the entire population and the smallest box represents the leadership group. The other boxes would represent smaller and smaller "recruitment pools" that supply people from the larger groups to the smaller ones. Recruitment is the gradual but continuous process of selection and elimination that narrows the large population to the few who hold the highest positions. Figure 8.2 is a diagram of that process showing four stages between the many and the few.

Legally Qualified Within the adult population there is a group of people who meet the legal qualifications for political officeholding. For instance, the Constitution sets minimum ages for some positions. Other legal qualifications include residency requirements (you must live in the state of which you would like to be a senator, for instance) and, for certain positions, professional credentials (especially for judicial offices, which are often limited to people with legal training). Legal qualifications, however, do not play a very significant part in political recruitment. Almost any adult citizen is legally qualified to hold public office. This has not always been the case. In the seventeenth century only property owners could stand for office; blacks were barred from office as well as from voting until after the Civil War; and women could not hold certain positions

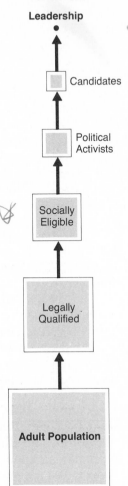

FIGURE 8.2
Recruitment Criteria for Political Leadership

until fairly recent times. One way to trace the growth of democratic principles in any society is through the progressive elimination of laws that bar particular groups from office.

Socially Eligible The next standard for choosing political leaders is that they be "socially eligible." A large percentage of leaders consistently come from particular social groups in the population. Leaders are not typical in their social origins, in their educational levels, and in their occupations before holding office.

Imagine that we were to study the way a tiny portion of your own generation will eventually come to hold the highest political offices. We might make up a list of people between the ages of 18 and 25 and then follow them through their careers until, say, thirty years from now, when a few of them will have risen to important positions. Suppose this list of younger citizens included the following:

- The son of a corporation lawyer who heads a law firm in Washington, D.C. He has just graduated from Princeton, where he was active in student politics and was editor of the campus newspaper. Next year he will enter Harvard Business School.
- A black longshoreman in San Francisco who is keenly interested in trade union affairs. He has already been elected secretary of his multiracial local. His formal education is limited to community college, but he is a good organizer and is popular with fellow workers. He has campaigned actively for local Democratic candidates.
- A student body president of a large state university in the Midwest. She is the daughter of a small-town mayor and has served her father as an unofficial consultant on ending sex discrimination in the town's schools and hospitals. Although she is known to be very sharp politically, her academic record is mediocre. Still, she has been admitted to the university's graduate school of education.
- A farmer's son who graduated with honors from Jerseyville High School but decided against further education. He was a football hero in the community and has recently joined the Elks, partly because some local businessmen have hinted that they would like him to serve on the town planning commission.

Now ask: What are the chances that thirty years from now any one of these four will have reached top government positions? We would rank their chances in the order in which they are listed, even though each has leadership skills. For every 100 people like the Princeton graduate perhaps one will end up in a top position; while for every 10,000 budding labor leaders only one is likely to get that far. However, this particular labor leader is black, which may be an advantage during a period when great attention is being given to racial equality. The next person on the list is disadvantaged by her sex and by the fact that she is taking advanced work in education rather than law or business. Finally we come to our high school hero, who, statistically speaking, has the lowest probability of reaching a high position.

Trying to predict which of these four 20-year-olds will become a national leader helps us see that leaders are chosen from a small portion of the general population. Coming from a wealthy family, being white and male, and attending a good university or college greatly increases the chances of moving into the circles from which leaders are selected. Consider two people on the list. The Princeton graduate has begun a career that often puts people with his background and ability in line for the highest positions in society. His family, his father's business associates, his Princeton classmates or Harvard professors would not consider it odd if he announced that his ambition is to become a member of the U.S. Senate or a well-known New York law firm.

The social setting of the farm boy is far different. It is less likely that he views himself as a future member of the highest political circles. There are few models for him to imitate and few contacts to help him on his way. His origins and social setting are not an absolute barrier to a political career, as Lyndon Johnson among others so effectively demonstrates. But it is more likely that the idea of success for a high school educated small town businessman is to become mayor. The point is clear: People eliminate themselves from the race for the few top positions as well as selecting themselves for those positions. Patterns of self-elimination and self-selection cannot be separated from social position. Some people are born with a foot on the ladder to power, but most are not.

Moreover, movement into leadership positions is always influenced by the judgments of people who already hold high office. This is true even if great stress is placed on "objective standards," for those standards can never be separated from the prejudices of the people who are responsible for them. No matter how talent is defined, it must be discovered by those who have already proved that they have it. Those who are already in leadership positions will encourage people with similar status and background. This selectivity from the top down contributes to a process in which certain social groups continue to supply recruits for the top political positions.

Social background, however, is only one among several factors that account for who reaches the top. All four of the people listed earlier have a chance, if for no other reason than that they have shown some leadership skill. In this way their chances are higher than those of schoolmates who have shown no such skill. Another Princetonian might come from the same social level, but he might have concentrated on chemistry for the past six years. He is now in graduate school and avoids activities that distract him from his academic work. This chemist is not a realistic candidate for a top political position.

Political Activists   Approximately one out of twenty adult citizens is a political activist, and it is from this group that leadership eventually comes. As Chapter 7 made clear, the activists pay close attention to political matters, serve on committees and work in campaigns, know and are known by the people who are actually in office, and are in positions that traditionally supply the recruits for

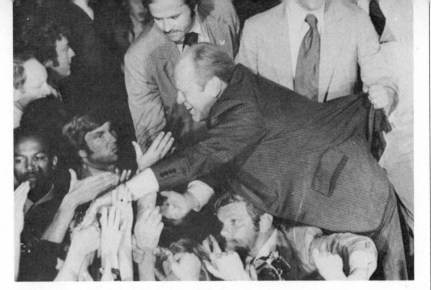

Candidates from top political office come from those who assert themselves.

public office. This group is largely, though not entirely, made up of middle- and upper-middle-class citizens.

The boundaries that separate the politically active from the less active are neither firmly established nor easily recognized. People move back and forth across these boundaries as their interests change, as their careers take them closer to or farther away from politics, and as their own ambitions respond to the chance to have a political career. In some important ways the active citizens are self-selected. There are no universal standards for entry into the loose network that supplies candidates for the highest positions. But political activists often come from families with a tradition of political involvement; they are exposed to politics early in life and simply carry these habits into their adult careers. Approximately one-third of the officeholders in the United States trace their earliest political involvement to the influence of the family. This may be seen in such families as the Roosevelts, Tafts, and Kennedys.

Candidates Within the politically active group is an even smaller number of people who become candidates for top leadership positions. This includes those who are actually nominated for elective positions as well as those whose names appear on lists when appointments are being made to the Cabinet, the Supreme Court, the executive agencies, and so forth. How some activists become serious contenders for the leadership positions and others do not is not well understood. One factor, however, is self-assertiveness. This is illustrated in President Johnson's view of the world as "a vacuum of non-wills in which the strong man with a 'will to power' automatically takes charge. Most people drop off the political ladder at the bottom and middle rungs; private values intrude; conflicts arise. The restless few who remain become the political leaders of the day." It was no accident that Johnson himself belonged to the rest-

less few: "As long as I can remember I've always been the kind of person who takes over in any group, who takes responsibility for calling the gathering together, setting the agenda for the meeting and carrying out the assignments."

Another factor is the attitude of people who are already in powerful positions. They can sponsor careers by the way they make opportunities available and fill key apprenticeship positions. For instance, when Johnson was Senate majority leader he greatly aided John F. Kennedy's career by helping the freshman senator gain appointment to the Senate Foreign Relations Committee. This gave Kennedy a platform from which he could launch his drive for the Democratic party's presidential nomination.

THE TEST OF ACHIEVEMENT IN LEADERSHIP SELECTION

The Chinese box puzzle shows how a very large population is gradually narrowed until a small number of candidates are competing for an even smaller number of top political positions. But this leaves unanswered the question of ability. Because so many leaders come from well-to-do families and are white males, some observers of American politics say that *who you are* is more important than *what you can do.* This is a hasty and incorrect conclusion. It is clear that social background provides advantages, but it can neither guarantee a place among the political leaders nor completely block entry to members of other social groups.

The people who govern American society are achievers. They have shown that they can manage large enterprises or direct the efforts of others or attract the loyalty of large numbers of people. Thus at any given time the President's Cabinet will probably include former chief officers of giant corporations, perhaps someone who has been the head of a foundation or a university president, a member of a leading law firm, an ex-labor union leader.

We appear to be inconsistent. First, leaders are largely white males from relatively high-status families. Second, they are able and talented people. It looks as if we have to conclude that ability and talent are concentrated among the sons of wealthy white families. But this conclusion is untrue. Some people have a greater opportunity to develop and display their abilities than others.

Display of Talent on a Grand Scale To be in line for national political leadership, it is necessary to show your ability on a grand scale. It is better to succeed at running Ford Motor Company than at selling worn-out Fords on the used-car lot, though the latter may involve greater skill than the former. It is better to be an innovative president of a well-known university than an innovative grade school teacher, though teaching a roomful of 8-year-olds may take more innovation than overseeing a university. It is better to be the popular vote-getting mayor of New York than the Mayor of Bellview, though it may take more popularity to turn out the vote in Bellview than in New York.

It is therefore not just achievement but very specific achievements that move one into leadership positions. This suggests why the wealthy provide so many of the top leaders. They have the education and contacts necessary to reach positions through which ability can be shown on a grand scale. The used-car salesman may be as skilled, personable, and hardworking as the president of the company whose worn-out products he sells. But the salesman was born into the working class, not the upper class. He attended a local junior college, not Harvard Business School. His friends also sell used cars; they don't direct the corporations that make them. He is sometimes active in precinct politics, but he does not give thousands of dollars to presidential campaigns. When the list of possible appointees to the Cabinet or possible nominees for the governorship or possible candidates for an ambassadorship is drawn up, it never includes the skilled, personable, hardworking used-car salesman, but often includes the head of the company whose cars he sells.

Top leaders are people who have achieved a lot. But the achievements that count are easier to display if you start life as a white male from a fairly well-off Protestant family. This is how you get the education and job opportunities that, in turn, launch the careers that take some people, but not many, to the top.

Ability to Win Elections   It is true that American politics often rewards with power those who have proved that they can direct the large institutions of commerce and business, banking, law, education, and philanthropy. But rewards also go to those with a very different kind of skill—the ability to win elections.

The electorate in a democracy necessarily controls entry into certain key leadership posts. Thus what matters is the basic achievement of winning elections. Nixon built on a series of election victories, starting with his campaign for the House of Representatives in 1946 and ending in his landslide reelection to the Presidency in 1972. Johnson also went from the House to the Senate to the Vice-Presidency to the Presidency. Of course not all major electoral victories build on a series of lesser victories. Eisenhower transferred his great popularity as wartime general into voter popularity and won the Presidency without ever having been active in politics. The former governor of California, Ronald Reagan, moved into that position directly from his career as a movie actor. Charles Percy was a corporation executive before being elected senator from Illinois.

Voter appeal can be used to advantage by people from any background. Indeed, in American politics it makes up for the lack of family wealth or a high-status education. Only one President out of the last seven (Kennedy, in contrast to Truman, Eisenhower, Johnson, Nixon, Ford, and Carter) started with the advantage of wealth.

We see, thus, that achievement is weighed in two different though sometimes related ways. There is the achievement shown by

Eisenhower transferred his great popularity as a wartime general into voter popularity and won the Presidency without ever having been active in politics.

becoming a corporation executive or a senior partner in a leading law firm or the president of a foundation or university. Such people are candidates for the highest political positions, as when Robert McNamara moved from head of Ford Motor Company to Secretary of Defense or Edward Levi moved from president of the University of Chicago to Attorney General. There is also the achievement of election victories.

How Much Agreement Is There Among Leaders?

There is, on the one hand, the argument that national leaders generally think the same way about public policy. Only small differences are allowed. Leaders are a cohesive group, and it is nearly impossible to introduce new ideas unless the "establishment" agrees to them. There is, on the other hand, the argument that leaders are very much divided into different and competing groups. Leaders have varying ambitions. They represent different economic groups, regions, or political movements. The important fact about leadership is not agreement but conflict. Which view is correct?

POLITICAL LEADERSHIP IN DISAGREEMENT

Leaders hold a great variety of viewpoints. Sharply different views are expressed on such issues as tax reform, inflation controls, defense expenditures, and so forth. It could not be otherwise. *The political recruitment process carries into leadership circles some of the basic conflicts and divisions of society.* This happens in many ways. For instance, we will see in Chapter 10 that Republicans and Democrats differ. In addition, leaders become spokesmen for the many political and social divisions in society: North versus South, Protestant versus Catholic, workers versus management. Then of course there are conflicts between state leaders and the federal bureaucracy, between Congress and the Presidency.

One example of disagreement among leaders can be found in Chapter 5, where we showed (in Table 5.6) that business leaders and labor leaders differ sharply on the causes of poverty, the business leaders thinking that poverty is the fault of the poor and labor leaders saying that it is caused by the system. Democratic and Republican leaders also differ on the causes of poverty.

There is a more general division among leaders, however, to which the disagreement on the causes of poverty points. This is the division between what we will call the *merchant class* and the *social engineers.*

The interests and institutions associated with the merchant class generally believe that the well-being of the society and of individual citizens is best promoted through the marketplace. Government action and interventions, while sometimes necessary, should be kept to a minimum. The unregulated marketplace will establish the conditions under which the private citizen can pursue individual goals. Leaders who hold to this belief are most likely to be found in

California Governor Jerry Brown differs sharply from many of the established leaders in America on a variety of the issues of the 1970s and 1980s.

banks and other financial institutions, in industry and business, and in the Republican party.

There is a variation on the views expressed by the merchant class, however. This variation also rejects government regulation and intervention, but it is not willing to grant that a totally free marketplace is in the public interest. Certain leading conservative economists and other academics believe that there should be incentives to make sure that private enterprise and the market economy do not pollute the environment or establish unsafe working conditions. To prevent these harmful effects of unregulated competition, there should be incentives such as lower taxes for firms that don't pollute.

In opposition to the merchant class and to those who would simply manipulate incentives are the social engineers. This group of leaders does not share the assumption that individual well-being and social progress are automatically produced by the workings of the competitive marketplace. They believe that social engineering should supplement the marketplace. This engineering normally takes place through government programs and interventions, for example, social-welfare policies. Both the merchant class and the social engineers worry about the well-being of individual citizens. But for the merchant class citizen well-being can be provided with economic rewards allocated by the occupational structure and exchanges in the marketplace. For the social engineers this is not enough. The market economy has to be supplemented with government grant programs such as public education, social security, medicare, and unemployment insurance.

Leadership for the social-engineering interests is most likely to be found in the upper levels of the government bureaucracy; in uni-

225

Leadership in the United States is not the exclusive male club it was a few years ago.

versities, research institutions, and foundations; in certain parts of the media, especially journalists; and in citizen action groups and political reform movements. Politically, the social engineers are more likely to be Democrats than Republicans.

Table 8.2 shows differences between leadership groups on whether the government should take action to reduce the income gap in the United States and whether it should see to it that everyone has a job. While only a few business leaders and Republicans favor such government action, a large majority of labor leaders and Democrats expect the government to reduce inequality and to actively promote employment. These differences illustrate the pattern of disagreement between the merchant class and the social engineers. It is not that the merchant class favors poverty and unemployment. Rather, these individuals feel that the income gap and unemployment are problems to be solved through the workings of the market economy.

TABLE 8.2
Leadership Differences on Government Action to Reduce Income Inequality and Unemployment

Government Should Take Action to Reduce Income Gap		Government Should Take Action to Provide Jobs	
Democratic leaders	75%	Democratic leaders	73%
Labor leaders	68%	Labor leaders	63%
Intellectuals	62%	Intellectuals	43%
Republican leaders	14%	Republican leaders	9%
Business leaders	14%	Business leaders	9%

Source: Sidney Verba, Gary Orren, Donald Feree, "The Meaning of Equality: A Leadership Survey." Conducted by the *Washington Post* and the Center for International Affairs of Harvard University, 1976.

Consensus among leaders emerge from shared backgrounds and shared experiences.

This distinction between the merchant class and the social engineers suggests the possibility of serious disagreements within the leadership class. But this is only half of the picture. There are also certain values and assumptions that are widely shared across the leadership class in the United States. For instance, social engineers as well as the merchant class believe that the United States should continue to be a capitalist economy. There is a high level of agreement on the importance of private ownership, different economic rewards for different tasks, labor mobility, and market competition.

Let's turn more directly to the question of agreement among leaders and how the recruitment process promotes it.

POLITICAL LEADERSHIP IN AGREEMENT

Leaders share many experiences. They often have similar backgrounds. They know how hard it is to get and use power. They worry about how to keep the economy working effectively and how to keep the government intact. Out of these shared experiences, backgrounds, challenges, and worries comes a form of leadership consensus. This is because leaders are recruited from the political *mainstream,* a term that has both a substantive and a procedural meaning.

Substantive Consensus The political mainstream includes the broad policies that most Americans actively support or at least willingly tolerate. Take military policy as an example. Most Americans agree that the nation should maintain military preparedness and that the United States should, if necessary, defend its national interests with military force. Most, but not all, citizens take this view. There are some who oppose the whole idea of military preparedness and believe that the United States should disarm. Such a view is considered to be outside the mainstream of American thinking. Equally outside the mainstream is the view that the United States should make nuclear strikes against its supposed enemies.

The recruitment process tends over and over again to select leaders from the political mainstream. One reason is that the electorate is not likely to support candidates whose viewpoints conflict with its own. This does not mean that every political leader is equally acceptable to every voter. A member of Congress elected by white rural Mississippians probably has views on race relations that are obnoxious to northern black voters. But while individual leaders may be disliked by particular electorates, the leadership group as a whole has policy views that go along with majoritarian, mainstream thinking.

There is, then, a certain consensus among the nation's leaders on the policies that the American public is willing to tolerate. Within the political mainstream, and thus within the leadership, are many divergent viewpoints. Take again the example of military policy. To say that there is broad agreement that the United States should be prepared to defend its interests is not to agree on the size of the budget for "preparedness" or on what is meant by "national interests." Despite these differences, the recruitment process bars from the top leadership circles views that strike most Americans as "extreme" or "going too far."

Procedural Consensus There is a second sense in which leaders reflect the political mainstream. Much that is important about American politics, or any politics, may be found in an oft-repeated phrase of the 1960s: "working within the system." Here the emphasis is on procedural consensus. There is an acceptable way of doing things and an unacceptable way. Political hostility toward peaceniks, eco-freaks, black militants, and hippies stemmed from the belief that without "the system" there is no hope for the goals sought by such groups — no hope for lasting peace, clean air, racial justice, cultural tolerance. Political dissidents can vote the rascals out, but they will not be allowed to destroy the system that permits a later group of rascals to be voted out; they can petition and demonstrate, but they cannot abolish the system that allows petitions and demonstrations; they can condemn acquisitiveness, but they cannot ruin the system that gives others the right to acquire.

Leaders agree on the importance of "working within the system," and in this way they reflect the political mainstream. Consensus on *how* to bring about change cuts across sharp policy disagreements on *what* changes, if any, are necessary. The recruitment process maintains this procedural consensus. The long climb to high office generally breeds commitment to the rules of the game, and the result is a common approach to governing despite different points of view.

Sometimes, however, political leaders fail to "play by the rules of the game." This sends shock waves through the political system, as in the Watergate affair. People in powerful positions were caught in such activities as illegal raising of campaign funds, political spying, and attempts to undermine the election process during the months before the 1972 election.

Perhaps those who were most disturbed by Watergate were certain elite groups that fully understood the implications of those activities. These groups — an independent judiciary, important media figures, and members of Congress — quickly saw the importance of ridding Washington of people whose ideas and methods conflicted with the procedural consensus on which successful political leadership depends.

National Leadership in Changing Circumstances

Membership in the national leadership group is not permanent, particularly for individuals, who leave in a variety of ways (e.g., defeat or retirement). Nor is it permanent for particular groups. New social forces—the women's movement, black power, consumer protest, labor unions—enter the scene, and very often they push aside some established groups. This is called *elite circulation*, a process through which new viewpoints, new groups, and new skills find a place in leadership circles.

THE CONTINUING SKILL REVOLUTION

The main job of leadership can be simply stated: Be prepared for the problems of society and solve them. This task is unevenly performed. Consider today's social problems: pollution of air and water; congested cities; inflationary costs of social services; racial, ethnic, and social-class tensions; finding new sources of energy. Would these problems be less severe if previous leaders had been more aware of the drift toward pollution, urban decay, and other current problems? To put the question another way, today are there signs of future problems that are not noticed by current leaders but will crowd the political agenda when today's college students are trying to raise their families?

Such questions are very hard to answer, but they point to an important issue for political recruitment. Leadership skills change as the problems facing society change. We ask, then, whether leadership skills have caught up to social problems. The struggle to keep up is what causes the continuing skill revolution.

The Political Agenda and Leadership Changes In the depression of the 1930s none of the traditional economic solutions seemed to work. Then in 1932 the Roosevelt administration took over. Dozens of new social reforms and programs were tried. The people who were in leadership positions had very different economic and social philosophies from preceding administrations. They had a new range of skills. Out of this "skill revolution" came the New Deal, a collection of government programs and social services and an attitude toward fiscal management that were unheard of a decade earlier.

This shows the link between a skill revolution and the political agenda. Pressing problems form the agenda. When the right skills are lacking, the problems get worse. When the right skills are provided, appropriate programs are begun. What are often called "national crises" occur during the lag time between the emergence of

229

Leaders are selected from among those who can adapt themselves to changing political agendas and conditions.

serious problems and the recruitment of people with the skills and outlooks needed to deal with them.

It is helpful to compare the past three decades with the present decade. In the thirty years from 1940 to 1970 the political agenda of the United States was dominated by issues of national security and international politics: World War II, the cold war, the Korean War, the North Atlantic Treaty Organization (NATO) and other mutual security alliances, the Berlin crisis, the arms race and nuclear stockpiling, the missile gap between the United States and the USSR, the Cuban blockade, and of course, the long-drawn-out Vietnam War.

This agenda of issues had a great effect on the skills and outlooks of the people who was recruited into top leadership positions. Thus, for instance, the man who was elected President in 1952, Dwight D. Eisenhower, had no record and few known positions on domestic policy questions. Indeed, *both* of the major parties had approached him about running for the Presidency. With national security and international politics dominating public attention, leadership fell into the hands of those who were skilled at diplomacy and military matters, people like John Foster Dulles, Eisenhower's Secretary of State, or, more recently, Henry Kissinger. The 1950s and 1960s produced the "military-industrial complex," but we should not be surprised that a nation with war, weapons, and security on its mind would turn to the Pentagon, the CIA, and the weapons manufacturers.

Now, however, the military-industrial complex is in disfavor. Americans are dissatisfied with the cold-war policies of the past decade, and they were disillusioned by the Vietnam War. Domestic political questions are demanding attention—pollution, drugs, crime, social services, taxes, inflation. This shift in the social-political agenda is, according to some observers, causing a transfer of political power from the military-industrial complex to the social services-industrial complex, and there is a demand for leaders who are able to solve problems in health and education, transportation, consumer protection, urban life, conservation, and environmental quality.

Thus, to sum up, we choose as our political leaders people from particular social groups and people who have proved their ability, but we also choose them from particular skill groups. The challenge of any society is to recruit the skills appropriate to the problems it faces. The drift into one crisis or another is due partly to the failure to recruit leaders who are able to prepare for and solve social problems. Otherwise the problems grow until they become crises, as when the "problems" of city life become the "crisis" of urbanized America. Some feel that it is past time for a major skill revolution, arguing that those who have managed America over the past decades have been concerned too much with national security and too little with the quality of life for American citizens.

THE EMERGENCE OF NEW SOCIAL GROUPS

Earlier we pointed out that some social groups provide most of our political leaders. National leadership has long been a white male club. But within this club some important changes have taken place over the years. Its social makeup is not completely fixed. The ministers, lawyers, and wealthy landowners who founded the nation did not expect that a century later the United States would be governed by men who had made their millions by building up giant industries. And the industrialists and bankers of the late nineteenth and early twentieth centuries did not expect that a few decades later they would be sharing power with the leaders of powerful labor unions. During this transition white males continued to dominate leadership positions, but the groups they represented changed dramatically.

Now, in the last quarter of the twentieth century, new social groups are getting into the club. Each year more blacks and women are counted among the national leaders. Table 8.3, for example, shows the number who have entered Congress over the past quarter-century. There are two women governors, and several large cities have black mayors. Changes are taking place in business, universities, newspapers, hospitals, and law firms as well. It is a slow process, but once started, it continues to put pressure on the leadership group.

231

Congress[a]	BLACK MEMBERS IN THE		WOMEN MEMBERS IN THE	
	Senate	House	Senate	House
80th		2	1	7
81st		2	1	9
82nd		2	1	10
83rd		2	3	12
84th		3	1	16
85th		4	1	15
86th		4	1	16
87th		4	2	17
88th		5	2	11
89th		6	2	10
90th	1	5	1	11
91st	1	9	1	10
92nd	1	12	2	13
93rd	1	15	0	14
94th	2	16	0	18
95th[b]	1	17	1	17

[a] Each congressional session lasts two years. There are a total of 435 members of the House and a total of 100 members of the Senate.
[b] November 1976 election. In 1978, Muriel Humphrey was appointed Senator from Minnesota to fill the remainder of the term of Hubert Humphrey, who died while in office.
Source: Based on data from *Current American Government* (Washington, D.C.: *Congressional Quarterly*, Spring 1973), pp. 25–26; and *Current American Government*, Spring 1975, p. 17.

Conclusions

A small group of people govern the nation. These are the people who have important positions in the dominant institutions of society. Through these institutions—banks, universities, government agencies, businesses, legislatures—the leaders decide how the resources of the society are to be used. The level of government spending on the military is such a decision; so is the interest rate on money borrowed by a homeowner, the tuition at colleges and universities, the type of scientific research that gets funded.

Leaders are recruited in a way that gives advantages to particular social groups. They share common experiences and backgrounds, though they do not agree about the kinds of policies the nation should be following. Moreover, the leadership group is under continual pressure to change, to allow new social groups to have a voice in the governing of the society, and to recruit new skills as the agenda of society changes.

controversy

Citizens have varying amounts of political influence and involvement. At the bottom are the inactive citizens who care little about political matters and do not even bother to vote. Then comes the mass of Ameri-

cans who vote and are involved in some political activity now and then. Then come the real activists, who are very involved in the political life of their community or of the nation. Then come those who try for public office: the candidates. Then come those who succeed: the officeholders. And these range from minor local officials up through the ranks to the top national leaders.

At each of these levels one finds a population that is more and more "elite" in social and economic terms. At each step upward the percentage coming from high-status families increases. At each step upward the percentage with higher levels of education increases. Some say that this reflects the proper working of American democracy. Others think of it as a major flaw.

One Side The fact that wealthier and better-educated citizens find their way to the top of American politics implies nothing bad about American democracy. They do so mostly because they choose to do so. Lower-status citizens are less interested. And if because of this they have less influence over the government than their wealthier fellow citizens, it is they who are to blame, not the system. As long as citizens are *free to participate* and *free to run for office,* democracy, is working. If some do not take advantage of these opportunities, it does not mean that democracy is not working well.

Furthermore, this situation has good results in terms of the kinds of people who are recruited to leadership positions. The higher you go, the more qualified the group you find. Recruiting skilled people is difficult under the best of circumstances. Turning to successful businessmen, lawyers, and civil leaders as candidates for high office means fewer mistakes. These people have shown that they can succeed where the competition is toughest. They have graduated from the hardest schools. They have achieved in highly competitive situations. They have proved that they can run the largest institutions in American society, and governing requires the skill to run such superinstitutions as the Pentagon or the Department of Health, Education and Welfare. We should recruit as our top leaders those who have shown such skill.

Earlier we described four young citizens: the Princeton graduate headed for a career as a corporation executive, the black longshoreman active in local politics, the politically skilled feminist preparing for a career in education, the popular small-town boy who will soon have experience in community planning. The chances of the corporation executive's reaching high political office are much, much greater than those of any of the other three. And he is likely to be the one with the background to grasp the complex problems of American society. The black trade union activist will know how to develop race relations programs that make sense for the docks of San Francisco. It is not clear, however, that he will have the experience necessary to create a broadly based program on the same issue. A creative program will have to take into account the race relations on Alabama farms, on army bases in Europe, in the sales forces of Boston insurance agencies. Moreover, it will have to be coordinated with a program for police colleges in the Department of Justice or a student exchange program with Africa planned by the Department of State. Perhaps the Princeton graduate—now an IBM executive who spent two years as a consultant in Nairobi, served on the Civil Rights Commission, is a member of the board of trustees of several colleges, and recently advised the Ford Foundation on its program for grants to inner-city schools—is the best person to direct a federal agency on race relations.

We should choose our leaders from the small group of citizens who have proved their ability. It is of course unfortunate that this small group is mostly white, mostly male, and mostly from wealthy and Protestant families. These facts should be changed, but they should be changed by ending race, sex, and class discrimination, not by recruiting unskilled citizens for leadership positions.

The color or sex or social background of leaders is not at issue. But the skills and outlook are. American society will suffer if it chooses as its leaders people of low achievement.

The Other Side   Democracy works only when all citizens have an equal voice; the more it fails in this respect, the less effective it is. The fact that the rich and better educated are more active in politics and more successful in climbing the political ladder is therefore a major flaw in American democracy. It is not fair to say that poorer citizens do not go far politically because they choose not to. The opportunities to participate are not equal across social groups. If lower-status citizens participate less than others, it is not because they don't care but because they lack resources. If election campaigns cost millions, those who cannot give large sums are not "equally free" to participate effectively. And they are even less likely to be able to run for office themselves.

Nor does this mean that only the "best" make it to the top leadership positions. Maybe they have more education, but there are important skills and outlooks that they may not have. The skills that might establish racial harmony, provide decent education and health care, and plan communities as places to enjoy life are not necessarily found in white upper-class males. Leaders should be drawn from the groups that have direct experience with the problems of American life.

The white corporate executive may have more organizational ability and more advanced education than the black union leader. But whose career is likely to develop the skills necessary to ease racial tension within the American working class? Might not the feminist be able to bring fresh approaches to the Department of Health, Education and Welfare? And might not the Jerseyville town planner be sensitive to protecting community well-being against urban sprawl?

American society may be shortchanging itself by always choosing leaders from the successful business and professional classes.

9
INTEREST GROUPS IN AMERICAN POLITICS

As we saw in Chapter 6, the United States is divided into many groups with different interests. We considered the reasons why some groups become politically powerful while others do not. Groups that are organized are likely to have a greater effect on government policy than those that have no organization. In this chapter we will look more closely at political organizations — organizations that try to influence government policy. How many interest groups or pressure groups are there in the United States? How powerful are they? What makes some groups powerful and others not?

The Role of Interest Groups

There is disagreement about the power of interest groups. Some students of politics have argued that all one needs to know about American politics can be learned by studying the role of such groups. Congress and the President, they argue, do not initiate policy. Rather, they respond to the demands of lobbies and organized interests. At best the government acts as a "broker" among such interests — seeing that each organized interest gets a little something in response to its demands. Thus the conflicting pressures from organized groups determine government policy.

Most writers on politics think this is an exaggeration. Government policy is not merely the sum of interest group pressures. Yet there is some truth to the view. Organized groups are not all-powerful. But interests represented by well-organized pressure groups are better able to pressure the government than unorganized interests. And this is important in determining who will benefit from government policy.

Observers also disagree as to whether the activities of such groups hurt society as a whole. Pressure groups serve the "selfish" interests of particular groups of citizens. Organizations lobby for the interests of clothing manufacturers, doctors, farmers. Nor are such "selfish" interests limited to the wealthy trying to get an even bigger share of the economic pie. Organizations press the claims of blacks, welfare mothers, labor. Their interests are "selfish" not because their demands are not justified but because they represent the specific interests of each group and do not take into account the needs and problems of other groups. Each group is out to "take care of its own."

Critics of pressure groups argue that they achieve their selfish interests at the expense of society as a whole. Pressure groups compete for the attention of government officials to obtain some benefit for their group. In this way the broader public interest is ignored. No one plans for the problems of society as a whole. Such a view of interest groups is reflected in the "muckraking" of writers like Lincoln Steffens at the beginning of this century. Such literature has revealed many cases of close association of specific interests with the government. Out of such close association comes a government policy that benefits particular interests and may hurt the rest of society. This position is strongly held by a number of the most serious students of American politics.

These critics make a further point. It is not only that the pressure group system ignores the interests of the nation as a whole in favor of particular selfish interests. It is also a fault of the pressure group system that only certain interests are communicated. In general, they agree, the interests of business and of the wealthier members of society are communicated in this way.

A different argument is made by other observers of American politics: that there is no conflict between the selfish interests of particular groups and some more general public good. Indeed, the public good, the argument goes, does not exist outside of and separate from the specific interests of groups of citizens. Rather, the public good represents the sum of the desires of those various groups, and out of the clash among those groups comes the most effective and responsive public policy.

Although those who defend the interest group system admit that not all groups are equally represented, they argue that the answer is more, and more equal, group representation. If some interests are well represented by interest groups and others are not, then the others should organize as well.

Does competition among organized interests hurt the general public interest? Or is it the most effective way of seeing that citizen interests are communicated to the government?

We will return to these questions later in this chapter, after we have discussed the role of organized groups in American politics.

How Much Organization?

America has often been called a society of joiners; foreign observers have been struck by the ease with which Americans form organizations and by the great numbers and far-ranging concerns of such organizations. And when we compare the United States to other nations we find a somewhat higher percentage of organization members here than elsewhere. Current figures indicate that about six out of ten adult Americans belong to some organization, a higher figure than in comparable countries, where a little less than half the adult population is likely to belong to some organized group.

WHO ARE THE MEMBERS OF ORGANIZATIONS?

Does the figure "six out of ten" mean that most Americans have some organization that takes care of their political interests? The answer is unclear. Although the data show that a majority of Americans belong to some organization, they also show a large minority—four out of ten—with no affiliation. More important, perhaps, is the fact that organizations do not represent all social groups equally. As we saw in Chapter 7, it is the upper-status citizens who are more likely to be organization members. If you are wealthy, if you have a college education, if you are white rather than black, then you are more likely to be an organization member. Thus not only is membership not universal in the United States, but what membership there is, is not spread equally across the society.

POLITICAL AND NONPOLITICAL INTEREST GROUPS

Furthermore, not all the organizations that citizens belong to have been formed to express political interests. (See Table 9.1.) Only 8 percent of the citizens belong to specifically political groups—political-party clubs; nonpartisan political groups like the League of Women Voters; and groups like the NAACP, whose purpose is to

TABLE 9.1
Types of Organizations to Which Individuals Belong

Type of Organization	Percent of Population Reporting Membership
Political groups such as Democratic or Republican clubs: political-action groups such as voters' leagues	8
School service groups such as PTA or school alumni groups	17
Service clubs such as Lions, Rotary, Zonta, Junior Chamber of Commerce	6
Youth groups such as Boy Scouts, Girl Scouts	7
Veterans' groups such as American Legion	7
Farm organizations such as Farmer's Union, Farm Bureau, Grange	4
Nationality groups such as Sons of Norway, Hibernian Society	2
Church-related groups such as Bible Study Group, Holy Name Society	6
Fraternal groups such as Elks, Eagles, Masons, and their women's auxiliaries	15
Professional or academic societies such as American Dental Association, Phi Beta Kappa	7
Trade Unions	17
School fraternities and sororities	3
Literary, art, discussion, or study clubs such as book review clubs, theater groups	4
Hobby or garden clubs such as stamp or coin clubs, flower clubs, pet clubs	5
Sports clubs, bowling leagues, etc.	12

Source: Based on data from Sidney Verba and Norman H. Nie, *Participation in America: Political Democracy and Social Equality* (New York: Harper & Row, 1972.)

pressure the government. Most organizations are formed for other purposes. They are related to recreational interests (fraternal groups, sports and hobby clubs); economic interests (unions, professional associations, farm groups); particular community concerns (parent groups, service clubs); or specific citizen identifications (nationality groups, religious groups).

But it would be a mistake to think that only groups with a political purpose communicate citizen interests to the government. All of these types of groups may become politically active, and some are active all the time. Indeed, it is hard to draw a line between political and nonpolitical organizations. Since all groups may at times be affected by government activity or require some response from the government, any group may become politically active. A good example is the National Rifle Association (NRA). Essentially organized as a recreational group for hunters and sportsmen, it became a major political force when it felt its interests challenged by supporters of gun control legislation. And the same can be said for every other type of group. Church-related groups do not have political goals, but they become involved in conflicts over the issues they see affecting their interests—abortion laws, school prayers, or any other issue that they take seriously. And groups that represent economic interests are constantly involved with the government.

Lobbies

Some organizations are more active in trying to influence the government than others. They have offices in Washington or in state capitals, and they have professional staffs that have close contact with the government. The range of organizations that are active in this way may be seen in Table 9.2, which is taken from a congressional report on lobbying organizations. Of the hundreds of such groups registered in Washington, it lists those that report the largest expenditures to influence Congress.

The data do not necessarily show which groups are most active in Washington; the Lobbying Act is vague on the subject of who has to

TABLE 9.2
The Top Twenty-Five
Spenders[a]

Organization	1973	1972
Common Cause	$934,835	$558,839
International Union, United Automobile, Aerospace and Agricultural Implement Workers	460,992	[b]
American Postal Workers Union (AFL-CIO)	393,399	208,767
American Federation of Labor-Congress of Industrial Organizations (AFL-CIO)	240,800	216,294
American Trucking Associations Inc.	226,157	137,804
American Nurses Association Inc.	218,354	109,642
U.S. Savings and Loan League	204,221	191,726
Gas Supply Committee	195,537	11,263
Disabled American Veterans	193,168	159,431
The Committee of Publicly Owned Companies	180,493	[b]
American Farm Bureau Federation	170,472	180,678
National Education Association	162,755	[b]
National Association of Letter Carriers	160,597	154,187
National Association of Home Builders of the United States	152,177	99,031
Recording Industry Association of America Inc.	141,111	88,396
National Council of Farmer Cooperatives	140,560	184,346
American Insurance Association	139,395	82,395
The Farmers' Educational and Co-operative Union of America	138,403	113,156
Committee of Copyright Owners	135,095	[b]
National Housing Conference Inc.	125,726	77,906
American Petroleum Institute	121,276	38,656
American Medical Association	114,859	96,145
Citizens for Control of Federal Spending	113,659	[b]
American Civil Liberties Union	102,595	73,131
National Association of Insurance Agents Inc.	87,422	50,924

[a] The top 25 spenders of the organizations that filed lobby spending reports for 1973, with the amounts they reported spending in 1973 and 1972.
[b] No spending record.
Source: Congressional Quarterly Weekly, July 27, 1974. Reprinted by permission.

register and is not firmly enforced. Indeed, published reports of organizational spending are usually described as the tip of the iceberg. It has been estimated, for instance, that the AMA spends about $8 million a year on its political activities, well above the $114,859 listed for 1973. Common Cause, the "public-interest lobby," comes out on top of the list in Table 9.2, not because it spends the most but because, since it favors greater control over lobbying, it feels a responsibility to list its spending fully.

But the list does show the types of organizations that are active. Some organizations represent particular parts of the business community: truckers, the home-building industry, the oil and gas industries, insurance companies. Some represent professional groups with particular interests, like the AMA or the National Education Association. Groups of workers are represented by their unions: postal clerks, letter carriers, auto and aerospace workers. And some organizations represent groups of citizens who are interested in particular political principles. Common Cause, for example, is a liberal group that is interested in environmental protection, social-welfare legislation, and government reform. The Citizens for Control of Federal Spending is a more conservative group that is interested in keeping taxes down.

The list shows the wide range of groups that try to influence the government. It also illustrates the main principle that explains why some groups are active while others are not: Groups become politically active when government policy affects them, that is, when they want the government to stop some activity that they feel is harmful or to take some action that they feel is beneficial. Thus it is no wonder that some of the most active groups are the ones that depend on the government because they are direct employees of the government (postal clerks, letter carriers, teachers). Nor is one surprised to find such businesses as truckers, savings and loan associations, or insurance associations on the list, since they are heavily affected by federal and state legislation. Where government activity is important, citizens and groups are likely to be active.

Business Lobbies Probably the main lobbying activity in Washington comes from business organizations that have full-time staffs in Washington to deal with government and public affairs. The major defense contractors and large multinational corporations are quite active.

In addition, there are a large number of trade associations. These include organizations for industries that are dominated by a few large firms, such as the oil industry, as well as organizations like the National Association of Retail Druggists, which represents tens of thousands of drugstores around the country. There are also large "peak" associations that try to organize many different kinds of businesses. The most important are the National Association of Manufacturers (NAM) and the U.S. Chamber of Commerce.

These organizations focus on specific interests. The representatives of the oil industry worry about oil imports or regulation of offshore drilling; the representatives of textile manufacturers are active when it comes to tariffs on foreign textiles. But some of these groups take stands on more general issues. The NAM, for instance, has been active against welfare legislation.

Labor Unions Traditionally, the American labor movement has been less "political" than those in other nations. In the United States unions are not formally affiliated with political parties, as they are in many European countries, and they put most of their energy into collective bargaining with employers for better wages and working conditions rather than into political activity. But unions are major political factors as well. Their economic goals depend on government policies that protect their ability to bargain effectively with management, as well as policies that affect their members directly.

Some unions, such as the United Automobile Workers and the United Steel Workers, have been particularly active in politics. The AFL-CIO has a large staff in Washington that lobbies on matters concerning its members, such as the wages paid on federal projects, as well as things like trade, tariffs, and welfare legislation. A branch of the AFL-CIO—the Committee on Political Education (COPE)—is active in political campaigns.

Professional Associations Most of the major professional groups in the United States—doctors, dentists, lawyers, teachers, scientists, and so forth—have professional organizations that spend a lot of time and effort lobbying for their members. The AMA is perhaps the best known of these because of its long opposition to federal medical-care programs, an issue on which it began to change its views in 1975. In addition, the National Education Association (NEA) lobbies for more spending on education, and the American Association for the Advancement of Science lobbies for more spending on scientific research.

Citizen and Consumer Lobbies It used to be said that interest groups representing producers were better organized than those representing consumers. Oil companies were well organized and were represented by professional lobbyists; drivers and those who heat their houses with oil were less well represented. The milk producers were better represented than the milk consumers. The reason, again, is intensity of concern. For milk producers the price of milk is of great concern; their economic well-being depends on it. The price of milk is important to consumers as well, but milk is only one of many items in a consumer's shopping basket. The average consumer is more likely to be active and concerned as a producer than as a consumer—trying to raise his or her income rather than trying to lower the prices in the supermarket.

The same is true of environmental interests. Many citizens want

Loggers believe that environmentalist groups want to protect scenery at the expense of the loggers' jobs.

to preserve open spaces and forests for recreation, but these consumer interests are rarely as intense as those of producers — the lumber or paper or mining interests that want to use these natural resources for profit. Similarly, all citizens might be affected as "consumers" of polluted air, but their concern is less intense than those of the manufacturing firms whose profits may be reduced if they have to invest in pollution control. In general, the interests of small special-interest publics have been better organized than those of large and widespread publics.

In recent years, though, consumer groups and "citizens' lobbies" have become important. The largest such group is Common Cause. It is active in a variety of areas ranging from consumer protection to reform of campaign financing. In addition, there are groups, such as the Sierra Club and Ralph Nader's The Public Citizen, that have become active on many government policies that used to be the subject of more one-sided lobbying. With their professional attitude and willingness to pursue the battle in Congress and in the courts, these organizations have been quite successful. Consider the following examples: The Alaska pipeline was delayed for four years despite the fact that the oil industry supported it, as did the administration in power. The lobbying of Ralph Nader was crucial in obtaining seat belt legislation for cars against a formerly untouchable automobile industry. The lobbying of Common Cause was instrumental in the passage of campaign reform laws.

Not that these groups act alone or are solely responsible for these laws. They have (and need) allies in Congress and the bureaucracy. But they represent a new and effective lobbying force.

Are these new organizations, representing consumer interests, environmental concerns, and other noneconomic interests, different from other pressure groups in that they work for the public welfare rather than for narrow, selfish interests? Or are they different from other pressure groups only in that they lobby for an alternate set of selfish interests — consumer interests rather than producer interests, scenery-lover interests rather than mining interests? Groups like Common Cause describe themselves as working for the "people's interest" and against the "special interests" that ordinarily dominate politics.

Here, however, is how one American business leader describes environmentalists and consumer groups:

> The political system is out of balance . . . We find our fate increasingly in the hands of a few relatively small but highly vocal, selfish, interest groups . . . These groups . . . pursue their own interests with complete disregard for the impact of their wants on the rest of the economy . . . And while they shout about the environmental impact of almost everything, they have no concern whatever for the economic impact of their corrective legislation.[1]

[1] *Consumer Reports,* January 1975, p. 53.

Consumer advocate Ralph Nader meets with a group of Nader's Raiders who have been studying nursing home abuses.

Citizen groups describe the business lobbies in the same words. Whether citizen groups represent a new type of selfish interest or the broader public interest is unclear. But in either case the citizen's lobbies are a new addition to the system of organized groups in America.

Beneficiary Groups Whenever the government helps one group or another, it creates a number of "beneficiaries." Members of such groups have an interest in seeing that government support and aid are continued and perhaps increased. Many of the organized groups that try to influence the government are of this sort: Farmers lobby for price supports or import controls; veterans lobby for veterans' benefits; welfare recipients press for continued or increased welfare benefits. In this way these groups act like business lobbies. (Indeed, we could have listed the farmers with business groups.)

Special-Interest Groups Many organizations have a particular policy goal: civil liberties, civil rights, opposition to abortion, support for abortion laws, and so forth.

Organizations as Pressure Groups

It is clear that there is much organized activity in America. But how does this activity affect government policy? Does it have any impact? And if so, who benefits from that impact?

Putting pressure on government is of course the best-known role of organized interests; they act as lobbies in Washington, in state capitals, and in local governments. Observers of the activity of lobbyists have sometimes concluded that the government is dominated by lobbies. They describe government policy as if it were the mechanical result of a "parallelogram of forces," the pressures placed on the government by organized groups. In such a situation the public as a whole plays no role. Nor does the government itself.

Environmental groups are a new addition to organized groups.

The role of government is merely to react to group forces or, at most, to act as a broker among them.

Such a description of policy making—in Washington or in state capitals—greatly exaggerates the power of organized groups and plays down the other forces acting on the government. One close study of Washington lobbyists concludes that "there is relatively little influence or power in lobbying per se. There are many forces in addition to lobbying which influence public policy; in most cases these forces clearly outweigh the impact of lobbying."[2] These other forces include public opinion and the feelings of members of Congress about the next election. Above all, one must note the dominant role of the executive branch of the government. Furthermore, as one congressman points out in the study just mentioned, members of Congress have their own opinions. Although they like to hear the views of lobbyists, they are not necessarily moved by them.

Organized interests are not all-powerful. But they are far from weak. Groups vary in degree of effectiveness. Thus it is useful to consider what kind of group is likely to be effective, on what issues, and where.

ORGANIZATION RESOURCES

Organizations are effective when they have the resources to influence the government. What are some of these resources?

Financial Resources Lobbying is expensive. The major lobbies have large, full-time staffs in Washington and in state capitals. They sometimes conduct expensive campaigns to influence Congress or the public. During its campaign against President Johnson's medicare legislation the AMA spent over $1 million in three months. One of the major areas of organizational spending is political campaigns. The milk producers' lobby was severely criticized when the Watergate investigations showed that it had contributed heavily to President Nixon's 1972 campaign in return for an alleged agreement to raise price supports for milk. But this did not stop the milk producers from giving $2,200,000 to 1974 congressional campaigns.

People Organizations with a mass membership that can get their members involved in political activity are also likely to be effective. The number of members is not as important as is their willingness to give time and effort to the organization. An organization with members who pressure government officials can be very effective.

One of the strongest lobbies is the NRA, which has blocked gun

[2] Lester W. Milbrath, *The Washington Lobbyists* (Chicago: Rand McNally, 1963), p. 54.

Some groups are organized around a specific policy goal.

control legislation for many years. It has 1,050,000 members in 12,000 state and local gun clubs across the country. (It also has at least 35 members in Congress.)

A million members is a large number, but not all that large. Public-opinion polls show that about four out of five Americans favor some kind of gun control; this means that the NRA members are outnumbered by over 100 to 1. The effectiveness of the NRA comes from the fact that its members really care about the issue, while the majority that favors gun control is weaker in its concern. The NRA keeps its members informed about gun control activities through its monthly *American Rifleman* as well as separate mailings of legislative bulletins. For example:

> If a state legislative committee, for instance, plans a hearing on a gun control bill, every NRA member in that state will receive a bulletin with the time and place of the hearing, the text of the proposed measure, and the name and home cities of all the legislators on the committee.[3]

As a result the hearings are jammed with NRA members.

Expertise Lobbies have one important resource that ordinary citizens or even members of Congress don't usually have. They have full-time skilled staffs who specialize in the subject in which the lobby is interested. Thus they often have much greater technical knowledge than members of Congress, who have many other problems and issues to consider. The National Education Association has all the relevant information on educational finance and research on new teaching methods. Representatives of the textile industry know the number of yards of goods imported from Hong Kong each month. The National Association of Retail Druggists can tell you the rate of failures among drugstores. These groups have a special voice in policy making because they know what policies they want to influence and what changes are important to them. Furthermore, they often have more information than the government officials

[3] *Wall Street Journal,* May 24, 1972.

The National Rifle Association is a powerful lobby, because it can mobilize its members.

involved. Government officials often depend on these organizations for basic information.

This is one of the reasons that producer interests tend to be better represented than consumer interests. Producer groups—business organizations in one field or another—have full-time professionals whose job is to know about the laws affecting their industry. Consumer groups tend to be "amateurs," working in their spare time and without the knowledge of the professionals. The new "citizens' lobbies" try to get full-time professionals working on the other side.

A good example of this situation is recent activity on environmental issues. Most citizens have some interest in preserving natural beauty or open park lands or clean rivers. But when it comes to decisions on the development of public lands, the groups that can put in a lot of time and energy usually carry the day. And these are usually the business interests who favor a particular use for public lands—mining, private development, cattle grazing. These groups are professionally concerned; they have the ability to use government agencies and the courts for their purposes, and because it is their job to do so, they put in the time and energy needed to be effective. An unorganized public is ineffective against them. What organizations like the Sierra Club do is to put professional skills and energy on the other side by having a full-time legal staff whose job is to fight against private development of public lands.

Access Organizations may develop another resource that can make them particularly effective: access to government officials. All citizens have the right to contact their representative in Congress or write a letter of complaint to a government office. But full-time professional lobbyists can develop close ties with government officials who are particularly relevant for their concerns. Their knowledge helps in this, and they work at it very hard. The job of the lobbyist is made easier by the fact that he or she may have to work with only a small number of government officials. In Congress most business is done in committees. The good lobbyist develops a close relationship with the chairperson and a few key members of the relevant committee, as well as with the government agencies that are active in his or her area.

MOBILIZING THE MEMBERS

Effective pressure groups must be able to depend on their members. For one thing, they must maintain their membership. Not all doctors belong to the AMA; in fact only about half of them do. Similarly, only about half of the lawyers in America belong to the American Bar Association. An organization that tries to speak for a group will want to have a fairly high portion of that group as members. Furthermore, it needs membership dues to carry out its many activities. And if it can get its members to be active—to write to the government, to campaign for the candidates it prefers—it can increase its influence.

Organizations are most effective when they offer many rewards to their members. Some people join a group because of their interest in its policy goals, that is, the policies the organization tries to get the government to support. But, as we saw in Chapter 6, this may not be enough. If the policy goal of a group is a collective good that is available to all whether or not they worked for it, the rational citizen will let others work for it and benefit from a "free ride." A doctor will save the cost of AMA membership dues and still benefit from the lobbying of the AMA on medical matters.

Most successful organizations offer many other things. They offer *selective* benefits that are available only to members. Business and professional organizations offer their members technical publications, insurance programs, and many other services. Doctors join the AMA not because they believe in the policies that the AMA supports (though they may) but because the AMA gives them services (e.g., aid in malpractice suits) and sends them medical publications. Or consider the American Bar Association. The following are among the benefits available to its members.

- lawyer placement service
- retirement income plans
- group life insurance program
- dependents' life insurance program
- group disability insurance program
- in-hospital insurance program
- specialized information on all sections of the law
- legal publications and reports; the *American Bar Association Journal*; the *American Bar News*

Services of this sort are important in keeping members in such organizations. (One of the authors of this book joined the American Association of University Professors so that he could take its reduced-fare flights to Europe.) And members who join for these reasons provide the base for a politically powerful organization.

Public-interest groups are faced with the same need to motivate supporters. Some groups provide selective benefits to members. The members of one of the largest consumer groups, Consumers' Union, receive the monthly *Consumer Reports,* which rates various products for safety, durability, and the like. Sierra Club members have access to publications, wilderness trips, and the like. But other citizens' lobbies offer few selective benefits. As a student of citizens' lobbies phrases the question: "Why do 275,000 persons send $15 to $20 a year to Common Cause, when they receive nothing in return but thank-you letters and an eight-page monthly newsletter? The 100,000 persons who send an average of $11 a year to Nader's Public Citizen, Inc., get a five-page progress report and a pamphlet, but no thank-you letter (to save money)."[4]

[4] Andrew S. McFarland, *Public Interest Lobbies: Decision-Making on Energy* (Washington, D.C.: American Enterprise Institute, 1976), p. 4.

250

The public-interest organizations offer few selective benefits, but they do have wide support. Why do citizens support such groups? The answer is that selective benefits are an important way in which interest groups motivate people to pay dues or to give time and effort to the group. But it is clear that citizens can be motivated because they believe in the policy goals of an organization. There are a number of reasons why the public-interest groups have been able to rally support from a large and widespread public, a public that has been traditionally difficult to organize. For one thing, the number of active and educated citizens has been growing, largely with the spread of higher education. Public-interest movements are more likely to appeal to college-educated citizens. In addition, the public-interest groups have had effective leadership in figures like Ralph Nader (founder of The Public Citizen) and John Gardner (founder of Common Cause). These leaders, who have been able to make a convincing case for their organizations, have appealed for support by arguing in favor of "civic balance." Special interests, they argue, have always been well organized in America. As a result they have usually defeated less well-organized groups attempting to work in the "public interest." Therefore, citizens must organize as well.[5] Apparently this argument is effective with a substantial number of citizens.

ISSUES ON WHICH ORGANIZATIONS ARE EFFECTIVE
The narrower and more technical the issue, the more effective organized groups are likely to be.

The Two Levels of Policy Making The policy-making process — a subject that we will deal with more fully later — goes through many steps. On the one hand there is the making of general policy, which is done in Congress and results in broad policy guidelines. But much of this policy making is symbolic.[6] It sets a general direction for policy, but the actual policy depends on specific features worked out in congressional committees and subcommittees, in the application of the legislation by government officials, or in the interpretation of the legislation in the courts.

The point is that while the broad guidelines of legislation seem to be most important, it is often the specific way in which the law is administered or the courts' interpretation of the law that really counts. The rules set down by Congress are so general that they have little impact until their details have been settled.

In the struggle for major legislation pressure groups are active, to be sure, but they are not at their greatest advantage. In such public activities Congress must keep its eye on the public; in turn, the

---

[5] Ibid., pp. 4–24.
[6] See Murray Edelman, *The Symbolic Uses of Politics* (Urbana: University of Illinois Press, 1964).

mass media are keeping their eye on Congress. But the specific details of a bill—worked out in committee or in some agency of the executive branch—are a better place for pressure groups to work. In such cases they can use their professional knowledge and access to government officials.

Tax Legislation   A good example of the two levels of policy making —the broad statement of principles and the detailed working out of practices—is found in tax legislation. The principle of progressive tax legislation is found in the Sixteenth Amendment. The idea is to tax those who can pay more at higher rates. This could have major effects on income distribution in America. Few argue with the general principle of a progressive tax. And there is no need to argue because the principle is hardly ever applied.

Although attempts have been made to reform income tax laws several times in the past few decades, the results are almost always the same. Congress sets some broad guidelines, and then the House Ways and Means Committee or the Senate Finance Committee (the committees in which tax legislation is worked out) approve a number of exemptions. These range from attempts to help a particular individual (the famous Louis B. Mayer amendment was designed to help the aging movie magnate protect his retirement benefits) to broader exemptions (such as the even more famous 22 percent depletion allowance for oil companies, which gave oil producers a big tax benefit). At the hearings on the major tax bills one will find hundreds of groups making statements on what seem to be very small issues, but they are issues that affect them closely. On each specific issue there is no one to oppose them.

The result, of course, is that though there is never any direct challenge to the principle of a graduated tax that falls most heavily on the wealthy, tax policy does not work out that way. As many observers have noted, the tax law allows for a maximum rate of 70 percent, but few people pay as much as 50 percent.[7] This is not the result of a decision by some government body—say, Congress or the Treasury Department—that a rate of 70 percent is too high. Rather, the principle of steeply graduated taxes holds, but the practice is to allow so many exemptions—for tax-free municipal bonds, depletion allowances, capital gains, real-estate transactions—that the principle never takes effect.

Tariff Legislation and Business Regulation   This pattern of principle and practice in policy making can be found in many fields. Tariff legislation has long been an area in which general tariff bills are watered down by a variety of decisions on specific goods. Another example is business regulation. Congress will enact general legislation to regulate some business practice, such as the quality of food products, the amount of pollutants allowed into waterways,

[7] See William L. Cary, "Pressure Groups and the Revenue Code," *Harvard Law Review*, 68 (1955), 745–780.

FIGURE 9.1
A Specific Interest Group
Confronted with the Opposition
of Many Citizens

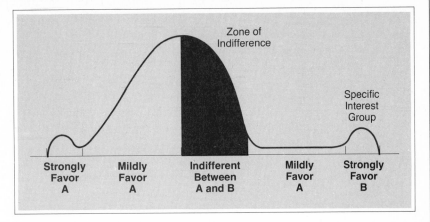

Zone of
Indifference

Specific
Interest
Group

| Strongly Favor A | Mildly Favor A | Indifferent Between A and B | Mildly Favor A | Strongly Favor B |

and the flameproofing of fabrics. The general principle will be clear
—Sell pure food, don't pollute, manufacture only fireproof fabrics.
But the details of the regulation—How pure? Is a little pollution all
right? What about slow-burning fabrics?—are usually worked out
with representatives of the businesses to be regulated. This is not
necessarily a bad thing, since only the businesses involved have the
necessary information on which the detailed regulations have to be
based. But it does give businesses a special voice in setting the terms
of their relationship with the government.

One of the reasons for this may be seen if we return to some of the
patterns of division described earlier in Chapter 6. When it
comes to broad issues in which a group with a specific interest
wants something that many other citizens oppose in principle, the
pattern of division will look something like Figure 9.1. On the
right—strongly favoring position B—would be the specific interest
group, small in number but firm. On the left would be the people
who are generally opposed to the policy that the small interest group
favors, and they will probably include a number of citizens who feel
strongly about the principle. In such a case the specific group that
wants B could win only after a public fight. And it would probably
lose, since most of the citizens could become involved. Members of
Congress might listen to the interest group, but they listen more
closely to election predictions.

If, for instance, representatives of top management in large corporations tried—through the NAM or the U.S. Chamber of Commerce—to have Congress pass a law severely reducing their rate of
taxation and made statements criticizing the principle of a graduated income tax, they would face strong opposition and would
probably lose.

If, on the other hand, the House Ways and Means Committee
approves a stock option plan in which profits from sales of stock
received under such plans can be treated as capital gains if they are

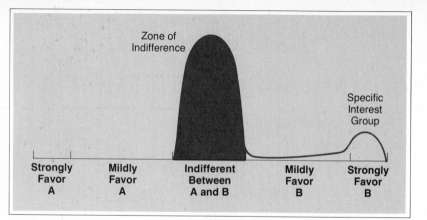

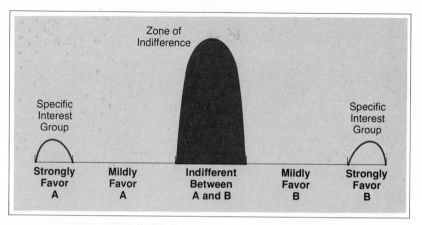

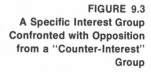

sold at least two years after the grant of the option and six months after the transfer of the stock, the public is unlikely to be aroused. As one observer noted after looking at many examples of tax exemptions won by specific interest groups, "In each instance the character of the relief afforded is so technical as to make a simple explanation impossible. Being obscure or downright incomprehensible to the layman, it is not recognized as an outright favor to one individual or a highly selected group."[8]

When it comes to a technical issue, the pattern of division is likely to be as shown in Figure 9.2. A deeply interested and technically skilled group favors a position. The position looks like a technical issue about which the public has little knowledge or concern. Thus there is no opposition. In such circumstances the specific interest group can be quite effective.

Citizens' lobbies try to convert the situation shown in Figure 9.2 into that shown in Figure 9.3: one lobby opposing another. The knowledge and activity of, say, the timber interests is offset by the professional staff of an organization like the Sierra Club. In the area

[8] Ibid.

of taxes, attorneys working for The Public Citizen or Common Cause watch over the detailed process by which tax loopholes are written into the law and try to lobby against them. The battle is not always equal; there are many more special interests and many more special-interest lawyers than public interests and public-interest lawyers. It is hard to know how many situations in the United States resemble the situation illustrated in Figure 9.3. Despite the rise of the new citizens' lobbies, it is likely that the situation shown in Figure 9.2, where an interest group is not opposed by any other group, is still a dominant pattern.

Where Are Pressure Groups Active?

Our discussion of the kinds of issues on which pressure groups can be most effective also tells us something about where they are most likely to be effective. One way in which they are active is in trying to arouse the public through campaigns in the media or through support of candidates in elections. In this way they try to influence public policy at the most general level—by affecting what the public wants and who is elected to office.

CONGRESSIONAL COMMITTEES

Interest groups are probably much more active and more effective in dealing with specific committees of Congress. Here they can develop close relationships with individual senators or representatives—who often come from districts where that particular interest is well represented—and with committee staff members. They often provide the information needed for the drafting of specific bills.

THE EXECUTIVE BRANCH

Interest groups may develop close ties with the agencies of the executive branch that regulate their affairs: farm interests with the Department of Agriculture, businesses with the Department of Commerce, labor unions with the Department of Labor. In particular, quite close ties may be formed between independent regulatory agencies and the businesses that they are supposed to regulate: between trucking interests and the Interstate Commerce Commission, radio and television interests and the Federal Communications Commission, airlines and the Civil Aeronautics Board.

THE COURT SYSTEM

The real impact of government policy is often felt through the courts' interpretation of laws or of the Constitution. And interest groups have been active in this area as well. Organizations provide the attorneys and professional skills to prepare cases; they often carefully choose the test cases; and they appear in those cases by filing *amicus curiae* ("friend of the court") briefs. Perhaps the most dramatic example is the long series of cases prepared and carried

Men supporting farmer's strike stand near Capitol building in Washington D.C.

through by the National Association for the Advancement of Colored People (NAACP), the school segregation cases being the best known of these. Besides the Supreme Court case of *Brown* v. *Board of Education of Topeka* (see Chapter 15), the NAACP was involved in dozens of cases preceding and following it—in lower courts as well as in the Supreme Court—that round out the Brown decision.

Groups whose interest is in some right that they believe is guaranteed by the Constitution—civil liberties, civil rights, or the separation of church and state—are particularly active in the federal courts. (See Chapter 16.) Thus one finds such groups as the American Civil Liberties Union, the Emergency Civil Liberties Committee, the NAACP, the Congress of Racial Equality (CORE), and the Protestants and Other Americans United for the Separation of Church and State most active in this way.[9]

Economic organizations play a similar role, sponsoring and supporting litigation on matters that are of concern to them. Again we see how particular interests can be most effective. Litigation is a slow, costly, and technically difficult process. We hear of major court decisions, but the real impact of court action often comes through a large number of narrower cases in the lower courts. And it is here that specific interest groups can be effective because they have the necessary interest, skill, and staying power.

Here again is an area in which the citizens' lobbies have tried to put "civic-balance" theory into effect. They have used the courts quite effectively, suing government agencies for failure to enforce regulations or suing to prevent the construction of nuclear plants or dams until environmental-impact studies have been completed. The larger citizen groups have the resources to carry cases through the long, complicated, and expensive process of litigation.

[9] See Clement E. Vose, "Interest Groups, Judicial Review and Local Government," *Western Political Quarterly*, 19 (March 1966), 85–100.

ELECTION CAMPAIGNS

Organized groups are also very active in election campaigns, supporting the candidates they believe will favor them. We have mentioned the large-scale campaign contributions of the milk producers in the 1972 presidential race and in the 1974 congressional races. As the president of the Mid-American Dairymen put it, "I have become increasingly aware that the soft and sincere voice of the dairy farmer is no match for the jingle of hard currency put in the campaign funds of the politician."[10]

Many interest groups have special branches for campaign activity. The AFL-CIO makes campaign contributions through COPE, the AMA through AMPAC (the American Medical Political Action Committee), the milk producers have C-TAPE (the Committee for Thorough Agricultural Political Education). In each case large sums of organizational money are given to favored candidates. The groups listed are but a few of those that make big contributions; among the agricultural interests, besides the milk producers, cattle, rice, cotton, and soybean interests also have political-action groups.

In 1976 private groups gave more than $20 million in campaign contributions to candidates for the House and the Senate. The money came from business groups, labor groups, and other interest groups. The amount given by labor groups on the one hand and business and professional groups on the other balanced out in 1976. Common Cause estimated that union election committees gave $8.2 million while business groups gave $7.1 million.

What are these campaign contributors buying with their money? Are they trying to get special treatment? They probably are. These campaign committees, as one observer put it, "generally distributed the money to promote what they saw as their best interests: making new friends, retaining old friends, perhaps softening up old enemies."[11] Senators and representatives who receive such contributions—they can run as high as $10,000 per candidate—are likely to give the donors special access when they are considering laws that affect those groups. Large contributors expect and can usually get a special hearing when their interests are concerned.

These special-interest campaign committees tend to concentrate their support where it will do the most good: They contribute most heavily to party leaders, to the chairpersons of major committees, to members of such key committees as the Senate Finance Committee or the House Ways and Means Committee.

Interest Groups as Quasi-Governments

There is one last, and important, way in which private-interest groups play a political role in America. This is by taking on directly

[10] Quoted in "Dollar Politics," *Congressional Quarterly*, 2 (1974), 13.
[11] Warren Weaver, Jr., *New York Times*, March 13, 1977.

the functions of government. Government, as we said in the introductory chapter, exists whenever binding decisions are made for a collectivity, that is, decisions that have the force of law and about which citizens have no choice. This definition is useful because it allows us to see where private organizations perform the governmental function of making such binding decisions. Private organizations are often given the power to make such decisions in their area of concern.

CONTROLLING ENTRY INTO A PROFESSION

Many professional and craft groups control entry into the occupations they represent. Medical associations have control over examinations and accreditation, bar associations over the bar examination, craft unions over apprentice programs, educational associations over accreditation. Furthermore, these associations may control access to important facilities such as hospitals, labor exchanges, and the like.

This activity is control in the governmental sense in that it is binding on citizens. One cannot practice law or medicine without accreditation; one cannot get work as a plumber without union membership (and that, in turn, requires completion of an apprenticeship program). In this sense the private associations that control entry into the profession act as governments.

Much of this activity, one can argue, is merely technical. Everyone wants a way to accredit doctors or lawyers, some way to judge them as professionals so that people who need medical care or legal advice can trust them. And who but members of the profession itself can judge?

But control can be used for other purposes as well. It can be used to keep members of a profession in line with the policies favored by the leaders of that profession. The fact that the AMA controls entry into the medical profession and, often, access by doctors to hospitals means that it could control the behavior of doctors. It could, for instance, discourage group and cooperative practices that it did not approve of. Indeed, the AMA has used its power to keep doctors in line behind its policy on national medical care.

Similarly, becoming a lawyer depends on passing a bar examination in each state. The examination, particularly the part that deals with "character," has been used in various states to keep out people with radical outlooks. And craft unions—plumbers, electricians, and the like—have used their control over accreditation to keep out blacks.

Citizens who oppose these controls can of course challenge them in the courts or appeal to Congress or state legislatures for a change. But this does not change the fact that they have the force of law.

CONTROLLING STANDARDS AND MAKING REGULATIONS

In a variety of fields the power to set industry-wide standards is given to a trade association or to some other private group. Again the logic is that such regulations require the skill and knowledge of those who are most involved. Furthermore, those who are most involved and are likely to be most affected are given a bigger voice. But this system also turns over control to those who are supposed to be controlled.

CONTROLLING THE ALLOCATION OF PUBLIC FUNDS

Many public programs are carried out by private groups that allocate government funds. Of course the government sets broad guidelines, but the control is essentially in the hands of the private group; moreover, the guidelines are often so vague that the private group is fairly free to do as it sees fit.

There are many examples from all fields of government activity. Urban-renewal funds are often controlled by private developers; funds for hospitals and other welfare activities are often controlled by private charitable groups; and funds for much of the antipoverty program were controlled by local groups.

This setup results in the participation of many more citizens who are familiar with local conditions. But it also gives private groups—which are not as accountable to the public as government officials and may not really represent the people they are supposed to represent—day-to-day power over government resources.

For Whom Do Interest Groups Speak?

Formally organized interest groups are most effective in pursuing specific interests. But it is not completely clear whose interests these are.

DOES THE INTEREST GROUP SYSTEM SERVE THE RICH?

One of the criticisms of the interest group system in the United States is that it serves the more affluent segments of society more than it serves the poorer people. Citizens have an equal right to form groups and organizations, but social and economic inequalities may prevent all citizens from benefiting equally from this right. As we have seen, wealthy and better-educated citizens are much more likely to belong to organizations. Citizens who are economically disadvantaged—slum dwellers, migrant workers, the unemployed— are likely to fall outside of the organizational system. A recent study found that 43 percent of the employed workers were members of some organization while only 25 percent of unemployed workers were organization members.[12] The conclusion is clear. Many of the people who need government assistance the most do not have organizations to speak for them.

The situation is made more extreme by the fact that business and professional organizations have been successful in speaking for

[12] Kay Lehman Schlozman and Sidney Verba, *Insult to Injury: Unemployment, Class, and Political Response*, forthcoming.

Many citizens—often economically disadvantaged ones—fall outside the interest group system.

their clienteles. The fact that labor unions and citizens' lobbies are also potent reduces somewhat this bias in favor of the more affluent groups in America. But even here an upper-status bias appears. Labor unions tend to speak most effectively for the better-paid and more secure workers. Unionization is most complete in industries that employ highly paid, skilled workers. Unskilled workers, workers in jobs with little security, and migrant workers are less likely to be members of labor unions. Nor do most of the citizens' lobbies recruit members from the more disadvantaged groups in America. A study conducted by the Massachusetts branch of Common Cause in 1974 found that the average family income of its members was $20,000. The typical Common Cause member had advanced education beyond a college degree. Such groups may speak for a wide constituency (or believe that they do), but their membership is hardly a cross-section of the American public.

Lastly, though the fact that traditionally well-organized business interests are opposed by citizens' groups in many instances gives more "balance" to the expression of interests, the opposing sides are often very different in terms of the resources they can muster. When a crucial business interest is at stake, business lobbies can often far outspend their opponents. In 1976, for instance, a Massachusetts environmental-protection group gathered enough signatures to place on the ballot a referendum to ban nonreturnable bottles and cans. If it had passed, it would have required that all soft drinks and beer be sold in containers for which a deposit would be paid. This, the environmentalists believed, would reduce littering and save resources, since the containers could be recycled.

The group was organized well enough to get the signatures needed to get a referendum item on the ballot. It spent $32,000 during the campaign. It was opposed by a lobby of container manufacturers and bottlers organized as the Committee to Protect Jobs and the Use of Convenience Containers. The business lobby spent $2.25 million dollars; 70 times as much as the environmental group. The referendum came within 12,000 votes of succeeding, but the overwhelming advertising campaign mounted against it by the business lobby led to its defeat.

INTEREST GROUPS AND THEIR MEMBERSHIP

When an interest group takes a position, it is said to be that of the members of the group—the AMA claims to speak for doctors and the NEA for teachers. Do they in fact do so? We often do not know. Early in this century the Swiss sociologist Roberto Michels wrote of the "iron law of oligarchy," by which he meant the tendency for organizations to be run by a small group of leaders who are unresponsive to the demands of the members. This may not be an "iron" law, but the tendency is often seen.

Most organizations are run by a small number of members who give time and effort to organizational activities. These members, furthermore, tend to become a special group—professional leaders. Trade union officials are professional officials, not workers who just happen to become leaders. AMA executives are professional officials, not practicing physicians. Indeed, the AMA is a classic case of an organization that is closely controlled by a leadership group.

Until recently opponents of the AMA claimed that it did not speak for the medical profession; the AMA claimed that it did. In fact it is unclear for whom the AMA spoke, since the profession as a whole was not active in Washington. And this is true of most associations. The members meet rarely, if ever, and control over the activities of the association is in the hands of a few elected officers — a board of directors — and, above all, a professional staff.

The fact that organizations are generally controlled by a small group leads one to question whether they represent the interests of their members. On the other hand, central control enables organizations to plan campaigns with a specific purpose, so that when they *do* speak for their members they can speak more effectively.

Furthermore, central control of an organization often develops because the members are not interested enough. When some group wants to challenge the leaders, it can often have quite an impact. In recent years, for instance, the conservative leaders of the AMA have been challenged by younger, more liberal doctors. The latter have not taken over the organization, but they have had an impact.

How Powerful Are Interest Groups?

Some observers of American politics, as we have pointed out, claim that public policy is simply a reflection of what organized interests want. They talk of a "hidden government," meaning that interest groups dominate all decisions. A close look at the way government policies are made will show that this is an exaggeration. Interest groups are not all-powerful. But they are not weak, either.

Interest groups are most powerful when they operate quietly on issues that do not arouse public concern. But when it comes to major clashes over public policy, they become only one voice among many. Lobbies may support candidates, but members of Congress do not respond only to particular interests. And the media often arouse the public and Congress when interest groups get too much power.

Consider the AMA and Medicare. If the AMA were all-powerful, we would not have a Medicare program because the AMA was firmly opposed to it. We do have such a program. Yet the AMA was successful in delaying Medicare. The United States was many years behind comparable societies in setting up a national health system, and the AMA also played a major role in shaping the program.

Interest groups cannot act alone. They need support and cooperation from within the government. The groups that are most effective often form close relationships with the parts of the government that are most relevant to their own goals — usually a congressional committee that is active in relation to their interests and a bureaucratic agency working on the same problem. Sometimes a tight triple alliance is formed among the interest group, the relevant congressional committee, and the government agency. When this happens the interest group will have an important say over policy, but only because it has the close cooperation of the government. (We'll discuss this further in Chapter 14.)

In recent years there is some evidence for a decline in the easy dominance that special interests have had over the government. For one thing, as we will see in Chapter 14, the federal bureaucracy has grown not only in size but also in the extent to which it takes the initiative in making policy. Many of the tasks that were once performed by interest groups outside of the government—watching over particular areas of policy, keeping an eye on the interests of particular segments of the population—have been taken over by government agencies. These agencies become "interest groups" within the government.

Furthermore, the rise of citizens' lobbies dedicated to "civic balance" means that special interests are more often opposed by organized groups on the other side. However, we ought not to assume that in these cases selfish interests are opposed by citizen groups speaking for the whole public. The citizen groups do not lobby for their own narrow economic interests, it is true. And in this sense they bring into the public clash of interest groups a new and broader view. On the other hand, it is not always clear which side represents the broad public interest. Citizens' lobbies have been effective in delaying, if not blocking, the construction of nuclear power plants. In so doing they speak for what they consider to be the public's interest in nuclear safety and in environmental protection. But those who favor such plants speak for what they consider to be the public's interest in increased energy resources. There is no clear answer as to which is in "the public interest." But it is probably true that the public is better served when competing interests are expressed. In this sense the competing lobbies do create a more balanced interest group system.

controversy

The extent to which interest groups contribute to the public good is problematic—meaning that the issue is unsettled.

One Side Interest group politics communicate specific citizen interests to the government. Without such groups, policy makers would not have the information they need to be responsive to them. Such activity, particularly when it works at the level of interpretation or application of policy, allows government policy to be "fine tuned" to specific circumstances. In a society as complex as ours this is needed if government policy is to take account of the great variety of citizen needs.

Pressure groups do not discriminate against any particular group of citizens. It is true that all are not equally organized or equally active, but all have the right to organize and to petition the government. The fact that a group is organized and active indicates that it has interests about which it is serious. If other groups do not organize to pressure the government, it means that they do not really care enough.

The close ties between government and interest groups are a way of applying the skills and energy of professionals to the formulation of government policy. In this sense the quality of policy improves.

Further, when citizens voluntarily work with the government in formulating regulatory policies, it follows that they will voluntarily comply with those policies. This is all to the good — the less force used, the better off everyone is.

Finally, the policy that results from the clash of specific interests does not hurt the common good — for the common good is the sum of the interests of specific groups.

In short, interest group politics produces the best overall government policy. It represents the views of specific groups and best serves the needs of the country as a whole.

The Other Side Interest group politics does not always represent the most important interests of citizens. Many groups with serious needs are unorganized. It is not necessarily lack of interest that keeps particular parts of the society inactive; they may lack the resources to organize. As a result the interests that are represented are those of upper-status groups, particularly those of the well-organized business community. And the interests of other groups are represented to varying degrees; unionized workers do better than nonunionized ones, though the latter may need government protection more. The result is a conservative tendency in government policy; policy tends to aid the privileged. This situation is made worse when power is given to those whom the government should be regulating, making the regulation less effective.

Interest group politics may be voluntary, but progress and social change may require force — at least they may require that citizens be forced to accept changes that they do not want. A major change in American society — a change that many feel is needed — requires stronger action by the government. And it is in this area that interest group politics is weakest; no one is concerned with the broader public interest, which is not simply the sum of the interests of specific groups. To solve the serious problems facing American society the government will have to listen to other voices besides those of narrow, selfish interests.

Which side is right? This question is fundamental to the way politics works in America. And whether one believes that interest group politics benefits the general public or not, it is a current fact of American political life.

HOW WE FIND OUT ABOUT POLITICS: III
policies and leaders

An earlier discussion of how to study politics focused on the sample survey, which uses interviews and questionnaires. Although the sample survey is a very useful tool for studying the opinions and behavior of the American public, it is not much help in answering many important questions about politics.

In studying public policy—both the institutions in which policy is made and the people who make it—many political scientists do what can be called *documentary research.* This includes a variety of research activities in which the records that the government keeps about itself and the records that others outside the government publish about government activities and personnel are used to answer questions about politics.

Those who make important decisions in our technological society, whether in the public or the private sector, need a lot of data if their decisions are to be rational. Therefore much information is gathered and stored in our society. Thus the political scientist doing documentary research can work with a great variety of records about the government and its activities, some of it gathered by the government itself, the rest by nongovernmental agencies that are concerned about various government activities.

The government describes its personnel, activities, and policies in hundreds of documents and reports. In addition, it describes the personnel, activities, and policies of other areas of American life. You can learn from government documents the number of scientists being trained in various universities, the number of private airplanes sold every year, the number of American businessmen living in Mexico, and the number of beds in private nursing homes. Very few activities in society, whether public or "private," escape the scrutiny of some government agency.

Furthermore, because the government is involved in such a wide range of activities, many nongovernmental agencies keep records about the government. The AFL-CIO, for instance, publishes the voting records of members of Congress on all questions of importance to the labor unions. The American Association for the Advancement of Science, a private, nonprofit professional association, reports the budget and policies of the National Science Foundation in its journal.

Thus there is a large "documentation deposit" that describes in detail the agencies and institutions that make public policy. Although this documentation is extensive, it should be used carefully. There are several things that a political scientist who uses these documents should keep in mind.

1. *The Institutional Bias:* Many government records are products of self-reporting. The records of campaign contributions are kept by the political parties that collect the contributions. Crime statistics are made available by the FBI and local police. An evaluation of the welfare reform program is published by the Department of Health, Education and Welfare, under whose direction the program was begun.

Self-reports are often biased. They exaggerate facts that work to the credit of the reporting agency and underplay facts that would discredit it. For instance, a corporate executive contributes $25,000 to a political party but does so by sending 25 checks of $1,000 each to 25 different committees and candidates. If the party wants to stress that it depends on many small contributions instead of a few large ones, it reports this as 25 separate contributions. A city police department that feels itself short-handed and wants a budget increase might report crime statistics in such a way as to show an increase in crime. Perhaps it calls every loss of property "suspected theft." Another police department that has just had a large budget increase and wants to justify it will want to report statistics showing a decrease in crime. It might report only cases in which theft clearly took place.

This institutional bias of government agencies is easily understood. To stay in business an agency must show that it is doing what it is expected to do and that it could do even better if its budget were increased. But while it is understandable from a political point of view, the institutional bias poses a problem for the researcher working with public documents. A careful researcher will try to recognize possible bias.

2. *Durability:* Some records are more durable than others; some last while others are lost or destroyed. The researcher who depends on documents for data may discover that the records he or she needs were destroyed in a fire or were never even kept in the first place. Suppose you wanted to compare turnout in city elections with turnout in national elections for the past 100 years. You would have no trouble finding the data for national elections, but for some communities you might be able to find records of turnout in local elections only for the past 10 or 20 years. Or say you wanted to study colonial regimes in East Africa. It is easy to get records on how England, for instance, administered its colonies in East Africa between 1920 and 1960. It is almost impossible to get records on the many African movements that opposed the colonial government. The records kept by opposition movements of their own activities (their members, their resources, their plans) disappeared as the movements themselves were put down. And the records kept by the colonial government on those movements were destroyed by the colonial officials just before the African nations gained independence.

3. *Secrecy:* In a democracy the business of government is supposed to be public. And compared with many nations the amount of information the U.S. government makes public about itself is considerable. Yet even in the United States much government business is conducted secretly. This is obviously true — for understandable reasons — in matters involving national security. Governmental secrecy, however, goes far beyond military and security agencies. Nearly everything that goes on inside the White House has traditionally been made public only at the discretion of the President or his staff (except in the dramatic case of the Watergate investigations). Although floor debate in Congress is public, congressional committees and subcommittees sometimes meet in private for the important sessions that finish the drafting of legislation, though the recent passage of "sunshine laws" requiring open meetings has reduced privacy in Congress. Supreme Court decisions are of course announced publicly, but the meetings of the justices take place in private. Anyone can read the budget proposed by the OMB, but few can go to the meetings at which the arguments for and against particular programs are considered.

In short, it is much easier to get information on the finished product of a legislative, executive, or judicial agency than to get information on the political process leading to that product. And thus the study of public documents is always to some extent the study of what the government chooses to let the outsider know.

Thus although we can learn a lot about the institutions and people of government and about the policies they make through careful study of government documents and similar materials, we must be aware that there are limits to what we can expect to learn from the public record. To give you an idea of the types of studies that can be carried out using these kinds of materials, we list a few examples of such research in the following paragraphs.

1. *Political Representation* It is possible to combine several kinds of data to give an overall picture of political representation. Census data can provide a profile of the citizens in a congressional district showing whether they are generally poor or wealthy, Catholic or Protestant, rural or urban. Using such profiles we could make some guesses about how the elected representative might vote on various public policies. We might guess, for example, that members from rural districts would favor farm subsidies while members from urban districts would favor rapid-transit subsidies. And of course, because there are records of the actual votes, we would be able to check our hunches. We could enlarge our study by including data—again from the public record—on whether a given district has strong party competition or is generally safe for one or the other of the political parties. On the basis of these data on the social makeup of the population, on how the elected representatives vote on legislation, and on the strength of the political parties, we could put together a picture of the representation process.

2. *The Legislative Process* Congress is a thoroughly documented institution. A particularly useful source of information about Congress is the weekly *Congressional Quarterly*. It reports the roll call votes of all members of Congress. It also gives a variety of information about major bills: their subject matter, their sponsors, the content of committee hearings, the action on the floor of Congress, and the results of any Senate–House conferences. It describes who heads various committees, what lobbyists are active on which bills, and how any given legislation fits into the President's program.

This kind of material is valuable for studying a great variety of questions about the legislative process. Is a committee headed by a southern Democrat likely to handle a civil-rights bill differently than a committee headed by a northern Democrat? Which pressure groups are most likely to get legislation favorable to their point of view? Are cohesive subcommittees more successful in getting their bills passed than divided subcommittees?

Political scientists have used documentary data on Congress to study all of these issues. Out of these investigations has come a very detailed understanding of the legislative process. Similar studies have been carried out in state legislatures and even in city councils, though the public record on legislative actions at the state and local levels is not as complete as it is for Congress.

3. *The "Power Elite"* For those who want to know about the people who lead our society, a great deal of descriptive material about the social and educational backgrounds and the careers of people who reach the top offices is available. Such biographical information may be found in a variety of publications, such as the *Congressional Directory*, the State Department

Biographical Register, Who's Who in America, or various biographical directories of special groups such as blacks, lawyers, or corporate directors.

Using such information we could answer several kinds of questions. We could try to figure out how much overlap there is between the various power groups in American society. For example, do the same people who serve on the boards of trustees of large universities also hold major corporate directorships? And are these the same people who move in and out of government, serving from time to time as advisers to important political leaders? Or we could use such information to find out the social backgrounds of leaders. We might want to know, for example, whether a large percentage of the members of Congress graduated from Ivy League colleges, or whether there are more top diplomats who are black or female than there used to be, or whether the percentage of lawyers in the Senate has changed since the nineteenth century.

4. *Priorities in Public Policy* Government budgets and reports give detailed data about public policy. This kind of information is important, since budgetary data show the priorities assigned to different programs. We know, for instance, that for some time military and security affairs have claimed more than two out of every five dollars spent by the federal government, leaving all other federal programs to be funded out of the remaining 60 percent. We could also use this kind of data to compare priorities across government units. For example, to see whether some states stress elementary education more than others we could compare the per-pupil spending of different states and the percentage of the state tax dollar spent on elementary education.

5. *Correlates of Government Expenditures* We could also use data from the public record to find out what kinds of political or social factors correlate with different priorities. For example, in the area of elementary education we could try to explain why some cities in Illinois spend more on elementary education than others. Perhaps cities in which businesses pay a large share of the property taxes tend to spend more; perhaps communities in which the citizens are relatively wealthy or well educated tend to spend more. We could find the data we need to test these hunches in the public record.

We might also look at some political factors to see, for example, whether state spending on elementary education is correlated with voter turnout, party competition, or turnover of elected officials. These data, too, are part of the public record.

Conclusions These notes touch on only a few of the ways in which political scientists have used the "documentation deposit" to find out about politics and government in the United States. But they show how much information is available and the importance of this information to systematic study. The sample survey is a powerful research tool but is far too costly to be used every time a researcher wants to learn something about government or public policy. Indeed, we use the sample survey primarily for studies of the entire population of the country because it is the only way we can get data on public opinion or general political participation. But when we turn our attention away from the population at large and concentrate on specific groups or political institutions, the data best suited to research are often found in documents, records, budgets, and the like.

10
POLITICAL PARTIES

Organizing the Weak Against the Strong

Most people, when they think about democratic politics in the United States, think first of our two major parties: the Democratic party and the Republican party. Each of our major parties brings together the energies of a large number of citizens who as individuals have very little power but as participants in a mass political organization have much more influence over political life. It is frequently said that parties organize "the weak against the strong." The citizen acting alone cannot easily challenge established arrangements and policies, nor can the individual citizen force one set of leaders out of office and install new ones. It takes organization if the "weak" are to challenge the "strong." Political parties are supposed to provide this organization. It is interesting that the Constitution makes no mention of political parties, nor did the writers of that document anticipate them. With hindsight we can see how significant this omission was. Political parties emerged fairly quickly after the founding of the Republic. They became and have remained crucial institutions in American democracy. It would indeed be difficult to imagine democratic politics in the United States — or in any democracy — without political parties. Democracy implies popular control over the government. In representative democracies such as the United States this takes place through elections. Political parties should play a major role in this process of citizen control through elections. They "organize" the public by providing the citizenry with choices at election time. And they "organize" the government by taking control over the legislative and executive branches when their candidates are elected. In this way the preferences of the citizens, expressed in elections, are converted into control over the government.

In this chapter and the following one on elections we attempt to learn how well the American party system provides an organized way for citizens to control their government. There is reason to be skeptical. In this chapter we will learn American political parties are fragmented organizations. In the next chapter we will see that increasing numbers of Americans are refusing to align themselves with either of the two major parties.

An American Invention: Mass Political Parties

Political parties began as groups or factions of like-minded legislators. These factions appeared in the U.S. Congress in the decade after the writing of the Constitution as members of Congress organized either to support or to oppose Alexander Hamilton's economic policies. The Federalists (as the supporters of Hamilton called themselves) and the Republicans (as the opposition, led by Jefferson and Madison, called themselves) soon became cohesive groups. Legislative factions such as the Federalists and Republicans had existed previously in England, where Parliament was organized into the Whigs and the Tories. But the legislative factions in the new United States soon took on broader activities outside of Congress. They became organizations for gaining the support of voters. In the first few decades of American history the parties became institutions with mass followings organized to contest elections. Such institutions had not existed previously. Thus the political party as we know it today was invented in the United States. It represents a major political innovation.

The Constitution did not mention political parties. But the formation of the parties nevertheless depended heavily on the Constitution. In the first place, the freedoms of speech and assembly guaranteed in the First Amendment made it possible for parties to organize. Secondly, the requirement of elections made it necessary that leaders of factions in Congress develop some organizational means of gaining voter support. Though the founders did not anticipate political parties, the Constitution they wrote may have made the invention of parties inevitable.

Party Systems in American History

The way the Democratic and Republican parties are currently structured and their bases of support have evolved during the past 190 years. Political scientists have analyzed these changes in terms of five historical eras. Each is characterized by changes in the structure of and support for the parties.

The Founding Period The first party system is generally dated from the beginning of the Republic until around 1824. There were two parties during this era: the Federalist party and the Democratic-Republican party. However, these were not mass-based parties. Because of the legal restrictions on who could vote (landowning white males over the age of 21) and because of the small role that popular elections were given in the system, the parties were elite organizations, formed to organize political support among leaders within the government. Only secondarily, and in a minor way, were the parties useful in elections.

The Federalist party drew most of its support from the North, particularly the commercial and mercantile class along the northern coast. It stood for a strong central government and for a strong Presidency. The Democratic-Republican party's supporters were farmers and small-town dwellers who opposed a strong federal government. After 1800, when the first Democratic-Republican became President, the Federalist party went into a decline, as might be expected of a party based on support from a city-dwelling commercial class in a society that still consisted almost entirely of farmers.

Jacksonian Democracy Beginning in the mid-1820s, and very much aided by the election of Andrew Jackson to the Presidency in 1828, political parties began to take on a character that is familiar today. They ceased to be small, elite groups, differing perhaps on important issues but generally agreed on the importance of a government conducted in a dignified manner by gentlemen. Political parties became mass-based electoral organizations. Voting rights were extended, primarily by the elimination of property qualifications. Voter participation increased dramatically. Presidential candidates were nominated by party conventions rather than by congressional caucuses.

Jackson was the first presidential candidate to be nominated by a party convention. He helped popularize mass political activity in the United States. The interests that he represented were in large part those of the Jeffersonians, whose followers eventually became known as the Democratic party. In reaction to Jackson a new party was formed, the Whig party, composed of manufacturing interests and New Englanders who were hostile to slavery.

Strong feelings on the slavery question, which set northern business interests against southern plantation interests, eventually destroyed the party system of the 1830s and 1840s. The forces of free labor versus those of slave labor generated a conflict that could not be managed by the political parties. The result was a new party alignment as well as a civil war.

The Civil War and Its Aftermath The third party system extends from the mid-1850s nearly to the beginning of the twentieth century. The parties that we know today as the Republicans and Democrats can be traced back to this period. The Republican party was the party of the North. It was opposed to slavery and represented the interests of a commercial class based on free labor. In 1860 the election of Abraham Lincoln as a Republican President led to the Civil War. The Democratic party was based primarily in the South, though it attempted to draw support from every region. The northern victory made it difficult for the Democrats to win national elections, and the post-Civil War period was one of Republican dominance.

During this period the Republicans established themselves as the party representing business interests. They favored policies that encouraged the massive industrialization of America — building railroads and canals, protecting monopolies, hindering the growth of labor unions, promoting economic development through private ownership.

Initially the Democratic party favored the same business interests. But by the 1890s the Democrats began to abandon their support of big business and to turn instead to a coalition of southern and western agrarian interests. William Jennings Bryan was their presidential candidate, but his firey antibusiness sermons never won him electoral success.

Political Reforms and the Progressives The fourth party system extends from the mid-1890s to the early 1930s. In response to pressure from a reform-minded minor party, the Progressives, several major changes in party politics took place. The reforms were intended to eliminate political corruption, but they actually weakened political parties as mass-based organizations. The reformers were bothered by the purchase of votes and the use of political patronage (control over jobs), especially in city politics. To protect politics from the "wrong sort," they introduced such reforms as voter registration and nonpartisan ballots. What they accomplished was to make it harder for voters to participate and parties to organize.

The target of most of the political reforms was the growing number of industrial workers living in the cities, many of whom were recent immigrants. Some interpretations of this period in American history stress that the industrial elite feared the radicalism of these urban voters. The elite weakened the parties so as to reduce the chances that popular majorities would be mobilized against the interests of the business and commercial class.

It is certainly true that during this period the Republican party firmly established itself as the party that favored business interests. The Democrats continued to oppose industrialization, but they also remained true to their rural constituency by opposing urbanization. Neither of the parties paid much attention to the great bulk of immigrant urban dwellers. Their numbers swelled the potential voting population, but compared to other groups they did not vote in significant numbers. When the Democrats tapped this block of voters in the early 1930s, the fifth party system came into being.

Today's Party System The fifth party system began in the 1930s, and it is more or less the party system that exists today. In the late 1920s the basis of support for the Democratic party began to shift from agrarian interests to urban industrial workers. Then, with the Great Depression of 1929, these workers began to vote, and to vote for the Democrats. The Democratic party continued to get support from the "Solid South," but now it also drew heavily upon voters in the northern industrial states. The party began to take positive positions on social welfare, government intervention, and civil rights. The Republicans remained the party of business, but it also began to draw more support from the farm regions of the Midwest.

Since this party system began over forty years ago, some changes have come about. These have caused political scientists to ask whether this system has ended and a new one has emerged. For example, the South is no longer solidly Democratic; neither party has dominated the White House in the past twenty years; and the issue positions of the parties have shifted. We will discuss these changes more fully in the next chapter.

Party History and Social Cleavages

Our review of party history points up two important facts about American political parties. First, political parties represent different clusters of interests and different kinds of social and occupational groups. More evidence is provided on this topic later in the chapter.

Second, our historical review tells us something important about what has *not* happened in American politics. Political-party systems, especially in European nations, often reflect sharp social cleavages. In societies where there are deep divisions along religious lines, say between Protestants and Catholics, parties based on religion are likely to emerge. Similarly, parties can reflect cleavages between rural and urban interests, among regions, or among ethnic and linguistic groups. In many societies parties emerged to reflect a basic cleavage between workers and management. This happened in most European countries when industrial workers organized into socialist parties to challenge the political and economic positions of the owner and managerial classes.

The parties that emerged early in the history of the United States did not reflect sharp social cleavages. American society was relatively homogeneous. It was not deeply divided on the basis of religion or language. In addition, America had no feudal history; in the early days of the Republic most Americans were farmers who owned their own land. There did not exist in the United States, as there did in many European nations, a landowning aristocratic class against which a landless peasant class or a rising business class had to struggle. As many foreign observers noted, the most distinctive aspect of American life was its relative equality. The political parties reflected these characteristics of American society. They did not represent closed, antagonistic social groups.

Note that American society was relatively homogeneous and equal only if one ignores the black slave population in the South. Indeed, that is what the American political process did at the time. What might have been a major political cleavage—a cleavage between the races—was suppressed by the fact that blacks were barred from political life.

Political parties were established early in the nineteenth century; so was universal suffrage (at least for white males). The fact that parties and universal suffrage came early in the history of the Republic had a major impact on the nature of American parties. The parties began while the United States was a relatively homogeneous agrarian society. During the nineteenth century it became a more heterogeneous industrial society. New immigrants entered the country; an urban working class was formed. In many European nations, a large urban working class became a political force *before* workers gained the right to vote and *before* the organization of worker political parties was fully legal. As a result workers organized *outside of* and *in opposition to* the existing party system. When they were given the vote they entered politics as a cohesive block—usually as supporters of a working-class socialist party. In the United States, rather than forming a separate, antagonistic party, the American working class—together with immigrant groups (often the same people)—was eventually incorporated into the existing system.

Third Parties

The composition of the Democratic and Republican parties has been and continues to be affected by *third parties.* Third (or minor) parties are political organizations that are similar to that of the two major parties in structure and purpose. They usually attempt to win elections for their own candidates at the local and state levels and sometimes have enough support to challenge the major parties in presidential elections. The most recent example of a third-party challenge was George Wallace's 1968 campaign as the candidate of the American Independent party. At the state level, the Liberal and Conservative parties in New York and the Farm-Labor party in Minnesota are examples of minor parties.

Third Parties and Social Change   As a result of changes in society—changes in the economy, shifts in the population—new problems come about that the various social groups in society want to have solved to their satisfaction. Some of these social groups are new, developing as a result of these changes, and some existed before the changes. One possible result of these developments is the creation of a third party. The goal of these parties is to bring new issues and new ways of looking at old issues to the political agenda by electing people to state and national governments.

The two most successful parties of this kind were the Populist Party in the 1880s and 1890s and the Progressive party at the beginning of the twentieth century. The Populist party, for example, was founded by farmer groups in the Midwest and West who were upset by the corporate monopolies and trusts that developed at the end of the nineteenth century. It also agitated (like the Progressive

Third Parties, such as La Raza Unida, are important sources of political and social change in American society.

party) for direct election of senators, the primary system instead of the convention method of nominating candidates, women's suffrage, and similar political reforms. Over time these reforms became law.

Splinter Parties　A second type of minor party breaks away from one of the major parties when compromise fails to hold together the many factions that make up any large party. Theodore Roosevelt's Bull Moose party of 1912 was a breakaway party resulting from a split in the national leadership of the Republican party. More recent examples are the largely regional parties of the South, often led by "states' righters" within the Democratic party. In 1948 Strom Thurmond (now a Republican senator from South Carolina, having switched parties) led the Dixiecrats, a group of southern Democrats who were dismayed at the nomination of Harry Truman. George Wallace's American Independent party split off from the liberal northern wing of the Democratic party that nominated Hubert Humphrey to run against Richard Nixon.

Third-party presidential candidates have little chance of being elected. But they can have an impact on the outcome of an election. A third party with a strong regional base can win electoral votes by gaining the largest share of the vote in certain states. Thurmond did this in 1948 and Wallace in 1968. If they had received enough electoral votes to deny a majority of the electoral college to either of the major candidates, the election would have had to be decided by the House of Representatives, and the third-party candidate could have wielded considerable power in deciding whom to support. In fact, however, third parties have never succeeded in doing this. No election has gone to the House since 1824.

Eventually most third parties have become absorbed by the major parties. As a result each of the kinds of third parties that we have mentioned affects the composition of the Democratic or Republican parties. Sometimes, as the minor parties succeed in forcing new policies on the established parties, they tend to disappear as the established parties "steal their thunder." Norman Thomas, the

The Prohibition Party has campaigned against the selling of liquor for one-half of a century, but it is less a political party than an interest group.

perennial Socialist presidential candidate, said that he quit running for office because the New Deal adopted most of the Socialist party's program. At other times the breakaway third parties serve as a conduit or way station for groups that are transfering their support from one of the major parties to the other. As a result of this switching, the composition of each of the parties changes.

Third Parties in 1976 Despite their inability to achieve major electoral success, third parties remain popular in American politics. In the 1976 election, for instance, thirty-seven different parties, including the Democrats and Republicans, nominated political candidates for Congress, governorships, or the Presidency. (They are listed in Table 10.1.) Third-party activity ranged all the way from the Communist party to the White Power party. It is evident that many political interests and impulses are not being serviced by the two

**TABLE 10.1
Names of Third Parties
Contesting Offices in
the 1976 Election**

American	Liberal
American Constitution	Libertarian
American Independent	Labor Party
Conservative	La Raza Unida
Concerned Citizens	Liberty Union
Co-Equal Citizens	Mayflower Party
Communist	Nonpartisan
Constitutional	National Democratic Party of Alabama
Democratic	Owl Party
Democratic Socialist	Prohibition
Free Libertarian	Peace and Freedom
George Wallace Party	People's Party
Human Rights	Republican
Independent American	Revolutionary Workers
Independent Conservative	Socialist Labor
Independents for Godly Government	Socialist Workers
Independent	United States Labor Party
Independent Party	Workers
	White Power Party

major parties. But the very small number of votes earned by any of these third parties indicates how hard it is to compete against the dominant parties.

Some third parties are really interest groups in disguise. They do not expect to gain political office, but they use the election process as a way to publicize their views. The Prohibition party, for instance, continues to campaign against the selling of liquor. By running candidates in local or national elections it gets press coverage and citizen attention.

Political Parties Within the Government

American history as well as the structure of American government influence the role political parties play within the government. In fact *as parties* they play very little role. Political parties do not formulate a coherent program that members who happen to hold elective office then legislate and administer into public policies. A Republican member of Congress, for instance, does not take orders, or even advice, from something called the Republican party. A Democratic President does not worry much about checking his ideas with the leaders of the Democratic party. In short, political parties do not operate as meaningful organizations within the government; they are not found formulating policy alternatives, seeing that appropriate legislation is passed, disciplining members of Congress who fail to vote the party line. The lack of disciplined, programatic parties in American government is explained by the facts that we have already reviewed. First, there are too many viewpoints within each party; this is a result of how the parties originated and developed. Second, the parties are too decentralized and fragmented; this a result of government structures as well as party development.

A VARIETY OF VIEWPOINTS

Each of the major parties is a collection of different and often disagreeing groups rather than a single-minded organization. To begin with, there are a variety of political viewpoints within each party. As we have already discussed this is largely a result of historical development. For a number of years the Democrats were divided between a northern liberal wing and a southern conservative one. In recent years the conservative South has become less conservative and has loosened its ties with the Democratic party. But the Democrats remain a party with many different viewpoints. One important split is between a more liberal wing supported by blacks and liberal intellectuals and a more conservative wing supported by unions and white factory workers.

The Republican party has also been shaped by history. Partly because it was the party of the North immediately after the Civil War, it became the party of the commercial and industrial class in the Northeast. But the Republican party also won the support of Main Street America and the frontier West, and thus today the Repub-

Roosevelt built a strong Democratic Party with the support of the working class and trade unions.

licans have a liberal northeastern wing as well as a more conservative southwestern wing.

The Republican party differs, however, from the Democratic party. Though each party seeks and receives support from groups with varying viewpoints, the Republicans tend to be a smaller and more homogeneous group with a decided tilt in the conservative direction. The Democrats are a bigger, more heterogeneous party with significant support from groups all across the political spectrum—though the dominant tendency in the party is in the liberal direction.

The variety within each party puts a large barrier in the way of cohesive party programs. The issue that most unites Republicans is the desire to defeat Democrats, and vice versa. Each party tolerates many viewpoints. Conflicts *within* the parties can be as sharp and divisive as struggles *between* the parties.

Party Structure

Parties in the United States are *national* without being *hierarchical.* By this we mean two things. First, both the Democratic and Republican parties are organized at local, state, and national levels, but there are few structural ties between these levels. Second, within the government there is little party discipline. It is not at all unusual, for example, for a Democratic President to find congressional members of his own party voting against his programs, despite the fact that the President is the accepted head of the party. Several features of the structure of American government help explain why the parties are such *decentralized* political units.

"Winner-Takes-All" Elections   In the United States elections are run on a single-member district, "winner-take-all" basis. Only one member of Congress is elected from each district; the candidate

279

with the most votes wins the election. Senate elections are conducted on the same basis. In any election year only one senator is elected from any state. The presidential elections are run on a winner-take-all basis as well. In each state all the electoral votes go to the candidate with the largest popular vote. This system differs substantially from a system of *proportional representation,* in which legislative seats are allocated to parties in proportion to the amount of votes they win in the nation as a whole or in large regions of the nation. A party that gets 10 percent of the vote gets 10 percent of the seats in the legislature. Under proportional representation smaller parties gain a share of the seats in the legislature, while in a winner-take-all system all the representation goes to the largest party in the district.

Winner-take-all elections have three consequences. In the first place, they make local and state party organizations more important. If only one person from a certain area can be elected, the national party is dependent on the local party organization to nominate the right person and get out the vote. The national party organization does not have the resources to promote candidates when there is little chance of a payoff. This is often the case in winner-take-all elections.

In the second place, parties tend to be large and heterogeneous. In order to win any representation at all a party must be the largest in the district. It therefore must win support from a wide variety of groups. If it appeals only to a narrow group of like-minded citizens, it will remain permanently out of power.

The third consequence of a winner-take-all system is a *two-party* system. Again it is not hard to see why. Most voters want to vote for a candidate who has a chance of winning. Smaller parties have no chance. Voters therefore are unlikely to "waste" their votes on a sure loser. The result is that they support one or the other of the large parties that have a chance of winning. Furthermore, the two major parties are constantly on the lookout for new sources of support, since they have to be bigger than the opposition to win. If a significant third party appears, one or the other of the major parties is likely to try to capture its voters by appealing to whatever interests the third party expresses.

Separation of Powers The Consitution carefully separated the executive and legislative branches of the government. This, too, worked to limit the extent to which the American political parties could be centrally controlled. The President and Congress are elected separately (unlike the case in parliamentary systems, in which a legislature is elected and the head of the government is chosen by the legislature). The result—as the founders intended—is that the two branches are independent of each other. There is an inevitable rivalry between Congress and President, a rivalry that extends to the question of who controls the political parties. The President is usually considered to be the head of his party, but members of his party in Congress do not necessarily follow his lead.

Primary elections, as well as general elections, are based on the "winner-take-all" principle, as both Jimmy Carter and Henry Jackson knew when they campaigned for the Democratic Party nomination in 1976.

The fact that the President and Congress are elected separately creates the possibility that the legislative and executive branches will be in the hands of rival parties. This has become quite common in recent years. In 14 of the 26 years since 1952, a Republican President has been in office while both houses of Congress were controlled by Democratic majorities.

Federalism The U.S. government has a federal structure. Power is shared between the national government and the state governments, and there is a tradition of strong local government. As a result the American parties developed as state and local organizations. There are in fact 50 separate Republican parties and 50 separate Democratic parties—more if we include some of the strong, nearly independent organizations at the county or city level. The state and local parties are loosely linked together by a national committee, but the organizational charts that show lines of communication from precinct to ward to county or district to state to national headquarters are misleading.

The reason for this may be seen by looking at the three levels of party organization. At the local level the parties have city or county committees that are based on townships, precincts, or wards. The famous political "machines" with their "bosses" (e.g., Pendergast in Kansas City or Daley in Chicago) are examples of these committees. Through their ability to deliver votes on election day for candidates for national and state offices these committees are able to wield considerable power.

At the top of the state structure is each party's state central committee. Its members are chosen locally in counties or other election districts. They organize state party conventions, coordinate campaigns, and raise funds. State organizations tend to be weak except when a dominant leader—the governor or a big-city mayor—is able to attract organized support.

The highest-level body of each party is its national committee. It consists of one man and one woman from each state, the District of Columbia, Puerto Rico, and certain U.S. territories. The Republican national committee also includes state chairpersons from states that voted Republican in the last state or national election. The only person of consequence on this committee is the national chairperson. However, this person is usually the political handmaiden of the President or the titular head of the party and therefore does not have much power.

The national party headquarters has little control over what is done in its name at the state or local level. Party control is decentralized. The active units of the party, where there *are* active units, are at the local level. This contributes to variety—the Democratic party of Biloxi, Mississippi is a different political animal from the Democratic party of Palo Alto, California. Within the party a process of compromise and negotiation goes on whenever a decision affecting the party as a whole must be made, such as the nomination of a presidential candidate. On other types of decisions each unit goes its own way, not worrying about what another county or state party might be doing. For example, the nomination of congressional candidates is entirely under the control of the local activists, or the local voters if they participate in a primary. There is no effective chain of command with instructions and policies formulated at the top and passed down the line.

The fact that nominations and election support are controlled within states and localities—even for a national office like senator or representative—has an important implication for the kind of role the parties play *within* the government. In countries where nominations and campaigns are controlled by a central party organization, the elected candidates are dependent on that organization after the election. The party has greater resources for disciplining its members in the legislature—it can see that they vote with the party. In the United States, members of Congress are not subject to such discipline. They are freer to vote as they please and do not necessarily follow party direction. This is largely because they are not dependent on the national party leadership for nomination or election.

Even the President often cannot command loyal party support in Congress. And again the reasons are to be found in the structure of American politics. The President is nominated and elected by a national constituency. He tries to respond to that constituency by stressing themes that unite many regions, groups, and viewpoints. But a member of Congress has a local or state constituency. To win reelection he or she must serve specific needs and respond to particular issues: a dam to provide flood control, a military contract to provide jobs in the district, a new junior college. If the presidential program does not help the member of Congress in the district or state that elected him or her, then the President is not likely to have the support even of members of his own party in Congress.

Party workers and loyalists are the activists of the party organization.

Because of the large number of local organizations, we must qualify our description of the United States as a two-party system. We do not mean that there are only two major party *organizations.* Rather, we mean that there are only two major party *labels.* Elections take place between two groups of candidates: one running under the label of the Republican party and the other under the label of the Democratic party. Elections are not fought by two unified organizations. Each party is a loose coalition held together by the goal of gaining office.

How Different Are the Two Major Parties?

The major parties are divided internally; they do not present to the public the clear, unambiguous differences in program and ideology presented by party systems in some other nations. Are there real differences between the two parties? Despite their internal divisions, are there elements that make it possible to distinguish the Democratic party from the Republican party? Or is there, as George Wallace claimed in his third-party campaign, "not a dime's worth of difference" between them? To put the question another way, does it make any difference who wins? When the conservative senator from Arizona, Barry Goldwater, won the Republican nomination in 1964, he promised the voters "a choice, not an echo." Goldwater insisted that the two parties had become so alike in outlook that the American voters had no choice between competing viewpoints. Many people agree, claiming that a two-party system actually reduces choice because each party must attract and hold the support of a wide variety of groups and individuals. The parties are coalitions, and coalitions cannot be held together unless they are flexible. Besides, this reasoning goes, the big prize for each party is the White House. Because there can be only one winner, it is natural for each party to design its strategy with that prize in mind. This means that they must tend toward the middle, where most of the voters are—especially the independent and undecided voters. This pattern is illustrated by the normal bell curve in Figure 10.1.

Other observers disagree. They say the parties reflect the basic conflict between haves and haves-nots, property owners and those without property, businessmen and workers, producers and consumers. Electoral competition, they argue, is a form of democratic class struggle. This pattern is illustrated in Figure 10.2.

Which is correct—a picture of the parties as more or less the same in outlook or a picture of the parties as reflecting conflicting policies? Let us turn to three kinds of evidence:

1. whether the parties draw electoral support from different social groups
2. whether party leaders differ in their policy views
3. whether support for legislation differs between the parties

FIGURE 10.1
The American Electorate

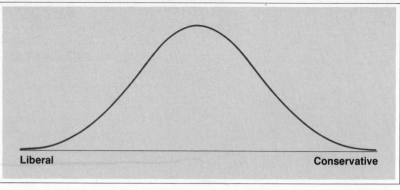

FIGURE 10.2
Party Differences as Reflection
of Class Antagonisms

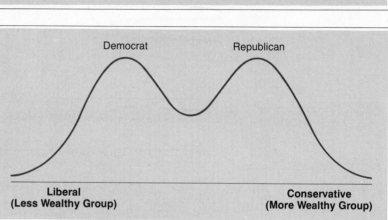

DIFFERENT SOCIAL GROUPS
SUPPORT THE TWO MAJOR PARTIES

There are differences between the social groups that support the major parties. These can be traced to the coalition formed by Democratic President Franklin D. Roosevelt during the depression of the 1930s. During that period the Republican party remained close to its traditional principles of fiscal responsibility and individual effort and thus kept the support of business and commercial interests and more affluent voters. Meanwhile the Democrats introduced such public-welfare measures as social security, unemployment insurance, and public aid and thus became the party of blacks, immigrant workers, the poor, and the unemployed. There were also religious differences between the parties: Catholics were more likely to be Democrats, northern white Protestants more likely to be Republicans. The parties came to differ in social class, too. The Democrats, however, maintained the support of the white South (southern blacks being effectively barred from voting). This attachment was based not on class but on regional sentiments.

The difference between the class bases of the Republicans and the Democrats can still be seen today. In general, Republicans tend to be of higher socioeconomic status than Democrats. They tend to have higher-status occupations, higher incomes, and more formal educa-

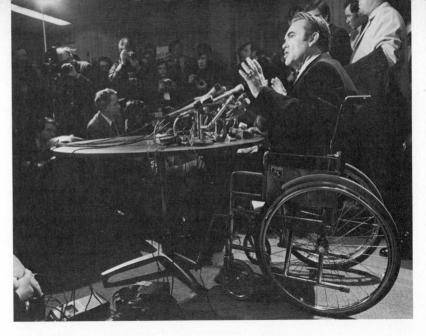

George Wallace claimed that there was "not a dime's worth of difference" between the two major parties, and twice led a third-party movement in the Presidential elections.

tion. However, important changes are taking place in the composition of the parties. The coalitions of the 1930s are not as clear as they once were. Workers are still likely to be Democratic, but now they are more willing to listen to Republican candidates. The same is true of Catholics. Similarly, the Republican dominance among northern white Protestants has weakened. But the various groups are not *switching* their affiliation from Democrat to Republican or vice versa. They are abandoning party ties. This is especially true among younger voters, about half of whom identify themselves as independents, as we review in the following chapter.

DEMOCRATS AND REPUBLICANS
DIFFER IN POLITICAL PHILOSOPHY

Neither of the parties has a dominant philosophy to which all of its supporters subscribe. But studies confirm that there are differences between the political beliefs of Democrats and Republicans. The differences are relatively mild among rank-and-file party members, those whose attachment to the party does not go beyond self-identification. But when one comes to the party activists the differences become greater.

A study of the political opinions of delegates to the presidential nominating conventions in 1956 concluded that the Democratic party "is marked by a strong belief in the power of collective action to promote social justice, equality, humanitarianism, and economic planning, while preserving freedom," while the Republican side "is distinguished by faith in the wisdom of the natural competitive process and in the supreme virtue of individuals, 'character,' self-reliance, frugality, and independence from government." Although the fit is not perfect, "the American parties do tend to embody

these competing points of view and to serve as reference groups for those who hold them."[1] The same researchers found a tendency for Democratic and Republican voters to differ in similar ways, but the differences were not nearly as sharp.

Research done two decades later, in 1976, found the same pattern, only perhaps more pronounced. Members of the national and state party committees and county party chairpersons were surveyed. Democrats differed from Republicans along the same philosophical lines found earlier. "Who," they were asked, "is to blame for poverty in America? Is it that the system does not give everyone an equal break or are the poor themselves largely to blame?" Democratic party leaders blamed the system by five to one; Republican leaders blamed the poor by four to one. "Should the government guarantee a job for all Americans who are able to work?" By six to one, Democratic leaders said yes; by ten to one, Republican leaders said no.[2] The leaders of the two parties also differed on the importance of national goals. Democrats are most interested in reducing unemployment and believe that reducing the role of government is the least important of ten goals about which they were asked. The Republicans were more interested in reducing the role of government (they rank this goal second in importance after curbing inflation) and rank the reduction of unemployment quite low. (See Table 10.2.)

These differences are striking. They suggest an important point about American elections. Some critics of the American party system have claimed that the parties try to sound as different as possible during elections but that their candidates do not differ when they take office. These critics seem to have the situation backwards. The evidence is that the parties often try to sound the same when campaigning for office, since they both want the support of the undecided voters who are likely to be middle-of-the-roaders. But in office their members may behave quite differently. The people that a Republican administration brings to Washington do differ in their beliefs from those that a Democratic administration would bring.

DO DEMOCRATIC AND REPUBLICAN MEMBERS OF CONGRESS DIFFER?

When it comes to votes in Congress, neither party can enforce strict party loyalty. The President and party leaders in Congress can put pressure on party members, but they can go only so far. The Republican or Democrat in Congress is relatively independent of his

The Democratic Party is more likely to be supported by workers and the Republican Party by businessmen and businesswomen.

[1] These findings are taken from a study of the delegates to the 1956 presidential nominating conventions of both parties. The delegates come from every part of the country and from every level of party and government. For a full report see Herbert McClosky, Paul J. Hoffmann, and Rosemary O'Hara, "Issue Conflict and Consensus Among Party Leaders and Followers," *American Political Science Review*, June 1960, p. 420.

[2] Data from an unpublished study of American leaders conducted by the *Washington Post* and the Center for International Affairs of Harvard University, April 1976. Questions are paraphrased.

Republican leaders, especially those in agreement with the conservative economic policies of Ronald Reagen, argue against government intervention in the economy.

or her party. Members of Congress are more sensitive to the voters back home and to those who provide financial support at election time. They also follow their own philosophies. Hence, if there are differences between the parties in terms of congressional votes, these reflect major differences in philosophy between the parties.

Political scientists have studied how the parties vote in Congress and have reached two conclusions: (1) There is much cohesion within each party and there are major policy differences between the parties, and (2) deviations from these patterns are due almost entirely to the influence of constituents. Thus if a Democrat votes differently in Congress from fellow Democrats, it is usually because of pressure from the voters back home or, more likely, from an important interest group in the home district.

TABLE 10.2
How Party Officials View the Importance of Ten National Goals
Question: Party officials were asked to rank, in order of importance, ten major problems.

Republicans	Democrats
1. Curbing inflation	1. Reducing unemployment
2. Reducing the role of government	2. Curbing inflation
3. Maintaining a strong military defense	3. Protecting freedom of speech
4. Developing energy sources	4. Developing energy sources
5. Reducing crime	5. Achieving equality for blacks
6. Reducing unemployment	6. Reducing crime
7. Protecting freedom of speech	7. Giving people more say in government decisions
8. Giving people more say in government decisions	8. Achieving equality for women
9. Achieving equality for blacks	9. Maintaining a strong military defense
10. Achieving equality for women	10. Reducing the role of government

Source: Based on a survey by the *Washington Post* and the Harvard University Center for International Affairs. *Washington Post*, September 27, 1976.

Differences in voting records between the two parties may be seen in roll call votes in the House of Representatives. Table 10.3 lists votes on selected legislative proposals over the past quarter-century; the striking contrast between Republicans and Democrats is evidence that there are differences between the parties. On balance, the Republicans have been economic protectionists and the Democrats economic protestors. The Republican party has opposed government regulation of the economy and income equalization and social-welfare programs, and has favored policies that create jobs and economic growth through free enterprise and private initiative. The Democrats introduced Keynesian economics, with its emphasis on greater government intervention in the economy; they have tried to reduce income differences through tax reform; and they have favored social-welfare policies. In addition, they are more concerned about unemployment.

Political Parties and Conflict

Politics implies conflict. Citizens differ in their preferences: in what they expect the government to provide, in who they think should pay for these government services, in how they believe the government should be organized. Governments, depending on their programs, their taxation policies, and their procedures, benefit some citizens and deprive others, reward some citizens and punish others.

Because the government has such enormous powers to help or harm, the struggle to control the government is by no means a trivial one. Great energy and large sums of money are directed toward seeing to it that one group of interests rather than another gets control of the government. Much of this competition over who controls the government is organized by and through the political

TABLE 10.3
Party Differences in the House of Representatives, 1945–1976

Year	Selected Legislation	Democrats in Favor	Republicans in Favor
1945	Full Employment Act	90%	36%
1947	Maintain Individual Income Tax Rates	62	1
1954	Increase Unemployment Compensation	54	9
1961	Emergency Educational Act	67	4
1964	Antipoverty Program	84	13
1969	Tax Reform	86	22
1971	Hospital Construction	99	41
1973	Increase Minimum Wage	88	27
1974	Federal Aid to City Transit Systems	81	23
1975	Emergency Jobs for the Unemployed	92	13
1976	Block Deregulation of Natural Gas	70	10

Source: Based on data from Robert A. Dahl, "Key Votes, 1945–1964," *Pluralist Democracy in the United States* (Chicago: Rand McNally, 1967), pp. 238–242; *Labor Looks at the 91st Congress*, an AFL-CIO Legislative Report, 1971; *Labor Looks at Congress 1973*, an AFL-CIO Legislative Report, 1974; *Labor Looks at the 93rd Congress*, an AFL-CIO Legislative Report, 1975; *Labor Looks at the 94th Congress*, an AFL-CIO Legislative Report, 1977.

parties, as we have seen in this chapter and will see from a different perspective in the next chapter.

Here we can conclude by emphasizing the major function of political parties in the United States. The parties manage the transfer of power from one set of interests to another. And they do so peacefully. This is a major achievement. Given the very high stakes associated with who controls government, it would not surprise us to learn that people who have power would not want to give it up. This is indeed the case in many nations. It takes a military coup or an assassination or a revolution to exchange one set of leaders for another set. The transfer of power is brought about by violence.

For nearly 200 years this has not been the experience of the United States. There has of course been violence in American politics: labor violence, racial violence, political-protest violence. And there have been political assassinations. But routine transfer of government power from the Republicans to the Democrats, or from the Democrats to the Republicans, has not been a direct result of acts of violence. Nor has this transfer of power been accompanied by violence.

Political parties establish the rules and habits of behavior that regulate the competition for political office. In so doing they establish the practice whereby the losers accept the outcome of the competition and allow the winners to peacefully take over positions of power.

HOW INSTITUTIONS WORK: II
how our political parties are organized

What is the organizational basis of American political parties? Our political parties can be thought of in terms of layers of organization. Each layer—city or county, state, national—is concerned chiefly with elections within its own area. The ties that link party organizations across these layers are more formal than real. Party structure is most often described as *decentralized*, which means that the parties are less organized at the state level than at the local level and least organized at the national level. Indeed, so decentralized and fragmented are the parties that, depending on the time and place, they may hardly be organized at all.

How are the parties organized at the national level? The highest-level body of each party is its national committee. It consists of one man and one woman from each state, the District of Columbia, Puerto Rico, and certain U.S. territories. The Republican national committee also includes state chairpersons from states that voted Republican in the last state or national election. Committee members are chosen in various ways in the states and rarely meet as a group. In fact the national committee amounts to little more than the national chairperson and the party staff in Washington.

What role does the national chairperson play in party affairs? Although he or she is formally elected by the national convention, the national chairperson is really the choice of the party's presidential nominee. Thus Jean Westwood was named Democratic chairperson by candidate George McGovern 1972 but was replaced in the power struggle that followed McGovern's defeat. This points to the national committee's primary purpose of raising money and helping coordinate the presidential campaign every four years. But even this role is small, since presidential candidates usually either take over the national machinery and make it their own or, like Nixon in 1972, may create a separate organization such as the Committee to Re-elect the President and use it to run the campaign.

Are there any other party structures at the national level? Both Republicans and Democrats have congressional and senatorial campaign committees chosen by the party members in each house. They are independent of the national committee and serve to channel money and assistance to House and Senate candidates.

What is the shape of party organization at the state level? At the top of the state structure is each party's state central committee. Its members are chosen locally in counties or other election districts. They organize state party conventions, coordinate campaigns, and raise funds. Like the national committees, state organizations tend to be weak except when a dominant leader—the governor or a big-city mayor—is able to attract organized support. Even in these situations the basis of strength is usually personal and cannot be translated into an ongoing political organization.

Patterns of political strength at the state level vary widely. It is estimated that there is serious competition between the parties in about half the states, with the others having either one-party or modified one-party systems. And even where there is two-party competition the pattern of organization may be very uneven. In Michigan, for example, the Democratic party organization is centered in Detroit and Wayne County while Republicans dominate much of the rest of the state.

Why do some party organizations operate more successfully than others? Successful party organization in America takes place at the local level. The basic unit is the precinct or election district, containing from 300 to 1000 voters. The key position is that of precinct captain, responsible for getting out the vote; the captain and the ward leaders may be volunteers or may be chosen in the same primaries in which candidates for office are nominated. In any event they serve as the building blocks of the larger district, city, and county organizations that make up the local layer of party structure. Such political "machines" are rare today, though the Cook County organization (Democratic) continues to function in this way. Generally speaking, areas where local political units are well organized tend to be dominated by one party — and for good reason. Effective party strength depends on money, organizational skills, many hours of work, and in some cases political control over jobs. These are scarce resources that usually can't support two well-organized parties within the same political space.

11
ELECTIONS IN AMERICA

Periodic elections are central to democratic government. They represent one of the major ways—perhaps *the* major way—in which the citizenry keeps ultimate control over political leaders. The political parties play a crucial role in the electoral process; they select the candidates to run for office, they organize the election campaign, they provide the American public with a choice between alternatives. At least that is what parties traditionally did in the United States. In recent years the role of the parties in the electoral process has declined somewhat. An increasingly important role has been played by the mass media, by candidates acting independently of the political parties, and by voters who vote independently of the parties. In this chapter we will look at the electoral process in America to learn about the changing role of political parties and to assess the meaning of the changes that are occurring.

As we will see in the chapter on federalism (Chapter 17), there are over 18,000 government units in America. This means many times that number of elected officials. Most government units are run by an elected head or an elected board or council. Furthermore, we elect to office many officials who would be appointed in other countries: judges, sheriffs, dogcatchers, coroners. The most crucial election in America, however, is the presidential election. In this chapter we will concentrate on that election, but we will also look at congressional elections.

Presidential Hopefuls

In 1976 a former governor of Georgia who had no national political experience and before his campaign was virtually unknown to the American people engineered a stunning political victory by winning 17 out of 30 statewide presidential primaries during the winter and spring of that year, capturing his party's nomination on the first ballot at its convention in July, and defeating the incumbent President in the November election. In a few short years Jimmy Carter had come a long way from his peanut farm in Plains, Georgia. To many people his success seemed nothing less than a "phenomenon," and for good reason. With the exception of popular military leaders like Dwight Eisenhower, presidential politics had long been the preserve of nationally known party leaders. Carter was neither a military hero nor a party leader. Why, then, was the election of a

Jimmy Carter possible in 1976? Have the rules of the electoral process really changed, or was Carter's success a fluke caused by the anti-Washington mood that prevailed during the immediate post-Watergate period of American politics? To answer these questions we must follow the road to the White House.

Only a very small number of people in the suitable age bracket can seriously hope to become President. Carter's success notwithstanding, most serious presidential candidates are likely to come from national political life. Governors of large states, especially New York, Pennsylvania, Illinois, and California, fall into this small group. So do forceful, articulate senators. Members of the House of Representatives are not usually included in this group, but Morris Udall's respectable showing in the race for the Democratic party nomination in 1976 indicates that this may be changing. Popular war heroes, if the war was a popular one, might count. A widely known college president might be mentioned but is not likely to be nominated unless there was an important government position somewhere in his career. And of course Vice-Presidents are in the pool.

There is no single road to the White House—as Jimmy Carter's candidacy makes clear. However, in recent elections the Senate has been the most fertile source of presidential candidates. In the five presidential races since 1960, more than half of the candidates had served in the Senate. Four of them—Kennedy in 1960, Goldwater in 1964, Humphrey in 1968, and McGovern in 1972—entered the race directly from prominent positions in the Senate. Lyndon Johnson went from the Senate to the Vice-Presidency and succeeded to the White House when Kennedy was assassinated. And Richard Nixon had served as a senator from California before running for the Presidency in 1968 (though he did not come to national prominence in the Senate; rather, he became nationally known as a congressman in the 1950s and then as Vice-President under Eisenhower). Furthermore, many of the leading contenders who did not make it to the nomination, as well as many vice-presidential candidates, have been senators.

Why has a career in the Senate replaced a career as governor of a major state as the most frequently traveled road to the White House? This change reflects a more general change in the nature of electoral politics in the United States. Governors of large states used to be likely candidates because they controlled large blocks of electoral votes in their own states and because they had behind them the resources of powerful state party organizations. The base of their political power was essentially within their own state. Senators enter the race for the presidential nomination from a more national forum. Their political strength depends less on control of a state organization than on national prominence achieved as the head of a major Senate committee. The change in the main source of presidential candidates parallels other changes that we will discuss; all involve the decline in importance of political-party organizations.

Members of the "In-Party" It is convenient to call the political party of the current President the "in-party." The number of presidential hopefuls in the in-party varies, of course, depending on whether the current President can succeed himself. Presidents are limited to two terms by the Twenty-Second Amendment (passed after Franklin D. Roosevelt had been elected to the Presidency four times). If the President cannot succeed himself, then the field is open, unless a particular person, such as the Vice-President, is clearly the front runner. The most recent case of a President serving out his two terms was Eisenhower, who left office in 1960. And in that year Eisenhower's Vice-President for eight years, Richard Nixon, faced almost no serious challenge for the Republican party nomination.

Traditionally, the current President was renominated by his party without serious opposition. But one of the most fascinating things about American politics in recent years is the crumbling of this tradition. In 1968 Democrat Lyndon Johnson was President; legally he could serve another term. Yet he was challenged within his own party in the primary elections. First Eugene McCarthy and then Robert Kennedy openly declared themselves candidates for the Democratic party nomination. They gained such support that Johnson decided that he would not seek renomination. A President had been forced from office by a serious challenge from within his own party. Eight years later another incumbent President—this time Republican Gerald Ford—was challenged by a fellow party member, Ronald Reagan. Reagan may have failed to win the nomination, but his near success seems to confirm that the value of incumbency is no longer as great as it once was.

Members of the "Out-Party" In the other major party the number of people who seriously hope to become President can grow to a dozen or two. In both 1972 and 1976 the Democrats fielded a large number of candidates. The number tends to be largest in the fall and winter preceding the first presidential primaries. By January of 1976, for example, twelve Democrats had entered the race: five senators and one former senator, one member of the House of Representatives, two governors and two former governors, and a previous vice-presidential nominee. The "winnowing process," as one unsuccessful candidate described it, began shortly after the first state primaries. Within a few months only a handful of the original twelve remained serious contenders. There was the possibility, of course, that no one would win the nomination on the first ballot at the convention and that someone who had not even entered the primaries would be selected as the nominee. But in the end Carter prevailed.

Nominating the President

In a strong, centralized party system the national party would control all nominations for office: for the Presidency, for Congress, and for local offices. This has never been the case in the United States; the national party never controlled local nominations. Even nomination for the Presidency has always involved some bargaining in which state and local party organizations took a major part. Powerful state and local party organizations—particularly those with a large block of delegates—often dominated the national party conventions. And these organizations had complete control over nominations in their states and localities.

In recent years state and local party organizations have declined in power. The Chicago Democratic machine under Mayor Richard Daley was one of the last of its breed. It controlled political life in Chicago, determining who got nominated and who got elected. It delivered delegate votes at the Democratic convention and citizen votes in the general election. But the Chicago machine appears to be a lot weaker than it once was. In 1976 it could not deliver Illinois for the national Democratic ticket, nor could it elect some of its own local candidates in Cook County. And the death of Mayor Daley may have weakened it more. Most other party machines have long since disappeared.

Though their importance has diminished somewhat, the two major parties remain central to the nomination of the presidential and vice-presidential candidates. Indeed, it is only as convention time draws near that the parties come together as national institutions.

The nomination process has gone through a long evolution since 1800. We will describe that evolution briefly before turning to a discussion of how candidates are nominated today.

King Caucus　The earliest political parties were nothing more than small groups of men meeting in party "caucuses" to determine which party members would become candidates for public office. Nominating caucuses for governorships and other state offices were generally made up of like-minded party members in the state legislatures. Congressional caucuses nominated the presidential candidates, who then took their case to the voters.

"King Caucus," as this system was called, did not last long, but it was the first step in the process leading to party domination over access to public office. The second step also has to do with nominating candidates. "Jacksonian popular democracy," a social movement of the 1820s named after Andrew Jackson, the seventh President, attempted to broaden the bases of participation in American politics. One of its notable successes was the replacement of the caucus system of party nominations with conventions. Conventions were made up of delegates selected by state and local party organizations and thus were supposed to be more broadly representative than caucuses.

Primary Elections   Throughout the nineteenth century nomination for nearly all public offices was done by party conventions. Today nominating conventions are important primarily for presidential candidates. Candidates for most governorships, state and national legislatures, and many local offices are now nominated in direct primaries.

Primaries—party elections that precede the general election—were introduced in order to reform "nondemocratic" politics. At the turn of the century various reform groups charged that party conventions had come under the control of political bosses and that candidates were controlled by special interests. The reformers felt that a larger dose of democracy would cure this ill, so they proposed primary elections.

Primary elections are a means of involving party members in the nomination process. From among numerous candidates who are members of the same party the supporters of that party choose the person whom they consider best qualified to run in the general election. At least this is the theory. Some form of primary election has now been adopted in every state, though the form and importance of primaries vary considerably from state to state. We cannot review all the different kinds of primaries; instead, we must satisfy ourselves with two very general conclusions.

On the negative side, the primary as a means of nominating candidates has many flaws. Voter turnout is always low. The choices presented are often not clear, resulting in considerable confusion among voters. At the same time, the costs in terms of both money and effort can be very high, using up resources needed for the general election. And the primaries have not brought about mass participation in the nomination process. On the positive side, the primaries have reduced the control of a small group of people over nominations. They provide a channel by which an opposing group can put its candidate forward.

Presidential Primaries   One of the biggest changes in the process of electing a President that has occurred in recent years is the increasing importance of the primaries. As recently as 1968 Hubert Humphrey won his party's nomination without even entering the primaries. But in 1976 it was clear that the long primary route had become *the* road to the nomination. Thirty states held primary elections over a 3½-month period, compared to 23 in 1972 and 17 in 1968. On the Democratic side, Carter was so successful in the primaries that his primary victories alone gave him nearly enough convention votes for the nomination. In any case he was so far ahead of his competitors that the party unified around him in the weeks before the convention. On the Republican side, the expanded 1976 primaries gave Ronald Reagan the opportunity to mount a serious,

Primary elections begin in New Hampshire long before the summer nominating conventions.

sustained challenge to incumbent Gerald Ford. In this case, however, the primaries did not settle the nomination; they ended in a virtual tie. What they did was to allow the challenger to take his case directly to the party rank and file.

Of course 1976 was not the first year in which the primaries played a decisive role in the nomination process. In 1960, for example, John Kennedy's victory in the West Virginia primary was a major boost to his candidacy, proving that a Catholic could win in a heavily Protestant state.

No longer are the presidential primaries just so many test cases for the benefit of the party regulars to measure the appeal of various candidates to different kinds of electorates. Instead, the primaries have begun to compete seriously with the nominating convention and the party regulars as the effective selector of the party nominee. If the current trend continues, they may replace the convention as the main instrument of nomination. Without consciously deciding to do so, we have been moving steadily toward a kind of national presidential primary, though it is administered in numerous places over a 3½-month period. This has opened up the electoral process to outsiders, like Carter, who strike a responsive chord with the American people.

Primaries reduce the control of party organizations over the nomination process. The primary system allows candidates to emerge who are not tied to regular party organizations. Jimmy Carter had no strong party organization behind him. He owed his success in 1976 to his victories in a number of early primaries.

Regulars vs. Purists Primaries reduce the power of party organizations in another way. They undercut the importance of the *party regulars.* Party regulars are members of local parties; they are committed to the party as an organization. They want to see the party win; what the candidate stands for matters less than the candidate's chance of winning. Why do they care so much for victory and so little for what the candidate proposes to do? Often it is because they are officeholders whose jobs depend on their party's being in power. The Democratic machine in Chicago, and most others, were based on such support.

Party regulars usually have the dominant voice in local party conventions and caucuses. Primaries provide a voice for a different kind of political activist: the amateur politician or *political purist.* True, they are interested in finding a winning candidate. But they are more interested in finding a candidate whose proposals they can support. The conservative Republicans who nominated Goldwater in 1964 or fought for Ronald Reagan in 1976 had strong commitments. The supporters of McCarthy in 1968 or of McGovern in 1972 were often of this sort. They supported their candidates because they believed deeply in the importance of the policies the candidates stood for: commitment to free enterprise in the cases of Goldwater and Reagan; opposition to the Vietnam War in the cases of McCarthy and McGovern.

The Democratic party has been troubled by a split between party regulars and purists. The regulars succeeded in nominating Hubert Humphrey in 1968; Humphrey lost partly because of lack of support from the more liberal wing of the party, where many of the purists are found. The purists defeated the regulars in 1972 and nominated McGovern. Again the party lost, this time because many of the regulars sat out the election or voted for Nixon. One of the secrets of the success of Jimmy Carter may be that he received a good deal of support in the primaries from people who were not party regulars, who were impressed with his position as an outsider campaigning against the failings of previous administrations. At the same time, his policy positions were not such as to alienate the party regulars. In addition, the weakness of the party organization allowed Carter to build his own organization.

PRESIDENTIAL NOMINATING CONVENTIONS

Every four years the Democrats and the Republicans, as well as minor parties, meet in convention for the purpose of nominating a presidential ticket. Party conventions are remarkable gatherings; they provide hours and hours of TV entertainment for the American public. Several hundred party members meet in a city selected by the national party organization (in close consultation with the television networks) to debate and formulate a "party platform" and choose a presidential nominee. When the two party conventions have finished their business, two people out of an adult population of more than 100 million Americans are serious contenders for the White House. In this sense the choice of the President is predetermined. Only the two nominees of the major parties have a realistic chance. Yet at the same time the choice is meaningful, for the party nominating process has given the electorate manageable alternatives.

How Delegates Are Selected   Delegates to the presidential nominating convention are selected in a variety of ways. Some states have presidential primaries that bind the delegates to the candidate who wins the primary election; other states have primaries that allow the voters to show their preferences but still leave the delegates some independence. In still other states the primary election chooses unbound delegates. In some states the voters choose some delegates but other delegates from that state are chosen by district or state party committees. All told, the use of some form of presidential primary accounts for the selection of three-quarters of the delegates to the nominating conventions. But a sizable number of states still rely on party caucuses or conventions to select convention delegates.

Although the primaries now account for the selection of a substantial majority of the convention delegates, delegate selection in the caucus states is not unimportant. In a close race like the Ford–Reagan contest in 1976 every vote counts. Reagan saw that he could offset some of Ford's success in the early primaries by concentrating on delegate selection in the caucus states. For a different reason Carter campaigned vigorously for support in the Iowa caucus that preceded the primaries. This was not so much to garner the few votes at stake as it was to generate favorable national publicity by gaining an early victory.

Who Are the Delegates?   Convention delegates are a cross-section of the political party. Included among them will be many office-holders, members of Congress, governors, mayors, state legislators. There will be party activists and contributors. In both major parties the delegates have tended to be white, male, and wealthier than the general population.

Both parties, though especially the Democratic party, have reformed their delegate selection practices in recent years so as to provide a more balanced convention. In 1970 a report of the Democratic party reform commission reported that too many delegates were selected at "secret caucuses" and "closed slate-making meetings." It also reported that minorities, especially blacks, Chicanos, women, and youth, were discriminated against. The number of minority delegates to the Democratic party convention in 1972 showed a marked increase from 1968 levels. In 1976, however, the percentage of minority delegates was down from the 1972 peaks, though still quite a bit higher than in 1968. Many women and blacks were not content to let the gains achieved in 1972 slip away. Blacks managed to get the party's Rules Committee to adopt a resolution calling for affirmative action to increase minority representation at future conventions, and women obtained acceptance of a resolution calling on the state parties to move toward equal representation of the sexes in future state delegations.

The Convention Chooses   In 1976 the Democratic party held its convention in New York City in July, followed by the Republican party in Kansas City in August. When the conventions were over

Conventions are less important than they once were, but close-fought contests still occur.

there were two national tickets. But did the delegates who poured into New York and Kansas City in the summer of 1976 actually decide anything? Or were they there only to confirm what had already been decided? Although the Democratic and Republican conventions displayed a striking contrast between an easy victory and a close-fought contest, in both cases it is clear that all but a handful of delegates made up their minds, or were obligated to vote in a certain way, before the convention began. Especially on the Democratic side, the convention functioned less to choose a party leader than to confirm a choice that had already been made.

It has not always been so. Past conventions have been meetings in which negotiating, compromising, and "deals" have resulted in an unexpected nomination. And other conventions have seen intense factional battles, with the outcome depending on how the undecided delegates finally voted. Today, however, much of the struggle that used to occur in the conventions has been shifted to the preconvention period—the presidential primaries and the state and local meetings where delegates are selected.

Still, the primary process may fail to produce a clear front runner. If the party is fragmented and there are many candidates fighting it out in the primaries, it is possible that by convention time no single person will dominate. Many people thought this would happen in 1976. But the fact that it did not happen then does not mean that it will not happen in the future. In such a case the convention would really have to choose its candidate.

The Presidential Campaign

Two major presidential candidates, and their vice-presidential running mates, will be left in the race at the end of the party primaries, delegate selection caucuses, and nominating conventions. Now starts the great democratic ritual of American politics: the presidential campaign.

If anything political attracts the attention of the American public, it is the presidential campaign every four years. The image and voice of each candidate bombard the citizen from billboards, bumper stickers, newspaper advertisements, radio spots, and most of all, television. A citizen may not care about the results, but it is not easy to avoid the campaign. Walk past a newsstand, and a half-dozen different pictures of one or both of the candidates smile from magazine covers. Turn the television on, and sooner or later comes a spot announcement telling the viewer how much *this* election means and how the candidate can solve the country's problems.

More than national holidays, more than public ceremonies, more than patriotic songs and speeches, the presidential campaign is the event that reaffirms what democracy is supposed to be about.

Candidates are faced with many possible campaign strategies when the campaign begins. Some of these have to do with the organization and financing of the campaign. How much should the candidate spend on television spot announcements? How much on billboards? How much effort should go into travel and personal appearances? How much into studio-based television speeches? Candidates also try to decide which parts of the country require their campaigning most. They spend less time in areas where they cannot win as well as in areas where they cannot lose. The winner-take-all rule of the Electoral College—whereby the candidate with the most votes in a state gets all its electoral votes—plays a role here. If a candidate is sure of victory in a particular state he gains nothing more from increasing his popular vote there; he gets all the electoral votes anyway. Similarly, if he is a sure loser in another state he gains little by increasing his vote if he still comes in second. Therefore candidates give their greatest efforts to states where the outcome is uncertain, especially if they are large states.

Appealing to the Voters

Political campaigns, it is often argued, should give the public a choice and should also educate the public. Each candidate should present his positions clearly, spelling out why they differ from those of his opponent. The candidate should offer the public a choice between two clearly delineated positions and explain to the public why his position is better. In fact, however, campaigns do not work that way. In every campaign we hear complaints about the low level of the debate, the lack of clarity of issues, the lack of a true choice. Why is this the case?

Candidates have to decide how to appeal to the voters. It is this set of decisions that sometimes results in a campaign that is less edifying than many people would like. Candidates can appeal to voters on the basis of party affiliation, personal characteristics, or positions on political issues.

PARTY AFFILIATION

As we will see when we look more closely at the American voter, many citizens have long-term party identifications. They consider themselves Democrats or Republicans and often have felt that way for their entire adult lives. Candidates can appeal to voters on this basis—the Democratic candidate asking for votes from Democratic supporters and the Republican candidate asking for the votes of Republicans. This tactic is more likely to be used by a Democratic candidate because there are more Democrats than Republicans. Recent polls have found that about 40 percent of the electorate consider themselves Democrats but only 20 percent considers themselves Republicans. Therefore a Democrat gains more if voters choose on the basis of party identification.

In many nations elections are run largely on this basis. People vote for the candidates of the party they have always supported. The candidates try to win the votes of those who are committed to their party. They do not appeal to the voters who support opposing parties.

In the United States, on the other hand, candidates do not appeal only to the supporters of their own party. They make a broader appeal. For one thing, a crucial block of voters is independent. About 40 percent of the public has no party identification. Furthermore, voters who identify with one party can often be lured over to vote for the presidential candidate of the opposition party. Republican candidates, because of their status as the candidate of the minority party, are under particular pressure to make a nonpartisan appeal. Millions of Democrats crossed party lines to give presidential victories to the Republican candidate in 1952 and 1956 (Eisenhower) and in 1968 and 1972 (Nixon).

In addition, the growing importance of the mass media—particularly television—reduces the extent to which candidates will use partisan appeals. When campaigns were conducted through personal appearances, candidates knew that they were usually addressing voters who supported their own party. Democrats came out to see the Democratic candidate, Republicans to see the Republican candidate. The candidate could safely appeal to partisan loyalties. But when a candidate faces a national television audience on prime time he knows that he is speaking to supporters of his party, supporters of the opposing party, and millions of independents. He is likely to downplay partisanship. Thus in the 1976 television debates, when each candidate faced a vast national audience of voters of all persuasions, there was little reference to partisanship.

PERSONALITY

Candidates also appeal to voters on the basis of their personal characteristics. They try to paint themselves as trustworthy, competent, more capable of running the government. In the wake of the Watergate scandal, for example, both President Ford and Jimmy Carter tried to stress their personal honesty. The candidate who appeals on the basis of personality does not ask the public to support him as a Democrat or Republican or because of his position on the issues. He asks voters to vote for him not for what he will do but for what he is as a person. Perhaps as important as the candidate's attempt to portray himself as trustworthy or competent is his attempt to characterize the opponent as irresponsible or incompetent. In 1964 the Johnson campaign used some incautious statements by Senator Barry Goldwater on nuclear weapons to label him irresponsible in such matters. In 1972 the Nixon campaign labeled Senator George McGovern an incompetent using some evidence of his indecision (in his choice of a vice-presidential candidate and in his plan for a tax rebate for poor people) as the reason. In each case the campaign appears to have had some success.

It is often said that people are irrational if they vote for a candidate on the basis of personal characteristics. This is probably true if the choice is made on the basis of the candidate's smile, but it is certainly not irrational to choose a candidate who gives evidence of trustworthiness or ability. Such characteristics are hard to judge, but they are far from irrelevant.

ISSUES

Candidates also appeal to the public by taking positions on political issues. There are many kinds of issues on which they can take positions.

Consensual Issues On some issues there is little disagreement among the public as to what the goal for America should be: All Americans want peace; they all want prosperity. On issues of this sort candidates will not differ from each other. No candidate is going to come out for war or recession. They debate such issues in terms of which candidate can do a better job in solving a particular problem. An example of such an issue is governmental corruption, which was a major topic in 1976. Both candidates agreed that government power had been abused in previous administrations. Each claimed that he would do a better job of cleaning things up than his opponent.

Intense Issues Another type of issue is that on which there is a special, intensely concerned public. In Chapter 6 we illustrated some patterns of issue conflict. The kind we have in mind here was illustrated in Example 5 on page 182. A relatively small group of citizens is deeply concerned about a particular issue while the rest of the public is only moderately concerned. There are many such issues. We have used the example of gun control. A small group of Americans is strongly opposed to any gun control legislation. Most Americans take the opposite position, but they do so with little intensity. Abortion is a similar issue, with a small, intense minority succeeding in delaying or reversing legislation permitting abortion despite the fact that many people favor such a policy.

How do candidates handle such an issue? Often they try to avoid taking a stand on it. If a candidate takes a stand in opposition to the intense minority, he loses votes. The intense group will vote against him no matter what his positions are on other issues. For this intense group only one issue counts. If the group is large enough and located in the right states, it can be a potent voting block. If an intense group is opposed by a moderately concerned majority, the candidate will worry about the intense minority. The less involved majority will not vote on the basis of the candidate's position on that issue.

Issue Alternatives A third type of issue is one on which there are alternate positions and the public is divided. This pattern is illustrated in Examples 1, 3, and 4 on pages 177, 179, and 181 of Chapter 6. In some cases most of the public takes a relatively moderate position on one side or the other; in other cases there are intense publics on either side. There are many such issues on which the public is divided: How much commitment should the government make to welfare spending? Ought there to be a guaranteed

Candidates often try to avoid issues on which groups feel intensely.

annual income? Should children be bused to foster integration of the public schools? These are the issues on which one expects political candidates to stake out clear positions and give the public a real choice. But that does not often happen. An analysis of election strategies in a two-party system will explain why.

STRATEGY ON ISSUES

Imagine an issue scale similar to the ones we used in Chapter 6. Citizens can take positions on the left or the right or in the middle. Assume also that citizens will vote for the candidate whose position is closest to their own. Where will the candidate who wants to win the most votes position himself? The answer is that in an electoral system like ours the candidate who wants to maximize his chance of winning will take a position as close to the middle of the road as possible.

The impact of our system of elections on the way candidates for office campaign is profound. As we saw in Chapter 10, we have a *winner-take-all* system. In presidential races the candidate with the most votes wins (subject to some strange things that can happen in the Electoral College, to be discussed shortly). The same is true in races for Congress. The candidate with the highest vote wins the seat. Those who come in second get nothing. This, as we have shown, differs from the system of proportional representation used in many nations with parliamentary systems, where the number of seats won by any party is proportional to the party's share of the electoral vote.

If a party that receives, say, 20 percent of the vote can get some share of government power by winning seats in the parliament, it may choose to direct its appeal to a small proportion of the public. It can take a position on the left or on the right, receive the votes of the minority that shares its views, and elect some members of parliament. But if only one candidate can win, the winning election strategy is to try to attract a large number of voters, indeed the *largest* number of voters. And this means that a candidate will move toward a compromise, middle-of-the-road position.

This situation is illustrated in Figure 11.1. Imagine an issue (e.g., welfare spending) on which one can take a left, center, or right position; that is, one can favor spending a lot, a moderate amount, or nothing. The voting public is spread out along the scale—some citi-

FIGURE 11.1
Issue Scale

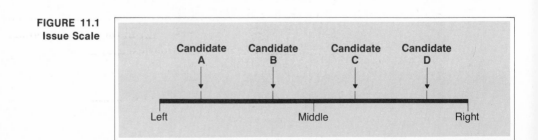

zens are on the left, some in the middle, and some on the right. If a candidate takes a position on the far left (call him candidate A) and runs against a candidate only slightly to the right of center (call him candidate C), it is clear that there are more voters close to C than to A. Similarly, if a right-wing candidate (candidate D) runs against a candidate slightly to the left of center (candidate B), B will get more votes. If the Democratic candidate (who is usually to the left) wants to maximize votes and the Republican candidate (who is usually to the right) wants to do the same, they will probably wind up close to the center, near the positions of B and C. The farther either candidate moves from the center, the more that candidate risks losing votes to his opponent.

Usually candidates who want to maximize their vote stick close to the middle. In some elections, however, a political party has nominated a candidate who is farther from the middle of the road. In 1964 the Republicans nominated Barry Goldwater, a self-styled conservative. He was opposed by Lyndon Johnson, who took a position closer to the center. Goldwater suffered a resounding defeat as many Republicans deserted him to choose the more moderate Johnson. In 1972 a similar thing happened on the other end of the political spectrum. The Democrats nominated George McGovern, who took a position toward the left end of the political scale. He too went down to defeat as Democrats crossed over to vote for Nixon. In each case the losing candidate was the one who presented the clearest electoral alternative. Goldwater's campaign slogan in 1964 was to give the American people "a choice, not an echo." He did. And the American public demonstrated that, given a choice, it would take the echo.[1]

The Special Position of Party Activists The preceding discussion suggests that candidates who want to win should take a middle-of-the-road position on most issues. But the situation may be more complicated for the candidate. As we saw in the previous chapter, each of the political parties is divided internally, with the party activists likely to take positions farther from the center of the politican spectrum than the views of ordinary party supporters. Democratic activists are more liberal than rank-and-file Democrats; Republican activists are more conservative than rank-and-file Republicans. The candidate who moves to the middle of the road to maximize his vote may alienate some of his most active supporters—the people who contribute time or money to a campaign. Furthermore, party activists are most important in the nomination process. They are more likely to vote in primaries; they are more likely to wind up as convention delegates. In order to win the nomination a candidate

[1] See Norman H. Nie, Sidney Verba, and John R. Petrocik, *The Changing American Voter* (Cambridge, Mass.: Harvard University Press, 1976), Chap. 18, for data on the subject.

may have to take a strong liberal or conservative position. To win the election he may have to take a more moderate one.

The complexity of this situation puts great pressure on the candidate to find a position that will gain the support of party activists and at the same time maximize his appeal to the public at large. The difficulty of this balancing act was seen during the 1976 election. President Ford chose Senator Robert Dole as his vice-presidential candidate. He did this in order to maintain the support of the large number of active conservative Republicans who had supported Ronald Reagan and were very active in the Republican party. Many observers felt that Ford should have chosen a more liberal running mate in order to compete better with Jimmy Carter in the general election. Some observers feel that the choice of Dole as a running mate made Ford less attractive to the electorate. In trying to satisfy conservative activists in his party (whose support he needed) he lost some votes (which he also needed).

The dual goal that a candidate is called upon to pursue sometimes leads to inconsistencies during a campaign. Often the activists who work for the nomination of a candidate are disappointed by his campaign. He does not sound as committed to a policy position that they like (a liberal or conservative one) as he was before the nomination. The reason is that the candidate is modifying his stand in order to appeal to as wide a range of voters as possible.

There are a number of strategies that a candidate can use in trying to maximize his vote in a situation in which the middle position is the winning one. The one that we have already discussed is to take a moderate position on the issue. Another strategy is to try to make the public think the opposing candidate is far from the middle of the road; that he is on the extreme left or right. As a glance at Figure 11.1 will show, it is to a candidate's advantage if he can make the public think his opponent is at the end of the issue spectrum. In 1964 Johnson characterized Goldwater as extremely conservative, and in 1972 Nixon characterized McGovern as a leftist.

Another possible approach is deliberate ambiguity. If a candidate is far from the center, voters may vote against him. They cannot do this if they do not know where he is. An example of successful use of ambiguity is found in Richard Nixon's 1968 campaign. Vietnam was a major issue. The public was unhappy and tired of the war but divided on what it wanted done. Nixon wanted to exploit the unhappiness, much of which was directed at the incumbent Democratic administration, without alienating voters who wanted to escalate to win the war or those who wanted to withdraw our troops. His solution was to announce that he had a plan but that he could not reveal it.

PARTIES IN AMERICA

Political parties used to play a major role in organizing political campaigns. A candidate for office must somehow convince thousands or even millions of voters that he is the best person for the job.

How to make the case? Either the candidate himself or his campaign workers must see that speeches are planned, publicity material distributed, advertisements put in newspapers, radio and TV announcements made, and when possible, individual voters contacted. Political campaigning is very complicated. It can also be expensive.

The political parties provided a skeleton organization that came to life around election time. "Coming to life" meant that party officials opened temporary election headquarters, volunteer workers licked stamps, and contributors were asked to write checks.

In recent years party control over campaigning has dwindled. The presidential campaign is no longer organized by the political parties. It is under the control of the candidate's personal group of advisers. Richard Nixon, for instance, ran his campaign through an organization—the Committee to Re-elect the President (CREEP)—that was independent of the Republican National Committee. Jimmy Carter's campaign was managed by the group of political advisers from Georgia that had carried him through the primaries, rather than by any regular Democratic party organization. This tendency to use personal organizations has reduced the significance of the political parties.

CAMPAIGN FINANCE

Before 1976, political campaigns had become prohibitively expensive. The 1972 campaign for the Presidency cost the candidates and the parties more than $100 million. Senate and House races had soared in cost as well. Naturally the candidates needed all the money they could get. The Watergate scandal revealed widespread abuses in campaign contributions. Direct contributions from corporate funds, unlawful since 1907, were among the abuses discovered in the Watergate investigations. Corporate executives were pressured by leading members of the Nixon administration. Claude C. Wild, former vice-president of Gulf Oil Corporation, who pleaded guilty to making an illegal contribution of $100,000 to the Nixon campaign, told the Senate Watergate Committee: "I consider it considerable pressure when two Cabinet officers [Attorney General John Mitchell and Secretary of Commerce Maurice Stans] ask me for funds—that is just a little bit different than somebody collecting for the Boy Scouts." By late 1974, 13 corporations had admitted making illegal contributions to the Nixon campaign, including American Airlines, Associated Milk Producers, Goodyear Tire, Minnesota Mining and Manufacturing, and Northrop.

The Republican party has also received major support from officials of corporations with large federal contracts. Table 11.1 lists 1972 campaign giving by officers and directors of various corporations heavily involved in Department of Defense, Atomic Energy Commission, and National Aeronautic and Space Administration (NASA) contract work. The advantage of the Republican party is clear.

TABLE 11.1
Campaign Contributions (1972)
from Officials of Corporations
with Large Federal Contracts

Corporation	Contributions to Republicans	Contributions to Democrats
Litton Industries	$277,709	$ 500
Hughes Aircraft	248,500	5,700
AT&T	132,560	103,991
Northrop	197,500	3,000
RCA	191,352	8,148
Westinghouse Electric	183,850	3,800
LTV	139,142	16,250
General Dynamics	149,906	750
Ford Motor	112,176	36,620
General Motors	127,628	6,207

Source: Based on data from *Dollar Politics*, vol. 2 (Washington, D.C.: *Congressional Quarterly*, 1974).

CAMPAIGN FUNDING REFORM

The abuses revealed by the Watergate investigations led to major legislation in 1974 and 1976 that tried to control campaign funding. There are three main parts to the legislation: (1) limits on the amount of money an individual or an organization can give, (2) limits on how much candidates for various national offices can spend, and (3) provision for public funding of Presidential elections. (See Figure 11.2) Under the law individuals may contribute no more than $1,000 to any one candidate per election and no more than $25,000 to all candidates in any single year. The massive contributions of 1972 are no longer possible.

FIGURE 11.2
Major Provisions of Campaign
Finance Reform

Contribution Limits. $1,000 per individual for each primary, runoff, and general election, and an aggregate contribution of $25,000 for all federal candidates annually; $5,000 per organization, political committee, and state party organization for each election.

Candidate and family's contributions: $50,000 for President; $35,000 for Senate; $25,000 for House.

Individual unsolicited expenditures on behalf of a candidate limited to $1,000 a year.

Cash contributions of over $100 and foreign contributions barred.

Spending Limits. Presidential primaries—$10 million total per candidate for all primaries.

Presidential general election—$20 million.

Presidential nominating conventions—$2 million each major political party, lesser amounts for minor parties.

Senate primaries—$100,000 or eight cents per eligible voter, whichever was greater.

Senate general elections—$150,000 or 12 cents per eligible voter, whichever was greater.

House primaries—$70,000.

House general elections—$70,000.

The first government subsidy of campaign costs in American history. Checks go out to eleven primary candidates in 1976 election.

It may be too early to tell what the overall effect of campaign finance reform on the parties will be. In some ways it weakens the parties. The campaign funding law provides matching funds for primary candidates who qualify by demonstrating fairly widespread support—the ability to raise $5,000 in small contributions in each of 20 states. But once past that hurdle, candidates receive a big boost from the public funding to which they become entitled. This boost may be particularly useful to candidates without regular party support. It is generally agreed that public funding helped Jimmy Carter, an outsider with little party support, to win the nomination.

In addition, the limitation on spending imposed on presidential campaigns by the law may reduce the amount a candidate will put into campaign organization. In 1976 the law imposed a spending ceiling of $21.8 million on each of the candidates as a condition for acceptance of the public funds. This was a good deal less than had been spent in previous years. The result was a cutback in the activities traditionally organized by political parties. There were fewer bumper stickers, buttons, billboards, posters. There were fewer storefront campaign headquarters. And because the money to finance the campaign came from the public treasury, there was less need for the fund-raising dinners and picnics that political parties used to organize. All in all, there were fewer reasons for the local Democratic or Republican organization to be active.

The campaign finance law reduced the organizational role of the parties; at the same time, it encouraged other organizations to take greater part in the election. The campaign law protects the right of labor unions to communicate with their members in the interest of a political candidate—by mail, telephone, and door-to-door canvassing. The Democratic candidates benefited from this manpower. The law gave corporations parallel authority for partisan campaigning among their executives and stockholders, but few exercised this right in behalf of the candidacy of President Ford.

On the other hand, public funding also aids the two major parties, not at primary time but in the presidential election. There are several reasons for this. For one thing, it gives the two established parties some advantage over third parties. The two major parties qualify for public funding before the election campaign begins because they were major contenders in the previous election. A new party has a harder time obtaining public funds. It is entitled to funds if it received 5 percent of the vote in the past election. If it did not, or if it is just starting up, it receives no support during the campaign. After the election it is reimbursed for expenses if it receives 5 percent of the vote. But the funds are not there to help it achieve the necessary electoral success.

The limitation on spending makes it difficult for new and unknown candidates to reach the electorate. This, it is argued, helps incumbents who are already known and who have the resources of their offices to help get their message across. This argument is uncertain: Incumbent candidates already had the advantages of being in office and being better known before the campaign funding reforms went into effect. They also had advantages in raising private funds, advantages that the new laws reduce.

CAMPAIGN STRATEGY AND THE ELECTORAL COLLEGE

A candidate for the Presidency must decide where to put his time and effort. Should he campaign in every state, concentrate on the most populous states, or concentrate on states where the election is going to be close?

These are exactly the kinds of questions that must be answered by the campaign strategy. They are important because of the Electoral College. The writers of the Constitution intended the Electoral College to serve as a method of choosing a President and Vice-President using a small group of respected citizens. Alexander Hamilton states the case in *The Federalist* (No. 68). The choice of a President "should be made by men most capable of analyzing the qualities adapted to the station. . . . A small number of persons, selected by their fellow citizens from the general mass, will be most likely to possess the information and discernment requisite to such complicated investigations." This small number of persons, the Electoral College, was to be chosen by the state legislatures.

This ancient institution still plays a major role in presidential selection, though not the role the founders intended. It has become an institution of popular democratic control. Each state has a number of electoral votes equivalent to the size of its congressional delegation. This number ranges from 45 (California) to 3 (6 small states and the District of Columbia have only 3 votes each). Electoral votes are bound by the unit rule; that is, all of the electoral votes of a state go to the presidential candidate who wins a plurality of the votes in that state. This rule makes the largest states—the urban, industrial states—most important politically. For instance, the candidate who can win the two largest states (California and New York) has nearly one-third of the electoral votes he needs to win the Presidency (86 out of 270).

This situation has had a major impact on twentieth-century politics. Because large states can be so much more important than small ones (the electoral vote of California is worth the combined electoral votes of 13 small states), the large states tend to dominate the nomination process. This bias carries over into the campaign as both parties concentrate on winning the large states. For the Democrats this means making a special appeal to party supporters in the large cities in these states, especially the ethnic groups and minorities. Thus a new Democratic President, mindful of the importance of these groups to his election, is anxious to represent their interests in the national government. For the Republicans, who have a different national constituency, the political effects of the Electoral College system are less pronounced.

The Electoral College makes it possible that the candidate with the most votes may not win the presidential election. This has happened three times. John Quincy Adams in 1824, Rutherford B. Hayes in 1876, and Benjamin Harrison in 1888 entered the White House despite the fact that they ran second in the popular vote. In 1976 Carter won 50.1 percent of the popular vote compared to 49.9 percent for Ford. However, if, for instance, Ford had won the state of New York (which he came close to doing) he would have won a majority of the electoral vote, and thus retained the Presidency, even though Carter had the largest popular vote. Indeed, in the 1976 election the shift of only 9245 votes in Ohio and 3678 votes in Hawaii would have led to the reelection of Gerald Ford, despite the fact that his opponent received more than 1½ million more votes.

The possibility that the candidate with the largest popular vote will lose the presidential election is the most serious criticism of the Electoral College. There are other objections. These include the winner-take-all system, whereby a candidate who carries a state, even by the narrowest of margins, gets all of that state's electoral votes. Many people feel that this disenfranchises those who vote for other candidates. These voters elect no members of the Electoral College. Furthermore, the electors are legally free to vote for whomever they want. Though electors are pledged to vote for a particular candidate, technically any elector can violate that pledge and thereby thwart the public's will.

The last important objection is to the provision that if no candidate receives a majority of the electoral vote the members of the House of Representatives choose among the three top candidates. Each delegation casts one vote, and a majority of the states is needed for election. (This happened once, in 1824.) A House that is controlled by one party can overthrow a popular preference for the candidate of the other party. The provision also makes it possible for a third-party candidate to prevent either major-party candidate from winning in the Electoral College and, in turn, play a crucial role in determining who wins in the House by giving his support to one of the candidates. Many observers thought that George Wallace would play such a role, but he never had the opportunity.

Reforming the Electoral College   In 1977, in response to this criticism Senator Birch Bayh, with the active support of President Carter, introduced an amendment to the Constitution. The proposed amendment provides for direct popular election of the President. This would eliminate many of the problems associated with the Electoral College. Under the amendment the presidential candidate with the largest popular vote would be elected. However, if no candidate won 40 percent of the vote the decision would pass to a joint session of Congress, with each member having one vote.

Though the plan eliminates many of the failings of the Electoral

College, it is opposed by many people who prefer the present system. They argue that we should not exchange a system that has worked quite well for a new one that may have unanticipated problems. Representatives of important voting blocks in some large states also oppose the change. It would deprive them of the special position they enjoy when they can swing a state and all its electoral votes in one direction or another.

Leaders of some small states fear that they will lose the slight additional power they receive under the Electoral College system. Under the present system each state receives a number of electors equal to the number of its senators and representatives. Small states such as Alaska, Vermont, Nevada, and Delaware would lose strength if their vote was only proportional to their population. Lastly, many argue that the Electoral College strengthens the power of the two main parties by making it more difficult for a third-party candidate. Such a candidate has to carry an entire state to have any chance of success in the Electoral College. Given the weakness of the parties, the critics of change oppose the new system because they do not want to see the parties further weakened.

At this writing the amendment has a long way to go. Even if it were approved by Congress, it would have a difficult time obtaining support in the required three-fourths of the state legislatures. Enough states stand to lose electoral influence under the new scheme so that its chances of making it through the long amendment process are slim.

The American Voter

We have discussed how candidates present themselves to the voters. But how do voters respond? The voting behavior of the American public has been closely studied by political scientists for many years.

Detailed survey studies of the American electorate began in the 1950s. The classic study was conducted by a group of University of Michigan scholars and reported in their book, *The American Voter.* They found that the American voter was quite different from the "rational voter" of democratic theory. The rational voter is one who has clear views on the issues of the day, knows where the candidates stand, and votes for the one who stood for policies that the voter wants.

The American electorate of the 1950s was not like this. For one thing, the public was relatively poorly informed on political matters. It often lacked the information about the positions of candidates that would be needed in deciding which candidate to support. Even more striking was the fact that citizens did not appear to have well-formed opinions on a large number of public issues. They might give researchers answers to questions on all sorts of issues, but the answers usually were not carefully formed opinions. (In one study a researcher asked a sample of Americans their opinion on the

"Metallic Metals Act." The act did not exist, but 70 percent had an opinion for or against it.)[2]

Furthermore, these studies showed that most Americans did not think about politics in ways that were familiar to better-informed citizens. Journalists, scholars, and politicians themselves are likely to have consistent positions on many issues. One can call them "liberal" or "conservative" or "radical" because they will take a consistent stand on a variety of political matters. Thus a liberal is someone who takes the following positions: He or she favors faster school desegregation and supports programs to reduce segregation in housing; on matters of social welfare he or she favors increased federal spending; on foreign affairs he or she favors a more conciliatory attitude toward the communist world. And the conservative would hold the opposite position: He or she would want to go slowly on integration, reduce welfare spending, and take a hard line in foreign affairs. In each case the person's positions on specific issues would be part of a more general outlook.

The studies of the American public conducted in the 1950s and early 1960s found that the average American rarely held such clear political views. People rarely thought in liberal or conservative terms when they evaluated candidates. Most striking was the fact that there was almost no relationship between a citizen's position on one issue and his or her position on other issues. If the average citizen was conservative on matters of race, he or she was as likely to be liberal as conservative on matters of welfare policy or foreign policy. Any one position could not be predicted from other positions.

This had important implications for American politics. It meant that the results of elections did not depend on the issues, since the public was uninformed about where the candidates stood on the issues and, in any case, did not hold consistent positions on those issues. The lack of clear positions on issues also meant that there was less chance of a sharp division of the American people into conservative and liberal camps. The citizen who was conservative on one matter was likely to be liberal on another—and therefore would not fit easily into one camp or another.

Thus it is no wonder that citizens were not rational voters. They could not vote for the candidate whose position they favored because they did not have information about the positions of the candidates and, worse, did not have clear and consistent opinions that could guide them in voting.

The Party-Oriented Voter Why did they vote the way they did? Voters can choose on the basis of one or more of three considerations: the party affiliation of the candidate, the candidate's position

[2] Stanley J. Payne, *The Art of Asking Questions* (Princeton, N.J.: Princeton University Press, 1951), p. 18.

on the issues, or the candidate's personality or character. Here is the view of a "party" voter: "I am a loyal Democrat, just as my parents were. The Democrats have always been the best for working people like me. I don't know much about that Jimmy Carter. But he's the Democrat and he'll get my vote." Here is an "issue" voter: "The nation is going to have to do something about inflation. Carter talks about it, but he's really for big spending. Ford is more likely to do something about inflation. If prices keep going up, my paycheck won't be worth anything. I'll vote for Ford." And here is a voter focusing on personality or character: "We need someone we can trust in the White House. He's got to be fair and honest. I'm just not sure about Carter. But Ford is a really level and honest person."

Of the three factors, party identification was the best predictor of how an individual would vote. Seventy-seven percent of the public identified with one or the other of the major parties. This identification appeared to be a long-term and stable one. Most citizens inherited such identification from their parents (just as one might inherit one's religion) and kept it throughout their lives.

Furthermore, party identification was a key to the vote. Most citizens voted for the candidate of the party they identified with. This was especially true in congressional races. In 1956, 91 percent of the voters stuck to their party in the congressional race. Voters might leave their party to vote for a popular presidential candidate—millions of Democrats voted for Eisenhower in 1952 and 1956. But they did so because of his personal popularity, not because they agreed with his issue positions. And though they crossed the line to vote for the candidate of another party, they continued to think of themselves as Democrats.

Studies done during the 1950s found the American voter quite different from the model of the rational voter. Voters identified with a political party and voted along party lines. If they left that party, it was not because they disagreed with the candidate of their own party.

In Chapter 5 we distinguished between two ways in which citizens can act in politics: on the basis of *cultural commitments* or on the basis of *rational calculation of interest*. The early voting studies found that citizens voted on the basis of long-term commitment to a political party. They did not calculate their interest in having one candidate win over another.

But the 1950s were an unusual period in American history: A popular World War II hero, Dwight Eisenhower, was in the White House; there were no serious domestic or foreign problems; and political conflict was relatively calm. In periodic studies since then we can trace some important changes in the public.

THE CHANGING AMERICAN VOTER

In the years since the 1950s citizens seem to have become more issue oriented. More and more citizens have relatively consistent political attitudes. If they are conservative on one issue, they are conservative on other issues; if they are liberal on one, they are liberal on others. Political opinions are less random than in earlier years. Furthermore, citizens more often judge candidates on the basis of their issue positions. In each presidential election since 1952 the University of Michigan Survey Research Center has asked citizens what they liked and disliked about the candidates. Some people mention the personality of the candidate; some mention the party of the candidate ("I like X because he is a good Democrat"); others talk about the issues the candidate stands for. Figure 11.3 shows the percentage of the public in each of the elections since 1952 that mentioned the personality of the candidate, his party, and his issue positions. Note that citizens still give a lot of attention to the personality of the candidate. About 80 percent mention this in each election year. But the striking change is the fall in the percentage of citizens who like or dislike a candidate on the basis of their party affiliation coupled with the rise in the percentage of citizens who judge candidates by their issue positions.

There are many indications that political parties are no longer as important as they used to be. In 1956 almost all Americans—77 percent—had a long-term commitment to one or the other party; by 1974 the percentage had fallen to about 60 percent. A majority still identified with one or the other party, but the portion had fallen quite a bit. More important, perhaps, young voters coming into the electorate at the end of the 1960s and early 1970s were as likely to call themselves independents as to identify with one of the major

FIGURE 11.3
Frequency of Evaluation of Candidates in Terms of Party Ties, Personal Attributes, and Issue Positions

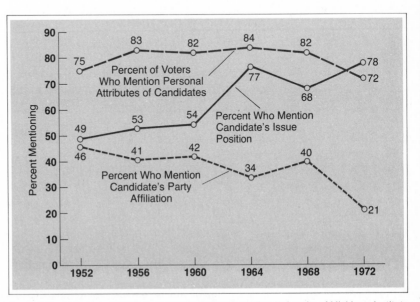

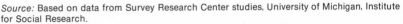
Source: Based on data from Survey Research Center studies, University of Michigan, Institute for Social Research.

parties — a big change from earlier times. And even among those who continued to identify with a party, more and more were voting for the other party's candidate or splitting their tickets.

Issue Voting As the importance of party as a guide to the vote has gone down, the importance of issues has gone up. Figure 11.4 shows the correlations between the issue positions of citizens and their vote and between their party identification and the vote. The higher the correlation between issue position and the vote, the more it means that citizens vote in ways that are consistent with their issue positions (that is, they vote for a liberal candidate if they are liberal themselves, for a conservative if they are conservative). The higher the correlation between party identification and the vote, the more it means that citizens vote in ways that are consistent with their party affiliation (vote for a Democrat if they are Democrats, for a Republican if they are Republicans). Note how as the correlation between party identification and the vote declines the correlation between issue position and the vote goes up.

This does not mean that the average voter carefully weighs the issue positions of candidates before deciding how to vote. Studies continue to show that the public often lacks basic political information. In 1972 only about half of the citizens (53 percent) knew the name and party affiliation of *one* of their senators; only 36 percent could name both senators and identify their parties. And even when issues become more important, as Figure 11.4 illustrates for recent elections, the correlation between issue position and the vote is still weaker than that between party identification and the vote. In short, citizens are voting on the issues and are less closely tied to their parties. But this does not mean that citizens are finally living up to the model of the rational voter.

Party identification is less important, but it still plays a role. Candidates can count on a high portion of the vote from those who identify with their party. This is especially true when there are no

FIGURE 11.4
As the Correlation Between Party Identification and the Vote Has Gone Down, the Correlation Between Issue Position and the Vote Has Gone Up

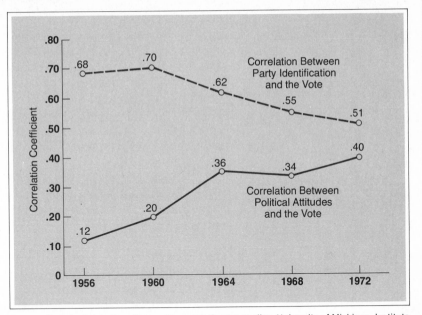

Source: Based on data from Survey Research Center studies, University of Michigan, Institute for Social Research.

other forces—a particularly popular or unpopular candidate or a particularly important set of issues—that would lead a voter to vote for the opposition party's candidate. In the 1972 election only 67 percent of the self-identified Democrats voted for George McGovern, the Democratic candidate for President, largely because of dissatisfaction with him as a person and disagreement with his issue positions. But in 1976, when there was less negative reaction to Jimmy Carter as a person and less reason to reject him because of his issue positions (which were not distinctive in the eyes of the electorate), Carter received about 8 out of 10 Democratic votes. And Gerald Ford received a similar portion of the votes of Republicans.

Party identification, furthermore, plays a bigger role in congressional elections. Congressional candidates are less well known than the presidential candidates. The issues they stand for and their personal characteristics count for less.

In sum, a changing American electorate has reduced the importance of parties. More voters are independent; more voters choose candidates for reasons other than their party. Parties continue to supply labels for the candidates, but the labels mean less. Voters are more likely than they once were to vote for the candidate rather than for the party label. Nevertheless the labels remain important in one respect. Republicans are increasingly willing to vote for a candidate under a Democratic label and Democrats to vote for a Republican. But most voters reserve their votes for a candidate who runs under one of the two major party labels.

The Mass Media in Campaigns

One effect of campaign finance limitations on the presidential campaign is to encourage the use of the media — particularly television — as the main campaign communications channel. As the media grow in importance party influence declines. The spending limits in the 1976 election compelled each of the candidates to concentrate resources on television and other forms of advertising rather than on other forms of campaigning. One estimate calculates that Ford spent $12 million on television, or more than half of his total budget. Carter's media expenses also amounted to approximately half of his spending.

The television debates contributed to the decline in the importance of the parties. The presidential opponents had three widely publicized and widely watched television debates, viewed by 75 to 80 million Americans. Much of what the public learned about the candidates was learned from the debates.

Why did the debates reduce the importance of the parties? To answer this question we must remember the three criteria voters use in making up their minds about whom to support: party loyalty, the issue positions of the candidates, and the personal qualities of the candidates. We saw that party voting has traditionally been used by voters who are reluctant to make the effort to learn a great deal about the candidates. The easiest thing is just to vote according to your party loyalties.

But the advantages of party voting are reduced when there is as much media exposure as there was in the 1976 election. A great deal of information about the candidates and their positions on issues is as close as the TV on-off switch. The typical voter is now less dependent on party leaders to supply information about the candidate.

The media are particularly important when the voters are in a mood to stress personal qualities in making their choices. Television allows the voters to take a good look at a candidate and to form a judgment about the kind of person he is. Does he speak with conviction? Is he the kind of person who can be trusted? Does he seem to care about people like me? Does he have leadership qualities? In asking these kinds of questions the voter emphasizes the personal qualities of the candidate and not his party.

Furthermore, the nature of the audience for television differs, as we have suggested, from that of the audience for in-person political rallies. The rally audience is likely to be partisan and candidates can stress partisan positions. The TV audience is made up of voters from both parties as well as independents. Candidates will downplay party when talking to them.

Congressional Elections

When scholars first studied congressional voting — the first major study was of the 1958 election — they found a pattern similar to that found in presidential elections. Voters knew little about the issue

About 80 million Americans watched the debates between the presidential candidates in 1976.

positions of candidates, but the picture of an unaware public was even more dismal when it came to congressional elections. As we have shown, about half of the voters (not half of the people, but half of those who are interested enough to vote!) had neither read nor heard anything about either candidate. The voters could hardly be blamed for this, however. The same study looked at local newspapers and found that the congressional race was covered in a very scanty way.

In this sense the situation differed from that found in presidential elections. If voters were not well informed about the issue positions of presidential candidates, they at least knew who the candidates were and had views about their personal characteristics. When it came to congressional elections neither the issues nor the candidates' personal characteristics seemed to make any difference. The main determinant of the vote seemed to be party affiliation — Democrats voted for the Democratic candidate, Republicans for the Republican candidate. Congressional elections were party elections to a greater extent than presidential elections were. Since voters had no clear sense of who the congressional candidates were, there was little chance for a popular congressional candidate to capture votes from the opposite party the way Dwight Eisenhower captured Democratic votes in his presidential race.

Though the public has grown more concerned about issues at the presidential level, there is less evidence of change at the congressional level. Recent studies show that the public remains fairly ignorant of congressional races—of the candidates as personalities as well as their issue stands. The mass media have taken a dominant position in informing voters about the election. But television focuses on the President. It does not expose the public to congressional candidates.

The result is that congressional races have remained partisan contests to a much greater extent than presidential races. The Democratic party, as we have seen, enters an election with a lead. There are twice as many Democratic-identifying as Republican-identifying voters in the electorate (about 40 percent to 20 percent). At the presidential level a Republican candidate can overcome this disadvantage. Voters know who the candidates are and can evaluate them independently of their party affiliation. At the congressional level the candidate's party affiliation is a more important cue to the voter.

As a consequence, while the Presidency has switched from party to party, the Democrats have had uninterrupted control of Congress for the past quarter-century. They have had a two-to-one margin in recent congressional elections, and it looks as if they will continue to enjoy this advantage.

Recent studies have found, however, that congressional voting is not simply a partisan matter. But what else can guide voting in congressional elections if voters know little about the individual candidates? The answer, according to the research, is that voters react to general forces in the nation as a whole. If the economy is doing well, if the President is seen as doing a good job, the voters reward the party of the incumbent President when it comes to congressional voting. It is an interesting fact that when voters deviate from their partisanship in voting for members of Congress they seen to respond not to the individual candidates but to general national forces. The effect of these national forces is felt most in congressional elections in a year when there is a presidential election as well. Congressional candidates suffer if there is an unpopular presidential candidate from their party; they benefit by riding on the "coattails" of a popular presidential candidate. In midterm elections the effect of presidential popularity and performance is still felt, but not as strongly.

SUMMARY: ARE THE PARTIES IN CRISIS?

Many observers describe the American party system in gloomy terms. It is easy to see why. Party loyalties have declined. The groups that formed the stable base of support for the parties can no longer be counted on. Party organizations are growing weaker. At the same time, the United States is faced with a new set of issues: equality between the races and the sexes; the environment; energy. Can the parties deal with these issues?

One way in which the American party system has adjusted to social change in the past is through party realignment. Can this happen now?

Party Realignment

MAINTAINING AND DEVIATING ELECTIONS

Most elections reaffirm the pattern of support that the public gives to the two major parties. These are called *maintaining* elections. Voters choose on the basis of party affiliation, and the distribution of party support determines the outcome. In other elections, sometimes called *deviating* elections, voters temporarily abandon their party to vote for a popular candidate or one whose issue position they prefer. Many Democrats voted for Eisenhower in 1952 and 1956 but remained Democratic. Many Republicans voted for Johnson in 1964 but remained Republicans. Maintaining and deviating elections leave the basic distribution of party loyalties unchanged.

THE NEW DEAL REALIGNMENT

From time to time an election or a series of elections brings about a major, permanent change in the composition of the political parties, as well as a shift in which party is dominant. The last such change took place during the Great Depression. Herbert Hoover was decisively defeated in 1932, ending a long era of Republican dominance in presidential politics. A new political coalition formed around the New Deal. It was based, as we have seen, on the urban workers in the North, many with immigrant backgrounds. The movement to the Democratic party had actually begun in 1928, when the Democrats ran Governor Al Smith of New York for the Presidency. He was the first Catholic chosen to run for the Presidency, and he greatly enhanced the appeal of the Democratic party to Catholics—mostly urban workers in the North—permanently attached themselves to the Democratic party during the 1930s. At the same time, the Democratic coalition kept control of the Solid South.

Recent research shows that the New Deal realignment depended on two factors: new issues and new voters.[3] The new issues were those of economic reform. The Democratic party stood for more active government involvement in regulating the economy and providing social welfare. But the new issues were not enough to create a new Democratic majority. What was also needed was a large group of voters who were not yet attached to a political party, voters who could be mobilized to support the Democratic party. These voters were found among the many young voters—often the children of immigrants—who entered the electorate in the 1930s as well as among many voters who had come of age in the 1920s but had never bothered to vote. It was not so much that many people abandoned the Republican party to become Democrats. It was that there were unattached voters ready to be tied to the Democratic party because of the new policies of the Roosevelt administration.

[3] Norman H. Nie, Sidney Verba, and John Petrocik, *The Changing American Voter* (Cambridge, Mass.: Harvard University Press, 1976). See Chap. 5 by Kristi Andersen.

REALIGNMENT TODAY: IS IT POSSIBLE? *YES 1992*

Can the crisis of the party system be turned around by a new party alignment? Many writers expect a reshuffling of the voters into a new liberal coalition opposed by a new conservative one. Others expect a re-creation of the old New Deal alignment rather than some new alignment.

If the realignment in the New Deal era depended on new issues and new voters, we would appear to be ready for another realignment. Many new issues have come onto the political agenda in recent years. There was the burning issue of Vietnam and the continuing concern about America's proper role in the world. There are the continuing issues of racial equality, sexual equality, the environment, and energy, not to mention traditional economic issues like unemployment and inflation.

Furthermore, there are new voters: the large portion of the electorate, mostly young, without partisan ties. Can they be molded into a new party coalition?

THE 1976 ELECTION: THE NEW DEAL RECREATED?

In many respects the 1976 election looked like a rebirth of the New Deal coalition. Carter received the votes of groups that have been loyal to the Democratic party for the past forty years: blue-collar workers, especially union members; blacks and other racial minorities; Jews and Catholics; the less well-off members of society. And he won the support of practically every southern state. In contrast, Ford was winning the votes of the western and midwestern states, which are more often Republican strongholds. And he gained the votes of farmers, professional and business groups, wealthier citizens, Protestants, and a majority of whites.

But there is little reason to believe that the coalition forged by President Carter represents the beginning of a new, stronger party system. Why not? Because there were new issues, changes in party support, and greater emphasis on the candidate as a person.

The New Issues In the New Deal era the two political parties offered a clear issue choice: The Democratic party was for the New Deal reforms, the Republican party opposed. The new issues that have arisen in the 1960s and 1970s are not ones on which the parties have offered clear alternatives. Vietnam was a bipartisan war, conducted first by a Democratic administration and then by a Republican one. Many new voters were concerned about the war, but they found neither party offering a clear choice. The result was not new party ties but a rejection of both parties. Race was another major new issue. But it, too, was not one that found the parties clearly arrayed one against the other. Racial conflict cuts right through the Democratic party.

Moreover, the issues crosscut each other. A Democratic coalition can unite working-class voters behind the issue of unemployment.

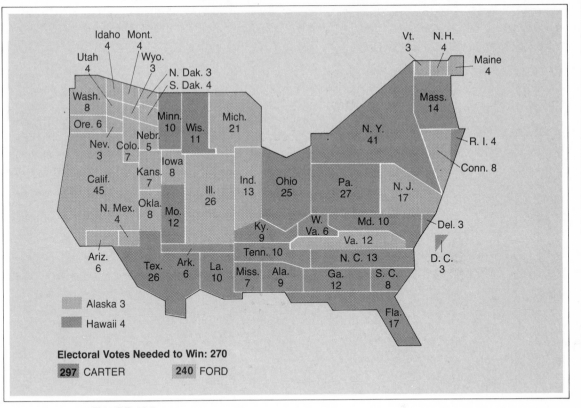

FIGURE 11.5
The Electoral Vote, 1976

But the workers split into blacks versus whites when it comes to issues such as busing to achieve school or housing integration or affirmative-action plans. A candidate like Carter can put together a temporary coalition—particularly if the issues of the election are such vague ones as honesty in government or opposition to big bureaucracy—but it may not have the permanence of the New Deal coalition. The New Deal era created deep commitments to the Democratic party. There is little evidence that such commitments were created in 1976.

The Party Supporters   The 1976 election found the groups that had supported the Democratic and Republican parties during the time of the New Deal coalition back in place, each supporting the proper party. But the support is a lot weaker today. The "solid" support that Carter appeared to receive in the South was not as solid as it had been in the New Deal days. Carter's victory there was based on heavy black support; he did not carry the majority of white voters in the South. (Figure 11.5 shows how the electoral votes were divided.) Aside from blacks, who are heavily Democratic, most of the social groups that previously formed the basis of support for one or

325

the other of the major parties are now more divided and less reliable in their support.[4] Carter carried the Catholic vote, but not as strongly as most earlier Democratic candidates had. More important is the fact that the vote may have been less for the party than for the person. Such voting does not form party commitments.

The Candidate, Not the Party The major way in which voters find out about candidates is through the media (rather than through party channels). The candidates run their campaigns through their personal organizations (not a party organization). All this means that a presidential victory is a victory for a particular candidate, not for his party. Whatever coalition was created is not likely to survive into the next election.

Parties and the Future

It may well be that we are in for a long period of weak political parties. Voters will vote as individuals, not as supporters of a particular party. Candidates will run as individuals, not as representatives of their party. What will be the consequences?

For one thing, there will be less continuity and predictability in American politics. We may see more candidates who are outsiders, as Carter was. Voters will judge them as individuals. The image they present through the media will play an important role in their success.

For another thing, the ability of the American public to hold political leaders accountable may be weakened. The political scientist V. O. Key claimed that voters hold elected officials to account *retrospectively*. They do not vote for particular policies that they hope to see enacted in the future. Rather, they make some evaluation of how things have gone in the past four years. If they like what they have seen, they reward the party that was in power by voting for it; if not, they vote against the previous administration.

This is an excellent way for citizens to maintain some control. It means that elected officials must constantly be on their toes; they have to "perform" or they will suffer the consequences in the next election. But these retrospective evaluations depend on some continuity in who is running for office. One has to be able to hold the candidates responsible for the actions of past administrations. This is still possible if one of the candidates is the incumbent, as Ford was in the 1976 presidential election. Otherwise the fact that candidates run as individuals, and not as party representatives, makes it difficult for voters to hold them to account. This is why Jimmy Carter deliberately dissociated himself from past Democratic administrations.

Political parties never played a very effective role in offering the public choices in elections. They did not offer programs that they

[4] See Nie et al., Chap. 12.

would carry out if their candidates were elected. But they provided the public with a basis for choice that had continuity from one election to the next. In future years the ability of the public to hold leaders accountable may be substantially weaker if our party system continues its decline.

A large number of citizens have withdrawn from any kind of electoral participation. Barely more than a majority of the eligible citizens even bothered to vote in 1972; in the 1974 congressional contests the number voting dropped to less than 40 percent. This low voting turnout is certainly a sign of dissatisfaction.

The American public is showing displeasure at the ways in which the two parties have responded to the social problems facing the

327

country. The major parties will attempt to accommodate them-selves to the new groups on the political scene. They will try to deal with the political agenda of inflation, recession, consumer protection, tax reform, social welfare, and street crime. They will not remain unchanged. And if they cannot absorb the new groups and deal with these issues, the two-party system as we have known it will fade. The inflexible party is a doomed party. But historically the party system has shown flexibility more than once.

controversy

In choosing its presidential ticket should a political party concern itself primarily with winning or should it stress the differences between the two parties? More often than not the two major parties nominate "centrist" presidential candidates; that is, they nominate candidates who can appeal to the middle ground in American politics. In doing so they smooth over important differences in political outlook between the Republicans and the Democrats. Most of the time the major parties purposely provide more echo than choice.

One Side The American voters respond favorably to presidential candidates who stand midway between a broadly conservative and a broadly liberal outlook. Since the job of political parties is to win elections, they should give the voters what they want. Recent nominations of "extreme" candidates have resulted in serious defeats. In 1964 the Republican convention nominated Senator Barry Goldwater, a spokesman of the conservative wing of the party. Goldwater led the Republican ticket to a major defeat as the Democratic nominees, Johnson and Humphrey, won more than 60 percent of the presidential votes. The election of 1972 was a repeat performance, except that this time the Democratic party chose a candidate, Senator George McGovern, who spoke for its liberal wing. McGovern's defeat by Nixon and Agnew was similar to Goldwater's defeat eight years earlier — and for many of the same reasons. A presidential candidate whose views are well to the left or right of center leads many voters to switch to the other party. This shows that voters prefer candidates, at least presidential candidates, who are middle-of-the-roaders.

Besides, crushing defeats like those suffered by Goldwater and McGovern can have unfortunate results if the winning party feels that the landslide victory has given it the right to do whatever it wants.

The Other Side While it is true that voters seem to prefer middle-of-the-road candidates, the major parties have a responsibility to values other than winning. They should give the voters a clear choice and use the presidential election as a chance to express different goals and policies for the nation.

Such a choice is especially important in a presidential campaign. Most American citizens pay attention to politics only at this time. If there is to be meaningful participation by the typical citizen, it can best occur during a presidential election year. If the typical citizen is going to think seriously about the alternatives facing society, he or she will do so in response to debates between presidential candidates. When the presidential campaign smooths over major differences about how to handle the problems of the nation, the democratic process is not working. The "me-too-ism" of most presidential campaigns denies the opportunity to have a national debate about significant issues.

A candidate who clearly differs from his opponent plays an important educating role, even if he loses. He reminds the nation that alternative policies are possible. This is part of the responsibility of leadership. In 1972, for instance, McGovern's strong antiwar stand might have contributed to his defeat, but perhaps it also contributed to the urgency with which the Nixon administration pursued peace negotiations that year. McGovern himself saw it this way: "There can be no question at all that we have pushed this country in the direction of peace, and I think each one of us loves the title of peacemaker more than any office in the land."

When the political parties fail to provide alternatives, they fail to provide leadership, and in this way they fail the American public.

12
CONGRESS: REPRESENTATION AND LEGISLATION

Article 1, Section 1 of the U.S. Constitution declares that "all legislative Powers herein granted shall be vested in a Congress of the United States, which shall consist of a Senate and a House of Representatives." Thus was created Congress, and in the remainder of Article 1 the duties, powers, and responsibilities of that body are set forth in detail.

The Roots of Congress

In creating a Congress the writers of the Constitution followed an ancient practice. In pre-Christian Greece and Rome special assemblies were chosen to make laws for the entire community. And if we stretch the language a bit, the tribal elders gathered around the chief in primitive societies resemble a legislative assembly. Americans, however, trace their legislative assembly to medieval British parliaments, the true ancestors of modern-day legislatures. In these medieval parliaments a selected few noblemen and clergymen met with the king to present the complaints of the estates for which they spoke. In its earliest days parliament was only a representative assembly: It *re*-presented the viewpoints of the important groups in society to the king. But it did not make laws. Only the king and his advisers could do that. Parliament did not become a legislative assembly until later, and this role was not firmly established until the eighteenth century.

By the 1780s, however, the American colonies had a lot of experience with their own legislative assemblies. And they liked what they had. The attempt of King George to whittle away the authority of these legislatures spurred the independence movement, for in the eyes of the colonists the royal governors (appointed by the king) in each colony were being given too much control, especially over economic affairs. Thus was born the effective political slogan "No taxation without representation." At first this was a rallying cry only for those who were demanding greater representation in the Parliament of England and greater independence for the colonial legislatures. When these demands were rebuffed the rebel movement became an open demand for independence.

After the war had been fought and won, the new nation had to set up political institutions that would avoid the excesses and arbitrariness of executive authority, whether that authority was a king or a governor or a president. The result was the separation-of-powers system, in which Congress cooperates with the executive but also stands against it. The power of political executives, the founders believed, is too often arbitrary and antidemocratic. A Congress would institutionalize a "counterelite," an independent group of leaders who would owe their careers and authority to popular election. It would check the excesses of executive power and at the same time remain close in its thinking to the voters it represents.

Representative Assemblies in the United States

"Representation is the grand discovery of modern times," wrote the Scottish philosopher James Mill, and his feeling is widely shared. Political representation is seen as a happy, workable compromise between the dangers of hereditary leadership and the difficulties of participatory democracy. This compromise is based on a belief in popular rule, but it recognizes that the people cannot actually govern themselves. Thus, as stated in *The Federalist*, political representation is an efficient "substitute for the meeting of the citizens in person."

THE POPULARITY OF REPRESENTATIVE GROUPS

Representative assemblies have been popular in the United States. In addition to Congress, there are state legislatures; village, township, and city councils; school boards; special-district commissions; and various county-level boards and commissions. All told, there are about 80,000 representative assemblies in the formal government structures in America. More than a half-million American citizens hold office as elected representatives. Representative principles have spread well beyond formal government. We find them throughout our economic and social life. Stockholders elect a board of directors to represent them and protect their interests against the managers of the firm. Union members elect officials who are supposed to govern the union in a manner that reflects member preferences. Voluntary associations in the thousands are led by elected representatives. We are introduced to political representation at an early age, as when we elect classmates to represent the homeroom on the student council. No political ideal, with the exception perhaps of majority voting, is as deeply a part of our political culture as the principle of representation itself.

Congress: The Responsive Branch

Of the three major branches of government—executive, legislative, judicial—the legislative branch, Congress, is supposed to be the most responsive to the public. Consider the Supreme Court. It has only nine members, who are appointed for life. It meets in secret; it is guided by the Constitution and by legal precedent; it announces major decisions in a technical language. The Supreme Court is remote from the hustle and bustle of everyday politics.

The executive branch is not as remote as the Supreme Court, but it is not completely accessible. It is often mysterious to the common citizen. The most visible and powerful part of the executive branch, the White House, keeps its distance. There is no visitor's gallery, as there is in Congress, where any citizen can walk in and watch the President and his advisers in action. Press conferences are held when the President wants to hold them. Carter campaigned on the promise that government would be more open than in the past. This promise has been hard to keep. It still takes a lot of attention by the press, members of Congress, and citizen groups to find out what is going on inside the White House.

Congress is very different from the Supreme Court and the White House. It is not nearly as solemn as the Court, nor is it as bureaucratic as the Presidency. It is made up of 535 men and women, all of whom want to be in the news. They come from every corner of the nation, and they carry with them the concerns and demands and hopes of a very complicated society. Congress is anything but remote from the hustle and bustle of everyday politics. It is at the center of those politics, the meeting place of journalists, lobbyists, protestors, and plain citizens.

CONGRESS AND DEMOCRACY

The burden of protecting the basic principles of democracy falls mainly on Congress. It is a big job. In the social and economic conditions of the twentieth century the ideas of popular rule are difficult to maintain. Huge nation-states, big defense budgets, industrialization, the mass media, and complicated social and economic issues make nonsense of the claim that people can govern themselves. At the least, democratic principles have been undermined by the growth of huge bureaucracies and the steadily growing role of the state in organizing and regulating (and manipulating) social life. The fascist governments of Europe shattered the belief that democracy was safe from tyranny. Stalinism killed the hope that communism as an economic system would somehow protect democracy where capitalism had failed. And the growth of the military-industrial complex has caused many people in the United States to question whether our political arrangements can keep power from shifting to the small number of individuals who manage the giant economic and political bureaucracies. Centralized organization and concentrated powers can too easily produce mass manipulation; democracy becomes the facade behind which the few direct the society. These are not groundless fears. Political representation is a major weapon against this tendency. If a democratic nation can protect its representative assembly, then the trend toward concentrated power is checked. The legislature is rooted in popular choice. If we cannot have government by the people, at least we can have government of and for the people.

How well is Congress doing its job? Many feel that it is failing.

Congress Under Attack

No institution of American government has received as much sustained criticism during the past several decades from political scientists, journalists, and even its own members as the U.S. Congress. Lethargic, labyrinthine, parochial, reactionary, inefficient, powerless, misguided, undemocratic—these are but a few of the words that have been used to describe Congress. Here we review some of the major charges.

A LOCAL INSTITUTION DEALING WITH NATIONAL ISSUES

Dissatisfaction with Congress has been based in large part on the complaint that the *institution* has not kept up with the *issues*. The issues with which the American government must deal are national in scope; Congress is essentially a local institution.

American society has become a national society. The issues that count are those that affect the whole society: transportation, housing, legal justice, national security, education. The nationalization of issues has occurred hand in hand with the nationalization of social institutions. Consider the institutions that matter in our society: the *National* Council of Churches, the *National* Baseball League, the *National* Association of Manufacturers, the *National* Education Association, the *National* Federation of Independent Business, the *National* Broadcasting Company. The Main St. Methodist Church remains, as do the community baseball team, the local shoe factory, the Horace Mann PTA, the corner drugstore, and the town radio station, but such local institutions have nowhere near the political importance of the huge national organization, a product of the twentieth century.

The federal government has both encouraged and suffered from the trend toward nationalization. Federal agencies and activities have grown in response to social problems that are national in scope. As transportation has become *trans-* and even *inter*national, the government has had to organize agencies such as the Federal Aviation Administration (FAA) to protect the safety and well-being of users. Medical research has implications for the entire nation, so

The busy day of a congressman leaves little time for recreation or exercise.

the government has created the National Institutes of Health and the National Science Foundation to fund and regulate this research. For every important issue one can think of—fiscal policy, unemployment, civil rights, highway safety, consumer protection—there are federal agencies and programs.

It is often said that Congress is ill equipped to play a serious role in formulating *national* programs. Yet Congress is supposed to represent and legislate for the American public. When you are bothered about the quality of life in America—traffic congestion, consumer prices, racial injustice, polluted rivers, street crime, mediocre schools, war spending—you are in fact bothered about issues that Congress has the constitutional authority to deal with.

THE CAREER OF A MEMBER OF CONGRESS

Although they serve in national office, members of Congress are closely tied to one particular part of the country. Most members have lived their entire life in the district or state they represent. They were educated at a local college or the state university. And if they went to law school, as more than half of them have, it was often to a local institution. If their career was business, it was not as an executive of a national corporation who was often transferred but, rather, in a business headquartered in their hometown.

The typical congressional career involves working through local office and perhaps the state legislature. At the turn of the century, three-fourths of the members of Congress had held state or local office; six decades later, despite the great changes in American society during that period, this career pattern was still true of two-thirds of the members. In contrast, while in 1900 about one-half of the top administrative leaders had held state or local office, in 1960 fewer than one-fifth of them had.

If recruitment stresses local ties, so does the continuing career. A member of the House of Representatives must stand for reelection every two years. He or she is hardly off to Washington before it is time to come home and campaign again. As the writers of the Constitution intended, this makes sure that representatives will not quickly forget their election promises. It also keeps them in close contact with local interests and local campaign organizations. Actually, however, members have rather long careers in Congress. Nine out of every ten who stand for reelection are successful. Being a representative or a senator is a career in itself; some people serve for their entire adult lives.

This pattern, it is claimed, contributes to the isolation of Congress from the changing issues of society. It leaves Congress under the control of people who first put together their winning coalition two or more decades ago. As long as these veterans continue to satisfy the narrow interests of a few key groups in their home districts or states, they can continue their congressional careers. The longer they stay, the easier it is to take care of voter interests, for it is the old-timers who, because of the seniority system, control the allocation of defense contracts, federal loans, funds for road construction, and similar "pork barrel" items. This leads to further isolation from national problems.

As summarized by Senator Richard Neuberger, "If there is one maxim which seems to prevail among many members of our national legislature, it is that local matters must come first and global problems a poor second—that is, if the member of Congress is to survive politically." A member of the House says, "My first duty is to get reelected. I'm here to represent my district. . . . This is part of my actual belief as to the function of congressmen. . . . What is good for the majority of districts is good for the country. What snarls up the system is these so-called statesmen-congressmen who vote for what they think is the country's interest . . . We aren't . . . paid to be statesmen."[1]

THE COMMITTEE SYSTEM AND THE SENIORITY RULE

Writing about the Congress of the late nineteenth century, Woodrow Wilson maintained that "there is one principle which runs through every stage of procedure, and which is never disallowed or abrogated —the principle that the Committees shall rule without let or hindrance. And this is a principle of extraordinary formative power. It is the mould of all legislation."[2] The critics argue that this characterization is as true of Congress today as it was in Wilson's day. The problem with committee dominance is that it gives a small group of members virtually total control over all legislation within a certain field. Though they legislate for the nation, these members are not accountable or responsible to the national citizenry but are accountable only to their local constituents. As a result congressional policy may not correspond with the preferences of a majority of the American people. In this sense the committee system is held to be undemocratic.

The critics also charge that the defects of the committee system are aggravated by the use of the seniority rule. This informal rule of the House and Senate requires that when a committee chairperson-ship—the most powerful formal position on a committee—becomes vacant, the successor should be the member from the majority party who has the longest continuous service on that committee. A member of Congress becomes chairperson simply by outlasting his or her colleagues. Thus the seniority system rewards length of committee service over ability. This is recognized in a revealing comment by Senator Byrd of Virginia: "Seniority of service and committee rank have importance over and above the capabilities of the

---

[1] The quotation from Senator Neuberger appears in Samuel P. Huntington, "Congressional Responses to the Twentieth Century," in David B. Truman, ed., *The Congress and America's Future* (Englewood Cliffs, N.J.: Prentice-Hall, 1965), p. 15. The second quotation appears in Lewis A. Dexter, "The Representative and His District," as reprinted in Theodore J. Lowi, ed., *Legislative Politics U.S.A.*, 2d ed. (Boston: Little, Brown, 1965), p. 86.

[2] From Woodrow Wilson, *Congressional Government* (first published in 1884).

members." (The fact that a member of Congress gains seniority through committee service, rather than through length of congressional service, strengthens the tendency of members to burrow deeper and deeper into a single legislative area rather than change committees.)

Seniority rewards age as well as long service, for the two cannot be separated. Congressional power passes into the hands of people in their sixties and seventies, many of whom built their winning coalitions around the issues of the 1930s and 1940s. Sometimes these individuals grow with the times, adjusting to new groups and new issues. But sometimes they do not. Reelected from safe, one-party districts, they can easily ignore a changing national political agenda. William Poage, a Texas congressman in his mid-seventies, was until 1975 chairman of the House Agriculture Committee. In committee hearings on a food stamp program for the poor, he asked a witness from the liberal Urban Coalition why he was "so concerned in maintaining a bunch of drones. You know what happens in the beehive? They kill those drones. That is what happens in most primitive societies. Maybe we have just gotten too far away from the situation of primitive man." (As we will see in a later discussion, recent reform of the seniority rule cost Representative Poage his chairmanship.)

There is a tendency for the committee and seniority systems to bias legislative policy in the direction of the views of a few individuals in each policy area, views that may run counter to the wishes of a national majority. It is charged that this tendency was responsible for the defeat of much of President John Kennedy's legislative program in the early 1960s — many major congressional committees were then controlled, and often chaired by, a conservative coalition of southern Democrats and Republicans.

SECRECY
Another major criticism of Congress has to do with the secrecy with which much of its business is conducted. This extends both to committee sessions, especially "executive sessions" (in which bills are put into final form) and floor voting (in which many decisions are reached without a record of individual votes). This secrecy makes the member of Congress less accountable for his or her actions, allowing him or her to take one stand in public while acting differently in private.

INSUFFICIENT STAFF
A frequently cited reason for poor congressional performance is insufficient staff assistance. It is argued that if Congress is to confront contemporary national problems it needs the assistance of numerous full-time, professional experts in such areas as housing, transportation, health care, and economics. In the past Congress has been most reluctant to increase its staff, fearing that voters will view this as fiscal irresponsibility, and has relied instead on experts in the executive branch. The critics maintain, however, that this

Congressional abuse of public position received much attention when Elizabeth Ray disclosed that she was being paid a government salary as a secretary, but that her duties were not secretarial.

makes Congress unduly subservient to the Presidency; furthermore, allowing present problems to go untreated will be, in the long run, far more expensive than making the modest investment necessary to increase Congress' technical competence.

PRESIDENTIAL DOMINATION

The concern that the legislature has become unduly subservient to the executive branch is a more recent criticism of Congress. It results from the events of the late 1960s and early 1970s: the Vietnam experience, in which the Presidency dominated Congress; the clash over domestic policy during the Nixon administration; the Watergate scandal; and revelations of abuses by the FBI and the CIA, both formally parts of the executive branch. The critics charge that Congress has become a mere responder to presidential initiative and has failed to exercise its responsibility to oversee the operation of government. They call on Congress to reassert its proper constitutional role as the principal policy-making organ of American government. (We will have more to say about the conflict between Congress and the Presidency in later chapters.)

CONGRESSIONAL ETHICS

One of the continuing criticisms of Congress is the charge that many members abuse their public position to satisfy their personal desires. Overseas vacations, or "junkets" — officially called fact-finding trips and subsidized by the taxpayers — have long been a target of attack by reformers. These charges were brought into sharp focus with the sex scandal of 1976, when Elizabeth Ray, nominally a secretary to Congressman Wayne Hays, chairman of the House Administration Committee, disclosed that she was being paid her government salary not to perform secretarial duties but to provide sexual favors to Hays. Within days of Ray's disclosure similar abuses surfaced, some of which apparently violated criminal statutes. In the past only extreme cases such as that of New York City Congressman Adam Clayton Powell in the 1960s had moved Congress to impose sanctions. (Powell was accused of improperly using public funds for foreign travel, falsifying expenditure reports, and making illegal salary payments to his wife.) Acting on the findings of a special committee, the House of Representatives refused to seat Powell in the 90th Congress (1967–1968). But in the mid-1970s, in the aftermath of Watergate, political ethics were a matter of increasing concern to the public. The House of Representatives responded by establishing an Ethics Committee to investigate charges of improper conduct. Congress is apparently making a serious attempt to clean its house.

CONGRESSIONAL OUTPUT

A final complaint about Congress is that it has not been a productive institution and is becoming even less so. In recent years there has

Planning strategy in the halls of Congress.

been a sharp decline in the number of laws passed by Congress. "The downward shift began in 1959 and has continued unabated from that point to the present with no indication that the present Congress will alter the trend."[3] However, balanced against this decline in the number of laws passed is an increase in the length of laws that are passed. Whereas twenty years ago the typical bill passed by Congress took only two pages to write out, today the typical bill will be more than five pages long. Table 12.1 presents data on both the decline in number of bills and the increase in length of bills.

Taken together, the two trends illustrated in Table 12.1 suggest that Congress may be spending more time on complex policy matters than on traditional and more routine business. The more complex the bill under consideration, the more parts it has and the longer it will be when it is finally passed. For example, an energy bill is likely to include sections on everything from speed limits to solar research, from price regulation to tax incentives. The more time that Congress spends debating and deciding on complex policy questions, the less time it has for routine bills; and the total volume of legislation will decrease.

Of course this raises the additional question of whether Congress is effectively organized to review, debate, and finally pass complex legislation. We will return to this issue later in the chapter when we talk about congressional committees.

Our Changing Congress

Congress is not a static institution. When it first came into being in 1789 it numbered only 81 members—59 in the House and 22 in the Senate. Sessions lasted only a few months, and after each session the part-time legislators returned to their regular occupations. The more important legislative issues were debated and resolved by the full houses. The nontechnical nature of the legislation, the breadth of experience and learning of the legislators, and the ample time for thorough deliberation made special standing committees and professional staff assistance unnecessary.

Our contemporary Congress is a far different institution indeed. Its 535 members, 435 in the House and 100 in the Senate, are now full-time legislators who are in session year-round. Most of the real legislative work is now done by committees; the full houses could not possibly study and debate the thousands of bills, some highly complex and technical, introduced during each session. And the day has long since passed when members of Congress could rely solely on their own knowledge and experience to make far-reaching policy decisions; expert information and advice are now essential to the legislative process.

[3] Donald Eilenstine, David L. Farnworth, and James S. Fleming, "Trends and Cycles in Legislative Productivity," unpublished paper. Cited in Allen Schick, "Complex Policymaking in the United States Senate," Commission on the Operation of the Senate (Washington, D.C.: GPO, 1977).

**TABLE 12.1
Public Bills Enacted,
1955–1974**

Congress	Years	Number of Public Laws	Average Number of Pages per Public Law
84	1955–56	1,028	1.8
85	1957–58	936	2.6
86	1959–60	800	2.2
87	1961–62	885	2.3
88	1963–64	666	3.0
89	1965–66	810	3.6
90	1967–68	640	3.6
91	1969–70	695	4.2
92	1971–72	607	3.8
93	1973–74	649	5.3

Source: Congressional Research Services prepared by Arthur Stevens. Cited in the Commission on the Operation of the Senate, *Policy Analysis on Major Issues* (Washington, D.C.: GPO, 1977).

In the context of this major historical change it might seem that Congress is not much different today than it was a decade ago: The size is the same; the Democrats remain in control; and the same standing committees dominate the legislative process. But this surface similarity is deceptive, for the 1970s have witnessed a series of major congressional reforms. *Congressional Quarterly,* a highly respected journal that covers the Washington scene, assesses the reforms enacted through the first session of the 94th Congress as follows:

> Over a six-year period from 1970 to 1975, Congress ended or revised long-established practices that critics claimed made it the most ossified of the nation's governmental institutions.
>
> The changes . . . produced a Congress that was much different at the end of 1975 than at the beginning of the decade.
>
> The changes produced a basic upheaval in the manner that power is held and exercised in Congress. Almost absolute authority had been vested through the seniority system in representatives and senators who had served longest. Their power was exercised primarily through the committee system and rarely was challenged successfully.
>
> The 1970–75 revisions overturned these traditional power preserves.[4]

Consider the following discussion of congressional reforms in the context of the major criticisms leveled against Congress. Does the Congress of the late 1970s warrant the same complaints that were directed against the Congress of the 1950s and 1960s? If some of the earlier criticisms are now out of date, are others still relevant?

THE REFORM OF THE SENIORITY SYSTEM
We have seen that the seniority rule made the selection of committee chairpersons in the House and Senate automatic. This had

[4] *Congressional Quarterly Almanac 1975,* 31 (1976), 26.

the effect of insulating the chairperson from control by the party leadership or the party caucus. As long as his position was secure he had no need to follow party policy. But this came to an end in January 1975, when the House Democrats deposed three committee chairmen including William Poage of Texas who was removed as head of the Agriculture Committee and Wright Patman, 82 years old and a congressman with 46 years of service, who was stripped of his powers as head of the Banking and Currency Committee.

Not since 1925 had anything like this happened. The first step took place within the Republican party in 1970, when the Republicans in the House decided to use secret ballots to determine the highest-ranking Republican on each House committee. But because the Republican party does not control the House, this reform did not affect the selection of chairpersons.

In January 1973 the Democratic party used a similar method, but no committee chairpersons lost their positions. The seniority rule was not broken until after the congressional election of 1974, the first election after Watergate and the fall of Nixon.

The 1974 election brought to Washington the largest number of newcomers in many years—92 freshman representatives. Because Democrats could take advantage of voter anger at Republicans, the majority of these freshmen (75) were Democrats. They provided the votes that led to the downfall of several once-powerful committee chairpersons.

In most cases seniority *has* been followed in selecting committee chairpersons in the House and the Senate, and it probably will continue to be followed. However, the threat of removal by the caucus forces the chairpersons to pay greater attention to the wishes of the congressional party.

THE RESURGENCE OF THE HOUSE DEMOCRATIC CAUCUS

The selection of committee chairpersonships is not the only way in which the House Democratic caucus has exercised a new and important role in the legislative process. For the first time in nearly half a century the caucus has taken a stand on policy matters before the House. Though it does not bind members to vote in a certain way, the caucus has on several occasions instructed House committees how to act on pending legislation. Most Democrats on these committees feel an obligation to support the party's policy, thereby giving the caucus a real influence in the legislative process. (In the background is the unspoken threat that the caucus could strip members of their committee positions and deny them their seniority privileges.)

The significance of this resurgence of the party as a policy instrument is that it counteracts the domination of the legislative process by the standing committees. Although a legislative body organized on the basis of powerful, independent committees can develop expertise and competence in a variety of specific policy areas, the decentralization of power that this entails makes the development of a comprehensive, integrated legislative program virtually impossible. Many people see the majority party caucus in the House and Senate as offering a way to develop such a legislative program and securing its enactment. The minority party, in turn, would offer an "opposition" program, thus giving the voters a clear choice between policy alternatives every two years. It is an understatement to say that the American national legislature has not been characterized by these features, which are typical of parliamentary governments. The new authority of the party caucus, however, raises the possibility of a move in this direction.

THE INCREASING INDEPENDENCE OF SUBCOMMITTEES
Another change that has decreased the power of committee chairpersons in both the House and the Senate is the strengthening of subcommittees as independent legislative units. In the past a subcommittee's jurisdiction, membership, and resources were determined completely by the chairperson of the full committee. This gave the chairperson a substantial influence over the fate of proposed legislation. But in recent years both houses of Congress have reduced the chairperson's authority in these areas. Subcommittee structure and membership are now determined by the party caucus on each committee, and subcommittee chairpersons now have the authority to hire their own staff. The result has been a greater decentralization of power within congressional committees.

GOVERNMENT IN THE SUNSHINE
Concerned that the legislative process is not sufficiently open to public scrutiny and accountability, many legislators have waged a vigorous campaign for more "government in the sunshine." Their successes have been striking. Most remarkable is the almost complete elimination of secret committee meetings in a few short years. Throughout the 1950s and 1960s about 40 percent of the committee meetings held each year in the House and Senate were conducted in secret. But by 1975 the number of secret committee meetings had dropped to only 7 percent of the total. House committee meetings have been further opened to public scrutiny by the decision for the first time to allow radio and television broadcasting of committee hearings. (Senate hearings were already open to these media.) There is currently substantial support in both houses for a policy of allowing radio and television coverage of floor debates. Finally, a rule change governing voting on the House floor ended the practice whereby some important and controversial decisions were made by a voting method that recorded the totals "for" and "against" but not how each voted. Now representatives must go on record on all important votes.

WEAKENING THE SENATE FILIBUSTER
One of the most frequently criticized rules of the U.S. Congress is that which allows senators to debate legislation on the floor of

Most congressional committees now meet in open, public sessions.

the Senate without time limits. This right of unlimited speaking is one of the Senate's oldest and deepest traditions, dating back to the first session in 1789. Its purpose was to provide an opportunity for thorough consideration of issues. In the twentieth century, however, this privilege of continuous speaking was often employed by a minority in the Senate simply to prevent the passage of legislation it opposed. Critics denounced the "filibuster" as undemocratic and pushed for reform.

Until 1917 even a single senator, speaking continuously, could prevent a majority from acting. But in that year a change in the rules made it possible for two-thirds of the senators present and voting to end debate. This two-thirds rule prevailed without interruption (though for a while it was changed to two-thirds of the *full* Senate) until 1975. In March of that year the first major change in over half a century was effected when the Senate reduced the number needed to shut off debate to three-fifths of the full Senate (60 senators). This compromise was intended to protect the right of a determined and sizable minority to force a full and thorough debate while recognizing that a majority as large as three-fifths should be allowed to work its will.

EXPANSION OF THE CONGRESSIONAL STAFF

The past two decades have been a period of staff expansion in Congress, as Table 12.2 shows. The total number of staff aides assigned to the Senate has increased from less than 2000 to well over 5000, and similar growth has taken place in the House.

Equally important has been the expansion of the supporting agencies that work for and answer directly to Congress. For example, the Congressional Research Service, the research arm of the Library of Congress that employs experts in a wide range of policy fields, increased from 219 employees in 1965 to 703 in 1975. In addition to the General Accounting Office, which dates back to 1921, Congress is assisted by the Office of Technology Assessment, established in 1972 to evaluate the technological impact of proposed legislation, and the Congressional Budget Office, which began functioning in 1975 to provide Congress with an independent expertise on budgetary matters.

TABLE 12.2
Growth of Senate and House Staffs, 1955–1975

	Senate	House
1955	1962	3623
1960	2643	4148
1965	3219	5672
1970	4140	7134
1975	5543	9951

Source: U.S. Civil Service Commission, as cited in *Inside Congress* (Washington, D.C.: Congressional *Quarterly*, January 1976), p. 19.

Expansion of congressional staffs has led to overcrowding in the halls of the congressional office buildings.

There are two major reasons for the substantial increases in congressional staffing. First, policy making has become more complex in the past two decades. It takes a great deal of staff work to sort out all the implications of tariff legislation or a public-employment bill. A member of Congress will be assisted by as many as eighteen staff aides, many of whom have advanced training and specialization in particular policy areas. In addition, members can call upon the Research Service or the Congressional Budget Office. Second, Congress has added staff in an attempt to match the considerable resources of the executive branch. With additional staff it can at least attempt to review policy alternatives with the same care that the Executive Office puts into this task. The congressional staff can also be a source of policy initiatives, making Congress less dependent on how the executive branch formulates various policy possibilities.

SUMMARY

In many different ways, then, Congress is a different institution than it was a decade ago. Legislation is less under the control of the standing committees and their chairpersons. New and younger members now have greater influence in the legislative process, both at the subcommittee level and in the party caucus. The functioning of the House and Senate is now much more open to public scrutiny. In the Senate obstructionist minorities are less able to thwart the majority will. Finally, the expansion of independent, professional staff assistance has made Congress a more technically competent institution.

But changes in organization and procedure do not tell us how well this new, reformed Congress is actually performing its central functions of representation and legislation. To this question we now turn.

The Member of Congress as a Representative

Political representation is a complex issue. Are representatives supposed to carry out the wishes of those who elected them, or are they to use their independent judgment? One view holds that a representative who does not closely follow the instructions of his or her constituency is not a representative at all. The opposing view asks: If every representative is bound by the instructions of his or her constituency, why bother to have a legislature? Why not simply decide public policy by public vote? But democracy by public-opinion poll would be foolish; it would ignore the benefits of an assembly that can formulate a policy representing the general interest rather than being a hodgepodge of disconnected and local concerns.

The case for the legislator as an elected but nevertheless independent agent was forcefully presented by Edmund Burke two centuries ago:

> Certainly, gentlemen, it ought to be the happiness and glory of a representative, to live in the strictest union, the closest correspondence, and the most unreserved communication with his constituents. . . . It is his duty to sacrifice his repose, his pleasures, his satisfactions, to theirs; and, above all, ever, and in all cases, to prefer their interest to his own. But, his unbiased opinion, his mature judgment, his enlightened conscience, he ought not to sacrifice to you, to any man, or to any set of men living. These he does not derive from your pleasure; no, nor from the law and the constitution. They are a trust from Providence, for the abuse of which he is deeply answerable. . . . Parliament is not [where] local prejudices ought to guide, but the general good, resulting from the general reason of the whole.[5]

In fact most members of Congress steer a middle course between the two viewpoints. They either mix them, depending on the issue at hand, or they lean toward the independent position, except in cases that clearly affect the well-being of their home area. This can be seen by considering how members represent individual citizens of their home area, how they represent the voters, and how they represent organized interests.

REPRESENTING THE INDIVIDUAL CITIZEN

Some descriptions of Congress picture interested citizens with problems that they expect their elected representatives to solve. These mythical citizens write, call, or visit their representatives in Congress, and the latter try to take care of the citizens' needs, not only because the citizens represent votes but because such efforts are a representative's duty. Unrealistic as this picture appears, it holds a great deal of truth.

The reason is simple. The federal bureaucracy touches the life of the individual citizen in dozens of ways: military draft, social-security payments, income tax laws, small-business loans, medicare, public employment, regulation of working conditions, consumer protection, and so forth. When citizens are mistreated by an executive agency or need some government service, they turn to their representatives in Congress for help. So the job of a member of Congress includes running errands for citizens or acting as an intermediary between a citizen and the bureaucracy. It is difficult to

[5] Edmund Burke, "Speech to the Electors of Bristol" (1774), *Works, II,* 11.

**CONGRESSMAN DRINAN SETS
BROOKLINE OFFICE HOURS**

Any Brookline resident who has experienced a problem in dealing with any part of the federal government is invited to meet Congressman Robert F. Drinan at the Brookline Post Office, 1295 Beacon Street, on Saturday, March 25. From 10 a.m. to noon and from 1 p.m. to 3 p.m., Congressman Drinan will be available to meet with any Brookline citizen who needs assistance.

If you need help cutting through federal red tape, come talk to the Congressman at the Brookline Post Office. Please call 890-9455 for an Office Hours appointment.

judge the amount of time a representative or a senator spends in this way, though some estimates go as high as 50 percent. It is certainly true that his or her staff spends much of its time on these individual problems.

Senator Vance Hartke, a Democrat from Indiana, once inserted the following statement in the *Congressional Record* (no doubt so that he could have it copied and mailed to Indiana voters):

> My office in Washington is a Hoosier headquarters. We receive an average of 275 phone calls a day, most of them from Indiana. We had nearly 6,000 visitors during the past year. . . . We received 45,938 letters and mailed out 50,678 letters. . . . We had 300 inquiries from people from Indiana who work for the Federal Government and wanted assistance with something pertaining to their jobs.
>
> The defense buildup has resulted in a great number of service and veteran problems. Since January 1, we have handled 709 of these problems, with the number growing daily. We assisted 261 Hoosiers with social security problems, 27 with draft board problems, 18 with railroad retirements, and 711 who sought patronage employment.
>
> I have helped also with 61 immigration cases who could be helped within the framework of the present law. Fifteen private immigration bills were introduced to assist those people who were worthy and who could not be helped through existing legislation. . . .
>
> It is my sincere conviction that I am in Washington to serve.

There is some concern that errand running takes up so much energy and time that Congress may be swamped and could decline as a legislative assembly. Representative Reuss makes this point when he describes a member of Congress as harried and remarks that "the days are hardly long enough for him to think and act soundly on all the great issues of war and peace, national prosperity and civil rights," especially when the days are shortened by "the requests and demands from voters that require him to serve as their mediator with the Federal Government."

Few members neglect these requests, however. Reelection can depend as much or more on your reputation as "available and helpful" than on your votes in Congress. Errand running creates a bond between citizen and legislator, but this bond has relatively little to do with public policy. A request for help in dealing with the Internal Revenue Service need have nothing to do with tax reform or income distribution; a request for help in getting a small-business loan need have nothing to do with government fiscal policy.

The gap between citizen request and public policy can lead to a great deal of independence for members of Congress. If they solve citizens' problems, they can be reelected regardless of how they vote on tax reform or fiscal management. Thus while members of Congress are paying very close attention to citizens' *problems*, they are paying less attention to citizens' *viewpoints*. Of course members are aware of the general viewpoint of their state or district, but as we will see in the next section, there is little reason to think that this has a strong effect on their actions.

REPRESENTING THE VOTERS

It is often hard for a member of Congress to represent voters accurately. When he was a senator from Massachusetts John F. Kennedy wrote:

> In Washington I frequently find myself believing that forty or fifty letters, six visits from professional politicians and lobbyists, and three editorials in Massachusetts newspapers constitute public opinion on a given issue. Yet in truth I rarely know how the great majority of the voters feel, or even how much they know of the issues that seem so burning in Washington.

This feeling has been called *mandate uncertainty*. Most members of Congress are very uncertain about how to interpret election victory. Partly this is because voters do not have very well-informed viewpoints and do not participate in politics in great numbers. On the average, fewer than half the eligible voters bother to vote in congressional elections. Turnout is especially low in "off-year" elections. It takes a presidential campaign to attract attention even to Senate contests. How can successful congressional candidates interpret their victory if fewer than one-quarter of the eligible voters in their districts supported them? This situation is worsened by the fact that the average voter knows very little about his or her representative. Even in competitive congressional races fewer than one-fourth of the voters know *anything* about either of the candidates and almost none know anything about their policy positions.

Mandate uncertainty is also caused by the large number of issues in any campaign. Candidates declare themselves for or against a lot of separate policies. They may support a negative income tax and revenue sharing with the state government; they may oppose continued space exploration and federally funded cancer research and be largely silent on foreign policy issues. Did such a candidate win because of the issues he supported? Or because he came out against certain policies? Or because he veered away from foreign policy and concentrated on domestic questions? Maybe the winner did not gain votes by his stands as much as his opponent lost votes by *her* stands. Or perhaps personal qualities such as integrity, religious convic-

tions or racial or ethnic identity were more important than issues.

In addition to mandate uncertainty, the sheer pressures of time and the complexity of congressional business make it impossible for the elected representative to translate voter preferences into public policy. The range of issues before Congress is huge: fiscal matters, civil rights, foreign treaties, funds for space exploration, wage and price policy, welfare programs, revenue sharing, tax reform, energy programs, and so on. No senator or representative checks with his or her constituency before every roll-call vote, and of course none check before a vote in committee or subcommittee, where most legislation is actually written. Only a tiny fraction of the voters have the vaguest idea about the bills that are pending in Congress, let alone any information about what their representative is doing.

Still, it is wrong to conclude that the policy views of the electorate have *no* bearing on how a member of Congress votes. Citizens may not have detailed information about specific legislation, but they are not usually neutral about the major issues of war and peace, inflation and unemployment, civil rights, and so forth. Members of Congress know the general tendencies in a district or state, this puts limits on the policies they support. The civil-rights voting record of Shirley Chisholm, a liberal black congresswoman from New York, is very different from the voting record of William Poage, an ultraconservative Texas Congressman, but a person with Chisholm's views would not be elected in Poage's district in Texas, nor would someone with Poage's views stand a chance of being elected in Chisholm's district.

Unfortunately, very few studies have compared the policy views of members of Congress with those of the voters they represent. One such study, however, shows a high correlation between the way members vote and the preferences of their constituencies on bills having to do with civil rights and race relations.[6] The study found that congressional districts with a population that is generally liberal on civil-rights issues are represented by members who vote in favor of civil-rights measures, and that districts with a more conservative population are represented by members who oppose such measures.

This can be explained in two different ways. The member's own attitudes may be nearly identical to those of the voters, in which case he or she need pay no attention to voter preferences. Or perhaps the member may not always see eye to eye with the voters but fears to differ with them, at least on an issue as major as civil rights and race relations. The evidence shows that the latter explanation is more nearly the case: Members of Congress appear to change their own views about race questions to accord with those of their con-

[6] The study cited here and in the next two paragraphs is from Warren E. Miller and Donald E. Stokes, "Constituency Influence in Congress," *American Political Science Review*, 57 (1963), 45–57.

stituents. Furthermore, members are quite accurate in judging how the voters feel about civil rights.

When voters and members of Congress were asked about foreign-policy and social-welfare issues, it was apparent that the attitudes of members of Congress were not often in accord with those of their constituents. On foreign policy in particular, senators and representatives seem not to be affected by the viewpoints of voters. Perhaps they sense that voters feel less secure in their views about foreign policy and are willing to give Congress and the Presidency much more leeway in this area.

REPRESENTING INTEREST GROUPS

Although a member of Congress may be uncertain about the views of the several thousands and even millions of individual voters in his or her district or state, he or she is not as uncertain about the views of the major groups back home, especially when legislation is pending that directly affects the interests of those groups. The contact that members of Congress have with their constituents is most often with the active and organized parts of the community: the interest groups.

Blocks of voters are more critical than the individual voter. The representative aiming at reelection must keep in mind the general policy preferences of groups that represent sizable voting power. And it's not hard to learn those views. Organizations with a standing interest in legislative matters support a full-time staff in Washington whose job begins and ends with lobbying members of Congress. Such organizations inform, persuade, and sometimes threaten in order to get favorable treatment from "their representative in Washington." What they offer, of course, is electoral support, either campaign contributions or votes. It is generally accepted, though, that group leaders cannot easily control the voting choices of group members. But they do control campaign funds, and they distribute publicity to group members about the area's representatives in Congress. Nearly all the political pressuring that takes place in Washington comes through organizations. If a member of Congress receives a mass mailing on a labor issue, it is because the union has organized that mailing; if the member is asked to speak to parents who are concerned about school busing, it is because a civic group has organized the meeting; if the member is asked to let a group of farmers present a petition on wheat prices, it is because a farmers' association has collected the signatures. This type of pressure group activity is particularly important if there are only one or two major interests that dominate the district or state. Thus automobile manufacturers and the auto unions are listened to carefully by members from Michigan, while a fruit growers' association will be especially important to a member from Florida.

A Difference Between the House and the Senate One of the important differences between the Senate and the House of Representatives is suggested by this point. The constituency of a senator is

Senator Kennedy has been an active promoter of health legislation.

nearly always more varied than that of a representative. Seldom will a single interest so dominate a state that its senators are in effect representatives only of that interest, though the influence of oil in Texas and of mining in Utah has at times been almost that strong. For the most part a senator will build a winning electoral coalition from a variety of groups and interests. It is for this reason that the Senate is said to have a constituency similar to that of the President. The constituency of a senator, especially one from a populous, urban state, is closer to that of the entire nation than that of a member of the House. Most senators will have to deal both with liberal labor unions and civil-rights groups and with more conservative business and agricultural organizations. Many representatives, however, are selected from districts dominated by one or two interests.

Two Forms of Group Politics In one respect this discussion of group politics and representative behavior is somewhat misleading. Organizations are active in two ways. First, as we have suggested, they are active as local pressure groups attempting to persuade a member of Congress to support legislation that will benefit his or her area. This is the case of the businessmen of a community trying to control the route of a federal highway, of a trade union trying to get a big contract for a local industry, of a large university trying to obtain a federal research center, of a farmers' association trying to get more favorable soil bank terms. These are specific groups using political influence to direct benefits to their area. They do not compete with any other interest in the area, and they usually have no difficulty getting the help of their representative in Congress. The struggle takes place *within* Congress, because more than one part of the country wants to affect the route of the highway, wants the same defense contract, wants the same research center, or wants favorable treatment from the Department of Agriculture. Members of Congress are judged by how successfully they negotiate within the federal government on such matters. Listen to no less an authority than President Johnson:

> At the March 2, 1968, rollout ceremony for the giant C-5A cargo aircraft at the Lockheed Aircraft plant at Marietta, Ga., President Johnson warmly complimented the Georgia congressional delegation for helping

to land the contract for their state. "I would have you good folks of Georgia know that there are a lot of Marietta, Georgias, scattered throughout our fifty states," the President said. ". . . All of them would like to have the pride [and cash inflow, we might add] that comes from this production. . . . But all of them don't have the Georgia delegation."

In contrast, groups can also compete with different groups, both sides trying to influence broad legislative policy or bills that may affect the well-being of an organization with a national membership. For example, members of Congress often hear from such powerful national organizations as the political agencies of the AFL-CIO, the AMA, the American Farm Bureau Federation, the American Legion, and the NAM. These organizations claim to speak for members across the entire nation. With less cause, they claim to speak in the national interest.

When the national headquarters of mass organizations try to affect legislation, the results are very different from those that occur when a local interest group contacts its representatives in Congress, because the issues that involve the national organizations are nearly always divisive in one way or another. As the battle shapes up between business and labor, between farmers and consumers, or between minority groups and states'-rights organizations, Congress itself is the battlefield, and its members are pressured from both sides.

Group Politics and Geographic Representation   National organizations influence the congressional process and even affect political representation. Clearly, national organizations have a large impact on a representational system that is formally based on geography. The Constitution makes residence the basis for electing members of Congress, but geographic representation has its drawbacks. Doesn't a doctor in St. Louis have more in common with a fellow doctor in Dallas than with his or her nextdoor neighbor, a grocery store owner? It depends on the issue. Politics is such a complex mixture of interests and issues that any election arrangement will sometimes make odd bedfellows.

Consider the alignment of three citizens on issues:

	Citizen A	Citizen B	Citizen C
Residence	Chicago suburb	Chicago suburb	Small town in Kansas
Occupation	Retired military	Public-school teacher	Shop owner
Race	White	Black	White

On an issue that is directly related to residence, we would find citizens A and B aligned against citizen C, but on other types of issues the alignment might well shift. For instance, it might look like this:

Issue	Alignment of Citizens
Federal support for urban transit	A and B vs. C
Increased veterans' benefits	B and C vs. A
Compensatory hiring of minority races	A and C vs. B

In this hypothetical case residence aligns citizens in a meaningful way on the issue of federal support for urban transit but not on veteran benefits or racial issues. By the same token, representation based on occupation does not make much sense on issues that directly benefit particular sections of the country or on issues that have to do specifically with race. And race is inappropriate as a basis for representation on issues that involve residency or occupation.

In any case the election of representatives on a geographic basis is a permanent part of our politics. No alternatives to this system have been given serious attention. Bearing this in mind, we can see the great importance of national organizations in the legislative process. On many issues they crisscross arbitrary geographic boundaries and provide an umbrella under which citizens may gather on issues that affect them in their occupational roles or because of their sex, age, race, background, language, or social outlook. The AMA collects the energies, resources, and viewpoints of doctors from Honolulu to Huzzah, from Mississippi to Maine. The National Council of Senior Citizens does the same thing for older citizens, no matter where they live and regardless of their sex or race. The memberships of such organizations are in one way narrow, focused on a single set of issues, but they are broad in their national base. This combination adds strength to national organizations.

Organizations with national memberships introduce an element of functional representation that cuts across sectional boundaries and counteracts the local focus that results from purely geographic representation. Insofar as Congress is responsive to national organizations on national issues, it is being much less local in outlook than some critics have claimed.

CHARACTERISTICS OF MEMBERS OF CONGRESS

A former Democratic congresswoman from New York, Representative Bella S. Abzug, insisted in a speech to the National Women's Political Caucus that in a truly representative Congress half of the members would be women and 11 percent blacks; there would be more younger and working-class people and greater numbers of teachers, artists, and members of other unrepresented occupations. She correctly described Congress as dominated by men, mostly white men, who have much more advanced education than the general population and are either from the professions (mostly law)

TABLE 12.3
Membership of the 95th
Congress, 1978

House		Senate
	Party	
292	Democrats	61
143	Republicans	38
	Independent	1
	Sex	
418	Men	99
17	Women	1
	Age	
27	Youngest	34
77	Oldest	80
49	Average	54
	Religion	
255	Protestants	69
107	Catholics	12
18	Jewish	5
4	Mormons	3
51	Others	11
	Profession	
215	Lawyers	65
81	Businessmen and bankers	13
45	Educators	6
14	Farmers and ranchers	6
22	Career government officials	0
24	Journalists, communications executives	4
2	Physicians	0
1	Veterinarians	1
0	Geologists	2
6	Workers and skilled tradesmen	0
25	Others	3
	Ethnic Minorities	
17	Blacks	1
2	Orientals	3
4	Spanish	0

Sources: "Congressional Directory," National Democratic and Republican Congressional Committees, Associated Press. Cited in *U.S. News & World Report,* January 10, 1977, p. 29 Reprinted from *U.S. News & World Report.* Copyright (1977) U.S. News & World Report, Inc.

or from the business and commercial sectors of society. The membership of the present Congress, the 95th, is shown in Table 12.3.

Congress clearly does not mirror the population that it is supposed to represent. Although blacks account for nearly 11 percent of the population, they had only 1 percent of the Senate seats and 4 percent of the House seats. There is one woman senator (appointed to office in 1978, when her husband Hubert Humphrey died in office) and only 17 women in the House of Representatives, yet women account for more than half the total population. This lack of demographic representation in Congress has long bothered critics who speak in the populist tradition.

Despite recent gains by minority groups and by women, Congress remains largely the preserve of white, male Americans.

What the reformer counts on is the likelihood that changing the composition of Congress will change the social policies it pursues. When civil-rights organizations campaign for black candidates, it is because they think blacks can best speak for the concerns of racial minorities; when the Women's Caucus demands more congresswomen, it assumes that the feminist viewpoint can be more forcefully presented by females than by males; when the U.S. Chamber of Commerce organizes political action groups, it is because it feels that businessmen in Congress will favor commerce.

But just because a person works in a factory does not guarantee that he or she has the interests of the working class at heart; not all women believe equally in the feminist movement; and a black skin may cover the political views of an Uncle Tom or of a black power advocate. Conversely, being born into the middle class does not always mean hostility toward the working class; some men care about women's liberation; some whites, including white members of Congress, have been active in the civil-rights movement. It was a white middle-class Congress representing a predominantly white middle-class nation that passed the landmark civil-rights acts of the 1960s.

Moreover, demanding that the U.S. Congress be a mirror image of the groups that make up American society seems to reduce the common good to the sum of individual group interests. Many people, however, believe with Edmund Burke that "the general good, resulting from the general reason of the whole" ought to guide the legislative process. (We will have more to say on this issue in the Controversy at the end of this chapter.) And if we really wanted our Congress to be a mirror image of American society, then selection of members of Congress by lot would seem to make more sense than popular election of senators and representatives. The purpose of the electoral process is to select people for public office who *stand out* from their fellow citizens, people who are so much *above* average that they are chosen over all competitors. And though it does not always work this way, there is clearly a widespread feeling among the American people that the leaders they select should be individuals of high (not average) competence, experience, and integrity. Such leaders, it is thought, will be better able to promote the good of all the people.

THE COST OF CONGRESS

Maintaining a Congress of 535 members plus 15,000 staff aides, additional employees in the Library of Congress, the General Accounting Office, and similar agencies of Congress, is expensive. In fiscal year 1976, for instance, Congress appropriated $827.5 million for its own operations, an increase of nearly $60 million from the appropriation for the previous year. Table 12.4 lists the costs of some of the items that contribute to the cost of Congress, though the figures vary from one member to another depending on how far the home district is from Washington, D.C. The figure of approximately $364,000 is for a typical member of Congress from the Midwest.

SUMMARY

Critics say that Congress is not fulfilling its representational responsibility. It is too much an institution of the nineteenth century, whereas the problems of American society belong very much to the twentieth century. Congress is local, middle class, conservative, and cautious — unable to play a creative role in formulating national programs. There is some truth to these criticisms. But they do not take full account of the changes Congress has undergone in the past few years, nor of the many ways in which members of Congress do represent their constituents. As a direct result of growing federal programs and activities, individual citizens make a large number of requests to their representatives in Congress, who (with their staffs) respond enthusiastically. Moreover, in a general if vague manner members of Congress do pay attention to what they believe the voters think about major policy questions. Certainly there is no one-to-one correspondence between congressional voting and voter viewpoints, but voter preferences are not ignored. Finally, members of Congress are responsive to organized pressure. They try to satisfy important groups in the district or state, at least on matters that affect them directly. And in a broader sense legislative policy on national issues partially reflects the preferences of national organizations.

TABLE 12.4
The Average Cost of a
Member of Congress

The member's salary	$ 57,500
Salary allowance for eighteen staff aides	255,144
Travel to home district	10,000
Rent for office in a home district	10,000
Equipment lease	9,000
Telephone, stationery, and other communication costs	19,750
Official expenses	2,000
Intern	1,000
	$364,394

Congress: The Legislative Branch

Is Congress an effective law making institution? Have the reforms of the past decade really contributed to making Congress a more competent legislative body? Ever since the demise of the Nixon Presidency, Congress has been exerting great efforts to provide affirmative answers to these questions.

THE ORGANIZATION OF CONGRESS

The Constitution separated Congress into two houses, the Senate and the House of Representatives. But the Constitution is silent on how the two houses should organize themselves. How Congress selects its leaders, divides responsibilities and duties, debates and votes on issues, and manages its affairs are matters to be settled by the members themselves.

DIFFERENCES BETWEEN THE SENATE AND THE HOUSE

Size   The Senate is the smaller and more prestigious group. Numbering only 100 people, two from each of the 50 states, it has a more informal way of working than the House. "The Senate of the United States is a small and special world," writes one student of Congress. "The chamber is quiet. It must be, because there is no public address system and business is conducted in conversational tones. It is dignified: somber-suited men, a few quite old, move in the perpetual twilight of its high ceiling lights." This small and special world is "ingrown and not wholly immune from narcissism, yet its nerve ends are in the great world outside, and its reaction to events can be instantaneous."[7]

In contrast, there are 435 members of the House of Representatives, the number from each state depending on its population. The most populous state, California, has the largest delegation, 43; a half-dozen small states send only one representative each. Legislative business in the House is carefully regulated by a complex set of procedures, and although power in the House is more widely distributed now than it was a decade ago, it is still concentrated in a smaller portion of its membership than is the case in the Senate.

Prestige   The Senate is more nearly a club of equals. The senator's term of office is six years, in contrast to only two for the representative, and thus even a new senator will be in Washington long enough to be noticed. The House member needs to be reelected several times before he or she begins to be noticed. Many senators are as well known as state governors, and a few are nearly as well known as the President himself. Indeed, four of the past seven Presidents (Truman, Johnson, Kennedy, and Nixon) were formerly senators.

[7] Ralph K. Huitt, "The Internal Distribution of Influence: The Senate," in Truman, p. 77.

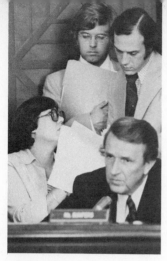

Staff support is critical for the member of Congress.

Only in very unusual circumstances will a member of the House gain a national reputation, though it can happen, as in the long, powerful career of Speaker Sam Rayburn of Texas and the appointment of former representative Gerald Ford to the Vice-Presidency and then to the Presidency.

The Senate is generally more visible to the public. Senate debate, for example, receives more attention from the press and TV than House debate. This is partly because Senate debate is unlimited except when closed by the members themselves, and the practice of filibustering can sometimes extend debate on a single issue over days or even weeks. The legislative debate in the House is much less dramatic; the time given any individual is sharply limited, usually to five minutes, and only a certain number of pro and con speakers will debate a particular issue. The daily workings of the House have much less flair and drama than those of the Senate.

Powers Although individual senators have on the average more power and prestige than individual representatives, this does not mean that the House as a collective body is less powerful than the Senate. Both parts of Congress share fully in the power to legislate, and bills must receive the stamp of approval in both the Senate and the House before passing into law. Certain powers are assigned to only one of the houses. Most notable among these are the power of the Senate to confirm such presidential appointees as Supreme Court justices (hence the involvement of the Senate in the defeat of two controversial Nixon appointees), ambassadors, and heads of major executive agencies, and the power of the Senate to ratify treaties. These special Senate powers are more than compensated for by the power of the House to originate all money bills, including those by which revenue is raised (tax bills and tariff legislation, for instance) and those by which money is appropriated to run the federal government. The "appropriation power," as it is sometimes called, is only the power of initiation, for even revenue-raising and appropriation bills must pass the Senate as well as the House. But the power to originate is the power to set the agenda, giving the House considerable influence in this, perhaps the most significant aspect of legislation.

LEADERSHIP IN THE HOUSE

The member of the House with the greatest formal power is the *Speaker*. The Speaker presides over floor debate and can sometimes influence legislation by recognizing or ignoring particular members. The Speaker also appoints members of select committees that do special jobs and nominates his party's Rules Committee members. However, the Speaker does not appoint members of other standing committees, a power lost in a major reform in 1910.

The Speaker is always a member of the majority party. Indeed, he is the recognized leader of the majority party. This, more than formal powers, is what gives the position influence and authority in House politics. The Speaker is chosen at a meeting, often called a *caucus,* of the majority party held before the official opening of a new congressional session.

Working closely with the Speaker are the majority party *floor leader* and the majority party *whip,* who help plan strategy for getting bills through the House. The floor leader negotiates with congressional chairpersons and with members of the House Rules Committee. This committee controls what bills will be brought before the House; no bill can be debated without a "rule" that specifies how much debate will be allowed and whether amendments can be added. Assisting the floor leader is the party whip, along with deputy whips, who are responsible for knowing how many party members are likely to support particular legislation. The whips also try to round up members in time for important votes. (The term *whip* is derived from English fox hunts, in which the man who is supposed to keep the hunting dogs from straying is called a "whipper-in.")

LEADERSHIP IN THE SENATE

According to the Constitution, the person who presides over the Senate is the Vice-President, but it is an unusual day when the Vice-President appears in the Senate. In his absence the formal leadership of the Senate belongs to the *president pro tempore,* but this position is more ceremonial than powerful.

The *Senate majority leader,* elected by the majority party, is the recognized leader of the Senate. His powers derive from his position as head of the party as well as whatever personal skills he brings to leadership. Montana Democrat Mike Mansfield, who served as majority leader from 1961 to 1976, did not push his views on his colleagues. When some senators complained that he was not forceful enough as a leader, Mansfield responded: "I am neither a circus ring master, a master of ceremonies of a Senate nightclub, a tamer of Senate lions, nor a wheeler and dealer."

His predecessor, Lyndon Johnson, was a bit of all the things Mansfield claimed not to be. Johnson was a forceful leader. He persuaded and threatened, traded and compromised, and most of all, counted votes. He knew who might support what version of which bill. And he used his knowledge and resources to shape legislation.

The contrast between Mansfield and Johnson holds an important lesson. It is often not the formal position but the personality and the drive of the person in the position that determines how much leadership will be exercised. This is especially true in a group of only 100 people, where power is exercised, if at all, in face-to-face settings.

MINORITY PARTY LEADERS

In both the House and the Senate the leadership structure of the majority party is matched by leadership in the minority party. One important role played by minority party leadership is linkage with the White House when the President belongs to the party that is not in control of Congress.

Legislation by Committee

It is impossible for 535 people to come together, debate dozens of complicated issues, and easily reach a collective decision. Even separating these people into two groups, one of 435 and one of 100, does not solve the problem. Even if all their other commitments (running errands for constituents, fulfilling ceremonial functions, meeting with organization leaders, electioneering, doing political party work) allowed enough time for the legislators to meet and discuss each bill, none of them could be even reasonably informed about the variety of things that require congressional action. How, for instance, is the single legislator to learn enough about each subject to be able to deal, in turn, with a flood control system for the Northwest, tariff policy on textile imports, wiretapping by the FBI, immigration quotas for Asian nationals, and a mutual-defense treaty with Canada? To make matters more complex, each of these broad issues can be subdivided into dozens of small but important questions: Should the flood control program be tied in with an irrigation project in the Southwest? Should there be matching funds from the various states, or should it be wholly federally financed? Is it the case, as conservationists have claimed, that a proposal made by the Army Corps of Engineers will destroy a wildlife habitat?

STANDING COMMITTEES OF CONGRESS

The more complicated the policy issue, the more complicated must be the legislation that deals with it, and the more necessary it is to give the drafting of the legislation to a small group of experts. Of this necessity was born the *standing committees* of Congress. When a situation calls for division of labor, the typical response is the committee. And this has been the response of Congress.

Standing committees in both houses have stated areas of responsibility. These responsibilities include reviewing all bills referred to the committee, consulting relevant executive agencies about possible effects of the bills, writing and rewriting the actual legislation, holding public hearings if necessary, and finally, sending the "finished" bill to the House or Senate *with the committee's recommendations.*

The committees are where legislation takes place and where proposals for legislation are blocked. Thus, insofar as Congress does govern the nation, it does so through committees. Table 12.5 lists the standing committees of Congress in order of importance.

Subcommittees of Congress Because the responsibilities of any single committee can include many issues and because the membership of even the committees themselves can be so large (the House Appropriations Committee has 50 members), there is need for a subcommittee structure. As we have seen, subcommittees have grown

**TABLE 12.5
Standing Committees
of Congress (in Groups,
in Order of Importance)**

Senate (18)	House (22)
I Appropriations Finance Foreign Relations	Appropriations Rules Ways and Means
II Agriculture and Forestry Armed Services Budget[a] Commerce Judiciary	Agriculture Armed Services Budget[a] Government Operations International Relations Interstate and Foreign Commerce Judiciary
III Aeronautical and Space Science Banking, Housing and Urban Affairs Interior and Insular Affairs Human Resources Public Works	Banking, Currency, and Housing Education and Labor Interior and Insular Affairs Public Works and Transportation Science and Technology Small Business
IV Government Operations Post Office and Civil Service Veterans Affairs	Merchant Marine and Fisheries Post Office and Civil Service Standards of Official Conduct Veterans Affairs
V District of Columbia Rules and Administration	District of Columbia House Administration

[a] New committees with important formal powers but not yet clearly established policy influence.

in importance over the past several decades; there are now nearly 250 subcommittees in Congress. Table 12.6 lists the subcommittees of the Senate Committee on Foreign Relations and those of the House Committee on Appropriations.

COMMITTEE ASSIGNMENTS

In the House of Representatives each member is normally assigned to only one or two standing committees, although he or she may serve on several subcommittees. Senators, in contrast, usually have three or four committee assignments and perhaps ten or more subcommittee assignments. This, by the way, increases the influence of the House because, being so much larger, it can divide up legislative tasks more effectively than the Senate. As a result House members often develop great expertise in a legislative area — fiscal policy, say, or farm price supports. The harried senator is less likely to be a subject matter expert, having to rely more on his or her staff than the representative. The greater expertise of the House member is particularly valuable in conference committees, which are joint House-Senate committees formed to negotiate an acceptable version of a bill that has passed both houses in different forms.

Assignments to the standing committees of the House and Senate are made by special party committees, which reflect the regional

Senate Committee on Foreign Relations	House Committee on Appropriations
African Affairs	Agriculture and Related Agencies
Arms Control, International Organizations, and Security Agreements	Defense
	District of Columbia
European Affairs	Foreign Operations
Far Eastern Affairs	Housing and Urban Development— Independent Agencies
Foreign Assistance and Economic Policy	Interior
Multinational Corporations	Labor, Health, Education, and Welfare
Near Eastern and South Asian Affairs	Legislative
Oceans and International Environment	Military Construction
Western Hemisphere Affairs	Public Works
	State, Justice, Commerce, and the Judiciary
	Transportation
	Treasury—Postal Service—General Government

and ideological distribution of the congressional delegation. The party leaders usually exercise considerable influence on these decisions. Committee seats are distributed between the parties according to their relative strength in each house. Thus if two-thirds of the senators are Democrats and one-third are Republicans, each committee (and, less exactly, each subcommittee) will be about two-thirds Democrats and one-third Republicans.

Positions on the more powerful committees are highly prized. This gives party leaders one of their major sources of power. Assigning new members to committees and filling committee vacancies gives party leaders a chance to reward those whom they approve of and punish those who don't play by the rules. Newcomers to the House have difficulty getting appointed to the important committees. "It would be too risky to put on a person whose views and nature the leadership has no opportunity to assess," said one veteran. A freshman representative who was lucky enough to be appointed to the powerful House Appropriations Committee recalled how it happened: "The Chairman I guess did some checking around in my area. After all, I was new and he didn't know me. People told me that they were called to see if I was — well, unstable or apt to off on tangents . . . to see whether or not I had any preconceived notions about things and would not be flexible — whether I would oppose things even though it was obvious."[8]

Reelection to Congress can often depend on one's committee assignment. Thus a representative from a rural district tries to get a seat on the Agriculture Committee, the better to serve his area and

[8] Cited in Richard F. Fenno, Jr., "The House Appropriations Committee as a Political System: The Problem of Integration," in Leroy N. Riselbach, ed., *The Congressional System* (Belmont, Calif.: Wadsworth, 1970), p. 194.

keep a watch on the Department of Agriculture. It is not uncommon for a member of Congress to claim that his or her seniority on a committee that directly benefits the home area is itself a good enough reason to return him or her to Washington. The opponent would go to Washington as a powerless and inexperienced freshman. Such campaign claims reflect considerable truth.

Committee positions become the basis of power within Congress, as illustrated in the career of the late Senator Robert S. Kerr, a Democrat from Oklahoma. Although he was not a formal leader in the Senate, Kerr was certainly one of its three or four most powerful members.

> The base of Kerr's power was never his major committees. Rather, it was his chairmanship of the Rivers and Harbors Subcommittee of the Public Works Committee, an obscure post that makes few national headlines, but much political hay. Kerr not only used it to consolidate his position in Oklahoma by festooning the state with public works but placed practically all Senators under obligation to him by promoting their pet home projects. He never hesitated to collect on these obligations later, when the votes were needed.[9]

Of course party leaders can try to hurt congressional careers by purposely assigning "unwanteds" to committees that isolate them from the concerns of their constituents. Freshman Representative Herman Badillo of the Bronx was initially appointed to the Agriculture Committee, where he felt unable to do much for his urban supporters. As he told Speaker Carl Albert, "There isn't any crop in my district except marijuana." Outspoken liberal Shirley Chisholm, a black congresswoman from Brooklyn, also was initially assigned to Agriculture. She remarked that "apparently all they know here in Washington about Brooklyn is that a tree grew there." Both appointments were changed in response to pressure from the New York delegation.

The request of a senator or representative to serve on a committee that is related to the concerns of his or her constituents is reasonable, but it does contribute to the local outlook that critics complain of. There is a price to pay for appointing lawyers to Judiciary, farmers to Agriculture, businessmen to Banking and Currency, urban dwellers to Education and Labor, or westerners to Interior. Committees become the property of specialized interests, and public policy making becomes the result of compromises among small groups that are more concerned with satisfying narrow constituencies than with dealing with national issues.

The Agriculture Committee of the House of Representatives is a good example of the tension between particular voter preferences and broader national programs. This committee, until recently chaired by a conservative rural Texan, W. R. Poage, had long been

---

[9] Nelson W. Polsby, *Congress and the Presidency* (Englewood Cliffs, N.J.: Prentice-Hall, 1964), p. 38.

When the House Agriculture Committee began to legislate about such programs as school lunches, liberal, urban representatives led a reform which changed its membership.

dominated by representatives from the nation's farm belt. People elected from rural districts wanted seats on the Agriculture Committee, and as we just saw, people from urban districts fought to stay off the Agriculture Committee. But the Agriculture Committee has jurisdiction over proposed legislation that is of concern to more than farmers. In recent years, for example, this committee has heavily influenced federal school lunch and food stamp programs. Such legislation has not been to the liking of members of Congress from urban districts, where the need for hot school lunches and food stamps is greatest.

It finally became clear to the liberal, urban representatives that the House Agriculture Committee needed a very different outlook if food and farm programs were to benefit consumers as well as producers. In 1975, in a major effort at reform, the Democrats in the House voted to remove Poage from the chair of the Agriculture Committee, despite his seniority. Moreover, twenty new members came onto the Committee, many of them liberal and consumer oriented.

BASES OF COMMITTEE POWER

Committee power comes from four factors: (1) the committees' control over the flow of legislation, (2) the expertise of members and the resultant division of labor among committees, (3) the ties committees form with executive agencies and interest groups, and (4) public hearings.

Control over the Flow of Legislation Control over the legislative process is a direct result of congressional rules as well as custom. It is the factor that is most often attacked by congressional reformers, but generally to little effect. What Woodrow Wilson observed ninety years ago needs only a slight change to be equally correct today: "The practical effect of this Committee organization of the House is to consign to each of the Standing Committees the entire direction of legislation upon those subjects which properly come to its consideration. As to those subjects it is entitled to the initiative, and all legislative action with regard to them is under its overruling guidances."[10] Today the legislative agenda is often set by the executive branch, but Wilson's description is still accurate.

Expertise The second base of committee power, expertise, is a natural outcome of the committee structure itself. Any organization that subdivides itself into working committees is simply recognizing the need for such expertise. Because all members cannot be equally informed about all issues, this is a practical arrangement. If, as is the case in Congress, these working committees are permanent and the same people remain on them for a long time, then it is hardly surprising that each committee develops considerable expertise in its area. This is true as well of the subcommittee structure; thus the Foreign Relations Subcommittee on African Affairs will develop extensive knowledge of that continent but have only a slight understanding of issues in Canadian-American affairs. On many matters of public policy a system of division of labor among committees and subcommittees develops. A member of Congress goes along with the recommendation of a committee with the comment, "They are the experts in this field, and usually know what they are doing." In the great majority of cases the recommendation of the subcommittee is accepted by the full committee and the recommendation of the full committee is accepted by the House or Senate. It is inside the committee, or even subcommittee, that one must look for sharp debate, lobbying, negotiations with the executive agency, and the final shaping of legislation.

Relationships with Interest Groups and Executive Agencies The third base of committee power is the ties it forms with relevant interest groups and executive agencies. The facts that the committee is concerned with a certain subject and that some of its members (the more powerful ones) stay on the committee for a long time makes it easy to form close ties with the groups in society that are most affected. The two Agriculture Committees, for instance, will be led not only by members from rural states but probably by members who have long received campaign and electoral support from the American Farm Bureau Federation. The bond is made stronger by a close relationship with the Department of Agriculture. Each of these three partners is attentive and supportive toward the other two, protecting them from "enemies" who might threaten their power either individually or collectively. Similar arrangements are common in the committees that deal with labor, commerce, finance, welfare, education, space, defense, and nearly every other aspect of American life.

[10] Wilson, *loc. cit.*

The three-way partnership among a congressional committee, an executive agency, and a pressure group strengthens the control of committees over legislation. Programs that are formulated in this way are not likely to be overriden on the floor of Congress.

Public Hearings Congressional committees and subcommittees can hold public hearings on legislation under consideration. These hearings perform several broad functions. First, they help members of Congress collect information and opinions from interested groups. This helps Congress formulate legislation, and it gives groups and individuals a way to try to influence policy. A public hearing on, say, price controls will call a large number of "expert" witnesses. Of course their testimony will clash, but members of Congress, who are often lawyers, use conflicting testimony much as a judge or jury uses it in a court case. Thus one expert may argue that price controls will hurt the economy, while another will claim that controls will halt inflation and thus benefit the economy.

Witnesses before congressional committees often represent an executive agency, perhaps one of the President's senior economic advisers. They may also speak for major interest groups that are affected by the proposed legislation. Sometimes a committee wants testimony from an individual who does not wish to appear. In such cases it can issue a subpoena.

One of the most complicated issues of the 1970s is the question of whether the executive branch can refuse to testify before Congress on the grounds of "executive privilege." This issue was brought into sharp focus during the Watergate hearings. The special Senate committee on Watergate received wide press coverage, including live television. This had the purpose of educating the public about the need to reform laws regulating political campaigning, but it also dramatized the issues that separate Congress and the Presidency. Such public hearings can add to the influence of a congressional committee and, as in the case of Watergate, contribute to the power of Congress as a whole.

How Legislation Is Passed

How is a bill passed? As shown in Figure 12.1, a bill must first be introduced in both houses of Congress; it is then referred to a committee. The committees, and perhaps the relevant subcommittees, hold hearings and then do the work of detailed formulation of legislation. If a committee "reports out" a bill, it is placed on the legislative agenda. It is then debated, perhaps amended, and passed or defeated. If the House and the Senate pass different versions of a bill, a conference committee consisting of members from both houses of Congress works out a compromise bill. If this compromise version is passed by both the House and the Senate, the bill goes to the President. If he signs it, the bill becomes law. If he vetoes it, the bill can still become law if it is passed once again by a two-thirds majority of both houses of Congress.

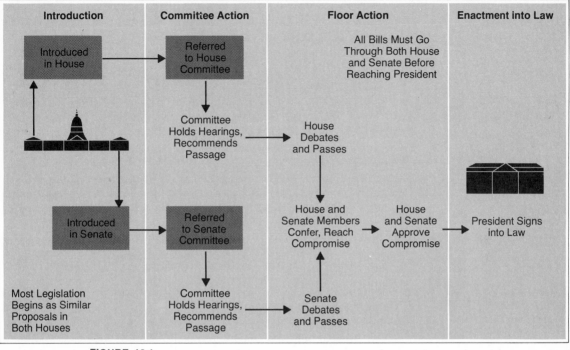

FIGURE 12.1
How A Bill Becomes a Law

If the President fails to act for ten days, the bill automatically becomes law—if Congress is still in session. If, however, Congress has adjourned, the bill is not enacted, having become the victim of a "pocket veto." This may seem a mere technicality, but since a great deal of legislation is passed in the hectic days before adjournment the pocket veto is important.

Thus a bill faces many barriers. It might be referred to an unfriendly committee, where it will be watered down or simply left to die; it might get bottled up in the all-important House Rules Committee, which must pass on legislation before it can be acted upon by the House; or it might be subjected to a Senate filibuster, that is, killed by prolonged debate.

There are many points at which a bill can be killed, but the real moment of truth is when it is put to a vote. Therefore if we are to understand how Congress works we must consider the various factors that influence congressional voting.

FACTORS AFFECTING CONGRESSIONAL VOTING

Many things affect congressional voting: prior agreement with an executive agency or fear of presidential anger; career hopes both inside and outside Congress; the individual's principles; instructions from party leaders; campaign promises; favors owed to lobbyists; thorough staff briefings; friendships; bargains and compromises; guesses as to probable voter responses; and of course, committee loyalties.

Sometimes the outside observer is dismayed at the seeming casualness of it all, of great issues of state being decided on what appear to be the flimsiest of reasons. Here is one description:

> All but four of the one hundred senators' desks are unoccupied this afternoon. The debate on the pending amendment is sputtering along. In the visitors' galleries, groups of tourists, initially awed, then perplexed, have been filing in and out at the 15 minute intervals prescribed by the attendants. Now, after whispered consultations below, the debate ends and the voting bell sounds, reverberating through the vast Senate complex of Capitol Hill buildings. Scores of senators begin to converge upon the chamber.
>
> Possessed of the prima donna's disdain for peers, compelled by their profession to fight one another on issues, they have often measured each other as enemies. But they are conscious, too, that they are brothers, that ambition makes them endure the same indignities, wage the same lonely struggle for career survival. And so they compensate for the mutual hostility inherent in their situation with the kind of exaggerated cordiality that is evident as they enter the doorways together.
>
> But, as the senators approach their desks, the cordial glow is fleetingly interrupted by a look of perplexity — what the hell is the vote about this time? . . . To men so skilled, the minute remaining before the roll call should be adequate to identify the issue and divine the safe vote.
>
> Covertly, they case the situation through the particular stratagem each has worked out over the years. Some have aides who now come forward to whisper a 30-second summary of the 3-hour debate. Some just follow their party leader, who has minions stationed about the floor to pass the word "aye" or "nay" to the faithful. Some, who are not faithful, follow the lead of their particular Senate guru. . . . Some, particularly those who are committee chairmen or near-chairmen, automatically support the position of the chairman who has jurisdiction over the measure — for they expect the same hierarchical support when they are piloting their own bills through the Senate.
>
> And, too, there is a last-second vote hustling on the floor. "Give me a vote, Bill, if you can," the sponsor of the pending amendment will say to an undecided senator he has given a vote to in the past; and, if this is not one of those red-flagged issues of particular interest back home, the vote may well be given for "friendship's sake," with the donor carefully filing the incident away in his memory for future repayment.
>
> Thus, by a variety of means most of them substitute for personal study and decision, the senators work their will, and the votes are counted.[11]

Although this is a good description of much congressional voting, there are times when an issue is debated and investigated by all members. One such occasion was the Senate vote in 1969 on President Nixon's plan to deploy the Safeguard antiballistic missile (ABM). A marathon debate lasting nearly five months involved dozens of congressional witnesses, extensive media coverage,

[11] James Boyd, "A Senator's Day," in Charles Peters and Timothy J. Adams, eds., *Inside the System* (New York: Praeger, 1970), pp. 101–103.

serious study by many senators, and intense lobbying on both sides. The critical vote was a 50–50 tie, allowing Spiro Agnew (who as Vice-President officially presided over the Senate) to vote in favor of the administration's proposal. A few days before the vote Senator Pearson, a Kansas Republican, said, "You know, this issue will come as close as any to turning on the quiet conscience of the individual senators. The Senate would be a powerful instrument if all the issues were debated in this manner."[12]

Harried men and women, having to consider dozens of major bills and hundreds of minor ones, seldom can afford the time for thorough debate. What are some of the factors that influence voting?

Bargaining   Often a vote reflects outright bargaining: "You help me this time, and I'll give you a vote when you need it." Here is an exchange that took place during a 1956 debate on support for burley tobacco:

> MR. LANGER (North Dakota): We do not raise any tobacco in North Dakota, but we are interested in the tobacco situation in Kentucky, and I hope the Senator will support us in securing assistance for the wheat growers in our state.
>
> MR. CLEMENTS (Kentucky): I think the Senator will find that my support will be 100 percent.
>
> MR. BARKLEY (Kentucky): Mr. President, will my colleague from Kentucky yield?
>
> MR. CLEMENTS: I yield.
>
> MR. BARKLEY: The colloquy just had confirms and justifies the Woodrow Wilsonian doctrine of open covenants openly arrived at. (Laughter.)[13]

Friendship   Friendship also helps build winning coalitions. In August 1971 the Senate prepared to vote on a bill to bail Lockheed Aircraft Corporation out of its financial difficulties by giving federal guarantees to a huge loan. One senator who was determined to vote against the bill was Lee Metcalf, a Montana Democrat, who had told his staff that he was opposed to "big-business slush funds." "But as he approached the floor he was cornered by his friend Alan Cranston of California, home of potentially unemployed Lockheed workers. Senator Cranston beseeched his Democratic colleague not to throw thirty thousand people out of work. Metcalf, weakened, finally chose employment over ideology and voted for the Lockheed loan, which slipped by the Senate 49–48."[14]

Economic Interests   Of course some members of Congress are interested in the legislation at hand. Mississippi Democrat James

---

[12] Cited in Nathan Miller, "The Making of a Majority: Safeguard and the Senate," in Peters and Adams, p. 158.

[13] *Congressional Record*, February 16, 1956, pp. 2300–2301.

[14] Mark J. Green, James M. Fallows, and David R. Zwick, *Who Runs Congress?* A Ralph Nader Congress Project Report (New York: Bantam, 1972), p. 211.

Eastland sits on the Agriculture Committee and repeatedly votes against ceilings on farm subsidies. Perhaps it is not a coincidence that in 1971 his wife received $159,000 in agricultural subsidies for farmland held in her name. Russell Long of Louisiana, chairman of the Senate Finance Committee, long opposed any changes in oil depletion allowances. And well he might. Between 1964 and 1969 his income from oil was $1,196,915, of which more than $300,000 was tax free. Reasons Long about the possible conflict of interest: "If you have financial interests completely parallel to [those of] your state, then you have no problem." In 1969 the *Congressional Quarterly* estimated that 183 members of Congress held stock or other financial interests in companies doing business with the federal government or subject to federal legislation.[15]

Committee Recommendations Bargains, friendships, and economic interests undoubtedly influence some of the votes some of the time. But in the long run the most effective factors are committee recommendations, political party affiliations, and voting constituencies. A careful study of the 84th Congress found that if a large majority of the committee in charge of a bill support it, then its chances of full Senate approval are nearly perfect. Indeed, 51 bills received at least 80 percent support in committee; every one of them passed. In 37 cases committee support was between 60 percent and 80 percent; 32 passed. A recommendation from a divided committee passes only about half the time.[16]

Party Ties It has often been said that our congressional parties are "undisciplined," which means that individual party members are free to vote against the wishes of party leaders. In this way our political parties are very different from, say, those of Great Britain, where disloyal voting by party members is a vote of no confidence in the leadership and can bring down the government.

The lack of party discipline in the British sense does not mean that there is no relationship between party identification and congressional voting. This we already saw in Chapter 10, where Democrats and Republicans in the House were compared on major legislative issues spanning a quarter-century. All things being equal, which they seldom are, members of Congress prefer to vote with their party rather than against it. Usually this means that members who belong to the same party as the President try to support administration programs while the "opposition" party attempts to block those programs. Northern Democrats in the House, for instance, supported President Kennedy on 84 percent of the domestic legislation he favored. Southern Democrats were not quite as enthusiastic, giving him 57 percent support. Republicans, however, trailed with

[15] Evidence for this paragraph comes from ibid., p. 140.
[16] Donald R. Matthews, *U.S. Senators and Their World* (New York: Vintage, 1969). p. 170.

34 percent.[17] Students of Congress have concluded that party pressure, whether it is direct or indirect, is the most effective influence on congressional voting.

Voters Back Home When members of Congress regularly vote against their party, the reason is usually to be found in *perceived constituency preferences*. We have stressed the fact that citizens know little about their senator or representative, let alone how he or she might be voting on a complex tariff amendment in a subcommittee meeting. Yet there are times when voters do know a great deal about the stands taken by their representatives in Congress. A representative from Seattle, where many people depend for employment on the Boeing Aircraft Company, would not have been likely to vote against federal funding for the supersonic-transport plane that was once being built there. No senator who depends on his state's labor unions for campaign funds and workers would support a bill that outlawed the right to strike. A representative from a white, rural Alabama district need not ask how constituents feel about compensatory hiring of blacks; he or she knows how they feel and how he or she will vote on any such bill.

Thus constituency opinion does matter—not always, not even usually. But it seems to matter most on the questions that matter most to the people back home.

Caucuses In the past decade there has been a spurt in the formation of special caucuses within Congress. One of the best known is the Black Caucus, made up of sixteen black members of the House of Representatives, which frequently reviews bills that affect black citizens and then votes unanimously on these bills. There is also a Women's Caucus, a Rural Caucus, and several regional caucuses, including the 216-member Northwest-Midwest Economic Advancement Coalition, which attempts to steer federal projects away from the Sunbelt and the East Coast and toward the areas represented in the coalition.

One of the most recently formed groups is the Blue Collar Caucus, thirteen members of the House who come from working-class rather than professional or business backgrounds. The founder of this caucus, Edward P. Beard, a Democrat from Rhode Island, earned $9000 a year as a house painter before coming to Congress in 1975. He observes that the caucus members do not agree on all issues, "but when the little guy stands to get the short end, that's when the blue collar caucus speaks as one."[18]

Membership in a caucus, then, becomes another pressure in con-

---

[17] See Lewis A. Froman, Jr., *Congressmen and Their Constituencies* (Chicago: Rand McNally, 1963), Table 7.1, p. 91.
[18] *New York Times*, June 23, 1977.

sidering how to vote on issues. And since these caucuses frequently include members of both political parties, their presence in Congress tends to weaken the hold of party leaders over congressional voting.

Pressure from the White House Yet another factor which influences congressional voting is pressure from the White House, especially on legislation that the President or his staff have proposed. In the next chapter we review the Presidency as a source of legislative initiative and as a pressure on Congress.

Conclusions

Our discussion of Congress has covered much ground, and for good reason: Congress is at the center of our representative form of government. Some observers are unhappy about this, for they see in Congress the bankruptcy of democracy. Other observers believe the critics exaggerate the weaknesses and overlook the strengths of Congress. In this book we can give no final answers to our two major questions: How well does Congress represent? How well does it legislate? But the reader should think about these questions in the light of the material in this chapter. More analysis is to come on the second question; we will discuss the role of the President and even the Supreme Court as "legislators" or lawmakers. And on the first issue—how well does Congress represent—we present a controversial question to help you think through your answer.

controversy

There has been much debate over *whether* Congress represents or not, but this misses the point. When members of Congress try to get a pork-barrel federal program for their district, they are representing. Even when they favor policies that give tax advantages to wealthy constituents they are representing. At issue is not whether Congress represents but whether members of Congress should represent the interests of those who support and send them to Washington or the broader public interest.

One Side   Members of Congress should vote for their constituents' interests, at least insofar as they know what those interests are on a particular bill. Not only should they concern themselves with the voters back home, they should try to represent the groups and organizations that supply them with campaign funds. Someone who represents a wealthy community should try to whittle away at the progressive income tax, just as a colleague whose district is crowded with poor people should try to make taxes more progressive. If funds for the supersonic transport brings employment to your home state, your job is to fight for those funds. No one expects a black congresswoman from a northern city to prefer farm subsidies for Montana wheat growers over an educational head start program, and no one should expect her Montana colleague to favor the head start program over wheat subsidies. A senator who receives campaign funds from the AMA should oppose medicare, just as a representative who accepts campaign help from the Senior Citizens should favor it.

Take the case of Jamie Whitten, a Democratic representative from the hill country of northern Mississippi. He is the powerful chairman of the House Appropriations Subcommittee on Agriculture. From this strategic position he forced the Department of Health, Education and Welfare (HEW) to leave Mississippi out of the National Nutrition Survey, the first effort by the federal government to investigate malnutrition in the United States. He has delayed and blocked various programs that would provide surplus food to schoolchildren or other hungry citizens. He opposes any attempt to study how technological changes in farming might affect the livelihood of farm workers or sharecroppers. His record as an opponent of social-reform measures is consistent. And his record seems to impress his constituents, for he has been reelected continuously since 1941!

Reelection—this is the true test of democracy. Members of Congress are supposed to seek reelection, for this is the major check that voters have over them. To seek reelection is to favor policies that directly benefit local constituents or are of particular concern to groups that provide campaign funds. But this is what an elected representative assembly should do—represent those who send him or her to Washington.

The Other Side   Not everyone agrees with the congressman who insists that he isn't paid to be a statesman. The argument against representing narrow constituency interests was effectively voiced two centuries ago by Edmund Burke in a famous speech to the Electors of Bristol:

> Parliament is not a [collection] of ambassadors from different and hostile interests, which interests each must maintain, as an agent and advocate, against other agents and advocates; Parliament is a deliberative assembly of one nation,

with one interest—that of the whole—where not local purposes, not local prejudices, ought to guide, but the general good, resulting from the general reason of the whole. You choose a member, indeed; but when you have chosen him, he is not a member of Bristol, but he is a member of Parliament.[19]

Burke's observations deserve careful reading. He believed that there is more to representative democracy than satisfying the immediate needs of your supporters. Someone must be thinking about the whole picture. Someone must try to figure out which policies are best for the entire nation. The best place for this to happen is in an elected, deliberate assembly. In our government this would be the U.S. Congress.

Let us again consider Jamie Whitten. During World War II some people in the federal government began to ask how the black GI returning from the battlefields would adjust to conditions in the South. They thought it would be useful to plan a study that would help the government prepare for the range of social and economic difficulties that were likely to be faced by the returning war veterans. Whitten killed this proposal. As he saw it, the Department of Agriculture's job was to help cotton planters, not to help the rural poor. His view no doubt reflected the feelings of his supporters.

But in killing the proposed study and blocking many similar ideas, Whitten may have contributed to the massive rural—urban migration that has changed American society so much since the immediate post-World War II years. Northern cities, unprepared for the inflow of rural poor people and southern blacks, have faced the huge problems of urban decay and have not had the resources to handle those problems.

It would be foolish and incorrect to say that Whitten somehow "caused" the urban crisis of the 1960s. It is not foolish and not incorrect to say that creative government programs started in the 1940s but looking toward the 1960s might well have eased the sufferings caused by the rural—urban migration. A Congress full of representatives concerned primarily with narrow and immediate constituency preferences is not likely to think up and fund such creative programs. But this is what a truly representative legislature would do.

[19] Burke, *loc. cit.*

HOW INSTITUTIONS WORK: III
a bill becomes a law

Where do bills originate?   Any member of the House or Senate may introduce a bill, except that all revenue bills must originate in the House. Because no bill can become law unless it is passed by both the House and the Senate, the general procedure is for identical bills to be introduced at about the same time in both houses of Congress.

What is the difference between "public" and "private" bills?   A public bill affects general classes of citizens, while a private bill is for the relief of individual citizens.

What is the next step after a bill has been introduced?   The bill is referred to the appropriate committee, depending on the subject matter involved. Private bills, however, are referred wherever their sponsors indicate they should go.

Why is the committee so important to the life of a bill at this point?   As the figures in Table 12.7 indicate, each session of Congress faces far more bills than it can possibly handle. So do most committees. It is the committee chairpersons who decide which bills the committees will take up. And it is at this point that 80–90 percent of all bills introduced in Congress die without any action having been taken on them. Committees eliminate far more bills by ignoring them than by voting them down. Bills that have been set aside in committee are said to have been "pigeonholed." They can be rescued by a discharge petition signed by a majority of the House members or by a special resolution of the Senate, but such attempts are rare.

If a committee does decide to take up a bill, what are the stages that follow?   The bill is first scheduled for consideration by the committee or sent to a subcommittee. It is then studied and, if it is important enough, hearings are held. These may be either public or private. The subcommittee then amends, rewrites, or "marks up" a bill and sends it back to the full committee. The committee then votes on whether to report the bill to the House or the Senate. This is another critical stage of the life of a bill be-

TABLE 12.7
Bills Acted upon by the 90th Congress, Both Sessions

	House of Representatives	Senate	Total
Bills introduced and referred to committee	20,587	4,199	24,786
Bills reported by committee	1,319	1,403	2,722
Bills enacted into law	1,133	1,286	2,419

Source: Adapted from Nelson Polsby, *Congress and the Presidency* (Englewood Cliffs, N.J.: Prentice-Hall, 1971), p. 90.

cause the committee can effectively kill a proposal with an unfavorable vote or by simply not acting at all.

If a bill is favorably reported by a House committee, how is it then brought to the floor for a vote? The procedures used in the House at this stage are somewhat complicated. A bill coming out of committee is placed on one of several legislative calendars. Bills coming out of a certain few committees (Appropriations and Ways and Means, for example) are given privileged status and can be reported to the full House at any time for action. All other important public bills are assigned to the House Calendar. They need a "special rule" from the House Rules Committee before they can be sent to the floor for debate.

Why is the Rules Committee so important in conducting the business of the House? The role of the House Rules Committee has been compared to that of a traffic cop directing the flow of pending legislation. This committee not only determines the order in which bills get to the House floor but also sets the conditions under which they will be debated. The process works as follows: Normally when a bill is voted out of a House committee and entered on the calendar, the next step is for the committee chairperson to ask the Rules Committee for a special rule taking the bill off the calendar and putting it before the House. The Rules Committee usually holds hearings on this request at which both the managers and the opponents of the bill in question argue for or against the granting of a special rule. The question of a special rule is not just a formal procedure; members of the Rules Committee consider bills on their merits and with an eye toward party strategies. Any bill that fails to clear the Rules Committee has probably been derailed for good.

Is there no way in which a bill can be brought to a vote if it is blocked by the Rules Committee? There are several maneuvers, including the discharge petition, by which the Rules Committee can be forced to send a bill to the floor. But they are seldom used.

It should be pointed out that although the Rules Committee does sometimes block important legislation, the majority of the bills killed by the Committee are not of major importance. The Rules Committee does not control all bills reported from House committees. Most of the measures brought to the floor each session are noncontroversial and are handled in routine fashion via the "consent" and "private" calendars. Here the Rules Committee plays no part. There are perhaps only 100 bills during each session of Congress that are controversial enough to warrant at least moderate debate on the House floor. It is for these bills that the Rules Committee is important.

If a bill is reported by a Senate committee, how is it brought to the Senate floor for a vote? There is only one legislative calendar in the Senate, so bills reported out of Senate committees are all placed on the calendar of business. And in the Senate the power to schedule floor action is held by the majority party's Policy Committee.

These more simplified procedures for getting a bill onto the agenda illustrate one of the major differences between the House and the Senate: The House, a large, unwieldy body, operates according to rigidly defined schedules. The Senate, on the other hand, conducts its affairs less rigidly and with more room for informal agreements on procedure.

What are the rules by which floor debate is carried out? The ground rules for House debate are usually laid down in the special rule that has come out of the Rules Committee. This states how long a bill may be debated and whether it may be amended on the floor. If floor amendment is not allowed, the bill is considered under a "closed rule," which permits only members of the committee that reported it to make any changes in language. When amendments are allowed from anyone on the floor, this is an "open rule."

As might be expected, debate in the Senate is less restricted. Senate debate is allowed to run far off the legislative track. Debate is usually unlimited, a tradition that has given rise to the filibuster, in which senators who are opposed to a given bill engage in marathon speechmaking in order to tie up the Senate for days or weeks and stall action on other legislation. The hope is to force concessions on the bill against which the filibuster is directed or to get the bill set aside. Filibusters can be broken only by a three-fifths vote of the senators present, and although filibusters are infrequent, successful attempts to end them are even rarer.

What happens if the House and Senate pass different versions of a bill? If the differences are slight, one house may simply agree to the other's version. But if the differences are great it is necessary to appoint a conference committee staffed by interested senior members from the House and Senate committees that managed the bill. They work together to iron out language acceptable to both, but a majority vote of each group is needed for approval. If the Conference is successful, the final text of the bill must still go back to each house for final approval.

After a bill has been passed by Congress and sent to the White House, what choices does the President have? The President is faced with four possibilities. He can simply sign the bill. Or, if he fails to sign it within ten days and Congress is in session, the bill becomes law without his signature. However, if Congress has adjourned, the President's failure to act constitutes a "pocket veto" and the bill does not become law. Finally, the President can veto the bill by refusing to sign it and returning it to Congress. Congress can then reconsider the bill but must pass it with a two-thirds majority in both houses for it to become law. Otherwise the bill dies.

What does the series of steps necessary to make a bill into a law tell us about power in Congress? Power in Congress is essentially negative. Any bill that is introduced must get over a series of hurdles. If a piece of legislation stumbles at any point along the way, it is very likely out of the running: You can clear the first five tests, fail on the sixth, and thus lose the entire effort. The result of such a system is that interest groups and political opponents have numerous points of access to the legislative process. They can tie up, rewrite, or defeat a bill at many points along the way, adapting their strategies and shifting their forces accordingly. As a result the kind of power required to maneuver a bill through Congress is the power to shape formulas that are acceptable to the majorities in the subcommittee, in the full committee, on the floor, and in conference. It is the power to combine politics with procedure without one strangling the other, and it rests largely with the President and his congressional supporters, with the leadership of the House and Senate, and with the managers of bills in committee.

13
THE PRESIDENCY

Presidents and the Presidency

No institution in American government is more difficult to describe than the Presidency. This may seem an odd thing to say. Isn't the President the most watched and written-about person in the United States, if not in the world? Probably so, but this fact adds to our problem rather than solving it. We know so much about individual Presidents that it is tempting to tell stories about them: about Jimmy Carter's surprising election victory as an outsider; about Richard Nixon's corrupt use of office and the Watergate scandal; about John Kennedy's sudden, violent death; and so on all the way back to the Presidents who are now more myth than man: Lincoln, Jackson, Jefferson, Washington.

Stories about individual Presidents do not necessarily add up to much in the way of political explanation. There is a good reason for this. While Presidents are of interest to us because they have considerable power under our form of government, their powers amount to little unless they are transformed into policies by the institutions of government. Thus in our explanation we must go beyond the individual to the institution, beyond the President to the *Presidency*.

The Cabinet, the Executive Office, the White House Staff, and certain independent commissions make up the Presidency. It is from this network of organizations that the President gets *information* and *advice.* This information and advice leads to presidential policies, which then must be translated into concrete policy programs. *Policy formation*, then, also derives from the Presidency. Having settled on a policy, to whom does the President turn to have it carried out? As with policy formation, with *policy implementation* too the Presidency is critical. But of course policies cannot be carried out unless they are authorized and funded by Congress. So an additional task of the Presidency is to seek *permission* to carry out the President's program.

All of these tasks—policy advice, formulation, permission, and implementation—are necessary if the modern President is to leave his mark on history, and most Presidents very much want to leave such a mark. Our chapter, then, will have to consider the President and the Presidency. We will start with the major powers granted to the President by the Constitution and then turn to the growth and organization of the Presidency.

The Constitution and Presidential Powers

Shortly after winning the 1960 presidential election John Kennedy expressed his idea of the Presidency: "The history of this nation — its brightest and its bleakest pages — has been written largely in terms of the different views our Presidents have had of the Presidency itself." Perhaps this claim is exaggerated; a good deal more has gone into American history than how three dozen men have defined their duty. But some truth remains in Kennedy's comment. More than other men, by a wide margin, the President of the United States can affect — though not control — history. What else did Kennedy think about the Presidency? Here are some excerpts from his speech:

> He must above all be the Chief Executive in every sense of that word. He must be prepared to exercise the fullest powers of his office — all that are specified and some that are not. He must master complex problems. . . . He must originate action. . . . It is the President alone who must make the major decisions of our foreign policy. That is what the Constitution wisely commands. And even domestically, the President must initiate policies and devise laws to meet the needs of the nation. And he must be prepared to use all the resources of his office to insure the enactment of that legislation. . . .
>
> But the White House is not only the center of political leadership. It must be the center of moral leadership — a "bully pulpit," as Theodore Roosevelt described it. For only the President represents the national interest. And upon him alone converge all the needs and aspirations of all parts of the country, all departments of the Government, all nations of the world.

Kennedy, an energetic President, undoubtedly claimed more powers for the Presidency than the Constitution intended. This is in the tradition of such strong nineteenth-century Presidents as Jefferson, Jackson, and Lincoln, a tradition carried on in the twentieth century by Wilson, both Roosevelts, Truman, Johnson, and Nixon. These men have poured much meaning into the ambiguous language of Article 2 of the Constitution: "The executive power shall be vested in a President of the United States of America."

The Constitution does more than assign executive powers to the Presidency, though not much more. Section 2 of Article 2 states that the President shall be Commander-in-Chief; in Section 3 the President is told to inform Congress on the state of the Union and to recommend legislation. These duties have served as the basis for the huge growth of the executive branch of the government. At the center stands the President, who, along with close advisers and department heads, has control over the extensive military, economic, and personnel resources of the executive branch.

In 1957 a federal court order directed the Little Rock, Arkansas school system to desegregate its public schools. The white citizens of Little Rock, the school officials, and even the governor of Arkansas refused to obey. When a federal court order is disobeyed, what is the President to do? In this case the President acted as Commander-in-Chief. Eisenhower sent federal troops to Little Rock. In a radio and television address to the nation, he explained his action.

> For a few minutes this evening I want to speak to you about the serious situation that has arisen in Little Rock. . . . In that city, under the leadership of demagogic extremists, disorderly mobs have deliberately prevented the carrying out of proper orders from a federal court. . . . I have today issued an executive order directing the use of troops under Federal authority to aid in the execution of Federal law at Little Rock, Arkansas. . . . Unless the President did so, anarchy would result.

The same powers and responsibilities were cited five years later by President Kennedy in response to a threat from outside the nation's boundaries. In October 1962, as Kennedy was having breakfast, his chief of staff for national security affairs arrived with bad news. The Central Intelligence Agency had evidence that the Soviet Union was arming Cuba with intermediate-range ballistic missiles that could destroy nearly any city in the United States. A week of intensive and very secret meetings between the President and his advisers resulted in the Cuban blockade, a military act that prevented Soviet ships from landing and installing the missiles. The President went on national television to announce his decision:

> Now, therefore, I, John F. Kennedy, President of the United States of America, acting under and by virtue of the authority conferred upon me by the Constitution and statutes of the United States . . . do hereby proclaim that the forces under my command are ordered . . . to interdict, subject to the instructions herein contained, the delivery of offensive weapons and associated material to Cuba.

WAR POWERS

The wisdom of sending troops to Little Rock or blockading Cuba might be questioned. The authority of Eisenhower and Kennedy to act as they did is not questionable, for clearly the Constitution states that the President is Commander-in-Chief of the armed forces.

But there is a paradox here. The Constitution gives Congress the right to declare war. It might be supposed, then, that the President's authority as commander of the armed forces would come into play when a war has been declared. This is not the case. There was no war in Little Rock when Eisenhower sent in troops. And we were not at war with either Cuba or the Soviet Union when Kennedy ordered the blockade.

Thus the President's powers as Commander-in-Chief are very much greater than they appear at first glance. The President can act

militarily whether there is a declared war or not. Indeed, Congress
has declared war only five times since 1789: the War of 1812, the
Mexican War, the Spanish-American War, World War I, and World
War II. And during this time U.S. forces have been involved in overseas military action more than 150 times. William Rehnquist, now
an associate justice of the Supreme Court, wrote in 1970: "The
United States may lawfully engage in armed hostilities with a
foreign power without a congressional declaration of war."

This view has been challenged by members of Congress. Congressional resolutions on Cambodia and Vietnam have limited the
kinds of military action the President is allowed to take. But these
resolutions have not changed the basic fact that military action and
war are not the same thing.

The distinction between military action and war has been basic
to the growth of presidential powers in the twentieth century.
President Roosevelt drew on this doctrine in 1940, when he gave
military protection and supplies to Britain in the months before
Pearl Harbor. The United States was formally neutral at the time
but was clearly aligning itself with Britain against Germany. Other
cases are the military action in Korea in 1950 and the stationing of
seven U.S. divisions in Germany in 1951, actions taken by President Truman without a declaration of war by Congress.

More recently, we have had the Bay of Pigs invasion of Cuba
(under Kennedy), the marine military action in the Dominican Republic and the attacks on North Vietnam (under Johnson), the
bombing and invasion of Cambodia and Laos (under Nixon), and the
attack against Cambodian forces to free the crew of the captured
merchant ship *Mayaguez* (under Ford). The history of the twentieth
century makes it clear that the President's power as Commander-
in-Chief is in fact the power to make war, and that this power has
greatly increased the role of the President in domestic and international affairs.

The Power to Declare "Peace"   Most cases of presidential war making throughout our history have had widespread popular support and at least implicit congressional approval. The Vietnam experience, however, convinced many people that checks must be placed on this potentially unlimited power. As a result in 1973 Congress overrode a presidential veto and passed the landmark War Powers Act. For the first time strict limits were placed on the President's authority to commit U.S. armed forces to combat. Basically, the law requires that the President report to Congress any commitment of military forces within 48 hours and that the forces be disengaged after 60 days unless Congress expressly authorizes further action.

The War Powers Act in effect gives Congress the right to declare a war effort over, to declare "peace" if it believes that the presidential action is misguided. President Nixon vetoed this act, denouncing the new law as "both unconstitutional and dangerous to the best interests of our nation." He maintained that it would "seriously undermine this nation's ability to act decisively and convincingly in times of international crisis." We do not yet know whether the War Powers Act will have any such effect, but it stands to future Presidents as a statement that they do not have unlimited power to engage in armed conflict.

THE PRESIDENT'S FOREIGN-POLICY POWERS

Tradition as well as the Constitution has made the federal government the sovereign power in foreign affairs and established the President as the nation's chief diplomat. Foreign policy has been carried out by the President, especially in the past half-century. Only the President is in "continuous session," and for this reason, if for no other, many foreign-policy powers are his to claim. It is often said that the world has shrunk in the twentieth century. Things happen quickly, and what happens in one part of the world affects what happens elsewhere. The business, military, and diplomatic empire of the United States is scattered around the world. A language riot in India, a border incident in Latin America, a monetary crisis in Europe, a new security pact in the Arab world—these and thousands of other happenings affect American programs and people. They require quick attention and action.

The President is in a position to act. He has authority over the network of ambassadors and consulates and technical-aid offices throughout the world; he is responsible for the nation's military forces; he has direct access to a huge international intelligence operation that provides the information on which foreign policy is based. In his actions as Commander-in-Chief and chief diplomat, the President cannot avoid making policy. Nixon's dramatic visit to China in 1972 is a case in point. This visit was planned in strict secrecy. Congressional approval was not necessary. The American public was not informed until the final arrangements had been made. Yet the policy significance of this visit was perhaps greater than that of any other single action by Nixon in his first term. The visit had an immediate effect on China's admission into the United

Nations, on U.S. military and technical aid policy toward India, on security pacts with Japan, and on summit talks with the Soviet Union later in the year. The visit had longer-term effects on our trade and tariff policies, our nuclear strategy, and our balance of payments.

But we do not react with surprise on learning that the President can change our military stance and our foreign relations. After all, this role is assigned to him by the Constitution. Most modern-day Presidents have been only too willing to engage in summit politics. Few seem able to resist the temptation to "remake" the world, or at least to make sure that the enormous military, economic, and diplomatic resources of the United States are felt worldwide.

Executive Agreements   The President does not have unlimited control over foreign policy. Congress periodically tries to assert its influence primarily by threatening to shut off funds for foreign programs of which it disapproves. It can also refuse to agree to treaties, but the President has a way of getting around this congressional power. *Executive agreements* between the United States and another nation are formulated by the State Department and put into effect by the President. Such agreements do not need congressional approval, and they can include such major arrangements as the location of military bases and the types of technical and military programs undertaken by the United States.

THE PRESIDENT AS INITIATOR OF DOMESTIC POLICIES

The Constitution says that the President "shall from time to time give to the Congress information of the State of the Union, and recommend to their consideration such measures as he shall judge necessary and expedient." On this basis all forceful Presidents have announced their own legislative programs: Franklin Roosevelt's "New Deal," John Kennedy's "New Frontier," and Lyndon Johnson's "Great Society" are examples of such programs. Legislative proposals are put forth in the State of the Union Address, the Budget Message, and the Economic Report. (President Nixon added a State of the World Message in which he outlined his foreign-policy goals.) In addition to these formal speeches, the President can and does send special messages to Congress at any time, as President Carter did in the case of energy policy and economic programs.

The State of the Union Address   The annual State of the Union Address is most often used to announce a presidential program. A good example is Nixon's 1972 address, in which he proposed specific legislation in eighteen different policy areas: technology, trade and monetary affairs, welfare reform, social services, environment, health care, hunger and nutrition, aging and the elderly, civil rights, women's rights, veterans' benefits, youth, farmers, the cities, transportation, crime, consumer protection, and school financing. In each area he referred to legislative proposals made during his first administration or promised to make specific proposals over the course of the coming year.

Presidential proposals and special messages become the legislative agenda. In one year, for instance, President Johnson asked for congressional action on 469 separate proposals. And as recently as 1968 the Democratic Congress was complaining that the Republican administration was not sending over enough new legislative proposals to keep it busy. Since then, however, Congress has become very sensitive to the charge of presidential domination and has taken a more active role in reasserting its legislative authority. It is no longer true that "the President proposes and Congress disposes."

The Domestic–Foreign-Policy Connection   Earlier we stressed the considered powers of the President in foreign policy making. Now, in considering his role in domestic policy making, we take note that Congress is at least a coequal branch, for reasons that were outlined in the preceding chapter. We need also to realize that many so-called foreign-policy questions are actually domestic issues in disguise. And on those questions the autonomy of the President is severely restricted by Congress and by the role of interest groups in American politics.

A good example of a "foreign policy" that is as much domestic as foreign is tariff policy. What, if any, taxes should be imposed on goods imported from foreign nations? Should there be taxes on Sony TV sets from Japan or on Volkswagen cars from West Germany? On the one hand, these questions involve delicate trade negotiations with Japan and West Germany and other nations. On the other hand, these are issues that are of great importance to American manufacturers and trade unions. They are of concern not only to TV and auto manufacturers, who would prefer high tariffs to keep competitive products out of the United States, but also to American manufacturers who export to Japan and West Germany and do not want to face high tariffs in those countries.

The President as a negotiator of tariffs and trade relationships has much less autonomy than the President as a negotiator of security

or defense matters. President Carter has much more room to maneuver in arriving at a strategic arms limitation treaty than he does in changing the terms of a tariff treaty. And of course even security questions can become so visible and symbolic that the President is subject to pressure from public and congressional opinion. President Carter found this to be the case with his Panama Canal Treaty, as President Nixon had with his policies designed to end the Vietnam War.

Establishment of the Presidency

A President's national-security and domestic policies are products not of a single individual but of the large number of people who make up what we have called the Presidency. The modern-day Presidency has roots that go back to the founding of the nation. The writers of the Constitution provided that the President "may require the Opinion, in writing, of the Principal Officer in each of the executive Departments," which, during the administration of George Washington, meant an Attorney General and the Secretaries of the first three Departments: State, Treasury, and War.

Initially the President needed a few advisers and people he could rely on for information about conditions requiring his attention. A small staff was adequate. Gradually, as matters of state became more complex and more demanding, the number of departments grew and the advisory staff expanded. We can trace the history of the Presidency in terms of three major institutions: the Cabinet, the White House staff, and the executive Office.

THE CABINET

Traditionally the Cabinet is composed of the chief executive secretaries of the major departments in the executive branch of the government. In 1789 there were only three departments, each responsible for one of the major tasks of government: the task of national security and war preparedness was assigned to the Department of War (now the Department of Defense); the task of coining money and providing for a means of economic exchange was assigned to the Department of the Treasury; and the task of dealing with foreign nations and taking care of important documents of the new government was assigned to the Department of State. In addition, there was an Attorney General, though as yet there was no Department of Justice.

At present there are twelve Departments, eight more than when the nation was founded. These departments were formed in response to the evolution of new governmental functions and the formation of new groups in the society whose needs had to be met. In the nineteenth century the Interior Department was formed to manage the western lands, mining rights, and the like, and the Agriculture Department was formed to meet the needs of farmers.

Shortly after the beginning of this century the Commerce and Labor Departments were formed to deal with the problems of business and labor that had been created as the nation became industrialized. New social problems led to the creation of new departments. The Department of Health, Education and Welfare (HEW) was formed out of a large number of separate agencies that provided social services to citizens. Other departments created in recent years are Housing and Urban Development, Transportation, and in 1977, Energy. They clearly reflect the issues and problems of modern America.

Today the nation is served by two departments that are responsible for national survival—State and Defense; two departments that exercise basic control functions—Treasury, which has control over the money supply, and Justice, which is responsible for public order; four departments that provide services to specific economic interests; and four departments that administer social welfare and attempt to provide programs for an urbanized America. All of these departments of course belong to the executive branch of the government.

Many of the departments grew up in response to the needs of social groups for government services. In most cases the departments have close ties with these groups. The departments often represent the interests of their clienteles: The Agriculture Department works closely with farm groups, the Labor Department with unions, the Commerce Department with business, HEW with doctors and educators. These close ties sometimes make it hard for the President to exercise control over the departments. They are often more responsive to their clienteles than to presidential directives.

The heads of the departments, as well as other top-level officials, are appointed by the President. The departments are responsible for gathering information, advising the President, outlining policy alternatives, negotiating with Congress, and executing the laws and programs passed or authorized by Congress.

There was a time when the Cabinet actually functioned as a Cabinet, that is, as a group that met with the President and reviewed various policy alternatives. Votes would be taken, with the President's vote equal to that of any other cabinet member. But two things happened. First, the President became more powerful. This is illustrated by a story told of President Lincoln. After being unanimously outvoted by his Cabinet, Lincoln announced the vote as "seven nays and one aye—the ayes have it." Second, the Cabinet has practically ceased to function as a group of advisers. It is not difficult to see why. Here a close adviser to President Johnson explains why Johnson turned to his personal staff rather than his Cabinet for advice:

> Power, in the Presidential sense, is a very personal thing. It is invested in one man in the White House. Since power is his greatest resource, it is the instrument by which he works his will. It is not something he is likely to invest in people whose first allegiance is not to him. He is not

likely to share what is his most precious resource with people whom he does not know well. Many Cabinet officers are men who are not well known to the President personally prior to his inauguration. They also become men with ties to their own departments, to the bureaucracy, to congressional committees, rather than exclusively to the President, as is the case with White House assistants.[1]

This quotation suggests why it is difficult for the President to use the heads of departments as a functioning Cabinet for advice on general policy. Each Cabinet member is normally in charge of a government department. Thus there is a Secretary of the Treasury, of Commerce, of Defense, and so forth. The people chosen to head the major government departments usually come from the President's party; they nearly always have had extensive experience; and that experience is normally in the area the department is responsible for. The Secretary of Agriculture, for example, will have long been active in farm matters and will be acceptable to the group his or her department works with, including the large farmer organizations.

It is sometimes said that the Cabinet should meet at regular times, coordinate government strategy, and advise the President on policy matters. Few Cabinets have done this. It is rare to find a department head who does not have what a general once termed *localitis:* "the conviction ardently held by every theater commander that the war was being won or lost in his own zone of responsibility, and that the withholding of whatever was necessary for local success was evidence of blindness, if not of imbecility, in the high command."[2] Most Cabinet members struggle to expand programs in their own departments. And though this is expected of department heads, it keeps the Cabinet from becoming a useful advisory group. Most Presidents use Cabinet meetings to inform one department of the government what other departments are doing. For actual advice on policy matters Presidents use smaller, hand-chosen groups.

Intragovernment Conflict Most of us who do not think too much about government tend to assume that a given presidential group must be pretty much in agreement on major issues. There are many examples in this chapter that suggest how wrong this assumption is. One of the major reasons for intragovernment conflict is that very different interests are represented by the different executive departments.

---

[1] Bill Moyers, taken from an interview conducted by Hugh Sidney, reprinted in Charles Peters and Timothy J. Adams, eds., *Inside the System* (New York: Praeger, 1970), p. 24.

[2] This remark is attributed to General George C. Marshall in Arthur M. Schlesinger, Jr., *The Age of Roosevelt: The Coming of the New Deal* (Boston: Houghton Mifflin, 1958), II, 520.

A revealing instance of this situation is the conflict between the Department of Agriculture and the Department of Health, Education and Welfare over the perils of smoking. HEW is deeply concerned about preventive medicine; and most of the doctors and scientists who work in HEW support the position that "Cigarette Smoking Can Be Dangerous to Your Health," the warning that appears on all cigarette advertisements. Yet at the same time that the government is warning us against smoking it is providing nearly $80 million a year to tobacco growers in the way of subsidies. This support to the tobacco industry is administered by the Department of Agriculture, whose present Secretary, Robert Bergland, has observed that "The Department cannot involve itself in the health aspects of tobacco." Here we have the government using taxpayer dollars to support an industry product that other government scientists, who are paid with taxpayer dollars, have concluded is likely to produce cancer. The government is also, of course, heavily involved in cancer research.

This example further illustrates the difficulty of using the Cabinet as an advisory group, for the head of Agriculture and the head of HEW would immediately be insisting on mutually contradictory policies. The conflict between department heads is avoided by allowing them each to pursue their own particular policies. When President Carter, a nonsmoker, was urged by a member of his staff to take a stand against the tobacco subsidies, he responded: "I refuse to be drawn into this fruitless issue."[3]

THE WHITE HOUSE

By the late 1930s the President was surrounded by so many executive departments and agencies that he found it difficult to coordinate their activities. There was concern about the lack of effective control by the President over his own branch of the government. Accordingly, in 1939 a major step was taken toward creating the modern Presidency. Two new units in the executive branch were created: the White House Staff and the Executive Office of the President.

The White House Staff The White House Staff is the group of advisers who are closest to the President. They work in the same building as the President—the White House itself. They generally have access to the President and provide him with much of the information he uses in making decisions. Some members of the White House Staff are close personal advisers as well, but this tends to depend more on their personal relations with the President than on a particular title. The main task of the White House Staff has been to carry the President's message to other parts of the executive branch and to summarize the information that comes from the

[3] This quotation, together with the previous quotation by Bergland, appears in *Science*, 197, no. 4302 (July 29, 1977), 443.

departments and agencies as well as from Congress, the public, and interest group leaders.

At the beginning of Jimmy Carter's administration the White House Staff consisted of about 550 people. The members of the staff have titles such as "special counselor," "special adviser," or "assistant to the President." They are responsible for a wide range of areas from international security to social security to science and technology. They also deal with crises or problems that arise unexpectedly or cannot be handled by existing agencies.

Every President approaches the task of staffing and managing the Presidency somewhat differently. FDR encouraged overlapping lines of communication and jurisdiction, sometimes giving the same job to two separate agencies. He did this in order to keep close control over the separate units of the Presidency. Eisenhower organized the Presidency in almost the opposite way. Drawing on his military experience, he established a firm hierarchy of responsibility; only the most important issues were supposed to reach his desk. Kennedy had a habit of calling together small, informal groups to work on particular issues until a decision had been reached or a program formulated. Nixon relied heavily on a few key advisers, as we will see later in the chapter when we discuss Watergate.

Although there are differences in style from one President to the next, there are certain common problems in the relationship between President and staff. To get information and intelligent advice on dozens of matters, the President surrounds himself with experienced advisers. It is natural to expect that these advisers have firm ideas of their own. Yet the temptation to say what "the Chief" wants to hear is very great indeed. For while the President expects independent ideas from his staff he also expects loyalty to himself and the administration's program. From the President's point of view his strong-minded staff must never undermine the policy goals he has set. Early in his first term Nixon fired a Cabinet member, Walter Hickel (Secretary of the Interior), for writing a letter complaining that the Nixon administration was not sensitive to the demands of college youth. As far as Nixon was concerned the line between loyal dissent and disloyal opposition had been crossed by a member of the team, and off the team he went.

THE EXECUTIVE OFFICE OF THE PRESIDENT

Originally the Executive Office was simply the Bureau of the Budget, now called the Office of Management and Budget (OMB). But the Executive Office is today a much expanded and very diverse part of the Presidency. The entire Executive Office numbers about 6000 people and is housed in a building across the street from the White House. While these people do not work with the President as closely as the White House Staff, they greatly affect the President's thinking. The President will draw some of this top advisers from the heads of his Executive Office agencies. More and more these agencies are collecting information, drawing up policies, and implementing them. These are responsibilities that were once reserved for the Cabinet and the independent agencies.

In addition to the OMB, the most important agencies in the Executive Office are the National Security Council and the Council of Economic Advisers. These agencies do about what you would expect from their titles. The National Security Council is heavily involved in foreign policy and related security matters. The Central Intelligence Agency (CIA) is part of the Council. It provides the President with intelligence about other nations and, at least until recently, was often involved in carrying out secret actions abroad. The invasion of Cuba during John Kennedy's Presidency was in large part planned and executed by the CIA.

The Council of Economic Advisers is less dramatic but no less important. This group supplies the President with information about how the economy is performing and advice about what to do if that performance is poor. The policy proposals of these advisers can directly and sometimes substantially affect levels of employment, rates of inflation, and patterns of business investment.

THE OFFICE OF MANAGEMENT AND BUDGET

Presidents have long tried to coordinate the executive branch through the budget. Each year the President sends a budget to Congress, listing the programs he wants supported and the amount that would be spent on each.

The Bureau of the Budget was set up to coordinate budget requests from the various departments and fit them into the overall presidential program. During the Nixon administration its name was changed to Office of Management and Budget. The purpose of the new agency is to coordinate all parts of the executive branch, not only in the preparation of the budget but in the actual administration of policies.

The OMB gives the executive branch a new tool. But it will hardly solve all problems of coordination. It has been criticized by particular agencies for interference in the administration of programs. The bureaucrats in the operating agencies (the agencies that carry out particular programs) claim that the bureaucrats in the OMB are not well informed about the programs they are trying to control. This shows that the struggle within the executive branch between the Office of the President and the various departments will continue. The former tries to coordinate, the latter to maintain some independence. It is a struggle that neither side can win, though the balance may shift one way or the other.

SUMMARY

The important features of the Presidency have now been described: executive departments, independent agencies, and, especially, the White House Staff and the Executive Office. It is the Presidency that largely provides information and advice to the President, helps formulate and then implement policies, and establishes contact with such critical actors as Congress, the media, state and city leaders, and important interest group leaders.

The President: Pressures Toward Activism

It is very difficult for modern Presidents to resist the temptation to create new programs and expand the government. There is a simple reason for this: "The expansion of government tends to go hand in hand with the type of rhetoric and oratory needed to get elected, whereas the contraction of government tends to sound unappealing, unimaginative, negative."[4]

The candidacy of Jimmy Carter illustrates this principle. Shortly after his election Carter's chief policy adviser for domestic issues put together a mimeographed volume called *Promises, Promises,* a collection of all the things Carter promised the electorate during his long campaign for the White House. Promise after promise stresses the need to act, to initiate, to promote, to regulate, to help, to provide, to reform, and to increase. Carter won the Presidency by promising to do more, not less.

And once in the White House Carter did initiate many actions. It would be surprising to learn otherwise. Carter the President is, after all, surrounded by energetic and ambitious people. And out of this Presidency comes pressure for new solutions to old problems. Let us look more closely at this process.

HOW PROPOSALS ORIGINATE AND DEVELOP

Many proposals come directly from close presidential advisers. A good example is the role of Henry Kissinger, who served as special national-security adviser to Presidents Nixon and Ford. At first Kissinger was brought to the White House to give attention to long-term security and foreign-policy questions. He was given funds to support a highly professional group of personal advisers and researchers. His own group numbered about fifty people chosen on the basis of great achievement in security, military, and diplomatic matters. Once assembled, Kissinger and his staff were soon involved in the day-to-day decisions of foreign policy. Kissinger was respon-

[4] Tom Bethell, "The Need to Act," *Harper's,* November 1977, p. 38.

sible for setting up the China and Russia summit meetings, personally negotiated the end of U.S. involvement in the Vietnam War, and took part in the Middle East peace talks.

The White House staff does not have sole responsibility for the presidential program. A specific proposal can come from a variety of sources within the executive branch—and can be greatly modified or even blocked long before it reaches the President and his closest advisers. Although no overview can describe how the executive program comes to be, the following is one fairly common route.

A department or agency within the executive branch begins to formulate a new program or modify an existing one. It may consult with a relevant congressional committee even at this very early stage, though this is usually done informally. The agency might also check with any interest groups that normally have a position on such programs. If the Department of Health, Education and Welfare has a group of people working on a program for federally financed university scholarships, for example, it is likely that they would be in touch with the staffs of the congressional committees that normally handle bills on education. They would also be in touch with relevant organizations such as the American Association for the Advancement of Science. The program would begin to take shape, including some provisions (e.g., low-interest loans) but dropping others (e.g., support for graduate teaching assistants) in response to actual or imagined opposition. As the proposal took shape, it would be sent to the OMB.

The OMB is the chief clearinghouse of the executive branch. It is responsible for coordinating the hundreds of programs that are proposed by various executive agencies. It also has the power to suggest to the President or his staff advisers that a proposed program cannot be fitted into the budget this year. A proposal that does not get through the OMB has very little chance of reaching the President's desk, let alone becoming law. And the OMB is in constant contact with congressional leaders, keeping informed of what legislation might be developing in a particular committee. Sometimes the OMB will advise an executive agency to shelve its program because a group on Capitol Hill already has congressional support for a similar project.

Even when an agency proposal gets through the OMB, it will not necessarily become part of the President's own legislative program. The executive agency may, however, be given the green light to try to get congressional action on its own. Franklin D. Roosevelt did this as early as 1935. To protect his own programs from various agencies in the federal bureaucracy, and to protect agencies from sniping at one another, he divided proposals into three categories:

> First, the kind of legislation that, administratively, I could not give approval to—[clearance] will eliminate that; secondly, the type of legislation which we are perfectly willing to have the department or agency press for, but at the same time we do not want it put into the [third] category of major Administration bills. Obviously I have to confine myself to what the newspapers called last year "the comparatively small list of *must* legislation." If I make every bill that the Government is interested in *must* legislation, it is going to complicate things . . . very much; and where I clear legislation with a notation that says "no objection" that means you are at perfect liberty to try to get the thing through [Congress], but I am not going to send a special message for it. It is all your trouble, not mine.[5]

Of course from the President's viewpoint there is *must* legislation, and it is these proposals that receive his attention and effort. Yet we should not attribute too much of the President's legislative program to his own ideas. For the most part a President's personal policy views are only vaguely formulated. He does not have the time to think through all the details of legislative proposals. However, his advisers, staff, party leaders, and executive heads do have strong interests in specific policies. Most of the proposals sent to Congress by the White House come from these sources. And these "high-energy" advisers are themselves in touch with a larger network that includes members of Congress, governors and other state officials, big-city mayors, powerful interest group leaders, and media people. Presidential proposals, then, reflect at least some shared outlooks.

This illustrates the importance of the types of people and interests that a new administration brings to Washington. A President understandably wants to win a place in history. To do so he depends

[5] This statement was made at a meeting of the National Emergency Council, as recorded in the *Proceedings of the Twenty-Second Meeting,* January 22, 1935, p. 2.

Roosevelt was the first President to use the airwaves to go directly to the people, and his lead has been followed by every President since.

heavily on a staff that can shape a set of legislative proposals that is likely to receive support in Congress.

TACTICS FOR GETTING PROGRAMS ENACTED

What a President sets out to get and what he actually gets are two different things. It is true that the chief executive and his staff have many resources. Some of these we have named: executive agreements in foreign policy, party leadership and control over jobs, a huge bureaucracy to give him information and proposals, the status of Commander-in-Chief, and ready access to the news media.

In addition, the President can put pressure on important members of Congress. Johnson and Kennedy, who had both served in the House and the Senate, relied heavily on this tactic. Johnson was in close contact with members of Congress when Presidential measures were at stake. Here is how one influential member of the House Rules Committee commented on a telephone call from the President:

> What do you say to the President of the United States? I told him I'd sleep on it. Then the next day I said to myself, "I've always been a party man, and if he really wanted me of course I'd go along even if the bill wasn't set up exactly the way I wanted it." Probably I took half a dozen guys with me. We won in the crunch by six votes. Now, I wouldn't have voted for it except for this telephone call.[6]

Presidents use the prestige of the office to put pressure on Congress in a second way. They sometimes go on national radio or TV to speak directly to the public and to urge the public to pressure Congress in behalf of presidential programs. Franklin Roosevelt did this in his famous fireside chats. Here is Roosevelt in 1942 asking for price controls:

> Today I sent a message to the Congress, pointing out the overwhelming urgency of the serious domestic economic crisis with which we are threatened. . . . I have asked the Congress to pass legislation under which the President would be specifically authorized to stabilize the cost of living, including the price of all farm commodities.

Roosevelt expected action within three weeks. If Congress didn't act, he pledged to act anyway, giving the war as a cause:

> In the event that the Congress should fail to act, and act adequately, I shall accept the responsibility, and I will act. The President has the powers, under the Constitution and under Congressional Acts, to take measures necessary to avert a disaster which would interfere with the winning of the war.

Whether Roosevelt actually had those powers was never tested in the courts, for Congress acted.

Recent Presidents have followed Roosevelt's lead. Nixon was under congressional pressure to deescalate the Vietnam War when

---

[6] *Newsweek,* August 2, 1965, p. 22. Copyright 1965 by Newsweek, Inc. All rights reserved. Reprinted by permission.

he sent troops into Cambodia (1970) and later mined the harbor of Haiphong (1972). Both times he went on national television to plead for public support. Nixon later used television in an attempt to sway public opinion during the Watergate affair. In this attempt he was quite unsuccessful; his popularity rating had fallen to an all-time low just before he resigned. Carter used television to generate support for his energy program, again without much success.

THE PRESIDENTIAL PROGRAM: RESTRAINTS

To review the role of the Presidency in formulating programs is not to say that Presidents always, or even usually, get what they want. The President is restrained because he shares powers with Congress and also by the difficulty of starting new programs and, even more important, by the difficulty of stopping old ones.

CONGRESS AS A RESTRAINT ON PRESIDENTIAL PROPOSALS

The press often exaggerates the power of the Presidency in making public policy. It refers to Johnson's War on Poverty or Carter's National Energy Plan. But seldom is a major presidential program passed without any changes. An executive proposal sent to Congress is reworked, and the final bill is a compromise between congressional and presidential wishes.

The Influence of Strong Congressional Leaders When Congress doesn't like a President's program, not much of it will become law. Running for the Presidency in 1960, Kennedy proclaimed his New Frontier in speech after speech. Perhaps that slogan helped him win, but it did not affect the victories of a half-dozen conservative southern senators who headed major Senate committees. James Eastland, a powerful Democrat, won his Senate seat with 91 percent of the vote in Mississippi while Kennedy was winning the Presidency by only 0.1 percent. Senators like Eastland had strong positions in Congress and voter support back home. Once in office, Kennedy had little success instituting his New Frontier program against such powerful congressional leaders as Eastland. The President was unable to push through any civil-rights legislation, for instance, and had to leave that issue to the courts and the Attorney General's office.

One source of congressional strength, as already noted, is its roots back home. The Washington community, especially the executive branch, is more isolated from "public sentiment" than is generally thought. As one long-time observer of Washington politics concludes:

> Congressional sentiment tends to be officialdom's pragmatic substitute for "public opinion" because it is on Congress, not the general public, that officials must depend, day after day, for legislation and for funds

to keep programs and personnel alive. And bureaucrats are not the only ones who make that substitution. For comparable reasons it is made, much of the time, by diplomats of many countries, officers of every state, representatives of private interests, local party leaders, and even congressmen themselves.[7]

Congress' Legal Power over the Executive Branch Congress also has very specific legal powers over the executive branch. The four most significant powers held by Congress are the following:

1. *Organization* The departments and agencies of the executive branch are created by acts of Congress.
2. *Authorization* Executive agencies operate within boundaries and on programs established by congressional legislation. For example, NASA cannot design just any space program it wants to; its programs and its very existence depend on congressional authorization.
3. *Financing* Congress controls the purse strings, and programs that are not funded cannot be implemented. In a bitter battle between President Nixon and Congress in 1970, Congress refused to provide funds for the development of a supersonic transport (the SST). Nixon had no choice but to let the project drop.
4. *Review* The executive agencies are subject to inquiry by Congress. Public hearings by a hostile congressional committee can embarrass an agency and do much to change administration policy.

In recent decades, Congress has not used its powers to the fullest. This has led some observers to conclude that Congress no longer checks the executive branch. "No matter how hard the Congress may struggle on one issue, it is overwhelmed by the vastly greater forces of the presidency. Whether Congress wins or loses, the President ends up on top" is the conclusion reached by the Ralph Nader Congress Project.[8] There is evidence to support this conclusion.

For instance, even when Congress passes legislation that the President doesn't like, the battle is not over. The President has the power to veto the legislation simply by refusing to sign the bill into law. The veto power was included in the Constitution primarily as a presidential check on unconstitutional or undesirable legislation. But usage has transformed it into an important policy tool of the President; he can threaten to veto acts of Congress that don't suit the presidential program. Here is Nixon in a special message to Congress as it prepared to vote on major health and education bills:

> I will simply not let reckless spending of this kind destroy the tax reduction we have secured and the hard-earned success we have earned in the battle against inflation. . . . With or without the cooperation of the Congress, I am going to do everything within my power to prevent such a fiscal crisis for millions of our people. . . . Let there be no misunderstanding, if bills come to my desk calling for excessive spending which threatens the federal budget, I will veto them.

[7] Richard F. Neustadt, *Presidential Power* (New York: Wiley, 1962), p. 89.
[8] Mark J. Green, James M. Fallows, and David R. Zwick, *Who Rules Congress?* (New York: Bantam Books, 1972), p. 94.

Congress can override the presidential veto with a two-thirds vote. Such a majority is not easy to get. Franklin Roosevelt vetoed 631 separate congressional measures; only 9 were overriden by Congress. Eisenhower vetoed 181 bills; only 2 of them were overridden. Recent Presidents have had more effective opposition, though.

The growth of the executive branch, coupled with the apparent weakness and disorganization of Congress, has led some observers to claim that the executive branch is taking over more and more of the legislative initiative that traditionally (and constitutionally) belongs to Congress. Yet three things should be kept in mind. First, what Congress gives, Congress can take away. Presidential initiative depends on a large and energetic White House staff and executive agencies. Authorization and funds for these come from Congress. Should Congress decide to reassert its full control over legislation, there is nothing the Presidency can do. Students of politics believe that the power balance between the legislative and executive branches moves in cycles. It was just a little over a decade ago that critics of the legislative branch were complaining about how *effective* Congress was in blocking the New Frontier legislation of President Kennedy. The tug of war between the two branches goes on, and certainly it is too soon to pronounce one branch dead.

Second, in the preceding chapter we reviewed many of the ways in which Congress has begun to reorganize itself in the past decade. Congressional staffs have grown and have become more professional. A congressional budget office has been established. The research arms of Congress have been given increased funds and more demanding tasks. These reforms substantially increase the effectiveness of Congress in dealing with the executive branch.

There is a third point to keep in mind. The complaint that the executive branch has supplanted Congress as the major force in American politics comes largely out of the years when defense and security issues dominated headlines. There is a longstanding tradition that defense and national security can best be handled by the President, along with the National Security Council, the Joint Chiefs of Staff, and the expertise of the State Department and the Department of Defense. In matters of warfare only the President can act quickly and decisively; in matters of diplomacy, only he can act with the necessary secrecy.

Even in matters of security and defense, however, recent events have limited the powers of the President. We noted that the "power to declare peace" or to end military action has been covered by the War Powers Act. And the oversight function of Congress has been applied more aggressively to the Central Intelligence Administration. We have also noted that the powers of the President in foreign affairs are less when the foreign policy has direct domestic consequences — such as tariff policy. It is accurate to conclude, however, that though Congress has had more foreign-policy influence in recent years, it has rarely managed to substitute its own will for that of the Presidency.

Congress, on the other hand, plays a bigger role in the bread-and-butter domestic issues. No President, for instance, could expect to push through tax reform legislation on his own. As columnist Russell Baker has noted: "No power is kept so zealously locked in the congressional safe as the power to decide who gets soaked and who gets the boons on April 15." It is to Congress and not the President that we look for final disposal of domestic welfare questions such as revenue sharing, an education bill, or a minimum-wage policy.

The Difficulty of Starting New Programs When Gerald Ford became President he inherited serious economic problems: unemployment, recession, and steep inflation. Central to these problems was the rapidly increasing cost of energy, which accounted for about 50 percent of the annual increase in the cost of living. Energy costs were linked to great increases in the price of imported oil. In just one three-month period (October–December 1974) the price of imported oil had increased by 400 percent.

It was a difficult time to become President. Shortly after taking office Ford spoke to a world energy conference: "It is difficult to discuss the energy problem without unfortunately lapsing into doomsday language," he said. "Exorbitant prices can only distort the world economy, run the risk of worldwide depression and threaten the breakdown of world order and safety."

With such big problems demanding to be solved, we might expect a wide range of innovative economic policies and energy programs. Nothing of the sort emerged during the two-year Ford Presidency. Why not? Because innovative policies and programs are not easy to think up, and when they are thought up they are not easy to put into effect. Even the powers of the Presidency and the prestige of the White House cannot always attract exactly the right talent, let alone ensure a cooperative approach. And if an innovative policy is formulated, it is not easy to put it into effect. A program as sweeping as would be necessary to solve the energy problem would necessarily affect the habits and well-being of millions of people, thousands of businesses, and dozens of already functioning government programs. In a later discussion (Chapter 18) we will give more attention to the difficulties of formulating and putting into effect major public programs. Here we stress that the President's powers are great, but not so great that he can easily cut through the barriers between a major problem and a workable solution. Thus Carter faced the same energy problems that Ford hoped to solve.

The Difficulty of Stopping Old Programs If things are hard to start, they are often even harder to stop. Government programs have great momentum, for individuals' careers and vested interests are always linked to any ongoing program. Just because a new President comes to town there is no guarantee that established programs can be easily changed. Most policy is made by adding to or subtracting from what

Carter is struggling with the same energy problems that President Ford before him tried to solve.

has gone before. Every President wishes to leave his mark on history, but every President must adjust to the personalities, quarrels, values and commitments, and inertia of the present day.

Eisenhower, a Republican, did not dismantle the New Deal programs begun by Democratic administrations from 1932 to 1952. Nor did the eight years of Democratic control of the White House following Eisenhower's eight years in office result in a sharp break in public policy—though many new programs were added. President Nixon tried to cut spending for programs that had been started during earlier administrations, but the job was nearly impossible. Here is his 1972 campaign pledge:

> We would like to operate the federal government at less cost, and we think we know how to do it. . . . We are for lower costs, for less function in the federal government. . . . My goal is not only no tax increase in 1973, but no tax increase in the next four years.

As one commentator observes:

> But where can the Administration cut enough to make its next budget consistent with this pledge? Roughly 40 percent of the projected budgets are allocated to defense, space and related activities—and it is clear the Administration does not want to cut here.
>
> Of the domestic budget, well more than half goes directly to people, either in cash benefits (Social Security, unemployment insurance, veterans' pensions, welfare, civil-service retirement, etc.) or in kind (Medicare, Medicaid, public housing). These people have real needs, real votes and real representatives on Capitol Hill. It is inconceivable that the President would propose legislation to cut these benefits back or that the Congress would pass it.
>
> Contractual obligations of the Government, such as interest on the debt, cannot be tampered with, and no one really wants to cut out such services as national parks or fish and wildlife preservation.[9]

Nixon did reduce federal spending on certain social-welfare programs, but as Figure 13.1 shows, the trend toward more spending was not halted. The growth of the federal budget has continued whether the President was a Democrat or a Republican. Clearly, it is very hard to stop federal programs once they are started.

The President as a Symbol

The government is a collection of institutions, organizations, laws, and policies. The nation is more than this. It includes the idea of political community. The members of the community share a "we feeling," as in "We are all Americans." This sense of shared community cuts across differences of opinion about particular policies

[9] Alice M. Rivlin, "Dear Voter: Your Taxes Are Going Up," *New York Times Magazine,* November 5, 1972, pp. 113–114. © 1972 by The New York Times Company. Reprinted by permission.

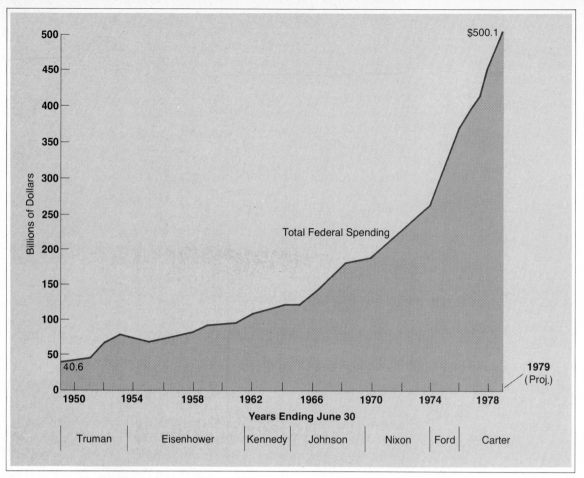

FIGURE 13.1
The Federal Budget Under Seven Presidents

Source: U.S. Office of Management and Budget.

or personalities. To see oneself as an American is to be psychologically separated from citizens of other nations, just as they are separated from Americans by their own sense of political community.

The political community of any nation is felt through symbols and ceremonies, a shared past and common heroes, public holidays and public monuments. Our 1976 bicentennial celebration was an expression of the symbols and ceremonies that try to capture what we mean when we talk about the political community.

The President is the primary symbol of the political community and the main actor in many public ceremonies. It is the President who proclaims National Codfish Day, who dedicates a national arts center, who is the central figure in bicentennial celebrations, who annually speaks on the State of the Union, and who toasts foreign dignitaries in the name of the United States. In these ways the President shows that he can speak for the entire political community. And he is looked upon in this way by the American public. Most of us first experience our nation in terms of its most dramatic

The important symbolic role of the President was dramatically revealed in the public response to Kennedy's sudden death.

personalities, and the most dramatic of all personalities is the President.

In the speech by President Kennedy quoted at the beginning of this chapter, the White House was compared to a pulpit. This would make the President a minister, priest, or rabbi. These are not far-fetched analogies. When Nixon became President in 1969 he called our national difficulties a "crisis of the spirit" and promised that his administration would meet that crisis with an "answer of the spirit." Somewhat later the widely read newspaper columnist James Reston commented on American society in similar terms. He presented a bleak picture of America as "a divided and selfish nation, dominated by powerful special interest groups that have no common concern for the national interest." He went on to say:

> In such a situation, the role of the Federal Government, and particularly of the President, is critical, for in a secular society that is full of doubt about the church, the university and the press, the White House is still the pinnacle of our civil life and the hope of some moral order and presiding national purpose. . . . More than anybody else, the President has the power to establish the standard and set the model, to direct or manipulate the powerful forces of the nation, to encourage the best in us.

The Watergate affair dramatically raised the issue of moral leadership. The President of the United States, revealed as foulmouthed, tolerant of petty criminal activity, and a participant in discussions that led to the criminal convictions of some of his close associates, clearly had let the country down—not because his policies were failures but because he failed to measure up to the moral standards imposed on the major figure in the American political community. Confidence in Nixon declined rapidly as the Watergate scandal unfolded. Figure 13.2 shows how sharply his popularity dropped during this period. It is no coincidence that over the same period the American people increasingly came to distrust all government leaders and even to lose confidence in nongovernmental institutions.

403

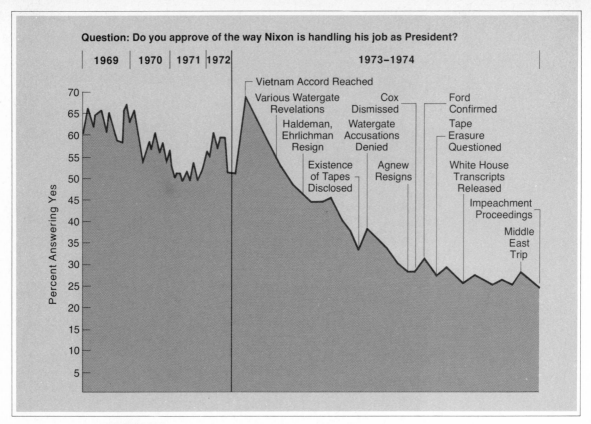

Question: Do you approve of the way Nixon is handling his job as President?

1969 | 1970 | 1971 | 1972 | 1973–1974

Percent Answering Yes

Vietnam Accord Reached

Various Watergate Revelations

Haldeman, Ehrlichman Resign

Existence of Tapes Disclosed

Cox Dismissed

Watergate Accusations Denied

Agnew Resigns

Ford Confirmed

Tape Erasure Questioned

White House Transcripts Released

Impeachment Proceedings

Middle East Trip

FIGURE 13.2 Source: Based on data from the Gallup poll.
Nixon's Popularity Ratings

Presidents: What Manner of Men?

When the noise and politics of nominations and campaigns are over, one man, and only one, is suddenly on top. How he handles pressure, how he works with advisers, how he speaks to the public, and how clearly he thinks about problems have a large impact on life in this and other societies. Nixon had the creativity to ease tensions with China and the Soviet Union, and thereby increased the chances of peace in the world. He had the arrogance to think he could fool most of the people most of the time in the matter of Watergate, and thereby reduced the confidence Americans felt in their government and even in themselves. Johnson had the energy and forcefulness to enact new civil-rights, welfare, and medical-care programs, and thereby improved the lives of some of America's poor and oppressed groups. But the same energy and forcefulness led him into the thicket of the Vietnam War, from which neither he nor American society could escape unscarred. Today President Carter struggles with a host of economic problems, not quite knowing whether a

given tax program or spending policy will make things better or worse. If Carter and his advisers make wrong choices, many will suffer. If they make right choices, fewer will suffer and for a shorter period. The stakes are high.

Only 38 people in America's history have had the chance to make —or avoid—such huge mistakes. And these 38 people have approached the task differently, depending on the political habits they brought to the office and on their outlook toward their own life. One student of presidential character has attempted to classify Presidents along these lines, using the term *style* to describe their habits of governing and the term *character* to describe their attitude toward self.[10]

Presidential style can be roughly divided into *active* or *passive* categories. For example, William Howard Taft, Republican President from 1908 to 1912, took a very restrictive view of his duties as President. "The President," he remarked, "can exercise no power which cannot be fairly and reasonably traced to some specific grant of authority." This reflects the classic passive style of presidential authority, a style that in many ways was repeated by Dwight Eisenhower, Republican President from 1952 to 1960. Eisenhower disliked much of the nitty-gritty of politics. He was uninterested in using the vast patronage powers of the Presidency; he refused to meddle in congressional politics; he did not like speechmaking; he ignored the press as much as possible; he avoided summit politics in international relations. On the latter topic, for instance, Eisenhower said, "This idea of the President of the United States going personally abroad to negotiate—it's just damn stupid." Other Presidents have favored vigorous presidential action. Kennedy, as mentioned earlier, viewed the Presidency as the "vital center of action in our whole scheme of government." Rejecting the passive role, he argued that the President must "place himself in the very thick of the fight."

Presidential character refers to whether the man in the White House seems generally happy and optimistic toward himself and his duties or moody, irritable, weighed down by the burdens of office. Although it is hard to characterize Presidents in such terms, this kind of analysis is useful if it can uncover something about the personality of the President. Johnson, for example, became increasingly negative and unhappy as opposition to his Vietnam War policies rose, until toward the end of his term he was complaining that "everybody is trying to cut me down, destroy me" and asking, "Why don't people like me?" A sense of persecution was even stronger in Nixon; he became moody, withdrawn, and irritable as impeachment for his role in Watergate became more certain.

[10] James David Barber, *The Presidential Character: Predicting Performance in the White House* (Englewood Cliffs, N.J.: Prentice-Hall, 1972).

405

PERSONALITY: DOES IT MAKE A DIFFERENCE?

The attempt to identify "personality types" in the White House seems fruitless to many observers of American politics. Decisions are made in the context of demanding situations and conditions; no matter who is in the White House, the same decision will be made. It is pointed out, for example, that Johnson was under such pressure to escalate the Vietnam War that there was really no alternative. When Johnson became President there was an existing framework within which foreign policy, including policy toward Southeast Asia, was being made. The assumptions of this framework, shaped by previous Presidents and their advisers, included a belief that saving South Vietnam from communist domination was important to America's national security. This view was shared in 1965 by nearly all of Johnson's advisers, by leading foreign-policy experts both inside and outside of the government, and by leading commentators in the universities and the media. Within this context, how could Johnson have acted differently? He escalated the war because that was the logical thing to do if one assumed that South Vietnam was vital to American security.

Such an analysis leaves little room for personality. The President is seen as responding to conditions and pressures. But this poses a different question. Johnson's way of handling the war—his choice of bombing targets, his dealings with congressional critics, his secretiveness, and his response to the antiwar movement—allowed for variation. And even small variations (e.g., refusing to meet with congressional critics) could take on great political significance. As these variations take on political meaning, we begin to see the importance of the character and personality of the man in the White House.

Watergate brought this lesson home with a force that was unimagined even during the difficult days of Vietnam. Nixon's secrecy and isolation and moodiness made him a target for those who were determined to get to the bottom of Watergate. If early in the cover-up he had simply confessed the poor judgment of his advisers and the lack of candor he had shown in earlier statements, it is likely that he would have been forgiven. But Nixon saw himself as a fighter against huge odds. He paid a high cost. And so did American society, showing once again that it is the President who stands at the very center of American politics.

The Watergate episode and the resignation of Nixon from the Presidency illustrate several important aspects of the role of the President in American politics. We will therefore conclude our discussion of the Presidency with a review of Watergate and its aftermath.

Watergate and Presidential Domination

In the years since the 1930s, we have seen a great rise of presidential power. Indeed, our era has been considered one of presidential domination. The growth of presidential power is not due to power-hungry Presidents. There are many other reasons for this growth. The Great Depression of the 1930s resulted in an increased role of the federal government in the domestic economy. The executive branch became the "manager" of the U.S. economy. World War II and the resulting deep involvement of the United States in the affairs of the rest of the world also increased the President's power. Only the executive branch had the technical skills and organization to formulate the national domestic and foreign policies that were needed.

PRESIDENTIAL POWER UNDER NIXON

President Nixon added further to presidential powers. But he pushed those powers so far as to come into conflict with the other branches of the government. For example, Nixon asserted the right to "impound" funds, that is, not to spend money that had been appropriated by Congress if he believed the appropriation was unwise. By impounding funds the President effectively refused to execute laws passed by Congress.

But it was not impoundment of funds or clashes over policy that led to Nixon's resignation. Rather, it was a series of illegal abuses of power that combined to cause his downfall.

One set of abuses related to the electoral process. The Watergate scandal began with the discovery of an attempt to wiretap the offices of the Democratic National Committee, an attempt that was later linked to the President's own campaign committee. In addition, there was evidence of plans for a number of "dirty tricks" during the campaign. And there was also evidence of campaign contributions that had illegally solicited in return for favors. These included contributions by milk producers' cooperatives in return for higher price supports for milk and from International Telephone and Telegraph in return for favorable action on an antitrust suit.

It was also revealed that the administration had tried to use the powers of the executive branch to harass its "enemies." The President and his aides pressured the Internal Revenue Service to audit the tax returns of people who were politically opposed to the administration.

Furthermore, the executive powers of the President were used in an attempt to cover up the Watergate break-in. The President and his aides tried to manipulate the CIA and the FBI to limit investigation of the break-in.

The Watergate hearings and trials revealed a large number of ways in which the Nixon administration had abused executive powers. Evidence was produced of the so-called Huston plan to keep an eye on domestic radicals. The plan included illegal wiretaps, break-ins, and disruption of radical organizations. That plan was not carried out but later it was shown that the CIA — which is supposed to have no domestic role — had been checking on radicals.

Finally, the President claimed absolute executive privilege when it came to the documents and tapes associated with the case. He claimed that the need for secrecy in executive actions is so great that only the President can decide what information to reveal to the public or to the other branches of the government.

"High Crimes and Misdemeanors," Not Policy Differences The abuses that we have described formed the basis of the actions that were carried out against President Nixon in the courts and by Congress. It is important to note that the movement to impeach the President did not grow out of differences between Congress and the President on *policy* matters. Nixon, a Republican, had been reelected by a large majority in 1972 and with some definite policy ideas. The majority of the members of the Congress that was elected at the same time were members of the Democratic party.

Under such circumstances sharp conflicts over policy are likely, and there were a number of such conflicts during Nixon's second term. In a parliamentary system of government, in which the executive officer (the prime minister) is elected by the legislature, such conflicts often result in the overthrow of the executive by the legislature through a "vote of no confidence." In our presidential system, by contrast, Congress cannot vote a President out of office because it disagrees with his policies. If there is a clash over policy, the result may be a stalemate. Congress may refuse to pass laws that the President wants, or the President may veto laws that Congress passes. But the President remains President.

The abuses of Presidential power included in the articles of impeachment voted by the House Judiciary Committee were, according to the Committee, illegal actions on the part of the President, not specific policies with which it disagreed. The Committee voted down an article of impeachment based on the President's action in ordering the bombing of Cambodia during the Vietnam War. The argument of those who opposed the inclusion of this particular article of impeachment was that the President was carrying out his legitimate function as Commander-in-Chief, and though they may have disagreed with his action, it was not an impeachable action. (Those who favored impeachment for the bombing of Cambodia agreed with the general principle that the President could not be impeached for carrying out a foreign policy that they disagreed with. But they argued that he was acting illegally in this case because he kept the bombing secret from Congress.)

REMOVING A PRESIDENT FROM OFFICE

Nixon was reelected by the largest majority in U.S. history. He was at the head of the most powerful office in the world, the American Presidency. He had under him a huge executive branch whose activities affected all areas of American life. And he was determined to use his executive powers fully (his critics would say ruthlessly) to accomplish his goals. Yet less than two years later he resigned from office under the threat of almost certain impeachment by the

House of Representatives and conviction by the Senate. How did this come about?

To find the answer we turn back to the Constitution. As *The Federalist* puts it, we would need no controls over government "if angels were to govern men." But the writers of the Constitution believed that our public officials were not likely to be angles. Internal and external controls over their conduct would be needed. The Watergate scandal shows how correct their judgment was; the Nixon administration was not run by angels, and the controls devised in the Constitution were put into effect in order to limit their abuse of power. The Watergate events show clearly how a government made up of *independent* powers can limit abuse by any one branch.

The Role of Congress   Our presidential system of government is, as we have seen, different from a parliamentary system. The head of the executive branch is not elected by the legislature, nor can the legislature vote him out of office when it disagrees with him. The President of the United States is elected by the people. He is not chosen by Congress.

But Article 1 of the Constitution does give Congress the power to remove a President. The power to impeach a President is given to the House of Representatives; the power to conduct a trial of the President after impeachment is given to the Senate. The Chief Justice of the United States presides at such a trial, and a two-thirds vote is needed to convict a President. The Constitution also makes clear that such removal should not be a punishment for unpopular policy. A President can be removed only if he is convicted of "Treason, Bribery, or other high Crimes or Misdemeanors" (Article 2, Section 4).

These terms are ambiguous, and much of the debate over the possible impeachment of Richard Nixon had to do with their interpretation. Some people argued that the President had to have committed a crime for which an ordinary citizen would be convicted in court. Others argued that a President could be impeached for gross misconduct in office, even if the acts of misconduct were not in themselves felonies.

The latter position appeared to prevail. The accusations in the articles of impeachment voted by the House Judiciary Committee in July 1974 included not only activities that would have been criminal if they had been committed by a private citizen but also other misconduct – such as failure to supervise the activities of subordinates – that would not be criminal acts.

The constitutional impeachment process was not completed in 1974; Nixon resigned after the House Judiciary Committee had voted three articles of impeachment against him. These were recommendations from the Committee to the entire House of Representatives. The next step in the process would have been a vote by the House on these articles. If a majority of the House had voted for impeachment, the Senate would have tried the President.

Although the impeachment process was never completed, it is clear from the historical record that it was the threat of impeachment that led to Nixon's resignation. It was only when he was sure that he would be impeached and convicted that he decided to resign.

The Role of the Judicial Branch The court system also played a major role in the Watergate affair. Many of the important revelations of Watergate were brought out in the trials conducted by Judge John Sirica of the federal district court.

At times of constitutional crisis the key interpretations are often made by the Supreme Court. Note the important role the Supreme Court played in the Watergate events. A major conflict arose over a set of tape recordings of presidential conversations. They had been subpoenaed as evidence in the trial of some of Nixon's aides, who were accused of taking part in the Watergate break-in and cover-up. President Nixon claimed that only he could determine whether such presidential materials would be released to the courts. He cited the doctrine of executive privilege, claiming that the President could not function as the nation's executive head unless he could maintain the secrecy of his records.

The case went to the Supreme Court. The Court ruled that there was indeed an executive privilege; the President could keep secret records if those were needed to carry out his work. But executive privilege was not absolute. If records were needed in a criminal case, the President could not hold them back.

What the Court was saying was that no branch of the government is above the law. It affirmed that the President had wide powers under the Constitution and that he needed such powers. But it also affirmed that those powers were not unlimited.

This decision was an important step in the process that led to the President's resignation. He had resisted a number of efforts to get the tapes, but he could not ignore the Supreme Court. A number of members of Congress made it clear that the President would face certain impeachment and conviction if he defied the Court. (Note how the powers of Congress and the Court combined to limit the power of the President.) When the tape transcripts made it clear that the President had known about the Watergate cover-up for a much longer time than he had admitted, he lost the rest of his support in Congress.

The independence of the judicial branch is underlined by the fact that of the eight Supreme Court justices who voted against the President (one justice took no part in the case), three had been appointed by Nixon. The power to appoint justices of the Supreme Court does give the President some control over that body; it is, indeed, one of the ways in which the Court's power is limited under the system of checks and balances. And the President had used that

Investigatory reporting by two Washington Post reporters, Bernstein and Woodward, contributed to the downfall of the Nixon Presidency.

power to appoint a number of justices whose constitutional views were close to his own. But justices are appointed for life and are not under the control of the President. Throughout American history the Supreme Court has acted quite independently of the other branches of the government.

The Fourth Branch of Government *The Federalist Papers* talk of external as well as internal checks on the powers of the government. We have seen how the power of the President was checked by other branches of the government. But outside forces are also important in controlling those who govern. Full public disclosure of the Watergate events would not have been possible had it not been for the relentless digging of a few journalists, particularly reporters for the *Washington Post* and the *New York Times.* Their pursuit of the facts was protected by the First Amendment. In only a handful of nations could newspapers have played as full and aggressive a role. Even in democratic nations like Great Britain the press would have been legally barred from publicly exposing the details of Watergate.

Watergate and the Constitutional Process

The Watergate affair illustrates some important ways in which general constitutional provisions such as separation of powers meet new circumstances. As we have seen, there are many silences and ambiguities in the Constitution. These give it the flexibility to adjust to new circumstances.

The process of adjustment is not a mechanical one in which members of Congress or Supreme Court justices read the clear words of the Constitution and apply them to the case. The words of the Constitution need interpretation. The meaning of *impeachment* is by no means clear, and executive privilege is not mentioned in the Constitution at all. How do the members of Congress decide the actual meaning of impeachment? And how do Supreme Court justices decide the actual meaning of executive privilege?

Nixon's last day as President.

For one thing, they look at the Constitution itself. What does it say on the subject? But where the Constitution is unclear, they look further. They consider the writings of those who wrote the Constitution, as well as the debates at the Constitutional Convention, to see what the founders had in mind. In addition, they consider the earlier historical uses of the word. When the founders used a term like *impeachment,* they were probably influenced by earlier legal practice.

Perhaps most important of all, those who want to interpret the meaning of the Constitution will consider how others have interpreted it in the past. They will look, in other words, for precedents. How has impeachment been carried out in the past? The members of Congress spent a good deal of time considering the one previous example of a presidential impeachment: the impeachment and trial of President Andrew Johnson after the Civil War. And the Supreme Court considered the way earlier Presidents and earlier courts had dealt with executive privilege.

Finally, one must mention political forces. Even though the debate over impeachment was conducted in legal terms, the fact that the President was a Republican whose policies were objectionable to many Democrats cannot be ignored. It is hardly an accident that the members of Congress in favor of impeachment were more likely to be Democrats, those opposed more likely to be Republicans. And the members of Congress pay attention not only to constitutional precedents but also to the views of their constituents. The fact that Nixon's public support faded during the summer of 1974 probably played a role in their decisions.

What is the balance between constitutional interpretation and the political calculations of members of Congress? Some critics claim that the proceedings were a purely political process. President Nixon's press secretary accused the House Judiciary Committee of being a "kangaroo court," that is, of paying little attention to law or evidence but acting on a political basis. Members of Congress, on the other hand, sometimes talked as if their task were purely legal.

In fact, most of the major constitutional crises in our history have combined both forces. The words of the Constitution and constitutional precedents play a role; so do contemporary political forces. Both could be seen in the Watergate case. But the seriousness of the debate on the nature of impeachment, and the fact that the final pressure for the President's resignation came from conservative members of his own party who decided that Nixon's legal position was untenable, suggest that the Judiciary Committee was not a political kangaroo court.

Under our uneasy balance of government powers there will be future clashes between the various branches. We can be sure that Congress and the President will differ over their powers in the future, and that the Supreme Court may be called upon to mediate. When this happens the Watergate decisions will be taken into consideration. Thus Watergate has become, in its turn, a precedent for the future.

AFTER WATERGATE

Some observers believed that the Watergate scandal would lead to a major change in the internal structure of the national government. Some indeed thought it would destroy the Presidency as an effective political force.

The result was not that dramatic. A strong Presidency is needed in the modern world. No sooner had President Nixon left office than President Ford and his administration were managing foreign policy and trying to cope with the domestic economic crisis. The main reason was simply that those problems required presidential action and initiative.

On the other hand, the Watergate events seem to have had a profound effect on the balance of power among the branches of the government. For one thing, the crisis reaffirmed the independence of the various branches. Congress called on its ultimate power — impeachment — and the President resigned. The Supreme Court and the President came into direct conflict over the extent of presidential power. Would the President obey an order from the Supreme Court to turn over the tapes of conversations for which he claimed exectuive privilege? When Nixon and his attorney were asked this question while the case was before the Court, the answer was usually evasive. But when the Court ruled that the President had to turn over the tapes, he obeyed.

HOW INSTITUTIONS WORK: IV
the federal budget

What is the significance of the federal budget?   The annual budget serves to order the nation's priorities by establishing how much money the government will spend and for which purposes. Figure 13.3 shows how President Carter's 1978 budget proposed to spend $500.1 billion. But the budget is also a tool of fiscal policy. The budget may, for example, be reduced in order to fight inflation, or a budget surplus or deficit may be planned in order to slow down or stimulate the economy.

What is the "budgetary process"?   The budgetary process is the ongoing planning, implementation, and auditing of all federal spending. Both the executive branch and Congress are deeply involved.

Who formulates the annual budget?   The federal government operates for accounting purposes on a fiscal year that starts on October 1 and ends on the following September 30. Each spring the agencies and departments begin drawing up their budget requests for the fiscal year starting some sixteen months later. These requests are then sent to the Office of Management and Budget, which oversees the executive budget. After reviewing the budget requests the OMB sends them to the President, who by now has also been provided with economic forecasts and revenue estimates for the coming year. The President coordinates this information to set budget guidelines. Within these guidelines the individual agencies then submit detailed budget requests, which are analyzed by the OMB and passed on to the President. Although intense bureaucratic in-fighting may occur and although agencies may appeal directly to the President, it is the OMB that largely decides how much money will be spent for each program. The final budget proposal is submitted by the President to Congress, usually in January or February.

What role does Congress play in the budgetary process?   The President's budget proposal is actually only a request, for only Congress can vote to spend federal funds. It does so in a two-step process. First it enacts *authorizations,* or legislation that authorizes a particular program and puts a ceiling on funds to finance it. Then it passes *appropriations* bills to grant the actual funds approved by authorization bills. An authorization without an appropriation is meaningless. In fact, however, close to 70 percent of the spending in any fiscal year is locked into the budget by previous congressional decisions and is not subject to annual appropriations.

How is Congress organized with respect to budget decisions?   By custom the President's budget requests are considered first by the House Appropriations Committee. After an appropriations bill has been passed by the House, it is transmitted to the Senate Appropriations Committee for similar consideration. Traditionally, the Senate has served as a court of appeals for agencies seeking to restore budget cuts made in the House. But there have been obvious problems with this pattern. Congress has typically spent several billion dollars more each year than the President requested, leading

414

**FIGURE 13.3
The Budget Dollar: Where It
Goes (Fiscal Year 1978
Estimate)**

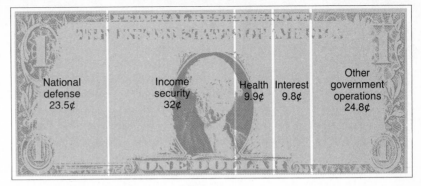

National
defense
23.5¢

Income
security
32¢

Health
9.9¢

Interest
9.8¢

Other
government
operations
24.8¢

Source: U.S. Office of Management and Budget

to charges of "fiscal irresponsibility." Moreover, the fragmented structure of Congress itself has led to piece-by-piece consideration of the budget without ever really looking at the budget as a whole. Therefore in 1974 Congress passed legislation designed to reform its budget procedures.

What are the principal changes called for in the budget reform law? The reform act creates new House and Senate Budget Committees aided by a new Congressional Budget Office staffed by experts. New procedures call for the Congress to (1) pass a joint resolution early in each session setting an overall target for spending, and then, after the customary appropriations process has been completed, (2) reconcile any differences between the target total and the sum of the parts.

Is there any check on whether the funds approved by Congress are spent as directed and within the budget. Each executive agency is responsible for making sure its outlays comply with legislation. The OMB also oversees each agency's spending. Congress gets an independent audit of all expenditures through the General Accounting Office.

Does the President have to spend the full amount appropriated by Congress for a given program? There has been much controversy over this question, especially during the Nixon years, when the President "impounded" funds for certain programs and refused to spend the full amount intended by law. To avoid long court battles over impoundments, the new congressional budget act requires congressional approval of all Presidential impoundments.

Can the executive get more funds from Congress in special circumstances? Yes, such requests can be made in the form of supplemental appropriations.

14
THE AMERICAN BUREAUCRACY

We have looked at some of the major institutions of American politics: the Presidency, Congress, the Supreme Court. These were established by the Constitution and play a dominant role in American politics. They form the three main branches of American government. There is, however, another branch of the government, larger and in many ways more powerful than the others. This is the vast administrative apparatus of the federal government, as well as its counterpart administrative departments and agencies in state and local governments. The ordinary citizen sees the President on the evening television news or reads about him in the newspaper. Citizens read about their senators and representatives; sometimes they even meet those individuals. But the real contact that most citizens have with the government is with bureaucrats: with the clerk in the post office, with a government inspector checking whether a business meets safety standards, with a tax examiner at the Internal Revenue Service.

The very word *bureaucracy* conjures up images of red tape; long, complicated forms to be filled out; indifference to human needs; waste and inefficiency. The United States has experienced repeated waves of antibureaucratic feeling. In recent years the intensity of that feeling appears to have increased. In the 1976 election candidates from both political parties took an antibureaucratic stance in their campaigns. Ronald Reagan, who challenged President Ford for the Republican nomination; Jimmy Carter, who won the Democratic nomination; and George Wallace, who tried for the Democratic nomination as an anti-Establishment candidate—all attacked the government for interfering in the lives of citizens. Even Ford, who as President was in charge of the government's administrative structure, attacked big government. The attack on the bureaucracy came from both liberal and conservative candidates: Both sides complained about too much government.

Everyone attacks the bureaucracy, yet no one believes that it can be eliminated. A complex, modern state needs a large administrative structure. Jimmy Carter as candidate complained about the size of the administrative apparatus in the Executive Office of the President. Jimmy Carter as President did not cut the size of the presidential staff—according to some estimates he increased it.

What Is a Bureaucracy?

Modern industrial societies contain a large number of big, complex organizations. Some are private organizations such as business firms, universities, and labor unions. But in most modern states the biggest and most complex organizations are found within the government. The army, the navy, the police, the post office, the school system, the government agencies that provide social services, the agencies that regulate the economy—these are all large, complex bureaucratic organizations.

Bureaucracies can be thought of as organizational machines. Just as complex machines such as jet planes, computers, or construction equipment allow societies to carry out difficult mechanical tasks that individuals and groups could not accomplish otherwise, so bureaucratic organizations allow societies to carry out social tasks that could not be accomplished by individuals or by informal groups. It takes a complex bureaucracy to deliver the mail, to provide social services, to design and produce military weapons, to conduct foreign policy.

Bureaucracies have a number of characteristics. Each can be thought of as an advantage of bureaucratic organization (something that helps it carry out its functions). At the same time, each poses a problem (it leads to "pathologies" that help explain why there is so much criticism of bureaucracies). What are these characteristics?

Bureaucracies Are Hierarchically Structured Organizations They have a chain of command extending from the top officials down to subordinate offices and agencies. *Advantage:* Top officials can maintain control of subordinates and thus make sure organizational goals are carried out. In government agencies this is how the bureaucracy is controlled by the officials who have been elected by the people. The President can issue directives to the heads of the executive departments, who, in turn, can issue directives to their subordinates. *Problem:* Such chains of command can be long and inefficient. Furthermore, most organizations that appear to have a clear structure of command do not in fact work that way. Subordinate agencies often have a lot of freedom. (We will discuss the reasons for this shortly.) This freedom introduces flexibility into what would otherwise be a rigid system, but it reduces control over the bureaucracy by the President and his appointed department heads. The principle of a hierarchical structure, therefore, does not eliminate a major "pathology" of bureaucracies: the possibility that they may be uncontrolled.

Bureaucracies Are Based on Specialization They are ways of bringing together a large number of technical experts, each of whom understands some aspects of the complex problems faced by govern-

419

The biggest and most complex bureaucracies are found in modern governments.

ment organizations. The Food and Drug Administration is staffed by chemists and biologists who test new drugs, by specialists in the inspection of manufacturing plants, by communications specialists, and by numerous other specialized workers. *Advantage:* In this way technical expertise is brought to bear on complex social problems. No single individual has all the knowledge that is needed to deal with most problems. Bureaucracies organize a large number of specialists so that they can work together on the same problem. *Problem:* Experts are sometimes narrow; they don't see the larger problems. Moreover, those who do not have similar technical competence, such as elected officials, do not find it easy to control technical experts. This reinforces the pathology of an uncontrolled bureaucracy.

Bureaucracies Operate on the Basis of Impersonal Rules Bureaucrats are supposed to carry out the decisions made by policy makers in a fair and impersonal manner. In government bureaucracies this means that they carry out the laws of Congress or the executive orders of the President; they do not make policy themselves. Furthermore, they treat each citizen or group that they deal with equally and impartially on the basis of rules provided by congressional or presidential policy. *Advantage:* Congress and the President have government agencies to carry out their policies. Citizens and groups deal with a predictable and fair government. *Problem:* It does not work quite that way. Bureaucracies often make policy. (We'll look at some ways in which they do so and discuss why this happens.) And when bureaucracies apply policy to individual cases they often have discretion; they do not act with mechanical impartiality.

Summary Bureaucracies are supposed to be efficient, impartial organizations that carry out policies made by elected officials. To some extent they function this way. At the same time, they are not easily controlled. They have discretion to make policy. This poses a serious problem for a democracy. Bureaucrats have autonomy; they make policy. Yet they are not elected. How can this fact be reconciled with democracy, in which citizens are supposed to have ultimate authority through their elected representatives? As we will see, there is no easy answer to this question.

THE GROWTH OF THE FEDERAL BUREAUCRACY

Early in our nation's history the federal government was small. A study of the federal government in 1802 found that it had only 2875 civilian employees. The "Washington Establishment" at the time numbered 291. The President had one clerk.[1]

The federal government grew during the nineteenth and early twentieth centuries. As we have seen, new departments were added to the executive branch. Much of the growth occurred in wartime — during the Civil War and World War I. But these increases were temporary. When the war ended, the government would shrink again.

The most significant growth of the federal government dates from the era of the New Deal. At that time the government took on some important new functions: provision of social services for citizens and regulation of the economy. Until the Great Depression of the 1930s, the federal government's expenditures were equal to about one-fourth of state and local government expenditures. By 1939 — after the New Deal reforms had been instituted — the federal government was spending more than the states and localities. By 1949 the federal government accounted for 70 percent of all government spending.

The number of federal employees is another indicator of the growth in the size of the federal bureaucracy. If in 1802 there were 2,875 federal civilian employees, in 1977 there were almost exactly 1,000 times as many: 2,862,000. (See Figure 14.1.) Perhaps the best indicator of the increase in the size of the federal government is not the amount of money it spends or the amount of people it hires but the number of different branches and agencies that exist. With the founding of the Department of Energy, there are now 12 executive departments. But that is the tip of the iceberg. Each of the departments has many subparts. The massive Department of Health, Education and Welfare has 11 main divisions and 76 separate agencies within it. In addition to the executive departments, there are the Executive Office of the President with 18 separate units; 121 non-Cabinet Executive agencies (e.g., the independent regulatory commissions); and 61 advisory agencies containing a staggering 1,179 committees.

[1] James S. Young, *The Washington Community: 1800–1828* (New York: Columbia University Press, 1966), p. 29.

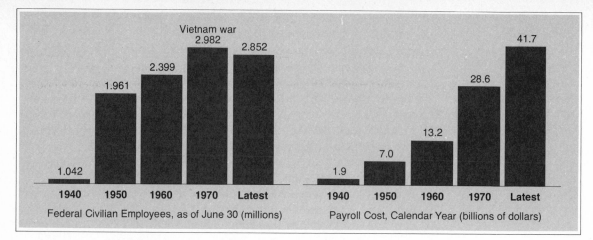

FIGURE 14.1
The Trend Upward
Source: U.S. Civil Service Commission.

Herbert Kaufman, a political scientist, has written a book with the provocative title *Are Government Organizations Immortal?*[2] He found that they are not immortal but are very long-lived. Further, Kaufman found that many new agencies have been created recently: 246 in the past 50 years. Of the 27 major regulatory agencies, 21 were created since 1930, 9 of them in the past 10 years.

The number of agencies is so large that President Carter's executive assistant in charge of reorganizing the government could not find out how many there were. "We were," he wrote, "unable to obtain any single document containing a complete and current listing of government units which are part of the federal government."[3]

The number of bureaus is matched by the variety of types. Some agencies regulate things: the safety of business, the purity of drugs, the quality of the environment. Others provide services: health care or educational benefits. Others support or carry on research. The agencies of the American government are characterized by specialization; each has a different task. In part this grows out of an American commitment to specialization as the most "scientific" way to run the government. In part it grows out of the tendency for each group in America to seek a government agency to represent its interests. In this way departments such as Agriculture or Commerce were formed. They, in turn, are divided into separate agencies that deal with different kinds of agriculture or different businesses.

COORDINATING THE AGENCIES
The multiplicity of separate agencies in the government creates a need for coordination among them. Agencies and departments that

[2] Herbert Kaufman, *Are Government Organizations Immortal?* (Washington, D.C., Brookings Institution, 1976).
[3] W. Harrison Wellford, quoted in the *Washington Post,* May 8, 1977.

are working on overlapping problems have to cooperate with each other. This leads to the creation of more agencies to do the coordinating. Hence, there are now a large number of interagency coordinating committees. In 1970 there were 850 such committees. One observer noted: "Nobody wants them, but everybody has them. Committees seem to thrive on scorn and ridicule, and multiply so rapidly that attempts to weed them out appear futile."[4]

One of the main reasons for the increase in size of the Executive Office of the President is the President's desire to improve his ability to coordinate the government.

> No President sets out to build the largest White House staff in history, although ultimately each one from 1933 through 1974 earned this distinction. The presidential establishment has grown in four decades from a White House staff of 37 to over 500, with thousands more employed in satellite staffs that also service the presidency. This corresponds to the increased size of the other parts of the national government. There has been a similar growth in Congress, for example, where members' and committee staffs totaled 2,443 in 1947 and now total 10,786.[5]

Within the executive office of the President, the major units were created expressly to coordinate government activity in one field or another. The National Security Council made up of the top officials in foreign and military policy attempts to coordinate that area. A similar function is performed by the Domestic Council.

Bureaucracy: The Real Problem

The fact that the government now employs more people or has a larger budget than in the past is not itself the cause of a "bureaucratic problem." Our nation after all is much larger than it was in the nineteenth century. Traditional and noncontroversial government services now require more money and personnel. For example, a larger and more literate population writes more letters and pays more bills by mail. This requires more letter carriers and more postal clerks. The volume of mail and the size of the Post Office do create problems of efficiency. Delay in the delivery of mail is a problem. But that is not the essence of the "bureaucratic problem."

Similarly, a growing population of schoolchildren or a desire for smaller classes creates a need for more teachers as well as for more school administrators. This too creates a larger government budget and more people working for the government. It may also create an unwieldy and inefficient school administration. It does not create a "bureaucratic problem."

---

[4] Harold Seidman, *Politics, Position and Power,* (New York: Oxford University Press, 1975), p. 171.
[5] Stephen Hess, *Organizing the Presidency* (Washington, D.C.: Brookings Institution, 1967), p. 150.

As long as the services that the government provides—such as delivering the mail or teaching classes—involve little discretion on the part of government employees, there is little chance of an uncontrolled bureaucracy. The Post Office has little discretion in what it does; it may hire more people to deliver the mail or sell stamps; it may carry the mail by jet plane rather than by pony express. But its basic job is the routine one of delivering the mail. It does not decide who should write what to whom or who is qualified to buy stamps.

BUREAUCRATIC DISCRETION

A "bureaucratic problem" arises when government bureaucrats have discretion, that is, when they are free to shape government policy. This can come about in a number of ways.

Writing Legislation   Government bureaucracies often take an active role in writing legislation. Though laws are passed by Congress, the advice and cooperation of bureaucratic agencies is often sought. In providing this advice the agency involved does not act merely as an "objective" technical consultant. The agency is likely to have a particular interest that it wishes to advance and will try to get Congress to follow its advice. Congress of course, has the final say. But it is dependent on the bureaucracy for information and for expert advice. This gives the bureaucracy power to shape legislation.

Writing Guidelines   After laws are passed by Congress, the task of writing precise regulations to carry out the law is often left to the bureaucracy. Congress may pass an act requiring that businesses pay more attention to job safety, but the government agency empowered to carry out the law (the Occupational Safety and Health Administration) has to write the safety regulations. It has a good deal of discretion in this matter. Similarly, Congress has established various standards that must be met by local school systems if they are to receive federal aid. These require the schools to provide special programs for handicapped children or to make special efforts to hire minority teachers. But it is the bureaucratic officials in the Department of Health, Education and Welfare who write precise guidelines as to what kinds of programs are to be established for the handicaped or what kinds of procedures are to be used in hiring members of minority groups.

Applying the Laws and Regulations   The possibility of discretionary power on the part of government officials does not end when laws are passed and regulations written. There is often a good deal of discretion left in the hands of the government official who carries out the law. Officials have to decide how a law or regulation applies to a particular case, and often they have a good deal of flexibility in doing so. The agent for the Internal Revenue Service, for instance, must decide whether a particular tax deduction really fits into one of the categories of allowable deductions.

Bureaucrats often write legislation and guidelines for carrying out laws.

We have used the letter carrier as an example of a government worker with little discretion. The letter carrier's job is very precisely defined. Not all government jobs are like this. The police officer on the beat is, like the letter carrier, carrying out government laws and regulations. But the job of a police officer cannot be precisely defined; the officer must often decide who looks suspicious, how carefully to check on possible illegal activities, whether to intervene in a family fight. Studies have shown that officers on the beat vary greatly in how they interpret the rules under which they operate. In this sense the officer shapes government law enforcement policy.

DISCRETION THROUGH REGULATION

In recent years more government activities have given bureaucratic officials discretionary power. This has come about as the government has taken a more active role in *regulating* the activities of Americans, especially the activities of American businesses. Businesses have come under a large number of safety, environmental, and consumer product regulations. But the government regulates the lives of many citizens, especially when access to government services — welfare payments, unemployment benefits, and the like — requires that citizens conform to government regulations as to eligibility. In addition, the federal government regulates state and local governments. For instance, as federal support for education has increased, so has the volume of federal regulation over school administration at the local level.

THE GROWTH OF GOVERNMENT REGULATION OF THE ECONOMY

Government intervention in the economy is not new. Throughout the nineteenth century the government intervened in the economy, but the goal of its intervention was usually to protect the autonomy of business (e.g., from challenges by labor unions) and to foster its activities by providing subsidies such as grants of land to railroads.

Government regulation of the economy began in the late nineteenth century with the formation of the Interstate Commerce

425

Officers on the beat have discretion in how they apply the law.

Commission to regulate railroad rates. During the early decades of the twentieth century the government moved into other areas of business regulation. During the 1930s it responded to the Great Depression with the series of social reforms associated with Franklin Roosevelt and the New Deal. The volume of regulation increased substantially. The Securities and Exchange Commission was created to regulate the securities market that had been abused in the boom of the 1920s. Banking laws were tightened. The Federal Power Commission, the Civil Aeronautics Board, and other agencies came into being to watch over abuses in other industries.

Most of the regulatory agencies have been set up as independent regulatory commissions. Although they deal with different areas, the commissions have a number of things in common. They are not directly under the control of the President or Congress. The goal was to make them "nonpolitical." These commissions were intended to be free from partisan politics. Their boards of directors must be bipartisan, and their members are appointed for fixed terms so that they can't be removed by a change in administration.

These agencies represented a new level of government intervention. And they generated many complaints about big government. The regulations, were still limited in scope, however. They tended to outlaw various abusive business practices, but the government did not attempt to intervene in the internal operations of business. There were few regulations that told businesses how to run their day-to-day operations.

In recent years the government has begun to intervene more directly in business practices. The government often intervenes when there is some social value to which business will not respond without government intervention. The market system does not respond to demands for solutions to such problems as equal opportunities for women or minorities, environmental pollution, unsafe jobs, unsafe or ineffective drugs. Since the early 1960s the government has intervened more and more in these areas. Such intervention involves regulation of the day-to-day operation of businesses. Affirmative-action programs require close regulation of hiring practices; environmental-protection requirements lead to regulation of the manufacturing process in plants; health and safety regulations for workers involve detailed regulation of the work place; laws requiring that manufacturers of new drugs demonstrate that they are effective in curing what they claim to cure lead to detailed requirements for drug testing by manufacturers.

New agencies have arisen to deal with these problems: the Environmental Protection Agency, the Occupational Safety and Health Administration, the Consumer Product Safety Commission, the Equal Employment Opportunity Commission. These and other agencies involve the government in new areas of detailed regulation.

The increase in regulation has been dramatic. Many people complain of the costs of regulation. Businesses claim that they spend an inordinate amount of time and money trying to comply with government regulations. Controversial decisions, such as the ban on saccharin by the Food and Drug Administration (because of evidence that it could cause cancer), have led to demands for fewer regulations. On the other hand, the regulators can point to the successes of regulation, such as a cleaner environment and safer products. It is clear that the controversy over how much regulation there should be and at what cost will continue for some time. (Table 14.1 lists some of the major regulatory agencies and indicates their functions.)

TABLE 14.1
The Grand Scale of Federal Intervention
Hundreds of federal departments, agencies, divisions, and bureaus regulate the nation's commerce to varying degrees. The following is a list of some of the most powerful and pervasive of the U.S. government's economic and social regulators.

Agency	Vital Statistics	Major Functions	Special Characteristics
Older Agencies			
Interstate Commerce Commission	Created in 1887, has 2,100 employees, 79 field offices, and a $57 million budget	Regulates rates and routes of railroads, most truckers, and some waterway carriers	The oldest and most hidebound independent regulator; spends most of its time adjudicating motor carrier tariffs and operating rights; is deeply committed to keeping competition among carriers in delicate balance
Antitrust Division (Justice Department)	Since 1890 has grown to 900 employees, 8 field field offices, and a budget of $27 million	Regulates all activity that could affect interstate commerce, from trade restraints and illegal agreements to mergers	Enormously influential because of the criminal and financial sanctions it can obtain through the courts; is a factor in every company's strategic planning but has not managed to stem industry concentration
Federal Trade Commission	Created in 1914, has 1,700 employees, 11 field offices, and a budget of $55 million	Has very broad discretion to curb unfair trade practices, protect consumers, and maintain competition	Once so absorbed in trivia that there were serious plans to disband it, but is now both aggressive and innovative in fulfilling its mandate; still stumbles because of its complex procedures
Food & Drug Administration	Founded in 1931, fields a staff of 7,000 with a budget of $240 million	Responsible for the safety and efficacy of drugs and medical devices and the safety and purity of food; also regulates labeling; oversees about $200 billion worth of industrial output	Known as an entrenched bureaucracy notorious for caution and close identification with the industries it regulates; recently becoming bolder under new administrators and with new, more rigorous laws to enforce

TABLE 14.1
(continued)

Agency	Vital Statistics	Major Functions	Special Characteristics
Federal Communications Commission	Created in 1934, has 2,100 employees, 24 field offices, and a budget of $60 million	Regulates broadcasting and other communications through licensing and frequency allocation, and interstate telephone and telegraph rates and levels of service	One of the most heavily "judicialized" of the independent commissions; takes forever to reach decisions; is bogged down in new radio station license applications; is considered to lack resources to deal effectively with AT&T's bureaucracy
Securities & Exchange Commission	Created in 1934, has 2,000 employees, 18 field offices, and a budget of $56 million	Regulates all publicly traded securities and the markets on which they are traded; administers public-disclosure laws and polices securities fraud	Most prestigious of the independent agencies; has a reputation—occasionally unmerited—for aggressive police work and zealous protection of investors; *current preoccupations:* foreign bribes and creation of a national securities market
Civil Aeronautics Board	Created in 1938, has 800 employees, 8 field offices, and a $22 million budget; also administers $80 million in subsidies to airlines	Regulates airline fares and and routes	Its enforcement of laws that limit competition in the airline industry has built substantial pressure for reform that would ease restrictions on fare and route decisions; a reform bill is in Congress
Federal Aviation Administration	Created in 1958, has 5,000 employees operating on a budget of $228 million; the bulk of its money—$1.3 billion—goes to operate the nation's air traffic control system	Regulates aircraft manufacturing through certification of airplane airworthiness; also licenses pilots	A tough enforcer, but officials tend to be chummy with top aircraft industry executives; *result:* some big flaps, such as the DC-10 cargo door controversy

Newer Agencies

Agency	Vital Statistics	Major Functions	Special Characteristics
Equal Employment Opportunity Commission	Created in 1964, employs 2,500, maintains 39 field offices, and will spend $70 million this year	Investigates and conciliates complaints of employment discrimination based on race, religion, and sex	Although it has filed—and won—some big court cases involving millions of dollars in back-pay awards, is essentially without power or real authority; it may be folded into a unified antidiscrimination agency.
National Highway Traffic Safety Administration	Created in 1970, has 800 employees, 10 field offices, and a $100 million budget; also administers $129 million in grants to states	Regulates manufacturers of autos, trucks, buses, motorcycles, trailers, and tires in an effort to reduce the number and severity of traffic accidents	An aggressive young regulator, has promulgated hundreds of regulations from auto bumpers to mandatory seat belt installation; its new administrator comes from Ralph Nader's organization

Agency	Vital Statistics	Major Functions	Special Characteristics
Environmental Protection Agency	Founded in 1970, employs 10,000, maintains 10 regional offices, and operates more than 20 laboratories, spending $865 million; administers more than $4 billion in sewage treatment construction grants	Develops and enforces standards for clean air and water, controls pollution from pesticides, toxic substances, and noise; approves state pollution abatement plans and rules on environmental-impact statements	Preoccupied with developing standards and writing broad rules, prefers negotiating compliance to twisting arms; under an active new administrator likely to be a tougher enforcer in the future
Occupational Safety & Health Administration	Created in 1971, employs 2,400, runs 125 field offices, and spends $128 million	Responsible for regulating safety and health conditions in all work places—except those run by governments	Few regulators have been the target of as much vituperation and antagonism; both labor and business have accused it of everything from triviality to harassment; major administrative reforms are expected
Consumer Product Safety Commission	Established in 1972, employs 890 on a budget of $39 million and maintains 13 field offices	Its mission is to reduce product-related injuries to consumers by mandating better design, labeling, and instruction sheets	Criticized for concentrating on trivia, has been reorganized to stress clearer priorities; its administrators' effort to reach into too many new areas sometimes means poor follow-up

Source: Adapted from *Business Week,* April 4, 1977, pp. 52, 53, 56.

Vague Laws Bureaucracies come under attack in relation to this new volume of regulation because they have discretionary power. A major source of this power is the vagueness of the laws passed by Congress in the regulatory area. Congress often is not equipped with the expert and detailed knowledge needed to write precise regulatory laws. The bureaucracy has this knowledge. One of the sources of its discretionary power is its possession of expert knowledge in the area of regulation. Regulations have to be adjusted to fit different industries; they are often complicated and require scientific and technical knowledge. The creation of such detailed regulation is left to the bureaucracy. Furthermore, Congress often writes vague laws because it is politically incapable of agreeing on more precise regulations—regulations that may upset constituencies at home. By leaving the task of detailed regulation writing to the bureaucracy, Congress avoids the political heat that would come from an offended industry.

This approach to the writing of law is not new. One of the first regulatory acts, the law setting up the Federal Trade Commission (FTC) in 1914, said that "unfair methods of competition in com-

Many complain about the burdens of government regulation, but regulators say they are needed if we want to solve problems like pollution.

merce or unfair or deceptive acts or practices in commerce are hereby declared illegal." But what is "unfair" or "deceptive"? The answer was left to the FTC and to the courts. In a similar manner recent legislation on the environment or on occupational safety mandates general concern with the issue but leaves to the bureaucratic agency the discretion to write the precise regulations.

Bureaucratic Behavior

Bureaucracies, as we pointed out earlier, can be thought of as organizational machines. They allow societies to carry out complex tasks that could not be carried out by individuals working separately. They allow specialization; they are organized to foster hierarchical control; they are methodical and predictable. Yet bureaucracies are organizational machines run by humans. They do not operate in as rigid a manner as bureaucratic theory would lead one to believe.

In theory, bureaucracies have no goals of their own. Policy makers provide a bureaucracy with goals; the bureaucracy carries out those goals. Thus Congress is expected to pass laws, which then become government policy. Bureaucratic agencies simply administer the law. Many theorists writing about bureaucracy have stressed the distinction between policy and administration. The former is supposed to be made by elected officials; the latter is the task of bureaucracy.

In fact, it does not work that way. Bureaucratic organizations do not simply administer laws that are handed down to them. They play a major role in setting policy. Policies often begin in bureaucratic agencies. Much of the legislation for federal medical care was written in the executive branch by civil servants who had long been concerned with the problem. They worked in close contact with the members of Congress who were to sponsor the legislation. Furthermore, as we have seen, much actual policy is made after congressional legislation has been passed as bureaucrats fill in the details of the legislation. Thus in many ways bureaucrats shape the policy goals of a government agency. They do not merely follow the directives of policy makers higher in the hierarchy.

BUREAUCRATIC POLITICS

In addition, bureaucracies have goals over and above the policies that they are supposed to carry out. One goal is to maintain and enhance the organization itself. Another is to protect established ways of doing things.

Maintaining and Enhancing the Organization Bureaucratic organizations are engaged in a power struggle with other bureaucratic organizations. Each agency of the government tries to protect the power it has and, if possible, to increase its power. Agencies try to increase their budgets, to increase the number of people they employ, to increase the scope of the programs under their control. If they cannot increase budgets, personnel, and power over programs, they will at least try to keep what they have. They will resist budget cuts, personnel reductions, and any attempt to cut back their programs.

There are many reasons why bureaucrats act to protect what they have and try to get more. For one thing, their jobs depend on this effort. A budget cut may mean the loss of one's job. For another, the *importance* of one's job depends on it. Bureaucratic rank and prestige depend on the size of one's program. Bureaucrats try to have their programs increase in size because their own status within the bureaucracy will rise accordingly.

Lest bureaucrats are made to sound like power-hungry officials with no interests but their own jobs and security, we must add that bureaucratic officials are usually deeply committed to the programs whose administration they are in charge of. The officials of the agency that is assigned the task of administering the federal highway safety program are engineers who are committed to highway safety. If they struggle for increased funding for their program or for more autonomy to carry out the program, it is in large part because increased funds and increased autonomy will, they believe, allow them to do a better job and save more lives on the highways, and they believe that, because they are experts, they know best how to do this.

As advocates of their own program, the bureaucrats in a particular agency often come into conflict with other bureaucrats. The Arms Control and Disarmament Agency in the Department of State works on problems of disarmament. Its commitment tends to be to arms limitation. This often brings it into conflict with the Defense Department, whose officials are less likely to have such a commitment.

Within the Defense Department, the Air Force and the Navy clash over weapons systems. It will come as no surprise that the Navy favors more funding for missile-carrying submarines, the Air Force more funding for supersonic manned bombers.

In domestic matters, the Environmental Protection Agency comes into conflict with other government agencies when it tries to get them to live up to environmental regulations. Or it may come into conflict with agencies in the Department of Energy that are more interested in preserving energy resources than in protecting the environment.

Standard Operating Procedures Bureaucratic agencies are often accused of being rigid in their methods; they require too many forms, too much red tape. To some extent this criticism is unfair. If we want agencies to be impartial and accountable, a certain rigidity in the way they operate is necessary. Red tape often infuriates those who deal with such agencies. But the existence of red tape—precise procedures that have to be followed in carrying out a governmental

Bureaucratic agencies are often accused of being rigid in their methods.

function—is often an indication that the agency is not acting arbitrarily.

Agencies develop standard operating procedures (SOPs). These too create rigidity. During the Cuban missile crisis in 1962 President Kennedy wanted to block Russian ships from carrying missiles to Cuba. However, he also wanted to limit the confrontation with the Russians. His plan called for a naval blockade, but one that was close enough to Cuba so that the Russians would have time to reconsider and turn around before confronting the American naval ships. The standard operating procedure in the Navy, however, was for a blockade to be set several hundred miles offshore to give ships enough room to maneuver. Kennedy had quite a struggle trying to get the Navy to modify its usual way of doing things for the special circumstances of the Cuban missile emergency.

Bureaucrats and Their Clientele

Bureaucratic agencies are often established to regulate particular parts of the American economy. The Food and Drug Administration was established to regulate drug manufacturers, the Civil Aeronautics Board to regulate the airlines industry, the Interstate Commerce Commission to regulate the railroads. (The ICC later came to regulate inland water transportation as well as trucking.) Over time these agencies often form close, cooperative relationships with the industries that they are supposed to regulate. Rather than regulating the industries in the public interest, they represent the interests of the industry. In some cases observers have referred to the "capture" of an agency by the regulated industry.

The extent to which agencies are "captured" by the industries that they are supposed to regulate is sometimes exaggerated. But there are clear examples of agencies that cooperate closely with their clientele. The Federal Aviation Agency works closely with the airlines industry; the Interstate Commerce Commission for many years worked closely with the railroads; the Food and Drug Administration was for many years closely identified with the drug industry. The close relationship between an agency and its clientele is often enhanced by a "revolving-door" system in which top officials of the agency are appointed to their positions from the industries that they are about to regulate, and many agency employees move on to lucrative positions in the industry they have been regulating after they leave their government position. Defense-related industries—weapons manufacturers and other contractors for the armed forces—frequently hire ex-military officers and ex-Defense Department officials.

There are other reasons why agencies develop close ties with those whom they are supposed to regulate. Agencies need the support of their clientele in dealing with other branches of the government. The Federal Communications Commission can more effectively defend its programs in Congress if the powerful voice of the media is raised to support it. The Interstate Commerce Commission

The Job Exchange Between Private Firms and the Public Bureaucracy (FEA = Federal Energy Administration)

FEA ATTORNEY

Major oil company in Houston, Texas has position available for attorney with a minimum of two years full-time FEA practice. Salary commensurate with experience. Send resume to:

　　Box T-556, The Wall Street Journal

Equal Opportunity Employer

Source: Wall Street Journal, October 23, 1977.

benefits from the support of the powerful trucking industry. Moreover, the agencies are in close and constant touch with the industries they regulate. Their officials meet often; they attend the same social events. The agency can easily come to share the perspective of the industry it is regulating.

The close connection between the regulating agency and the regulated industry comes up in other areas besides business regulation. The bureaucrats in the Labor Department work closely with their clientele, the labor unions, the Agriculture Department with farm groups, the Office of Education with the National Education Association; the officials in the National Science Foundation with university scientists.

The close cooperation between industry and regulatory agency also grows out of the fact that many industries welcome government regulation as something that benefits them rather than a nuisance imposed upon them. Government regulation often protects the firms in an industry from the entrance of new competing firms by setting difficult standards for entering the industry. Government regulation also limits competition among firms by setting prices. When the administration of President Ford suggested eliminating regulation from the trucking industry, the industry itself protested. As the chairman of the American Trucking Association put it, "We have adequate trucking primarily because of legislation providing for federal regulation of interstate motor transportation wisely enacted by Congress in 1935."[6] Similarly, the telephone, banking, television, airline, and other industries actively lobby for government regulation of their industries—particularly regulation that limits competition.

One of the most important developments in recent years is a movement away from such cozy relationships between the regulating agency and its clientele. Regulating agencies are getting tougher; they are becoming more independent from the industries they regulate. Many of the newer agencies have been quite active in their regulatory activities. The Environmental Protection Agency,

[6] Lee R. Sollenberger, in the *National Journal*, July 24, 1976, p. 1052.

the Consumer Product Safety Commission, and the National Highway Safety Administration are zealous—the industries involved would say overzealous—in enforcing their regulations. And some older agencies—the Federal Trade Commission and the Food and Drug Administration—have become more autonomous.

Bureaucracy and Accountability

One of the hallmarks of democracy is the accountability of those who govern to those who are governed. The main mechanism by which this is accomplished is the periodic election. If elected officials are not responsive to the people, they are likely to be voted out of office the next time around. Bureaucrats, however, are not elected. They stay in office for extended periods. Many are protected by civil-service laws and can stay in their positions for life. They carry out many of the major functions of government. How can this be compatible with democracy?

If bureaucrats implemented clear laws without discretion—if they merely delivered the mail and distributed social-security checks—they would pose no problem for democracy. Much bureaucratic activity is routine. But as we have seen, bureaucrats do have a good deal of discretion. They make policy by "filling in the details" of vague congressional laws; and they have discretion in the application of those laws. Bureaucrats have real political power. One cannot solve the dilemma of the power exercised by nonelected officials by denying that they have power.

Another way of resolving the dilemma of a powerful and nonelected bureaucracy is to keep the bureaucracy under control of elected officials—under the control of the Congress or the President. If the performance of bureaucratic agencies is closely controlled by elected officials, the existence of a powerful bureaucracy is not inconsistent with the basic democratic ideal of popular control over the government. Certainly the writers of the Constitution did not intend that there be a fourth branch of government over and above the three that they specified in that document—the executive, the legislature, and the judiciary. Yet there are a number of reasons why the bureaucracy is not easily controlled by the elected branches of the government.

Size The very size of the bureaucracy makes it impossible for elected officials to control it closely. The obvious person to control the bureaucracy is the President. He is the head of the executive branch and is empowered under the Constitution to see that the laws are carried out. But he (or someday she) is only one person. The amount of supervision he can give is limited. He might increase the size of the White House Staff to help him in this job. But even the White House Staff cannot supervise all aspects of the bureaucracy. And indeed, as the White House Staff grows to aid the President in this task it becomes a large bureaucracy that is also in need of supervision. We saw this when we examined how the need to coordinate government bureaucracies only creates more bureaucracy.

Congress, as a body made up of elected representatives, might also supervise the bureaucracy and thereby bring it under popular control. Congress has more hands available for the job, there being 535 members of Congress. This allows more supervision by elected officials, but it does not ensure popular control. The President is elected by the entire nation; individual members of Congress are elected from particular districts or particular states. Congress as a whole can be thought to represent the public, but individual members cannot. As we will see, there is a good deal of control over the bureaucracy by individual congressional committees, but this does not always translate into effective public control.

Complexity   Another reason why the elected branches of the government have difficulty controlling the bureaucracy is that much of what the bureaucracy does depends on special technical knowledge that is not shared by elected officials. Few members of Congress have the training to understand the complexities of nuclear-weapons technology, drug testing, water pollution control, and so forth. Furthermore, even if they have the needed skills, they are dependent on bureaucratic agencies for technical information. Bureaucratic agencies collect the data on which policy is based — the FBI collects crime statistics; the Bureau of Labor Statistics collects data on unemployment; the Federal Aviation Administration collects information on new airplane safety devices. This enables bureaucracies to limit congressional control.

Separation of Powers   The nation's founders set up three branches of government; they did not intend to set up a separate bureaucracy. But the fact that they created three independent branches of the federal government made it more likely that the growing government bureaucracy would be relatively independent of the elected branches. The reason the separation of powers into three branches fosters the formation of a relatively independent fourth branch — the bureaucracy — is that bureaucracies learn to play one branch against another. In this way they enhance their independence.

The examples are numerous. The branches of the armed forces are supposed to be under presidential control. The President is Commander-in-Chief of the armed forces under the Constitution. However, the armed forces have close connections with the congressional armed forces committees. They are often able to get what they want from these committees even if the President opposes them. For instance, they can procure weapons for which the President has not asked. Similarly, the FBI was for many years almost totally immune from control by the President and by the Attorney General, the Cabinet officer who is legally in charge of it. The independence of the FBI was buttressed by congressional support.

435

Independent Commissions As we have seen, many agencies are set up in such a way as to be—at least in part—independent of presidential control. At least fifty government agencies are set up this way. These include the major independent regulatory commissions such as the Interstate Commerce Commission and the Federal Communication Commission. They also include very large agencies such as the Postal Service and the Veterans' Administration, which by law are independent from the executive branch. In addition, such agencies as the FBI and the Army Corps of Engineers, though they are technically under the control of one of the executive departments, have developed a position of substantial independence over the years.

Institutional Loyalty and Secrecy One reason bureaucracies may be hard to control is that bureaucrats will often rally to defend each other from outside interference. Those who work in an agency develop a loyalty to their agency and to their fellow workers; they become protective of their agency. Therefore they will often suppress information about mismanagement within the agency. The penalty for the government official who violates this self-protective norm of government agencies can be severe. Consider the case of Dr. Stanley Mazaleski, a government scientist:

> In the Spring of 1974, Dr. Mazaleski . . . began complaining about the sluggish pace in which his agency had set about designing safety standards for industrial workers exposed to carcinogenic chemicals. The following winter, Mazaleski's criticisms were leaked to the newspapers. Within a few months he was fired . . . Mazaleski belongs to a haunted little tribe of Federal employees who have transgressed against the bureaucracy—who having seen something seriously wrong in a government operation, made a noise about it.[7]

Congress and the Bureaucracy

As we saw in Chapter 13, Congress has a number of powers that give it control over the bureaucracy: It creates agencies, authorizes their activities by legislation, finances their activities, and maintains a general oversight over bureaucratic agencies through hearings and reviews. Heads of such agencies spend much of their time testifying before congressional committees and subcommittees or preparing for such testimony. The effective agency head is one who knows the members and staff of the congressional committee that watches over his or her agency and who manages to maintain good relations with them.

The relationship between Congress and bureaucratic agencies is, however, not usually one of tight control by the former over the latter. Rather, it is best described as a close, cooperative relationship. Supervision of bureaucratic agencies is not carried out by

[7] *New York Times Magazine,* October 30, 1977, p. 41. © 1977 by The New York Times Company. Reprinted by permission.

Congressional committees often work closely with the government agencies that they are supposed to supervise. Here the Secretary of Defense testifying before the House Armed Services Committee.

Congress as a whole but is done by individual committees and sub-committees of Congress. Members of Congress tend to be appointed to committees that supervise programs with which they are sympathetic. Members from agricultural districts are likely to wind up on committees dealing with agricultural matters; members with a particular interest in military matters may be assigned to the Armed Forces Committees in the Senate or House; and so forth. Over the years these members form close ties with the bureaucratic agencies that they are supposed to supervise. They become specialists in the subject matter of the agency; in fact they often become advocates for the agency. The staff of the congressional committee often plays a crucial role as well. Staff members often develop cordial and comfortable relationships with the heads of agencies.

The bureaucratic agency and the congressional committee supervising it often form a close alliance with another group—the interest group that the bureaucratic agency is empowered to regulate. Thus there may be a close "triple alliance" among the House Armed Services Committee, the Defense Department, and the major arms manufacturers. Similar alliances exist among the House Education and Labor Committee, the Labor Department, and the AFL-CIO as well as among the House Agriculture Committee, the Department of Agriculture, and farm groups.

All three participants in a triple alliance benefit from it. The agency is protected from attempts to cut its budget or reduce its jurisdiction. Congress conducts most of its business through committees. Therefore an agency that has a close association with a committee and its staff is shielded against any damaging action by Congress. Members of Congress who are dissatisfied with the performance of a particular agency often find themselves in no position to exercise any control because they do not belong to the committee that is empowered to deal with that agency.

Similarly, the agency is protected in its relations with other parts of the executive branch. The triple alliance makes it difficult for the President or his Cabinet secretaries to maintain close control over the agency; the congressional committee can protect the agency from too much control by the executive branch.

In addition, the alliance between a congressional committee and an agency makes it difficult for the President to reorganize the executive branch. Various Presidents have wanted to change the structure of the executive branch. They might want to change the jurisdiction of an agency, to merge several agencies for greater efficiency, or to abolish an agency. Often such changes are blocked in Congress because of the vested interest of a congressional committee or subcommittee in its close connection with a particular agency.

The triple alliance also benefits the members of Congress who are involved in it. The agency can often do favors for those members. It can provide facilities or services for the member's district or for some of the member's constituents. It can hire people who have been recommended by the member. A contributor to the member's campaign will receive quick and courteous attention from an agency that is supervised by a committee on which that member serves. (Campaign contributors know this well and will give their support to members of Congress who sit on the committees allied with the agencies that deal with problems that are of interest to the contributor.) In a number of ways a compliant bureaucratic agency can help a member of Congress maintain his or her position with the voters and with campaign contributors.

Lastly, the alliance benefits the interest group that is regulated by the agency. Its close and cooperative relations with the agency and the committee mean that its interests receive careful consideration.

Congressional Oversight   Though congressional committees have close relations with particular agencies, Congress does not simply let agencies have their own way. In many cases congressional committees supervise agencies quite closely. Such congressional control is referred to as *congressional oversight.* Congress is often criticized by the agencies for supervising them too closely in the management of their day-to-day business. The agencies would rather have Congress set general guidelines and give them the independence to carry out the details of any given policy. Some congressional committees appear to be more interested in the details of administering a policy than in the broad contours of the policy. Often this is the case because individual members of Congress are mostly interested in seeing that the agency serves the specific needs of their districts.

The President and the Bureaucracy

The President is constitutionally in charge of the executive branch, but in practice he is lucky if he knows what is taking place in even a tiny part of it. Consider the following news item, datelined Notasulga, Alabama, July 27, 1972:

In 1932, Charlie Pollard, then a 26-year-old Macon County farmer, took advantage of a public health official's offer of a free blood test and was told a few days later that he had "bad blood."

"They been doctoring on me off and on ever since then," Mr. Pollard, now 66, said yesterday. "And they give me a blood tonic."

Mr. Pollard did not know until Tuesday that for the past 40 years he has been one of a constantly dwindling number of human guinea pigs in whose "bad blood" the effects of syphilis have been observed.

U.S. Public Health Service officials revealed Tuesday that under a Public Health Service study, treatment for syphilis has been withheld from hundreds of afflicted Negroes for the 40-year period. For the past 25 years, penicillin has been generally available to treat it. The purpose of the study was observation of the course of the disease in untreated persons over a long period of time.[8]

This study had been carried out by officials of the U.S. government and supported with public funds. It spanned the Presidencies of Roosevelt, Truman, Eisenhower, Kennedy, Johnson, and Nixon, all of whom headed the executive branch, of which the Public Health Service is a small part. Any one of them would probably have stopped the program immediately had it come to their attention. But how can one man know what is taking place in the name of the U.S. government in hundreds of offices, laboratories, agencies, bureaus, departments, programs, and projects? Kennedy, it is said, was surprised to learn that the U.S. government, represented by the CIA, was planning to invade Cuba. Nixon claimed to be surprised to learn that, contrary to orders, U.S. pilots had continued to bomb restricted parts of North Vietnam.

When we think of a top executive like the President of the United States and the bureaucratic agencies under him, we imagine that the President issues orders and the agencies obey. Most Presidents have found that this is not the case. When Dwight Eisenhower, whose previous career had been as a top military officer, took over the Presidency in 1953, Harry Truman, his predecessor, remarked: "He'll sit there . . . and he'll say, 'Do this! Do that!' *And nothing will happen.* Poor Ike—it won't be a bit like the army. He'll find it very frustrating."[9] Or consider the description by Franklin Roosevelt:

The Treasury is so large and far-flung and ingrained in its practices that I find it almost impossible to get the action and results I want—even with Henry (Morgenthau) there. But the Treasury is not to be compared with the State Department. You should go through the experience of trying to get any changes in the thinking, policy, and action of the career diplomats and then you'd know what a real problem was. But the Treasury and the State Department put together are nothing compared with the Na-a-vy. The admirals are really something to cope with—and I should know. To change anything in the Na-a-vy is like punching a

[8] *New York Times,* July 27, 1972, p. 18. © 1972 by The New York Times Company. Reprinted by permission.
[9] Richard Neustadt, *Presidential Power* (New York: Wiley, 1960), p. 110.

439

feather bed. You punch it with your right and you punch it with your left until you are finally exhausted, and then you find the damn bed just as it was before you started punching.[10]

Or Nixon: "We have no discipline in this bureaucracy. . . . This fellow deliberately did not . . . carry out an order I personally gave."

We have already seen how the close relationship between bureaucratic agencies and Congress limits the President's control over the bureaucracy. But there are other sources of such limitation. Top officials can be terribly dependent on their subordinates. The President depends on his subordinates for two important things: information and compliance.

Information   The federal agencies are the only ones close enough to their own field to know what programs are working and what programs are not. Consider foreign policy. The State Department, the CIA, and the military have people on the spot. The President has to rely on them for information. The same is true in domestic affairs. The bureaucrats in the Agriculture Department have the facts and figures on grain production; the officials in the Nuclear Regulatory Commission have the details on nuclear power plant safety.

Control of such information can give subordinates power over their superiors. Information can be distorted to serve the interests of the one who is sending the information. Agencies of the government that want more money for their programs will give information showing why additional appropriations are needed. Or they can try to make their programs look more successful than they are. The messages sent by field commanders during the Vietnam War made things look a lot better than they were.

Similarly failures can be covered up. An official investigation of the My Lai killings during the Vietnam War—in which a large number of civilians were killed by American troops—found that the number of victims reported became lower as the information was reported upward through the army. By the time it reached the top officials it didn't look bad at all.

Bureaucrats have good reason to send distorted information up the executive ladder. Their careers depend on looking good to their superiors. In addition, agencies of the government want to protect their programs; they want to see that they receive enough money each year. They will often adjust their reports to serve these needs.

Compliance   The President is given the constitutional duty to see that laws are "faithfully executed" (Article 2, Section 3). But the actual execution of laws usually takes place at a much lower level. Congressional law directs that there be safety regulation for air travel; the President executes that law. But the detailed regulations are prepared by the Flight Standards Service of the Federal

[10] Ibid.

440

Aviation Administration, which is a branch of the Department of Transportation. The quality of the safety regulation depends more on the rules worked out at the lower level than on the general rules laid down by Congress. Indeed, it may depend on how carefully inspectors check aircraft maintenance or pilot qualifications.

One criticism of many government programs is that much effort goes into designing programs and little into seeing how they are carried out. The result is that many programs are ineffective or have results other than those intended by Congress and the President.

Similar problems exist in foreign affairs. The President sets down broad foreign-policy guidelines. But the actual administration of policy takes place at the "country desks" of the State Department (where a government official deals with our policy to Italy or Burma or Kenya) and in embassies around the world.

The size of the government and the fact that the lower levels control a good deal of information make it impossible for the President (or the Executive Office) to know what is going on in all parts of the government and to make sure their directives are complied with. Many Presidents have complained that they had no real control over parts of the government: Kennedy complained that he could not count on the State Department to carry out his foreign-policy directives. No matter what he wanted, they acted in their established ways. And most Presidents have made similar complaints about one or another branch of the government.

THE CIVIL SERVICE

One major way in which presidential control over the bureaucracy is limited is that most positions in the federal government come under civil-service regulations. The employees have job security; they cannot be fired by a new administration.

During most of the nineteenth century federal jobs tended to be filled by the spoils system. The main qualification was membership in the party that was in power. When a new administration came into office, it replaced government workers with its own supporters. As William Seward (later Lincoln's Secretary of State) said in 1849, when Zachary Taylor took office: "The world seems almost divided into two classes: those who are going to California in search of gold, and those going to Washington in search of office." The spoils system bred corruption and inefficiency because officials were hired for their political loyalty, not because they were qualified for the job.

In 1883 the Pendleton Act was passed. It replaced the spoils system with the civil-service system. The new system rested—and continues to rest—on two principles: (1) Selection is on the basis of merit, usually performance on civil-service exams; (2) jobs in the civil-service would be secure even if the administration changed. These two principles were intended to eliminate political criteria as qualifications for office.

The first two principles required a third one: (3) The civil service was to be responsive to the political leaders of the day. It was supposed to be neutral, with no political views of its own.

To a large extent the civil service works as it is supposed to. Most government positions—about 2 million federal employees—are included in the system. Civil servants have job security. An incoming President can appoint only about 2000 of his own people.[11] Of this group, only about 700 are top executives; the rest are assistants to these executives, ranging from confidential advisers to cooks and chauffeurs.

The civil service, however, reduces presidential control over the bureaucracy. As one top official in the Department of Health, Education and Welfare put it: "The system is rapidly bringing the government to a state of paralysis." He listed the following complaints: It is virtually impossible to fire an employee for incompetence; the seniority system (whereby those who have been in office longest rise to the top) makes it impossible for a new administration to reorganize a bureau.[12]

The civil service gives the government continuity as administrations change. However, it also creates a lot of inertia, making change difficult. The civil service was supposed to be the neutral servant of whatever administration came into power. But it is a servant with ideas of its own. New administrations find it hard to control.

Political Appointees and Career Officials   When a new administration comes to power, the President appoints a number of top officials. Some are appointed to the Executive Office of the President, but many are appointed to the operating departments. These include the Cabinet members who are heads of the major departments. But it also includes a large number—700 or so—top level officials: assistant secretaries, heads of agencies, bureau chiefs. These appointees are supposed to help the President take control of the bureaucracy. But it is not easy for such appointees to take effective control.

They are usually new to the job, while the agency they are put in charge of is staffed by long-term career civil servants. These career employees have more expertise and more long-term commitment to the programs and procedures of their particular agency. It is hard for a political appointee to take control. Furthermore, the turnover in jobs among such appointees is fairly rapid. They average two years on a particular job, hardly enough time to find one's way around.[13]

Richard Nixon, frustrated by what he felt was "bureaucratic subversion," tried to gain control of the bureaucracy after his election in 1972 by appointing people who were totally loyal to him to ad-

[11] This figure does not include ambassadors, U.S. attorneys, and members of various commissions.

[12] Anonymous official quoted in the *National Journal,* April 23, 1977, p. 617.

[13] Hugh Heclo, *A Government of Strangers* (Washington, D.C.: Brookings Institution, 1976).

A major problem faced by any President is coordinating the government.

ministrative posts throughout the government. He never succeeded, in part because of Watergate. Other Presidents have been reluctant to try to create an "administrative Presidency" with a bureaucracy totally under its control. If they tried, they would not be likely to succeed.

Though Presidents and their political appointees may be frustrated by a bureaucracy that is not responsive to their direction, the independence of many government agencies from direct political control is important to the functioning of the government. If there is to be an effective federal program to support research on cancer, it is important that decisions on what research to support are made by qualified experts who are independent of political demands that research funds be spent in one congressional district rather than another.

The civil-service laws and the tradition of an independent bureaucracy help protect agencies from control by elected officials for partisan purposes. The Bureau of Labor Statistics would resist any effort by the White House to tailor the unemployment rate to the needs of a President running for reelection. When Nixon tried to use the Internal Revenue Service to harrass his political enemies, it refused. Though many observers of government prefer a bureaucracy that is under the control of elected officials when it comes to carrying out general government policy, few want a bureaucracy that is subservient to the partisan political needs of the President.

Public Control over the Bureaucracy

If elected officials have trouble controlling the bureaucracy, can the public itself have any direct control? Americans often complain about unresponsive bureaucrats who pay little attention to the needs of citizens. One way in which citizens can keep bureaucratic officials responsive to their needs is through their member of Congress. As we have shown in the chapter on Congress, one of the main activities of representatives is individual "casework." Congressional staffs spend much of their time dealing with complaints from constituents or answering requests for special treatment.

In addition, government programs are sometimes set up so as to involve citizens in their administration. A number of "Great Society" antipoverty programs under President Johnson included provisions for participation by the urban poor in carrying them out. Similarly, farmers have participated in the administration of federal soil conservation programs for many years. In general, observers have found that such participation is relatively ineffective. Few citizens take part; they are often unrepresentative of the people who are affected by the program; and they usually have little impact on the administration of the policy.

Recently Congress passed the "Government in the Sunshine Act." This requires that federal agencies and commissions hold

Director   Your address
Federal Bureau of Investigation   Your phone number
10th and Pennsylvania Avenue, N.W.   Date
Washington, D.C. 20535

Dear Sir:

This is a request under the Freedom of Information Act as amended (5 U.S.C. paragraph 552).

I write to request a copy of all files in the Federal Bureau of Investigation indexed or maintained under my name and all documents returnable by a search for documents containing my name. To assist you in your search, I have indicated my Social Security number and date and place of birth below my signature.

As you know, the amended Act provides that if some parts of a file are exempt from release that "reasonably segregable" portions shall be provided. I therefore request that, if you determine that some portions of the requested information are exempt, you provide me immediately with a copy of the remainder of the file. I, of course, reserve my right to appeal any such decision.

If you determine that some or all of the requested information is exempt from release, I would appreciate your advising me as to which exemption(s) you believe covers the information which you are not releasing.

I am prepared to pay costs specified in your regulations for locating the requested files and reproducing them.

As you know, the amended Act permits you to reduce or waive the fees if that "is in the public interest because furnishing the information can be considered as primarily benefiting the public." I believe that this request plainly fits that category and ask you to waive any fees.

If you have any questions regarding this request, please telephone me at the above number.

As provided for in the amended Act, I will expect to receive a reply within ten working days.

                                           Sincerely,
                                               Name
(Write on the envelope: Social Security Number
Attention: Freedom of   Date of Birth
Information Act Unit)   Place of Birth

their meetings and hearings in public and give adequate notice as to when and where they will be held. The purpose is to allow more citizen participation. Some agencies, such as the Environmental Protection Agency, regularly hold open hearings when they are considering certain regulations. It is too early to tell how effective such laws will be in increasing public control over the bureaucracy.

THE FREEDOM OF INFORMATION ACT
AND CITIZEN CONTROL

Public control over the bureaucracy has often been hampered by lack of information. Agencies traditionally had a good deal of discretion in withholding information; their files were closed to the public. In 1966 Congress passed the Freedom of Information Act in an attempt to increase disclosure of information to the public. However, agencies were allowed a good deal of discretion in deciding what they wanted to release. The agencies could also delay in responding to requests for information and charge high fees for the information they provided. The result was that the act was ineffective—a good example of how bureaucratic agencies can protect themselves from attempts to bring them under greater control.

In 1974 Congress amended the act to make it more effective. Agencies have less discretion in deciding what they will release; they have to respond within a fixed time; and they have to charge reasonable fees for the material. The new law has been much more effective. Public-interest groups, academics, and citizens in general have made extensive use of the law. Their requests have focused on such agencies as the Department of Defense, the FBI, and the CIA, agencies that have rarely been brought under public scrutiny. The requests have brought out detailed information on government spying on domestic political groups such as the Socialist Workers Party and on black and feminist groups. The law brought out information from the files of the CIA on the agency's 25-year program of research on mind control drugs. In 1976 alone there were about 150,000 requests for information under the act.

Though the Freedom of Information Act was supported by public-interest groups who thought that it would enable them to oversee the activities of the bureaucracy in the name of public causes, the largest user of the law has been American businesses. They have been particularly active in seeking information from the Federal Trade Commission and the Food and Drug Administration. The motives behind corporate use of the Freedom of Information Act range from seeking information about competitors and trade secrets to attempts to paralyze regulatory agencies beneath an avalanche of requests.[14] This heavy use by business—which was not anticipated by those who originally favored the act—illustrates a point that we have made before: Those who have the most resources (in this case money and legal advice) can take the greatest advantage of government laws and regulations.

The Freedom of Information Act has given citizens some control over bureaucracies—at least in some areas. The act has been criticized as making it difficult for agencies to operate effectively. They complain about the burden of time and personnel needed to handle requests from citizens. And they claim that many requests—especially to the CIA and the Defense Department—lead to the release of information that violates national security.

[14] *Washington Post,* July 25–29, 1976 (Series on the Freedom of Information Act).

National park rangers are part of the federal bureaucracy.

Professionalism and the Bureaucracy

The influence of professionals—people with advanced technical training—on the American bureaucracy is great. This can create special problems of public control, but it can also sometimes make bureaucracies more independent from control by special interests.

When the "spoils system"—whereby most bureaucratic jobs went to loyal partisans of the newly elected President—was abolished, the alternative that replaced it was government by professionals. As new agencies were created to deal with new problems, they were turned over to professional specialists such as educators, engineers, doctors, chemists, foresters, agronomists, and the like. Thirty-six percent of all the people listed by the Census Bureau as having "professional, technical and kindred" occupations are employed by the government. As one observer put it: "The character of the public service . . . which seems to be most significant today is professionalism."[15] (See Table 14.2.)

Professionals have a distinctive orientation. They believe, probably rightly, that they understand the problems of their area of specialization better than people with no professional training. Doctors have special knowledge of medical problems, engineers of engineering problems. Professionals tend to share professional standards with other members of the same profession; they judge themselves and other professionals by how well they live up to such standards. Above all, they seek autonomy from control by nonprofessionals. "A basic drive of every profession . . . is *self-government* in deciding policies, criteria, and standards."[16]

The fact that so many agencies are controlled by professionals makes it harder for elected officials or the public to control them. As Daniel Patrick Moynihan has put it: "Professionals profess—they profess to know better." This can challenge the very foundation of presidential authority. Presidential authority is based on the fact that the President is elected by the people and stands for the popular will. Professionals profess to know best—better than the people themselves—what is really good for them.

This may make such agencies hard for the public to control, but it can also make them effective servants of the public interest. In recent years a number of older regulatory agencies that used to be closely tied to particular industries have become more effective regulators of those industries. The recent more stringent regulation of the drug industry by the Food and Drug Administration is an example, as is the more vigorous Federal Communications Commission. A major reason for the change has been the increased role of professionals—chemists, engineers, communications specialists—in these agencies. The professionals respond less to pressure from the industries than to the standards of their professional colleagues

[15] Frederick Mosher, *Democracy and the Public Service* (New York: Oxford University Press, 1968), p. 101.
[16] Ibid, p. 124.

TABLE 14.2
Professionals Employed by
the Federal Government

Occupation	Number of Federal Workers
Engineers (all types)	146,940
Scientists (all types)	85,501
Nurses and nurses' aides	67,904
Personnel administrators	35,331
Accountants	31,780
Teachers	26,284
Air-traffic controllers	26,005
Internal Revenue Service agents	21,155
Investigators	21,133
Inspectors	17,427
Forestry workers	14,624
Mathematicians and statisticians	13,550
Attorneys	12,761
Computer operators	11,602
Doctors	8,033
Librarians	6,643
Economists	4,798
Writers and editors	3,577
Psychologists	3,099
Photographers	3,061
Veterinarians	2,284
Pharmacists	1,439
Dentists	925
Chaplains	461

Source: U.S. Civil Service Commission. Data as of October 1974.

in universities and in other agencies. Similarly, many new government agencies such as the Consumer Product Safety Commission and the Environmental Protection Agency have been vigorous enforcers of standards despite industry opposition because they are staffed with professionals.

Direct vs. Indirect Regulation

In recent years the volume of detailed regulation issued by the government has come under increasing criticism. Agencies such as the Environmental Protection Agency or the Occupational Safety and Health Administration (OSHA) send out detailed instructions on water and air pollution or on safety regulations for factories (OSHA's regulations on the use of stepladders run to twenty-six pages). The government attempts to reduce water and air pollution or to reduce industrial accidents by creating detailed regulations on how wastes should be treated before they are dumped into our rivers and by writing specific regulations on how jobs are to be performed so as to minimize accidents. Such direct regulation requires active government intervention: Precise requirements for water quality or safety standards must be spelled out in detail; government inspec-

447

New policies such as a switch to the metric system require a lot of regulation that some citizens resent.

tors must observe and control the processes by which businesses conduct their day-to-day operations. Such regulations, critics complain, reduce the flexibility that would enable businesses to find better ways of doing things.

Some people have argued that regulation would be less burdensome and more efficient if the government used a less direct approach. The government could provide incentives for good results without specifying how a firm achieved those results. Consider an early example of such regulation. The famous code of law created by Hammurabi, king of Babylon in the eighteenth century B.C., contained the first recorded regulation of this sort: If a dwelling fell down and killed an occupant, the builder was put to death. The regulation did not specify how to build a house. It did not detail what materials or mode of construction must be used. But it clearly gave builders an incentive to be careful about the materials they used. Modern forms of regulation by incentive are not as dramatic. But the principle is the same if a firm is informed that it will have to pay a fee to the government on the pollutants that it emits from its factories or that it will have to pay a tax if it has a bad safety record. The regulation does not specify in detail how the firm will eliminate the pollutants or reduce accidents. The firm has flexibility, and the government does not have to write detailed regulations. But the firm knows that its self-interest requires that it do the best it can to reduce pollution or accidents. Though government inspectors are needed to monitor the pollution or accidents, the inspections can be simpler.

Many observers of government regulation believe that the goals of such regulation — cleaner air and water, greater industrial safety — are important and cannot be achieved without some intervention on the part of the government. But they find the cost of such regulation excessive and the results inefficient. An incentive approach to regulation might achieve the desired goals while limiting the extent of bureaucratic control over individual citizens and firms.

Whether such an approach will be taken and whether it will be effective remains uncertain. But the search for alternate approaches to regulation illustrates the concern many feel about the problems of bureaucratic control. However, even if such schemes were to reduce the extent of bureaucratic control they would only marginally reduce the size and importance of the government bureaucracy. A large bureaucracy, only imperfectly controlled by elected officials and the public, is an inevitable feature of any modern democracy, including the United States.

controversy

How far should the government go in regulating the lives of its citizens? This question arises very often when the government sets up some regulation to protect citizens from harm or injury. Certain kinds of regulations cause little controversy. No one objects if the government sets stringent criteria for the safety of commercial aircraft. The average traveler has no way of judging whether the plane is safe or not and must rely on government inspectors to protect the interests of the traveling public.

But what if the harm represents a risk that the citizen is aware of and chooses to take? How far should the government go in preventing him or her from taking that risk? Government policy is inconsistent on these matters. People may legally buy cigarettes even though studies show that they increase the risk of cancer; saccharine was outlawed because it has been shown to increase risk of cancer. The government ruled at one time that cars had to have seatbelt interlock systems so that they could not be started if the seatbelts were not fastened. The rule was later repealed, though cars must still have belts and warning buzzers. Often the decision as to how closely to regulate a dangerous practice is made on political grounds. The seat belt interlock requirement was repealed because of public reaction against it.

Consider a law that is on the books in many states requiring motorcycle riders to wear crash helmets. Many motorcyclists have protested against this law.

One Side The government has no business telling motorcycle riders that they must wear crash helmets. It is, after all, *their* heads that are at stake, and they have the right to risk injury. Such regulation interferes with their freedom. It is not as if this were a speeding law; forcing motorcycle drivers to obey speeding laws protects not only their lives but also the lives of others. Here the government is interfering in a decision that affects only their own safety. Furthermore, like all government regulations this one is costly to enforce. Traffic police spend a lot of time stopping bareheaded motorcyclists when they could be doing more important things like catching people who drive in such a way as to endanger others.

Laws like the crash helmet law are an example of the government meddling where it ought not to meddle.

The Other Side A law that prevents people from hurting themselves is perfectly appropriate. Studies have shown that crash helmets reduce injury and fatality in motorcycle accidents by a substantial amount. The average citizen may not realize this, which is one reason why safety experts make such studies and translate them into law. Moreover, it is not quite true that the motorcycle driver who goes without a helmet is risking only his or her own head. Suppose there is a serious injury and the state is responsible for medical care. Suppose the driver is killed and his or her children go on welfare. In either case the taxpayers have to pay for the driver's negligence. In a modern welfare society the health of all people is a social matter, not merely a personal matter.

15
THE SUPREME COURT IN AMERICAN GOVERNMENT

What Do Courts Do?

"Scarcely any political question arises in the United States that is not resolved, sooner or later, into a judicial question." De Tocqueville made this observation about America 150 years ago, but he would probably say the same thing today. What does it mean to make judicial questions out of political issues?

For one thing, our Constitution established a very complicated government, with three branches (legislative, executive, and judicial) and two layers (federal and state) and all sorts of crisscrossing checks and balances. Quite often, and on very serious matters, one unit of government has political differences with another unit. President Nixon, for example, did not want to turn the Watergate tapes over to a congressional committee, claiming that executive priviledge allowed him to withhold them. Such conflicts have to be settled by an umpire, and the courts play this role.

Secondly, Americans have a habit of taking their differences to court. This is true of everything from simple liability cases—I'll sue you for medical costs, because I broke my leg when I slipped on the ice on your sidewalk—to the sweeping reforms that have so transformed American society: the right of workers to form unions, of blacks to vote, of state governments to impose income taxes.

Finally, the United States probably has more "judge-made" law than any other nation in the world. On the one hand, we have laws made by legislators, Congress, and the fifty state legislatures as well as local councils. These are laws made in accordance with the principle of "popular sovereignty." On the other hand, we tolerate judicial interpretation and even reversal of legislature-made law. More than this, we allow judges to propose and even to administer specific social reforms, school busing plans being a recent example.

Courts, especially the Supreme Court, do these three things then: umpire the relations between contending units of a complicated government; resolve disputes or adjudicate conflicting political interests; and make law, sometimes even in opposition to democratically elected representatives of the majority will.

A Complicated Government Needs an Umpire

In earlier chapters we learned that the writers of the Constitution intended to create a government that would protect itself against the temptation to become a political tyranny. To achieve this protection the Constitution lays down two great principles: separation of powers and federalism, which between them spread the powers of government all over the place. As we will see shortly, however, the Constitution does not make clear what should happen when one part of the government differs from another part. Such differences are not infrequent in our political history. Once these differences became so severe that a bloody and destructive civil war was fought. Other differences, however, have been resolved more or less peacefully. Something called judicial review has served as the umpire that sorts out squabbles between Congress and the President, or between state laws and national laws.

THE POWER OF JUDICIAL REVIEW

The power of judicial review is the power of the courts to decide whether a legislative act is constitutional or not and to declare it void if it is deemed unconstitutional. This is what is generally meant by the term *judicial review.* However, the term also means the power to review and overrule lower-court decisions. It is the power of the courts to review the constitutionality of legislative acts that has made American courts (and particularly the United States Supreme Court) so politically powerful, and much more powerful than courts in most other countries, where they do not have this power. (Since World War II several countries, including India, West Germany, and Italy, have introduced the system of judicial review.)

It is strange indeed that judicial review, which has become one of the most important features of the operation of the American Constitution, is not even mentioned in that document. This may have been intentional. The founders knew that not all controversial questions could be settled at a single convention. Had the delegates at Philadelphia proposed to give a few judges appointed for life the authority they now have, the convention might very well have broken up. States' righters would have opposed giving a national court the power of judicial review of state supreme courts and state legislative actions, and many populist democrats no doubt would have opposed judicial review of congressional acts. However, if they had failed to provide for a federal Supreme Court with broad, if vague, responsibilities for guarding the Constitution, the federalists and the constitutionalists would not have been satisfied. All things considered, therefore, the best solution was to resort to obscure language, allowing each faction to read its own views into it. Hence the creation of a guardian umpire of great but uncertain potential, to be defined and shaped in the political conflicts of the future.

Those conflicts were not long in coming. In order to establish judicial review the Supreme Court had to overcome two significant sources of opposition. First there were those who felt that Congress, as the constitutionally established legislature for the Republic, was the institution that was best suited to pass final judgment on the meaning of the Constitution. Second there were those who were committed to state "sovereignty," who believed that the state supreme courts were fully empowered to interpret the Constitution in relation to the laws of the various states. Two issues had to be resolved, one stemming from the ambiguities in "separation of powers" and the second stemming from ambiguities in "federalism." The first was resolved in favor of the Court over Congress, the second in favor of the federal government over the states. We will review these landmark decisions in the following pages.

Judicial Review of Acts of Congress

When the first Congress provided for a Supreme Court and for several lower federal courts (in the Judiciary Act of 1789), it had nothing to say about judicial review of congressional acts, although it did give the Supreme Court power to review state court decisions in certain types of cases. It was up to the Supreme Court itself to decide whether it was to have such power. The Court's initial history did not seem to suggest that it was going to be an agency with any real power and influence. When John Marshall was appointed Chief Justice in 1801, there were few cases before the Court and Marshall's political enemies were capturing control of the other two branches of the national government. In fact the Court was caught up in a bitter political fight. Yet within two years Marshall cleverly managed not only to save the independence of the Court but successfully to assert the power of the Court to invalidate acts of Congress.

THE CASE OF MARBURY V. MADISON[1]

As early as the mid-1790s two factions were trying to win the Presidency. One faction, the Federalists, was led by John Adams (who became President in 1796); the other was led by Thomas Jefferson. In the election of 1800 Jefferson won a big victory. The outgoing President, Adams, appointed the outspoken Federalist John Marshall as Chief Justice of the Supreme Court, and in the last hours before Jefferson took over the Presidency he appointed many Federalists to positions in the federal judiciary. For these so-called "midnight appointments" Adams was accused of trying to entrench in the judicial branch the Federalist views that he had been unable to get accepted in the elected branches of the government.

In its last-minute haste to pack the judiciary with Federalists, the Adams administration had not been able to deliver to one William Marbury his commission as justice of the peace for the District of Columbia. President Jefferson's Secretary of State, James Madison, refused to deliver the commission, and Marbury turned to the Supreme Court for a writ of *mandamus* compelling Madison to do so. (A writ of *mandamus* is an order to an official to carry out a duty which the law has placed on him or her.) Marbury based his

[1] Cranch 137 (1803).

Chief Justice John Marshall.

claim for such a writ on a congressional law (the Judiciary Act of 1789) that had authorized the Supreme Court itself to issue such writs.

Marbury's suit placed the Marshall Court in an awkward position. It seemed to face two alternatives. It could order Madison to deliver the commission, but if Jefferson and Madison refused to comply with the order, as the Court suspected they would, it would advertise its own powerlessness to the world. Or it could refuse to issue the writ, which would have been to concede Madison's right to withhold the commission and again show the powerlessness of the Court. Marshall avoided this apparent dead end by creating a third alternative, an alternative that in fact gave the Court a much greater power than Marbury had asked it to exercise, namely, the power of judicial review.

What Marshall did was to declare unconstitutional the law on which Marbury's suit was based. Section 13 of the Judiciary Act had given the Supreme Court the power to issue writs of *mandamus* in original jurisdiction. *Original jurisdiction* means the power to decide a case in the first instance, that is, without another court having decided the case first. But Article 3 of the Constitution provides that the Supreme Court should have original jurisdiction in only two kinds of cases: cases affecting ambassadors and consuls and cases in which a state is a party. Therefore, reasoned Marshall, Section 13 was contrary to the Constitution and was null and void. The Court had no jurisdiction and could not hear the case.

Before Marshall ruled on this jurisdictional question he gave a lecture to President Jefferson and Secretary of State Madison. He asserted that Marbury did have a legal right to the commission, that Madison had wrongfully withheld it, and that the federal courts (though not the Supreme Court in original jurisdiction) had the power to order Madison to deliver the commission. Marshall deviated from the normal practice of ruling first on the question of whether the Court has the right to hear and decide a case. Had he followed this practice, he would not have been able to assert that the executive branch was subject to judicial control. It was precisely this part of the Court's statement that infuriated Jefferson and his followers. It was this particular assertion that was protested and debated. The exercise of judicial review over Congress in the form of setting aside a part of a congressional law went almost unnoticed. In addition, Marshall had introduced the notion of judicial review in a case in which its exercise had made his political adversaries in the executive branch appear victorious in the particular case at hand: After all, the Court had not ordered Madison to deliver the commission.

So much for Marshall's political skills. What about his legal justification for holding that the Court had the power to invalidate congressional laws if it found them to be in violation of the Constitution? Contrary to most Court cases, the Marbury decision did not cite a single judicial precedent; and while it referred to the "original intention" of the Nation's founders, it did not attempt to document that intention by citing statements by contemporary statesmen who had been in the Constitutional Convention or in the ratifying state conventions. Instead, Marshall's method was an exercise in logic. "It seems only necessary to recognize certain principles," he said, "supposed to have been long and well-established, to decide it."[2]

There are three principles that make up the basic theory of judicial review: (1) The Constitution is superior to congressional law; (2) it is the function of the Court to determine what the Constitution means; and (3) laws that conflict with the Constitution must be declared void and inoperative by the courts. Let's take each of these three principles and see how Marshall constructed and supported them.

"The people have an original right," Marshall stated, "to establish such principles of government as shall most conduce to their own happiness." This "original right" of the people to lay down a system of government for themselves and future generations echoed the so-called social-contract theory of the Englishman John Locke, which had recently been used by the American patriots to justify revolution against the British.

As for the second major principle, that the Court has the power to interpret the Constitution, Marshall held that the judicial function is not only to apply the law but also to say what the law is. He reasoned that:

1. The judicial power is the power to say what the law is.
2. The Constitution is law.
3. Therefore the judiciary has the power to say what the Constitution is.

By now the groundwork had been laid for the third major principle, that laws that are contrary to the Constitution must be thrown out by the Court. Marshall was not content with simply proving that the Constitution is superior to congressional law and showing that a law that conflicts with the Constitution is void. He felt that he also had to prove that a congressional act that is in conflict with the Constitution and therefore void should not be carried out by the courts. For the courts to give effect to congressional acts that are in conflict with the Constitution would be, he said, "to overthrow in fact what was established in theory." The very concept of limited government, which is the foundation of all written constitutions, implies and dictates that laws that go beyond the limits prescribed by the Constitution shall not be permitted to become legally operative. Also, if two laws, that is, both the Constitution and a congressional law, apply to the same case, and they are in conflict with one another, the Court must apply the superior law, namely, the Constitution.

This is how judicial review came to America. Two kinds of con-

[2] Ibid., p. 176.

troversies have raged about this power ever since the Marbury case. Historians have carried on an argument concerning whether this was a usurpation of power by the Court or was simply carrying out the intention of the founders. Political theorists have argued over whether judicial review is compatible with democratic government or not. These problems are unsolvable. On the first question the evidence is too scanty, and on the second question differences exist as to how to define democratic government. What is certain is that judicial review is generally accepted by the American people, even though particular applications of such review may lead to dissatisfaction and controversy.

Actually, the number of judicial vetoes of congressional acts is not that great. Only 85 acts or parts of acts have been declared unconstitutional in the 176 years since *Marbury* v. *Madison.* Some of these acts have been very important ones, but many constitutional scholars believe the significance of judicial review lies not so much in the statutes declared unconstitutional as in the threat of a Supreme Court veto.

There is one kind of judicial review power that the Court has exercised much more frequently: its power to review and veto actions of state governments. How did the Court achieve this power? This will be the subject of our next inquiry.

Judicial Review of State Court Decisions – National Supremacy

Nowhere in the Constitution is there any specific grant of authority to the United States Supreme Court to review and set aside the verdicts and rulings of the highest courts of the states. Nevertheless one of the very first things the newly established Congress did was to give the Court that authority, which is known as *appellate power.* Under Section 25 of the Judiciary Act of 1789, appeals could be taken to the Supreme Court whenever the highest state court that had jurisdiction over a case ruled against the constitutionality of a federal law or treaty, or against a right claimed under the Constitution or federal law. Such appeals could also be taken in cases in which the state courts had ruled in favor of a state law that was claimed to have been in violation of the Constitution, treaties, or national laws.

Thus contrary to judicial review of congressional laws, which the Court itself had to infer directly from the Constitution, the power of judicial review of state court decisions was granted to it by an act of Congress. This did not mean that the Court did not have to legitimize and justify this form of judicial review through reference to and interpretation of the Constitution. For twenty-six years the Court was able to exercise this power over state courts without serious opposition. But then, in 1815, came a very serious challenge to the Court's appellate power.

MARTIN V. HUNTER'S LESSEE[3]

The first important challenge to the Court's appellate jurisdiction over state courts came from Virginia. That state had enacted a law denying aliens the right to inherit real property. One of the richest landowners in Virginia had willed his estate to a British relative. Virginia refused to let his English heir inherit the estate and proceeded instead to sell the land to its own citizens. When the heir sued in the courts of the state to regain title to his land, arguing that the state law was in violation of a treaty with Great Britain that guaranteed certain rights of British citizens in the United States, the Virginia Court of Appeals upheld the state law. The Englishman then appealed to the Supreme Court of the United States, which reversed the ruling of the Virginia court and sent a mandate to it ordering it to execute the reversal decision.

The Virginia judges, in a unanimous opinion, refused to obey the Supreme Court's mandate, declaring that it was a violation of state sovereignty to subject the Virginia Court to the authority of another sovereign body.

Virginia's refusal to obey caused the case to be taken once again to the Supreme Court. The Supreme Court met this challenge to federal judicial power in the famous case of *Martin* v. *Hunter's Lessee.* In this case the issue was: Did the United States Supreme Court have appellate power over state courts? The Supreme Court argued that the Constitution was established not by the states but by "the people of the United States." The people had established the Constitution to obtain certain common objectives, and they had a right to deny to the states any powers whose exercise would be incompatible with this general purpose. It was not inconsistent with "the genius of our government" that the Constitution operated directly on the states in their corporate capacities. Many provisions specifically limited the powers of the legislatures of the states, and the Supreme Court could set aside state laws and executive actions if they were found to be contrary to the Constitution. Therefore, the Court concluded, the power of appellate jurisdiction over state courts would be equally compatible with the spirit of the Constitution.

Moreover, federal appellate jurisdiction over state courts was necessary in order to ensure national uniformity in the interpretation of federal laws and treaties and of the U.S. Constitution. Otherwise federal laws and treaties would come to mean different things in different states and, the Court said, "The public mischiefs that would attend such a state of things would be truly deplorable."

A federal treaty was upheld and a state law set aside, and a state court order had been reversed by the Supreme Court of the United States. The Martin case clearly had sustained what the nation's founders had intended: supremacy of national law and federal judicial review over state courts in cases when this authority was needed to protect national supremacy, as outlined in Article 3. Al-

---

[3] 1 Wheaton 304 (1816).

though the Supreme Court has had to respond to other challenges to this power, the Martin case was the key decision. It made the Supreme Court, in effect, the umpire or arbiter in conflicts between the states and the federal government. Although the Court has been able to act as an impartial umpire at several points in our history, the fact that the Court is a part of the national government may have something to do with the fact that in most federal–state conflicts the national government has tended to prevail.

Judicial Review of State Laws and National Supremacy

Three years after the Martin case the Court was confronted with the challenge of reviewing a state law that was claimed to be in conflict with national law. The Court put teeth into the "national supremacy" clause (Article 6, Section 2), first, by resolving the immediate issue in favor of the national government, and second, by formulating general guidelines that would protect the legal supremacy of the national government and its agencies in future cases of federal–state conflict. Let's review how it happened?

McCULLOCH V. MARYLAND

The congressional chartering of the second Bank of the United States in 1816 was a most unpopular act. Also, certain branches of the Bank had engaged in reckless speculation and were accused of fraudulent financial practices. In order to protect state banks and private banks from competition from the national bank, several states levied taxes on the operations of the United States Bank. The State of Maryland was among these states: The legislature had levied a heavy tax on the Bank's Baltimore branch. McCulloch, the cashier of the Baltimore branch, refused to pay the tax, arguing that it was unconstitutional. When the state took legal action against McCulloch and the state courts upheld the state law, the bank appealed the decision to the United States Supreme Court.

There were two constitutional issues in this case: Did Congress have the power to charter a national bank, and if so, could a state tax such a bank? (Note that the Court no longer considered the Court's appellate power over state court cases as debatable.)

The Power to Tax Is the Power to Destroy   Chief Justice Marshall wrote the opinion for the Court. While he conceded that the state's power of taxation was of vital importance, he declared that it was not unlimited. Thus the Constitution had specifically prohibited the states from laying any duties on imports or exports. Though there was no specific provision in the Constitution that prohibited the states from taxing federal agencies and instruments, such prohibition could be inferred from the nature of the system of federalism and was implied by the "national supremacy" clause. The power to tax implies the power to destroy, Marshall held, and if federal functions could be taxed by the states they would be dependent on the will of the states. This would alter the charter of the American union and would, if applied generally, make the states "capable of arresting all the measures of the government, and of prostrating it at the foot of the states." The Constitution had instead created a system in which the operation of the national government was not to depend on the good will of the states.

The McCulloch decision once again proved that the Supreme Court was to be the umpire that would speak with final authority in constitutional issues involving conflicts between the national and state governments. Furthermore, the Court had laid down general principles and guidelines that gave the supremacy clause some clout. No state had any power to "retard, impede, burden, or in any manner control, the operations of the constitutional laws enacted by Congress." In other words, when Congress has entered a field where it has constitutional authority, its legislation cancels all incompatible state regulations.

The Implied-Powers Doctrine Did Congress have the power to charter a United States Bank? The counsel for the State of Maryland argued that the government of the United States was a government of delegated powers, that is, a government with only powers that are specifically granted to it in the Constitution; nowhere was there any mention of the power to charter a bank. Hence, to charter a bank was to exceed the authority granted the Congress by the Constitution. Marshall responded by referring to general principles as well as to the language of the Constitution. First, it follows from the general nature of things that a government must have all the powers it needs to carry out its responsibilities. Second, Article 1, Section 8, Paragraph 18 of the Constitution states (after having listed a series of delegated powers) that Congress shall "have the power to make all laws which shall be necessary and proper for carrying into execution the foregoing powers." The inclusion of this clause clearly indicated that the founders intended Congress to have other powers than those that were expressly mentioned, Marshall reasoned. In other words, express powers implied the exercise of other powers for their implementation. Or, as Marshall put it:

> Let the end be legitimate, let it be within the scope of the Constitution, and all means which are appropriate, which are plainly adapted to that end, which are not prohibited, but consistent with the letter and spirit of the Constitution, are constitutional

Applying this principle to the case at hand, Marshall held that the *ends* of borrowing money, raising an army, and regulating interstate commerce (delegated powers) made it convenient or necessary for the national government to resort to the *means* of chartering a national bank.

The introduction of the implied-powers doctrine was yet another victory for the forces of nationalism, as it allowed the national government to reach and regulate areas that were not specifically delegated to it. For example, the national government regulates matters of labor–management relations even though the Constitution does not authorize it to do so.

SUMMARY

We started out by saying that a system of government as complicated as ours needs an umpire. Under the doctrine of judicial review the Supreme Court has become this umpire. It is the Supreme Court that decides whether an act of Congress is constitutional. It is the Supreme Court that can step in and settle disputes between different branches of the government, as we saw in the discussion of Watergate in the preceding chapter. And it is the Supreme Court that sorts out differences between the federal government and the various state governments.

What we have not yet made clear is how courts go about resolving differences, whether those differences are between units of government, between individual citizens, or between a citizen and the government. We are going to break into our discussion of the Supreme Court and take a look at something called *adjudication,* which is a technical term for what courts do when they settle disputes. Once we have a better understanding of adjudication we will return to the role of the Supreme Court in our political history and concentrate on some of the major issues that have been settled by the Court.

What Do We Mean by Adjudication?

Adjudication is the power to interpret and apply the law in cases of legal dispute. One citizen says that a law prohibiting school segregation means that public schools cannot discriminate against racial minorities. Another citizen says that this law means that the school board must take action to bring about racial integration in the classroom. What does the law "really" mean? Once it is known what the law "really" means, then people (or school boards) who are not in compliance with the law can be punished or otherwise made to comply. Adjudication, then, not only finds out what the law means but also finds out whether individual citizens or government agencies have broken the law.

To understand adjudication and how the courts operate, it will help to look at the idea of judicial power, rules of court operation, and what we call the adversary process.

JUDICIAL POWER

Judicial power is the authority to interpret the law with the understanding that whoever or whatever is affected by the interpretation has the legal obligation to accept the Court's version of the law as final.[4] Without this understanding, the act of discovering what the law means would be without consequence. It is "the law" that the courts deal with. The law is the source of the court's power as well as a result of the exercise of the court's power. "The law" is an abstraction, however. There are actually several kinds of law: constitutional law, statutory law, administrative law, and common law.[5]

Constitutional Law The concept of a "higher law" controlling and limiting legislation is a very old one. In the medieval period the "higher law" was the law of God. Beginning in the eighteenth century it became the law of nature or of reason. What the writers of the U.S. Constitution did was to transfer this concept from the realm of theory to that of law. Hence, the Constitution was declared to be supreme law. Constitutional law, therefore, is the Constitution proper plus the many decisions rendered by the Court when it has had to interpret the meaning of the Constitution. It is this work of the Court that constitutes the bulk of what is known as constitutional law. The most important aspect of constitutional law is that it is superior to other kinds of law.

Statutory Law Statutory law is law enacted by a legislature, such as Congress. Statutes are attempts to solve social problems and set down certain general principles or rules covering defined situations. Although the principles stated in statutes are not as general as constitutional principles, they still have to be interpreted and clarified by the courts. Thus statutory law consists of the statutes themselves plus what the courts have had to say about them.

Administrative Law This is a body of rules and regulations made by administrative agencies in the executive branch in order to carry out the objectives of legislative programs. Although these rules are not made by lawmakers, they have the effect of law. They cannot be in conflict with the statutes that authorized the legislative program involved. Examples of administrative law would be the rules and regulations made by the Federal Communications Commission.

Common Law Common law is judge-made law. It originated in England after the Norman Conquest. Judges were asked to solve conflicts basing their decisions on custom or common sense or reason in the absence of statutes or other legal codes. Early decisions served as precedents for subsequent analogous problems; that is, judges came to consider themselves bound by previous court cases in this area (this is called the rule of *stare decisis*). Common

---

[4] Another attribute of judicial power is the power of the courts to punish people for contempt of court. This power exists in order to protect the processes of the court.
[5] There is also what is known as *equity*. This is the power of the courts to prevent a person from committing an act that would obviously injure another person or damage his or her property.

law can be overriden by statutory or constitutional law, however.[6] Since common law looked so much to the past for guidelines, it could be effective only in a static society. After the Industrial Revolution new problems arose and past guidelines became inapplicable. Hence the emergence of more statutory law and the rise of a more dynamic lawmaking body—the legislature. Common law still governs the legal relations among Americans, particularly in the area of tort actions (in which we can sue a person who has injured us or damaged our property through carelessness).

RULES OF OPERATION

Cases and Controversies   When confronted with a social problem a legislature can initiate remedial action in an effort to solve it. Courts, on the other hand, must wait for someone else to bring a case or controversy to them. What constitutes a case or controversy? The Supreme Court has ruled that the following characteristics must be present before a conflict or dispute will be considered to be a case or controversy that may be resolved in a court of law: First, there must be an *actual conflict* with two parties having adverse interests. This again means that the courts will not render advisory opinions, for example, opinions on the constitutionality of proposed laws. Nor will it deal with cases in which the parties have feigned a controversy in a friendly suit. Second, one must have a *standing to sue.* Not everyone with money and an axe to grind can bring a suit before an American court. In order to be able to do that (in other words, to have a standing to sue, an individual must have a sufficient interest in a controversy. Basically, he or she must prove, first, that the interest he or she claims is a personal one, not simply some interest he or she shares with citizens generally, and second, that the interest he or she wants defended is a legally protected interest, or a right, that is threatened or placed in jeopardy.

No "Political Questions"   A case or controversy that has all the characteristics just mentioned will not be resolved in a court if it involves a "political question." The refusal to touch such issues is implied from the system of separation of powers. When it would be inappropriate to override congressional or presidential decisions (e.g., in the area of foreign affairs, particularly military action) or whenever there is a lack of satisfactory legal criteria for a judicial determination, the controversy is said to involve a political question and the Court will not intervene. But of course it is the Court itself that decides whether something is political in this sense. Cynics have stated that this is simply a convenient way to pass the buck on

---

[6] It was called "common" because it applied to all of England, thus overriding local customs or rules (an important early step toward the "nationalization" of government).

issues that are too hot to handle. The provision in the Constitution that the United States "shall guarantee to every state in this Union a Republican form of government"[7] will not be enforced by the Court, which has held that whether a state has a "republican form of government" or not is a political question to be decided by the political branches of the government.[8]

THE ADVERSARY PROCESS

The Role of the Lawyer The role of the lawyer is often misunderstood. Lawyers do not necessarily sympathize with the goals of their clients. But it is central to the lawyer's creed that the client receive the most forceful representation of his or her interests as possible.

The lawyer does not search for "justice" or "the truth." These objectives will be secured, it is assumed, if lawyers on both sides of a case present their positions as forcibly and effectively as they can and a third, independent agent makes the truth-finding decision. This system is called the *adversary process.*

The Role of the Judge Unlike continental European judges, the American judge is not expected to investigate or do research about a case. Rather, he or she is expected to make a decision — or instruct the jury to make a decision — solely on the basis of arguments and evidence presented in the court by the opposing parties. The judge is responsible for making sure that a proper adversary proceeding is carried out: that legally correct claims and charges are entered; that each party is given a chance to present his or her case; that irrelevant testimony is kept off the record; that illegally obtained evidence is not used.

It can be seen from this description that the adversary process has two major stages: first, the active argument by the disputing parties' lawyers, both motivated by self-interest or the interest of their clients; and second, the disinterested evaluation by the judge, the umpire, who is not actively engaged in eliciting or bringing out the truth (as opposed to finding the truth in what has been brought out by the disputing lawyers).

It is often argued that in our adversary system no one has the duty actively to bring out the truth and that justice therefore will not be dispensed. The answer to this criticism is threefold: (1) Admitting that the adversary system is not flawless or perfect, neither is any alternative. If we instead had a disinterested inquisitor or judge, what would happen if that person was oppressive, lazy, unjust? (2) Though lawyers are expected to fight for the self-interest of their clients, they are also bound by certain ethical rules. They are "officers of the court" in addition to being fighters for their

---

[7] Article 4, Section 4.
[8] *Luther* v. *Borden* 7 Howard 1 (1849).

464

A judge is expected to make decisions on the basis of evidence presented in the adversary process.

client's interests. (3) Whatever their motives, lawyers' arguments must focus on the principles of justice or on the law, and they must prove that their client's claim is just or is supported by the law.

Room for Policy Making

The power to adjudicate, to decide what the law really means, provides the Court ample room for policy making. Indeed, in no other country do the courts have such a great amount of policy-making power. This must be puzzling to students in an introductory American-government class. First they learn that the courts constitute the judicial branch of our government and that the judicial power is the power to interpret and apply the law, after having learned that the power to make laws belongs to the legislature, and then, all of a sudden—without warning—they are told that the courts are also policy makers. How can this be?

Briefly speaking, the answer is that laws are (and by their very nature must be) general in their formulation. Constitutions must be stated at a high level of generality. Broad, ambiguous words such as *unreasonable* (no unreasonable searches or seizures) and *equal* (equal protection of the law) and *due* (due process of law) appear in our Constitution. Anyone who has the task of interpreting such generally stated principles has the power not only to apply what already exists but to decide what *does* exist as a matter of law. No wonder, then, that the Supreme Court has been able to hold that the constitutional principle of equality (equal protection) *did not* prohibit the states from establishing a racially segregated public school system and later that it *did* prohibit this without a single word having been added to or subtracted from the Constitution.[9]

But the power to interpret statutes passed by a legislature also leads to the power to fill in the details, to stretch the law, or—in some cases—to alter the intent of the legislators. Although the power to make policy by interpreting statutes is more subtle and less dramatic than the making of policy by interpreting the Constitution, it must nevertheless be taken account of if one wants to understand the overall role of the courts in the American political system.

It is becoming quite fashionable for political scientists to describe the Court as another political body (as contrasted with the traditional description of the Court as a legal body). This is partly because the Court has policy-making power. This is to label the

[9] A fuller description of how the power to interpret the Constitution gives the Court the power to make constitutional law can be found in Chapter 14. What one should constantly bear in mind in this regard is that many constitutional-law decisions could have reasonably gone the other way. Often a minority of the Supreme Court justices *did* argue the other way.

Court by its output. But judging from the other end, so to speak—
that is, from what goes into the Court's decision-making processes
—we can see that the Court operates in response to other pressures
besides those described in our discussion of the adversary process.
The Court does not simply rely on reason or logic or past decisions
when it seeks guidelines for its rulings. It often operates in a context of social pressures and demands, pressures that it sometimes
cannot or will not ignore. Behind the various possible constitutional interpretations are choices among competing social, economic, or political interests and policies. Since this is true, one
should not be too surprised to learn that the courts find themselves
in the center of social-policy conflicts. They too have their constituencies.

Who are these actors and how do they operate? Among others,
they are special-interest groups of various kinds and the thousands
of lawyers and legal scholars who keep close watch on the actions
of our courts. Special-interest groups use adjudication as a means
of pursuing their political objectives in four ways: (1) They organize
in order to collect the money needed to take an issue all the way to
the Supreme Court. (2) They recruit individuals who have standing
in a court to raise the issue in the courts.[10] The NAACP is one
organization that has been able to use the judicial route to accomplish changes in social policies favored by its members. (3) In addition to sponsoring (and financing) test cases, special-interest groups
gain access to judicial decision making by entering a case as a
"friend of the court" *(amicus curiae)*. This is sort of "lobbying"
whereby special-interest groups can state their policy interest before
the court, expressed of course in legal terms in written briefs.[11]
(4) Special-interest groups also attempt to influence the selection of
judges (where judges are appointed; where judges are elected the
group becomes active in the elections). Special-interest groups will
attempt to block the appointment of a judge whom they believe to
be opposed to their particular interest.

Lawyers are a primary element in the Court's constituency. The
American Bar Association in particular has an important role to
play in the selection of federal judges as well as judges in many
states. Legal scholars write articles in law reviews that analyze
important court decisions. A well-written law review article may

---

[10] A person can bring a suit in a federal court on behalf of himself or herself and all
others who are "similarly situated." This right has been narrowed as a result of a
recent court case, however.

[11] Thus, in a recent case in which the Court once again struck down some form of
government aid to parochial schools in Ohio, the case was brought by Benson
Wolman, a citizen and taxpayer of Ohio, sponsored by the American Civil Liberties
Union of Ohio and supported by several groups that appeared as "friends of the
court," such as Americans United for Separation of Church and State, the National
Coalition for Public Education and Religious Liberty, and a coalition of various re-
ligious and civil liberties groups. *Wolman* v. *Walter*, decided June 24, 1977, cited in
United States Law Week, 45, 1977, 4861.

persuade some judges to alter their views; and sometimes the Supreme Court itself refers to such scholarly articles for support of a decision.

The Supreme Court and Public Policy

The power to adjudicate can also be seen as the power to make public policy. In establishing this principle we have ignored two very interesting questions. First, is judicial policy making compatible with democracy? Second, what kinds of public policies have been made through court action? We will start with the second question and they try to sort out what it all means for democratic theory.

HISTORICAL OVERVIEW

In some sense policy is made in thousands upon thousands of specific court cases, and we can hardly talk about more than a few of them. Here we will review three general headings, the first of which has already been discussed.

1. *Establishing a National State* The early decades of the nineteenth century saw the Marshall Court develop the concept of judicial review. As we have noted, judicial review was used to promote the centralization of power in two ways: by shielding the national government from state obstructionism and by giving a broad and liberal construction to the powers of the national government. Marshall's judicial nationalism served for a long time as a check against the tendency toward state sovereignty and localism. It also set the stage for another era in political-constitutional history.

2. *Establishing a Capitalist Economy* In the nineteenth and early twentieth centuries political thought, as reinforced by the Supreme Court, nurtured the idea that the economic interests of business should be protected against government action. Many state laws that regulated economic activities were struck down (often because they violated the constitutional powers of the national government). Since the national government had little interest in exercising all the power that the Court said it possessed, the end result was that an economic system could emerge both on a national scale (without state restrictions) and of a capitalist nature (without control by either state governments or a regulatory national government). In the next section we will review the constitutional foundation for this system of capitalism.

3. *Establishing Social Citizenship* The constitutional doctrine that the government should leave citizens alone to work out their own economic salvation came to an end in the 1930s. As we saw in Chapters 3 and 4, the political philosophy that accompanied the New Deal announces that the government has an obligation to

Until the 1930s, the Supreme Court ruled that business practices such as child labor could not be prevented by government laws.

provide the rights of social citizenship: to meet the basic needs of citizens for shelter, security, jobs, education, and health care. From the middle of the 1930s to the present time the Supreme Court has been caught up in the enormous transformation of the United States into a welfare state. Accommodating the Constitution to the demands for equality and social citizenship has severely strained the resources of our court system. This we will see after reviewing constitutional doctrine and the establishment of capitalism.

Judicial Activism in Defense of Capitalism (1890–1937)

The Civil War removed a major obstacle to the growth of a powerful industrial economy. It destroyed the notion that the United States could have two different economic systems, a plantation economy based on slave labor and an industrial economy based on the principle that people are "free" to sell their labor power. In the latter part of the nineteenth century the industrial revolution shifted power from the countryside to the cities, from the small businessman and farmer to the bankers and captains of industry. This new industrial elite often abused its powers, and both state and national governments began to place legal restrictions on economic activities. The industrial elite turned to the Court for protection, and the Court, committed to the ideology of economic individualism, came to its rescue.

THE DOCTRINE OF SUBSTANTIVE DUE PROCESS
The constitutional provisions that allowed the Court to elevate the capitalist principle of free competition into constitutional law were the "due process" clauses of the Fifth and Fourteenth Amendments. The latter amendment prohibited the states from depriving "any

person of life, liberty, or property without due process of law," and the former contained the same prohibition against the national government.

The "due process" clause can be traced to the guarantee embodied in the *Magna Charta* that "no freeman shall be taken or imprisoned . . . or in any manner destroyed . . . except by a legal judgment of his peers or by the law of the land." When the "due process" clause was included in the Bill of Rights, its meaning was clear: The government could not deprive people of their personal or property rights without following proper procedures.

In the last decade of the nineteenth century the Court read into "due process" an altogether different meaning. The concept of *substantive* due process became a check on what the government could do instead of on the process it had to follow in order to do it, as the phrase had traditionally been defined. Any law that the Court felt was an unreasonable restraint on property and liberty could be declared unconstitutional. The application of such a vague judicial test turned the Court into a superlegislature, which overturned laws by the Congress and by the states that had sought to bring under control some of the questionable practices of big business. Legislatively determined rates for public utilities and railroads, laws that provided for minimum wages, maximum hours, and price regulations were among the kinds of legislation that the Court felt constituted unreasonable interference with liberty and property.

Not all the justices of the Supreme Court adhered to the substantive due process view. One of those who did not was Justice Oliver Wendell Holmes. Dissenting in the case of *Lochner* v. *New York*,[12] in which the Court had overthrown as unconstitutional a New York law that limited hours of work in bakeries to 10 per day and 60 per week, Holmes observed:

> This case is decided upon an economic theory which a large part of the country does not entertain. If it were a question whether I agreed with that theory, I should desire to study it further and long before making up my mind. But I do not conceive that to be my duty . . . A Constitution is not intended to embody a particular economic theory, whether of paternalism . . . or of *laissez faire.*

THE COURT VS. THE PRESIDENT: THE END OF SUBSTANTIVE DUE PROCESS

In a normal period the Court would perhaps have gone unchallenged. But in October 1929 the stock market collapsed, and with it the economic certainties of American capitalism. The idea of corporate immunity to government control was thrown on the defensive as ruined speculators, bankrupt merchants, unemployed laborers, and farmers facing foreclosure joined in the demand for sweeping government action.

[12] 198 U.S. 45 (1905).

469

As the economic crisis deepened, a governmental crisis grew. The reform administration of Franklin Roosevelt introduced laws to deal with the crisis, but these new laws often ran into the roadblock of the Supreme Court. By 1935 the Court was rejecting as unconstitutional most of the major innovations of the New Deal. Between 1935 and 1937 it set aside a total of twelve congressional statutes—nearly one-seventh of all the federal laws it had declared unconstitutional in nearly two centuries. It overturned statutes designed to bring relief to the nation's farmers, the oil industry, the coal industry, and other groups.

The Court reasoned that it had no choice; these laws clearly went against constitutional provisions. It appeared to believe that it could ignore the rising tide of public disapproval, congressional annoyance, and presidential frustration. In other words, the Court believed that it was above politics and was merely carrying out the "automatic" task of comparing laws with the Constitution and rejecting those that did not fit its provisions. In fact, as events showed, it was wrong on both counts. It could not ignore political currents, nor were its decisions inevitable. Other justices would see things differently.

Roosevelt's "Court-Packing" Scheme The lifetime appointments of the Supreme Court justices seemed to protect them against popular sentiment; but in the end their power rested on the acceptance of their legitimacy, and this legitimacy was now fraying rapidly. President Roosevelt, fresh from his second election victory, tried to "pack" the Court by means of a law allowing him to add new justices. The bill that the President proposed to Congress early in 1937 provided that whenever a federal judge aged 70 or older refused to retire, an additional judge could be appointed to that court. The maximum size of the Supreme Court was set at fifteen. If the bill had passed, it would have allowed the President to "pack" the Court with pro-New Deal judges and swing it over to his side. The Constitution is silent both on the matter of retirement of judges and on the size of the Supreme Court.

Strictly speaking, it was not unconstitutional for Congress to change the size of the Supreme Court. This had been done six times. However, many people felt that this was an unconstitutional attack on the integrity and independence of the judicial branch. Thus many members of Congress objected to the President's plan, Democrats as well as Republicans, New Dealers as well as anti-New Dealers. Many members were, then as now, lawyers who had been conditioned in their law schools to look upon the institution of the Supreme Court with reverence and respect.

A Switch in Judicial Philosophy The President's "court-packing" scheme failed, but it was a mere skirmish in the greater battle over policy-making supremacy. That battle was lost by the anti-New Deal judges and their conservative supporters when the "swing men" on the Court, Justice Roberts and Chief Justice Hughes, decided to make, in the newspaper language of the day, "the switch in time that saved nine."

Laws hardly distinguishable from those that had been found unconstitutional by 6–3 majorities were now upheld by a majority of five justices. On March 29, 1937, while the debate over the "court-packing" scheme was at its height in Congress, the Court found that the Fourteenth Amendment's due process clause no longer stood in the way—as it had in New York barely a year before—of a minimum wage law in the state of Washington. Two weeks later Chief Justice Hughes declared that Congress had the right to establish a National Labor Relations Board to deal with conflicts over union organization and collective-bargaining rights. Four dissenting justices pointed out that in a long train of decisions, including several in the past two years, the Court had ruled so sweeping a grant of power unconstitutional; but the Chief Justice simply said, "These cases are not controlling here."

The change in the Supreme Court signified a return to the judicial nationalism of the Marshall Court. Once again the Court gave a broad construction to the powers of the national government, and the doctrine of implied power replaced the substantive due process approach. But the Marshall Court had used judicial nationalism primarily as a bulwark against state laws; it was now used to uphold the exercise and use of the powers of the national government. In other words, while Marshall's nationalism had the effect of protecting *laissez-faire* capitalism, the judicial nationalism of the late 1930s opened the way to wide national regulation of the economy.

Judicial Activism in Favor of Reform

The next major chapter in constitutional history starts shortly after World War II and extends more or less to the present. It will be convenient to discuss the Warren Court (1954 to 1969), so called because Earl Warren was Chief Justice, separately from the Burger Court (1969 to the present), named after Chief Justice W. E. Burger.

The Warren Court was known as an activist court, implying a willingness to break with precedents and to challenge congressional interpretation of what is constitutional. The judicial activism of the Warren Court promoted, rather than stopping or delaying, social reform. Again and again the Warren Court took the initiative as the agent of reform when Congress, the President, and state governments were either unable or unwilling to act. This can be seen in the area of racial segregation.

RACIAL DESEGREGATION
In the southern states the law demanded segregation of the races in public schools and other public services such as libraries, parks, swimming pools, and the like. This racial segregation had been in

In the 1950s and the 1960s, the Supreme Court ruled that school segregation was unconstitutional, but it sometimes required federal troops to enforce the Court's rulings.

operation since 1896, when the Supreme Court had held that such a policy did not violate the equal-protection clause of the Fourteenth Amendment to the Constitution. This clause states that "no state shall deny to any person . . . the equal protection of the law." The Court had then been asked to throw out as unconstitutional a Louisiana law that required racially segregated railroad facilities. Instead, it came up with the so-called separate-but-equal doctrine, holding that the principle of equality had been complied with as long as black people gained access to the same types of facilities or services that were provided for the white people.[13]

For the next half-century the law concerning racial segregation remained unchanged. However, the status of black Americans did not remain unchanged. As they became better educated and as they gained political experience and influence through the ballot box and through organization, they became more assertive of their right to full equality. World War II also greatly changed the status of black citizens as blacks moved northward in large numbers from southern tenant farms to get better-paying jobs in defense industries.

The NAACP, convinced by experience that Congress could not be made responsive to its demands, decided to expand its longstanding fight in the courts by launching a series of carefully chosen suits to widen the range of constitutionally protected civil rights. One of these suits was the famous *Brown* v. *Board of Education of Topeka*.[14] The NAACP believed that it had at last found the ideal test case for making the Court reopen the constitutional status of the separate-but-equal doctrine.

The schools for black children in Topeka, Kansas were equal to the white schools in all respects—physical plant and equipment, courses available, qualifications and quality of teachers. This fact allowed the question to be openly raised as to whether legally enforced segregation of students on the basis of race was compatible with the constitutional principle of equality. In 1954 a unanimous

[13] *Plessy* v. *Ferguson* 163 U.S. 537 (1896).
[14] 347 U.S. 483 (1954).

Court ruled that "in the field of public education the doctrine of 'separate but equal' has no place." The Court asserted that "separate educational facilities are inherently unequal."

With this decision the Supreme Court reshaped the agenda of modern American politics. Racial discrimination by law could no longer be thought of as consistent with the constitutional principle of equality before the law. For another ten years, however, the judiciary was left to struggle practically alone with the huge job of implementing the nation's newly defined legal and moral responsibility to black citizens. The executive branch did little, and only in 1964 did Congress begin to respond positively.

Desegregation of the schools is a highly sensitive, complicated problem that cannot be easily and readily solved. It is far from being settled, as the controversy at the end of this chapter makes clear. What is settled, however, as a matter of constitutional law, is that our governments cannot by law set up or dictate the establishment of racially segregated institutions or services.

ONE PERSON, ONE VOTE

Another area in which the Warren Court broke with precedent was that of congressional and state legislative apportionment. State legislatures had for a long time drawn the boundaries of congressional and state legislative districts with little regard for the number of people in a given district. A legislator elected from a rural district might represent only 25,000 voters while one from an urban area might represent ten times that many voters. For more than a generation reformers had attempted to have the Court intervene in the area of apportionment, but it had consistently refused to do this, holding that the matter was a "political issue" and therefore could not be resolved by a court of law.

In a precedent-shattering case[15] the Warren Court now ruled that apportionment issues were justiciable after all, and began to take jurisdiction in cases involving unfair apportionment systems.

The Court's decision in *Baker* v. *Carr* unleashed an avalanche of apportionment litigation along with the political efforts by many state legislatures to redraw their election districts to meet the new constitutional standards. The new constitutional standards were that the "seats in both houses of a bicameral state legislature must be apportioned on a population basis." "Simply stated," said the Court, "an individual's right to vote for state legislators is unconstitutionally impaired when its weight is in a substantial fashion diluted when compared with votes of citizens living in other parts of the state."[16] Thus the "one person, one vote" rule came to apply to both houses of state legislatures, throwing out the practice in

[15] *Baker* v. *Carr* 369 U.S. 186 (1962).
[16] *Reynolds* v. *Sims* 377 U.S. 533 (1964).

some states of assigning seats in one house according to population and in the other according to other criteria (such as units of local government) as bases for representation.

The political impact of the Court's intervention in the area of reapportionment, and its application of the "one person, one vote" rule, has been tremendous. It has broken the domination of many state legislatures, by rural and small-town voters and increased significantly the political influence of the voters in our big cities and suburbs at both the state and national levels.

REFORMS IN THE AREA OF LAW ENFORCEMENT

The egalitarian spirit embodied in the Court's handling of the racial-segregation and reapportionment issues was also evident in the Court's reforms in the area of law enforcement. Several major extensions of procedural rights were of particular benefit to the poor and the weak. The procedural rights (that is, the rights of people suspected or accused of crimes to a fair treatment) contained in the Bill of Rights were intended to apply only to the national government. The Fourteenth Amendment had protected people's procedural rights against the states, but only in a general way (life or liberty could not be taken away except through "due process of law"). In the 1930s the Court had begun to incorporate some of the procedural protections of the Bill of Rights into the "due process" protection against the states (after having rejected the attempt to have the entire Bill of Rights incorporated into it). What the Warren Court did was to substantially increase the number of procedural rights that should be brought under the protective umbrella of the Fourteenth Amendment against the states. To say the same thing differently, the Warren Court brought a much greater portion of state criminal procedure under federal judicial supervision.

Before the Warren Court, it was possible in some states to be sentenced to prison without benefit of counsel, as many defendants were too poor to be able to hire a lawyer. The adversary system applies to the criminal-justice area, which means that the prosecutors and defenders are the active finders and presenters of facts. The judges and jurors are not fact finders but have to select the facts from those that are brought out by the two parties to the case. Without a counsel for defense, an ordinary person would be handicapped in his or her investigation of facts as well as in his or her self-defense in the courtroom, cross-examination of witnesses, and so forth. The other side (i.e., the police and the prosecutors) would have vast resources to conduct investigations and expertise in courtroom procedures. The Warren Court refused to tolerate this kind of situation, and in the famous case of *Gideon* v. *Wainwright*[17] it threw out Gideon's conviction, which had been procured without benefit of counsel for the defense. A counsel for the defense, said the Court, is "fundamental to a fair trial," and, if need be, a state has to provide a defendant with one.

[17] 372 U.S. 335 (1963).

Not only did a defendant have the right to counsel at the trial: he or she should have access to counsel in the pretrial stages, such as the arraignment and preliminary hearings. As a matter of fact, in the controversial *Miranda* v. *Arizona*[18] case the Court held that before they can start to question a suspect in custody the police must inform the suspect of his or her right both to have counsel present and to remain silent. In this case the right to counsel had become a necessary means of guaranteeing the protection against self-incrimination. The Miranda decision revealed the Court's distrust of convictions based upon mere confessions. The adversary system starts with the assumption that a suspect is innocent until proved guilty, and it is the state's responsibility to prove that he is guilty. The protection against self-incrimination means that a defendant has no duty to help the state build a case against him or her. Without giving the "Miranda warnings," the police may too easily be tempted into tricking or coercing a suspect into incriminating himself or herself.

Early in the twentieth century the Court had ruled that if the police had collected evidence against a suspect in violation of constitutional rights (e.g., without a proper search warrant), such evidence could not be introduced in a federal court. This became known as the *exclusionary rule*. However, such evidence could still be used in state courts. The Warren Court ended this inconsistency, holding that the exclusion of illicitly obtained evidence is the only effective means of discouraging violations of the law by the police. As a result of these reforms in criminal law, the Court has to some extent become the supervisor of the activities of thousands of state and local law enforcement officers, who all of a sudden have had to consider the Supreme Court one of their bosses in a new and unprecedented fashion.

The Burger Court: A Break in Judicial Activism

The Warren Court had broken with precedents and initiated reforms in other areas besides segregation, reapportionment, and criminal law. But in these three areas in particular the Court provoked a storm of criticism, protest, and even overt defiance. Thus on two occasions the President of the United States had to call out federal troops in the South to come to the aid of the newly established law of racial desegregation in the public schools. And President Nixon was aided in his bid for the Presidency in 1968 by the so-called white backlash vote and by his promise to put "law and order" judges on the Supreme Court.

Shortly after Nixon's election he was given a chance to fulfill his campaign pledge. Chief Justice Warren resigned from the Court

[18] 377 U.S. 201 (1966).

and President Nixon was able to choose a Chief Justice who would reflect his own political and judicial philosophy. He selected Warren Burger, a man who had clearly and persistently spoken out against the activism of the Warren Court. Within the first three years of his Presidency Nixon was able to make three more appointments to the Court. (See Table 15.1) After Nixon's departure from the Presidency his Republican successor had the opportunity to appoint yet another new justice to the Court, making the veteran Warren Court members a minority of four.

Long before that, however, the Nixon appointees had succeeded in causing the Court to strike a different judicial posture from that of the Warren Court, a posture of judicial restraint and caution. There has been one striking exception to this tendency: the Burger Court's decision that states could not constitutionally forbid women to have abortions during the first six months of pregnancy.

Apart from the abortion case, the Burger Court has not shown much eagerness to solve America's pressing problems by becoming the nation's reformer, though it has from time to time extended the reforms of the Warren Court and made innovations of its own on a piecemeal, pragmatic basis. For example, the Burger Court has extended the right to counsel for the poor to misdemeanor cases (the *Gideon* case had granted this right in felony cases); it has made it much more difficult for the states to use capital punishment than before and has decreased the number of crimes that can be punished by capital punishment; it has ruled that private nonsectarian schools may not refuse to admit black children because of their race; it has accented the concept of busing as a tool of desegregation of our schools; it decisively (8–0) turned down the Nixon administration's efforts to use wiretaps and other bugging devices in cases involving political dissident groups without a judicial search warrant; and it rejected Nixon's claim that the Watergate tapes were protected by executive privilege. (The latter ruling was important in Nixon's decision to resign.)

Even though the Burger Court has not overturned the Warren Court's major reform work, it has from time to time slowed the momentum or modified and, in some areas, gravely weakened the

TABLE 15.1
Members of the
Supreme Court, 1978

Member	Appointed by	Year
William J. Brennan, Jr.	Eisenhower	1957
Potter Stewart	Eisenhower	1959
Byron R. White	Kennedy	1962
Thurgood Marshall	Johnson	1967
Warren E. Burger	Nixon	1969
Harry A. Blackmun	Nixon	1970
Lewis F. Powell, Jr.	Nixon	1971
William H. Rehnquist	Nixon	1971
John P. Stevens	Ford	1975

impact of the Warren rulings. For example, the Burger Court has allowed variations from the one person, one vote reapportionment principle (though it accepts the right of the Court to take jurisdiction in such cases); it has told lower courts that they must limit system-wide solutions to racial segregation in schools to cases in which system-wide violations are found; and it has ruled in a housing discrimination case from a Chicago suburb that predominantly white communities have no constitutional duty to change their zoning laws in order to provide low-income housing for blacks unless the laws were deliberately enacted to bar blacks. And in the area of criminal law enforcement the Burger Court has been more sympathetic to the problems of law enforcement than to the claimed rights of suspects.

The Court Intervenes:
Judicial Authority Expanded

An entirely new chapter in constitutional history is being written. It is a chapter that goes well beyond the judicial nationalism that prevailed when the country was founded, the judicial protectionism that developed when industrial capitalism was being established, and the judicial activism that has prodded a new egalitarianism into being.

Federal and state courts are taking over the day-to-day operation of prisons, hospitals, and school systems. They are issuing court orders of great specificity. They are requiring state legislatures to raise new taxes in order to build or upgrade specific facilities.

An example from Jacksonville, Florida will illustrate this new form of court interventionism. A federal district Judge, Charles R. Scott, found the conditions in Jacksonville jails to be intolerable: cells without windows, inhabited by rats and roaches as well as suspects, and strewn with filth, including urine and vomit. Sleep was nearly impossible, and muggings and homosexual rape were common. Inmates were not allowed to shower, shave, or brush their teeth. Scott found the jail conditions to be cruel and inhuman punishment, and he ruled that prisoners were also being subjected to "arbitrary, capricious and unlawful summary discipline" by prison guards.

Scott directed sweeping improvements, "from reduction of the prison population to hiring of additional correction officers and nurses." He ordered the construction of recreation facilities and the purchase of hot trays for food. Moreover, "he threatened city and county officials with contempt if they failed to follow the order." And he appointed a U.S. marshal to ensure that the reforms took place.

State legislators in Florida argued that Scott was doing things that only the state legislature was allowed to do. He was usurping the legislature function. Scott answered that if Jacksonville "chooses to operate a jail, it must do so without depriving inmates of their rights guaranteed by the Federal Constitution."[19]

What Scott set out to accomplish in Jacksonville, other judges have tried in St. Louis, Baltimore, New Orleans, New York City, and elsewhere. Judges are also running state hospitals in Alabama, Louisiana, and Mississippi and a school district in Boston. Many observers believe that we are on the verge of a wave of such court interventions. They argue that this represents the most far-reaching extension of judicial authority since *Marbury* v. *Madison* and the doctrine of judicial review.

Serious reservations have been voiced. Governor George Wallace of Alabama, for instance, believes that the courts are taking over the functions of the legislative and executive branches of the government and thereby destroying the principle of separation of power. "It is government by the judicial branch. The judges, in their robes, lean back and say, 'You spend this money.' They don't say how to raise it."

Sources of Judicial Interventionism

Judicial interventionism should be seen in historical perspective. The idea that the government is responsible for the dignity, equality, and liberty of the citizens arose in the 1930s and greatly accelerated in the 1950s and 1960s. Before the 1930s the task of law had been to prevent the government from interfering with the citizen. This was the doctrine of limited government. But now the task of law is to ensure that the government is meeting its obligations to citizens.

This necessarily involves the Court in deciding whether the government is satisfying its obligations. If the government passes a law promising clean air, then the citizen can file suit against the government for failing to enforce its own law if the air doesn't get cleaner. If the government promises equal schooling, then it had

[19] Quoted by Martin Tolchin, "Intervention by Courts Arouses Deepening Disputes," *New York Times,* April 24, 1977. © 1977 by The New York Times Company. Reprinted by permission.

better deliver or it will find itself answering in court for its own failure.

Time and again in recent years the citizen has taken the government to court. Not, as in the past, because the government was unconstitutionally harrassing the citizen, but because the government is "unconstitutionally" failing to help the citizen. Often these cases are filed by public-interest groups, such as consumer protection groups or environmental clubs. And they often are class action suits, in which the person challenging the government does so on behalf of a "class" of people who are equally affected by the condition in question.

The expansion of judicial authority must be viewed against the broader changes in American society. District Judge Frank Johnson makes the point effectively. "In an ideal society," he observes, humane decisions "should be made by those to whom we have entrusted these responsibilities. But when governmental institutions fail to make these judgments and decisions in a manner which comports with the Constitution, the Federal Courts have a duty to remedy the violation."[20] He is echoed by Chief Justice Burger of the United States Supreme Court. When asked whether it was dangerous for lower federal courts to take over the virtual administration of prisons and hospitals, he replied: "If a State is running its prisons or its mental hospitals in a way that violates the civil rights of the inmates of those institutions, then it is a judge's duty to act."[21]

The Supreme Court and American Democracy

To some observers the Supreme Court has always been an anomaly. What place has a body of officials appointed for life in a government based on accountability through elections? And in a system of checks and balances what place has a tribunal with "supreme" power to interpret the Constitution and set aside the actions of the legislative and executive branches? Who guards the guardians? As the Court's history makes clear, the Supreme Court is by no means all-powerful. We have already learned some of the limitations on the power of the Court. It is time to summarize them and spell out some others.

LIMITATIONS ON THE POWER OF THE COURT
The Constitution Even though the power of the Court to interpret the Constitution gives it broad discretion, as the Constitution is often couched in general and ambiguous terms, the Court does not have a totally free hand. It may decide what the limits of freedom of

[20] Ibid.
[21] Quoted in *U.S. News & World Report*, December 19, 1977, p. 27.

The Supreme Court Justices
take a break.

speech are, but it cannot rule that the Constitution does not guarantee freedom of speech of any kind.

Precedents The Court usually follows past decisions and uses them as guidelines when it has to deal with problems that are similar to those covered by these earlier cases. This is the principle of *stare decisis*, a principle that leads to an important ingredient in a system of government by law: continuity in, and certainty of, the law. Occasionally the Court will not follow past decisions, but then it will either look for distinguishing features, pretending that precedents have not been overturned, or face the heavy burden of proving the need for a new ruling principle.

Political Restraint As has already been explained, the justices, even though they have some independence of the partisan politics of the day, cannot cut themselves off from the currents of American politics. For one thing, they are appointed by Presidents who are interested in certain policies. Both Franklin Roosevelt and Richard Nixon, to single out two, appointed justices who they believed would interpret the Constitution in a manner they preferred.

Overrule by Amendment The Court's interpretation of the Constitution can be overturned by constitutional amendment. For this reason the Court's decisions may not be final after all. Three constitutional amendments have been brought about in a deliberate effort to overrule Supreme Court decisions, namely, the Eleventh, Fourteenth, and Sixteenth.[22]

[22] When, for example, the Supreme Court ruled that the national government could not levy taxes on income, the Sixteenth Amendment was passed.

Avoidance of Compliance   Since the Supreme Court cannot enforce its own decisions, it is dependent on the executive branch of government for enforcement. As we have already seen, this makes it possible for the President to sabotage Court decisions. This can be done by means of a go-slow policy or delaying tactics rather than by a direct and total refusal to comply. State and local officials can successfully limit the effect of a Court ruling, particularly when they know that Congress and the President are not eager to carry out the Court's decisions. This happened in the years immediately following the school desegregation case.

Power to Impeach   The power of Congress to impeach justices and remove them from office constitutes a restraint on the Court's powers. Though this power has not been used very frequently, the knowledge that such a power does exist might have a deterrent effect on judicial misbehavior.

Public Acceptance   A distinguished constitutional scholar writes that "the most important quality of law in a free society is the power to command acceptance and support from the community so as to render force unnecessary, or necessary only upon a small scale against a few recalcitrants."[23] Government in general and the courts in particular will command this respect only when they perform in an authorized fashion the functions that are assigned to them.

This observation brings us to our last restraint on the Supreme Court. The Court can be an effective institution only if it has the acceptance of the community. But this leaves unclear what it is that the Court must do to earn and keep this acceptance. Two somewhat contradictory principles must be balanced.

The Court cannot get too far ahead of the nation for too long a time, nor may it lag behind the popular will. Thus public opinion is a restraint on the Court. One instance of this is the switch in judicial philosophy that took place in the 1930s, in which the Court shifted from judicial protectionism of economic interests to judicial cooperation with the New Deal. Another instance is the way in which the Burger Court modified the criminal protection policies of the Warren Court. Both instances suggest that the Court "follows" public opinion.

Yet a Court that mirrors public opinion too closely may also, paradoxically, lose respect from the community. For it is the aspiration of the Court to reach for justice, and in so doing to appeal to our better selves. Justice is an ethical goal, not easily reached but worth the effort. If the Court bends to the wishes of current public opinion, it may lose contact with the ethical principles that also serve to legitimize the Court's work and, ultimately, the role of the Court in our system of government.

[23] Archibald Cox, *The Role of the Supreme Court in American Government* (New York: Oxford University Press, 1977), p. 103.

controversy

In the early 1970s the Supreme Court as well as the other federal courts became involved in an explosive controversy over the courts' attempts to have schoolchildren bused in order to achieve desegregation of schools. *Brown* v. *Board of Education of Topeka* had ruled that legal segregation of the public schools violated the Constitution. But as the years passed it became clear that abolishing legal segregation would not necessarily eliminate segregated schools. The reason was obvious. In many parts of the country housing patterns had developed in which black Americans and other minority groups lived in separate sections of metropolitan areas — usually in the center of the city — while whites lived in other neighborhoods and in the suburbs. If children went to neighborhood schools, they usually went to schools that were de facto segregated. Some courts, therefore, decided that only by busing schoolchildren from one neighborhood to another, or even from one community to another, could segregation be eliminated.

One Side Busing schoolchildren is a major way of ending de facto segregation. Under the Brown doctrine segregated schools violate the Constitution whether they are a result of state laws or of housing patterns. To put an end to de facto segregated schools, white pupils must be bused into black neighborhoods, or even from community to community, and black students must be bused into white areas.

There is also the question of which branch of the government should enforce desegregation of the schools. It is the constitutional duty of the courts to do so. The President, Congress, and state legislatures are powerless to act effectively because of the political pressures on them. To be sure, the courts may not be the best place to formulate regulations for school desegregation, but in the absence of action by the other branches of the government they are the only place where such action can be taken.

The Supreme Court is well aware of the complexity of the problem — it has taken on a big job that it has to do alone, with little aid from the executive and legislative branches of the government — and in several cases it has written enforcement decisions on desegregation. Admittedly the Court has not made a definitive decision on desegregation, but perhaps this is due to judicial sensitivity to the complexity of the issue and the intense feelings surrounding it. And it may be that in view of the opposition to busing the Court is following its own directions to the federal district courts in the Brown decision: Require local and state officials to move toward integration "with all deliberate speed."

The Other Side The only way to end de facto school segregation is to break down the barriers that force blacks and other minority groups to live in separate areas. The solution is to get rid of the ghettos. Under the Brown doctrine de facto segregated schools do not violate the Constitution. Some courts have ruled to this effect: The Brown decision, they have decided, applies only to cases in which segregation is a result of *discrimination by intent*.

The legislature and the executive should enforce desegregation — not the courts. If the courts rule that a local district has to bus children from one neighborhood to another to achieve racial balance — or even from one community to another, as some court decisions that demanded the merging of central-city and suburban districts would have required — the courts

The legal and political fights over school integration are not yet over.

are taking over the lawmaking role of the legislature, ignoring the opinions of the community, and reading the Constitution as they see fit, influenced perhaps by the personal preferences of the justices.

Further, issues such as redrawing school boundaries and making plans for busing children from one area to another are too sensitive and complicated to be handled by adversary proceedings in court.

Besides, court decisions can be avoided. Various members of Congress considered introducing a constitutional amendment barring the busing of children to reduce segregation. Laws were passed, such as the Higher Education Act of 1972, that attempted to restrict the use of busing for desegregation purposes. (The constitutionality of the laws still, of course, requires a court test.) And as might be expected in the light of his views on busing, President Nixon made new appointments partly in order to change the direction of Court decisions on desegregation. This made the Court more divided on the issue (though still leaning in the activist direction).

Then there is the role of the Supreme Court itself in enforcing desegregation. Granted, the Court took on a huge job when it made the Brown ruling. This is a sociological decision, and such decisions are hard to enforce; it is not easy to change a person's attitudes, beliefs, and way of living. And if, as some people think, the courts are the only place where movement toward desegregation can take place, why hasn't the Court made a definitive enforcement decision rather than, for the most part, leaving the responsibility to the lower courts?

This conflict brings to mind another time when the Supreme Court raised a tornado of anti-Court feelings. In the New Deal era of the 1930s the Court came under fire when it continued to defend big business against the wishes of the people (and their elected representatives) for regulation of the economy. Then, sensitive to the climate of opinion, the

Court reversed its position. As in the 1930s, the busing issue in the 1970s generated a series of attacks on the Court by many political forces: by Congress, by the state legislatures, by the press, and in political campaigns. And as in the 1930s, again the cry was "legislative usurpation."

Finally, there are the views of the majority of the citizens. Whether or not the courts are moving against the current of public opinion is not yet clear. If this is the case, we must ask the question, Has the Court the right to enforce busing to integrate the schools if such a policy goes against the will of the majority of the citizens?

HOW INSTITUTIONS WORK: V
the american court system

The American court system has two distinctive though overlapping parts: the federal judicial system and the state judicial systems. Figure 15.1 shows that the Supreme Court has appellate jurisdiction over both parts. We start with a description of the appeal process.

The Judicial Appeal Process

There are basically two major reasons for having courts of appeal. One is to prevent miscarriages of justice. Statistics show that a substantial portion of criminal convictions are reversed by appellate courts. The Warren Court took a great step forward when it rules that no state could refuse a defendant the right to appeal his or her conviction on account of inability to pay for a transcript of the records of the trial court's proceedings. A second reason is that appeals courts make the interpretation of laws and the administration of justice more uniform.

In a federal system a third reason should be recognized: Federal courts must have the power to review state court decisions involving federal questions in order to implement the principle of national supremacy.

Appeals courts do not operate under the same rules as trial courts. The appeals court does not retry the case being appealed but, rather, works from the record of the original trial, from the appeal briefs filed by the attorneys, and from the oral arguments presented. There is never a jury in an appellate proceding. Appeals are heard by a panel of judges, usually three. To win a case on appeal a litigant must normally show that the trial court misconstrued the case before it, made procedural errors, applied the wrong legal rules, or drew a clearly mistaken conclusion from the evidence.

The Federal Judicial System

The federal judicial system has three layers. The Supreme Court is the top layer; circuit courts are the middle layer; and district courts are the foundation. There are also special courts for cases involving customs, patents, and the military.

The Supreme Court

The Supreme Court has both original and appellate jurisdiction. You will recall from our description of the Marbury case that original jurisdiction means that cases can start before the Supreme Court. The Supreme Court has such jurisdiction in only two kinds of cases: (1) cases that involve ambassadors and other foreign diplomats, and (2) cases that involve disputes between states.

Appellate jurisdiction means that the Court can review cases that have already been dealt with by a lower court. The Supreme Court hears cases appealed from lower federal courts and from state supreme courts (though not all state supreme court decisions can be appealed to the Supreme Court).

Technically speaking, there are two procedures by which cases reach the Supreme Court from other courts: by appeal or by certiorari. Cases that come to the Court via the first route are appealable to the Supreme Court

FIGURE 15.1
The Judicial System

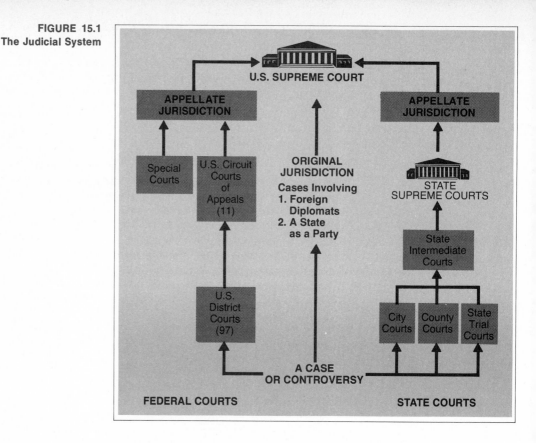

as a matter of right. The second route refers to cases that are appealable by a petition for a writ of certiorari (from the Latin *certiorari*, "to be made more certain"), which may be granted or rejected at the Court's discretion. Before 1925 a large category of cases were brought to the Court as a matter of right by the losing party in a lower court. In that year, however, Congress passed a law (known as the Judiciary Act of 1925) expanding the Court's certiorari jurisdiction. The Court had fallen behind in its work, and this law allowed it to hear and decide fewer cases. The philosophy behind the 1925 act was that the Court could no longer review cases that were of importance only to the private parties involved, but should restrict itself to cases that were important to the public at large. This fact has made the distinction between cases being "appealed" and cases coming up for a writ of certiorari essentially irrelevant. In both kinds of cases the Court makes a preliminary decision as to whether or not a case involves important enough issues for it to consider. If four or more justices vote in favor of hearing the case, it will be put on the docket. Otherwise the case is rejected and the decision of the lower court stands.

The Supreme Court can hear only a few of the thousands of cases that are brought before it. In the 1976 term, for instance, it took 176 cases and issued opinions on 136 of them—less than 5 percent of the 4000 cases that were filed with it.

This means that state supreme courts and federal circuit courts are in fact the courts that speak with finality in most cases over which the Supreme Court could have final say.

**Circuit Courts
of Appeals**

Most cases come before the Supreme Court on appeal from circuit courts. There are at present eleven such courts in the nation, each with jurisdiction over a particular area. The circuit courts were created in 1891 to ease the burden on the Supreme Court and to make the handling of cases in the federal judicial system easier. These courts have between 3 and 15 judges, depending on the number of cases generally tried in the circuit or region for which the court has responsibility. The circuit courts are called courts of appeal because they have no original jurisdiction; they hear only cases appealed from lower courts. Only the Supreme Court can review the decision of a circuit court.

District Courts

Ninety-seven district courts, along with four territorial courts (Canal Zone, Guam, Puerto Rico, and Virgin Islands), try the great majority of the cases that enter the federal court system. Populous states like California have as many as four district courts, but the normal arrangement is for a district court to coincide with state boundaries. A large district court might have as many as 24 judges, though the workload would be divided and often only 3 judges would hear a case. District courts hear cases that involve citizens from different states (an automobile accident involving an Iowa driver and an Illinois pedestrian, for instance, or a case of transportation of stolen goods across state lines). District courts also try cases involving violations of federal laws—immigration, counterfeiting, antitrust, food and drug, income tax, mail fraud, and so forth.

State Judicial Systems

In addition to the federal judiciary system, each state has its own system. Some of these systems are very complicated. State systems are often organized on a county or district basis, which leads to decentralization. Generally, however, a state court can be classified at one of the three levels.

Trial Courts

Called different things depending on the area, these courts try minor criminal cases: traffic violations, disturbing the peace, petty theft. In rural areas, these are the justice of the peace courts, often headed by people without formal legal training. In cities, these lower-level trial courts are called police courts, city courts, or municipal courts.

More serious crimes are heard in major trial courts, sometimes known as superior courts or county courts. Here the defendant might have a trial by jury. The jurisdiction of such courts is normally fixed by state legislatures. Murder, burglary, rape, and other felonies are tried in these courts.

**Intermediate Courts
of Appeals**

Larger states have courts of appeal, which review cases from trial courts at the county or municipal level and form a layer between trial courts and state supreme courts.

State Supreme Courts

Each state has a supreme court that plays a role similar to that of the United States Supreme Court. They hear cases on appeal from lower state courts and in some cases have original jurisdiction.

The Relationship Between Federal and State Courts

The citizen of the United States is confronted with more layers of courts of law than citizens of most other countries. This is due to the federal system, and to the opportunity for more appeals to higher courts than citizens elsewhere have. It should be pointed out that most cases of both a civil and a criminal nature are tried in state courts, as most crimes involve violations of state laws (the national government's criminal jurisdiction is quite limited) and most civil cases arise under either state statutory law or common law.

What kinds of cases come under the jurisdiction of federal courts? An answer to this question must begin with a look at the Constitution. Article 3, Section 2 outlines the jurisdiction of the federal courts. One class of cases comes to the national courts because of the nature of the subject matter involved: cases involving interpretations of the Constitution, congressional laws, or federal treaties, for example. A secondary category is based on the kinds of parties involved in a suit, regardless of what kind of subject matter or law is involved: cases between citizens of different states, cases between two or more states, between a state and a foreign state, and the like.

It would have been less confusing had the Constitution given the federal court system exclusive jurisdiction in all the cases enumerated in Article 3, Section 2. However, the jurisdiction of federal courts stated in the Constitution is only the potential jurisdiction of the courts of the United States. Congress has chosen to give the state courts concurrent jurisdiction with the federal courts over cases enumerated in Article 3, Section 2. The result is that we have a very complicated and confusing judicial system with federal and state courts having overlapping, competing, and sometimes conflicting jurisdictions. Perhaps one advantage of this is that it offers a choice of courts to someone who seeks a favorable court ruling.

As we saw in our treatment of the appellate power of the United States Supreme Court (*Martin* v. *Hunter's Lessee*), the fact that the Supreme Court can review state courts does help establish national supremacy. However, since the Supreme Court hears only a small fraction of the cases brought before it, the decision by the highest court of the state frequently becomes the final judgment — even in cases in which a federal question is involved. But if the Supreme Court wanted to and had the time, would it have the constitutional power to review all state supreme court decisions involving legal controversies? Contrary to the views of many people (including many college students), this is not so. The United States Supreme Court can review only state court cases that come under the judicial power of the United States as laid down in Article 3, Section 2. For example, questions of interpretation of a state law are settled with finality by the highest state court, and the question of whether a state law is contrary to the state Constitution is also settled with finality by the highest court in the state.

Selection of Judges

Because there are two distinct judicial systems, federal and state, there are two different kinds of judges. All federal judges are appointed by the President, though they must be approved by the Senate. The appointment of federal judges is usually done on a party basis — a Republican President appointing Republican judges and a Democratic President appointing Democratic judges. Table 15.2 shows the percentage of judicial appointments that comes from the political party of the appointing President.

Selection of judges at the state and local levels is done by appointment, election, or both. The most frequent arrangement, found in thirty-eight states, is popular election, with terms lasting anywhere from two years to life. In other states the judges are appointed by the governor with approval by the legislature. In some cases the judges are chosen directly by the legislatures. About a dozen states use a combination of appointment and

TABLE 15.2
Judicial Appointments, by
President: Roosevelt to Nixon
(Federal, District, and Court
of Appeals Judgeships)

TABLE 15.2
Judicial Appointments, by
President: Roosevelt to Nixon
(Federal, District, and Court
of Appeals Judgeships)

	Democrats	Republicans	Same Party as President
Roosevelt (D)	188	6	96%
Truman (D)	116	9	93%
Eisenhower (R)	9	165	95%
Kennedy (D)	111	11	90%
Johnson (D)	159	9	95%
Nixon (R)	18	220	93%

Source: Based on data from *Nixon: The Fourth Year of His Presidency* (Washington, D.C.: *Congressional Quarterly*, 1973), and updated from the *Chicago Tribune*.

election patterned on the arrangement introduced in Missouri in 1940 and called the Missouri Plan: (1) A nonpartisan commission made up of lawyers, citizens, and a judge nominate candidates for judgeships; (2) the governor appoints judges from the nominees; (3) voters approve or withhold approval after the judge has served an initial term on the bench.

Few people are satisfied with the way judges are selected in the United States, for it seems that no matter what the formal arrangement, it is the politicians who in fact select judges. Politically chosen judges, whether or not they are ratified by voters, are not always respected by citizens, and, as Presidential task force on justice has concluded, the quality of the judiciary largely determines the quality of justice.

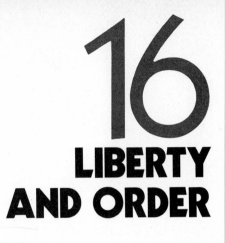

16
LIBERTY
AND ORDER

What is a democracy? A democracy is a government that allows individual freedom: Citizens in a democracy are free to speak as they wish and to worship as they wish; they cannot be arbitrarily put in jail for unpopular acts.

What is a democracy? A democracy is a government in which the majority rules: Laws and regulations are determined by the will of the majority.

Most citizens would agree that these two answers describe basic democratic principles: individual freedom and majority rule. Yet these two principles are often in conflict. In this chapter we will describe the way individual rights and majority rule are balanced.

Majority Rule: Some Modifications

If you asked the average citizen how political decisions are made in the United States the answer would very likely be "by majority vote." In some ways this answer is right. A basic "decision rule" of a democracy is majoritarianism. This is a decision rule to which children are introduced very early, often by a homeroom teacher: "Today we must elect someone to represent our class on the student council. We have two nominees, Jennifer and Geoffrey. Write your choice on a piece of paper." When the ballots are counted the teacher announces the results: "Jennifer gets 17 votes and Geoffrey gets 14. The majority decides, so Jennifer is our representative." But although majoritarianism is a basic decision rule in our political life, it is subject to modifications. There are five such modifications.

THE SPECIAL MAJORITY

There is the *special majority*. Some matters are so important that a "50 percent plus 1" majority is not large enough; a larger majority should favor the decision before it is made. For example, a special majority is required if Congress passes a bill by a simple majority vote, 50 percent plus 1, and the President vetoes it. Congress can then override the veto by a "special two-thirds majority. The Constitution does not give the President ultimate power over legislation. But it does weigh the President's disapproval seriously, and thus it requires a special majority to pass the bill over his veto.

492

THE VOTING UNIT

Another modification of the majority rule concerns the choice of the *voting unit*. Federalism, as we will see in Chapter 17, gives some responsibilities to units that are much smaller than the entire nation. Which voters should decide whether the schools in Richmond, Virginia are to be integrated—those of the Richmond school district, those of Virginia, those of the southern states, or those of the entire United States? By shifting a choice to the larger unit, you risk an outcome that differs from what would occur in the smaller unit. The battle over states' rights is not over majority versus minority rule so much as over the geographic area within which majority rule is to prevail. When the decision is left to the local community or to the state, majority rule at the national level may be violated. When the decision is shifted to the national level, the majority preferences of the local community may be swept aside.

PLURALITY RULE

A third modification of the majority rule is the *plurality rule*, which has an opposite effect from the special majority. Plurality rule allows the opinion of a group that is less than a majority to prevail, as long as that group is still larger than any other group. In 1976 Jimmy Carter received 50.1 percent of the popular vote, but this was more than Gerald Ford received (49.9 percent), so Carter won the election. However, since only 54.4 percent of the eligible adult population voted that year, Carter in effect was supported by about 27.2 percent of those who were entitled to vote. In fact Presidents are usually elected by a minority of the voting-age population. (See Table 16.1.)

THE INTENSE MINORITY

Another modification of the majoritarian decision rule results less from legal arrangements than from practical considerations. This is the modification introduced by the *intense minority*. Sometimes a small group of citizens feels intensely about an issue while the large majority doesn't feel as strongly. (See Chapter 6.) Since "the squeaking wheel gets the grease," government officials will often respond to the vocal minority rather than to the indifferent majority. In day-to-day politics this informal rule probably prevails more often than the constitutional rule of strict majoritarianism.

THE RIGHTS OF MINORITIES

There is a final modification of majority rule: *the constitutional rights of minorities*. This modification is so important in American politics that we will devote the rest of the chapter to it. The principle of minority rights has been in conflict with majoritarianism since the founding of the nation. If "50 percent plus 1" were the only rule for democratic decision making, the majority would be

Year	Percent of Voting-Age Citizens Voting	Percent of Popular Vote Received by Victor	Percent of Voting-Age Citizens Voting for Victor
1948	51.4%	49.6%	25.5%
1952	62.6	55.1	34.5
1956	60.1	57.4	34.5
1960	64.0	49.7	31.8
1964	62.9	61.1	38.4
1968	61.8	43.4	26.8
1972	63.0	60.7	38.2
1976	54.4	50.1	27.2

Source: U.S. Department of Commerce, Bureau of the Census, Statistical Abstract of the United States: 1974 (Washington, D.C., 1974).

free to do whatever it wished to a minority group—it could take away its members' livelihoods, their homes, their freedoms, even their lives. And it would all be, by definition, democratic.

The "Tyranny of the Majority"

Many writers have warned of democratic tyranny—the so-called tyranny of the majority. In some respects such tyranny is more to be feared than the tyranny of a smaller group. The chances of successful resistance are, of course, less if a minority has a majority united against it. Many foreign observers of life in America have commented on the power of public opinion, particularly over unpopular ideas and behavior. And when public opinion is coupled with the arm of government—that is, when one has a government carrying out the will of the majority—it becomes a force that a deviant minority cannot easily resist.

The writers of the Constitution were, as we have said, concerned with this problem. They designed a government that would curb the power of the majority in many ways. Federalism, checks and balances, and the Bill of Rights all help prevent the concentration of power in the hands of any one group—including the majority. In this the Supreme Court has been important. It symbolizes the limitations on the majority that are built into the constitutional framework. In this chapter we look at the role of the Supreme Court and the Constitution in relation to majority rule and minority rights.

Reconciliation of Majority Rule with Minority Rights

The reconciliation of majority rule with minority rights is one of the great dilemmas of democracy. If majority rule is not an easily acceptable absolute principle, neither is minority rights. Give all rights to all minorities—that is, give all minority groups in society the right to disobey the government—and one no longer has a society. Rather, one has a war of all against all. Each of us, after all, is a minority of one.

But where, then, does one draw the line? What minorities are to be respected and in relation to what rights? Much of the debate on the nature of democracy centers on this question. What rights are so important that they should be protected from the ordinary procedures of democracy whereby the wish of the larger number becomes the rule for all? Historically several kinds of rights have been singled out for protection from the wishes of the majority:

1. The right to freedom of speech, a free press, and freedom of assembly.
2. The right to freedom of religion.
3. The right to have one's property protected from arbitrary acts of the government.
4. The right to have one's person protected from arbitrary acts of the government.

Each of these rights has a somewhat different justification in democratic theory, and each has been given special recognition at one time or another.

Freedom of Speech, Press, and Assembly

Many people believe these three rights are the basic ones that must be protected from the majority if democracy is to survive. They are provided in the First Amendment to the Constitution: "Congress shall make no law ... abridging the freedom of speech, or of the press, or the right of the people peaceably to assemble...." These three rights are what is meant by *civil liberties;* they are also sometimes called First Amendment freedoms. The First Amendment protects these rights against acts of Congress. Over the years the Supreme Court has extended this protection so that state governments are also barred from curtailing these rights.

First Amendment freedoms are central to a democratic system because they are the key to effective majority rule. Effective majority rule depends on knowledge of alternatives and on the ability of people with minority views to try to convince others. Only if there is freedom to present all sides of an issue can there be a real choice.

And these freedoms are very important to the minority, for a minority cannot expect to carry the day if it is but a small part of the decision-making unit. If majority rule were the only accepted route to decision making, the minority's situation would be hopeless. But the guarantees of freedom of speech, press, and assembly give it a chance to convince others to join with it, thereby forming a new majority. Today's minority can become the basis of tomorrow's majority. To put it another way, First Amendment freedoms are supposed to prevent any given majority from becoming "frozen" and therefore too strong. The role of the Supreme Court is important. If the majority tries to put down opposition or outlaw picketing or censor the press, the Court is supposed to block it:

> When the channels of opinion and of peaceful persuasion are corrupted or clogged, political correctives can no longer be relied on, and the democratic system is threatened at its most vital point. In that event, the Court, by intervening, restores the processes of democratic government; it does not disrupt them.[1]

Considerations like these have given the First Amendment freedoms a special place in democratic thought. Some claim that they are "absolute" rights that must never be limited by the majority or by the government supposedly speaking for the majority. According to this view, the correction for unpopular ideas or speech is found in the "free marketplace of ideas." No one—neither a minority nor a majority—can legislate truth. Therefore a free society should never bar any group from expressing its views, no matter how unpopular those views are.

CONFLICTS OVER THE LIMITS OF FREEDOM OF SPEECH

"Free speech without limitations" sounds like the only acceptable democratic position. But there are arguments against it. For one thing, it clearly violates the idea of majority rule. Suppose a majority of the American people want to bar some form of speech. What is the "democratic" thing to do—bar the speech and thereby violate freedom of speech, or allow it and thereby violate the principle of majority rule? Such a situation is not merely hypothetical. As we saw in Chapter 5, majorities have at times favored the prohibition of speeches by communists or atheists. And public-opinion polls on obscenity make it clear that if matters were put to a vote a majority would oppose the distribution of many books and magazines found on newsstands or the showing of many movies currently seen in theaters.

These situations help us understand why conflicts over freedom of speech arise. They arise when the speech threatens some other value that is important to certain groups. Consider some examples.

Libel The right to say what one wants may be a value, but the right of the individual citizen to be protected against unjustified attacks is also a value. Thus limitations on freedom of speech are found in libel laws that protect citizens from such attacks.

But, as in most political issues, the general statement does not go very far in practice. One may agree in principle that speech and the press should be free up to the point at which they unfairly offend or hurt some individual. At that point expression should be limited by libel laws. But applying this principle is not so easy. For example, at what point does newspaper criticism of a public

---

[1] Robert H. Jackson, *The Struggle for Judicial Supremacy* (New York: Knopf, 1941), p. 285.

official become a libelous attack for which the official can sue the newspaper for damages? These are the issues that the courts—including the Supreme Court—are constantly working out.

On the issue of criticism of public officials the courts have recently leaned in the direction of allowing a wide range of criticism even if it might be damaging. The right to criticize public officials is basic to a democracy. Thus one risks some weakening of the individual's right to be protected from unfair attack in order to make sure the press is free to criticize government activities.[2] And the Court has leaned toward favoring a free press over the protection of the private citizen from libelous statements in the press.[3]

Obscenity Obscenity is another field in which the Supreme Court tries to balance conflicting interests. On one side is the right to publish what one wants (a First Amendment right). On the other side is the right of citizens to protect their children from exposure to material that they think will be harmful or to protect themselves from speech that they find offensive. On the one hand is the principle that free speech should be limited when it becomes pornographic; that is, all literature and movies ought to be allowed except those that appeal solely to "base or prurient" interests and have no "redeeming social value" or literary qualities. And on the other hand is the principle that all writings and movies should be allowed, regardless of their content.

Most states have some laws banning pornography, but it is hard to define what books and movies fall beyond the line of acceptability. Some people consider many great literary works so damaging to morals that they ought to be barred. In this difficult area the burden falls on the courts to draw the lines.

The Supreme Court has tried for a long time to define what may be barred by state and local pornography laws and what is protected by the First Amendment. At one time a work could be banned if it had "no redeeming social value." Then the Court proposed that a work that might otherwise be censored as obscene would be saved if it had "serious literary, artistic, political, or scientific value." The problem is that these terms have no clear meaning, and the Court found itself deciding what is obscene on a case-by-case basis.

In 1973 the Supreme Court took a new approach to the definition of pornography. It ruled that individual communities should have the right to decide for themselves what constitutes pornography and obscenity.[4] Communities, according to this ruling, could decide whether they wanted *Hustler* magazine sold or the movie *Deep Throat* shown. The new approach was aimed at creating diversity—a value that, as we will see in the chapter on federalism (Chapter 17),

[2] *New York Times* v. *Sullivan* 376 U.S. 254 (1964).
[3] *Gertz* v. *Robert Welch Inc.* 42 LW 5123 (1974).
[4] *Miller* v. *California* 413 U.S. 15 (1973).

is often associated with local control. What the public in New York or San Francisco might accept would be unacceptable in more conservative communities.

This decision has by no means settled the matter. There are still no clear guidelines as to how one determines what community standards are. Furthermore, there have been several controversial convictions of publishers of nationally circulated magazines. They have been prosecuted in conservative communities, despite the fact that the circulation of the magazine in that community was very limited. The publisher of *Hustler* magazine was convicted for selling an obscene publication in Cincinnati, Ohio even though the magazine is not published there, and the publisher of *Screw* was convicted on charges of distributing obscene material in Wichita, Kansas. *Screw* had only a few subscribers in Wichita. Opponents of the obscenity laws claim that the new rule established by the Court does not protect the autonomy of local communities to set their own standards. Rather, it allows zealous prosecutors to choose the locality where they can most easily convict those who are accused of obscenity. In this way any community can be used to set standards for the nation.

This complex issue is still unresolved. The law on pornography and obscenity is still vague. The Court continues to try to define the boundary between the competing claims of those who would limit pornography and those who claim the right of freedom of speech under the First Amendment.

Freedom of Speech and National Security

The major area of conflict over freedom of speech—and the most important one from the point of view of democratic politics—is the conflict between freedom of speech and national security. Freedom of speech is particularly important when it protects people with unpopular political opinions, especially opinions that are severely critical of government. But the right to express unpopular political opinions may conflict with another right: the right of the society to protect itself.

As with libel and obscenity, it is easier to state principles than to apply them. For instance, the First Amendment guarantee of freedom of speech does not give the citizen the right to commit sabotage or to use violence against government officials, and Congress can pass (and has passed) laws punishing those who commit or try to commit such acts. This principle should be easy to apply, but the boundary between speech and action is by no means clear. Speech, some people have argued, can itself be violent. And there is no doubt that speech can be used to incite violent action.

Consider sabotage. The government can arrest and prosecute those who commit or try to commit sabotage. But:

1. What if I plan an act of sabotage with someone else? I tell him where to plant the bomb and when to do it. I only "speak." He does the actual bombing. Is my "speech" protected by the First Amendment?
2. What if I make a speech at a public meeting saying that people should sabotage government operations? After the meeting some of those who heard me speak go out and plant bombs in government buildings. Is my "speech" protected?
3. What if I make a speech like the one described in Example 2 but no one acts? Is my "speech" protected?
4. What if I make a speech that merely says that "there are times when it would be justifiable to sabotage the government"? (That is, I do not directly advocate such sabotage.) Suppose someone hears the speech, decides that the current circumstances justify sabotage, and attempts it. Is my "speech" protected?
5. Suppose I write a book on the history of sabotage and treat some famous saboteurs sympathetically? Is my "speech" protected?

It should be clear from these examples that the clash between the principle of freedom of speech and the principle that the government can punish actions directed against it can arise in many circumstances. And at times it is unclear whether one is dealing with speech or action. For one thing, it is hard to determine when speech directly advocates action and when it does not. In Example 1 it would seem clear that it does; perhaps in Example 2 as well. But what if one says, as in Example 4, that "there are times when one must act"? Is that person advocating action?

And it's hard to tell whether speech in fact leads to action. Again it would seem clear that it does in Example 1. But can we be sure, in Example 2, that the speech led to the action? (What if the action comes a month later?)

In Example 1 the "speech" involved would probably not be protected by the First Amendment. It is clearly part of a criminal action and punishable without violating the Constitution.

Example 5 is a fairly clear case of "speech" that is protected under the First Amendment (even though it is possible that someone would read such a book and be motivated to imitate a saboteur).

Examples 2, 3, and 4 lie in between, and it is not clear whether the courts would consider the behavior involved to be *speech* protected by the Constitution or *activity* punishable as subversive. At times the courts have seemed to rely on the doctrine of "clear and present danger" first enunciated by Justice Oliver Wendell Holmes in 1919.[5] Under this doctrine speech is punishable only when it may lead straight to illegal action and when the connection between the speech and the illegal action is unambiguous. But the "clear and present danger" doctrine is just another way of stating the problem of deciding where speech ends and action begins. When does such a danger exist? The doctrine is not a clear principle that can be followed by the courts.

GOVERNMENT ACTIONS AGAINST CONSPIRACY AND SUBVERSION

Drawing the line between civil liberties and the right of the government to protect itself is made difficult by the fact that attempts to limit these liberties usually take place during times of national emergency—in particular, in time of war. At such times the dangers of sabotage and subversion loom large in the eyes of the government and the public. Civil liberties usually suffer. In the Civil War, for instance, President Lincoln suspended the writ of habeas corpus (a fundamental right guaranteed in the Constitution under which citizens cannot be held in jail without being brought into court or to trial). And in World War II all Americans of Japanese ancestry, whether there was evidence of subversive activity or not, were moved from the West Coast to "relocation centers" in the Midwest, where they were kept until the war was over.

In each case, the Supreme Court later reviewed the government's action, but in each case the review came after the war was over.

The Smith Act of 1940   In the three decades since World War II the issue of civil liberties versus national security has centered on a series of laws aimed at blocking conspiracy and subversion. These laws, and the court cases relating to them, arose when the nation was involved in a "cold war" with the forces of communism. The Smith Act, passed in 1940, made it a crime to teach or advocate the violent overthrow of the U.S. government. In 1951 the Supreme Court upheld the conviction of Eugene Dennis, head of the U.S. Communist party, under the Smith Act.[6] Critics of this decision (including the dissenting justices) argued that the defendants were convicted for speech, not action (for "teaching and advocating"), but the Supreme Court majority held that the government had the right to protect itself against the *actions* that the defendants taught and advocated. Therefore such teaching and advocacy was punishable.

In later cases the Supreme Court has generally upheld the provisions of the Smith Act. But it has put a heavy burden of proof on the

[5] *Schenck* v. *United States* 249 U.S. 47 (1919).
[6] *Dennis et al.* v. *United States* 341 U.S. 494 (1951).

government and has been narrow in its interpretation of the Act. In this way it has limited the extent to which the law can curtail speech without ever saying that provisions of the law violate the constitutional guarantee of freedom of speech.

The McCarran Act of 1950   The Court's indecision may also be seen in its interpretation of another post-World War II law — the McCarran Act of 1950 requiring registration of communist and communist front organizations — which Congress passed at the beginning of the Korean War. The Supreme Court held that although the registration requirements were constitutional, making the officials and other members of the party register would mean that they could be required to testify against themselves, and this would violate the freedom from self-incrimination guaranteed by the Fifth Amendment.[7] Thus the Supreme Court did not challenge the constitutionality of the registration requirements, but it did interpret them narrowly so as to limit the extent to which they curtailed freedom of association.

The Antiriot Bill   The most recent attempt by Congress to legislate against subversion came in response to the urban unrest and violence of the late 1960s. A 1968 antiriot bill made it a crime to cross a state line to incite riots or conspire to do so. This law was invoked in the trial of the "Chicago Seven," who were accused of conspiring to incite riots at the 1968 Democratic Convention in Chicago. No conspiracy was proved, but five of the defendants were convicted of crossing a state line to incite a riot. Those convictions were reversed in 1972 by a federal appeals court because of the way their trial had been conducted. But the court upheld the antiriot law itself. As with the Smith and McCarran Acts, the courts provide narrow interpretations that limit the impact of such laws on civil liberties but do not challenge the laws directly (which makes it possible for the laws to be used to limit freedom of speech).

Symbolic Speech   The Supreme Court has enlarged the definition of speech to include symbolic acts such as wearing armbands to show protest or hanging the American flag upside-down as a symbol

[7] *Communist Party* v. *Subversive Activities Control Board* 367 U.S. 1 (1961).

The "cold war" after World War II resulted in a number of court cases about the rights of communists to free speech.

Police challenge "Yippie" leader Abbie Hoffmann who is wearing a shirt made out of the American flag.

of political distress. In 1974, for instance, it ruled that someone who sewed the U.S. flag on the seat of his pants could not be punished under a Massachusetts law against abusing the flag. The law, according to the Court, was unconstitutionally vague.[8] And it similarly overturned the conviction of a student who protested the Vietnam War by attaching a peace symbol to the flag and hanging it upside-down. The interest of the state in protecting national symbols from abuse and ridicule, the Court reasoned, was not as great as the interest of society in free political expression.

The Free Press and the Pentagon Papers One of the most dramatic Supreme Court decisions on matters of freedom of speech grew out of the publication of the Pentagon Papers. The case pitted two of the best-known newspapers in the country, the *New York Times* and the *Washington Post*, against the executive branch of the government. It arose when the government tried to block publication of the Pentagon Papers, documents that contained top-secret information on the Vietnam War, in which the nation was still involved at the time.

The government was attempting *prior restraint;* that is, it was attempting to block the publication of material in advance. The government claimed that publication of the papers would do "grave and irreparable" damage to the national interest. This national-security interest was placed against the First Amednment guarantee of a free press. In previous cases the Supreme Court had struck down attempts at prior restraint, and in the Pentagon Papers case it reaffirmed that rule.[9] The newspapers were freed from restraint and continued to publish the papers. The papers revealed that the Kennedy and Johnson administrations had been involved in Vietnam long before the public or Congress knew what was going on.

This Supreme Court decision was hailed as a victory for freedom of speech over national security. But such victories are rarely clear-cut. The newspapers were able to continue publishing the Pentagon

[8] *Smith* v. *Goguen* 94 S. Ct. 1242 (1974).
[9] *New York Times Co.* v. *United States* 403 U.S. 713 (1971).

Papers and the prohibition against prior restraint was upheld. But the nine justices wrote nine separate opinions on the case—six in favor of the newspapers' position and three in favor of the government's. This shows how confused the law is on this subject. Most of the justices said that there could be cases in which prior restraint would be allowed if publication of some national-security material would "result in direct, immediate, and irreparable damage to our nation or its people." In this case they ruled that no such damage was likely. But the possibility of prior restraint in the future was not removed.

Furthermore, the Court left open the possibility that the newspapers would be prosecuted after publication for harm done to the national interest. In fact the newspapers were not brought to trial for this, though Daniel Ellsberg, who had leaked the papers to the press, was prosecuted for violations of national security. (His case, in turn, was dismissed when it was shown that the government had used illegal means to get evidence against him.)

Though the Pentagon Papers case resulted in no clear precedent for future cases, it remains an important example of the way the Supreme Court protects First Amendment freedoms. The administration used its strongest argument—national security—in attempting to block publication of the Pentagon Papers. In most societies (democratic as well as nondemocratic), governments would be able to bar publication for such a reason. In this case the Supreme Court said that the newspapers, not the government, had the right to decide what news to print.

FREEDOM OF SPEECH: NOT AN ABSOLUTE RIGHT

In sum, the freedoms guaranteed in the First Amendment are real but by no means absolute. Attempts by the federal government to use antisubversive legislation to limit those freedoms in the name of national security cannot obscure the fact that in the United States it is legal to express strong criticism of the government. But the antisubversive laws passed by Congress, the enforcement of those laws by the Justice Department, and the interpretation of those laws by the courts make it clear that the First Amendment freedoms are not absolute. At times of crisis or political conflict the government is likely to try to prevent subversive acts and in so doing to limit political dissent. The Supreme Court checks these limitations on freedom of speech. But it often does so rather late (when the damage may already have been done) and usually by restricting the government to narrow limits in its enforcement of these laws rather than by directly challenging their constitutionality.

Freedom of Religion

The same constitutional amendment that guarantees freedom of speech contains the equally basic guarantee of freedom of religion:

"Congress shall make no law respecting an establishment of religion, or prohibiting the free exercise thereof." Two provisions concerning religion are contained in these famous words of the First Amendment. The first, the "nonestablishment" clause, forbids the government from supporting any particular religious establishment. The second, the "free exercise" clause, bars the government from interfering with the freedom of Americans to worship as they wish. These provisions are related. If the government were to favor one religion over another, it would be reducing the freedom of some Americans to exercise their faith. This may be one of the cornerstones of civil peace in America. In a society with many religions severe conflict may arise if the government favors one over another. The First Amendment reduces this possibility.

Yet, as with freedom of speech, the wording of the First Amendment does not settle the issue. The words of the First Amendment are striking but ambiguous. The amendment was meant to bar a state-supported religion and permanently to separate church and state. But how wide that separation was supposed to be remains unclear.

The government cannot establish a church. But does this mean that it cannot give aid to parochial schools? Does it mean that it cannot provide buses for children going to such schools? What about police officers to direct traffic outside such schools?

The government cannot prohibit individuals from practicing their religion. But what if that religion involves polygamy or snake handling? Or forbids its members to pay taxes or serve in the armed forces or salute the flag? Are all activities justified if they represent "exercises of religion"? If not, has freedom of religion been limited?

As with freedom of speech, it can be seen that the Constitution leaves some questions unanswered. The result is a mixed, inconsistent system under which the government respects the separation of church and state in general, but not completely. It does not (under Supreme Court rulings) give aid to parochial schools, but it is allowed (also under Supreme Court rulings) to provide buses for children who go to such schools. Chapel attendance was required at the nation's military academies—West Point, Annapolis, and the Air Force Academy—until 1972, when the Supreme Court ruled it unconstitutional. But the federal government still supports chaplains in the armed forces, and the sessions of Congress open with prayer. Those who object for religious reasons can refuse to salute the flag. But citizens cannot refuse to pay taxes for religious reasons.

All of these seeming inconsistencies stem from the same general problem—the need to balance one value with other values. Consider the following aspects of church–state relations.

THE RIGHT TO WORSHIP AS ONE SEES FIT
Freedom of religion is clearly guaranteed in the First Amendment. The government can neither prohibit nor enforce any particular religion. Yet the boundaries of the free exercise of religion become controversial when a religious practice would violate some other

504

principle. In the nineteenth century the Supreme Court upheld the government's prohibition of polygamy even though this was a fundamental practice of the Mormon religion.[10] The Court reasoned that polygamy was so contrary to the American moral code that even though it was a matter of religious faith it could not be allowed to continue. One wonders what decision the Court would reach today, when views about the nature of marriage have loosened somewhat. But even if the Court decided that polygamy is no longer as shocking as it once was, there are certainly many other practices— such as public nudity—that it would continue to prohibit.

FREEDOM OF RELIGION IN THE FIELD OF EDUCATION

The field of education offers many examples of the delicate balance between freedom of religion and the requirements of the state. The Supreme Court has upheld compulsory-education laws even for members of religious groups that are opposed to education—the Amish, for example. But it has allowed parents to choose religious schools for their children as long as those schools meet state educational standards. However, religious schools are not able to get government support. Apparently the Court believes, on the one hand, that the interest of society in educating its citizens overrides the objections of some religious groups to compulsory education but, on the other, that there is no overriding need for such education to take place in state-controlled schools.

The Flag Salute Cases   The attempt to balance the rights of minority religious practices against obedience to general laws is found in the so-called flag salute cases. The Jehovah's Witnesses—whose firm rejection of secular authority has led to many run-ins with the law and to numerous court cases—oppose the worship of images. They do not allow their children to salute the flag. But many state laws required a flag salute ceremony at the beginning of the school day, the justification of such laws being that the state had the right to teach children respect for national symbols.

In 1940 the Supreme Court upheld such a law, saying that Jehovah's Witnesses could be required to salute the flag.[11] Three years later the Court reversed itself—with four justices who had supported the right of the state to require a flag salute now supporting the right of the minority group to refuse to do so.[12] The new reasoning of the Court was that the state's interest in a flag salute was not important enough to override the right of the minority to follow its religious convictions.

The 1943 flag salute case was a landmark in the attempt by the Supreme Court to locate the proper boundary between individual

[10] *Reynolds* v. *United States* 98 U.S. 145 (1879).
[11] *Minersville School District* v. *Gobitis* 310 U.S. 586 (1940).
[12] *West Virginia State Board of Education* v. *Barnette* 319 U.S. 624 (1943).

freedom of conscience and the right of the government to demand respect for its institutions. But open issues remain in drawing this boundary. Under a New Jersey law public-school students who did not wish to take part in the daily pledge of allegiance were required to stand at attention during the ceremony. In 1977 a federal court overturned the law as unconstitutional. The court ruled that students could remain seated as long as they were not unruly. This case illustrates the subtlety of the decisions that courts are called upon to make in drawing the line between the rights of individuals and the power of the state.

FREEDOM OF RELIGION FOR NONBELIEVERS

The provisions of the First Amendment were intended to prevent the government from favoring a particular religion over another. But might not the government favor those who were religious over those who were not? In many ways government policy seemed to do this. But in recent years the Court has curtailed such practices. We have mentioned the abolition of compulsory chapel attendance at the military academies. In addition, the Supreme Court struck down a longstanding provision of the Maryland constitution requiring that public office-holders say that they believe in God.

Conscientious-Objector Status Similarly, the Court has extended the right to refuse to do military service to those who do not belong to an established religion or say they believe in God. Before this ruling those who claimed conscientious-objector status had to prove their right to such status on religious grounds—usually membership in some religious group that traditionally opposed military service. But in 1965 the Court decided that this discriminated in favor of particular religions, and extended the right to conscientious-objector status to those who oppose war on ethical grounds.[13]

School Prayers Perhaps the most controversial problem of religious freedom is in the area of school prayers. Does it violate the freedom of nonbelievers if the government sponsors prayers in the public schools—even if the prayers are nonsectarian and not compulsory?

Many school systems around the country traditionally opened the school day with some prayer. In 1962 the Supreme Court barred such prayers.[14] It ruled that a school district in New York State violated the Constitution by requiring that classes be started with a nonsectarian prayer composed by the New York Board of Regents. The school board had specifically indicated that pupils could be excused at the request of their parents. Yet the Court held that such prayers violated the separation of church and state because they were required by the government. And in a similar case the Court

[13] *United States* v. *Seegar* 380 U.S. 163 (1965).
[14] *Engel* v. *Vitale* 370 U.S. 421 (1962) and *Abington School District* v. *Schempp* 374 U.S. 203 (1963).

barred a Pennsylvania law requiring that the Bible be read daily in the schools in that state.

There can be little doubt that the Court was taking the side of a small minority. Public-opinion polls have consistently shown that large majorities of the public favor school prayers. In 1962, the year that the Court ruled against school prayer, the Gallup poll found 79 percent of the public in favor of religious observances in the schools. And in 1975 another Gallup poll found that 77 percent favored amending the Constitution to permit prayers in the public schools. The parents who objected (and brought the case to the courts) were a small and generally unpopular group.

Here is an area in which the issue of separation of church and state is far from settled. Critics of the Supreme Court's decisions argue that while the minority who believe in no religion can expect tolerance for their views, such tolerance is adequately expressed in the fact that their children do not have to take part in the prayers. Supporters of the Court's position argue that the Constitution requires more than mere tolerance.

The Court decision does not settle the issue. There has been a good deal of agitation for a constitutional amendment to allow prayer in the schools, though the movement has thus far not been successful. Furthermore, Supreme Court decisions are not always followed in practice. Studies have shown that many school districts have continued to allow some kind of prayer despite the Court ruling.

GOVERNMENT AID TO RELIGIOUS SCHOOLS

Another major controversy is over government aid to private religious schools. Does it violate the separation of church and state if the government gives support to such schools? The argument in favor of such support is that these schools contribute to society by educating children. And since parents who send their children to such schools are also taxed to pay for the public-school system, those who choose a religious school, which they have to support as well, are doubly burdened because of their beliefs. Opponents of aid to religious schools say that it would represent discriminatory support for particular religions.

The Supreme Court's decisions in this area have been quite mixed. In a major decision in 1947 the Court upheld a New Jersey law providing payment for bus transportation for children attending parochial schools. The payments helped those children obtain religious training. The Court majority made a strong statement in favor of absolute separation of church and state: "The First Amendment has erected a wall between church and state. That wall must be kept high and remain impregnable. We could not approve the slightest breach."[15] It is evidence of the uncertainty of the Court's

---

[15] *Everson* v. *Board of Education* 330 U.S. 1 (1947).

position that this statement appears in a ruling that approved payment for busing to parochial schools.

The Court has drawn some complex boundaries. A state can provide transportation to parochial schools and pay for textbooks. It cannot pay for the maintenance or repair of such schools. On the other hand, state funds can be used for construction in church-related colleges. In 1972 the Court rejected as unconstitutional a "released-time" program allowing children to be excused from public school to attend religious training. Four years later it reversed the decision and allowed such a program. The "wall of separation" has become what Chief Justice Burger has called "a blurred, indistinct and variable barrier depending on all the circumstances of a particular relationship." The main principle that the Court appears to follow is that the government should not use its funds to support the teaching of any religious tenet. On the other hand, it cannot inhibit the right of citizens to exercise their religion freely by denying them ordinary government support and protection, such as police protection, when they attempt to practice their religion. Free transportation to parochial schools was defined as a program for the welfare and safety of children, not support for religion. Similarly, the Court allows government support for church-related schools at the college level but not at the elementary or secondary levels. The reasoning is that college training is less likely to involve actual indoctrination in a religion, while elementary and secondary education might.

The Right to Property

Throughout American history a large share of the national wealth has been in the hands of a fairly small minority. This condition has persisted despite the principle of majoritarianism, which would seem to give the poorer majority a means of using the government to redistribute wealth. As we saw in Chapter 4, this redistribution has not taken place. We reviewed some of the reasons in that chapter. Here we wish simply to stress that the Constitution helps protect the property rights of citizens.

In the 1780s, unlike today, there was no talk of property rights versus human rights. The rights for which the Revolutionary War was fought were the rights of political liberty and property. "The true foundation of republican government," wrote Thomas Jefferson, "is the equal right of every citizen, in his person and in his property." This did *not* mean that every citizen would have equal amounts of property. The delegates to the Constitutional Convention met not to redistribute property but to protect it.

PROTECTION OF PROPERTY RIGHTS

Protection of property rights was written into the Constitution and is established in legal precedent. For example, the Constitution prohibits any state from passing a law that would impair the obligations of contract. There is also a just-compensation clause. The nation's founders recognized that privately owned lands might be needed for public projects, but they were concerned that the costs of such a project should be widely distributed. Thus the property owner would be fairly compensated out of the public treasury. Other clauses restrict both federal and state governments from depriving a citizen of property without *due process of law*. Stemming from these comparatively simple constitutional provisions are many laws protecting private property, and standing behind them is, of course, the police.

What is meant by *property rights*? We have in mind the basic right to own something and to prevent others from using it. So we put locks on doors. We also mean the right to sell or trade the thing we own, be it tangible property such as a car or a house or intangible property such as stocks and bonds. And we mean the right to will property to chosen heirs. But the rights to own, sell, and give are limited. The courts and legislatures in the United States have put many restrictions on private property, restrictions that raise complicated questions about "minority rights" in a majoritarian democracy.

THE PROPERTY OWNER VS. THE PUBLIC INTEREST

Government restrictions on property often rest on the claim that the public interest overrides the rights of property. The owner of a 300-horsepower automobile cannot drive it at its highest speed because that would threaten "the public safety." The homeowner with a diseased elm tree is told to cut it down to prevent the disease from spreading. The contractor building a downtown apartment building has to include parking space in order to reduce the public nuisance of cars parked on the streets. In each of these cases one might well ask, "Who are they to tell me what to do with my property?" "They" is the government claiming to act in the public interest.

The task of defining and then applying something as vague as "public interest" is very complex. The definition of public interest varies from one area to another and from one time to another. Take billboards, for instance. The right of a property owner to lease land to a billboard company was not challenged through much of our history. And as a result our public highways are surrounded by private advertisements. But now, spurred by a different concept of "public interest," some local and state governments are restricting this practice. In this respect the United States is catching up with other nations. You can drive from one end of Canada to the other and never have the scenery blocked by a billboard.

THE PROPERTY OWNER VS. HUMAN RIGHTS

On the 1964 ballot in California there was a proposed state constitutional amendment guaranteeing the right of any property holder in California to sell, lease, or rent his property to anyone he chose. This seems a reasonable enough proposal and certainly is in line with property rights. The proposed amendment, however, was in fact in response to an open-occupancy bill passed by the California legislature. The open-occupancy law banned racial discrimination in selling and renting property. Here is a clear case of "property rights" (the right to do what one wants with one's own home) versus "human rights" (the right of black citizens not to be discriminated against). The voters of California passed the amendment, but it was later declared unconstitutional by the state supreme court, and this ruling was upheld by the United States Supreme Court.

The open-occupancy law in California shows how legislatures and courts restrict the uses of property when those uses violate other constitutional rights—in this case the right of equality before the law. When two constitutional rights are in conflict, it is the courts that must make a final decision. Sometimes this puts the courts on the side of the minority against the majority. Such was the case in California, when both state and federal courts overturned the clear preference of the majority. The property rights of the majority were restricted in favor of the human rights of the minority.

At other times it is the minority whose property rights are restricted in favor of the human rights of the majority. Progressive income taxes and inheritance taxes can be looked at in this light. A portion of the wealth of the richer groups in society is taxed. This leads to some redistribution from a minority to the majority. We saw in Chapter 4 that this does not go very far; it nevertheless shows some attempt to restrict the property rights of a wealthy minority.

But despite limitations on property because of the public interest or because of competing constitutional rights, there remains firmly planted in our heritage a strong respect for the rights of private ownership. It is remarkable that the restrictions on property are so few. In this way majoritarian democracy has been much less of a threat than many feared. John Dickinson, a delegate to the Constitutional Convention, warned that "the most dangerous influence" to public order was "those multitudes without property and without principle with which our country, like all others, will soon abound." But Dickinson was wrong on one very important fact: The multitudes have not been without property and, thus, have not supported any major challenge to the rights of private ownership. Thomas Jefferson saw the importance of widespread ownership of property when he remarked that "everyone, by his property, or by his satisfactory situation, is interested in the support of law and order." The support of law and order meant in Jefferson's time, as it does today, the use of the legal and police powers of the government to protect private property.

The Right of Privacy

Does the Constitution protect the individual citizen from the society and the state when it comes to his or her private life? This is a new and fascinating area of constitutional interpretation. Many states have laws regulating the sexual activities of citizens. At one time or another the laws have made so-called deviant sexual behavior or the use of any birth control device illegal. In addition, most states have had laws making abortions illegal.

In recent years the Supreme Court has begun to recognize a citizen's right to "privacy"—arguing, that is, that the state has no business regulating the intimate behavior of individuals. The "right of privacy" is not mentioned in the Constitution. But the Court has found that such a right is implied in other rights that are mentioned, such as the Fourth Amendment right against "unreasonable searches and seizures," the Fifth Amendment protection against "self-incrimination," and the broad but undefined "other rights" mentioned in the Ninth Amendment.[16]

The Supreme Court cited these rights in overturning a Connecticut law that made it illegal to use any drug or device to prevent conception.[17] Lower federal courts have cited the same right of privacy to challenge Virginia's sodomy statute, broadly ruling that states could not regulate the private behavior of individuals whether married or unmarried. As the Court put it, the right of privacy applies to "intimate sexual relations between consenting adults, carried out under secluded conditions."[18] And a similar decision by a federal district court recently held that a school district violated the right to privacy by barring the hiring of homosexuals. "The time has now come for private, consenting, adult homosexuality to enter the sphere of constitutionally protected interests."[19] In cases of this sort the courts expand the range of private activities that are protected from the control of the state—even though such activities may be looked upon with disfavor by a majority of the population.

ABORTION

The most controversial issue involving the right of privacy is that of abortion. In an important decision in 1973 the Supreme Court overturned antiabortion laws in forty-six states. It held that the right of privacy included the right of a woman to decide to terminate a pregnancy during the first three months.

Few Court decisions have aroused as much conflict. The Catholic Church opposes abortion, as do many other groups. The opponents of abortion claim to represent the constitutional rights of another group: unborn children. It is likely that this controversy will continue, for there are deeply felt interests on each side. Some anti-abortionists are seeking an amendment to the Constitution to overrule the Supreme Court.

[16] *Griswold* v. *Connecticut* 381 U.S. 479, 490–492 (1965).
[17] Ibid.
[18] *Lovisi* v. *Slayton* 363 Fed. Supp. 620, 625–626 (1973).
[19] 41 LW 2691 (1973).

The Supreme Court struck down anti-abortion laws, but the issue remains controversial.

In the meantime the Court has continued to expand the right of abortion. In 1976 it overturned a state law requiring that a married woman obtain her husband's consent for an abortion and another law requiring that a minor gain parental permission for an abortion. On the other hand, the Court did not rule unconstitutional a federal law denying medicaid funds for nontherapeutic abortions. A woman has the right to have an abortion, the Court is saying, but the federal government is under no obligation to pay for it, even if she cannot afford one.

Criminal Rights

The area of criminal rights may be the hardest one in which to balance individual freedom and majority concerns. Crime has grown to huge proportions in American society. The 1969 Uniform Crime Reports listed over 4.3 million crimes against property and nearly 700,000 violent crimes in that year alone, and much additional crime is unreported. A Gallup survey in 1972 showed that 1 out of every 3 center-city residents had been mugged, assaulted, or burglarized in the preceding 12 months.

Many people have blamed the growth in crime on Supreme Court decisions "coddling criminals." In 1968 Richard Nixon, campaigning for the Presidency, charged that the Court had put up a "barbed wire of legalisms . . . to protect a suspect from invasion of his rights [and] has effectively shielded hundreds of criminals from punishment." According to this view, if we put fewer restrictions on the police and the prosecutor we could rid society of more criminals.

Perhaps so, but a democratic society has other values besides protection from criminals. Citizens in a free society are protected from excessive and arbitrary use of police power. This raises the dilemma of buying greater security against crime at the price of greater insecurity against abuse of government power. For example, in the Drug Abuse Act of 1970 Congress authorized the use of "no-knock" search warrants by federal narcotics agents. Agents could break into homes without knocking if they could later show a magistrate that giving a warning would result in, for example, destruction of the drugs as evidence. But the result was that narcotics agents took advantage of the no-knock rule to break into homes in the middle of the night, harass innocent people, and destroy personal property—all without a warrant. Congress accordingly repealed the rule in 1974.

THE FOCUS OF CRIMINAL RIGHTS

Like the rights discussed earlier, the rights of criminals are rooted in our constitutional system. Common law assumes that a person is innocent until proved guilty and that the accused has the same rights as all other citizens and is similarly protected against violation of those rights. Here the due-process clause of the Fifth Amendment is basic; it affirms not only that the government itself is subject to the law but also that citizens cannot be denied legal recourse when their basic rights are violated.

But what are the particular rights at issue? It is useful to distinguish between the *substantive* and the *procedural* aspects of criminal rights. By substantive rights we mean the essence of what is protected: privacy and dignity, freedom of person and property, and protection against "cruel and unusual" punishment. Procedural rights involve the steps and standards that the government must follow before imposing punishment. These procedural rights, originally applicable only to the federal government, are guaranteed in the Bill of Rights. They have been elaborated by Supreme Court rulings and extended to the states as well. We turn next to a summary of these criminal procedures.

CRIMINAL PROCEDURES

Arrest To arrest a suspect for an offense, a police officer must have "probable cause" to believe that the person has committed or is about to commit a crime. Mere suspicion is not enough, although the line between suspicion and probable cause is not clear. Broadly speaking, the officer must have some tangible evidence. Most arrests are made without a warrant.

Protection against unreasonable arrest was affirmed in a case stemming from the May 1971 Vietnam protests in Washington. Hundreds of demonstrators had marched on the Capitol for a rally. While the protestors listened to the speeches of antiwar members of

The rights of the accused criminal are a subject of continued dispute.

Congress, police arrested 1200 of them and took them to a make-shift detention center. Of all those arrested, only 8 were actually tried, and the charges against them were eventually dismissed. The demonstrators went to court, claiming gross violation of their rights. In 1975 a Washington jury awarded them $12 million in damages—roughly $10,000 apiece. This is thought to be the first case in U.S. history in which damages were awarded directly to citizens for violations of rights that are guaranteed by the Constitution.

Search and Seizure "The right of the people," states the Fourth Amendment, "to be secure . . . against unreasonable searches and seizures, shall not be violated, and no warrants shall issue, but upon probable cause, . . . and particularly describing the place to be searched, and the persons or things to be seized." The interpretation of this right is so dependent on particular circumstances that Supreme Court rulings have varied almost as widely as police practices. In general, the Court has confined the area to be searched without a warrant to the person of the suspect and the immediate area under his or her control. If the authorities wish to look into a suspect's home or office, they normally must get a warrant. A police officer may carry out a search and seizure without a warrant, however, if there is probable cause to believe that a crime has been committed and there is no time to get a warrant, or if it is necessary to seize weapons or to prevent the destruction of evidence. These rules are easy enough to apply in many cases, but situations often arise in which decisions must be made on the spur of the moment and in real danger.

The Court has found it very hard to establish general principles on the application of "stop and frisk" laws in several states. The Court has approved of at least modified searches when there is enough cause to suspect criminal activity but no reasonable or probable grounds for arrest. For example, in 1968 the Court found it reasonable for a detective to question and then search three men whom he observed repeatedly casing a store. The Court then affirmed their conviction for carrying concealed weapons.[20] On the other hand, in the same year the same justices reversed a conviction on the grounds that the fact that the defendant was seen talking to a number of known drug addicts did not justify his being searched and convicted for possession of heroin.[21]

The Court has also moved to bring electronic eavesdropping within the scope of the guarantee against unreasonable search and seizure, saying that such eavesdropping is illegal without a court order.

In a further effort to discourage unauthorized search and seizure, the Court has banned the use in court of evidence obtained in this way. We noted earlier the dismissal of the Ellsberg case when it was shown that the government had used illegal means to get evidence against him.

THE RIGHT TO A FAIR HEARING

By judicial interpretation, the conditions that are necessary for a "fair hearing" have been included in the constitutional requirement of due process. Such rights include prohibitions against having to testify against oneself, unreasonable bail, and double jeopardy (a defendant can be tried only once for a single act). The Constitution also guarantees the right to a speedy and public trial, to an impartial jury, to be informed of the charges against one, to confront the witnesses against one, and to make favorable witnesses appear in one's behalf (the power of subpoena).

Moreover, as we saw in the preceding chapter, the Court has ruled that criminal defendants must be provided counsel at government expense if they cannot afford their own[22] and that the police must inform the accused of his or her constitutional rights, including the right to free counsel, before they can begin questioning.[23]

And though the Bill of Rights does not specifically mention a right to appeal, the federal government and all the states allow at

[20] *Terry* v. *Ohio* 392 U.S. 1 (1968).
[21] *Sibron* v. *New York* 392 U.S. 40, 64 (1968).
[22] *Gideon* v. *Wainwright* 372 U.S. 335 (1963).
[23] *Miranda* v. *Arizona* 384 U.S. 436 (1966).

least one such appeal as a matter of legal right. The appellate court examines the trial as a whole to make sure that it was fair to the accused in both substance and procedure; to ensure, for example, that the judge was unbiased, the jury was not improperly influenced, and a reasonable body of people could have concluded from the evidence that the defendant was guilty. Here too the Supreme Court has ruled that the government must give needy convicts free legal counsel in order to make good the right to an initial appeal.

CRIMINAL SENTENCING

In recent years a different part of the criminal process has come under sharp debate. What kind of sentence is appropriate to what kind of crime? Most criminal laws give the judge (or the judge and the parole board) a great deal of leeway in deciding whether to send a convicted criminal to prison. And if the penalty is to be imprisonment, there is leeway about how long the sentence should be: "from two to twenty years," or "a convicted burglar should be imprisoned for some time not to exceed thirty years."

The main justification for "indeterminate sentencing," which is the fancy name for this leeway, is that the judge can take into account the immediate facts of a case. The unemployed father who steals a loaf of bread to feed a sick child is not the same as the drug addict who repeatedly enters private homes to rip off whatever there is of value so as to maintain his drug supply. Sending the father to prison for three years might turn him into a criminal. Sending the drug addict to prison for three years might reduce house burglaries in the community. The judge and parole board try to make the sentence fit the crime *and* the criminal.

Indeterminate sentencing is part of a "rehabilitative" theory of criminal justice. Society puts people in prison in order to rehabilitate or reform them. The parole board should be able to release a person from prison as soon as the rehabilitation has taken effect. When the judge says "two to twenty," he or she is in effect turning over the length of the prison term to the parole board, which will determine when it is fair and safe to allow the convicted criminal to return to normal society. Notions of rehabilitation assume that the criminal can be cured. Prison, then, is a treatment. It would be just as silly to keep a "cured criminal" in prison as it would be to keep a "cured patient" in the hospital.

Reform of Criminal Sentencing   Recently, however, the rehabilitative theory of criminal justice has come under criticism. And the broad scope in the penalties associated with particular crimes has also been subject to discussion. Conservative critics cite the case of the armed robber or rapist released from jail after a very short sentence. Liberals are equally outraged when long prison terms are served by first offenders or by people who have been convicted of trivial offences such as possession of marijuana when they happened to be stopped for a traffic violation.

Major reform of criminal sentencing is under consideration. The reform would specify the sentence for each crime and reduce the discretion of the judge. One reason for this reform movement is the large number of studies showing that people convicted of similar crimes receive very different sentences, depending on the judge who hears the case. For instance, in the court system of Long Beach, California the chances that a burglar would go to prison were only one in seventeen if the case was tried by a lenient judge, but one in five if it was tried by a "hanging judge." Judges have different ideas about the seriousness of crimes.

WHAT DOES PRISON ACCOMPLISH?

A major question for those who would reform criminal sentencing is trying to figure out what sending people to prison is supposed to accomplish.

Protecting Society One argument is that we send people to prison because they are dangerous to society if they are not in prison. They have a record of attacking property or people. And they will steal or do violence again if they are not imprisoned. Public safety, then, is what criminal sentencing and prisons are all about.

But policy based solely on public safety will not get us very far in deciding what kinds of sentences to impose. If we used prisons simply to remove from society those who, if left free, would commit other crimes, "then white middle-aged, middle-class wife murderers should be released instantly and black, young, drug-addicted auto thieves should be kept locked up indefinitely. It is virtually a statistical certainty that the former will not kill again but that the latter will steal again." The author of this quotation, a perceptive student of criminal processes, concludes that such a policy is obviously silly. In effect we would be saying "that a human life is worth nothing, and a stolen car is worth everything."[24]

Deterrence A second reason for putting criminals in prisons is deterrence: The threat of prison is supposed to keep people from commiting crimes. It is as if society is saying, "We know you are tempted to cheat on your income tax or steal a car, but resist that temptation because if you are caught you are going to pay for it." Some critics of the criminal-justice system think that sentences are too light and that this is why crime is increasing. If sentences were more severe, and more certain, then those who are tempted to commit crimes would take notice and would be deterred.

However, there is little evidence that imprisoning criminals contributes much to deterrence. This is true whether one speaks of gen-

[24] James Q. Wilson, "Changing Criminal Sentencing," *Harper's*, November 1977, p. 20.

517

eral deterrence or of individual deterrence. General deterrence assumes that the example of punishment will be a lesson to others. Putting one criminal in prison will keep someone else from becoming a criminal. But except for white-collar crimes, the idea of general deterrence does not seem to have much effect on criminal behavior. Perhaps criminals do not learn by example; perhaps they believe that they will not get caught.

Individual deterrence assumes that if you catch someone at a crime and punish that person, he or she won't repeat the act. Here common sense is misleading. The number of criminal repeaters (the *recidivism rate*) is so high as to suggest that imprisonment does not have this individual deterrent effect.

This is not to reject the deterrence argument, but it is to warn against basing sentencing only on this criterion. For if deterrence were the goal it would be tempting for a society to impose harsher and harsher penalties as a way to reduce crime. Logic would even suggest making the penalties very visible. We would not only hang and torture but hang and torture in the city square.

Punishment and Justice There is another reason for prisons, one that goes beyond protecting society or deterring would-be criminals. Prisons punish people. They punish people who have done some wrong against society. Criminal laws constitute a moral code. They identify certain behaviors that society has decided are simply wrong. The criminal justice system, then, is supposed to find the people who have done these wrong things and make them pay for it. This is why the wife murderer, who is not likely to repeat his crime, is locked up along with the car thief.

In this argument punishment is justice and prisons do justice. Society punishes not out of a sense of revenge but in order to establish a moral order. "There is a sense of moral outrage when crimes go unpunished. This outrage can be disorganizing and destructive to the social system, which operates with the tacit understanding that there is—if not absolute fairness—some normal order in life. It simply seems wrong and unfair—almost unbearably so—for evil to triumph and good to be punished."[25]

APPROACHES TO CRIMINAL JUSTICE
The Adversary Mode As we have observed, in recent years the Supreme Court has moved aggressively to extend the Bill of Rights to cover all criminal proceedings at all stages. The goal has been to ensure equal treatment for all defendants, rich or poor, particularly by requiring that free legal counsel be provided to the poor. In making such a requirement the Court has not acted out of benevolence to the poor. Rather, it has acted in recognition of the fact that society has deliberately chosen the adversary system. As discussed in the previous chapter, the adversary system assumes that a vigor-

[25] Willard Gaylin, "Up the River, but Why?" *New York Times,* December 18, 1977. © 1977 by The New York Times Company. Reprinted by permission.

ous clash of opposing sides—the accused versus the prosecution—
is the best means of uncovering the truth. Since this necessarily involves complex rules of procedure and evidence far beyond the grasp
of anyone but a trained lawyer, each side must have enough resources to present its case if the truth is to emerge. It is because
society—not the individual defendant—has chosen the adversary
system that the Court has required legal counsel for all those accused. Otherwise the greater resources available to the government
would tip the scales of justice hopelessly against many defendants.

The Administrative Model   The fact remains that in the great majority of criminal cases the adversary model does not come into play.
Most cases—about 90 percent—never come to trial. Instead, they
are handled according to what can be called the *administrative
model* of criminal justice. The administrative model differs from the
adversary system in both assumption and purpose.

The administrative system of justice assumes that most defendants are guilty. This is based on the observation that the police
do not arrest people at random. The objective therefore is to determine the proper treatment for the defendant. This is done most
commonly through "plea bargaining," in which the prosecutor offers to reduce or drop certain charges against the defendant in return
for a guilty plea. Thus the defense and the prosecution are not adversaries but negotiators. The overriding concern that they share is

to maintain a smooth flow of cases and to avoid a breakdown of the court structure. As a Manhattan prosecutor put it, "Our office keeps eight courtrooms extremely busy trying 5 percent of the cases. If even 10 percent of the cases ended in a trial, the system would break down. We can't afford to think very much about anything else."[26]

Any defendant can of course insist on a trial. But if he or she is in fact guilty there may be little to gain from adversary proceedings. The administrative process encourages guilty pleas rather than requests for trial, notably by setting bail beyond what the accused can pay. The defendant may conclude that he or she has little to gain from a long delay in jail awaiting trial.

The administrative system of justice lacks formal safeguards for the accused. Whereas due-process rights are at the heart of the adversary process, administrative justice has few procedural restrictions. The important decisions are made in private between the prosecutor, the defense, and the judge. The administrative model is governed by the interest of all the parties involved in disposing of a case so that everybody gains something: a high conviction rate for the prosecutor, a reduction of charge and sentence for the accused, and a more efficient flow of cases through the court system.

It must be remembered that the adversary and administrative models of justice are not found in pure forms. In practice one model may be mingled with the other, and typically they coexist within the same courtroom. Nonetheless they do reflect a basic difference. The administrative process views criminal justice from the standpoint of society's interest in an effective, efficient system of arresting and sentencing criminals. The adversary process views it from the standpoint of the right to challenge before a judge any action of the government. This stress on individual rights is considered necessary to protect society against arbitrary use of police power.

controversy

The Constitution bars the government from favoring one religion over another. It is supposed to keep the government out of religion and religion out of the government. Yet this barrier has never been absolute. There are chaplains in the military; the sessions of Congress open with prayer; the Pledge of Allegiance was rewritten to read "one nation, under God."

A main area of controversy is prayers in public schools. The Supreme Court has generally ruled that such prayers are unconstitutional, but communities often try to get around these rulings.

[26] Albert W. Alschuler, "The Prosecutor's Role in Plea Bargaining," *University of Chicago Law Review*, 36 (1968), 55.

One Side   Communities should be allowed to require that school begin with a prayer. Some communities may not want to pass such laws, and that is all right. But some communities are quite religious, and if the local citizens feel that a prayer is a good way to begin the day, they should have the right to require it.

Furthermore, they can allow pupils who do not want to take part in the prayer to leave the room. And prayers can be nonsectarian. Thus no one loses any freedom. On the contrary, when it forbids school prayers the Supreme Court takes away the freedom of local communities to run their schools the way they want.

The Other Side   It is true that many Americans want the school day to open with prayer. And in many communities a large majority would favor this. But it is just such majorities against which the minority has to be protected. Prayer in the schools represents a breakdown of the constitutional barrier between church and state. It places the support of the state behind religion.

Nor is it adequate protection for the minority if the child who does not want to join in the prayer can leave the room. The Supreme Court was correct in overturning school prayer laws even when that protection was built in. The reason is that the child will feel pressure to be like the majority. Prayer does not belong in the schools.

17

WHITE HOUSE, STATE HOUSE, AND CITY HALL: FEDERALISM IN AMERICA

To understand the full complexity of government in America, it is important to note that one must talk not of American government but of American *governments*. A major fact of political life is that there are many governments in America. The federal government in Washington is of course the biggest and the most powerful. But it is just one of a large number of governments; there are also state governments and a great variety of local governments.

Unitary Governments, Confederations, and Federations

A nation may have a unitary government or may be a confederation or a federation. A *unitary government* is one in which all state and local governments are subordinate to the central government; the latter creates and, if it wishes, can abolish local governments. Policies are made centrally. Many European nations, such as France, have such unitary systems. At the other extreme is a *confederation*. In a confederation the central government is subordinate to the state governments. It has little direct power over the individual citizen; it acts only through the state governments. An example of a confederation is the government established by the Articles of Confederation in 1783.

A *federal* form of government is somewhere between these two types in a federation neither the central government nor the state government is subordinate. Each level of government is sanctioned in the Constitution and protected by it. Neither government can abolish the other, and each has a sphere of activity independent of that of the other. Both levels have direct power over citizens. In short, neither the central government nor the state governments are supreme.

What form of government do we have in the United States? The traditional answer is that we have a federal form of government, in contrast to unitary governments and confederations. But in practice it is difficult to fit the United States neatly into any category. (Note the confusion in our language: When we talk of a "federal form of government" we refer to the relations between the central government in Washington and the states. But the term *federal government* also means the central or national government in Washington.)

If a federal form of government implies that the central and state governments are somehow equal, the United States does not have such a form of government. The state governments are clearly subordinate to the federal government in Washington. If a federal form of government means that each level has certain powers that the other level cannot take away, the United States does not have such a form of government. The current interpretation of the Constitution by the Supreme Court is that national laws (that is, laws of the U.S. Congress) are the "supreme law of the land" and override any state laws that interfere. In these ways the United States resembles a unitary form of government.

But it is far from a unitary government in reality. For one thing, the states are not created by the federal government and cannot be abolished by it. The preservation of the states is, of course, meaningless if all their powers are taken away. But though under present constitutional interpretation the federal government could take over almost all state functions if it wished, the fact remains that it has not and is unlikely to do so. For several reasons state governments remain important and independent centers of power. The federal and state governments can each raise and spend money; each level has considerable control over our lives.

Can we, then, call the United States a federation? In some ways yes and in others no. It is a federation through the constitutional guarantee of the survival of the states. It is also a federation in the sense that real powers remain in the states. But it resembles a unitary government as well. The central government is clearly dominant and could be more so if it wanted to.

Perhaps it is more useful to consider the ways in which the nation and the states interrelate than to try to label the system. The important questions are: Where are decisions made? How is authority divided? How are the arguments of centralization and decentralization settled?

The delegates to the Constitutional Convention tried to deal with the question of division of powers by naming different areas in which the governments would be active. But there has never been a simple division of labor with the states dealing with some problems and the federal government with others. Rather, the history of the relationship between the states and the nation is one of constant change and complex interaction; it involves shared and overlapping powers more often than separate and distinct ones.

LOCAL GOVERNMENTS

The pattern of government in America would be relatively simple if one were dealing only with the national government and the states. Fifty-one governments are, after all, not that many. But there are many, many more governments in America—county governments, cities, towns, townships, as well as special districts for all

sorts of purposes from education to sewage disposal to recreation to mosquito abatement. Indeed, as one can see from Table 17.1, there are almost 80,000 government units in America today: 18,517 municipalities, 16,991 townships, 23,885 special districts, and 15,781 school districts.

Are these 78,000 units really governments? Some would say no. Only the federal government and the states are guaranteed existence and autonomy by the Constitution. This means that in certain ways their power is ultimate; it does not come from higher levels of government. The Constitution, on the other hand, does not guarantee the existence of cities or counties—and certainly not mosquito abatement districts. Rather, these smaller local governments are set up by state governments and, at least as far as the Constitution is concerned, are subordinate to the states.

Yet in fact these 78,000 units have many of the features of government. Some of them have guaranteed existence in state constitutions, though not in the federal constitution. Many cities have powers that have clearly been given to them by home rule laws. But above all, these political units are governments in that they have the power to raise money and spend it. Sometimes (like city and county governments) they raise funds and spend them on a wide range of programs; sometimes (like the special districts) they deal with specific problems. But even in the latter case the problems are important ones and the districts act as real governments.

Finally, cities, counties, and school districts are real governments because they are part of American political life. The states neither could nor would want to abolish them. Moreover, there is no hierarchy in which local governments deal with the states and the states with the federal government. Local governments deal directly with the federal government, with one another, and with the states. And to complicate things even more, there are also numerous intergovernmental agencies overlapping and combining various political units. The Port Authority of New York overlaps two states and seven counties in an attempt to organize some of the complex problems of transportation and commerce in the New York metropolitan

TABLE 17.1
Number and Types
of Local Governments, 1967

Counties	3,044
Municipalities	18,517
Townships	16,991
Special districts	23,885
School districts	15,781
All local governments	78,259

Source: U.S. Department of Commerce, Bureau of the Census, *Census of Governments,* (Washington, D.C., 1972).

area. As any observer of that powerful agency can tell you, it is also a quite independent government unit. Problems of pollution or control of water resources have led to many other such intergovernmental agencies in various parts of the nation.

The fact that many local governments are single-purpose governments (set up to control pollution, get rid of mosquitoes, build sewers, etc.) doesn't mean that they are not real governments. Education is, in terms of spending, the largest domestic government activity. Over four-fifths of American public schools are controlled by independent school districts—districts that are independent of other local governments even when they cover the same territory. These districts are run by independent school boards, often elected by the local residents or sometimes appointed by the local town council. These districts can levy taxes and float bonds to build and maintain schools and pay salaries. They have much to say about curriculum and special programs. It is true that they all must operate within guidelines set by the states (and federal guidelines if they receive federal funds). But they usually have much discretion. By almost any standard these school districts are real governments.

Thus instead of two levels of government—the federal government and the states—there are several levels covering the same territory and overlapping one another. One estimate is that there are about 1500 government units in the New York metropolitan area alone. These governments vary in size from small districts—with budgets of a few thousand dollars affecting some small part of the lives of a few hundred citizens—to governments like those of New York or Chicago—with budgets larger than those of most of the members of the United Nations.

Why so many governments? Why such a variety? How can they possibly get along with one another?

To answer these questions we will first consider rather generally why one might want a large government (like the federal government or the government of California) rather than a small government (like that of South Royalton, Vermont), and vice versa. And in the light of these general questions we will consider how the particular pattern of American governments evolved. We can then see how these governments get along (and why they sometimes don't) as well as the results of having so many governments.

Centralization vs. Decentralization

We can understand this issue if we start with the example of a major government activity: education. It used to be said that the Minister of Education in France could look at his watch and say with confidence: "At this moment, every sixth-grade child in France is doing the following problem in math. . . ." And he could tell you the exact problem they were working on. The story is an exaggeration, but it shows that French education is a highly centralized system in which schedules, curriculum, standards, and the like are all set by the Ministry of Education in Paris and then carried out in the local schools.

Compare this with the educational system in America. Suppose you wanted to find out what pupils were doing in the sixth grade in the United States. You could go to the Office of Education in the Department of Health, Education and Welfare in Washington. But you would not find out there. Matters of schedule, curriculum, standards, and so forth are not decided in Washington. The American tradition in education is local control. Such matters are generally in the hands of the states or the school boards of counties, cities, towns, or school districts. If you wanted to find out something about sixth-grade curriculum, you might have to visit 15,781 separate school jurisdictions.

THE ARGUMENT FOR DECENTRALIZATION

One can make a strong argument for this diversity. After all, pupils differ in different parts of the country. They have different interests, needs, backgrounds. If some central-government official tried to set up a uniform curriculum for the ghetto school in Harlem, the suburban school in Grosse Pointe, Michigan, and the rural school in Towner County, North Dakota, that curriculum would fit none of those places well. Only the local citizens and their school boards understand the educational needs of their own district and can create programs to fit those needs. And this argument would be made not only by the farmers of North Dakota who are jealous of their freedom from domination by the big cities or by the wealthy suburban residents of Grosse Pointe who are proud of their well-funded schools, but also by many residents of Harlem who are eager to have a curriculum focusing on their own particular needs and background.

Furthermore, the defender of this system would argue that local control lets the community decide how much it wishes to put into the school system; if the citizens in one community can afford a luxurious school system, shouldn't they be allowed to have it? Isn't that better than a uniform standard across the country? Finally, the defender of the system would point to the huge and complex bureaucracy that would be needed to run a nationwide school system —a bureaucracy that would place the schools beyond the control of parents. The supporter of localism could cite several studies of the American public showing that the average citizen feels that he or

FIGURE 17.1
Examples of Differences Among State Expenditures for Education

From State to State

$1809

$716

| New York Spends per Pupil | Alabama Spends per Pupil |

Within the Same State

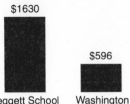

$1630

$596

| Deggett School District (Utah) Spends per Pupil | Washington County School District (Utah) Spends per Pupil |

Source: Based on data from *Financial Status of the Public Schools, 1974* and *National Education Association and State Review of Government in Utah, 1972.*

she understands local politics better than national politics and can have more influence on the local level. And, everything else being equal, citizens are more likely to be politically active where the political unit is small and relatively independent. In short, citizen control may be greater the more local the government.

THE ARGUMENT FOR CENTRALIZATION

But the defender of a centralized system might argue that a system of local control is chaotic and wasteful. For one thing, there are no national educational standards. And communities vary widely in their ability to provide such an education. The result is that some pupils get a much better education than others who happen to be born in the wrong place. New York spends about 2½ times as much on education as Alabama. In 1973–1974 New York spent $1809 per pupil, Alabama $716. And there are even greater variations within states—wealthy communities spend a lot more per pupil than poorer ones. (See Figure 17.1.)

The defender of centralization would add that many serious urban problems are due to the disparity in school quality. If suburban schools were no different from inner-city schools, we would not face the urban crisis caused by the fact that wealthy citizens often move to the suburbs for the better schools, leaving the cities to the poor.

The defender of centralization would be advocating greater attention to the value of *equality* and less attention to the value of *diversity*. The quality of education that a child can receive ought not to be determined by the "geographic accident" of where he or she is born. The defender of decentralization, in contrast, would argue for diversity, that is, the right of communities to choose how much to spend on education. He or she would oppose an equalization that would "drag down" the quality of education in the good schools to a uniform level.

The issue of equality versus diversity illustrates an important point about the debate between centralization and decentralization. Centralization is often advocated by those who want more equality —racial equality, equality in housing, equality in educational opportunities. As we will see, one of the main sources of pressure toward greater centralization of government has been the demands by various groups for equal treatment.

An argument for centralization could also be made on the grounds of educational efficiency. Local districts do not have the skills and specialists needed for a modern educational system; these could be provided by a centralized school system. A local school district cannot design a complex new physics curriculum, nor can it always afford laboratory facilities. The defender of centralization would also say that our system is totally uncoordinated. A degree from a French *lycée* (high school) means something specific—you know what the student has studied and what he or she can do. In the United States a high school diploma has no standard meaning. In some cases it means that a student is prepared to enter a university, in some cases not. How can you run a complex society that way?

Finally, the defender of centralization might warn his or her opponents that they may be mistakenly identifying decentralization with democracy. If decisions are made within a local community, there may be greater control by the average citizen, but this is only potential control. Local government may be democratic, with many chances for citizen participation and control. But it may also be run by a political "boss" or by a small group of wealthy citizens. In such a case more independence for the local community may mean less, not more, citizen control over government decisions.

James Madison, in *The Federalist* (No. 10), argued that small governments can be harmful to democracy. In a small community a single interest, such as a particular industry or the farmers growing a particular crop, is likely to dominate. The rights of other groups may be ignored. Madison argued for a larger political constituency — the kind one gets through relatively centralized government — so that there would be competing factions to prevent the tyranny of any one group over the others. Some recent observers go further. They argue that local control results not in domination by the local majority over other groups but in domination by a small local faction over the majority. Decentralization, they argue, enhances the power of local elites over the rest of the community.[1]

WHO IS RIGHT?

It is hard to say who is right. Some people may feel that the evidence favors local control; some may feel that the centralized system is better. Few would argue that there is not something to be said for each side. And one can imagine a similar debate about centralized versus decentralized control in many other areas. On some matters — such as libraries or recreational facilities — the evidence would favor decentralization. On others — such as transportation facilities that cross borders — more central control would seem desirable. But in all fields there are good arguments on both sides.

THE DILEMMA

There is a real dilemma when it comes to the issue of centralization versus decentralization — when one argues over federal power versus states' rights or big government versus local government. Almost any solution stressing decentralization and local control can be criticized: Coordination is lacking. Almost any solution stressing centralization and federal control can be criticized: It doesn't pay enough attention to local needs and desires. One can see this by supposing that one could create a government as big or as small as one wanted. It is clear that any proposal for a government bigger than,

[1] Grant McConnell, *Private Power and American Democracy* (New York: Knopf, 1966.)

say, the small town or neighborhood can be criticized as too big; there is little chance for effective citizen participation. But it is also clear that a government smaller than the whole world could be criticized as too small, for isn't the world one large interdependent system? It follows that any government of intermediate size—say, that of an American city or state or that of the United States—could be criticized as both too big and too small.

Indeed, one can almost predict that a centralized system will come under pressure to decentralize and vice versa. In the United States, with its decentralized school system, there is pressure from many sources for more centralization and coordination. In France, with its centralized system, there is pressure for more local control.

Tension between the two principles is almost automatic. And it may be seen in much of American political history and much of today's American politics. Indeed, the crazy-quilt pattern of American governments—the big governments in the state houses and large cities, the bigger government in Washington, the little governments overlapping and crisscrossing these, the intergovernmental agencies—can be viewed as one response to the dilemma of centralization versus decentralization. If neither solution is right, try both at the same time. In this sense there is reason for the variety of governments in America: some small ones (like school districts) to deal with local problems, some big ones (like the federal or state governments) to coordinate things and deal with problems that require larger government.

THE VARIETY OF GOVERNMENTS

The mixed pattern in America does not always work. The pattern of central government mixed into local government is not a result of careful consideration of what powers and functions should go to what levels. Rather, it is due to a long historical process, a process dominated less by theories about what form of government best fits what problem than by the *constellation of interests* prevailing at the time.

This point is important. The argument over centralization versus decentralization can be based on general principles: the interdependence of society and the need for coordination on the one hand and, on the other, the differences among areas and the desirability of local control. But in any particular circumstances specific interests may lead one group to favor federal control and another to favor local control, no matter what their general philosophy about big and little government. If variations among the states in the regulation of commerce hamper business activity, businessmen may argue for uniform federal standards. If on other matters they believe that they can more effectively influence state regulatory agencies than federal ones, they will argue for states' rights. Black leaders may want more centralization (federal involvement in local affairs) if they want to challenge the power of white-dominated governments or white-dominated school boards where they are a minority. In neighborhoods where they are a majority, they may call for local control. In general, a group will prefer to see power at the level that it believes it can influence most.

The history of federalism, and of local versus central government, is in large part the history of clashes between real interests. Since interests have pressed in both directions, the result has been the American mixture. To see how this has worked out, we must return to the Constitution.

The Constitutional Evolution

We saw earlier how the writers of the Constitution tried to shift the balance of power between the states and the federal government away from the state-dominated system of the Articles of Confederation. They created a federal executive, gave Congress the power to pass laws directly affecting the lives of citizens (including the power to tax and to regulate interstate commerce), and set up a federal court system to adjudicate disputes between the states and the federal government. Thus they created a truly national government. Yet at the same time they balanced the scale by setting limits on the central government such as equal representation for all states in the Senate. In addition, the first ten amendments limited the powers of the government.

The balance seemed to be a good one, and few criticized it at the time. In fact, however, the division of powers between the central government and the states was still to be worked out in numerous court decisions, in the drift of government powers in one direction or another, in the pressures of a changing America, and — in several basic areas — on the battlefields of the Civil War.

But the nation's founders could not foresee these changes; and even if they could, there was probably little that they could do about them at the time. The Constitution has lasted partly because some things were not completely worked out. The tensions built into the constitutional compromise between nation and states provided a framework within which future generations could work out the specifics of government and, in particular, the role of centralized versus decentralized government.

WHY THE DELEGATES GAVE UP
THE POWER OF THE STATES

Why were the delegates from the various states willing to give up the power held by their states to a central government? This is an important question. It is dangerous to give up power — it may be hard to get back; it may be used against you. For generations people have talked of a world federation, of a federation of Europe, of a federation of African states — new centralized governments that would replace the individual nations. Yet except for unions created by force of arms (in which the various parts do not *give up* their

Under the Constitution, the states give up the power to coin money.

independence but have it *taken away* from them), there are few successful voluntary federations. Why were the states willing to give up their power in 1787? There are several answers.

The States Gained from Union   The first answer has already been suggested. There was something to be gained from union. There had been commercial and administrative chaos under the Articles; trade among the states was hampered; trade with other nations was difficult without a central treaty-making power; the rich new territories on which the states bordered could not be used without some central authority. The delegates to the convention were men of affairs, and their affairs were not running very well. A central government would improve things.

The Society Was Homogeneous   As important as the gains that would come from union was the question of what losses might be suffered. When we discussed problems of conflict and competition among groups in America, we saw that no group is likely to give up power to another—be it the opposition party or a central government—if it feels that its *vital* interests will suffer. One thing that has prevented the union of nations throughout history is that they have different basic cultures—they speak different languages, follow different religions, have different ways of life. One independent political unit is unlikely to give up its independence to a larger unit if it feels that the latter will not respect these vital interests. If an independent unit has such interests, it will join a larger union only if it can be guaranteed that its interests will be protected, usually by limitations on the power of the new central government to legislate on such matters. And the more extensive such interests are, the more limited the central government will be and the less meaningful the union will be.

The answer to why the states were willing to join a new central government thus becomes obvious. They had few such vital interests to protect. They had a common language and a relatively common culture; they were not sharply divided on religion. In short, the Union was based on a relatively homogeneous society.

The States' Vital Interests Were Protected   But in areas in which there was potential conflict over interests that were seen by the states to be vital, they hedged the Constitution to protect those interests.

For one thing, the Constitution did not destroy the states. Quite the contrary. Although the founders knew that power was being shifted from the state level to the national level, they also saw the Constitution as preserving the independence of the states in many important matters. The states had, after all, existed before the Union.

Small states also feared that their vital interests would suffer in a union dominated by a few of the larger, more powerful states. Thus they pushed for a Senate in which each state, no matter what its size, would have equal representation. The convention spent a lot of time worrying about the large-vs.-small-state issue, though this has never become a major conflict in America.

The South's Interests Were Protected The most basic conflict of interest was between the economy and social system of the North and those of the South. The North had a growing economy based on manufacturing. The South had an economy solidly based on the cultivation and export of cotton, and organized around plantation slavery. The South (i.e., the southern delegates representing the white population) had a vital interest that they feared might be hurt by a government dominated by northern states.

To protect these interests certain clauses were included in the Constitution. One barred the national government from taxing exports, since the South depended on finding markets (often foreign ones) for its cotton. Another clause increased the representation of southern states in the House of Representatives by counting slaves among the population (at only three-fifths of their actual number, though many southern delegates would obviously have preferred a full count). And the Constitution barred Congress from interfering with the slave trade until 1808. This point is a good illustration of what a group may consider a vital interest. The southern delegates would not have compromised on slavery itself; this they considered vital. (In fact there is little evidence that northern delegates were anxious to raise this question anyway.) But the compromise that allowed future limitations on the slave trade was less vital, since the southern states could breed slaves.

The issue of North versus South and the related issue of slavery make it quite clear that the Constitution only temporarily settled the question of the relationship between the states and the nation. What the Constitution meant was not settled until the Civil War, and then only partially. Indeed, what the Constitution means and how the powers of the national and state governments are to be divided—on racial matters and on other matters as well—remains open.

State and Nation

As with so many other issues in American political life, the Constitution did not settle the issue of federalism. Rather, it provided a framework within which future changes would be worked out. The basic framework was the federal principle: a unified central government and a series of partially independent states. The Constitution established both principles—centralization and decentralization—without facing the fact that they were contradictory. And perhaps this has allowed the evolution of the federal system within the framework of the Constitution. The balance of power between the nation and the states has changed over time, but the framework of a central government and an independent set of states has survived.

The first era under the Constitution—from its writing to the Civil War—points up the tensions between the principles of centralization and decentralization. During this period a series of major Supreme Court decisions firmly established federal power over taxes and interstate commerce and in many other areas.

In 1819 Chief Justice John Marshall, ruling on the case of *McCulloch* v. *Maryland,* spelled out the doctrine of *implied powers.* Congress, he declared, was not limited in its powers to those that were *specifically* listed in the Constitution. Rather, it had all the powers that were *necessary to carry out* the specific powers listed. The decision made it clear that the federal government was indeed a government and not simply a creation of the states. At the same time, the Supreme Court established itself as the supreme interpreter of the Constitution.

THE PRINCIPLE OF CONCURRENT MAJORITIES

Meanwhile there was the pull of decentralization that was to lead to the Civil War. The issue centered on the question of the vital interests that particular areas wanted to see protected. During this era John Calhoun, a leading southern senator, developed the idea of *concurrent majorities.* According to this theory, no mere majority of the citizens of the United States, nor a majority of the states themselves, could tell the others what to do. Rather, policies had to be based on the agreement of majorities *within the regions involved;* that is, each section would have to agree on policies that affected it. As one might expect, this reflected the specific interests of Calhoun's region, interests that the South wanted protected from the rest of the nation. The principle was, of course, quite contrary to the idea of a strong federal government. Indeed, the reader will see that the principle of concurrent majorities is very similar to the veto power of members of the Security Council of the United Nations, by which any of the major powers can block decisions that it does not agree with.

The Civil War partially resolved the tension of centralization versus decentralization. It settled the issue of secession: Decentralization could never go so far as to let a state or group of states leave the Union. But, as with the writing of the Constitution itself, the war did not settle the issue of the central government versus the states. Nor did it do away with the issue of concurrent majorities. The notion of concurrent majorities survives, though it is described in other terms. Specific groups still have a strong voice—often a deciding voice—in policies that affect them. Often these groups are not specific states or regions but, rather, economic interest groups. But the principle of decentralization remains.

DUAL FEDERALISM

In the years from the Civil War to the revolution in constitutional interpretation that took place in 1937, the Supreme Court evolved a doctrine that has been labeled *dual federalism*. According to this doctrine, the states and the national government each had a specific area of jurisdiction. The Commerce Clause of the Constitution was interpreted as barring the states from regulating interstate commerce. The Tenth Amendment, on the other hand, was interpreted as limiting Congress by reserving powers to the states.

Dual federalism was a negative doctrine. Its main effect was to limit the power of both the national and state governments. National power was limited to protect state power; state power was limited to protect national power. The result was that the Supreme Court often blocked both levels from carrying out social-reform legislation.

NEW FEDERALISM

Court decisions since the late 1930s have completely changed this balance. The phrase in the Tenth Amendment that spoke of powers "reserved" to the states was dismissed by the Supreme Court in 1941 as a "truism." This meant that the states had only whatever powers the national government had not yet taken away.[2] There was no limit on what could be taken away. And in cases since then the Court has laid great stress on the clause of the Constitution that says national laws are the "supreme law of the land . . . anything in the Constitution or laws of any state to the contrary notwithstanding" (Article 6, Section 2).

State courts, on the other hand, have been much more restrictive with local governments. They have tended to follow the so-called Dillon rule (named after the state judge who expounded it most fully). The powers of local governments have tended to be interpreted quite narrowly. If a locality is given a specific power in a state law, it gets that power and nothing more. Thus federal court doctrine has allowed great expansion of federal power, but state courts have tried to hold local powers more closely in check.

Where Does Power Lie?

The Constitution, as currently read by the Supreme Court, does not treat the states and the nation as equals. The laws of the national government are clearly superior. If Congress passes a law that conflicts with a state law, the congressional law prevails. And there is no constitutional limitation on the kind of law that Congress can pass.

The only constitutional limitation on the national government in relation to the states is that Washington cannot abolish the states or change their boundaries without their consent (Article 4, Section 3). But clearly Congress could take all effective power from the states.

[2] *United States* v. *Darby* 312 US 100.

Expansion of Federal Power

The Constitution allows the federal government to expand its powers. Political and social forces that have prevailed since the New Deal era have led the federal government to take advantage of that opportunity. The federal government has become active in many areas where state law once ruled, and in those areas federal law replaces state law. The federal government is the major force in regulating the economy. Its regulations affect business and labor. Matters of ecology were once the concern of the states and local governments (if they were of concern to anyone); the federal government is now active in these fields. Civil rights were once a state and local matter; the federal government is now a major force in this area. Control over voting was once a state matter; federal law now plays a major role here, too.

These are areas that once were largely under state control. The states still play a role, but the federal government has moved in. Add the new programs that have become important since the New Deal—defense spending, atomic energy, the space program—that are completely run by the federal government, and you can see how the balance of government power has shifted toward Washington.

WHY HAS THE FEDERAL SYSTEM EVOLVED AS IT HAS?

No one reading the constitutional provisions that divide power between the federal government and the states—those that give the federal government certain powers and the Tenth Amendment, which seems to limit those powers—would be able on that basis alone to give an accurate description of which levels of government have what powers. This division depended on historical forces. Nor can we give a full analysis of the forces that led to the pattern of federal–state–local relations in every field. But we will discuss two broad aspects of the federal system.

Why has federal power grown so much beyond what the founders imagined? And why, despite the growth of the federal government, have state and local governments remained major sources of power?

The answer to the first question lies in the development of America as a nation. The writers of the Constitution wanted to create a unified nation, especially in the areas of interstate commerce and foreign affairs. And these were two basic powers, given the way the nation evolved. The more the United States became a large continental economy and the more it became a world power, the more federal power grew. Consider the federal government's power over interstate commerce. If the United States had remained an agrarian society that power would have been important, but not nearly as important as it became in a highly industrialized society whose economic growth depended on large internal markets. The more the nation needed a unified economy, the more the role of the federal government increased.

Development of a National Economy   The reason is that the development of a national economy makes it impossible for any one state to control it. The major economic problems of the United States are ones that affect the entire nation and need decisions at the national level. Inflation and unemployment do not stop at state borders. The goods in a Chicago supermarket come from all over the country; an energy crisis triggered by Middle East politics touches all parts of America; unemployment rises in Detroit when car sales fall in California, New York, and elsewhere; and unemployment in Detroit, in turn, affects employment in every state. The economy is a tightly interlocked system, and only national policy can deal with it.

One basic reason why states or local government cannot effectively regulate a national economy has to do with the *imbalance of costs and benefits* that would result if they tried. A state government or a local government that attempted to regulate business practice—that tried, for instance, to enforce a strict sanitary code for food producers or a strict antipollution law—would be doing something that benefited people beyond its borders as well as its own citizens. The consumers of the food product or those who benefit from the cleaner air and water might be located outside of the state or locality that was doing the regulating. But the state or local government would risk paying a large cost for that regulation. It can only regulate businesses within its own jurisdiction. Some businesses might move to another location where the laws are more lenient. Even if established businesses stayed, new businesses might be reluctant to move in, and economic growth would slow. State and local governments are therefore reluctant to regulate businesses. They bear all the costs of such action while the benefits are enjoyed by people who are outside of their jurisdiction. For reasons of this sort much regulation of business (antitrust legislation, standards for consumer goods, and so forth) has become a federal activity.

A similar situation exists in an area in which the drift toward centralization has not gone as far: welfare. If one state sets up a program with much higher welfare payments than other states, it may be swamped by poor families from other states. Yet under the Constitution the state cannot close its borders to citizens moving from other states. The one state that wants a better welfare program is part of the same national economy as the others. What other states do affects its own programs. Under such circumstances pressures build for federal standards.

Growth Through Defense Power   Another source of the growth of federal power is the role of the United States as a world power. Federal power has always grown in wartime, and the seemingly permanent high military budgets maintain that power. This shows why the constitutional definition of the powers of the federal government is not a good guide to its real powers. Imagine that the power over national defense were the only *specific* power given to the fed-

The American economy is a national one; the individual states cannot regulate it.

eral government. It is easy to see how that power could lead to all the other powers held by the federal government as long as there is a flexible interpretation of *implied* powers. The power to defend the nation is meaningless without the power to raise necessary funds; hence the taxing power. One cannot defend the nation without high technology; hence the federal government's involvement in education. Good defense requires good roads; hence the federal government's multibillion-dollar road-building program. And so forth and so on.

This hypothetical scheme is not completely imaginary. Federal power in many fields has grown along with defense power. The National Defense Education Act gave large amounts of aid to local school boards in the name of national defense. Federal involvement in transportation, space research, and health programs has often been defense related. The example of defense power also illustrates the more general principle that the specific powers given to the federal government in the Constitution can be stretched.

Group Pressures for Equal Treatment   As we saw in Chapter 4, one major issue in American politics is that of equality. Over the years more and more groups have called upon the government to enforce equality—between blacks and whites, between the sexes, between the voters in rural and urban areas. The pressure for equality almost always involves federal power. For one thing, the federal courts have greatly limited state and local powers in this area in enforcing the "equal protection of the laws" provision of the Fourteenth Amendment. This provision was used by the Supreme Court to ban school segregation,[3] to equalize voting rights,[4] and, in recent cases, by lower federal courts to equalize treatment of the sexes.[5]

Furthermore, groups seeking equality naturally turn to the national government. Since equality applies to citizens in all parts of the country, federal law is the most likely way to enforce it. And local governments are often more conservative in matters of equality, particularly racial equality. Thus recent decades have seen the growth of federal power in such areas as race relations, equal treatment of the sexes, and voter registration, which were once under state and local control.

One area in which the issue of equality is hotly debated is education. As we pointed out earlier, decentralization of the public schools often leads to inequality in education. The schools are supported by local property taxes. Wealthy communities can therefore afford to pay much more for the education of their children.

[3] *Brown* v. *Board of Education of Topeka* 347 US 483 (1954).
[4] *Baker* v. *Carr* 369 US 186 (1962).
[5] See the cases listed in Edward S. Corwin, *The Constitution and What It Means Today*, revised by Harold W. Chase and Craig R. Ducat (Princeton, N.J.: Princeton University Press, 1974), pp. 645–646, footnotes 235–244.

Local control of the schools
allows for variety as well as
wide differences in quality.

East Hamption, a wealthy community in Suffolk County, New York, has $285,302 in taxable property for each pupil in its public school system. The neighboring town of Brentwood has $24,814 behind each of its pupils. Naturally, East Hampton can afford a better education for its children.

Educational reform groups have attempted to change the system so that it will provide more equal schools. They have sued in federal and state courts, arguing that unequal schools violate the rights of pupils to "equal protection of the laws." In 1973 the Supreme Court rejected this argument.[6] The Court stated that local control over the schools was a fundamental principle of American government. School equalization under federal auspices would overthrow local control and undermine the balance of the federal system. Furthermore, the Court argued that the present system of local control encourages healthy experimentation and initiative in educational matters. Asked to choose between central control and equality on the one hand and decentralization and diversity on the other, the justices in this case chose the latter.

The advocates of greater equality among schools have had more luck in state courts. (The United States Supreme Court ruled that school equalization was not a fundamental right under the federal Constitution. This does not prevent state courts from ruling that such a right exists under state constitutions, many of which have clauses guaranteeing equal protection or equal education.) In New Jersey, Connecticut, and California the state courts have ruled that the state's system of finance discriminates against poorer districts. These states are actively searching for new ways to finance the schools. In other states similar suits are pending. The outlook for these suits is uncertain, but many educators believe that many states will reform school finance to foster greater equality among the schools.

On this issue the pressure for equality leads to reduced control on the part of local communities and an increase of control on the part of the states. In this case centralization does not mean federal control over school financing to eliminate inequalities both within and between states. If the Supreme Court had ruled that the equal-protection clause of the Constitution created a *federal* right to an equal education, there would have been pressure for centralization on the national level. As the situation now stands, the pressure for equality results in a decline of local control in favor of control in the state capitals.

THE FINANCIAL CRISIS OF STATE AND LOCAL GOVERNMENTS

The weakness of the state and local governments compared to the government in Washington is increased by the fact that the former

[6] *San Antonio School District* v. *Rodriguez* 93 S.Ct. 1278 (1973).

cannot raise enough money through taxes to meet their needs. There are three major kinds of taxes that citizens pay in the United States: income taxes, sales taxes (and other taxes on consumer goods), and property taxes. Each of the levels of government tends to rely on one form for most of its revenue. The federal government gets over four-fifths of its revenue from income taxes; state governments get about two-thirds of their revenue from sales taxes; and the localities get almost nine-tenths of their revenue from property taxes.

The federal income tax has a number of advantages over the state and local taxes based on sales and property. First, it provides more money, since it taps personal income directly. Second, it is progressive, since it falls more heavily on the rich—though not by very much. Sales and property taxes are regressive; they fall more heavily on the poorer citizens. Third, income taxes are more flexible; the amount they bring in goes up when the economy expands. Sales and property taxes respond more slowly to the economy.

Finally, sales and property taxes lead to inequality among the states and among localities. This is especially true in the case of property taxes. Wealthy communities or communities with industries located in them can raise much more in property taxes than poorer communities, though the needs of the poorer communities may be greater.

Many states have tried to get around this problem with income taxes of their own. But in most cases political pressures have kept the tax rates very low. State income taxes are unpopular largely because the federal government has already taken such a large bite out of income.

FEDERAL AID TO STATE AND LOCAL GOVERNMENTS

One way in which the imbalance between the national government and state and local governments is corrected is by the transfer of funds from Washington to the states and localities. State and local budgets have come to depend more and more on federal funds. In the decade between 1962 and 1972, federal aid to the states and localities rose from about $8 billion to over $35 billion per year. (See Figure 17.2.) In 1975 it was estimated that federal assistance provided 23 percent of all state and local revenues. Federal funds are used by the states and localities for a wide range of purposes: welfare programs, education, highways, environmental control, and mass transit.

There are many forms of federal assistance. The two main forms are grants-in-aid and revenue sharing. The difference between the two lies largely in the strings attached to the aid.

Grants-in-Aid   Grants-in-aid are given for specified purposes; they usually come with regulations as to how the funds are to be used. Grants-in-aid are of two kinds. *Categorical* grants are for narrowly defined purposes. There is usually little or no flexibility in the way the funds can be used. *Block* grants are also for specified purposes,

**FIGURE 17.2
The Increasing Dependence
of State and Local
Expenditures on Federal
Grants-in-Aid**

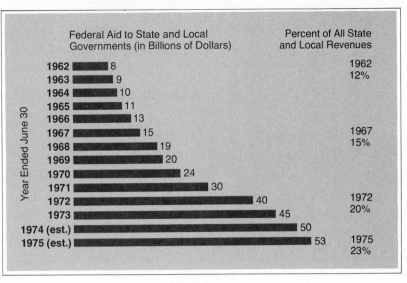

Source: U.S. Office of Management and Budget.

but they are more broadly defined and give the state or locality more power to spend the funds as it chooses. It is clear that categorical grants give more power to Washington.

Revenue Sharing Revenue sharing goes several steps beyond the block grant in giving states and localities freedom in the use of funds. The program began in 1972 as the cornerstone of President Nixon's "New Federalism." Under the program over $30 billion has been distributed to the states and to local governments with few strings attached, largely for the states and localities to use as they wish. Local governments are supposed to use the funds in priority areas such as health, public safety, and recreation. But these are general guidelines, and the localities have a lot of flexibility.

Revenue sharing has given states and localities needed funds. But what may be most important is the attitude it reflects. As George P. Schultz, Nixon's Secretary of the Treasury, put it, "revenue sharing is important less for the money it will provide than for the philosophy it contains. Revenue sharing will place the power and the resources back in the state houses and the city halls of this country."[7]

Revenue sharing is clearly an attempt to increase the powers of the states and localities relative to the federal government. And for just that reason it is controversial. Critics of revenue sharing — including some members of Congress — claim that the local governments do not give funds to important programs like health and welfare. One critic estimates that only 4 percent of the funds go

[7] Quoted in the *New York Times*, January 3, 1974, p. 30.

Senator William Proxmire, the head of the Senate Banking Committee, meets with the head of the New York teachers' union and the mayor of New York City.

to the poor and the aged.[8] Many local governments have not spent the federal funds on new projects but have used them to replace local funds and cut taxes. Also, civil-rights groups complain that the program does not include enough protection against racial and sexual discrimination.

In a sense revenue sharing has come under attack because it has succeeded in giving effective power to localities. The critics do not like the way that power is used. Local government officials, they claim, are likely to be conservative and less willing to listen to minority groups or citizens in need of welfare. It is at the national level that such groups have been most effective. To give funds to localities is to reduce the effectiveness of these groups.

The controversy illustrates two important points we have already made about federal–state–local relations:

1. Where someone stands on the issue of centralization versus decentralization will usually depend on where he or she stands on other issues. Many local officials prefer revenue sharing because it gives them flexibility. It also gives them a chance to lower local taxes (or to provide more services without raising taxes). And this pleases their most important constituents, the property owners. Some minority groups will prefer tighter national control over spending because they have greater influence on the national government.

2. When one gives power to the states and localities, the results depend on who is in power. Decentralization may or may not increase the power of the ordinary citizen. In some cases citizens are more effective at the national level. In general, some groups will benefit and some will lose from such programs as revenue sharing. A recent study found that revenue sharing has given local elected officials more discretion over the use of funds. On the other hand, the study found no broadening of citizen involvement in local affairs: The increased power given to local officials was not matched by increased participation by local citizens.[9]

[8] Ibid.

[9] Richard P. Nathan and Charles F. Adams, Jr., *Revenue Sharing: The Second Round* (Washington, D.C.: Brookings Institute, 1976).

In sum, revenue sharing seems to represent a genuine return of power to states and localities. What long-run effects it will have will depend on whether Congress continues its commitment to the program and whether Congress begins to restrict the use of the funds. Clearly state and local dependence on federal funds could lead to further federal domination. But such potential is not always used fully. The states and localities still survive and play important roles.

THE ROLE OF BUREAUCRACY IN CHANGING THE FEDERAL-STATE BALANCE

As federal grants to states and localities increased—particularly as narrow categorical grants to carry on a specific activity grew—there emerged an interlocked bureaucracy at the federal, state, and local levels. The specific federal agencies that dispense funds for a particular grant develop a close relationship with the state and local agencies that administer the grant. Often a federal grant requires that the state or locality create such a counterpart agency. The state and local agencies, once established, find that it is in their interest to cooperate with the federal agency to maintain the system of detailed categorical grants.

State and local elected officials are largely excluded from this process because the funds are provided for a narrow, specified purpose. In recent years state and local elected officials have demanded that the grant system be shifted toward heavier reliance on block grants and revenue sharing. They have formed such organizations as the National Conference of Mayors, the National Governors Conference, and the National Association of Counties. They believe that they can increase state and local control—as well as enhance their own power within the states and localities—by reducing the number of categorical grants controlled by bureaucratic agencies and by increasing block grants and revenue sharing.

State and Local Governments in Action

The federal government may be more and more important, but one would not want to write off the state and local units. Counting only domestic programs (that is, excluding spending on defense, foreign affairs, or space programs, which form a large part of the federal budget), states and localities account for over 60 percent of government spending. Moreover, the states and localities still have a lot of power over many of the most important areas of public policy: the protection of life and property; the establishment of domestic or "family" laws covering marriage, divorce, and abortion; the control of land use through eminent domain, zoning restrictions, and so forth. Indeed, most government activities that affect our daily lives are under the control of local or state governments.

States and localities build highways; they create and maintain most park and recreation facilities. Their decisions affect the environment. And as we have pointed out, the education of children is largely under state and local control. It is true that in each of these areas funds often come from the federal government, and with the funds come some controls. Nevertheless the states and localities have survived. Indeed, they have major legal and financial responsibility over policy areas affecting all members of the political community.

COOPERATIVE FEDERALISM

The complex mixture of federal, state, and local powers is called *cooperative federalism.* There is no clear division of powers; government functions are shared across the several levels. One student of federalism has described it as a marble cake rather than a layer cake.[10]

Consider public education, an area that has traditionally been under state and local control. And so it remains, with most of the funds for education raised and spent locally. Yet the federal government has been involved in one way or another from the very beginning. Before the writing of the Constitution, a 1785 statute provided for federal grants to local governments to build schools. Such federal aid continued in the nineteenth century; under the Morrill Land Grant Act of 1862, federal land grants were given to the states to set up agricultural land and mechanical colleges. In 1917 the Smith-Hughes Act provided similar grants-in-aid for vocational education.

Since then various federal programs have expanded federal aid to local education. During World War II legislation was passed to help "impacted" areas, that is, places where defense activity (e.g., a military base) put pressure on the local school system because of increased population or because federal use of local land reduced the tax base. In such cases federal funds were used to build, operate, and maintain local schools. These programs were continued after World War II. In addition, when the first artificial satellite, the Russian Sputnik, went into orbit, the federal government decided that a major effort should be made to keep up with the Russians in technological education. This led to the 1958 National Defense Education Act, which gave aid to local school districts to improve education in mathematics, science, and foreign languages plus funds to improve school administration. In addition, it provided scholarship and fellowship funds in colleges and universities. The big Elementary and Secondary Education Act of 1965 involved fairly large grants of federal funds to school districts with large numbers of pupils below the poverty line. And in 1974 a general education

[10] Morton Grodzins, "Centralization and Decentralization in the American Federal System," in Robert A. Goldwin, ed., *A Nation of States* (Chicago: Rand McNally, 1963).

bill extended the 1965 Act. Recent laws have further broadened the federal government's role here.

Sharing Functions   The history of government involvement in education illustrates a number of important general points about the way the states and the nation share functions. Despite the growth of the role of the federal government, it is too soon to say that state and local power over education has ended. The largest of all government domestic programs is still heavily state and local. During the 1960s the federal government's share of spending of public education almost doubled. But this involved a growth from 6.1 percent in 1960 to 10.6 percent in 1971 — showing that most spending for public education remains on the state and local level.

The increased federal involvement in education comes at least in part indirectly, that is, in response to other issues in which the government has always been involved. Thus one main expansion of federal aid to local education derived from concern with matters of defense: The defense system was putting too great a burden on some areas of the country. The educational system could not teach the skills needed for defense. Similarly, the most recent expansion of aid to education has been tied to the federal government's involvement in problems such as poverty.

One should not take this too literally. In part these bills were passed to aid education per se. But it is usual to justify the expansion of the government in one area in terms of more traditional federal activities.

Federal aid to education also shows how the nation and the states share functions. The federal government itself does not take over the schools. Rather, federal involvement takes the form of grants-in-aid to state educational commissions or local school boards. The states and localities continue to control the educational process itself. But most federal aid has strings attached, usually in the form of guidelines on educational practices or other issues, guidelines that must be complied with if the aid is to be given. How tight these strings are varies from issue to issue, but the guidelines imply some federal involvement in the educational process. However — just to complicate things and illustrate the tug in the federal–state relationship — the federal guidelines are often set up in close consultation with the states and with local school districts, so that in part they involve standards applied by the states and localities to themselves.

The debate over the role of the federal government in the educational process again shows how the general principles of centralization versus decentralization interact with more specific interests. Opposition to federal involvement in education is often stated in general terms. One argues that locally controlled education is better than education dominated by a remote Washington bureaucracy, and the argument comes back that national standards and equality of educational opportunity are more important values.

But one's position for or against federal involvement in education often depends not on these general principles of federalism but on where one stands on other issues. Thus federal aid programs to local schools sometimes include desegregation requirements. One's position on school desegregation is more likely to affect one's attitude toward federal school aid than the more general principle of central versus local control.

The result, in relation to education, is a mixed system. The federal government is involved through its grants and guidelines, but power over the educational system is certainly shared with the states. And this pattern can be found in many fields. The social-security system set up in the 1930s involves a sharing of power and responsibility between the federal government and the states. Consider the program for unemployment insurance: Is it a federal or a state program? In most cases it is a state program; the states levy a payroll tax, which is used to provide unemployment insurance. But the states are required to levy such a tax by federal law under which the federal government would levy the tax if the states did not do so. Thus all fifty states levy the tax, since it is to their advantage to do so. Furthermore, though they run their own programs, the states must meet federal standards. But the standards give the states considerable leeway.

If you are still not sure whether the unemployment insurance program is a federal or a state one, this is intentional. As with many programs, the actual situation is a complex pattern of shared powers and overlapping functions.

Federal–State–Local Relations What has been said about the sharing of functions between the federal government and the states applies as well to relations between those two levels of government and the more local governments—cities, counties, towns, school districts. Local governments also share functions with the federal government. In some cases they get federal aid indirectly through the state governments. But in many cases they enter into direct relationships with the federal government, with aid going directly to cities or to school districts. In this sense these local political units are full participants in the federal system.

What Preserves the States and Localities?

The Constitution puts no limits on federal expansion. The tax structure gives the federal government the resources it needs for continued growth, while the states and localities are financially weak. And more and more problems are national in scope. What, then, preserves state and local governments?

The answer lies mainly in the structure of American politics. One crucial component is the organization of the political parties. If the parties were—like those in some other countries—tightly organized and disciplined, the drift of power into federal hands would have happened faster and more thoroughly. It is possible for the states to be "swamped" by federal power. If the national administration controlled an organized party stretching down to the grass roots, the legal potential would become a political reality.

In fact, as we have seen, the American party system is quite the opposite. The political parties are basically state and local organizations. They may develop national unity for presidential elections, but this is only temporary (and not always very united). Moreover, the White House and the state houses (or city halls) are not always controlled by the same party. And even when they are, this does not mean that the local party is controlled by the party organization in Washington (which in fact hardly exists). In some countries the national party leadership decides who runs under the party label in local elections. If this were the case in the United States, governors and mayors would be under close control by the national party. In fact, however, decisions as to who runs in state and local elections —even who runs for Congress—are made locally, not nationally. And this gives the local party independence from national control. The result is that states and localities remain independent governments because they have *political power*, not because of the Constitution.

Financial considerations and recent constitutional interpretation would seem to make the U.S. government a unitary system, with the states and localities subordinate to Washington. But political reality tips the balance back and makes the federal government, at least in part, a product of the states and localities. Members of Congress are part of the federal government but are strongly aware that they represent particular areas. And even the two officials elected by the nation as a whole—the President and the Vice-President—must be aware of the importance of state parties in the nomination and election process.

The following example illustrates this point. When the social-security legislation of the New Deal was prepared in the 1930s, the original plan was for a fully federal program. The program had been planned in Washington, and many people felt that it would be more effective if it was administered from there. But the program passed by Congress involved a lot of sharing with the states. Much of the program was administered by the states within the framework of federal guidelines—a pattern found in many other areas. The main reason was that the Roosevelt administration knew that Congress would accept only a proposal that provided for the involvement of the states. If there had been tightly centralized party organizations in the United States, President Roosevelt as head of the Democratic party would not have had to worry about the doubts of members of Congress; he could have controlled their votes. But those members—though they are part of the federal government—are elected from their own localities and often act to defend those localities.

To take another example, in 1965 the federal Office of Economic Opportunity (OEO) decided that the city of Chicago was not following federal guidelines on school desegregation. Federal aid to the Chicago school system was needed to keep the system running. This was a case in which federal involvement in local school matters could mean federal control of local school operations. The OEO did cut off school aid to Chicago. But within a few weeks it had backed down. And in the process it had suffered a major blow to its prestige and authority within the government.

Why did this happen? The OEO did not go beyond its legal powers. It would probably have been backed up by the courts, which were pushing in the same direction. And it had the resources to back up its demand; the school district could not have functioned without federal aid. These two forces—the absence of court or constitutional limits on government power and its control over revenue sources—are what make the federal government so powerful.

But the one factor the OEO did not reckon with was the *political power* of the Chicago Democratic organization and its leader, Mayor Richard J. Daley. The Chicago political machine—one of the most effective such organizations in the country at that time—controlled a number of important resources such as the Democratic votes of a major state, numerous members of Congress, and an important block of delegates at presidential nominating conventions. On the basis of such real political power, local government survives.

Of course not all localities are as large as the city of Chicago; nor is power a matter of size alone, for few other cities have local governments as powerful as Chicago's was at the time. Yet the localities—even small ones—have some power over the federal government because of their political independence and because their representatives in Congress will defend that independence.

FEDERALISM AS AN ATTITUDE

We have seen that the fundamental beliefs of citizens help determine what kind of government we have. This is true in relation to the issue of centralization versus decentralization. It has been argued that Americans "think federally"; that is, they believe in the importance of state and local governments. This is especially true of elected officials, since their voter support is in a particular state or congressional district. Congress often provides for state and local participation in carrying out a law because it believes that such participation is a good thing.

Washington, the States, and the Cities

The greatest challenge to the American mixture of governments is found in the large metropolitan areas. Can a constitution written for a small agrarian society deal with the contemporary city? Within the urban areas we see all the problems of central versus local control, of multiple governments with overlapping functions, of federal–state relations, of federal–local relations. (See Figure 17.3.)

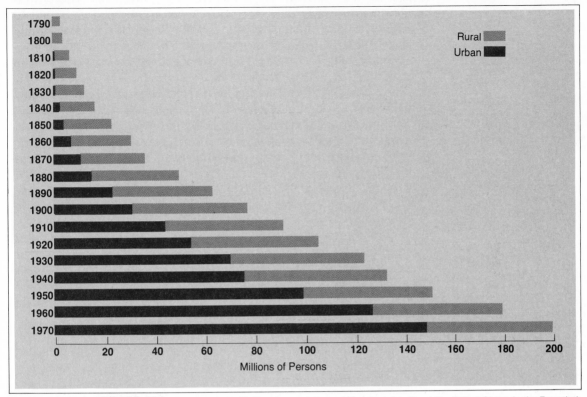

FIGURE 17.3
Urban and Rural Populations of the United States, 1790-1970

Source: Irene B. Taeuber and Conrad Taeuber, *People of the United States in the Twentieth Century* (Washington, D.C.: U.S. Department of Commerce, Bureau of the Census, 1971), and *Social Indicators: 1973* (Washington, D.C.: U.S. Office of Management and Budget, 1973).

METROPOLITAN AREAS

Consider the metropolitan areas. Two things are clear: They are socially and economically interdependent, and they are politically divided.

The very definition of a metropolitan area, as used by the Census Bureau, stresses its interdependence: "The general concept of a metropolitan area is one of an integrated economic and social unit with a recognized large population nucleus." And this interdependence takes many forms. People move easily from one part to another; they live in one area (perhaps a suburb) and work in another (perhaps the central city). The various communities in a metropolitan area share roads, public transportation, shopping areas. They are dependent on the same clean water, pure air, and space for recreation.

The term *spillovers* is used to describe the activities of a community that affect its neighbors. There are many spillovers. Smoke from a factory in one community pollutes the air of the next community; if one community has an effective mosquito abatement program but the next does not, the former will still suffer during the summer. If a suburb limits housing to single-family homes on large plots of land, it will effectively keep out poor citizens and, in turn, affect the population of other communities.

There can be beneficial spillovers. One community may provide parks and open them to all metropolitan residents. Or the central city may keep its streets clean, and those streets may be used by commuters who live in the suburbs.

One could go on pointing out areas of interdependence. The major point should be clear: The metropolitan areas are social and economic units that share problems. But overlaid on this is the disorder of American local government—that curious mixture of local governments with overlapping boundaries, of state government and federal government. As we have pointed out, it is estimated that there are about 1500 government units in the New York metropolitan area, and similar numbers may be found in most such areas. There is the government of the central city. There are separate governments for satellite cities and small and large suburbs. And these are overlapped and crisscrossed by county governments, special districts, and various state and federal jurisdictions.

The Advisory Commission on Intergovernmental Relations describes the result:

> Fragmentation of this kind may appear to bring government closer to the people, but it compounds the difficulties of achieving coordination within metropolitan areas. Political responsibility for governmental performance is divided to the point of obscurity. Public control of government policies tends to break down when citizens have to deal with a network of independent governments, each responsible for highly specialized activities. Even when good channels are developed for registering public concern, each government is so circumscribed in its powers and in the area of its jurisdiction that important metropolitan action is virtually impossible for local governments to undertake. If a few governments are prepared to agree on joint or coordinated programs, their efforts can be blocked by others that are unwilling to cooperate.[11]

What this means is that while problems cover a wide area, the solutions are applied within small parts of that area. This also often means a wide gap between those who pay for services and those who receive them. The central cities provide clean streets and generally pay for them out of the taxes paid by their residents. Those streets are then used by suburban residents, who pay their taxes to a suburban government. This helps explain why central cities try to tax suburban residents who work in the city, and since the cities do not always succeed in this, many cities have dirty streets and most do not have good mass transit systems.

The Crisis in American Cities Today's urban crisis is due (at least in part) to the fragmentation of government. The situation in the major American cities is by now quite clear. For a number of years

[11] Advisory Commission on Inter-Governmental Relations, *Metropolitan America: Challenge to Federalism* (Washington, D.C., 1966).

the white middle classes have been moving out of the central cities of metropolitan areas into the suburbs. They have been replaced by poor minority groups, mostly black. The 1970 census, for instance, shows that in the 1960s the white population of New York City decreased by 9 percent while the nonwhite population increased by 62 percent. There are many reasons for the movement to the suburbs. Partly it is due to the desire for fresh air, lawns, and the like. It is also due to the desire to leave the problems of the cities — especially those of the urban poor — behind and find peaceful, middle-class school districts.

The result is that the urban core of America is decaying and is filled with the largely nonwhite poor. The suburbs are white, wealthier — and fearful of the cities. This situation was used in the chapter on group conflict to show how a problem can potentially tear a society apart.

And consider how the overlapping boundaries of governments in the metropolitan area help create this situation. What is important is that members of the white middle class, when they leave the city, cross a political boundary into another community. They no longer vote or otherwise take part in the government of the city; they no longer share its problems; and above all, they no longer pay taxes to the city.

One result is great pressure on the central city to provide services for a growing population that needs such services badly — welfare services as well as the other needs of urban life. But the cities come under these pressures just when the tax base required to provide the services is declining. Another result is that the school-age population in the central cities includes larger and larger percentages of nonwhites. (See Table 17.2.)

This situation has two effects. It makes it hard to integrate the schools because there are not enough white pupils to go around. It also makes the problem worse as more and more whites flee what they see as ghetto schools.

Suppose the boundaries were different. Suppose the movement to the suburbs did not involve crossing the political boundary to another community. Surely that would not end the problems we have mentioned but things would look somewhat different. The tax base of the cities would not change as much. The suburbs would still be part of the same district. Similarly, it would be easier to integrate the schools if the entire population of the metropolitan area were considered at once rather than being divided between the central city and the suburbs. And that might weaken the drive among the white middle classes to leave the city — since it would make less difference in the schooling of their children if they did. In short, the cities would still have their problems — the nature of the boundaries does not cause urban problems. But the boundaries would not make the problems worse.

As the U.S. Commission on Civil Rights put it in February 1977:

TABLE 17.2
The Large Black Student
Population in the Big Cities

School District	Black Enrollment	Percent of All Students
Washington	133,638	95.5%
Atlanta	73,985	77.1
New Orleans	77,504	74.6
Newark	56,736	72.3
Richmond	30,746	70.2
Gary	31,200	69.6
Baltimore	129,250	69.3
St. Louis	72,629	68.8
Detroit	186,994	67.6
Philadelphia	173,874	61.4
Oakland	39,121	60.0
Birmingham	34,290	59.4
Memphis	80,158	57.8
Cleveland	83,596	57.6
Chicago	315,940	57.1
Kansas City, Mo.	35,578	54.4
Louisville	25,078	51.0

Source: U.S. Department of Health, Education and Welfare, *Directory of Public, Elementary and Secondary Schools in Selected Districts* (Washington, D.C., 1972).

The migration of blacks and minorities to the cities in search of opportunities and the suburbanization of whites has left the nation with a new racial separation, not merely of segregated school systems coexisting within the same metropolitan area. The problem is growing worse, not better . . . Increasingly, the boundaries between cities and suburbs have become not merely political dividing lines but barriers that separate people by race and economic class. Accordingly, the future of school desegregation in these large urban areas hinges upon whether the obligation to provide a remedy ends at the city line.

The Supreme Court has considered this issue. A lower court had ordered cross-busing between Detroit and its suburbs in order to achieve racial balance. In July 1974, in what may prove to be a landmark decision, it overturned the lower-court decision by a 5–4 vote. Detroit's schools are about 70 percent black. The lower court had reasoned that racial balance could be achieved only by involving the white suburbs. The Supreme Court, however, ruled in favor of another principle: local control of the schools. It is useful to quote the majority opinion, for it shows that centralization (in this case on a metropolitan basis) is far from the only trend in America: "No single tradition in public education is more deeply rooted than local control over the operation of schools; local autonomy has long been thought essential both to the maintenance of community concern and support for public schools and to the quality of the educational process."[12]

The Court ruled that a metropolitan-wide solution involving busing between the central city and the suburbs could be ordered

[12] *Milliken et al.* v. *Bradley* 42 LW 5249 (1974).

by the courts only when there was evidence that the suburbs *had intended* to discriminate against black students in drawing the lines of their school districts. The segregation in the Detroit metropolitan area was the de facto result of residential patterns and not a deliberate policy of the communities involved. Therefore the Court came down on the side of local school autonomy and against cross-boundary busing.

The Federal Government and Housing   Another possible solution is greater involvement of the federal government in the metropolitan areas. The federal government has a long history of involvement through its programs in urban areas, mostly in relation to housing. But the nature of that involvement is instructive. The first major federal program was the Housing Act of 1937, which set up the FHA mortgage insurance program. This allowed many more people to build and own their own homes than would otherwise have been the case. But such a program was of greatest value to middle-class homeowners. And indeed the FHA program helped speed the growth of the suburbs at the expense of the inner city. The FHA program was balanced by federal support for low-rent housing, almost always in the central city. In short, the federal programs have helped create the current urban crisis.

Or consider the involvement of the federal government in urban renewal, the major federal urban program of the past few decades. Its purpose was to renew central cities. Local officials were given federal money to buy up blighted property (usually downtown slums inhabited by nonwhites) and to clear the land. It was then sold to others for residential, commercial, or industrial development. The result did not help the poor population of the inner cities. What was supposed to be urban renewal turned out to be black removal.

These federally supported programs tended to increase rather than decrease housing segregation in metropolitan areas. Recently black organizations have used the courts in an effort to break this pattern. In a 1976 court case black tenants in Chicago housing projects sued to compel the Chicago Housing Authority (CHA) and the U.S. Department of Housing and Urban Development (HUD) to build housing on suburban sites. They argued that the CHA had always built housing projects in predominantly black areas in Chicago, thereby maintaining housing segregation, and that this policy had been supported by HUD, which had provided funds for the housing projects. The Supreme Court agreed with the tenants that new housing programs should be built in formerly all-white suburbs. They ruled this way despite the fact that there was no evidence that the suburbs themselves had actively discriminated against blacks. But the decision was on rather narrow grounds – the fact that HUD, a federal department, had jurisdiction in both the city of Chicago and its suburbs. The Court did not take the position that autonomous suburbs could be forced to build such housing

Washington, D.C. opens its first subway five years behind schedule.

projects. The Court did not fundamentally challenge local autonomy.[13]

URBAN BOUNDARIES

Where does this confusing situation leave us in terms of the "best" boundaries for metropolitan cities? Should they all come under direct federal control; should there be huge metropolitan governments; should there be local governments as there now are; or should there be even more localism involving neighborhood governments?

This book is not intended to suggest solutions to current problems—even if we knew them. Those problems would not be solved just by changing boundaries. But the situation of the metropolitan areas shows how all government units are too big and all are too small. Big units do not easily adjust to the problems of the local citizens, nor do they give them enough control. Small units need to be coordinated with the larger ones.

Let us see how this paradox applies to the cities. Suppose we have federal control or big metropolitan governments. Many of the problems of lack of coordination would be gone and tax bases could be equalized. But could such a government adjust its policies to the needs of citizens in various parts of the metropolitan area? Doesn't each part know best what it wants and have the right to run its own affairs? This question might be asked by a wealthy white suburban resident who would like to ignore the problems of the inner city, but it might also be raised by a black resident of the urban core who wants local control.

But will the opposite solution work—a small, fragmented system of governments like the one that already exists or one that is divided even further into neighborhoods? Certainly this would give the local residents more control over their own lives. Or would it? The problems they would have to deal with—transportation, housing, pollution, even education—extend beyond their neighborhood. Extreme localization of government would give the citizen more control over his or her government, but it would be over a government that could not deal with today's problems.

[13] *Hills* v. *Sautreaux* U.S. Supreme Court, April 20, 1976.

The best conclusion is that the dilemma of centralization versus decentralization is a real one and that the tension between the two principles will continue for many years. The solution tried at a particular point in time will depend more on the constellation of interests among the participants and their relative political power than on general principles about local or coordinated government.

controversy

Unlike schools in centrally controlled societies, the schools in America vary widely in quality. There are a number of reasons for this. The major one is the tradition of local control and financing. Some communities care more about education. Parents are willing to sacrifice more—for instance, to pay more taxes—to fund a good school system. Some communities can afford more. Their citizens are wealthy and own large homes, or the community has a lot of commercial property in it. Since schools are financed by property taxes, the community with a lot of taxable property can raise more money to support the schools.

Recently the variations among communities in the amount spent on schooling has come under attack. Some people want equal spending by all communities. Others defend the present system.

One Side The present system is fine. If there is variation in the quality of schools, that merely reflects the fact that some communities want better schools. They should be given the freedom to have them. If this means that children in poorer districts have worse schooling, that is no different from the fact that poorer people in America live less well in many ways than wealthier people. Complete equality has never been our goal. Furthermore, any attempt to make all schools uniform would eliminate the chance for schools to be innovative or for there to be variety among schools. American education would be characterized by bureaucratic sameness.

The Other Side Children have a right to equal educational opportunity. The type of community into which a child is born and the income of his or her parents should not determine the quality of the education that child receives. Even if it is not a matter of what a community can afford but, rather, that the parents in one community care more about education than the parents in another, our school policy should be made to suit the pupils, not the parents. The children don't choose their school. If equality is to mean anything in America, we cannot let artificial community boundaries determine who gets a good education and who gets a poor education.

HOW INSTITUTIONS WORK: VI
the role and organization
of state and local government

What is the legal and political framework of state government? The basic structure of each state government is set forth in a state constitution. All such constitutions are based on the principles of separation of power and checks and balances; all provide for executive, legislative, and judicial branches. The actions of state officials, the laws passed by state legislatures, and the decisions of state courts must conform to the federal Constitution and may be reviewed by the United States Supreme Court.

How are the three branches of government organized at the state level?

Executive
The chief executive in each state is the governor, who is elected for a two- or four-year term. Like the President, the governor submits the state's annual budget to the legislature and largely decides the legislative agenda. Most governors can call a special session of the legislature to deal with specific issues, and all but one have veto power. Nonetheless the role of the executive has traditionally been secondary to that of the legislature. And although executive power has been strengthened in most states during the past half-century, the office of governor remains weak in many states.

In almost all cases the governor shares executive power with elected officials other than the lieutenant governor. These typically include the secretary of state, treasurer, attorney general, auditor, and superintendent of education. These other officials may or may not be from the same political party as the governor; even when they are, they may still be political rivals. The result is a weakening of the governor's executive control. This is made more complicated when members of executive agencies and commissions are not directly responsible to the governor.

Legislative
All state legislatures except Nebraska's are composed of an upper house and a lower house. In accordance with Supreme Court rulings, seats in both houses must be assigned on the basis of population. The size of state legislatures varies widely, from fewer than 60 to more than 400 members. As in Congress, the legislatures work through committees, and except in Minnesota and Nebraska state legislatures are organized along party lines. The quality of the elected legislatures often is not high, for several reasons. Only about half the state legislatures meet on an annual basis, with the others meeting only every two years. Many states also limit the length of legislative sessions, pay low salaries, and provide little staff assistance. Thus, for the majority of state legislators public service is only a part-time job.

Judicial
Although no two states have identical court structures, most state judicial systems are organized along similar lines. At the bottom are justices of the peace and municipal courts; then there is a middle level of county or trial courts and specialized courts that handle juveniles, probate, and the like; at the highest level can be found courts of appeals or state supreme courts.

In two-thirds of the states judges are popularly elected. The other states select judges either by appointment or through a merit system combining both appointment and election.

What are the primary functions of state and local governments?   As discussed in the preceding chapter, the functions of government are increasingly shared by the three levels. But the states have major responsibility for education and public health, transportation, welfare, and the administration of justice. States also have authority over corporations, public utilities, and financial institutions, as well as in the regulation of political parties and elections. Responsibility for the delivery of these services and the enforcement of state regulations is shared with local governments. Together state and local governments annually spend more than $200 billion and employ over 10 million people.

What is the legal basis of local governments?   All local governments derive their existence and powers from the states. Municipalities have state charters, while other local units such as counties and special districts are either subdivisions of the state or creations of the legislature. They have only the authority granted by the state. However, about half the states have "home rule," in which municipalities may run many of their own affairs.

What are the three basic forms of city government?   Most larger cities use the *mayor-council* form of government, in which the mayor shares power with an elected city council. There are strong- and weak-mayor governments, depending on the actual distribution of powers. Council members may be elected in either partisan or nonpartisan elections. A second model is the *commission plan,* which calls for a small board of elected commissioners to serve both as a legislative council and as heads of the city departments. This form is usually nonpartisan and is popular in the West. There is also the *council-manager* plan, which separates politics from administration. In this form a nonpartisan council hires a professional city manager, who runs the city subject to the council's approval.

What are the other units of local government?   The other units consist of counties, townships, and various special districts. (See Table 17.1.)

Counties   County governments function in all but three states and are the most important unit of local government in rural areas. Intended as administrative and judicial units, counties are usually run by elected officials such as the sheriff, prosecutor, treasurer, and clerk and a board of commissioners.

Townships   Townships are unincorporated, usually rural units of government found in fewer than half the states. The principal governing body is a board of supervisors, but their governmental role has been declining steadily.

Special and School Districts   Unlike the units of local government that are multipurpose in nature, special districts have been created for special purposes. They handle problems that may cut across the boundaries of existing political units. Chief among them are school districts, which can tax, borrow, and spend public funds. There are also over 20,000 special districts to administer particular functions such as soil conservation, fire protection, and recreation.

18
THE POLICY PROCESS

Politics produces policies, and these policies affect the lives of all Americans. What the government does (or does not do) about pollution, the economy, mass transit, or public safety makes the lives of Americans better or worse. Not that government policies have the same impact on all citizens. Quite the contrary. Some policies make the lives of some citizens better without affecting others. Some make the lives of some citizens better while making those of others worse. This differential impact is what much of politics is all about. It makes it important to have access to the government, to influence its policies.

How is policy made in America? Who decides what the government does? Much of our book is about these questions; we have looked at the various actors and institutions in American politics from that point of view. What remains to be done is to tie all this together by looking at the way policy is actually made.

WHAT IS A POLICY?

The activity of the government can be understood in terms of *policies* and in terms of *decisions*. Policies are long-term commitments of the government to a *pattern of activity*. Decisions are particular points at which that pattern of activity changes. The United States had a *policy* toward China from 1949 to 1971, a rather hostile one stressing nonrecognition, limitations on trade and contacts, and support for the government of Taiwan. In 1971 President Nixon made a *decision* to go to Peking, one that meant a general change in the policy.

In some cases policies continue for a long time while no decisions are made about them. Sometimes policies are maintained through periodic decisions. The decision year after year to oppose the entry of China into the United Nations was part of the overall policy. And sometimes policies are constantly being changed by decisions. Government policy on busing to achieve school integration has been changed several times in recent years through decisions by the courts, by the federal executive, and by the states.

How to Understand Government Policy

To understand how government activities affect the lives of Americans one has to understand the roots of long-term policies as well as the sources of the specific decisions that change those policies.

Moreover, one may have to look quite broadly to see what government policy actually is. We defined a policy as a long-term commitment to a pattern of *activity.* We are interested in what the government actually *does* in a particular area, not just in what it says.

Study the Detailed Provisions Many of the general statements about policy may be hopes rather than descriptions of reality. If Congress passes a law stating that all children have the right to an equal education, that law has little meaning without funds to carry it out. Congress often passes laws with a high intent and a small budget. Furthermore, there is often a gap between the general statement of a law and its details. The preamble gives the overall intent of the bill, but the detailed provisions often lead to different results. Tax policy is an example. A major tax bill has general purposes: to raise revenue, to control inflation, perhaps to redistribute wealth. These are expressed in the preamble of the bill. But the real policy is found in the many specific clauses of the bill, and these may lead to a result that is quite different from the general statement.

Administration of a Policy In addition, one has to follow a policy from its initial statement right through to its administration. The formal descriptions of American government tell us that Congress makes policies and administrative agencies carry them out. But this is not always the way it works, for how the general directives are carried out may determine the effectiveness of a policy. For example, Congress may pass a law to improve inner-city schools; it may even appropriate funds for that purpose. But if the local school officials use those funds for other purposes, the effective policy is not one of helping ghetto schoolchildren. Local school districts have sometimes used funds from the federal government to replace their own contributions to the inner-city school, effectively leaving such schools in the condition they were in before the law was passed and making more funds available to schools in better neighborhoods.

A similar pattern could be found in urban renewal — as we saw in the preceding chapter. The overall purpose of urban renewal, as expressed in the preamble to the bill, was to improve conditions in the inner city by replacing slums with better buildings. But how that policy worked depended heavily on how the particular urban-renewal plan developed locally. The specific plan determined who was moved out and where, what was built in place of the removed buildings, and who ultimately benefited from the program. In many cases it was the builders and the program directors rather than the people themselves who benefited.

A policy, then, does not administer itself. Someone must carry that policy out. And in the process it can be changed. Congress often passes laws with vague meanings because it wants administrative agencies to really define them. This increases the need to observe a policy in action rather than the statement of a policy.

It is not unusual for laws passed to achieve high purposes to achieve little or nothing. But the failures may not be noticed. Policies are made in Washington with much fanfare; it is big national news when a voting-rights bill or a bill setting up a job corps is passed. The administration of the program in cities and towns all over the country receives a lot less attention. Many of Johnson's Great Society programs were criticized for putting more into development of the general policy than into implementation.[1]

The Supreme Court also makes important statements about policy, and like those of Congress, they do not always automatically go into effect. For example, in a variety of decisions the Supreme Court has cited the First Amendment on the separation of church and state to limit religious activities in the public schools. But individual school districts are sometimes slow to comply and quick to think of alternatives. As one specialist on education and the law wrote, "School systems in virtually every state violate in some way the legal principles concerning religious instruction in the public schools."[2] And if no one minds these violations, little is done about them.

To take another example, in 1964, ten years after the Supreme Court's 1954 decision outlawing school segregation, only 2 percent of the black children in the eleven southern states were in integrated schools. Since then more southern schools have been integrated, but only upon strict enforcement by the Justice Department.

In short, if you want to see government policy in a particular area, you have to see what is actually happening and not what congressional law or Supreme Court decisions tell you should be happening.

Implementation   The more complex the process of carrying out a law, the more likely it is that there will be a wide gap between the intentions of the law and its results. One study of various voting-rights bills passed in the late 1950s and early 1960s illustrates this. A voting-rights bill was passed in 1957, another in 1960, and another in 1965. Each had the same purpose: to outlaw voting discrimination against blacks, particularly in the South. The first law had little effect because its implementation required that blacks sue in federal court if they felt that their rights had been violated. This is a long, expensive, and cumbersome process, and few such suits were brought. The 1960 law made things a bit easier: The Justice Department was allowed to bring suits. But this too was cumbersome; each violation had to be taken to court. Few blacks were registered to vote under the 1960 law. The 1965 law, on the other hand, was much more effective. And one of the main reasons for this was that

[1] For a dramatic example of failure to implement a program, see Jeffrey L. Pressman and Aaron B. Wildavsky, *Implementation* (Berkeley and Los Angeles: University of California Press, 1973).
[2] Frank J. Soraug, "*Zorach* v. *Clausen:* The Impact of a Supreme Court Decision," *American Political Science Review*, 53 (September 1959).

it was easier to carry out — the Justice Department could enforce the law without having to go to court.[3]

Symbolic Response   One student of American politics has noted a number of cases in which demand for change — for a decision that would lead to a new policy — has been met by a *symbolic* response. A symbolic response is one in which the government, through a law passed by Congress or a major statement by the President, announces a new policy: "No more rotten meat shall be sold." "Railroads can no longer set fares to discriminate against some customers." "Our rivers and lakes shall be clean." But beyond the broad symbolic statement little is done to carry out the policy. The real policy may look little different from the situation that existed before the new "symbolic" policy was stated. However, such symbols can have important results, particularly if those who want change think such change has in fact taken place. Nothing is different, but they are content. Therefore this scholar calls such policies "symbols of quiescence."[4] This underlines our general point: To understant a real policy one has to look at how it is carried out.

Unintended Results   Not all policies work out the way those who design or administer them intend them to. Often they have additional results, which follow inevitably from the policy but were by no means planned. Policies of school districts on uniform testing were not intended to discriminate against blacks. But they have a discriminatory effect if the tests ask about aspects of life that are more familiar to middle-class whites than to blacks or if tests use language more in tune with that used in white homes than in black homes.

Or take the example of the impact on urban America of federal policies on housing, urban development, and roads. These policies were not intended to create a situation in which inner-city ghettos are surrounded by wealthier white suburbs. The Federal Housing Administration (FHA) program was intended to help citizens buy their own homes. In practice, however, it helped white citizens buy homes outside the city, where land was available and they believed they would find fresh air and green grass. The FHA did not have a policy against giving such loans to blacks. But blacks rarely could afford private homes. And even if they could, the FHA tended to guarantee loans only in neighborhoods that were not likely to become slums. The fact that a black family wanted to buy a home in a particular neighborhood (or was able to) made the agency feel that

[3] Frederick M. Wirt, *The Politics of Southern Equality* (Chicago: Aldine, 1970), chap. 3.
[4] Murray Edelman, *The Symbolic Uses of Politics* (Urbana: University of Illinois Press, 1964).

such a neighborhood would not be a safe bet. The purpose of the program: help citizens buy homes. The result: black ghettos.

It is, indeed, difficult to carry out a large-scale government program without creating consequences that are unintended. An excellent example is the massive interstate highway program. It began in the mid-1950s as one of the largest government projects ever attempted. Twenty years and $62 billion later, the nation was crisscrossed with 38,000 miles of limited-access highways. The goal of the program was to replace unsafe and slow roads with well-designed, fast highways linking all parts of the country. In this the program succeeded. The driving time between sections of the nation has been reduced substantially; the rate of highway accidents is much lower on the interstates than it was on the older roads.

There are, however, a number of other consequences. For one thing, many small towns that were bypassed by the interstate highways suffered economic losses as travelers sped past them. "They didn't dry up and blow away," said one observer, "but they are much like the towns left off the railroads 100 years ago."[5]

The impact of the interstates on big cities was no less severe and was equally unplanned. The interstates made it easier for middle-class city dwellers to move to the suburbs—or beyond the old suburbs to "exurban" areas—leaving behind them racially unbalanced and impoverished cities. Like the federal programs to support home ownership, the interstate highway program helped foster urban crisis.

Unintended results are not always bad. Sometimes a policy with one goal can achieve others at the same time. In response to the energy crisis, speed limits were reduced on the nation's highways. The purpose was to save gasoline. It also saved lives as the accident rate went down.

Creating Unintended Consequences   At times unintended consequences are created deliberately. This sounds contradictory. What we mean is that Congress or a state legislature will pass a law with one purpose in mind. A group with other interests will use the law to achieve goals other than those intended by the legislature. We saw an example of this in the chapter on bureaucracy (Chapter 14). Congress passed the Freedom of Information Act to allow citizens to check on the activities of government agencies. The act has been used by businesses to obtain government information that allows them to check on their competitors.

Or take another example: Laws have been passed requiring school systems to provide extra programs for pupils with "special" needs. The intention was to have schools provide remedial programs for pupils with learning disabilities, for handicapped pupils, and for pupils whose native language is not English. In some communities parents have called on the school system to provide enrichment programs for "gifted" children. In some cases they have gone to

[5] *New York Times*, November 14, 1976.

court to force the schools to provide such programs to meet the special needs of their children. The point is not that such programs do not deserve support. The point is that a law that is intended to aid disadvantaged pupils can be used to aid advantaged ones. Such a consequence was not intended, but the law was written in such a way that parents with gifted children could use it to obtain such programs.

Limitations on What the Government Can Do

Each of us is, at some point, dissatisfied with some aspect of American society, and we believe it can be improved by government action. We complain that there is poverty in the midst of plenty; that we lack good public transportation; that the schools are failing to educate our children. We complain about the failure of the government to act against these evils: Congress is too disorganized; there are not enough representatives who think the way we do; the President is not providing leadership. The failure lies in the absence of the political will to act.

The impact of the interstate highways on big cities has been severe.

Such complaints are in many cases justified. There are many policy areas in which the government seems unable or unwilling to make policy. But our discussion of implementation should suggest that making broad policy is not enough. There is a long and difficult road between the creation of general policy and the actual results of the policy. Let us consider some reasons why government policy does not always do what it sets out to do.

We Sometimes Do Not Have Clear Goals   Policy goals are sometimes vague. Often this is simply because Congress is uncertain as to what it is trying to accomplish. Or the goals of a law may conflict with other goals that are also of value. In recent years there has been a good deal of conflict over the means of achieving school integration, particularly the use of busing. The conflict is not between those who favor integration and those who are opposed (at least that is not how the conflict is phrased). It is, rather, a conflict between the goal of school integration and the goal of local control of the schools. In the 1973 education law, for instance, Congress tried to achieve both goals at once. But in fact this may be impossible.

Sometimes the conflict between a particular policy and other goals shows up only when the policy is carried out; the result is often a failure to implement the policy. Here is a description of an innovative program to build model communities on government-owned surplus land in metropolitan areas:

> Late in the summer of 1967, the Johnson administration started a program to build model new communities on surplus federally owned land in metropolitan areas. During the next year, the White House and the Department of Housing and Urban Development announced seven projects. Nearly three years later, the program had clearly failed. Three

of the projects were dead, and the rest were in serious trouble. Almost no construction had been initiated.

Why would anyone want to look a gift horse in the mouth? Why would anyone reject the benevolent efforts of President Johnson, the White House, and the Department of Housing and Urban Development to offer subsidies on federally owned surplus land in metropolitan areas for the laudable purpose of building new communities joining Black and White, rich and poor, living together in harmony with the new technology? Although initial agreement appeared—at least to the federal officials—to be widespread, disagreements rapidly came to the surface. A number of local groups strongly opposed low cost public housing; local officials preferred kinds of development that would yield more tax revenue; and conservationists were opposed to plans for construction. As apparent agreement rapidly yielded to pervasive disagreement, the program ground to a halt.[6]

We Sometimes Do Not Know How to Achieve Our Goals In 1975 the Ford administration proposed a tax cut. Its purpose was to increase consumer spending in order to stimulate the economy. There were two alternatives: a lump sum tax rebate or a reduction in monthly withholding from wages and salaries. The former would give people a large amount all at once; the latter would give them a bit more each month. Which would lead to more spending (rather than more money being put into savings accounts)? The economic planners did not know. Consumers were not predictable enough.

Take another example: The federal, state, and local governments have put a lot of money and effort into improving education in inner-city schools. Many programs have been tried: innovative curricula, smaller classes, open classrooms, traditional classrooms, and so on. Some programs have been successful; some less so. But we still do not know exactly what makes for successful education and what does not.

Some Things Can Be Changed More Easily Than Others Sometimes the diagnosis of a problem suggests a policy that is fairly easy to achieve; sometimes it suggests changes that are not so easy to achieve by government action. It is easier to reduce the size of classes in inner-city schools than to bring in better teachers (in part because one can measure the size of a class easily, but we are not sure what a good teacher is and how to find one). But it may be easier to improve the quality of teachers than to change the values that children learn in the home. If the values learned in the home are the basic factor determining success in school (it is by no means certain that this is the case, though some argue that it is), government programs can do little. Government programs will concentrate on class size, since something can be done about it, even though this may not get to the root of the problem.

[6] Pressman and Wildavsky, p. 91. The authors draw this example from Martha Derthich, *New Towns In-Town* (Washington, D.C.: Urban Institute, 1972).

Things That Can Be Changed Cannot Always Be Changed Much
Suppose studies showed that smaller class size does improve education. Class size can be reduced, but only within limits set by available budgets, teachers, and classrooms. Noticeable effects may come only if class size is reduced from 35 to 20. But because of limited resources class size is reduced only to 30 pupils. The local school board introduces the "right" policy, but not enough of it. The result is little measurable impact on learning.

Well-Intentioned Policies Can Fail When Other Conditions Are Wrong   The success of a policy often depends on other conditions that are outside the control of the policy maker. If the conditions are right, the policy works. If not, the policy fails. In recent years, for example, there has been an increase in government action to end job discrimination on the basis of race or sex. Business firms, universities, and other institutions have been required to take affirmative action to open more and better jobs to women and minority groups.

Such affirmative action programs are easier to carry out in a growing economy in which new jobs are constantly being created. The implementation of these programs in the mid-1970s was made more difficult by an economic slump that was beyond the control of the government officials in charge of carrying out the antidiscrimination laws.

It Is Often Hard to Tell Whether a Program Has Succeeded   Funds are allocated to a particular program. But is the program successful? It is often hard to tell. The standards of success may be unclear. The government sets up a retraining program so that workers laid off from one job can develop skills for a different job. What is the standard of success of such a program? The amount spent on training? The number of people who enroll in the program? The number who complete the program? The extent to which they actually learn new skills? Their success in finding jobs after completing the program? The permanence of such jobs? A program may be successful by one standard (lots of people graduate from the program) but unsuccessful under another (they cannot find jobs where they can use their new skills).

The problem of evaluation is made harder by the fact that those who carry out the program may have a stake in showing that it is successful. And the information that gets to higher officials may be biased to show more success than is actually achieved.

This list of "limitations" is not meant to suggest that all government programs fail. Quite the contrary. Many programs achieve what they set out to achieve, or at least something close to it. The point is simply that planning a policy and implementing it successfully are not the same thing.

The issue of bilingualism has recently come on the government's agenda.

Government Action and Inaction

To understand the full range of government policy one has to consider what the government does *not* do as well as what it does. If the government is inactive in some area, that is a policy as well, though not necessarily a planned one. There may never have been a decision to do nothing. But the lack of action has an impact nevertheless.

A visitor from another country like Belgium or Canada, where there is constant conflict over language policy, might ask about the policy of the American government in relation to the English language. "What do you mean by a language policy?" most Americans would reply. "There is no issue or problem here." Yet it is incorrect to say that we are a monolingual country. Most citizens speak English, but a large minority speak Spanish. The lack of an explicit policy on the subject does not mean that there is not an *implicit* policy. It means that government business is conducted in English, civil-service examinations are in English, literacy tests for voting are in English, and school teaching is conducted in English. And all of these work to the disadvantage of those whose native language is not English. (Indeed, though formerly the government's language policy was implicit, today a conflict of interests has been recognized, leading to explicit policies in New York City and California that recognize the multiplicity of languages spoken there.)

One could give many examples in which the lack of government activity is a policy. What is the government's policy on the length of vacations for workers? Surely we do not expect the government to have a policy on this subject, yet some countries do. In the United States, however, vacations are left to bargaining between employers and workers. We may believe that vacations are "in the natural order of things" not subject to government activity. But there was a time when we believed that wages were "naturally" a subject for private agreements among workers and management. Now of course we have many laws affecting wages. For many years the government was inactive in the area of medical care. This had the effect of a policy, for it meant the individual citizen had to pay his or her own medical expenses.

How Issues Become Issues: Setting the Agenda

The discussion of action and inaction points to a major factor in understanding the pattern of government policies. The first issue may be: What are the issues? The impact of government policy on the lives of citizens depends in part on how decisions are made about issues, such as whether the government provides funds for mass transit or for roads. But even more basic may be the question of how the issue of roads or mass transit gets on the agenda in the first place. How do roads become a subject of government decisions? Why should the government have a policy in that area? In trying to understand government policy we must ask why issues become issues.

The first political issue is the choice of issues; the first step in dealing with a problem is to recognize that it is a problem. Once a problem has been raised — "put on the agenda" — citizens can pressure the government; debate can take place in the press, in Congress, and in the executive branch; proposals can be made. Remember our stress on government inaction: When the government does nothing about health care or pollution or vehicle noise, that is in a real sense a policy. And nothing is done when an issue never gets the attention of the American people.

LACK OF PROCEDURAL RULES

Is there a "proper procedure" for putting problems on the political agenda? When we discussed Congress we dealt with the House Rules Committee, which is powerful because it controls the agenda of the House of Representatives. It decides what bills come to the floor, and it controls the debate. When it comes to American politics in general, no clear set of rules determines what gets on the agenda. The legal rules on who can bring up an issue are found in the Bill of Rights — they are freedom of speech and the right to petition Congress. In this sense anyone has the right to put a matter on the agenda — to write to his or her representative in Congress saying that something should be done. But not everyone does so with equal effectiveness.

The process by which problems come to the attention of the public and the government has not been studied much. One reason is that it is difficult to identify "nonissues," that is, problems that have not yet been recognized. (If it were easy to do so, the problems would be recognized.) Social scientists as well as political leaders have been surprised by the sudden eruption of issues. The women's movement caught most people off guard, as did many of the first black protest activities in the 1950s. Looking back, one can say that these were "natural" issues that were certain to arise sooner or later. But that is hindsight.

HOW PROBLEMS GET ONTO THE AGENDA

Does the Agenda Reflect Reality?   One view of how problems get onto the political agenda is that they do so automatically. If the economy is going badly, economic problems automatically get onto the agenda of politics; if it is going well, little attention is paid to them. In earlier days, when our rivers and streams were pure, pollution was not on the agenda. Now they are filthy, and pollution is a major political issue. (See Figure 18.1.)

This view has some truth in it. One cannot imagine pollution as an issue if the air and water are pure. In this sense an objective problem (dirty water) is a *necessary* but not a *sufficient* condition to get

FIGURE 18.1
The Issue of Pollution: Slow in
Getting on the Agenda but
Now a Major Government
Concern

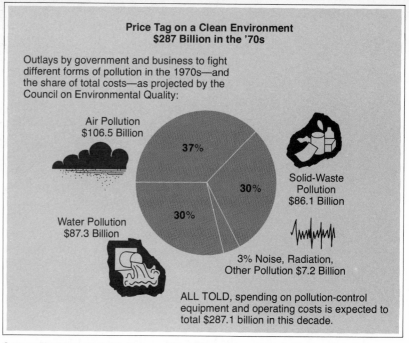

**Price Tag on a Clean Environment
$287 Billion in the '70s**

Outlays by government and business to fight
different forms of pollution in the 1970s—and
the share of total costs—as projected by the
Council on Environmental Quality:

Air Pollution
$106.5 Billion

37%

30%

30%

Solid-Waste
Pollution
$86.1 Billion

Water Pollution
$87.3 Billion

3% Noise, Radiation,
Other Pollution $7.2 Billion

ALL TOLD, spending on pollution-control
equipment and operating costs is expected to
total $287.1 billion in this decade.

Source: Reprinted from *U.S. News and World Report,* August 21, 1972. Copyright © 1972, U.S.
News and World Report, Inc.

a problem onto the agenda. The "political" agenda does not merely
reflect the "real" problems of a society. Our lakes and rivers were
polluted long before the current concern with the problem, well
back into the nineteenth century in some cases. Lake Erie became
almost hopelessly polluted without anyone showing much concern.
Now that the same thing is happening to some of the other Great
Lakes, it is an issue. Surely something besides the objective problem
is responsible.

In the 1950s and 1960s the issue of race relations exploded on the
American scene. Does this mean that there was less of a problem
earlier? Quite the contrary. Data show an improvement in the life
conditions of American blacks at the same time that their demands
for equal rights became stronger. What had to be added to the objective problems was subjective awareness of them.

There is another reason why the agenda of politics reflects more
than the objective problems of society. Each time a new problem
arises, it does not push the old ones off the agenda. It is often hard
for a new problem to get onto the agenda. One political analyst
found that the best way to find out what will be on this year's budget
is to look at last year's. Just as most organization meetings have
"old business" as the first item on the agenda, so does the American
political structure. Once a problem has been recognized, it tends to
become institutionalized; that is, a government agency is set up to
deal with it; it has a place on the government's budget; a congressional committee or subcommittee works on it. It is on the agenda,

Sometimes social problems take a long time to get on the agenda. Inadequate housing was a problem for many years, before it became a subject of governmental concern.

and year after year it stays there because the government agency and the congressional committee see to it. A new problem has no such support; it may have to wait in the wings for a long time—sometimes years and decades—before it is recognized.

Can Anyone Put a Problem on the Agenda? A second view is that anyone can put a problem on the agenda. In a way this is true, but it is also somewhat misleading. The Constitution guarantees the right to petition Congress or to form a political group. And these things are often done. But not all social groups are equally organized. And unorganized interests have less chance of getting their problems onto the political agenda than organized ones.

The fact that a serious problem exists does not make one active in trying to get the government to deal with that problem. This can be seen from a study of political participation that found that black Americans were more likely than whites to say they had serious problems that could be solved by government activity. And the problems that blacks mention are serious: lack of adequate jobs, income, housing. Blacks thus recognize their problems as political, that is, as problems that the government would be most likely to solve. But though blacks are almost twice as likely as whites to say they have problems requiring government action, they are less than half as likely to have contacted an official about such a problem. And when asked why they did not do so, the most frequent reason given by blacks was that they doubted their own effectiveness and the government's responsiveness.[7]

Of course even if a group raises an issue for the political agenda there is no certainty that it will be given serious consideration. The Constitution gives everyone the right to raise an issue; it does not guarantee a sympathetic reply. Thus just as citizens are not equally likely to raise issues, there is even greater inequality in the responses of the government.

[7] Sidney Verba and Norman H. Nie, *Participation in America: Political Democracy and Social Equality* (New York: Harper & Row, 1972), chap. 10.

Anyone has the right to put a matter on the agenda, but not everyone does so with equal effectiveness.

Can Any Problem Get onto the Agenda? A third point can be made about the political agenda. Just as some people are less likely to put their problems on the agenda, there are certain problems that are less likely to get onto the agenda. Our "free-enterprise" tradition makes it unlikely that an issue involving government ownership of industries will be raised or, if it is raised, will be taken seriously.

There are a number of reasons why such issues might not be raised. Quite simply, they may be considered so far "out of the question" that citizens would not think of raising them. Of course, what is "out of the question" may be hard to tell until a question is raised. Many major changes were once considered unlikely or impossible. The notion that some issue is "out of the question" can be a self-fulfilling prophecy. People think some issue is out of the question and therefore do not raise it. In this sense the political agenda has a lot of inertia built into it.

Another reason that such issues are not raised is that it may be risky to do so. This is particularly true for candidates for office, as Barry Goldwater learned in his 1964 campaign for the Presidency. The social-security system has become an accepted part of the American scene; it is no longer an issue for discussion. But in speeches and articles Goldwater had toyed with the idea of modifying social security. It was on this issue that the Democrats chose to "hook and hang" him, observes Theodore H. White in *The Making of the President, 1964*.[8] A television spot in which the fingers of two hands tore up a social-security card was shown over and over again during the campaign. By election day millions of elderly Americans were convinced that, as President, Goldwater would abolish social security and cut off their retirement checks. When they were surveyed after the election, delegates to the Republican Convention that had nominated Goldwater ranked the social-security issue as the second most important reason for their party's defeat.

Who Can Get Issues onto the Agenda?

Those who are politically active are more likely to get problems put on the political agenda. The reason is simple. Participation communicates to the government the views of the citizens. If the citizens do not participate, their views remain unknown. One study compared the views of citizens on the major problems of their communities with the problems that community leaders felt were most pressing and on which they were working. It found that the leaders tended to have on *their* agendas the problems expressed by the *active* citizens. Thus the first generalization is that one has to be active to get problems onto the agenda.

Activity, however, may not be enough. The study just mentioned also compared the effectiveness of political activity by upper- and

[8] Theodore H. White, *The Making of the President, 1964* (New York: Atheneum, 1965).

lower-status citizens. Among the active citizens it was found that those from upper social groups—the wealthy, the educated, those with high-status occupations—were very effective in getting items put on the political agenda. The lower-status citizens who participated actively were less successful; the agendas of community leaders did not match up very well with the preferences of lower-status citizens.

Why did lower-status citizens who were active still not succeed in communicating their views on the most pressing problems in the community to their leaders? There are three possible answers, each of which tells us something about setting agendas.

For one thing, the lower-status citizens who were active were socially very different from the community leaders. The leaders tended to be wealthy and well educated; the lower-status activists tended to be poorer and less well educated. These differences may have made the leaders less attentive to them. Second, the problems that the lower-status citizens wanted to put on the agenda were different from those that the upper-status citizens were interested in. The latter were interested in better community facilities and perhaps also (inconsistently) in lowering taxes. The former wanted basic issues of welfare placed on the agenda. Third, though the lower-status activists were as active as the upper-status ones, there were fewer of them. Thus their views were drowned out by a larger group of upper-status activists.[9]

This discussion should help make clear why some groups turn to more direct, sometimes violent, protest action to bring their problems to the attention of the government. Violent action, as we have suggested, is a *signal*, a way of getting the attention of political leaders. Violent outbursts, whatever their other costs, are effective in calling the attention of leaders to problems that they might otherwise ignore. It is a way of getting onto the agenda.

Agenda Setters There are also individuals and groups whom we can call *agenda setters*. Their specialty is seeking and publicizing new problems—a long tradition in this country. Around the turn of the century the muckrakers brought many social problems to public attention and got these problems onto the government agenda. Much of the legislation regulating business dates from that time. The job of bringing forth new issues is currently being done by the leaders of the consumer movement, the ecology movement, and the women's rights movement. In addition, investigative reporters often bring new problems to the attention of the public. An example is the revelation in 1975 that the CIA had been investigating the activity of Americans in the United States (by law it is required to limit its activity to foreign countries). The issue was raised by a series of articles in the *New York Times*. Once it had

[9] Verba and Nie, chap. 20.

In recent years, many senators have become agenda setters. Here Senator Mike Gravel pickets the White House to protest a nuclear test.

been made public, it was put on the political agenda; Congress and the executive branch set up committees to investigate the charges.

In recent years a particularly important type of agenda setter has emerged. Members of Congress — especially senators — often play an important role in bringing new issues before the public. The Senate, as we have pointed out, is now the most frequent source of presidential candidates. But how can a senator achieve the national prominence needed to enter the magic group of potential candidates? One way is to find an important public issue and use the committee that the senator chairs (each member of the Senate chairs at least one committee or subcommittee) to bring that issue before the public. It helps if the issue has a broad public appeal.

One of the first senators to follow this route was Estes Kefauver, who took on the drug industry in the 1950s. The result was closer regulation of that industry. Legislation on consumer protection, on the environment, and on automobile safety has had similar origins. Sometimes an agenda setter within the government works closely with one outside of the government. The legislation setting up the National Highway Safety Bureau grew out of investigations conducted by a Senate committee led by Abraham Ribicoff of Connecticut as well as out of the activities of Ralph Nader. The professional staffs of congressional committees are also important in this process. They help find issues and bring them before the public.

The role of agenda setters is especially great when it comes to policies that would benefit a large and unorganized group — a group such as consumers or citizens exposed to air pollution. As we have pointed out, the government has traditionally been more responsive to narrow, intense, and well-organized interests than to broad, unorganized ones.

The industry that must bear the cost of environmental legislation by buying expensive devices to clean the smoke coming out of its smokestacks can be expected to oppose such legislation with vigor. The public that would benefit from the purer air is harder to organize. No single citizen would have enough impact on the law or would receive sufficient benefit to make it worthwhile to take the time and effort to fight for the law. Furthermore, since all citizens would benefit from the clean air whether or not they

Sometimes groups try to keep government out of an issue. Here women protest regulation of abortions.

worked to have the law passed, it makes sense for the ordinary citizen to wait for someone else to push the legislation and then get a "free ride," taking advantage of the law even if he or she made no effort to have it enacted. The result is that little pressure emerges from a broad public.

Agenda setters, on the other hand, receive more direct and concentrated benefits from their activity. They can win national recognition. They also receive the gratification of doing a professional job well—and their profession is discovering and pushing new issues. This provides an important motivation to fight the more intense and narrow interests that are opposed to the law. We are not arguing that such agenda setters raise a particular issue simply to gain national stature. The senators and their staffs, as well as the agenda setters outside of the government, usually believe deeply in what they are trying to accomplish. But the additional motivation of obtaining recognition and satisfying their own professional norms helps make them active advocates of the legislation they favor.

Alternate Modes of Policy Making

Imagine a government official faced with a policy problem. Suppose he is trying to write legislation to deal with automobile pollution. There are two ways he can approach the problem. One we call the *comprehensive* approach, and the other we call the *incremental* approach.

USING THE COMPREHENSIVE APPROACH

In using the comprehensive approach the government official will consider all possible ways of handling the issue and all of their possible effects in relation to other problems. He will very clearly state the goal he is trying to achieve and relate it to other goals that he thinks are important. He will then choose the best possible means to achieve the goal.

Let us look at what a comprehensive approach to automobile pollution control might entail:

1. *The Past Is No Limit* The planner dealing with the problem of automobile pollution in a comprehensive manner will not allow himself to be limited by what has been done before. The past design of automobiles, the number of older automobiles on the road, the evolution of the automobile industry, and the pattern of use of the automobile will not interfere with a new comprehensive plan.

2. *All Possible Policies and Techniques Will Be Considered* The comprehensive planner will not stop at considering ways to modify current cars; he will consider all possible technologies. Nor will he limit himself to existing means of transportation. He may very well consider the possibility of replacing the car with mass transit.

3. *Connections with Other Policies Will Be Considered* The planner will see the linkage of his goal to other policies, and he will not be

577

afraid to plan for changes in those policies if they are related to automobile pollution. Does private ownership of cars lead to greater pollution? Then perhaps private ownership should be barred. Perhaps government ownership of the automobile industry would increase control over pollution. If so, that possibility should be considered as well.

4. *All Values Are Considered* The comprehensive planner, however, is not single-minded. He does not consider only how to curb auto fumes. Rather, he is fully aware that we have other values as well as a desire for less pollution. Pollution could be stopped by banning all cars, but that would hurt other values such as a functioning economy and full employment, or our desire to get from place to place.

The comprehensive planner does not ignore these other values but takes them all into consideration. How much do we value curbing pollution? How much do we value curbing inflation? How much do we value full employment? How much do we value limiting government control over the economy? All of these values are related to pollution. A comprehensive planner will weigh them against the gain that would come from curbing automobile pollution.

5. *The Comprehensive Planner Considers All the Effects of His Plan* What effect does it have on jobs, on housing, on other means of transportation? Maybe a reduction in pollution will improve health. The planner might even consider the need for new facilities for the aged, who will probably live longer in a pollution-free atmosphere.

USING THE INCREMENTAL APPROACH

Consider, on the other hand, the incremental approach to policy making. It differs from the comprehensive approach in every way. (See Figure 18.2.)

1. For the incremental planner, the past is a major constraint. She considers the current situation: how many cars are on the road, their economic importance, current patterns of automobile use. Past policies, such as the policy not to support mass transit, will be considered as "givens"—a framework within which she must work.

2. Rather than considering all possible ways of dealing with the problem, the incremental planner will consider cars as they are currently designed and the modifications that could fit into current technologies.

3. The planner will stick fairly closely to the technical problem of standards for automobile pollution and ignore larger changes in the economy. Such major changes as the banning of the private automobile or the nationalization of the automobile industry would probably not even enter her mind.

4. The incremental planner would not worry much about the effects of her plan in other areas. Her area of concern is automobile pollution. Let other government agencies worry about inflation or full employment. The planner will not consider all other relevant values and weigh them against that of cleaner air. Rather, she will ignore most other values and think only of the narrower task at hand.

The results of the two modes of policy making would be different indeed. The comprehensive planner could almost redesign the world from scratch. The incrementalist will create a policy that is narrowly designed to deal with a specific problem, modifying but not scrapping current practices.

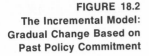

**FIGURE 18.2
The Incremental Model:
Gradual Change Based on
Past Policy Commitment**

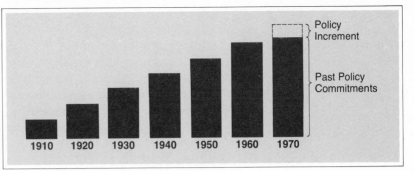

Source: Thomas R. Dye, *Understanding Public Policy,* © 1972. Reprinted by permission of Prentice-Hall, Inc., Englewood Cliffs, New Jersey.

The Government Uses the Incremental Approach

At first glance the comprehensive approach appears much more productive. Piecemeal solutions often accomplish little. And we have seen that failure to consider all the effects of a policy can lead to unforeseen and unwanted results. But despite the seeming advantages of the comprehensive approach, most government policy takes the incremental approach. Policies tend to be based on previously existing policies and are worked out step by step, narrowly focusing on one aspect of the problem. There are many reasons for this.

First, comprehensive planning is beyond the ability of planners. To consider all possible values and weigh one against the other is not possible. There is no precise way of saying (or knowing) how much one values clean air versus full employment. A plan that covered all relevant values and all possible effects of a decision could not be worked out, even with the aid of the most advanced computers.

Second, most government planners are not in a position to consider all aspects of a problem at once. The official who was assigned to work on automobile pollution control and came back with a plan that required vast funds for mass transit would be told to stick to his or her job. And that is what most public officials do. Of course there are institutions that are supposed to have a more comprehensive view of problems: the Presidency and Congress. But even here incremental planning may rule. Congress may make the broadest of legislation, but it itself is organized into committees that are geared to specific problems rather than planning comprehensively across all fields. And even the President, burdened with particular problems that have to be dealt with at a particular time, may have trouble taking a more general view.

Many Presidents have complained about the lack of time to deal with a problem comprehensively. In the area of foreign policy, for

579

instance, they have complained that the pressure to make decisions on emergency problems makes it impossible to deal with overall long-term policy. They have often been aware of the problem but unable to deal with it.

Another reason why policy making tends to be incremental is the weight of history. Policy makers cannot avoid past decisions. Once a course has been charted, one cannot easily change it without risking severe problems. If a government program of one sort has been set up, one cannot come along and start all over again without considering the status and effects of the existing program.

Furthermore, people become committed to existing programs and put pressure on the government to keep them going.

One major study of government spending on various programs, which we mentioned in passing earlier, asked how one could predict what any state or city would spend on various functions—welfare, health, education, transportation, parks, and so forth. What was the best predictor, the study asked: the party that won the last election? the social makeup of the locality? the changes in the problems the government faced? The answer was no. By far the best predictor of how a government will spend its funds this year is how it spent them last year. Changes there may be, but they will be *incremental* changes. Last year's budget tends to be the starting point for this year's.[10]

The weight of existing programs falls on all levels of government, high and low. After twenty years out of office, the Republicans elected a President in 1952. The previous two decades had seen the growth of huge government programs in the area of social welfare, programs that had been severely criticized by leaders of the Republican opposition. But none of these programs was ended. Some may have been changed somewhat, some cut. But those were incremental changes, not comprehensive ones. The weight of past decisions is also found in foreign policy. Each President inherits the policies of past Presidents. And though each moves in a different direction, this almost always makes a smaller difference than the public (or even the new President and his staff) expect. They may change course by 5, 10, or 20 degrees—but rarely by 180 degrees.

THE ARGUMENT FOR INCREMENTAL POLICY MAKING

Incremental policy making is a fact of American politics. This is how most policy is made. Its defenders argue that it is a most effective way of making policy. For one thing, they point out that focusing on one aspect of a problem is not a bad way to do things. It is not that other issues and other values are ignored. It is just that there are other government agencies worrying about the other problems. If the official who is concerned with air pollution does not face the issue of inflation, it does not matter. She would not have dealt with it well anyway. It is not her area and she has other problems to

[10] Ira Sharkansky, *Spending in the American States* (Chicago: Rand McNally, 1968).

worry about. Let some other part of the government worry about that. And if separate parts of the government worry about separate problems, every problem will be dealt with somewhere.

Furthermore, it is good to make policy without considering all possible effects. Otherwise one would never act; it would take a lifetime of study to consider all the possible effects of a policy.

The argument in favor of incremental planning is not without flaws. It assumes that somehow every possible value has a government agency worrying about it. But of course that is not the case. Certain interests are preserved by certain parts of the government; others aren't dealt with. It is only in recent years that a government agency has been set up to deal with consumer interests, and the organizational power of that agency is much weaker than that of most others. And while it is true that a comprehensive concern for all possible effects might lead to no policy at all, one can find too many examples in which unintended effects have made the results of a policy almost the opposite of what was planned.

But whether one approves of it or not, one has to understand policy making in America as a process that often goes on in an incremental way. This is reinforced by the tendency to *disaggregate* the policy-making process.

THE DISAGGREGATION OF POLICY MAKING

Incremental policies are accompanied by disaggregated decision making. This refers to a major tendency in American politics to divide the policy-making process into small units. In part this is reflected in the tendency to decentralize decision making into small government units—states, cities, towns, school districts. More generally, it is a tendency to fragment policy making. Policy is made by a narrowly focused government agency for a particular group on a fairly narrow range of issues. Policy is not made for the economy as a whole. Rather, different parts of the government specialize in particular aspects of the economy. The regulation of one part of the economy is done by one branch of the government (a bureau in the Department of Agriculture, the Interstate Commerce Commission, the Bureau of Mines) that works closely with those it regulates (the farmers growing a particular crop, the railroads, the mine interests).

Disaggregated decision making means that those who are to be regulated are likely to take part in the regulation. For example, President Nixon's Task Force for Business Taxation, appointed in 1969, was made up of four lawyers from corporate law firms, two New York investment bankers, three representatives of corporate accounting firms, two top officials of large industrial corporations, and three business-oriented economists. Policy is made within narrow limits. Each government agency is concerned with the problems of the particular part of the society whose problems it specializes in. It is not concerned with broader social issues. This disaggregation in the executive branch of the government is paralleled by disaggregation in Congress. The congressional structure of specialized committees and more specialized subcommittees makes for a similar narrow focus on the problems of a particular group.

Consequences of Disaggregated Policy Making   Policy making for narrow constituencies has important results. The top political institutions in the country—the parties, the President, Congress—have (or should have) broad rather than narrow constituencies. Their constituents come from all branches of the economy—workers and management, farms and industries. And they come from all kinds of farms and all kinds of industries, not just wheat farms or the aluminum industry. If policy is made by such institutions, it is likely to take into consideration many sides of a problem. If the constituency is broad, a suggestion for an increase in dairy prices would be considered not only from the point of view of the dairy farmers but also from that of the consumers who must pay for their products. But if the constituency is narrow—if policy is made in a bureau of the Department of Agriculture that deals only with dairy interests—policy will more likely be made with only the dairy interests in mind.

How Does Disaggregation Come About?   Disaggregation is in part a result of the organizational structure of the government. It happens when major policy decisions are made by specialized agencies or committees. Disaggregation also results because American political parties do not provide broad programs among which citizens can choose, and it is reinforced by the tendency mentioned earlier for laws of Congress to be general and vague. This leaves a vacuum when it comes to carrying out policy. Someone has to decide how the policy is to be applied, and this is left to administrative agencies with narrower constituencies.

Finally, the disaggregation of government policy is supported by a general belief that as much government activity as possible should be freed from "politics." This slogan is heard in a number of fields: "Let's keep politics out of the schools!" "The Federal Communications Commission should not be placed under political pressure!" "Don't make medicare a political football!"

Keeping "Politics" Out of Policy Making

The slogan calling for keeping politics out of government activity is somewhat self-contradictory, because politics exists whenever binding decisions are made for the society. Whatever the FCC does is, by our definition, political. Medicare, which involves federal spending for medical care, is political. Education, the largest domestic government program, is political. The confusion lies in the fact that our general "political science" definition of politics isn't what the slogans mean. And to understand this is to understand something very important about policy making in America.

When people talk about freeing some area of public concern—schools, communications policy, medicare—from "politics," they generally mean freeing it from *partisan politics*. They think this area should not be the concern of the political parties, with each party trying to use the policy to get votes. Similarly, the policy should be removed from the partisan control of Congress. Certain policies, in short, should not be subjects of partisan conflict.

How, then, should communications, education, or medical-care policy be made? The answer will be that such policies should be impartial, objective, decided by experts. Regulation of the airwaves is a very technical problem. It requires specialists in communications policy. The granting of a new TV license should not be a subject of partisan conflict, with the license going to the side that can get more congressional support. Education of children is a complicated business. It should not be subject to partisan pressures but should be controlled by specialists in education.

This attempt to remove policy making from politics (in the narrow sense of *partisan politics*) is found in the federal administration with its specialized agencies, in Congress with its specialized committees. It is found in the state governments, which have a similar structure. It is found at the local level.

But—and here our broader definition of politics becomes important—to remove some government function from partisan politics is not to remove it from politics more generally. The decisions of technical experts remain political as long as they have behind them the force of the government, as long as they involve regulation of behavior or the spending of tax money. What removing a matter from partisan politics does is to turn it over to a narrow constituency. Communications policy is not made in a vacuum. Removing that policy area from partisan politics means that the vacuum is filled by the interest that is most affected—the communications industry. It becomes the constituency of the government agency making that policy. The same is true of educational policy. The role of organized educational interests—colleges of education, the educational bureaucracy, teachers' organizations—increases as the pressures of a broader constituency decrease.

Those who approve of disaggregated decision making argue that it gives major control over policy to the specific groups that are most affected. The narrow constituencies that are closely tied to government agencies or congressional committees are just those that the policy affects most. Thus policies can be adjusted to the needs of particular groups.

The argument against such decision making should be familiar by now: Not all constituencies are equally served. Many do not have powerful agencies that they can contact. Educational policy may be adjusted to the needs of colleges of education more than to those of teachers, and may serve the needs of both better than those of pupils. The schools of education are better organized than the teachers; the teachers, in turn, are better organized than the pupils. Furthermore, broad concern with some more general public interest is missing when policy making is disaggregated.

Comprehensive and Centralized Planning

As we have often seen in American politics, one tendency is balanced by another: The forces of localism pull against the forces of centralization; Congress pulls against the President; individual liberties pull against national security. The same is true in policy making. The tendency in American politics toward policies that are incremental and disaggregated is in constant tension with attempts to develop more comprehensive and centralized planning.

Both Congress and the executive branch have tried to create institutions for comprehensive policy making, institutions that are more general than the committees of Congress or the departments of the executive branch.

COMPREHENSIVE INSTITUTIONS

The Office of Management and Budget (OMB)   This agency is directly under the control of the President. It is not a part of any department. Its purpose is to improve the coordination of government policy. It prepares the federal budget and, in so doing, tries to see that the budget proposals coming from the executive departments fit into the President's overall program. In addition, it tries to oversee the way programs are carried out.

The OMB represents an attempt to deal comprehensively with governmental programs. It is a powerful branch of the Executive Office and takes a more comprehensive view than the individual departments do. But often it is involved in a tug of war with the individual departments as the latter try to protect and develop their own programs.

The Council of Economic Advisers   This is a three-member body set up under the Full Employment Act of 1946. Its purpose is to help the President make overall economic policy. The members of the Council are usually professional economists, but they share the President's general economic views. In the economic crisis of the mid-1970s the Council played an important role in setting general economic policy.

The National Security Council   This body tries to coordinate U.S. foreign policy. It brings together the top officials of the various departments that deal with foreign affairs: the Department of State, the Department of Defense, and the CIA. Over the years it has grown from a committee of top officials to an agency with a large professional staff. It is an example of the way "coordinating" agencies are created to try to take control of what would otherwise be a disaggregated policy-making process.

Attempts by the government to create a comprehensive energy program have run into opposition from public utilities, consumer groups, and other interests.

Budget Committees in Congress Congress has also tried to increase its capacity for comprehensive planning. The process of making budget appropriations in the House and Senate has traditionally been incremental and disaggregated. The President would submit his annual budget to Congress. Separate committees would work on separate parts of the President's requests for authority to spend money. There was no committee that looked at the budget as a whole. In 1974 Congress set up new committees on the budget in the House and Senate. These new committees allow the members of Congress to look at the overall budget and set target figures before working on various parts of the budget.

The purpose of the new committees is to take a more comprehensive and centralized approach. It is hoped that this will increase the influence of Congress on the budgetary process and make the process less chaotic.

The new committees of Congress are intended to reform its traditionally decentralized ways of doing things. But it is not yet certain how they will work. As the *Congressional Quarterly* (a private magazine that comments on affairs in Washington) put it: "To make the design effective, Congress will have to overcome a lack of budgetary expertise, some committee jurisdictional jealousies, the temptation to waive budget-making deadlines and, occasionally at least, the personal political interests of 100 senators and 435 House members."[11] Or, as a former official of the OMB has suggested: "To make it work, Congress and its individual members will have to act a hell of a lot differently than they do now."[12]

Some members of Congress were less pessimistic about the new committees, but they agreed that it would take several years for them to work properly.

[11] "Current American Government" (Washington, D.C.: *Congressional Quarterly*, Spring 1975), p. 75.
[12] *Ibid.*

The Actors in the Policy-Making Process

Who might be among the influential actors on a particular policy? They can be individuals and groups within the government or outside it.

The Mass Public, Special Publics, Organized Groups   One potential actor is the *mass public*, or the part of it that is called the majority. Its opinion can be expressed in public-opinion polls and in letters to members of Congress, perhaps at election time. If public involvement takes a narrower form, *special publics* may be the actors. These so-called attentive publics are likely to have an interest in a particular policy: Union members, for instance, are likely to be an attentive public for labor legislation, farmers for farm legislation, doctors for medical-care legislation. Or the actors may be *organized groups*. And here we can make a useful distinction between groups with a broad constituency and those with a narrower one. A broad constituency would include a wide range of types of citizens and interests; a narrow one would cover a much more precisely defined group. A few examples will make the distinction clear: Groups with broad constituencies include the so-called peak business associations that represent interests from many parts of the business community: organizations like the National Association of Manufacturers or the U.S. Chamber of Commerce, representing industry as a whole, or the American Textile Manufacturers Institute, representing many branches of a particular industry. In the labor field there is the AFL-CIO, representing unions of all sorts. Other broad-constituency groups might include the National Council of Churches (representing many church groups), Common Cause (a lobbying group representing a loose coalition of liberals), or the Liberty Lobby (a parallel group representing conservatives).

More specific groups have narrower memberships. Particular labor unions—the Auto Workers, the Teamsters, the Postal Workers—fall into this category. So do groups representing specific industries or firms. The U.S. Savings and Loan League and the National Association of Retail Druggists speak for narrower interests than those mentioned earlier, as, of course, do U.S. Steel and International Telephone and Telegraph. Groups representing particular kinds of farmers—cotton growers, Wisconsin dairy farmers—fall into this category as well. We distinguish between interest groups in this way because it makes a difference, in terms of the policy-making process, which kinds are involved. The more disaggregated the policy, the more narrowly based the groups involved.

The Party System   Policy makers who come from the party system might include national party organs such as the national committee or groups like the Young Democrats or the Ripon Society (a group of liberal Republicans). They might also include state and local party groups.

State and Local Governments   The states, through their governors or other representatives, take part in federal policy making. And so do the cities and other local governments. At times it may be difficult to distinguish a state or local government as actor from a party group as actor. When, as we saw in Chapter 17, Mayor Daley of Chicago used his political clout against the Office of Economic Opportunity, was he acting as mayor of Chicago or as head of the powerful Cook County Democratic organization? The answer of course is that he was acting as both, and that's where the clout came from.

The Federal Government   The most important actors in the making of federal policy tend to come from within the federal government itself. The office of the President is crucial. This includes the President and his close advisers on the White House Staff as well as government bodies close to the White House such as the OMB, the Council of Economic Advisers, and the National Security Council. Other parts of the executive branch — the federal departments such as Agriculture, Commerce, State, and their various bureaus; the independent regulatory commissions such as the Interstate Commerce Commission and the Federal Communications Commission — all take part as well. The other two branches of the federal system — Congress and the courts — also play a major role.

This list of actors should be familiar to the reader. It is a summary of the groups that we have dealt with so far. Thus we already know a good deal about how they take part in the policy process. But we have dealt with each group separately. To see how they relate to one another, we shall have to see how they interact when making policy. We have introduced policy making in this chapter, but we have dealt with it on a rather general level. To better understand the policy making process, we turn to some specific areas of policy making in the next chapter.

19
PUBLIC POLICIES: DOMESTIC AND FOREIGN

In this chapter we present a few case studies of how policy is made. The federal government is active in almost all areas of our lives (and those of people in other countries). To see how policy is made we might have to look at thousands of issues and at the activities of hundreds of bureaus, committees, and groups. But since that is not possible we must choose a few policy areas to study.

Yet the choice is difficult, for studying the policy process in one area may not tell us much about how policy is made in other areas. How the government makes policy decisions on nuclear weapons may tell us little about how agricultural policy is made.

In this chapter we will consider a range of policies that provide an overview of the various ways in which policy is made and the actors involved. There is no single process by which policies are made, but the categories and distinctions discussed in the preceding chapter should serve as a useful framework for analysis.

Tax Policy

If one wanted to choose the one area of government activity that best represents the government in general, one could do no better than to choose the area of tax policy. Taxes are the key to all other government programs, providing the funds for almost everything else the government does. They touch the lives of all citizens. In terms of impact every American is a potential actor on tax policy.

PURPOSES OF TAXATION

The main purpose of taxes is to raise revenue. But taxation can have other goals as well. These include redistributing income and regulating the economy.

Redistributing Income   Taxes can be used to transfer wealth from one group in the society to another. The major way in which this is done is through the progressive income tax. The logic of a progressive income tax is that people with higher incomes can afford to pay a larger portion of that income in taxes than people with lower incomes. Look at a federal income tax form and you will see that the amount paid ranges from a tiny percent of the income of those in low income brackets up to 50 percent of the income of those earning over $100,000 a year. If these funds are then used for government programs that benefit poorer people more than the wealthy (welfare payments, public housing, etc.), or even if they are used to pay for programs that benefit all citizens equally, it is clear that there has been a transfer of wealth from richer citizens to poorer ones.

This has been the goal of much tax policy, particularly the federal income tax. And the evidence is that tax policy does lead to some redistribution of income. Those in lower brackets get more out of the government than they put in; those in higher brackets get out less than they put in. But as noted in Chapter 4, the extent to which such transfer of income takes place is much less than a quick reading of basic income tax rates would lead one to believe. If indeed the poor paid only 2–3 percent of their income in taxes while the rich paid 50 percent, there would be quite a bit of income transfer. In fact, however, the rich rarely pay as much as 50 percent of income. The tax laws are full of loopholes—exemptions for income from certain kinds of investments, deductions for certain kinds of expenses, lower rates for certain kinds of income. These loopholes tend to be used by upper-income citizens, for two reasons. First, they tend to apply to the kinds of income that are received by those with higher incomes: tax-free municipal bonds or capital gains. Second, the upper-income taxpayer is more likely to use professional help in preparing his or her tax return. The tax laws are very complicated, and only a professional can take full advantage of the many legal deductions and exemptions that the laws allow.

Indeed, the impact of income taxes on the rich and the poor clearly illustrates two of the principles of policy making that we have set forth: (1) To understand a policy you have to look beyond the law as it is written to how it is applied, and (2) policy making in the United States tends to include those who are being regulated as active participants.

The first principle is illustrated by the fact that a citizen's actual tax burden is by no means clear from the basic tax bracket in which he or she falls. One has to look carefully at that citizen's income, its sources, and the tax loopholes that he or she takes advantage of. Thus, despite the very high peak rates for taxes, it is estimated that very few citizens pay an effective rate as high as 50 percent. In 1969 it was discovered that a number of wealthy Americans took advantage of various loopholes to pay no federal income taxes. A "minimum tax" law was passed that year to see that at least some taxes were paid. But apparently some tax lawyer found loopholes in this loophole-closing bill, because in 1972 there were 500 individuals with incomes over $100,000 who paid no federal income taxes.

The second principle—that those who are being regulated participate in the regulation—is illustrated by the self-reporting of taxes. In the United States citizens calculate their own taxes, subject of course to audits by the Internal Revenue Service. What this means is that citizens may differ in the extent to which they take advantage of the tax laws. No one has made careful calculations along these lines, but it is likely that many citizens—particularly those who do not get professional help—miss chances to take deductions, while those who get such help (in most cases those with higher incomes) do take advantage of these loopholes. The federal government has tried to correct this situation by simplifying tax returns and offering to calculate the tax. But it is likely that there are great differences among groups in the extent to which they *participate effectively* in the taxing process, that is, take full advantage of the laws as written.

Note that there is nothing illegal here. We are not talking about cheating on taxes. Rather, we are talking about greater or less ability to take advantage of legal tax arrangements.

There is another reason why taxes do not redistribute income as much as the basic tax rates suggest they do. Income taxes are just one of the many forms of tax in the United States. They are the main way in which funds are raised by the federal government, and they are an increasingly important way for states and some municipalities. But there are many other forms of tax, some of them less progressive and some regressive. Sales taxes are a major way in which funds are raised for state and local governments. And such taxes tend to be regressive, which means that those with lower incomes pay a higher portion of their income in sales taxes than those with higher incomes, for the simple reason that poorer citizens spend a higher percentage of their income on taxable goods. In addition, much local activity is supported by real-estate taxes. These additional taxes greatly modify the extent to which the total tax system redistributes income from the rich to the poor.

Regulating the Economy In addition to the raising of revenue and the redistribution of income, taxes can be used for other purposes. Tax policy is used as a means of regulating the economy. Higher tax rates may be used to curb spending in times of inflation or too rapid economic expansion. Tax rates may be lowered to increase spending and stimulate business in an economic slowdown. The administration used a tax rebate for this purpose in 1974. Tax policy may be used as an indirect means of controlling certain activities. High taxes on alcoholic beverages and cigarettes reflect a government policy (not a very strong one) of limiting their use. Taxes on gasoline can be used for the same purpose. Taxes can be used to stimulate particular parts of the economy—by adjusting tax rates so that citizens will invest in those areas.

Tax policy as a means to regulate economic behavior has lately been receiving much attention by policy makers. The government might gradually begin to substitute tax incentives for more direct forms of regulation. When the issue of a clean environment was first addressed by the government, the standard government response was to issue regulations requiring that factories reduce their pollution. This led to the establishment of the Environmental Protection Agency, as well as dozens of state and local agencies trying to regulate factories and households (you cannot burn leaves in many U.S. cities). Reducing pollution through regulations has proven difficult. In addition it has added to the cost of government, because the regulations have to be applied and adjudicated when there are disputes about their meaning.

Tax policy is an alternative to detailed regulations. A factory that installs scrubbing devices to clean what it discharges into the air or waterways benefits from a lower tax rate. A similar principle has been suggested as a way to enforce energy conservation in private households. For example, rather than write detailed regulations about household insulation, simply give a tax deduction to the family that installs storm windows or insulates the exterior walls.

It is important to keep in mind that the power to tax is the power to redistribute wealth and to regulate social and economic behavior, as well as the power to raise revenue. These additional uses of taxation bring different actors into the policy process.

HOW IS TAX POLICY MADE?

At first glance tax policy doesn't look like a good area for disaggregated policy making. Taxes affect all citizens; they touch all parts of the economy. Insofar as they redistribute income they can become the subject of major clashes over the principles of free enterprise, over the proper role of the government in relation to the poor.

And indeed there are organized groups whose aim is to push general views of federal taxing policy—in particular, groups who want to limit that policy as much as possible. More important, the public is involved in taxes in a way in which it is not involved in the regulation of business. The public cares about taxes. In any election, national or local, tax rates are likely to be an issue. In public-opinion polls citizens are always against tax increases. And government officials are very wary about raising taxes—particularly when an election is coming up.

Even in this area one finds a tendency to disaggregate policy into a series of narrow decisions. One reason for this is suggested by the complexity of the tax system in the United States. Federal income taxes are the largest single item on the citizen's tax bill, but citizens pay many other kinds of taxes as well. And these tax burdens are decided in the states and localities, by special districts and by school districts. This disaggregated decision making has the usual results: Decisions are made for one narrow constituency without considering their impact on other groups. The tax decisions of one school district in a metropolitan area affect other parts of that area in that they may stimulate population movements into or out of the district, thereby affecting the policies of its neighbors. Indeed, as we have shown, one of the causes of the metropolitan crisis is differences among the school systems within metropolitan areas. Yet each school district makes its own tax decisions. (This system is being challenged in the courts because of the inequalities that it produces.)

Even federal income tax policy is subject to disaggregation into a series of particular decisions for small constituencies. We can see this by looking more closely at how federal tax policy is made. The public is involved in tax policy because of its concern about high taxes and because of the concern of government officials about how public attitudes will affect the next election. And the President is concerned as well, particularly when higher taxes are needed to support foreign or domestic programs that he favors or when he wants to use tax policy to slow down or speed up the economy. But in both cases the pressure is a rather general one — for higher or lower tax revenue. It doesn't involve a specific division of the tax burden among groups.

How Tax Laws Are Written   Numerous studies have been made of the process by which tax laws are written. They agree that tax laws are a series of specific decisions about specific types of income. Various industries, businesses, and other types of economic interests make requests for tax relief: exemptions, lower rates, special treatment for depreciation. In this they are often represented by a member of Congress with a strong interest in that area, usually because it is heavily represented in the member's state or district. In these matters most members of Congress tend to think of themselves as defending the interests of their constituents, and since all the other members are doing so, a member who does not play this role would be in danger of losing support.

The procedures for making tax law make it easy to respond to such requests. For one thing, the law is complicated and contains a great range of alternatives. Thus income can be taxed as regular income or as capital gains, the latter at a much lower level. It would be a major concession by Congress, which would lead to criticism in the press and by the public, if a certain kind of income were completely exempted from taxes or even given an arbitrarily lower rate. But to move one kind of income from regular salary to capital gains appears to be a much more technical decision, a decision to which others are less likely to object. And indeed most special tax advantages result not from changing the basic tax rate but from more subtle adjustments.

Second, the decisions are made on an "interest-by-interest" basis; that is, they are disaggregated decisions. When the question of tax relief for a particular kind of farmer comes up, Congress tends to deal with it in terms of what is equitable in that case. It often seems easy, and not harmful to others, to offer a particular group relief from a tax burden that it considers too high. But there are more general principles involved: Who will have to pay higher taxes to compensate for the lower taxes paid by this group? What social programs will be hurt by the reduction in revenue that result from the tax advantage just offered? Is the advantage given to this group equal to advantages received by others? But since each adjustment for each group is considered separately, these broader questions are not asked.

The system of adjustments for specific interests is also highly technical and does not get much public attention, despite the general concern about high taxes and despite the potentially hot issue of unfair tax advantages. The public can be aroused by high taxes or clear unfairness. But when the tax adjustments for some groups are hidden in the complexities of the tax law, little opposition can be aroused.

One result of all this is that special tax benefits go to wealthier citizens. They are more likely to pressure Congress for relief from taxes and more likely to have the kinds of earnings that benefit from special exemptions. As Table 19.1 shows, benefits from capital-gains exemptions are more likely to help those with high incomes.

Nor does Congress as a whole play much of a role. Over the years the House Ways and Means Committee has developed ways of pushing through the House, without hearings and with little debate, "minor" tax bills that often cost the Treasury large sums.

These bills come up as "members' bills" brought up to deal with specific cases of alleged tax inequity rather than to change general tax law. Each year the Ways and Means Committee brings a long list of such bills before the House. They are called up under a rule that allows them to pass by unanimous consent without debate. Only later is it discovered that some of these bills have given to a particular industry or firm a major tax break that is not available to others, a benefit that costs the U.S. Treasury millions of dollars. There is no better example of what we mean by a disaggregated decision.

The final result is a hodgepodge of separate benefits guided by no overall structure. This can be seen by looking at the oil depletion allowance, which for many years gave the oil industry a 22 percent deduction against gross earnings because of the depletion of its resources. The logic of this provision was that it would stimulate exploration for new sources of oil, which was needed for national defense, among other things.

TABLE 19.1 Capital Gains Benefit the Rich	Adjusted Gross Income	Average Amount Saved Through Capital-Gains Tax Exemption
	Under $3,000	$ 1.66
	$5,000–7,000	7.44
	$10,000–15,000	16.31
	$50,000–100,000	2,616.10
	Over $100,000	38,126.29

Source: Based on data from *The Washington Monthly,* January 1973.

Over time similar, though smaller, deductions have been allowed for other industries using natural resources that may disappear. Allowances are made for the gravel and sand industry, though no one has argued that we have to locate more gravel and sand for national defense. Allowances are made for the coal industry, and here the logic is opposite to that of the oil depletion allowance. It is not that we are running out of coal but that there is too much coal; it could not be sold because of competition from gas and oil. Indeed, the depletion allowance for oil (which led to the production of more oil) created the problem of the coal industry by increasing the availability of the competing product!

In short, the various allowances to the mineral industries follow no general plan. Rather, each represents an adjustment to that industry made in the light of its particular appeal.

Tax policy thus works out in ways that are not unlike the regulation of business. The public is somewhere in the background pushing for lower taxes. But its voice is absent when it comes to the details of the tax law and how it is applied. The President is involved when there is a need for more tax revenue or when the Treasury Department wants to use the tax power to regulate the economy. But this involvement is rather general as well, and does not determine how the tax burden is divided among groups. Congress is involved, but only in a general sense. It sets an overall framework within which tax law is made. The most effective actors — the ones who in some real sense make the tax law — are the businesses and other interests working closely with congressional committees and of Congress. A policy that seems hard to disaggregate winds up disaggregated to the nth degree.

The result of these various tax loopholes is that many billions of dollars of income are exempt from federal taxes. In 1972 it was estimated that $166 billion of income was exempt, and that the federal government lost $55 billion in tax revenue by not taxing that income. The exemptions for specific interests add up. (See Table 19.2.)

RETURNING TAX POLICY TO PUBLIC VIEW

In the preceding chapter we described the tension between disaggregated and incremental policies and more centralized and comprehensive policies. There are times when tax policies come before a wider audience; when concern for a more general "public interest" is placed against the narrow interests that ordinarily determine policy. In 1974 and 1975 a number of events took tax policy out of congressional committees and brought it to the attention of the public as well as the executive branch.

Three events combined to produce the more general concern with tax matters: (1) The energy crisis brought the oil industry and its 22 percent depletion allowance under public scrutiny; (2) the recession spurred the Ford administration to use tax policy to try to stimulate the economy; and (3) the revelation during the Watergate

TABLE 19.2
One Estimate of Income That
Escapes Federal Taxes

Tax Preference or Privilege	(BILLIONS OF DOLLARS)	
	Estimated Income Removed From Tax Base in 1972	Estimate Loss in Tax Revenue
Tax exemption for transfer payments, including social-security pensions	$ 55.1	$13.1
Special deductions, double exemptions for the aged and blind, and the retirement income credit	42.2	14.2
Special benefits for homeowners, including deductions of mortgage interest	28.7	9.6
Special tax treatment of capital gains on sales of securities, other things	26.0	13.7
Exemption of interest earned on life insurance investments	9.1	2.7
Tax exemption of interest on state and local bonds	1.9	1.2
Tax exemption of up to $100 in annual dividends per person	1.9	0.7
Excess depletion and depreciation allowances	1.1	0.6
Total	$166.0	$55.8

Source: "Individual Income Tax Erosion by Income Classes," a study by Joseph A. Pechman and Benjamin A. Okner, Brookings Institution, published by the Joint Economic Committee of Congress on May 8. Reprinted from *U.S. News and World Report,* May 22, 1972. Copyright © 1972, U.S. News and World Report, Inc.

hearings of President Nixon's attempts to avoid paying taxes led to public concern with tax reform. Under these circumstances the chances for more general tax reform increased. Jimmy Carter pledged during his campaign to institute major tax reforms. He did indeed send some proposals to Congress during his first year in the White House, but other issues demanded his attention and no general tax reforms were produced.

The general concern with tax policy that grew out of the events just mentioned tells us something important about disaggregated policy making: Policy making remains successfully disaggregated when few people pay attention to it. When some area of public policy becomes a matter of general public concern, the dominant position of narrow but intensely concerned interests is challenged. We will describe this situation more fully in the following section.

Medical Care

THE MEDICARE PROGRAM

In the early summer of 1965 President Johnson signed into law the medicare program — a program of government support for the medical expenses of citizens over 65. The program represented a major

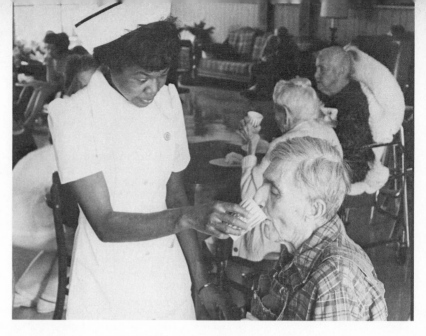

Medical care for the aged has been government policy since 1965.

step in a long battle over the role of the government in relation to medical expenses. The issue had been on the agenda for decades. Around the time of World War I, bills to set up state health insurance programs had been introduced in various state legislatures. In the early 1930s, the New Deal administration had considered adding health insurance to its social-security legislation. In 1948, Harry Truman had made government-supported health insurance a major part of his campaign program.

In each case the proposals came to nothing. A strong campaign was mounted by the American Medical Association, whose opposition to "socialized medicine"—as it labeled any program of government health insurance—had become a dominant feature of the public debate on this issue. The early state programs failed in the state legislatures; the New Deal program was never even submitted for fear that the addition of a controversial measure like health insurance would hurt the chances for passage of the rest of the social-security program. And Truman's program died in committee in both houses of Congress. It never even came to a floor vote.

Policy on medical care shows how the absence of government action is nevertheless a policy. Medical costs for the American population had been rising rapidly with the improvement of medicine and the increase in specialization. Paradoxically, the success of medical care was itself one of the sources of higher medical costs: People live longer, and medical expenses are particularly high for the aged. (See Table 19.3.) By the 1940s the United States had become the only industrialized nation in the world with no program of government health insurance, and many nations, such as Germany, had had such programs since the nineteenth century.

The program passed in 1965 was hailed as a great breakthrough for government health insurance. But it did not bring the United

TABLE 19.3
Health Care and People
over 65

With One-Tenth of the Population, the Aged Account for One-Quarter of Medical Spending

	Share of Population	Share of Health Spending
65 and over	9.9%	27.4%
Ages 19–64	54.4%	56.5%
Under 19	35.7%	16.1%

For Practically Every Type of Care, Bills Are Highest for the Aged

HEALTH SPENDING PER PERSON IN 1971

	65 and Over	Ages 19–64	Under 19
Hospital care	$410	$158	$ 41
Nursing home	151	2	—
Physicians' services	144	69	45
Drugs	87	37	20
Dentists' services	19	27	16
Other health services	50	30	18
Total	$861	$323	$140

Source: U.S. Department of Health, Education and Welfare. Also reprinted from *U.S. News and World Report*, January 22, 1973. Copyright © 1973, U.S. News and World Report, Inc.

States into line with other nations. The medicare program was limited to medical expenses for the aged. In several major ways the program is an example of incremental policy making. Although more comprehensive medical-care plans had been prepared, the program that was able to pass Congress was one that involved incremental modifications of existing programs. For one thing, government assistance to the aged was a well-established program. This made a medical-care program for the aged more likely to pass. Furthermore, it was set up as an insurance program, in which benefits become an "earned right" based on previous payments into the social-security program. This too was in line with past practices. In this way medicare became an extension of the social-security laws. It was a major step, but it was by no means a comprehensive program for medical care.

But one thing must be noted about incremental changes. Over time a number of small steps can add up to a comprehensive change. The supporters of federal medical assistance would have preferred a broader program. They supported the narrower one because its passage was possible by 1965 and because they felt it was a basis on which further small steps could be taken toward a comprehensive program. Each incremental step becomes a takeoff point for the next. And indeed the AMA shared this perspective, though its evaluation of the situation was much more negative. For the AMA the medical-care program for the aged was a cause of concern because it was a "foot in the door" for comprehensive medical care.

THE ACTORS IN MEDICAL-CARE LEGISLATION

Who were the major actors in this long history of medical-care legislation? In terms of impact the issue of medical costs touches everybody. Of course such expenses are a greater burden for poorer families. However, it was not just the very poor for whom medical care was a burden, for they could often get treatment in free clinics. The burden fell just as heavily on middle-income families, particularly when major illnesses hit them. And above all, medical costs were a major burden on the aged. Medical needs soar in one's later years, just when one's income is declining.

The Public at Large   For a number of years public-opinion polls had found the American people in favor—usually by two to one—of government health insurance plans, despite the AMA's campaign against them. But this public support can be thought of as only a vague and general pressure on the government. Much more is needed to carry a new social program through Congress.

The Aged: A Noncohesive Group   Interestingly enough, even after the issue began to focus on medical care for the aged there was little direct involvement of the aged as a cohesive group. There were some organizations associated with the aged—senior citizens' councils, golden-age clubs—but these were small compared with the major lobbying groups such as the AMA. This illustrates a generalization presented earlier—it's hard to get organized pressure from "consumer" groups. Although the aged were major consumers of medical services and would be greatly helped by this legislation, they did not represent a self-conscious and organized group.

Interest Groups   The major public actors were organized interest groups. The proponents included the AFL-CIO, other labor unions, and charitable organizations. The opponents were led by the AMA and included the American Hospital Association, the Life Insurance Association of America, and other more general organizations like the National Association of Manufacturers and the U.S. Chamber of Commerce. It was these organizations—because they were *organized*—who could carry on the battle, particularly in Congress.

But notice one major imbalance between the organizations that favored the medical-care program and those that opposed it. Those that favored it were well-organized and powerful groups such as the AFL-CIO. But these were organizations for whom medical care was only a side issue. Labor unions, after all, have many other purposes and are more directly involved in such matters as wages and labor conditions. When it comes to wages, the unions are *producers* of services; when it comes to medical expenses, they are *consumers*. And since citizens and groups become more active in relation to their interests as producers than as consumers, the unions are likely to be more effective and active on wage policy than on medical policy.

The contrast with the opponents of medical insurance is striking.

The opponent groups were led by the organizations representing the major producers of medical treatment—the AMA and the American Hospital Association. The Life Insurance Association of America was also involved as a producer, since medical-insurance programs would compete with private insurance. The involvement of these groups was much more intense and steady. And they were involved in many ways. For one thing, they claimed the special status of producer groups—the status of experts. In addition, the AMA conducted a long campaign to persuade the public that medical insurance was "un-American." In this way the debate rose to a more general level.

The AMA had several advantages. It was well financed. Medical problems were its main concern. And it could mobilize much of its membership. The nature of its membership is important. Doctors are members of a highly respected profession; they are spread throughout the country; and they are likely to be important citizens in their localities—just the kind of constituency to catch the attention of members of Congress.

The Presidency If the battle had been between the interest groups alone, the stalemate might never have been broken. But there were other important actors in the White House and in Congress. Much of the pressure for medical-care legislation came from the Presidency. Truman made medical insurance one of his major legislative goals. In this he had the support of some influential members of Congress, such as Senator Robert Wagner of New York, who introduced some of the major bills. Truman did not succeed. His program was blocked by a hostile congressional coalition of Republicans and conservative Democrats. But his support kept the prospects of medical insurance alive.

During the Eisenhower years the program had little White House support. But it came alive again under President Kennedy and culminated with the medicare bill under President Johnson. Without the strong push from the White House, no progress would have been made.

Government Specialists In this process a key role was played by the government specialists who shaped the legislation. Officials of the Federal Security Agency—people like Wilbur J. Cohen and I. S. Falk—had worked on medical-care problems for years. Over the years they had become the leading administrative spokesmen at congressional committee hearings. They played a major role in drafting the legislation and adjusting it in ways that would make it acceptable to Congress.

Congressional Committees As with tax legislation, the crucial arena for medicare legislation was Congress, or, rather, the relevant congressional committees. The two powerful committees in this case, as in the tax case, were the House Ways and Means Committee and the Senate Finance Committee, with the House committee and its chairman, Wilbur Mills, playing a major role. The annual hearings before this committee were the main public battleground in the war over medical insurance. It was here that the various interest groups testified. It was here that legislation would have to be initiated if it was to be successful in the House of Representatives.

The situation points up a key paradox of Congress' representative role. Congress is the institution that is most capable — in principle — of representing the views of the public: Its members are elected from all parts of the country; they consider themselves representatives of their constituents; and unlike the independent regulatory commissions, they have broad constituencies. Each member of Congress represents many interests in his or her district, and all the members together represent a wide range of citizens and groups. Thus Congress should be able to make policy according to the public's wishes.

But the organization of Congress is such that it rarely acts as a body. Rather, the key role is played by particular committee members. In 1961 President Kennedy, who favored a medical-insurance program, had a Democratic majority in Congress. But this majority was, as is often the case, not enough to push through a legislative program. It included many conservative southern Democrats, who often joined the Republicans in opposition to the administration. It was only when Representative Mills decided to support the medicare plan that it was passed. In his change of mind the public did play a role — though indirectly. The landslide victory of Lyndon Johnson in 1964 brought with it both a larger Democratic majority and an apparent demand from the people for some new legislation. "By changing from opponent to manager [of the medicare bill], Mills assured himself control of the content . . . at a time when it might have been pushed through the Congress despite him."[1]

CONCLUSIONS ON THE MEDICARE ISSUE

Of course, as we have seen from other legislative areas, what may really count is not the decision to enact legislation but the details of how that legislation is written and applied. And in working out these details Representative Mills "called on committee members, HEW officials, and interest group representatives to lend their aid in drafting a combination bill."[2] In this way interest groups like the AMA — though they may have lost the overall battle against the legislation — did have some influence in the writing of the bill. For instance, one of the effects of the bill has been a large increase in the income of doctors, primarily because the bill did not define what it meant by "reasonable charges." The result has benefited doctors, since they define that term as they wish.

[1] Theodore R. Marmor, "The Congress: Medicare Politics and Policy," in Allan P. Sindler, ed., *American Political Institutions and Public Policy* (Boston: Little, Brown, 1969), p. 53.
[2] Ibid., p. 52.

What can be said about the actors in the medicare issue? For one thing, it shows that no one is all-powerful. The AMA did not have its way; it would have preferred no legislation. The President— even when he had a majority of the same party in Congress, as Truman and Kennedy did—could not push through the legislation he wanted. The public, though according to the polls it favored some sort of medical-insurance program, was unable to make Congress act.

If any institution appeared to be all-powerful, it was perhaps the House Ways and Means Committee and its chairman. But even he was movable when the forces changed. And he would probably not have held out against a medical program as long as he did if he had not had the support of the AMA.

Yet the political efficacy of an organization like the AMA cannot be denied, particularly when it has powerful allies at strategic points in Congress. Such a combination can be a powerful force, especially when it is dedicated to holding the line against innovation. It is true that a bill was ultimately passed despite the objections of the AMA. But it held the line for a long time. Germany had a health insurance program in 1883!

Furthermore, by holding the line it also played a major role in setting the agenda of the debate on medical care. The bill that was passed was still quite limited, at least compared to other, more comprehensive plans that had been proposed. And this limitation was largely due to the belief—probably correct—among the proponents of medical insurance that nothing more extensive could be passed. In this sense the anti-medical insurance forces remained strong even when they seemed to have been defeated.

Medicare represented an incremental change in the government's involvement in health insurance. And as such it becomes the basis for the next step. The next step is likely to be a more comprehensive national health insurance program. A number of competing plans are currently under consideration. The AMA no longer opposes all such programs. Rather, the debate is on what kind of program—how comprehensive? paid for in what way? run by whom? These are not minor questions. As we have stressed, the details of a policy may be more important than its overall goals. But as one observer has put it, the issue is no longer "whether" but "what kind of" program to enact.

Desegregation of the Public Schools

The process of policy making on school desegregation differs from medical-care policy in one important way: The major consumers of medical services, who would benefit from new laws—the aged and their organizations—were not major actors in pushing for legislative action. The major "consumers" of education, who would benefit from desegregated schools—blacks and organizations represent-

Court enforced busing is the latest in a long line of policies designed to racially integrate public schools.

ing them — were major actors. In particular, the National Association for the Advancement of Colored People (NAACP) was important in pushing for change. This difference helps us understand the conditions under which groups can play a major role in the policy process. The aged do not form a cohesive and self-aware group. They are probably more divided by other social characteristics — religion, place of residence, race, income level — than they are united by their age. Blacks, on the other hand, though they are by no means a fully cohesive and organized group, have a greater basis for cohesion and organization. They have a common history, tend to live in racial neighborhoods, and throughout American history have suffered a special deprived status.

THE ROLE OF THE SUPREME COURT

Segregation in public schools was formally adopted as policy by about twenty states in the 1890s. State law explicitly declared that white and nonwhite pupils had to attend separate schools. Such laws — as well as many other laws requiring segregation in the use of public facilities — were coupled with legislation limiting black participation in politics. And these undercut any improvement in the status of blacks since the Civil War.

The laws requiring segregation in the schools were challenged in the Supreme Court as violating the equal-protection clause of the Fourteenth Amendment. But in 1896, in a famous 7–1 decision — *Plessy* v. *Ferguson* — the Supreme Court held that the Constitution did not bar separate schools as long as they were equal. The "separate-but-equal" doctrine was to be the law of the land for decades.

But as we have seen, the mere statement of a policy — even by a government body as respected and powerful as the Supreme Court — does not automatically put it into effect. To see what the policy means, one has to observe how it works in practice. In connection with the separate-but-equal doctrine, the Court's views went into effect only in part. The schools were indeed separate, but they were rarely equal. The "separate" doctrine was enforced, since that was the practice already and local officials were in favor of keeping the schools segregated. The "equal" doctrine was not enforced, because equal schools were costly, local officials were not really interested (since blacks had no political power, barred as they were from voting), and the Court had no way to check on the equality of facilities.

The Role of the NAACP   The first challenge to school segregation was led by the NAACP, an organization founded by a small group of educated blacks headed by W. E. B. DuBois shortly after the turn of the century. After attempting unsuccessfully to work through the legislative branch, the NAACP turned its attention to the courts. In Congress action could be stopped by a determined bloc representing the one-party, all-white politics of the southern states. The court was above such direct political pressures. Also, the wording of the Fourteenth Amendment, declaring that no state could "deny to any person within its jurisdiction the equal protection of the laws," seemed inconsistent with the practices of the southern states—though the Court had not yet ruled that way.

The NAACP's appeals through the courts followed the by now familiar incremental approach: trying to make step-by-step changes in the rules applying to segregation. At first they challenged the equality of the schools. In 1938 the Supreme Court ruled that the State of Missouri was not giving black students equal education by providing scholarships to an out-of-state law school, there being only an all-white law school in Missouri.[3] Equal education required that the state open a law school for blacks within Missouri. Note that the Court allowed for a separate school but was beginning to enforce equality.

In 1950 the Court went further, saying that separate law schools —one for each of the races—were inadequate. Their very separateness made them unequal.[4] In 1954 the Supreme Court handed down its landmark Brown decision: that segregation in the public schools led to unequal treatment of pupils and was unconstitutional.

The movement by the Court to the school desegregation decision was an incremental one. It dealt first with the issue of equality, only later with separation. It ruled first on graduate schools—not as hot an issue as the public schools—and only later on the public schools. And the school desegregation decision itself, with its call for "all deliberate speed" and allowances for delays in carrying out specific plans, certainly fits the incremental mold.[5]

The role played by the NAACP through the Supreme Court shows how a group can bypass the legislative branch of the government. The Court acted where Congress was unable or unwilling to

[3] Missouri ex rel. *Gaines* v. *Canada* 305 U.S. 337 (1938).
[4] *Sweatt* v. *Painter* 339 U.S. 629 (1950).
[5] *Brown* v. *Board of Education* 347 U.S. 483 (1959).

act. But a group that wants to do this needs many resources. For one thing, it has to be able to make a constitutional case. Without the Fourteenth Amendment, the NAACP would not have gotten far with this tactic. Another thing it needs is a lot of time and effort. The constitutional road is a long one; cases have to be carefully prepared and argued up from the lower courts. The NAACP's success took many decades of steady work. Finally, it needs a great deal of skill. The NAACP had this in a competent group of lawyers led by Thurgood Marshall, who later became the first nonwhite justice of the Supreme Court.

Our analysis of what happens to general statements of law—by Congress or by the courts—should warn the reader that the battle for equal schooling did not end with a statement by the Supreme Court that segregated schools are unconstitutional. Administration of the program was turned over to local school districts and to the states—all under the supervision of the federal courts. But, as with the regulation of business, this meant in effect that those who carried out the law were those who were to be regulated. After all, the local school districts and the states had been carrying out the segregation laws. These local districts dragged their feet, helped by the state legislatures in the South, which found various ways to block court-ordered desegregation. The result was that a decade after the Court decision less than 2 percent of black children in the South were attending integrated schools.

The slowness is in part a result of the separation of powers in America. Although the Supreme Court can interpret the Constitution and such interpretations are the "supreme law of the land," the power to enforce that law lies in the states and localities. They can effectively block federal action, especially if that action is a decision of the Supreme Court that is not backed up by the other branches of the federal government.

President Eisenhower had used the U.S. Army to keep Governor Orville Faubus of Arkansas from blocking the court-ordered integration of Little Rock High School, and in that way he had thrown the executive power behind the Supreme Court. But Eisenhower never spoke out directly on the issue of segregation and never pressed for legislation to follow up the Supreme Court's ruling. And Congress was inactive as well.

Progress toward ending legal segregation had to wait until other parts of the federal government could take action. Kennedy put his administration behind a bill enforcing school desegregation, and so did Johnson—with more force and success. The Civil Rights Act, sponsored by the Johnson administration, was passed in 1964. This Act put the power of the executive branch behind integration. The attorney general was given the power to initiate desegregation suits if asked to do so by local residents; the Office of Education had the power to survey the extent of segregation in a district. The federal government could thus become a powerful offset to local authorities.

TABLE 19.4
Percentage of Black Pupils Attending Schools That Are More Than 95 Percent Black

Chicago	85%
Baltimore	76%
Washington, D.C.	89%
Los Angeles	78%
Mobile, Alabama	85%
Nationwide	61%

Source: U.S. Department of Health, Education and Welfare.

DE FACTO DESEGREGATION—A MAJOR ISSUE

With federal support more progress was made toward ending de jure segregation in the South. But this of course did not end school segregation. What was becoming clear in the 1960s was that school segregation was only partly due to state law. By the 1970s there was more segregation in the North than in the South, because in the North segregated schools were a result of the segregated residential patterns that had evolved in northern cities over the decades. (See Table 19.4.)

De facto segregation may turn out to be harder to handle than de jure segregation. For one thing, it is deeply rooted in the social structure and geographic layout of American cities. School integration requires either a change in residential patterns—a long-term and difficult process—or large-scale busing of children. On the busing issue large groups of people, both black and white, tend to become emotional.

Unlike most of the issues we have been discussing, school desegregation has not been turned into a disaggregated issue. In America, as pointed out earlier, many policies are disaggregated; a policy is made to benefit a specific constituency—the railroads, say, or a particular type of farmer—without at the same time considering its effect on other groups in society. Such policy making produces little opposition because the benefits given to one group are not seen by others as costing them anything.

Matters of school desegregation, particularly those that involve busing, often involve direct conflict between those who favor integrated schools and parents who see busing as a direct cost to them. A policy seen as beneficial to blacks is seen as costly to some whites. Under such circumstances the number of relevant political actors increases. Disaggregated issues tend to be decided quietly; issues that involve clashes among constituencies are noisier. The press plays a major role too, since open conflict becomes news.

The courts are active, sometimes closely supervising the desegregation of the schools through busing. Local and state governments are active, since both levels have a role in education. The federal government is involved. Congress has tried to limit the use of federal educational funds for busing, a position that may put it at odds with the Supreme Court. And within the local community many parents and community leaders are active on each side.

In short, it is a policy with many, many actors. Out of such a conflict may come social change, but it is unlikely to come smoothly.

Energy Policy

President Nixon told the American people that "we must . . . face up to a very stark fact. We are heading toward the most acute shortages of energy since World War II." In an earlier chapter we quoted President Ford's comments to a world energy conference: "It is difficult to discuss the energy problem without unfortunately lapsing into doomsday language. Exorbitant prices can only distort the world economy, run the risk of worldwide depression and threaten the breakdown of world order and safety." President Carter's first major message to the nation declared the energy crisis to be "the moral equivalent of war."

Our last three Presidents have put the weight of the executive branch behind a comprehensive energy policy. But no such policy has emerged. There are many reasons for this. One is the sheer complexity of the problem. Second, until 1977 there was no executive agency fully in charge of energy policy. Third, Congress, under pressure from dozens of different constituencies, has picked apart every presidential attempt to formulate a comprehensive policy. Fourth, when it comes to energy policy the power of particular interests in America, and abroad, is awesome. And these interests are not in accord.

ENERGY: A COMPLEX ISSUE

A lot of factors make energy an unusually complex policy problem. Here we will concentrate on only three of those factors.

First, there is no way to separate the so-called energy issue from a broad range of economic-policy questions. American society is currently trying to find a way out of an economic condition that is frequently defined as *stagflation*, a stagnant economy with high unemployment and inflation taking place at the same time. An energy policy that conserved gasoline by imposing a high user tax would contribute to higher gas prices and therefore to inflation. An energy policy that emphasized the use of imported oil would be said to "export jobs" and therefore to contribute to unemployment. In these simple examples we see that energy policy cannot be formulated simply on its own terms but must be coordinated with a host of other policies designed to bring price inflation and unemployment under control.

Second, energy is neither a domestic nor a foreign-policy question. It is both. While this is also true of other policy questions, the energy crisis is particularly well suited to illustrate the complexity of policies that must take into account an uncertain international environment and a great many pressures and demands from domestic interest groups. For instance, the oil-producing nations of the Middle East increased the price of crude oil from $2.59 a barrel to $11.65 a barrel *in one year*, an increase of 350 percent. The Arab countries also used an oil embargo in late 1973 to pressure the industrial nations, heavy oil importers, to side with the Arab countries against Israel. The price increases and the embargo led the Nixon administration to declare Project Independence, a program intended to make the United States self-sufficient in energy sources by 1980. Project Independence, in turn, had many domestic ramifications, including conservation measures such as lowering

speed limits and production measures such as emphasis on nuclear power. Although Project Independence failed as a specific policy, many of the energy measures put into effect then continue to affect both internal and international politics today.

Third, energy policy has found itself surrounded by and often in serious conflict with another major policy thrust of the 1970s: environmental protection. Governments at the federal, state, and local levels have been making a determined effort to clean polluted water and air, preserve and expand open spaces, and protect ecologically vulnerable areas. Strong public-interest pressure groups such as the Sierra Club and the Wilderness Society have scored notable successes in forcing the enaction of environmental-protection laws. As energy policy began to be fashioned in the 1970s, it immediately confronted strong opposition from the environmentalists on such issues as offshore oil drilling, easing of automobile exhaust-emission standards (which led to about 5 percent increase in gas consumption), and nuclear power plants.

THE MANAGEMENT PROBLEM

When the pressures for an energy policy mounted in the mid-1970s it was quickly discovered that energy matters had no natural organizational home in the government. There was no single executive agency to provide leadership. There was no committee in either the House or the Senate where expertise in this area was concentrated. Thus the problem of what to do was compounded by the problem of who was to do it.

In late 1973 President Nixon and his advisers drafted an Emergency Energy Act, sending it to Congress with the urgent request that it be acted upon immediately. Among other things, this legislation provided for a Federal Energy Administration in the executive branch that would centralize energy policy making and implementation in the White House. The FEA was established in 1974, though Nixon's general policy plan did not escape the congressional process unscathed. Also established in 1974 was the Energy Research and Development Agency (ERDA), which over the next several years was to contract for millions of dollars' worth of research seeking to discover new sources of energy.

Nixon and his successor, Ford, made do with the two major executive agencies formed in 1974, but still found it difficult to bring together all the pieces of an energy policy. On taking office in early 1977 President Carter decided that even more coordination and centralization was necessary. Besides, he wanted the energy issue to have maximum visibility.

The Department of Energy   Carter, with congressional approval, established a Department of Energy. This new department brought together two major executive agencies that had been established by Nixon in 1974 in response to the initial energy crisis. It also incor-

Many hope that solar energy will reduce our dependence on oil and coal.

porated the Federal Power Commission, which since 1920 has had authority over electricity and natural gas.

The new department also picked up pieces of the energy puzzle that had been scattered across dozens of other executive agencies. For instance, federal coal policies had been the responsibility of five different bureaus within the Interior Department. The Department of Defense had its piece of the puzzle as well, being responsible for emergency oil reserves. Efficiency standards for home heating were under the authority of the Department of Housing; oil pipeline regulations were administered by the Interstate Commerce Commission; and other aspects of energy policy were being made by the Department of Transportation and the Securities and Exchange Commission. There was hardly an executive agency that did not have some say in energy policy.

It might be thought that the presence of a well-financed and strongly run new executive department would be able to get a comprehensive energy policy through Congress. At least in its first year, nothing of the sort happened. The Carter administration found Congress just as difficult to deal with on energy policy as the Ford and Nixon administrations had in earlier years.

PRESIDENTIAL INITIATIVE, CONGRESSIONAL RESPONSE

The history of energy policy in recent years underlines the important lesson that we learned in our discussion of the executive and legislative branches. Though the President has the edge when it comes to initiating complex and comprehensive policies, Congress has the last word. And thus far the "last word" has led to only piecemeal attempts to deal with energy issues.

Back in 1973 Nixon requested congressional approval of broad executive authority to reduce energy consumption through a series of measures, including the power to ration gasoline and oil, to lower speed limits, to impose taxes on excessive energy uses, and to exempt certain industries from controls imposed by the environmental-protection laws.

The Nixon proposals quickly got bogged down in Congress. The opposition was led by Senator Henry Jackson, who assumed the role of protector of consumer interests. Jackson, a Democrat with White House ambitions of his own, feared that Nixon would use such a broad grant of authority to benefit the oil industry. Three factors fed this fear: (1) Nixon was the beneficiary of substantial campaign contributions from oil executives in 1972—$82,000 from Standard Oil of California, $23,000 from Texaco, $36,000 from Standard Oil of Indiana, and more. (2) Nixon seemed to favor the suspension of antitrust and conflict-of-interest rules that would keep oil industry representatives out of the direct management of new government programs; (3) Jackson felt that oil industry lobbyists were directly involved in formulating administration proposals, commenting at one time to the press that "I can't distinguish the White House position from the oil industry's position."

Jackson argued that the administration's proposals would allow huge windfall profits for the oil industry, an argument that was supported by figures showing that oil companies were making profits of about 20 percent at the time, well above those of manufacturing as a whole. He insisted that any emergency energy act include a rollback on oil prices or provision for a tax on windfall profits. Jackson's view prevailed in Congress, and the bill sent to the White House directed the President to reduce the per-barrel price of domestic crude oil.

Nixon vetoed the bill, associating himself with the oil industry's claim that a price rollback "would only have aggravated the energy shortage by reducing the domestic oil supply and would have eventually resulted in higher prices . . . Congress should join the President in junking price concepts . . . and write [a bill] that lets free markets work to increase the energy supply."[6]

The sense of urgency drifted away as the Arab oil embargo ended and gasoline became more plentiful. No comprehensive energy plan emerged from the Nixon administration, which was soon busy defending itself against the many charges and investigations growing out of Watergate. President Ford inherited the same energy problems that Nixon had faced, but his two years in the White House produced only a few modest proposals.

Carter was determined to be more vigorous. But he too encountered a difficult Congress. A year after he had announced his comprehensive energy policy and established the Department of Energy, he was still waiting for congressional action. It is not that Congress failed to consider energy policy. It was simply that Congress could not decide how to choose among difficult and complex alternatives. Both Congress and the White House find themselves under intense cross-pressure from well-organized and forceful interest groups.

ORGANIZED INTERESTS

Energy policy, or the lack of it, has such a pervasive influence on American life that it is difficult to find an organized interest that does not have a hand in the policy pie. Automobile manufacturers want less restrictive pollution standards. Bird watchers want natural habitats protected. Truckers want higher speed limits. Friends of Israel want less cooperation with Arab oil producers. Multinational oil companies want tax credits for taxes paid abroad. Consumers want lower fuel prices. Environmentalists want strict controls on strip mining. Depressed areas want the jobs that nuclear power plants would provide.

[6] From an editorial in the *Oil and Gas Journal*, the official publication of the American Petroleum Institute, as cited in Harmon Zeigler and Joseph S. Olexa, "The Energy Issue," in Robert L. Peabody, ed., *Cases in American Politics* (New York: Praeger, 1976), p. 201.

Conflicting positions on the environment are taken by the lumber industry and public interest groups.

The list is endless, but two broad categories can be suggested. There is, on the one hand, a cluster of interests and organizations that believe that the best energy policy is to conserve what we have. There is, on the other hand, a cluster of interests and organizations that argue that aggressive development of energy sources is the solution to the energy crisis. Although many issues divide these two sets of interests, perhaps nothing is more illustrative of the differences than the issue of energy versus the environment.

Increasingly the goals of the environmental-protection movement are bumping up against economic realities. Offshore oil drilling, for instance, provides the United States with its best opportunity to reduce dependence on oil imports and to ease the energy shortage. It is estimated that nearly 200 billion barrels of oil may be recoverable—twice as much as the total produced from U.S. wells over the past century. The pressure to exploit this resource is intense. As John B. Connally, then Secretary of the Treasury, observed in 1972: "Let us start leasing, exploring, drilling, pipelining, shipping, refining and using more prudently the resultant clean energy this country needs to keep our people employed, our economy going, and our society alive and thriving." He is echoed by the powerful American Petroleum Institute, the oil industry's major trade association, as well as by numerous other business and manufacturing associations.

Lined up against the industrial interests are the environmentalists. They recall with bitterness the rupture of an oil well in the Santa Barbara channel in 1969. Thousands of barrels of oil blackened California beaches, killing birds and fish. Ecologists insist that the underwater and beach wildlife of the area has not yet returned to its pre-spill condition. The Santa Barbara oil spill stimulated the public concern that led to the National Environmental Policy Act, which was signed into law in 1970. This act requires federal agencies to assess the environmental impact of their decisions, including, of course, the granting of permission to explore for offshore oil.

Environmentalists have succeeded in halting or delaying millions of dollars' worth of projects. But economic interests are equally insistent. Thus after a long environmental fight oil and gas drilling off the coast of New Jersey began in 1978.

There will be no "final victory" in the ongoing battle between those who would sacrifice economic growth for environmental protection and those who would sacrifice environmental goals for more jobs or cheaper energy. The continuation of the battle itself is a major reason that President Carter, like those before him and no doubt those after him, may well find it impossible to fashion a truly comprehensive and coordinated energy policy.

Food Policy as Foreign Policy

It is increasingly difficult to maintain the distinction between "domestic policy" and "foreign policy." There is too much interdependence between what happens abroad and what happens at

Grain surpluses play a role in both domestic and foreign policies of the United States.

home. In the discussion of the energy crisis, for example, we saw that policy was shaped not only by what American political leaders wanted but also by what oil-producing nations demanded. Now we turn to another policy issue, food, and concentrate on its international dimensions.

To deal with food as a foreign policy issue seems odd at first. Isn't food policy really about how much farmers will earn when they grow wheat or fatten cattle, and how much the American family will have to pay for its bread and beef? Aren't the major actors the Department of Agriculture, the relevant committees in Congress, the various farmer organizations, the American consumers—typically thought of as part of the domestic political process, far removed from the State Department or the National Security Council?

Until the early 1970s considering agriculture and food strictly as part of the domestic political process was basically correct. Let us first review the agricultural policy of the pre-1970 period. Then we can see what changed it from a domestic issue into an international policy issue. Finally, we will look at the changes in the actors that are involved and in the issues that now constitute our food policy.

POLICY BACKGROUND

Agriculture policy centers on the production of grain—wheat, corn, soybean, rye, and so on. The American farmer has no difficulty growing enough grain to satisfy American appetites. Some of the grain is consumed directly in breads and cereals, but much of it is consumed indirectly. It is fed to the livestock that, in turn, puts meat on the dinner table.

The farmer's ability to provide enough, and even more food than is required for the American population, has traditionally caused an agricultural policy problem. This problem is overproduction. Producing food is not like producing manufactured goods. Whereas neither farmers nor manufacturers can anticipate the demand for their products, farmers cannot even predict how much they will produce because of the undependable nature of the weather. A late freeze or lack of rain can sharply decrease production. What are farmers to do in this uncertain environment? Planting against the prospect of poor growing conditions can lead to overproduction which drives crop prices down. Farmers find that they must sell their grain or their livestock for less than what it costs to produce them. This not only creates an economic hardship for farmers and in general for rural America, it also reduces the incentive for the farmers to grow grain in the future. This leads to grain shortages, thereby driving prices up and creating inflation and food shortages. Ultimately the American consumer suffers.

From the late 1940s to the early 1970s, the agriculture policy in the United States primarily dealt with the problem of grain surplus. The major features of this policy were: (a) payments made to farmers for not growing crops for which there was a surplus; (b) a complex system of price supports (known as the farm subsidies) that guaranteed a minimum price at which certain grains would be sold; (c) a program to subsidize the purchase of farm equipment in order to reduce the farmers' heavy investment in capital equipment; (d) a system of "target prices" in which direct payments were made to farmers in depressed markets.

None of these components of the agriculture policy were particularly foreign or international in conception or implication. They were hammered out by agriculture committees in Congress, by the Department of Agriculture, and by various interest groups representing farmers and large purchasers of farm products.

The only part of agriculture policy in the pre-1970 period that was directly international was the Food for Peace program. Under this program, the United States gives away a part of its grain surplus to other nations. For example, the government purchases approximately 20 percent of the U.S. rice crop and distributes it to nations around the world.

THE "FOOD CRISIS" OF THE 1970s

Several things began to happen in the late 1960s and early 1970s that transformed agriculture policy from a domestic issue to an issue mixing domestic and international interests. The most dramatic event was a severe drought-caused food shortage in many undeveloped nations of the world, leading to sickness and starvation in the Indian subcontinent and in the sub-sahara regions of Africa. As many as a billion persons were threatened with starvation. There was immense moral pressure on the food-producing nations, especially the United States, to shift their surplus food to the needy nations of the world. But this kind of shortage was only the most visible part of the international food problem.

The sharp increase in oil prices from the Middle Eastern nations, as discussed in an earlier section, had direct implications for food production and prices. First, it raised the price of oil-based fertilizers that are essential for massive crop yields. Second, it increased the costs of running mechanized farms that produce the greater amounts of grain and livestock. The end result was to increase the cost of grain in the world market beyond the financial resources of less developed nations. Since the wealthier nations of Western Europe and Japan were able to buy the grains at the higher prices, thereby sustaining the high market, the poorer nations were forced out of the market, adding severely to the food shortages they already experienced due to drought conditions.

U.S. FOOD POLICY IN THE 1970s

The production and distribution of food became major international issues in the 1970s. In the middle of these issues stood the United States, which had, because of its productivity, a dominant position in world agriculture. A few figures illustrate this dominance. The United States exports about 40 percent of its crop, enough to feed a quarter of the world's population one meal a day. Over 50 percent of all grain that is traded in the world comes from American farms. To be more specific: 70 percent of the grain used to feed the people and livestock of Israel comes from the United States; 60 percent of what Japan consumes comes from the United States; and even our "enemy," the Soviet Union, obtains about eight percent of its grain from American farmers. This dependence on U.S. farm products also exists in many other nations of the world.

When one nation is dependent upon another nation for the supply of something as critical as food, the supplier is tempted to use its position to meet its foreign policy objectives. Such has been the case for the United States. In the last decade, the "political" use of food has become part of the foreign policy process. One clear example has been the grain sales to the Soviet Union. In 1972, for example, the United States committed more than 30 percent of its wheat crop to the Soviet Union at prices well below the market. Selling cheap grain to the Soviet Union was part of the larger policy of detente with the Soviet Union formulated by the foreign policy advisors to President Nixon.

Another example is the Food for Peace program that, increasingly, has been directed to U.S. military allies, whether or not they were in need of food. In the early 1970s approximately 70 percent of the food distributed under the Food for Peace program went to South Vietnam and Cambodia. The governments of these nations used at least some of the food for military purposes, sometimes selling it in order to have cash to supply their armies. This arrangement was tolerated by the United States as part of the Vietnam War effort.

Exporting food also became part of the foreign economic policies of the United States. As early as 1971, the Nixon administration abandoned certain price supports for farm products. In addition, the government ceased to maintain grain reserves. It was thought that increased demand for American grown food in the world market would be adequate incentive for farmers to produce more, and the overproduction problem would be solved by exporting greater

United States' food helps feed many nations around the world and thereby becomes part of international power politics.

amounts of grain. Of course, it was recognized that this might lead to rapid price increases. It could also lead to fluctuations in supply and potential shortages, which might in turn cause havoc in the economies of nations dependent upon the United States for food. The federal government pledged to monitor grain sales by American farmers and grain traders in the world market in order to minimize any disruptive consequences of this change in policy.

ACTORS IN AGRICULTURAL POLICY

As agricultural policy began to be viewed as part of U.S. foreign policy, the agencies and interest groups involved in making policy changed from the 1960s. Of course, the Department of Agriculture remained a key actor. It defined its role as protecting the welfare of the American farmer. The State Department, under Henry Kissinger, had a different, though not necessarily conflicting, set of goals: to use American grain to promote closer relations with the Soviet Union; to supply military allies; and to create economic dependency on the United States. Because these goals led to wider markets for the U.S. farmer, conflict with the Department of Agriculture was minimized. However, there were differences about how to ship grain to the Soviet Union and about the role of international grain reserves. Outside of government, interest groups did challenge the new food policies that were taking shape. Consumers and business groups, for instance, feared the inflationary consequences of rising food prices. Thus, two traditional Republican groups, farmers and business, opposed each other. President Ford was caught in this squeeze in 1974 and eventually had to cancel grain sales to the Soviet Union.

There were also citizen interest groups concerned about worldwide starvation. They fought for two things: first, more food to needy nations, irrespective of military or ideological alliances with the United States; second, less grain for feeding livestock and more grain going directly to poor nations. On neither count were the humanitarian groups very successful. Americans are accustomed to having meat with their meals. The American farmer helps to provide this by growing grain that is primarily useful as animal feed. For example, about 90 percent of the corn grown is used to feed livestock. Since only one pound of meat is produced from 20 pounds of grain, meat turns out to be an expensive way to provide energy and protein for a population. But even against the backdrop of threatened worldwide starvation, agricultural policy in the United States remained tied to beef, pork, and poultry. It was easier to modify domestic agriculture policy to satisfy international military and security goals than to modify it to accomplish humanitarian goals.

SUMMARY

This brief review of food policy during the 1970s indicates the difficulty of drawing a line between "domestic" policy and "foreign" policy. We already saw that energy policy also has both domestic and foreign dimensions. In the next section, we will see that the war in Vietnam began as a military and security policy but quickly became the subject of intense policy disputes within the United States. This blurring of the line between domestic and foreign policy is producing new organizational structures and interests in the policy process. Government agencies that traditionally concerned themselves primarily with international matters (i.e., the State Department) and those that concerned themselves mainly with domestic matters (i.e., the Department of Agriculture) now find themselves having to take into account a new range of conditions and interests. Foreign policy is less likely to be made at the international elite levels and more likely to be shaped by domestic pressure groups. And domestic policy will increasingly accommodate itself to the national security and foreign policy goals of the nation.

Policy Making in Foreign Affairs: Vietnam

If there was a crisis in American politics in the 1960s and early 1970s, the two issues on which it centered were race and Vietnam. Race, as we have shown, is a "naturally" divisive issue, particularly if one race sees benefits that are given to the other as directly harmful to it. Usually a war has just the opposite effect. In most cases wars have led to national unity, as was true of the two world wars. And even the Korean War, which did not have as much popular support as the world wars, did not lead to the kinds of stresses that grew out of the Vietnam War.

This is not a book about Vietnam. The histories of U.S. involvement in the Vietnam War will be written and rewritten, and we can only touch lightly on the complexities of that issue. But the history of policy making on Vietnam can tell us a lot about government policy making. Vietnam shows how foreign policy is made in "ordinary" times and how it is made in the unusual situation in which a foreign-policy issue has aroused major public controversy.

Vietnam policy under President Kennedy and during the first

years of the Johnson administration was made the way foreign policy is usually made—with little public or congressional attention. Vietnam policy after 1964 or 1965 was a much more public issue. Yet even then it took quite a while for Congress to get much control over Vietnam policy.

VIETNAM UNDER PRESIDENT KENNEDY

Roger Hilsman, a leading student of foreign policy and Kennedy's Assistant Secretary of State for Far Eastern Affairs has said: "Any discussion of the making of United States foreign policy must begin with the President."[7] Despite the power over foreign affairs that would seem to belong to Congress—based on its power to declare war and to appropriate funds, as well as on the power of the Senate to ratify treaties—foreign affairs has traditionally been the province of the President. He—or rather his administration—oversees day-to-day foreign affairs; only the executive branch has the expertise and information needed for foreign policy making. Nor have the powers of Congress limited the President. President Truman sent American troops to Korea without a congressional declaration of war or even a resolution supporting the move. And the American involvement in Vietman took place largely through a series of presidential decisions.

It would be a mistake, though, to consider the President a free agent when it comes to foreign policy. To begin with, policies, as we have seen, have a history. At any moment a President must make decisions in the light of what has gone on in the past. Thus when Kennedy took office in 1961 he inherited commitments made under Eisenhower to support the government of South Vietnam. As early as 1961 there were several hundred American military men in Vietnam working directly with the South Vietnamese government.

The President is limited in another way. He is very dependent on the foreign-policy bureaucracy. The bureaucrats do not make decisions on foreign policy—at least not the major ones—but they can structure the President's decisions by the advice they give him, by the information they control. In "ordinary" foreign policy making, such as Kennedy's policy on Vietnam before it became a public issue under Johnson, the major actors are the Presidency and the agencies that give the Presidency information: the State Department, the CIA, the military.

Thus in 1962, using information from the CIA on the needs of the South Vietnamese government, President Kennedy ordered an increase in American troops in Vietnam from a few hundred men to 12,000 men. The nature of this step is important. It was considered a limited response to a particular issue, not an open-ended commitment to preserve the South Vietnamese government at any cost. At least there is no evidence that the administration foresaw the bombings and the half-million Americans who would be fighting in

---

[7] Roger Hilsman, *The Politics of Policy Making in Defense and Foreign Affairs* (New York: Harper & Row, 1971), p. 17.

Vietnam within a few years. In this way it was an incremental policy, one that modified an earlier policy.

But Vietnam policy was also guided by an overall strategy based on the desire to keep communism from spreading. According to the "domino theory," the loss of South Vietnam would topple the other Asian nations. Thus Vietnam policy in the 1960s took the form of small incremental steps guided by an overriding concern not to "lose" South Vietnam.

The Role of Congress in Vietnam Policy The role of Congress during this era is easy to summarize: It was minimal. In 1961, 1962, and 1963 Congress had little to do with Vietnam. It was busy with other problems. Its first major involvement came in the summer of 1964, during President Johnson's first year in office. In response to a presidential request that came on the heels of an alleged attack by North Vietnamese gunboats on two American destroyers, Congress passed almost unanimously the so-called Tonkin Gulf resolution. It expressed support for the President in Vietnam and allowed him "to take all necessary measures to repel any armed attack against the armed forces of the United States and to prevent further aggression."

The event illustrates the relative roles of the President and Congress in foreign affairs. The fact that the President asked for such a resolution shows that there is some sharing of power over foreign affairs. Otherwise such support would not be needed. Yet the resolution shows how little sharing there was. The President, as well as many members of Congress, felt that the resolution was not necessary; the President already had the powers that the resolution gave him. In other words, congressional support was not a necessity but, rather, a way to strengthen the President's position.

In short, then, the actors on Vietnam policy until late 1964 or early 1965 were fairly limited. Policy was made in the White House; the major actors were the President and his close foreign-policy advisers in the State Department, the Department of Defense, on the White House staff, and on the National Security Council, and all based their decisions on information from the CIA and the military. It is not clear when the decision to make a long-term commitment in Vietnam was made. But many believe such a decision was made fairly early in 1964, before the Tonkin Gulf incident. If this is the case, it was made largely in the White House. If there was opposition—and there is some evidence that there was—it came from within the administration itself, not from outside.

VIETNAM UNDER PRESIDENT JOHNSON

The "second stage" of the Vietnam war dates from sometime in 1965. There were two changes from the earlier stage. For one thing, the American involvement grew steadily, culminating in 1968 with over a half-million American troops in Vietnam, large-scale bombings, and what is generally agreed to have been domination of the war effort by American troops. At the same time, Vietnam came to public attention. In 1964, when the American people were asked in a survey to name the most important problem facing the nation, 8 percent mentioned Vietnam. By 1966 that figure had risen to 46 percent, and during the late 1960s Vietnam was consistently mentioned as the most important problem facing the nation. And public expression was not limited to public-opinion polls. Some groups showed their concern in a growing number of protest marches and demonstrations.

Protest against the war also moved to the floor of the Senate, where Senators Fulbright, McGovern, Kennedy, and McCarthy came out against Vietnam policy. And in 1968 first McCarthy and then Kennedy entered the presidential primary races against President Johnson. The result was the President's withdrawal from the campaign.

Public involvement continued after President Nixon took office. Student protest reached a new high after the President sent troops into Cambodia, and congressional critics spoke out.

But in some ways things didn't change much. Vietnam exploded as an issue in America. Congress was aroused, and many members were critical; the public was concerned, and large groups became active in opposition. Yet the major way in which Vietnam policy was shaped — by the President on the basis of the advice of his staff — did not change much. They operated in a new environment where policy was under close scrutiny and constant attack, an environment quite different from that of the early 1960s. The President, however, remained what Hilsman has called the "ultimate decider."

Consider how the roles of the various actors changed in the years after 1965. The Tonkin Gulf resolution represented the high point of Senate backing of the President in Vietnam. From then on the Senate — or, rather, certain senators — became more critical. A series of public hearings in 1968 brought out information showing that the administration had not been candid and had used the Tonkin Gulf incident to take advantage of the Senate. Various resolutions were introduced in the Senate expressing disapproval of presidential policy, calling for withdrawal of troops, and the like. But in all of these attempts the Senate acted as a critic of presidential activity. It did not intervene directly in the process of decision making on Vietnam. It could embarrass the administration — and indeed such pressure may have been a major factor in Johnson's decision not to seek reelection. But it did not shape policy. Nor did Congress use its power over appropriations to limit the administration. Vietnam appropriations were criticized but usually passed.

There are many reasons for the relatively weak position of Congress when it comes to foreign policy. For one thing, the constitutional balance of power lies in the direction of the President. The President's role as Commander-in-Chief of the armed forces was the main basis for sending troops to Korea and Vietnam. Once such

commitments have been made, Congress is reluctant to deny the appropriations necessary to support the troops.

More important than constitutional power is the administration's greater ability to coordinate policy, to get information on foreign affairs, to present its position to the American people. The President controls the bureaucracy in the State Department, the Defense Department, and the CIA, as well as the large White House Staff. Congress has few such resources.

Foreign affairs is only one of the many subjects that members of Congress must deal with, and for all but a few it is not the most important. Senators and representatives, as we have pointed out, are, first and foremost, representatives of their states and districts; they know local needs and problems. But that knowledge is not very helpful in foreign affairs. Foreign affairs take time and win few local votes.

Pressure from Congress   This is not to argue that the growing congressional opposition to the war did not have an effect on the policy makers in the White House. They were aware of the pressure to end U.S. involvement in the war. They also felt great pressure from the public, seen in negative ratings in public-opinion polls as well as in large antiwar demonstrations like those that followed the invasion of Cambodia in 1970. But despite these pressures the major decisions on Vietnam, right up to the "Christmas bombing" decision of the Nixon administration on the eve of the ceasefire agreement, were made by the White House.

VIETNAM'S IMPACT ON FOREIGN POLICY

As long as the United States was directly involved in the Vietnam War, Congress complained but did little to change the course of U.S. policy. After direct American military involvement ended with the ceasefire at the beginning of 1973, Congress took a more active role. It explicitly limited the use of American military forces in Vietnam and Cambodia. In 1973 it passed, over the President's veto, a law setting a limit of sixty days on the ability of the President to commit U.S. forces abroad without the consent of Congress. (In the Korean and Vietnam Wars the President had committed troops without the consent of Congress.) Furthermore, Congress' previous habit of complaining about but going along with administration requests for aid to Vietnam ended in 1975, when it refused a large request for emergency aid. Shortly thereafter the Saigon regime collapsed.

Congress was able to take a more active foreign-policy role because of the weakness of the Presidency during the Watergate investigations and the revelation that the administration had misled Congress and the public about the bombing of Cambodia four years earlier. Nor did Congress limit its foreign-policy activity to Southeast Asia. It limited the aid that the President could give to Turkey after the Cyprus conflict; it limited U.S. aid to such countries as South Korea and Chile. And it set limits on the trade agreement that the Ford administration was negotiating with the Soviet Union. It opposed sending troops to a series of trouble spots in Africa: Angola, Zaire, Ethiopia.

This all caused Secretary of State Kissinger to complain: "The growing tendency for Congress to legislate in detail the day-to-day or week-to-week conduct of our foreign affairs raises grave issues." He wondered whether the United States could carry out an effective foreign policy if it could not speak with a unified voice. He argued that Congress should limit its involvement in foreign policy making so as to give the administration the flexibility and consistency that are needed in the making of foreign policy.[8]

Many members of Congress were sympathetic to this position. Congress is not organized to supervise the day-to-day operation of foreign policy, nor is it effective in making more general policy. The information and skills needed are more often located in the executive branch. But Congress was so dissatisfied with the administration that it seemed unlikely to return the powers that it had taken away.

[8] *New York Times,* January 25, 1975.

Epilogue

In physics every action produces a reaction. In politics things do not happen in such a neat and balanced way. Yet political trends often produce, or are accompanied by, countertrends. Politics in the 1970s has been characterized by both trends and countertrends. The trend has been toward more and bigger government that takes more and more responsibility for the character of life in the United States. The countertrend has been a sense of disillusionment with the government and a desire to reduce the extent to which it intrudes into the lives of citizens.

Clearly, this is a kind of action producing a reaction. The more that the government tries to accomplish, the greater the number of regulations and the higher the cost of operations. The revolt against big government in this decade has been a revolt against exactly this—intrusive regulations and high taxes. It is likely that the trend and countertrend that has emerged in the 1970s will set the political agenda of the 1980s.

One of the main themes of this book has been the growth of the government. We have seen the bureaucracy grow, the office of the President grow, and the staff of Congress grow. This too has been action and reaction. One part of the government grows in response to growth elsewhere. One of the main reasons for the growth of the presidential office has been the desire to control the vast bureaucratic apparatus. And the growth of congressional staffs represents an attempt on the part of Congress to maintain its competitive position with the executive branch.

The growth of government personnel in all branches is, in turn, the result of the growth in government programs. The 1970s however, were not the beginning of large-scale government. As we have seen, government regulation of the economy began earlier in the century. In the 1930s, the New Deal brought a commitment on the part of the government to further regulate the economy and to sustain the welfare of its citizens. Since then government programs have grown. As new problems are defined, they require government action and regulation. Energy and environment are two examples. In the 1960s and 1970s we discovered that energy resources were not unlimited; that what had been left to the free market required government intervention. Indeed, a new executive department, the Department of Energy, was created to coordinate government activities in that area. At the same time, we discovered that our environment was seriously in danger and that government intervention in the guise of antipollution regulations was needed to protect it. Here, too, a new agency, the Environmental Protection Agency, was created.

Interestingly, the goals of increasing energy resources and protecting the environment can conflict. Drilling for off-shore oil to get new energy, for instance, creates environmental dangers. And the government has to reconcile this conflict—this leads to even more government.

Another major source of growing government is different groups in society desiring and fighting for equal treatment. This has been one of the major themes of our book. Demands for equal treatment have come from all sorts of groups: women, racial and ethnic minorities, gays, the handicapped, and the aged. And they want equal treatment in a number of areas: in jobs, schooling, health care, and access to facilities. Each of these demands, if it is to be met, requires government intervention. For example, equal access to jobs or education leads to government programs that enforce such equality. One such program, affirmative action, has become a very controversial issue. And if medical care is taken out of the private sector—as it has been for older citizens through Medicare and as it may for all citizens if a more comprehensive program for national health insurance is passed—government will grow even more.

Big government has always had its critics. As government has grown, so has the criticism. In part, it is a public reaction to government failures. The Vietnam War and the Watergate episode which greeted this decade led to a disillusionment with the government. In addition, a number of programs were launched with glowing names such as The Great Society, the War on Poverty, and Model Cities. These programs often promised more than they could accomplish. Although they did some good, they fell short of society's expectations and this, too, created a sense of disillusionment. Furthermore, a number of problems arose in the seventies such as the combination of recession and inflation (called stagflation) that the government did not seem capable of solving.

The critics of large-scale government are found in many places. The Republican party and big business traditionally harbor opponents of big government. Other critics are "neo-conservative" intellectuals who believe that government regulation is inefficient and who prefer free market mechanisms as a way of dealing with social problems. Opposition to big government also has come from groups of citizens. In June, 1978, the California electorate approved Proposition 13 which set upper limits on property taxes. The anti-tax revolt that this represented spread, and there was talk of "Proposition 13 Fever." In the November, 1978 elections, similar propositions were approved in thirteen states. Political candidates have also been critics of big government. In the 1976 presidential election both candidates campaigned on anti big-government platforms, each arguing that the government ought to interfere less in the lives of its citizens. And in the 1978 midyear elections more and more candidates for Congress, for governorships, and for local office ran on anti-tax programs.

Does the backlash against big government mean that the regulation and social service programs of the twentieth century are about to be scrapped? Unlikely. The revolt of the taxpayers *is* a real phenomenon, but many government programs cannot easily be scrapped. The problems we face with energy resources and environmental protection, for instance, will not go away. Nor can they be faced and solved without government intervention. The demands of social groups for equal treatment are also not about to disappear. So the pressures for an activist government remain.

We cannot say that the public wants an end to active government entirely. The polls show that citizens are opposed to waste in government and believe that there is a lot of it. The public is also opposed to the cost of government which it believes is too high. But it is not opposed — indeed it supports — the social programs that the government carries out. On Election Day, 1978, the New York Times-CBS poll found that a majority of Americans favored a federal program for national health care as well as a law requiring a balanced federal budget. The public seems to be saying "spend less but continue to provide the services."

All this means that big government will remain with us, but it will be surrounded with controversy. Demand for service will remain high as will demand for less spending. Some groups will continue to fight for greater equality; others will oppose these demands if the costs are high, or if they require too much regulation, or if they mean that privileged positions will have to be abandoned.

Thus the need for big government and the pressures for more government intervention come at the same time as public disillusionment with government grows. The result is that government power may grow, yet its moral authority may weaken. Can these contradictory trends be reconciled? It is a question high on the political agenda of the 1980s.

Bibliography

Chapter 1   Government and Politics in a Democratic America

Basic works on government and politics extend, of course, over the entire history of mankind. Classics relevant to contemporary political life include Thomas Hobbes, *The Leviathan* (1651); John Locke, *Essay Concerning Human Understanding* (1690) and his *Two Treatises of Government* (1690); Karl Marx, *Capital: A Critique of Political Economy* (1887, 1907, 1909); John Stuart Mill, *On Liberty* (1859) and his *Considerations on Representative Government* (1861); and the writings of the German political sociologist, Max Weber. Particularly relevant essays appear in *From Max Weber: Essays in Sociology,* translated and edited by Hans H. Gerth and C. Wright Mills (New York: Oxford University Press, 1947).

More recent works useful for understanding some of the basic processes of government and politics include Karl W. Deutsch, *The Nerves of Government* (New York: Free Press, 1963); David Easton, *A Systems Analysis of Political Life* (New York: Wiley, 1965); Herman Finer, *The Theory and Practice of Modern Government,* rev. ed. (New York: Holt, Rinehart & Winston, 1949); Carl J. Friedrich, *Constitutional Government and Democracy: Theory and Practice in Europe and America* (Boston: Ginn, 1950); and Harold Lasswell, *Politics, Who Gets What, When, How* (New York: McGraw-Hill, 1936).

Studies with particular reference to American democracy are cited throughout the bibliography, and need not be repeated here.

Chapter 2   The Constitutional Framework

The Federalist, originally written as newspaper essays urging the adoption of the new Constitution, under the authorship of Alexander Hamilton, James Madison, and John Jay, remains the most lucid interpretation of various constitutional principles. See also Max Farrand, *The Framing of the Constitution* (New Haven, Conn.: Yale University Press, 1926). Charles A. Beard, in his famous *Economic Interpretation of the Constitution of the United States* (New York: Macmillan, 1913), attempts to show that economic interests of influential delegates to the Constitutional Convention explain many of the Constitution's provisions. For refutations of Beard's thesis, see Forest McDonald, *We the People: The Economic Origins of the Constitution* (Chicago: University of Chicago Press, 1958) and Robert E. Brown, *Charles Beard and the Constitution* (Princeton, N.J.: Princeton University Press, 1956).

Two useful works on American political ideas are Louis Hartz, *The Liberal Tradition in America* (New York: Harcourt Brace Jovanovich, 1955) and Richard Hofstadter, *The American Political Tradition* (New York: Knopf, 1951). Robert A. Dahl, *A Preface to Democratic Theory* (Chicago: University of Chicago Press, 1956) deals in a more formalistic way with certain key ideas in democratic thought, including the Madisonian formulations that so substantially influenced the Constitution.

A readable and informative account of the Constitutional Convention and of the battles over ratification is Catherine Drinker Bowen, *Miracle at Philadelphia* (New York: Bantam, 1968). This book would make excellent light reading as background to our discussion.

Chapter 3   The American Economy and Political Life

A classic work on capitalism and democracy is Joseph A. Schumpeter's *Capitalism, Socialism, and Democracy,* 3rd ed. (New York: Harper & Row, 1950). For a less favorable view of similar issues, written from a Marxist point of view, see Paul A. Baran and Paul M. Sweezy, *Monopoly Capital: An Essay on the American Economic and Social Order* (London: Pelican, 1968) and Ralph Miliband, *The State in Capitalist Society* (New York: Basic Books, 1969).

Three works by John Kenneth Galbraith provide useful perspectives on American economic society. These are *The Affluent Society* (Boston: Houghton Mifflin, 1958), *The New Industrial State* (Boston: Houghton Mifflin, 1967), and *Economics and The Public Purpose* (Boston: Houghton Mifflin, 1973). A more general statement about the transformation of the American economy can be found in Daniel Bell, *The Coming of the Post-Industrial Society* (New York: Basic Books, 1973).

To examine the U.S. economy in comparative perspective, see Charles E. Lindblom, *Politics and Markets* (New York: Basic Books, 1978.)

A textbook by Paul A. Samuelson provides not

only basic facts about the American economy but also lucid interpretation; see his *Economics*, 9th ed. (New York: McGraw-Hill, 1973).

Current statistics on government programs and expenditures can be found in various publications by the Office of Management and Budget and in publications of the Congressional Quarterly Service. See, for instance, the latter's *Federal Income Policy*, a background report on economic developments and legislation.

Chapter 4 Political Equality, Social Inequality

The classic treatment of American egalitarian values is Alexis de Tocqueville, *Democracy in America*, ed. Phillips Bradley, 2 vols. (New York: Knopf, 1945), a report of this perceptive Frenchman's visit to the United States in the 1830s. Perhaps the most convincing essay ever written on citizenship is that of T. H. Marshall, "Citizenship and Social Class," as reproduced in his *Class, Citizenship, and Social Development* (Garden City, N.Y.: Doubleday, 1964). The distinction between legal, political, and social-rights citizenship used in our chapter is drawn from this essay.

Morris Janowitz, in his *Social Control of the Welfare State* (Chicago: University of Chicago Press, 1976) advances the interesting argument that citizenship is being transformed under the conditions of the modern welfare state. For a pessimistic account about the future of citizenship freedoms in "planned democracies" see F. A. Hayek, *The Road to Serfdom* (London: Routledge & Kegan Paul Ltd., 1962).

The literature on equality in America is very large indeed. Useful data can be found in Christopher Jencks et al., *Inequality: A Reassessment of the Effect of Family and Schooling in America* (New York: Basic Books, 1972). A collection of critical essays is in Maurice Zeitlin, ed., *American Society, Inc.* (Chicago: Markham, 1970). A small book by Arthur M. Okun, *Equality and Efficiency: The Big Tradeoff* (Washington D.C.: The Brookings Institution, 1975) very nicely poses the dilemma that the title announces.

Chapter 5 Political Beliefs in America

Two classics about American political belief systems are Alexis de Tocqueville, *Democracy in America*, ed. Phillips Bradley, 2 vols. (New York: Knopf, 1945) and James Bryce, *The American Commonwealth*, 3d ed., 2 vols. (New York: Macmillan, 1899).

Gabriel A. Almond and Sidney Verba, *The Civic Culture: Political Attitudes and Democracy in Five Countries* (Boston: Little, Brown, 1965) views the political beliefs in America compared to other democracies. It is the source for the comparative information in this chapter and for the data on education and attitudes. An in-depth study of citizen attitudes on politics is in Robert E. Lane, *Political Ideology: Why the American Common Man Believes What He Does* (New York: Free Press 1962).

Two other major works on the American public are V. O. Key, Jr., *Public Opinion and American Democracy* (New York: Knopf, 1961) and Angus Campbell, Philip E. Converse, Warren E. Miller, and Donald E. Stokes, *The American Voter* (New York: Wiley, 1960). Both are sources for many specific items in this chapter. Good coverage of the beliefs of Americans is also found in Kenneth M. Dolbeare and Patricia Dolbeare, *American Ideologies* (Chicago: Markham, 1972). Seymour M. Lipset's *The First New Nation* (New York: Basic Books, 1963) discusses the evolution of distinctive American beliefs in a new nation.

Recent controversies as to the interpretation of popular opinion are contained in Philip E. Converse, "Public Opinion and Voting Behavior," in *The Handbook of Political Science*, vol. 4, eds. Fred Greenstein and Nelson W. Polsby (Reading, Mass.: Addison-Wesley, 1975).

For the sources of political beliefs in the process of socialization, see Richard Dawson, Kenneth Prewitt, and Karen Dawson, *Political Socialization* (Boston: Little, Brown, 1977) and Kent Jennings and Richard Niemi, *The Political Character of Adolescents* (Princeton, N.J.: Princeton University Press, 1974).

Chapter 6 Social Origins of Conflict

Two of the best books on the group bases of American politics are V. O. Key, Jr., *Public Opinion and American Democracy* (New York: Knopf, 1961) and Angus Campbell, Philip E. Converse, Warren E. Miller, and Donald E. Stokes, *The American Voter* (New York: Wiley, 1960).

For an historical interpretation of the reason for the absence of class based politics in American see Louis Hartz, *The Liberal Tradition in America* (New York: Harcourt Brace Jovanovich, 1955). For an argument that class still plays a role see Richard Hamilton *Class and Politics in the United States* (New York: Wiley, 1972).

For material on ethnicity in America, see Nathan Glazer and Daniel P. Moynihan, *Beyond the Melt-*

ing Pot 2nd ed. (Cambridge, Mass.: MIT Press, 1970) and Andrew M. Greeley, *Why Can't They Be Like Us?* (New York: Institute of Human Relations Press, 1969). Michael Novak's *The Rise of the Unmeltable Ethnics: Politics and Culture in the Seventies* (New York: Macmillan, 1971) deals with white ethnics.

On American blacks, see the classic by Gunnar Myrdal, *An American Dilemma: The Negro Problem and Modern Democracy,* 20th Anniversary Edition (New York: Harper & Row, 1962); Donald R. Matthews and James W. Prothro, *Negroes and the New Southern Politics* (New York: Harcourt Brace Jovanovich, 1966); and Talcott Parsons and Kenneth B. Clark, eds., *The Negro American* (Boston: Beacon Press, 1967).

Chapter 7   Political Participation in America
For a study of the participation of American blacks, see Donald R. Matthews and James W. Prothro, *Negroes and the New Southern Politics* (New York: Harcourt Brace Jovanovich, 1966) and Alan A. Altshuler, *Community Control: The Black Demand for Participation in Large American Cities* (New York: Pegasus, 1970).

For a consideration of participation in America in comparative perspective, see Gabriel A. Almond and Sidney Verba, *The Civic Culture: Political Attitudes and Democracy in Five Countries* (Boston: Little, Brown, 1965) and Sidney Verba, Norman H. Nie, and Jae-on Kim, *Participation and Political Equality: A Seven Nation Comparison* (New York: Cambridge University Press, 1978).

For a discussion of violence in American politics, see Jerome H. Skolnick, *The Politics of Protest,* Staff Report to the National Commission on the Causes and Prevention of Violence (New York: Ballantine Books, 1969) and Hugh Davis Graham and Ted Robert Garr, eds., *The History of Violence in America: A Report to the National Commission on the Cause and Prevention of Violence* (New York: Bantam Books, 1969).

Chapter 8   Leadership Recruitment and Political Power in the United States
Important theoretical commentary, as well as useful if now somewhat out-of-date data, on the process of political recruitment into top positions in the United States can be found in C. Wright Mills, *The Power Elite* (New York: Oxford University Press, 1956). Elaboration of certain themes appearing in this chapter can be found in Kenneth Prewitt, *The Recruitment of Political Leaders* (Indianapolis: Bobbs-Merrill, 1970) and in Kenneth Prewitt and

Alan Stone, *The Ruling Elites* (New York: Harper & Row, 1973). The idea of "skill revolutions" is developed by Harold Lasswell in *Politics: Who Gets What, When, and How* (New York: McGraw-Hill, 1936).

For recent information on blacks in political office see James E. Conyers and Walter L. Wallace, *Black Elected Officials* (N.Y.: Russell Sage Foundation, 1976); and on women see Jeane J. Kirkpatrick, *Political Woman* (N.Y.: Basic Books, 1974). The work of G. William Domhoff also contains both argument and data. See his *Who Rules America?* (Englewood Cliffs, N.J.: Prentice-Hall, 1967) and *The Higher Circles* (N.Y.: Random House, 1970). Also relevant is Thomas R. Dye, *Who's Running America?* (Englewood Cliffs, N.J.: Prentice-Hall, 1976).

Chapter 9   Interest Groups in America
The classic statement of the benefits of interest-group representation is David B. Truman, *The Governmental Process* (New York: Knopf, 1951). The counter position is well expressed in Grant McConnell, *Private Power and American Democracy* (New York: Knopf, 1966) and in Theodore J. Lowi, *The End of Liberalism* (New York: Norton, 1969). E. E. Schattschneider's *The Semi-Sovereign People* (New York: Holt, Rinehart & Winston, 1960) is a critical analysis of the pressure system in the United States. A critical summary of the theories of interest group politics is in J. David Greenstone, "Group Theories," in Fred Greenstein and Nelson Polsby eds., *The Handbook of Political Science.* vol. 2 (Reading, Mass.: Addison-Wesley, 1975).

A subtle theoretical statement relevant to the dynamics of organization is found in Mancur Olson, Jr., *The Logic of Collective Action: Public Goods and the Theory of Groups* (Cambridge, Mass.: Harvard University Press, 1965). Murray Edelman's *The Symbolic Uses of Politics* (Urbana: University of Illinois Press, 1964) is relevant for the kinds of interests that can be served by group activity.

Lester W. Milbrath's *The Washington Lobbyists* (Skokie, Ill.: Rand McNally, 1963) covers the activity of lobbyists. James Q. Wilson's *Political Organizations* (New York: Basic Books, 1973) is a sophisticated analysis of how organizations motivate their members to contribute and what makes some successful. Public interest lobbies are discussed in Andrew S. McFarland, *Public Interest Lobbies: Decision Making on Energy* (Washington, D.C.: American Enterprise Institute, 1976) and Jeffrey M. Berry, *Lobbying for the People* (Princeton N.J.: Princeton University Press, 1977).

Chapter 10   Political Parties

The standard reference work on American political parties is V. O. Key, Jr., *Politics, Parties, and Pressure Groups*, 5th ed. (New York: Crowell, 1964). This work includes a detailed treatment of party organization, the nominating process, campaign techniques, party finance, and related topics. It also includes some historical discussion. For additional historical treatment as well as analytic interpretation, see the collection of studies in William Chambers and Walter Burnham, eds., *The American Party Systems: Stages of Political Development* (New York: Oxford University Press, 1967).

For the argument that our political parties are not sufficiently programatic and responsible, see the thesis developed in E. E. Schattschneider, *Party Government* (New York: Holt, Rinehart & Winston, 1942). For further analysis on the same topic the treatment of Austin Ranney, *The Doctrine of Responsible Party Government* (Urbana: University of Illinois Press, 1956) is very helpful.

The thesis that American political parties will converge toward a "centrist" position is well developed in Anthony Downs, *An Economic Theory of Democracy* (New York: Harper & Row, 1957). James L. Sundquist, *Dynamics of the Party System* (Washington D.C.: Brookings Institution, 1973) comprehensively reviews the processes of change in the political party system in the United States. Robert R. Alford, *Party and Society* (Skokie, Ill.: Rand McNally, 1963) places the U.S. party system in comparative perspective.

Chapter 11   Elections in America

The major analysis of American voting behavior is in two publications of the Survey Research Center at the University of Michigan: Angus Campbell, Philip E. Converse, Warren E. Miller, and Donald E. Stokes, *The American Voter* (New York: Wiley, 1960) and, by the same authors, *Elections and the Political Order* (New York: Wiley, 1966).

More recent trends are discussed in Norman H. Nie, Sidney Verba, and John R. Petrocik, *The Changing American Voter* (Cambridge, Mass.: Harvard University Press, 1976).

Presidential nominations in William R. Keech and Donald R. Matthews, *The Party's Choice* (Washington, D.C.: The Brookings Institution, 1976), while campaign finance is the subject of Herbert E. Alexander, *Financing Politics: Money, Elections and Political Reform* (Washington, D.C.: *Congressional Quarterly*, 1976). For material on electoral realignments see James L. Sundquist, *Dynamics of the Party System: Alignment and Realignment of Political Parties in the United States* (Washington, D.C.: The Brookings Institution, 1973) Everett C. Ladd with Charles D. Hadley, *Transformations of the American Party System*, 2nd ed. (New York: Norton, 1978).

On the role of the mass media, see Sidney Kraus and Dennis Davis, eds., *The Effects of Mass Communication on Political Behavior* (University Park, Pa.: Pennsylvania State University Press, 1976).

Chapter 12   Congress: Representation and Legislation

A provocative book on Congress, very much in the muckraking tradition, is the Ralph Nader Congress Project report, *Who Runs Congress?* (New York: Bantam, 1972). A more balanced though still critical review appears in the collection of essays edited by Senator Joseph S. Clark, *Congressional Reform: Problems and Prospects* (New York: Crowell, 1965). This book ends with Clark's own recommendations for "making Congress work." Published in the same year are the solid, informative essays in David B. Truman, ed., *The Congress and America's Future* (Englewood Cliffs, N.J.: Prentice-Hall, 1965).

Much of the scholarly literature on Congress, of which there is a great deal, appears in journal articles. These are often collected in readers. For a representative selection of articles, see Robert L. Peabody and Nelson Polsby, eds., *New Perspectives on the House of Representatives* (Skokie, Ill.: Rand McNally, 1963) and Leroy N. Riselbach, ed., *The Congressional System* (Belmont, Calif: Wadsworth, 1970). Monograph studies of importance include Richard F. Fenno, Jr., *Congressmen in Committees* (Boston: Little, Brown, 1973) and David R. Mayhew, *Congress: The Electoral Connection* (New Haven, Conn.: Yale University Press, 1971).

More general treatments appear in Randall B. Ripley, *Congress: Process and Policy* (New York: Norton, 1975) and Gary Orfield, *Congressional Power: Congress and Social Change* (New York: Harcourt Brace Jovanovich, 1975), the latter including several case studies which illustrate how a law is made.

Publications of *Congressional Quarterly, Inc.*, provide up-to-date material on the organization of Congress and the legislative politics of particular policy questions. See especially the *CQ Guide to*

Current American Government, published twice a year. Congressional Quarterly, Inc., is located at 1414 22nd St., N.W., Washington, D.C., 20037.

Chapter 13   The Presidency
A useful general book is Clinton Rossiter's The American Presidency (New York: Harcourt Brace Jovanovich, 1956). Two books written in the 1960s that make a case for stronger Presidential leadership are James M. Burns, Deadlock of Democracy: Four-Party Politics in America (Englewood Cliffs, N.J.: Prentice-Hall, 1963) and Richard E. Neustadt, Presidential Power (New York: Wiley, 1960). It is said that both of these works were closely read by John Kennedy and may well have been the inspiration for his ambitions for the Presidency, as illustrated in the quotation that begins this chapter. A very telling critique of the Burns and Neustadt proposals can be found in Garry Wills, Nixon Agonistes: The Crisis of the Self-Made Man (Boston: Houghton Mifflin, 1969), which includes as well some fascinating interpretive discussions of what the election of Richard Nixon to the Presidency tells American society about itself.

Presidents and the Presidency have, of course, long fascinated observers. Many journalistic accounts have been written, and some of them contain rich descriptive material as well as sound analysis. Often, however, the reader will find that the preferences of the author color his perspective. The weaknesses as well as the strengths of such accounts appear in two highly readable books written about the Kennedy years: Theodore C. Sorensen, Decision-Making in the White House (New York: Columbia University Press, 1963) and Arthur M. Schlesinger, Jr., A Thousand Days (Boston: Houghton Mifflin, 1965). On the Johnson Presidency, see Robert D. Novack and Rowland Evans, Lyndon B. Johnson: The Exercise of Power (New York: New American Library, 1966), which includes a useful account of his first years in office, when he managed to put through Congress much domestic legislation, but stops short of the years when Vietnam dominated his administration. For Johnson's own account of his Presidency, see his The Vantage Point (New York: Popular Library, 1971).

Nixon's Presidency, especially the final segment concerning the Watergate affair, will be the topic of many books, both popular and scholarly. For an account of how two Washington Post reporters helped uncover Watergate see Carl Bernstein and Bob Woodward, All the President's Men (New York: Simon & Schuster, 1974). Arthur Schlesinger's The Imperial Presidency (New York: Popular Library, 1973) deals with the growth of Presidential powers and their potential for abuse. Finally, for spontaneous, unrehearsed commentary on the workings of the Nixon Presidency, directly from the oval office of the White House, see The Presidential Transcripts (various editions, 1974), the transcript of the White House tapes that led to Nixon's resignation.

Stephen Hess, Organizing the Presidency (Washington, D.C.: The Brookings Institution, 1976) makes an effective case for reorganization of the White House and the presidency more general. Useful collections of articles on the presidency appear in Norman C. Thomas, (ed.) The Presidency in Contemporary Context (New York: Dodd, Mead, 1975) and Thomas E. Cronin and Rexford G. Tugwell (eds.), The Presidency Reappraised, 2nd ed. (New York: Praeger, 1977).

Chapter 14   The American Bureaucracy
The issue of bureaucracy and democracy is covered in Frederick C. Mosher, Democracy and the Public Service (New York: Oxford University Press, 1968); Francis E. Rourke's, Bureaucracy: Politics and Public Policy (Boston: Little Brown, 1969) deals with the formation of the civil service and the idea of a nonpolitical bureaucracy. Harold Seidman's Politics, Position and Power: The Dynamics of Federal Organization, 2nd ed. (New York: Oxford University Press, 1974) places the bureaucracy in the framework of American government.

For a discussion of the way in which major policy is made involving the bureaucracy see Aaron Wildavsky, The Politics of the Budgetary Process, 2nd ed. (Boston: Little Brown, 1974) and Morton H. Halperin, Bureaucratic Politics and Foreign Policy (Washington, D.C.: The Brookings Institution, 1974).

Hugh Helco's, A Government of Strangers (Washington, D.C.: The Brookings Institution, 1977) discusses the problems of the temporary appointee in dealing with the permanent bureaucracy. For the role of scientific advisors in government see Don K. Price, The Scientific Estate (Cambridge, Mass.: Harvard University Press, 1965).

Chapter 15   The Supreme Court in American Government
A standard work is Robert G. McCloskey's The American Supreme Court (Chicago: University of Chicago Press, 1960), as is Alexander Bickel's The Least Dangerous Branch (Indianapolis: Bobbs-Merrill, 1962).

Herbert Jacob, Justice in America (Boston: Little, Brown, 1965) covers many relevant topics not reviewed in this chapter, especially material on the organization of American courts and appellate proceedings. For a broad and provocative view of the role of law in American society, see the collection of essays edited by Robert Paul Wolff, *The Rule of Law* (New York: Simon & Schuster, 1971).

Richard Richardson and Kenneth Vines, *The Politics of Federal Courts* (Boston: Little, Brown, 1970) reviews the lower federal courts in the United States, and Henry Abraham, *The Judicial Process* (New York: Oxford University Press, 1968) includes in a discussion of the Supreme Court and judicial review useful comparative material about court systems in European countries.

There are numerous casebooks on constitutional law; a useful one is Alpheus T. Mason and William B. Beaney, eds., *American Constitutional Law* (Englewood Cliffs, N.J.: Prentice-Hall, 1965). See also Robert F. Cushman, *Cases in Constitutional Law*, 4th ed. (Englewood Cliffs, N.J.: Prentice-Hall, 1975) and, for special treatment of civil liberties cases, Lucius J. Barker and Twiley W. Barker, Jr., eds., *Civil Liberties and the Constitution*, 2nd ed. (Englewood Cliffs, N.J.: Prentice-Hall, 1975).

An essay by Archibald Cox, *The Role of the Supreme Court in American Government* (New York: Oxford University Press, 1976) is a lively yet balanced discussion of the role of the court in administering as well as adjudicating law.

Chapter 16 Liberty and Order

On the general problems of majority rule and minority rights, see the important analysis by Alexis de Tocqueville, *Democracy in America* (New York: Oxford University Press, 1947) and the illuminating treatment by Robert A. Dahl, *Preface to Democratic Theory* (Chicago: University of Chicago Press, 1965). John Stuart Mill's *On Liberty* (Englewood Cliffs, N.J.: Prentice-Hall, 1947), originally published in 1851, is the classic philosophical statement of the libertarian defense of freedom of speech. Henry David Thoreau's 1849 essay *On the Duty of Civil Disobedience* (New Haven, Conn.: Yale University Press, 1928) is a remarkable plea for the individual to resist unjust governmental authority.

A widely read history on American civil liberties is Zechariah Chafee, Jr., *Free Speech in the United States* (Cambridge, Mass.: Harvard University Press, 1941). A more recent work on the Bill of Rights and the court's interpretation of it is Henry J. Abraham, *Freedom and the Court: Civil Rights and Civil Liberties in the United States*, 2nd ed. (New York: Oxford University Press, 1977). The report of the Commission on Obscenity and Pornography (Washington, D.C.: Government Printing Office, 1970) covers this topic thoroughly. Anthony Lewis' *Gideon's Trumpet* (New York: Random House, 1964) covers a classic case involving the rights of accused criminals.

On the right of privacy see P. Allan Dionisopoulos and Craig R. Ducat, eds., *The Right of Privacy* (St. Paul, Minn.: West Publishing Company, 1976) and on the conflict over pretrial publicity see Twentieth Century Fund, *Rights in Conflict: Report of the Task Force on Justice, Publicity, and the First Amendment* (New York: McGraw-Hill, 1976).

Chapter 17 White House, State House, City Hall: Federalism in America

On federalism in America, see Morton Grodzins, *The American System* (Skokie, Ill.: Rand McNally, 1966); Richard Leach, *American Federalism* (New York: Norton, 1970); James L. Sundquist, *Making Federalism Work* (Washington, D.C.: The Brookings Institution, 1969); and Michael D. Reagan, *The New Federalism* (New York: Oxford University Press, 1972). William H. Riker's *Federalism: Origin, Operation, Significance* (Boston: Little, Brown, 1964) is a more systematic analysis than most.

For a discussion of the urban problem, see James Q. Wilson and Edward C. Banfield, *City Politics* (Cambridge, Mass.: Harvard University Press, 1963); Robert C. Wood, *1400 Governments: The Political Economy of the New York Metropolitan Region* (Garden City, N.Y.: Doubleday, 1964); and Michael Danielson, ed., *Metropolitan Politics* (Boston: Little, Brown, 1971). For a general discussion of community government, see Alan A. Altshuler, *Community Control: The Black Demand for Participation in Large American Cities* (New York: Pegasus, 1970).

Chapter 18 The Policy Process

A good account of how policy is made in the all-important area of budgeting is Aaron Wildavsky, *The Politics of the Budgetary Process*, 2nd ed., (Boston: Little, Brown, 1974). An explication and defense of incremental policy making are found in Charles E. Lindblom, *The Policy-Making Process* (Englewood Cliffs, N.J.: Prentice-Hall, 1968), p. 68. A critique of this mode of policy making is in Theodore J. Lowi, *The End of Liberalism* (New York: Norton, 1969).

On the ways in which policies can have symbolic rather than substantive meaning, see Murray Edelman, *The Symbolic Uses of Politics* (Urbana: University of Illinois Press, 1964), and Murray Edelman, *Politics as Symbolic Action* (Chicago: Markham, 1971).

On the problem of Policy implementation, see Jeffrey L. Pressman and Aaron D. Wildavsky, *Implementation* (Berkeley and Los Angeles: University of California Press, 1973). Theodore L. Beeker and Malcolm M. Feeley's *The Impact of Supreme Court Decisions* (New York: Oxford University Press, 1973) deals with the actual effects of Supreme Court decisions.

Chapter 19   Public Policies:
Domestic and Foreign

The literature on the policies discussed in Chapter 19 is vast. James L. Sundquist's *Politics and Policy: The Eisenhower, Kennedy and Johnson Years* (Washington, D.C.: The Brookings Institution, 1968) deals with the passage of social legislation under three Presidents.

A few works on each issue area: Tax policy: Joseph A. Peckman and Benjamin A. Okner, *Who Bears the Tax Burden?* (Washington, D.C.: The Brookings Institution, 1974) analyzes the impact of taxes on income distribution in the United States. A comprehensive account of medicare legislation is Theodore R. Marmon, *The Politics of Medicare* (Chicago: Aldine, 1973). Desegregation of the schools: A good collection of essays on race relations is *The Negro American*, ed. Talcott Parsons and Kenneth B. Clark (Boston: Beacon, 1967). See also Milton D. Morris, *The Politics of Black America* (New York: Harper & Row, 1975). Energy: A publication of Congressional Quarterly, titled, *Continuing Energy Crisis in America*, has much useful information (Washington D.C., Congressional Quarterly Inc., 1975); see also Barry Commoner, ed., *Energy and Human Welfare: A Critical Analysis* (New York: Macmillan, 1974) and *A Time to Choose: America's Energy Future, Final Report of the Energy Policy Project* (Cambridge: Ballinger, 1974). On food policy as it has recently changed see Pierre R. Crosson and Kenneth D. Frederick, *The World Food Situation: Resource and Environmental Issues in the Developing Countries and the United States* (Baltimore: The Johns Hopkins University Press, 1978). Vietnam: David Halberstam's *The Best and the Brightest* (New York: Random House, 1972) is a detailed account of the making of Vietnam policy in the White House. Roger Hilsman's *The Politics of Policy Making in Defence and Foreign Policy* (New York: Harper & Row, 1971) covers Vietnam policy making and the policy-making process more generally.

The Constitution of the United States

[Preamble]
We the people of the United States, in Order to form a more perfect Union, establish Justice, insure domestic Tranquility, provide for the common defence, promote the general Welfare, and secure the Blessings of Liberty to ourselves and our Posterity, do ordain and establish this Constitution for the United States of America.

ARTICLE 1
Section 1
[Legislative Powers]
All legislative Powers herein granted shall be vested in a Congress of the United States, which shall consist of a Senate and a House of Representatives.

Section 2
[House of Representatives, How Considered, Power of Impeachment]
The House of Representatives shall be composed of Members chosen every second Year by the People of the several States, and the Electors in each State shall have [the] Qualifications requisite for Electors of the most numerous Branch of the State Legislature.

No person shall be a Representative who shall not have attained to the Age of twenty five Years, and been Seven Years a Citizen of the United States, and who shall not when elected, be an Inhabitant of that State in which he shall be chosen.

Representatives and direct Taxes shall be apportioned among the several states which may be included within this Union, according to their respective Numbers, which shall be determined by adding to the whole Number of free Persons, including those bound to Service for a Term of Years, and excluding Indians not taxed, three fifths of all other Persons. The actual Enumeration shall be made within three years after the first Meeting of the Congress of the United States, and within every subsequent Term of ten Years, in such Manner as they shall by Law direct. The Number of Representatives shall not exceed one for every thirty Thousand, but each State shall have at Least one Representative; and until such enumeration shall be made, the State of New Hampshire shall be entitled to chuse three, Massachusetts eight, Rhode-Island and Providence Plantations one, Connecticut five, New York six, New Jersey four, Pennsylvania eight, Delaware one, Maryland six, Virginia ten, North Carolina five, South Carolina five, and Georgia three.

When vacancies happen in the Representation from any State, the Executive Authority thereof shall issue Writs of Election to fill such Vacancies.

The House of Representatives shall chuse their Speaker and other Officers; and shall have the sole Power of Impeachment.

Section 3
[The Senate, How Constituted, Impeachment Trials]
The Senate of the United States shall be composed of Two Senators from each State, chosen by the Legislature thereof, for six Years; and each Senator shall have one Vote.

Immediately after they shall be assembled in Consequence of the first Election, they shall be divided as equally as may be into three Classes. The Seats of the Senators of the first Class shall be vacated at the Expiration of the second Year, of the second Class at the Expiration of the fourth Year, and of the third Class at the Expiration of the sixth Year, so that one third may be chosen every second Year; and if Vacancies happen by Resignation, or otherwise, during the Recess of the Legislature of any State, the Executive thereof may make temporary Appointments until the next Meeting of the Legislature, which shall then fill such Vacancies.

No Person shall be a Senator who shall not have attained to the Age of thirty Years, and been nine Years a Citizen of the United States, and who shall not, when elected, be an Inhabitant of that State for which he shall be chosen.

The Vice-President of the United States shall be President of the Senate, but shall have no Vote, unless they be equally divided.

The Senate shall chuse their other Officers, and also a President pro tempore, in the Absence of the Vice-President, or when he shall exercise the Office of President of the United States.

The Senate shall have the sole power to try all impeachments. When sitting for that Purpose, they shall be on Oath or Affirmation. When the President of the United States [is tried] the Chief Justice shall preside: And no Person shall be convicted without the Concurrence of two thirds of the Members present.

Judgment in Cases of Impeachment shall not extend further than to removal from Office, and disqualification to hold and enjoy any Office of honor, Trust or Profit under the United States: but the Party convicted shall nevertheless be liable and subject to Indictment, Trial, Judgment and Punishment, according to Law.

Section 4
[Election of Senators and Representatives]
The Times, Places and Manner of holding Elections for Senators and Representatives, shall be prescribed in each State by the Legislature thereof; but the Congress may at any time by Law make or alter such Regulations, except as to the Places of chusing Senators.

The Congress shall assemble at least once in every Year, and such Meeting shall be on the first Monday in December, unless they shall by Law appoint a different Day.

Section 5
[Quorum, Journals, Meetings, Adjournments]
Each House shall be the Judge of the Elections, Returns and Qualifications of its own Members, and a Majority of each shall constitute a Quorum to do Business; but a smaller Number may adjourn from day to day, and may be authorized to compel the Attendance of absent Members, in such Manner, and under such Penalties as each House may provide.

Each House may determine the Rules of its Proceedings, punish its Members for disorderly Behaviour, and, with the Concurrence of two thirds, expel a Member.

Each House shall keep a Journal of its Proceedings, and from time to time publish the same, excepting such Parts as may in their Judgment require Secrecy; and the Yeas and Nays of the Members of either House on any question shall, at the Desire of one fifth of those Present, be entered on the Journal.

Neither House, during the Session of Congress, shall, without the Consent of the other, adjourn for more than three days, nor to any other Place than that in which the two Houses shall be sitting.

Section 6
[Compensation, Privileges, Disabilities]
The Senators and Representatives shall receive a Compensation for their Services, to be ascertained by Law, and paid out of the Treasury of the United States. They shall in all Cases, except Treason, Felony and Breach of the Peace, be privileged from Arrest during their Attendance at the Session of their respective Houses, and in going to and returning from the same; and for any Speech or Debate in either House, they shall not be questioned in any other Place.

No Senator or Representative shall, during the Time for which he was elected, be appointed to any civil Office under the Authority of the United States, which shall have been created, or the Emoluments whereof shall have been encreased during such time; and no Person holding any Office under the United States, shall be a member of either House during his Continuance in Office.

Section 7
[Procedure in Passing Bills and Resolutions]
All Bills for raising Revenue shall originate in the House of Representatives; but the Senate may propose or concur with Amendments as on other Bills.

Every Bill which shall have passed the House of Representatives and the Senate, shall, before it becomes a Law, be presented to the President of the United States; if he approves he shall sign it, but if not he shall return it, with his Objections to that House in which it shall have originated, who shall enter the Objections at large on their Journal, and proceed to reconsider it. If after such Reconsideration two thirds of that House shall agree to pass the Bill, it shall be sent, together with the Objections, to the other House, by which it shall likewise be reconsidered, and if approved by two thirds of that House, it shall become a Law. But in all such Cases the Votes of both Houses shall be determined by Yeas and Nays, and the Names of the Persons voting for and against the Bill shall be entered on the Journal of each House respectively. If any Bill shall not be returned by the President within ten Days (Sundays excepted) after it shall have been presented to him, the Same shall be a Law, in like Manner as if he had signed it, unless the Congress by their Adjournment prevent its Return, in which Case it shall not be a Law.

Every Order, Resolution, or Vote to which the Concurrence of the Senate and House of Representatives may be necessary (except on a question of Adjournment) shall be presented to the President of the United States; and before the same shall take Effect, shall be approved by him, or being disapproved by him, shall be repassed by two thirds of the Senate and House of Representatives, according to the Rules and Limitations prescribed in the Case of a Bill.

Section 8
[Powers of Congress]
The Congress shall have the Power To lay and collect Taxes, Duties, Imports and Excises, to pay the Debts and provide for the common Defence and general Welfare of the United States; but all Duties, Imposts and Excises shall be uniform throughout the United States.

To borrow Money on the credit of the United States;

To regulate Commerce with foreign Nations and among the several States, and with the Indian Tribes;

To establish an uniform Rule of Naturalization, and uniform Laws on the subject of Bankruptcies throughout the United States;

To Coin Money, regulate the Value thereof, and of foreign Coin, and fix the Standards of Weights and Measures;

To provide for the Punishment of counterfeiting the Securities and current Coin of the United States;

To establish Post Offices and post Roads;

To promote the Progress of Science and useful Arts, by securing for limited Times to Authors and Inventors the exclusive Right to their respective Writings and Discoveries;

To constitute Tribunals inferior to the supreme Court;

To define and punish Piracies and Felonies committed on the high Seas, and Offences against the Law of Nations;

To declare War, grant Letters of Marque and Reprisal, and make Rules concerning Captures on Land and Water;

To raise and support Armies, but no Appropriation of Money to that Use shall be for a longer Term than two Years;

To provide and maintain a Navy;

To make Rules for Government and Regulation of the land and naval Forces;

To provide for calling forth the Militia to execute the Laws of the Union, suppress Insurrections and repel Invasions;

To provide for organizing, arming, and disciplining the Militia, and for governing such Part of them as may be employed in the Service of the United States, reserving to the States respectively, the Appointment of the Officers, and the Authority of training the Militia according to the discipline prescribed by Congress;

To exercise exclusive Legislation in all Cases whatsoever, over such District (not exceeding ten Miles square) as may, by Cession of particular States, and the Acceptance of Congress, become the Seat of the Government of the United States, and to exercise like Authority over all Places purchased by the Consent of the Legislature of the States in which the Same shall be, for the Erection of Forts, Magazines, Arsenals, dock-Yards, and other needful Buildings—And

To make all Laws which shall be necessary and proper for carrying into Execution the foregoing Powers, and all other Powers vested by this Constitution in the Government of the United States, or in any Department or Officer thereof.

Section 9
[Limitation upon Powers of Congress]

The Migration or Importation of such Persons as any of the States now existing shall think proper to admit, shall not be prohibited by the Congress prior to the Year one thousand eight hundred and eight, but a Tax or duty may be imposed on such Importation, not exceeding ten dollars for each Person.

The Privilege of the Writ of Habeas Corpus shall not be suspended, unless when in Cases of Rebellion or Invasion the public Safety may require it.

No Bill of Attainder or ex post facto Law shall be passed.

No Capitation, or other direct, Tax shall be laid, unless in Proportion to the Census or Enumeration herein before directed to be taken.

No Tax or Duty shall be laid on Articles, exported from any State.

No Preference shall be given by any Regulation of Commerce or Revenue to the Ports of one State over those of another; nor shall Vessels bound to, or from, one State, be obliged to enter, clear, or pay Duties in another.

No Money shall be drawn from the Treasury, but in Consequence of Appropriations made by Law; and a regular Statement and Account of the Receipts and Expenditures of all public Money shall be published from time to time.

No title of Nobility shall be granted by the United States: And no Person holding any Office of Profit or Trust under them, shall, without the Consent of the Congress, accept of any present, Emolument, Office, or Title, of any kind whatever, from any King, Prince, or foreign State.

Section 10
[Restrictions upon Powers of States]

No State shall enter into any Treaty, Alliance, or Confederation; grant Letters of Marque and Reprisal; coin Money; emit Bills of Credit; make any Thing but gold and silver Coin a Tender in payment of Debts; pass any Bill of Attainder, ex post facto Law, or Law impairing the Obligation of Contracts, or grant any Title of Nobility.

No State shall, without the Consent of the Congress, lay any Imposts or Duties on Imports or Exports, except what may be absolutely necessary for executing its inspection Laws: and the net Produce of all Duties and Imposts, laid by any State on Imports or Exports, shall be for the Use of the Treasury of the United States; and all such Laws shall be subject to the Revision and Control of [the] Congress.

No State shall, without the Consent of Congress, lay any Duty of Tonnage, keep Troops, or Ships of War in time of Peace, enter into any Agreement or Compact with another State, or with a foreign Power, or engage in War, unless actually invaded, or in such imminent Danger as will not admit of delay.

ARTICLE 2
Section 1
[Executive Power, Election, Qualifications of the President]

The executive Power shall be vested in a President of the United States of America. He shall hold his Office during the Term of four Years, and, together with the Vice-President, chosen for the same Term, be selected as follows:

Each State shall appoint, in such Manner as the Legislature thereof may direct, a Number of Electors, equal to the whole Number of Senators and Representatives to which the State may be entitled in the Congress: but no Senator or Representative, or Person holding an Office of Trust or Profit under the United States, shall be appointed an Elector.

The Electors shall meet in their respective States, and vote by Ballot for two Persons of whom one at least shall not be an Inhabitant of the same State with themselves. And they shall make a List of all the Persons voted for, and of the Number of Votes for each; which List they shall sign and certify, and transmit sealed to the Seat of the Government of the United States, directed to the President of the Senate. The President of the Senate shall, in the Presence of the Senate and House of Representatives, open all the Certificates, and the Votes shall then be counted. The Person having the greatest Number of Votes shall be the President, if such Number be a Majority of the whole Number of Electors appointed; and if there be more than one who have such Majority, and have an equal Number of Votes, then the House of Representatives shall immediately chuse by Ballot one of them for President; and if no Person have a Majority, then from the five highest in the List the said House in like Manner chuse the President. But in chusing the President, the Votes shall be taken by States, the Representation from each State having one Vote; A quorum for this purpose shall consist of a Member or Members from two thirds of the States, and a Majority of all the States shall be necessary to a Choice. In every Case, after the choice of the President, the Person having the greatest Number of Votes of the Electors shall be the Vice-President. But if there should remain two or more who have equal Votes, the Senate shall chuse from them by Ballot the Vice-President.

The Congress may determine the Time of chusing the Electors, and the Day on which they shall give their Votes; which Day shall be the same throughout the United States.

No person except a natural born Citizen, or a Citizen of the United States at the time of the Adoption of this Constitution, shall be eligible to the Office of President; neither shall any Person be eligible to that Office who shall not have attained to the Age of thirty five Years, and been fourteen Years a Resident within the United States.

In Case of the Removal of the President from Office, or of his Death, Resignation, or Inability to discharge the Powers and Duties of the said Office, the Same shall devolve on the Vice-President, and the Congress may by Law provide for the Case of Removal, Death, Resignation or Inability, both of the President and Vice-President, declaring what Officer shall then act as President, and such Officer shall act accordingly, until the Disability be removed, or a President shall be elected.

The President shall, at stated Times, receive for his Services, a Compensation, which shall neither be encreased nor diminished during the Period for which he shall have been elected, and he shall not receive within that Period any other Emolument from the United States, or any of them.

Before he entered on the Execution of his Office, he shall take the following Oath of Affirmation: — "I do solemnly swear (or affirm) that I will faithfully execute the Office of the President of the United States, and will to the best of my Ability, preserve, protect and defend the Constitution of the United States."

Section 2
[Powers of the President]
The President shall be Commander in Chief of the Army and Navy of the United States, and the Militia of the several States, when called into the actual Service of the United States; he may require the Opinion, in writing, of the principal Officer in each of the executive Departments, upon any subject relating to the Duties of their respective Offices, and he shall have Power to grant Reprieves and Pardons for Offences against the United States, except in Cases of Impeachment.

He shall have Power, by and with the Advice and Consent of the Senate, to make Treaties, provided two thirds of the Senators present concur; and he shall nominate, and

by and with the Advice and Consent of the Senate, shall appoint Ambassadors, other public Ministers and Consuls, Judges of the supreme Court, and all other Officers of the United States, whose Appointments are not herein otherwise provided for, and which shall be established by Law: but the Congress may by Law vest the Appointment of such inferior Officers, as they think proper in the President alone, in the Courts of Law, or in the Heads of Departments.

The President shall have Power to fill up all Vacancies that may happen during the Recess of the Senate, by granting Commissions which shall expire at the End of their next Session.

Section 3
[Powers and Duties of the President]
He shall from time to time give to the Congress Information of the State of the Union, and recommend to their Consideration such Measures as he shall judge necessary and expedient; he may, on extraordinary Occasions, convene both Houses, or either of them, and in Case of Disagreement between them, with Respect to the Time of Adjournment, he may adjourn them to such Time as he shall think proper; he shall receive Ambassadors and other public Ministers; he shall take Care that the Laws be faithfully executed, and shall commission all the Officers of the United States.

Section 4
[Impeachment]
The President, Vice-President and all civil Officers of the United States, shall be removed from Office on Impeachment for, and Conviction of, Treason, Bribery, or other high Crimes and Misdemeanors.

ARTICLE 3
Section 1
[Judicial Power, Tenure of Office]
The judicial Power of the United States, shall be vested in one supreme Court, and in such inferior Courts as the Congress may from time to time ordain and establish. The judges, both of the supreme and inferior Courts, shall hold their Offices during good Behavior, and shall, at stated Times, receive for their Services, a Compensation, which shall not be diminished during their Continuance in Office.

Section 2
[Jurisdiction]
The judicial Power shall extend to all Cases, in Law and Equity, arising under this Constitution, the Laws of the United States, and Treaties made, or which shall be made, under their Authority; — to all Cases affecting Ambassadors, other public Ministers and Consuls; — to all Cases of admiralty and maritime Jurisdiction; — to Controversies to which the United States shall be a Party; — to Controversies between two or more States; — between a State and Citizens of another State; — between Citizens of different States; — between Citizens of the same State claiming Lands under Grants of different States, and between a

State, or the Citizens thereof, and foreign States, Citizens or Subjects.

In all Cases affecting Ambassadors, other public Ministers and Consuls, and those in which a State shall be Party, the supreme Court shall have original Jurisdiction. In all the other Cases before mentioned, the supreme Court shall have appellate Jurisdiction, both as to Law and Fact, with such Exceptions, and under such Regulations as the Congress shall make.

The Trial of all Crimes, except in Cases of Impeachment, shall be by Jury; and such Trial shall be held in the State where the said Crimes shall have been committed; but when not committed within any State, the Trial shall be at such Place or Places as the Congress may by Law have directed.

Section 3
[Treason, Proof and Punishment]
Treason against the United States, shall consist only in levying War against them, or in adhering to their Enemies; giving them Aid and Comfort. No Person shall be convicted of Treason unless on the Testimony of two Witnesses to the same overt Act, or on Confession in open Court.

The Congress shall have Power to declare the Punishment of Treason, but no Attainder of Treason shall work Corruption of Blood, or Forfeiture except during the Life of the Person attainted.

ARTICLE 4
Section 1
[Faith and Credit Among States]
Full Faith and Credit shall be given in each State to the public Acts, Records, and judicial Proceedings of every other State. And the Congress may by general Laws prescribe the Manner in which such Acts, Records and Proceedings shall be proved, and the Effect thereof.

Section 2
[Privileges and Immunities, Fugitives]
The citizens of each State shall be entitled to all Privileges and Immunities of Citizens in the several States.

A Person charged in any State with Treason, Felony, or other Crime, who shall flee from Justice, and be found in another State, shall on Demand of the executive Authority of the State from which he fled, be delivered up, to be removed to the State having Jurisdiction of the Crime.

No person held to Service or Labour in one State, under the Laws thereof, escaping into another, shall, in Consequence of any Law or Regulation therein, be discharged from such Service or Labour, but shall be delivered up on Claim of the Party to whom such Service or Labour may be due.

Section 3
[Admission of New States]
New States may be admitted by the Congress into this Union; but no new State shall be formed or erected within the Jurisdiction of any other State; nor any State be formed by the Junction of two or more States, or Parts of States, without the Consent of the Legislatures of the States concerned as well as of the Congress.

The Congress shall have Power to dispose of and make all needful Rules and Regulations respecting the Territory or other Property belonging to the United States; and nothing in this Constitution shall be so construed as to Prejudice any Claims of the United States, or of any particular State.

Section 4
[Guarantee of Republican Government]
The United States shall guarantee to every State in this Union a Republican Form of Government, and shall protect each of them against Invasion; and on Application of the Legislature, or of the Executive (when the Legislature cannot be convened) against domestic Violence.

ARTICLE 5
[Amendment of the Constitution]
The Congress, whenever two thirds of both Houses shall deem it necessary, shall propose Amendments to this Constitution, or, on the Application of the Legislatures of two thirds of the several States, shall call a Convention for proposing Amendments, which, in either Case, shall be valid to all Intents and Purposes, as Part of this Constitution, when ratified by the Legislatures of three fourths of the several States, or by Conventions in three fourths thereof, as the one or the other Mode of Ratification may be proposed by the Congress; Provided that no Amendment which may be made prior to the Year One Thousand eight hundred and eight shall in any Manner affect the first and fourth Clauses in the Ninth Section of the first Article, and that no State, without its Consent, shall be deprived of its equal Suffrage in the Senate.

ARTICLE 6
[Debts, Supremacy, Oath]
All Debts contracted and Engagements entered into, before the Adoption of this Constitution, shall be as valid against the United States under this Constitution, as under the Confederation.

This Constitution, and the Laws of the United States which shall be made in Pursuance thereof; and all Treaties made, or which shall be made, under the Authority of the United States, shall be the supreme Law of the Land; and the Judges in every State be bound thereby, any Thing in the Constitution or Laws of any State to the Contrary notwithstanding.

The Senators and Representatives before mentioned, and the Members of the several State Legislatures, and all executive and judicial Officers, both of the United States and of the several States, shall be bound by Oath or Affirmation, to support this Constitution, but no religious Test shall ever be required as a Qualification to any Office or public Trust under the United States.

ARTICLE 7
[Ratification and Establishment]

The Ratification of the Conventions of nine States, shall be sufficient for the Establishment of this Constitution between the States so ratifying the Same. Done in Convention by the Unanimous Consent of the States present the Seventeenth Day of September in the Year of our Lord one thousand seven hundred and Eighty seven and of the Independence of the United States of America the Twelfth In witness whereof We have hereunto subscribed our Names.

Go. Washington
Presidt and deputy from Virginia

New Hampshire	John Langdon Nicholas Gilman
Massachusetts	Nathaniel Gorham Rufus King
Connecticut	Wm Saml Johnson Roger Sherman
New York	Alexander Hamilton
New Jersey	Wil: Livingston David Brearley Wm Paterson Jona: Dayton
Pennsylvania	B. Franklin Thomas Mifflin Robt. Morris Geo. Clymer Thos. FitzSimons Jared Ingersoll James Wilson Gouv Morris
Delaware	Geo. Read Gunning Bedford jun John Dickinson Richard Bassett Jaco: Broom
Maryland	James McHenry Dan of St Thos. Jenifer Danl Carroll
Virginia	John Blair James Madison Jr.
North Carolina	Wm Blount Richd Dobbs Spaight Hu Williamson
South Carolina	J. Rutledge Charles Cotesworth Pinckney Charles Pinckney Pierce Butler
Georgia	William Few Abr Baldwin

AMENDMENTS TO THE CONSTITUTION
[The first ten amendments, known as the Bill of Rights, were proposed by Congress on September 25, 1789; ratified and adoption certified on December 15, 1791.]

AMENDMENT I
[Freedom of Religion, of Speech, of the Press, and Right of Petition]

Congress shall make no law respecting an establishment of religion, or prohibiting the free exercise thereof; or abridging the freedom of speech, or of the press; or the right of the people peaceably to assemble, and to petition the Government for a redress of grievances.

AMENDMENT II
[Right to Keep and Bear Arms]

A well regulated Militia being necessary to the security of a free State, the right of the people to keep and bear Arms, shall not be infringed.

AMENDMENT III
[Quartering of Soldiers]

No Soldier shall, in time of peace be quartered in any house, without the consent of the Owner, nor in time of war, but in a manner to be prescribed by law.

AMENDMENT IV
[Security from Unwarrantable Search and Seizure]

The right of the people to be secure in their persons, houses, papers, and effects, against unreasonable searches and seizures, shall not be violated, and no Warrants shall issue, but upon probable cause, supported by Oath of affirmation, and particularly describing the place to be searched, and the persons or things to be seized.

AMENDMENT V
[Rights of Accused in Criminal Proceedings]

No person shall be held to answer for a capital, or otherwise infamous crime, unless on a presentment or indictment of a Grand Jury, except in cases arising in the land or naval forces, or in the Militia, when in actual service in time of War or public danger; nor shall any person be subjected for the same offense to be twice put in jeopardy of life or limb; nor shall be compelled in any criminal case to be a witness against himself, nor be deprived of life, liberty, or property, without due process of law; nor shall private property be taken for public use, without just compensation.

AMENDMENT VI
[Right to Speedy Trial, Witnesses, etc.]

In all criminal prosecutions, the accused shall enjoy the right to a speedy and public trial, by an impartial jury of the State and district wherein the crime shall have been committed, which district shall have been previously ascertained by law, and to be informed of the nature and cause of the accusation; to be confronted with the witnesses against him; to have compulsory process for obtaining witnesses in his favor, and to have the Assistance of Counsel for his defence.

AMENDMENT VII
[Trial by Jury in Civil Cases]

In Suits at common law, where the value in controversy shall exceed twenty dollars, the right of trial by jury shall be preserved, and no fact tried by a jury, shall be otherwise reexamined in any Court of the United States, than according to the rules of the common law.

AMENDMENT VIII
[Bails, Fines, Punishments]
Excessive bail shall not be required, nor excessive fines imposed, nor cruel and unusual punishments inflicted.

AMENDMENT IX
[Reservation of Rights of the People]
The enumeration in the Constitution, of certain rights, shall not be construed to deny or disparage others retained by the people.

AMENDMENT X
[Powers Reserved to States or People]
The powers not delegated to the United States by the Constitution, nor prohibited by it to the States, are reserved to the States respectively, or to the people.

AMENDMENT XI
[Proposed by Congress on March 4, 1793; declared ratified on January 8, 1798.]
[Restriction of Judicial Power]
The Judicial power of the United States shall not be construed to extend to any suit in law or equity, commenced or prosecuted against one of the United States by Citizens of another State, or by Citizens or Subjects of any Foreign State.

AMENDMENT XII
[Proposed by Congress on December 9, 1803; declared ratified on September 25, 1804.]
[Election of President and Vice-President]
The Electors shall meet in their respective states, and vote by ballot for President and Vice-President, one of whom, at least, shall not be an inhabitant of the same state with themselves; they shall name in their ballots the person voted for as President, and in distinct ballots the person voted for as Vice-President and they shall make distinct lists of all persons voted for as President, and of all persons voted for as Vice-President, and of the number of votes for each, which lists they shall sign and certify, and transmit sealed to the seat of the government of the United States, directed to the President of the Senate; — The President of the Senate shall, in the presence of the Senate and House of Representatives, open all the certificates and the votes shall then be counted; — The person having the greatest number of votes for President, shall be the President, if such number be a majority of the whole number of Electors appointed; and if no person have such majority, then from the persons having the highest numbers not exceeding three on the list of those voted for as President, the House of Representatives shall choose immediately, by ballot, the President. But in choosing the President, the votes shall be taken by states, the representation from each state

having one vote; a quorum for this purpose shall consist of a member or members from two-thirds of the states, and a majority of all the states shall be necessary to a choice. And if the House of Representatives shall not choose a President whenever the right of choice shall devolve upon them, before the fourth day of March next following, then the Vice-President shall act as President, as in the case of the death or other constitutional disability of the President. — The person having the greatest number of votes as Vice-President, shall be the Vice-President, if such number be a majority of the whole number of Electors appointed, and if no person have a majority, then from the two highest numbers on the list, the Senate shall choose the Vice-President; a quorum for the purpose shall consist of two-thirds of the whole number of Senators, and a majority of the whole number shall be necessary to a choice. But no person constitutionally ineligible to the office of President shall be eligible to that of Vice-President of the United States.

AMENDMENT XIII
[Proposed by Congress on January 31, 1865; declared ratified on December 18, 1865.]

Section 1
[Abolition of Slavery]
Neither slavery nor involuntary servitude, except as a punishment for a crime whereof the party shall have been duly convicted, shall exist within the United States, or any place subject to their jurisdiction.

Section 2
[Power to Enforce This Article]
Congress shall have the power to enforce this article by appropriate legislation.

AMENDMENT XIV
[Proposed by Congress on June 16, 1866; declared ratified on July 28, 1868.]

Section 1
[Citizenship Rights Not to Be Abridged by States]
All persons born or naturalized in the United States, and subject to the jurisdiction thereof, are citizens of the United States and of the State wherein they reside. No State shall make or enforce any law which shall abridge the privileges or immunities of citizens of the United States; nor shall any State deprive any person of life, liberty, or property, without due process of law; nor deny to any person within its jurisdiction the equal protection of the laws.

Section 2
[Appointment of Representatives in Congress]
Representatives shall be apportioned among the several States according to their respective numbers, counting the whole number of persons in each State, excluding Indians

not taxed. But when the right to vote at any election for the choice of electors for President and Vice-President of the United States, Representatives in Congress, the Executive and Judicial officers of a State, or the members of the Legislature thereof, is denied to any of the male inhabitants of such State, being twenty-one years of age, and citizens of the United States, or in any way abridged, except for participation in rebellion or other crime, the basis of representation therein shall be reduced in the proportion which the number of such male citizens shall bear to the whole number of male citizens twenty-one years of age in such State.

Section 3
[Persons Disqualified from Holding Office]
No person shall be a Senator or Representative in Congress, or elector of President and Vice-President, or hold any office, civil or military, under the United States, or under any State, who, having previously taken an oath, as a member of Congress, or as an officer of the United States, or as a member of any State legislature, or as an executive or judicial officer of any State, to support the Constitution of the United States, shall have engaged in insurrection or rebellion against the same, or given aid or comfort to the enemies thereof. But Congress may by a vote of two-thirds of each House, remove such disability.

Section 4
[What Public Debts Are Valid]
The validity of the public debt of the United States, authorized by law, including debts incurred for payment of pensions and bounties for services in suppressing insurrection or rebellion, shall not be questioned. But neither the United States nor any State shall assume or pay any debt or obligation incurred in aid of insurrection or rebellion against the United States, or any claim for the loss or emancipation of any slave; but all such debts, obligations and claims shall be held illegal and void.

Section 5
[Power to Enforce This Article]
The Congress shall have power to enforce, by appropriate legislation, the provisions of this article.

AMENDMENT XV
[Proposed by Congress on February 26, 1869; declared ratified on March 30, 1870.]

Section 1
[Negro Suffrage]
The right of citizens of the United States to vote shall not be denied or abridged by the United States or by any State on account of race, color, or previous condition of servitude.

Section 2
[Power to Enforce This Article]
The Congress shall have power to enforce this article by appropriate legislation.

AMENDMENT XVI
[Proposed by Congress on July 12, 1909; declared ratified on February 25, 1913.]
[Authorizing Income Taxes]
The Congress shall have power to lay and collect taxes on incomes, from whatever source derived, without apportionment among the several States, and without regard to any census or enumeration.

AMENDMENT XVII
[Proposed by Congress on May 13, 1912; declared ratified on May 31, 1913.]
[Popular Election of Senators]
The Senate of the United States shall be composed of two Senators from each State, elected by the people thereof, for six years; and each Senator shall have one vote. The electors in each State shall have the qualifications requisite for electors of the most numerous branch of the State legislatures.

When vacancies happen in the representation of any State in the Senate, the executive authority of such State shall issue writs of election to fill such vacancies: *Provided,* That the legislature of any State may empower the executive thereof to make temporary appointments until the people fill the vacancies by election as the legislature may direct.

This amendment shall not be so construed as to affect the election or term of any Senator chosen before it becomes valid as part of the Constitution.

AMENDMENT XVIII
[Proposed by Congress on December 18, 1917; declared ratified on January 16, 1919.]

Section 1
[National Liquor Prohibition]
After one year from the ratification of this article the manufacture, sale, or transportation of intoxicating liquors within, the importation thereof into, or the exportation thereof from the United States and all territory subject to the jurisdiction thereof for beverage purposes is hereby prohibited.

Section 2
[Power to Enforce This Article]
The Congress and the several States shall have concurrent power to enforce this article by appropriate legislation.

Section 3
[Ratification Within Seven Years]
This article shall be inoperative unless it shall have been ratified as an amendment to the Constitution by the legislatures of the several States, as provided in the Constitution, within seven years from the date of the submission hereof to the States by the Congress.

AMENDMENT XIX
[Proposed by Congress on June 4, 1919; declared ratified on August 26, 1920.]
[Woman Suffrage]
The right of citizens of the United States to vote shall not

be denied or abridged by the United States or by any State on account of sex.

Congress shall have power to enforce this article by appropriate legislation.

AMENDMENT XX
[*Proposed by Congress on March 2, 1932; declared ratified on February 6, 1933.*]

Section 1
[*Terms of Office*]
The terms of the President and Vice-President shall end at noon on the 20th day of January, and the terms of Senators and Representatives at noon on the 3rd day of January, of the years in which such terms would have ended if this article had not been ratified; and the terms of their successors shall then begin.

Section 2
[*Time of Convening Congress*]
The Congress shall assemble at least once in every year, and such meeting shall begin at noon on the 3rd day of January, unless they shall by law appoint a different day.

Section 3
[*Death of President Elect*]
If, at the time fixed for the beginning of the term of the President, the President elect shall have died, the Vice-President elect shall become President. If a President shall not have been chosen before the time fixed for the beginning of his term, or if the President elect shall have failed to qualify, then the Vice-President elect shall act as President until a President shall have qualified; and the Congress may by law provide for the case wherein neither a President elect nor a Vice-President elect shall have qualified, declaring who shall then act as President, or the manner in which one who is to act shall be selected, and such person shall act accordingly until a President or Vice-President shall have qualified.

Section 4
[*Election of the President*]
The Congress may by law provide for the case of the death of any of the persons from whom the House of Representatives may choose a President whenever the right of choice shall have devolved upon them, and for the case of the death of any of the persons from whom the Senate may choose a Vice-President whenever the right of choice shall have devolved upon them.

Section 5
Sections 1 and 2 shall take effect on the 15th day of October following the ratification of this article.

Section 6
This article shall be inoperative unless it shall have been ratified as an amendment to the Constitution by the legislatures of three-fourths of the several States within seven years from the date of its submission.

AMENDMENT XXI
[*Proposed by Congress on February 20, 1933; declared ratified on December 5, 1933.*]

Section 1
[*National Liquor Prohibition Repealed*]
The eighteenth article of amendment to the Constitution of the United States is hereby repealed.

Section 2
[*Transportation of Liquor into "Dry" States*]
The transportation or importation into any States, Territory, or possession of the United States for delivery or use therein of intoxicating liquors, in violation of the laws thereof, is hereby prohibited.

Section 3
This article shall be inoperative unless it shall have been ratified as an amendment to the Constitution by conventions in the several States, as provided in the Constitution, within seven years from the date of the submission hereof to the States by the Congress.

AMENDMENT XXII
[*Proposed by Congress on March 21, 1947; declared ratified on February 26, 1951.*]

Section 1
[*Tenure of President Limited*]
No person shall be elected to the office of the President more than twice, and no person who has held the office of President, or acted as President, for more than two years of a term to which some other person was elected President shall be elected to the office of the President more than once. But this Article shall not apply to any person holding the office of President when this Article was proposed by the Congress, and shall not prevent any person who may be holding the office of President, or acting as President, during the term within which this Article becomes operative from holding the office of President, or acting as President during the remainder of such term.

Section 2
This Article shall be inoperative unless it shall have been ratified as an amendment to the Constitution by the legislatures of three-fourths of the several States within seven years from the date of its submission to the States by the Congress.

AMENDMENT XXIII
[*Proposed by Congress on June 17, 1960; declared ratified on May 29, 1961.*]

Section 1
[*District of Columbia Suffrage in Presidential Elections*]
The District constituting the seat of Government of the

United States shall appoint in such manner as the Congress may direct:

A number of electors of President and Vice-President equal to the whole number of Senators and Representatives in Congress to which the District would be entitled if it were a State; but in no event more than the least populous State; they shall be in addition to those appointed by the States, but they shall be considered, for the purposes of the election of President and Vice-President, to be electors appointed by a State; and they shall meet in the District and perform such duties as provided by the twelfth article of amendment.

Section 2
The Congress shall have power to enforce this article by appropriate legislation.

AMENDMENT XXIV
[Proposed by Congress on August 27, 1962; declared ratified on January 23, 1964.]

Section 1
[Bars Poll Tax in Federal Elections]
The right of citizens of the United States to vote in any primary or other election for President or Vice-President, for electors for President or Vice-President, or for Senator or Representative in Congress, shall not be denied or abridged by the United States or any State by reason of failure to pay any poll tax or other tax.

Section 2
The Congress shall have power to enforce this article by appropriate legislation.

AMENDMENT XXV
[Proposed by Congress on July 6, 1965; declared ratified on February 10, 1967.]

Section 1
[Succession of Vice-President to Presidency]
In case of the removal of the President from office or of his death or resignation, the Vice-President shall become President.

Section 2
[Vacancy in office of Vice-President]
Whenever there is a vacancy in the office of the Vice-President, the President shall nominate a Vice-President who shall take office upon confirmation by a majority vote of both Houses of Congress.

Section 3
[Vice-President as Acting President]
Whenever the President transmits to the President pro tempore of the Senate and the Speaker of the House of Representatives his written declaration that he is unable to discharge the powers and duties of his office, and until he transmits to them a written declaration to the contrary, such powers and duties shall be discharged by the Vice-President as Acting President.

Section 4
[Vice-President as Acting President]
Whenever the Vice-President and a majority of either the principal officers of the executive departments or of such other body as Congress may by law provide, transmit to the President pro tempore of the Senate and the Speaker of the House of Representatives their written declaration that the President is unable to discharge the powers and duties of his office, the Vice-President shall immediately assume the powers and duties of the office as Acting President.

Thereafter, when the President transmits to the President pro tempore of the Senate and the Speaker of the House of Representatives his written declaration that no inability exists, he shall resume the powers and duties of his office unless the Vice-President and a majority of either the principal officers of the executive department or of such other body as Congress may by law provide, transmit within four days to the President pro tempore of the Senate and the Speaker of the House of Representatives their written declaration that the President is unable to discharge the powers and duties of his office. Thereupon Congress shall decide the issue, assembling within forty-eight hours for that purpose if not in session. If the Congress, within twenty-one days after receipt of the latter written declaration, or, if Congress is not in session, within twenty-one days after Congress is required to assemble, determines by two-thirds vote of both Houses that the President is unable to discharge the powers and duties of his office, the Vice-President shall continue to discharge the same as Acting President; otherwise, the President shall resume the powers and duties of his office.

AMENDMENT XXVI
[Proposed by Congress on March 23, 1971; declared ratified on July 5, 1971.]

Section 1
[Lowers Voting Age to 18 Years]
The right of citizens of the United States, who are eighteen years of age or older, to vote shall not be denied or abridged by the United States or by any State on account of age.

Section 2
The Congress shall have power to enforce this article by appropriate legislation.

Glossary

accountability The principle according to which officials in a democracy are held responsible for their actions by those who elected or appointed them.

advice and consent Senatorial power, granted in Article 2, Section 2 of the Constitution, to approve presidential treaties and certain presidential appointments such as ambassadors and justices of the Supreme Court. Treaties require a two-thirds vote of the Senate for ratification.

agenda The list of items to be considered at a meeting or legislative session; more generally, the list of politically relevant issues.

amendment An alteration or addition to a bill, motion, or constitution. Congressional bills may be amended at virtually any point before they are passed. As specified in Article 5 of the Constitution, constitutional amendments may be proposed by a two-thirds vote of both houses of Congress or by a convention assembled by Congress at the request of the legislatures of two-thirds of the states. To be ratified, a constitutional amendment must be approved by the legislatures of three-fourths of the states or by conventions called for that purpose in three-fourths of the states.

amicus curiae brief Literally, a brief filed by a "friend of the court"; thus a brief filed by one who is not a party to a lawsuit — but who may be affected by its outcome — stating a legal principle for the consideration of the court.

appeal A legal proceeding in which a case is carried from a lower court to a higher court for review or reexamination.

appropriation A bill granting the actual funds for a program that has been authorized by Congress.

assimilation The process by which a minority is absorbed into the dominant social group. When a group is assimilated, its members lose their distinctiveness.

authorization Congressional legislation prescribing a particular program and putting limits on spending for that program.

Bill of Rights The first ten amendments to the U.S. Constitution.

budget A statement of estimated income and expenses. The President is responsible for preparing the annual budget of the federal government.

capitalism An economic system based on private ownership of land and natural resources and of the means of production, distribution, and exchange, in which there is a minimum of government interference in the economy.

centralization The gravitation of political power and decision-making responsibility from units or agencies that are geographically small or functionally specific to ones that are larger or more general (cf. decentralization).

checks and balances The principle according to which various government institutions exercise certain checks on the activities of other government institutions. Examples of this system include the President's power to veto acts of Congress and the courts' power to declare legislative acts unconstitutional.

citizen A member of a state, either native-born or naturalized, who owes allegiance to its government and enjoys the protection of its laws.

citizens' lobby An interest group that lobbies in behalf of the public welfare (e.g., consumer protection, conservation, political reform, etc.).

civil liberties Liberties guaranteed to the individual by the First Amendment to the Constitution: freedom of speech, press, and assembly.

closed primary An election in which a party's candidates are selected and in which the participants include only those who have declared themselves to be party members or supporters (cf. direct primary).

coalition A political union containing disparate political elements. American political parties, for example, are coalitions including members of many different ideological and social groups.

collective good A benefit available to everyone in society regardless of whether any particular individual worked toward the attainment of that benefit.

Commander-in-Chief The President's role, specified in Article 2, Section 2 of the Constitution, as supreme commander of the armed forces and of the state militias when they are called into federal service. Acting in his role as Commander-in-Chief, the President can deploy troops abroad without having received a congressional declaration of war.

commission plan A form of city government in

which a small board of elected commissioners serves both as a legislative council and as heads of the city departments.

communal activity Political activity in which citizens join together and act as a group to pressure the government. Communal activity may involve either ad hoc or formally structured organizations.

comprehensive planning A form of planning in which all possible ways of solving a problem are considered (cf. incremental planning).

concurrent majorities The idea that a majority of the citizens of the United States cannot determine the policy followed within a particular region; a majority of the citizens of that region must concur.

conference committee A joint Senate–House committee convened to reconcile the differences between the versions of a bill passed by the Senate and the House of Representatives.

confirmation The Senate's power to approve nominations made by the President for certain posts such as ambassadors or Supreme Court justices.

congressional caucus A meeting by the members of one party in either the House or the Senate in which various partisan decisions are made. Congressional party leaders – whips, floor leaders, candidates for presiding officer – are chosen in such meetings.

Connecticut compromise The agreement reached at the Constitutional Convention that Congress would consist of two chambers: the House of Representatives, in which the size of state delegations would be fixed according to population, and the Senate, in which each state, regardless of population, would be represented equally.

conscientious objector A person who refuses to serve in the military because religion or conscience forbids it.

conservatism A political philosophy stressing the importance of maintaining social stability and the need for strong political and social institutions to restrain natural passions; often, a political philosophy urging maintenance of the status quo (cf. liberalism).

constituency The district represented by a legislator; in broader terms, the set of interests represented by a government unit such as a congressional committee or an executive agency.

constituent A resident of a legislative district.

constitution The fundamental law – written or unwritten – that sets up the government of a nation, state, or any other organized group of people;

specifies the duties and powers of the various government agencies; and describes in detail the relationship between the citizens and their government.

cooperative federalism A system in which government powers are shared across the various levels of government – federal, state, and local (cf. dual federalism).

council–manager plan A form of city government in which a nonpartisan council hires a professional city manager, who runs the city subject to the council's approval.

decentralization The process of passing political power and decision-making responsibility from larger political units or agencies to ones that serve smaller geographic areas or narrower functional constituencies (cf. centralization).

decision The point at which a pattern of government activity changes (cf. policy).

de facto segregation Segregation that results from housing patterns in which different social groups live in different neighborhoods.

de jure segregation Segregation that is required by law.

deviating election An election that temporarily changes the balance of political forces (cf. maintaining election, realigning election).

direct primary An intraparty election in which the voters choose the candidates who will run on a party's ticket in the forthcoming general election (cf. closed primary).

disfranchise (or disenfranchise) To deny the privileges and rights of citizenship, especially voting.

dual federalism The doctrine that the states and the nation have separate areas of responsibility (cf. cooperative federalism).

due process of law The protection, guaranteed in the Fifth and Fourteenth Amendments to the Constitution, that acts of government that would deprive the individual of life, liberty, or property cannot be arbitrary but must be in accordance with established judicial procedures.

Electoral College The body of electors from each state who, after a presidential election, actually choose the new President and Vice-President. Each state selects a slate of electors in the November election. Normally they vote as a unit for the candidates who received a plurality of the vote in that state in the general election. The candidates who receive the majority of the electoral votes, who may or may not be the same as those who received the nationwide plurality of popular votes, become the President and Vice-President.

elite circulation The process by which established groups are gradually replaced by new ones so that new viewpoints and skills are represented in leadership circles.

ethnic group A group whose members share such traits as national background, religion, customs, culture, language, or historical experience. Catholic Americans of eastern or southern European origin are sometimes referred to as "ethnics."

executive agreement An international agreement made by the President that does not need senatorial approval to be operative.

extradition Transference of a person to the nation or state in which he or she has been accused of committing a crime by the government of another nation or state.

federalism A system of government in which power is shared between a central government and state or regional governments.

Federalist Papers A series of essays written by Alexander Hamilton, James Madison, and John Jay in defense of the newly drafted U.S. Constitution.

filibuster Obstruction of Senate action on a bill by the use of dilatory tactics. A common filibuster technique is to take advantage of the Senate's provision for unlimited debate in order to "talk a bill to death."

fiscal policy The use of economic tools—adjusting taxes, increasing or decreasing government spending on public projects, balancing the federal budget, or engaging in deficit spending—to stabilize the national economy or to spur economic growth.

floor leaders Party leaders, one from each party in each house of Congress, who are responsible for marshaling the party's forces in legislative battles.

gerrymandering Drawing the boundaries of legislative districts in an unnatural way in order to gain partisan advantage.

grandfather clause A provision, used in southern states to enfranchise whites who had been disqualified from voting by literacy tests or property qualifications, that held that disenfranchised people could vote if they or a lineal ancestor had been able to vote on January 1, 1867.

grant-in-aid A subsidy given by the federal government to a state or local government (or by a state government to a local government) to be used for some specified purpose according to prescribed standards.

habeas corpus A writ ordering an official who has a person in custody to bring that person to court and demonstrate why he or she is being held. The necessity of producing such a writ constitutes an important guarantee against arbitrary arrest.

impeachment A formal accusation of a public official for misconduct in office, made by the lower house of a legislature (a necessary step before the accused can be tried by the upper house of the legislature).

implied powers The doctrine that Congress isn't limited to the powers listed in the Constitution but has all the powers necessary to carry out those that are listed.

impoundment Literally, seizing and holding in legal custody; in the political context, refusal by the President to spend funds appropriated by Congress.

incremental planning A form of planning in which problems are approached one step at a time (cf. comprehensive planning).

independent regulatory commission An agency, such as the Securities and Exchange Commission, set up outside the major executive departments and responsible for regulating a given sector of the economy. An independent regulatory commission is generally shielded from partisan politics and from presidential control.

independent voter A voter who identifies with neither major political party and votes on a case-by-case basis according to the specific candidates or issues involved in a given race.

individualism The doctrine that the liberty and well-being of the individual are to be placed above those of society; also, the belief that the lot of the individual is a function of character and abilities rather than social forces.

inequality of distance A term that refers to the gap in income between the rich and the poor in a society.

inequality of scope A term that refers to the ways in which the rich are better off than the poor.

inflation An economic situation in which an increase in prices is accompanied by a loss of purchasing power.

interest group An organized group that uses various techniques to influence government policy; also referred to as a "pressure group" or "lobby."

Jim Crow law Any of a variety of laws passed by southern states requiring segregation of blacks and whites.

libel and slander Statements, either written (libel) or oral (slander), that defame the character of a person without justification.

liberalism A political philosophy emphasizing political, social, and economic changes in order to promote the well-being of the individual (cf. conservatism).

lobbyist An individual, often representing an interest group, who seeks to influence the contents of pending legislation, the outcome of legislative votes, or the decisions of executive agencies.

maintaining election An election that maintains the existing balance of political forces (cf. deviating election, realigning election).

majority rule The principle that the will of the greater number, a number over 50 percent, shall prevail in making political decisions and in choosing public officials (cf. plurality).

mandate uncertainty The difficulty experienced by elected officials in determining the preferences of their constituents.

mayor–council plan A form of city government in which the mayor shares power with an elected city council.

merchant class A group of leaders who believe that the well-being of citizens and of society as a whole can best be achieved by allowing the competitive marketplace to operate without government interference.

monetary policy Government efforts to manage the economy through changes in the money supply and interest rates.

patronage The power to make partisan appointments or to distribute, on a partisan basis, various jobs, franchises, contracts, or favors.

plurality The largest number of votes. When more than two strong candidates run for a given office, the winner will usually have a plurality rather than a majority (cf. majority rule).

pocket veto A presidential power that amounts to an effective veto over legislation passed at the end of a legislative session. If the President holds a piece of legislation without signing or vetoing it for ten days—and Congress adjourns during that time—then the bill does not become law.

policy A long-term commitment of the government to a pattern of activity (cf. decision).

political efficacy A citizen's belief that he or she can influence the affairs of government by his or her own actions.

political mainstream The broad policies that most Americans actively support or at least willingly tolerate; also, the belief in the importance of "working within the system."

political socialization The process by which young people learn basic political beliefs.

potential group A group with interests in common but little shared sense of group membership.

popular sovereignty The concept that political authority ultimately rests with the people.

president pro tempore The presiding officer of the Senate in the absence of the Vice-President. The President *pro tem* is always from the majority party in the Senate, regardless of the party of the Vice-President.

prior restraint The attempt to block publication of material (e.g., by a newspaper) in advance.

proportional representation An electoral system in which legislative seats are apportioned to parties or factions according to their approximate electoral strength.

radical A person who advocates immediate and sweeping political, social, or economic changes.

realigning election An election in which the party that had more faithful supporters than the second party loses its advantage and becomes the minority party. This happens when many new voters identify with what had previously been the minority party or when large numbers of voters change party allegiance (cf. deviating election, maintaining election).

revenue sharing A program under which federal funds are distributed to state and local governments for them to use in high-priority areas such as health care or public safety.

roll call vote A vote in Congress in which the legislators' votes of "yea" or "nay" are recorded.

segregation The separation of blacks and whites in public and private facilities—schools, buses, theaters, restaurants, and so on.

seniority rule The traditional congressional practice of awarding a committee chairpersonship to the member of the majority party with the longest uninterrupted service on that committee. A few successful challenges to this practice have occurred in recent years.

separation of powers The principle according to which government power is shared by the three branches of government—legislative, executive, and judicial.

social engineers A group of leaders who believe

that government programs must supplement the operations of the marketplace if individual and social well-being are to be achieved.

Speaker of the House The presiding officer and in general the most powerful member of the House of Representatives. The Speaker is elected by the entire House but is actually chosen by a caucus of the representatives from the majority party.

special district A local government unit that is created to provide a single service such as maintenance of parks or mosquito abatement.

spillover A term used to describe the activities of a community that affect its neighbors.

split ticket A ballot on which the voter has selected candidates of different parties for different offices (cf. straight ticket).

standing committee A permanent committee in the Senate or the House of Representatives.

stare decisis The principle that past decisions should be used as guidelines in ruling on similar cases.

State of the Union address An annual speech to Congress in which the President assesses the problems that face the nation and presents a legislative program to deal with them.

state sovereignty The principle, espoused by many people before the Civil War, that ultimate authority rests with the various states rather than with the national government.

straight ticket A ballot on which the voter has selected candidates of a single party for different offices (cf. split ticket).

tariff A tax on imports that protects domestic products from foreign competition by raising the prices of foreign products.

three-fifths compromise The agreement reached at the Constitutional Convention that slaves would be counted as three-fifths of one person in apportioning seats in the House of Representatives.

whip An assistant floor leader, selected in a party caucus in either house of Congress, who is responsible for acting as a liaison between party leaders and party members and for making sure party members are present for crucial votes.

writ of mandamus An order commanding an individual, corporation, or public official to perform some duty.

Index

OXFORD WORLD'S CLASSICS

EUGENE ONEGIN

ALEXANDER SERGEEVICH PUSHKIN was born in Moscow in 1799 into an old aristocratic family. As a schoolboy he demonstrated a precocious talent for verse and was recognized as a poetic prodigy by prominent older writers. In 1817 he received a nominal appointment in the government service, but for the most part he led a dissipated life in the capital while he continued to produce much highly polished light verse. His narrative poem, *Ruslan and Lyudmila* (publ. 1820), brought him widespread fame and secured his place as the leading figure in Russian poetry. At about the same time a few mildly seditious verses led to his banishment from the capital. During this so-called 'southern exile', he composed several narrative poems and began his novel in verse, *Eugene Onegin*. As a result of further conflicts with state authorities he was condemned to a new period of exile at his family's estate of Mikhailovskoe. There he wrote some of his finest lyric poetry, completed his verse drama *Boris Godunov*, and continued work on *Eugene Onegin*. He was still in enforced absence from the capital when the Decembrist Revolt of 1825 took place. Although several of his friends were among those executed or imprisoned, he himself was not implicated in the affair, and in 1826 he was pardoned by the new Czar Nicholas I and permitted to return to Moscow. By the end of the decade, as he sought to become a truly professional writer, he turned increasingly to prose composition. In the especially fruitful autumn of 1830, while stranded at his estate of Boldino, he completed *Eugene Onegin*, wrote a major collection of prose stories (*The Tales of Belkin*), and composed his experimental 'Little Tragedies'. In 1831, he married Natalya Goncharova and sought to put his personal and professional affairs on a more stable footing. The rest of his life, however, was plagued by financial and marital woes, by the hostility of literary and political enemies, and by the younger generation's dismissal of his recent work. His literary productivity diminished, but in the remarkable 'second Boldino autumn' of 1833 he produced both his greatest prose tale, *The Queen of Spades*, and a last poetic masterpiece, *The Bronze Horseman*. In 1836 he completed his only novel-length work in prose, *The Captain's Daughter*. Beleaguered by numerous adversaries and enraged by anonymous letters containing attacks on his honour, he was driven in 1837 to challenge an importunate admirer of his wife to a duel. The contest took place on 27 February, and two days later, the poet died from his wounds.

JAMES E. FALEN is Professor of Russian at the University of Tennessee, where he teaches nineteenth- and twentieth-century Russian literature and Russian language. He is the author of *Isaac Babel: Russian Master of the Short Story* (University of Tennessee Press, 1974) and has published translations of lyric and dramatic verse by Alexander Pushkin. He is currently working on translations of twentieth-century Russian poetry.

OXFORD WORLD'S CLASSICS

*For over 100 years Oxford World's Classics have brought
readers closer to the world's great literature. Now with over 700
titles—from the 4,000-year-old myths of Mesopotamia to the
twentieth century's greatest novels—the series makes available
lesser-known as well as celebrated writing.*

*The pocket-sized hardbacks of the early years contained
introductions by Virginia Woolf, T. S. Eliot, Graham Greene,
and other literary figures which enriched the experience of reading.
Today the series is recognized for its fine scholarship and
reliability in texts that span world literature, drama and poetry,
religion, philosophy and politics. Each edition includes perceptive
commentary and essential background information to meet the
changing needs of readers.*

OXFORD WORLD'S CLASSICS

ALEXANDER PUSHKIN

Eugene Onegin
A Novel in Verse

Translated with an Introduction and Notes by
JAMES E. FALEN

OXFORD
UNIVERSITY PRESS

OXFORD

UNIVERSITY PRESS

Great Clarendon Street, Oxford OX2 6DP

Oxford University Press is a department of the University of Oxford.
It furthers the University's objective of excellence in research, scholarship,
and education by publishing worldwide in

Oxford New York

Athens Auckland Bangkok Bogotá Buenos Aires Calcutta
Cape Town Chennai Dar es Salaam Delhi Florence Hong Kong Istanbul
Karachi Kuala Lumpur Madrid Melbourne Mexico City Mumbai
Nairobi Paris São Paulo Singapore Taipei Tokyo Toronto Warsaw

with associated companies in Berlin Ibadan

Oxford is a registered trade mark of Oxford University Press
in the UK and in certain other countries

Published in the United States
by Oxford University Press Inc., New York

British Library Cataloguing in Publication Data

Data available

Library of Congress Cataloging in Publication Data

Pushkin, Aleksandr Sergeevich, 1799–1837.
[Evgenii Onegin. English]
Eugene Onegin : a novel in verse / Alexander Pushkin ; translated
with an introduction and notes by James E. Falen.
Includes bibliographical references.
1. Falen, James E., 1935– . II. Title. III. Series.
PG3347.E8F35 1995 891.73'3—dc20 94–45634

ISBN 978-0-19-953864-5

21

Printed in Great Britain by
Clays Ltd, Elcograf S.p.A.

CONTENTS

INTRODUCTION

Alexander Pushkin (1799–1837) is the poet and writer whom Russians regard as both the source and the summit of their literature. Not only is he revered, like Shakespeare in the English tradition or Goethe in the German, as the supreme national poet, but he has become a kind of cultural myth, an iconic figure around whom a veritable cult of idolatry has been fashioned. This exalted status that Pushkin has been accorded in his own land has been something of a disservice to the living reality of his works, and it contrasts oddly with the more modest reputation that Pushkin has secured abroad. To many non-native readers of Russian literature the panegyrics of his compatriots seem excessive, and indeed, in their eyes, Pushkin has been somewhat overshadowed by the great Russian writers who came after him. They do not comprehend why these writers themselves generally grant him the first and highest place in their pantheon of artistic geniuses. For those who do not read Pushkin in his own language, the situation remains perplexing and the questions persist: just who is he and why, almost without exception, do the most perceptive of his compatriots regard him as one of the world's greatest artists?

Within the Russian tradition the scope of Pushkin's achievement is essentially clear and well established. He is unarguably a figure of protean dimensions, the author in his own right of a formidable and enduring body of work and at the same time the seminal writer whose example has nourished, enriched, and in large part directed all subsequent literature in the language. He came of age at a historical moment when the Russian literary language, after a century or so of imitation of foreign models, had been roughly shaped and readied for the hand of an original genius. Pushkin was to fulfil that role.

He began his career in an era when both the writers and the readers of literature belonged almost exclusively to the limited milieu of aristocratic society and at a time when poetry rather than prose was the dominant mode for high literature. Well read in both the ancient classics and in Western European literature, especially French literature of the seventeenth and eighteenth centuries, Pushkin was the most dazzlingly talented member of a younger generation of writers who were attempting, under the banner of romanticism, to reform and invigorate the language and the styles of poetry. If Pushkin's early work (he began composing as a schoolboy prodigy) was facile and conventional, consisting mainly of light verse suitable for the literary salons of the day (frothy Epicurean pieces, witty epigrams, album verse), it already displayed an impressive plasticity of language that was new in Russian literature; and quite soon he exhibited a mastery of virtually all the poetic genres and styles known to the writers of his era. The eventual range of his creativity was enormous, embracing not only all the prevailing forms of lyric verse (which he reshaped into his own freer medium of expression), but including brilliant examples of narrative verse as well. He also achieved stunning success in poetry based on the idioms and themes of Russian folklore, and he experimented fascinatingly in the field of verse drama, both on a large Shakespearian scale and in intensely concentrated, minimalist studies of human passions. He is, in sum, a poet of astonishing versatility. Possessed of a uniquely supple linguistic instrument, he is the master of an apparently effortless natural-ness, a seamless blend of appropriate sound, sense, and feeling.

During the last decade of his life, when literary activity was being democratized and commercialized, and when a larger, more broadly based readership was emerging, Pushkin turned increasingly to prose, which was fast outdistancing poetry in popularity, though it had yet to achieve the same high level of excellence attained by Russian verse. Pushkin's prose fiction, which is characterized by an unusual terseness and precision of expression, includes several masterpieces in the short-story form, one completed historical novel (as well as the beginnings of several others), and a number of unfinished drafts of a contemporary social novel. He also made significant contributions to Russian culture as a journalist, as a literary critic and editor, as an accomplished letter-writer, and as a gifted, if amateur, historian. He became in effect Russia's first complete man of letters.

All his creative life Pushkin suffered from the indignities and impositions of an autocratic state: exile in his youth, the frustrations of police surveillance and a grossly interfering censorship in his later years, the constant and onerous obligations of government service, and the continuing humiliation of having to rely on imperial favour. In an effort to secure his independence from such state control over his affairs he gave his political allegiance to a kind of 'aristocratic party', seeing in the old Russian landed gentry, the class to which he himself was born, the only viable check on the arbitrary power of the autocracy. This aligned him as well, in a literary sense, with the notion, prevalent among the educated members of 'élite' society, that the writer's appropriate role was that of the gentleman *littérateur*, a view of the artist that probably hindered Pushkin in his effort, during the last decade of his life, to transform himself into a truly free and independent professional writer. He never succeeded, finally, in escaping from either the constraints of court pressure or his own persistent allegiance to a fading aristocratic culture. His further development as an artist was abruptly terminated by his death in a duel at the age of 38.

In both his poetry and his prose Pushkin was a profound innovator. He brought to its successful conclusion the revolt against the tenets of French neoclassicism, which, with its rigid divisions and classifications of genres, had dominated the literature of the eighteenth and early nineteenth centuries. Life, in Pushkin's view, was wilder and more various than these conventions would allow, and, although he always retained a rather classical respect for balance and proportion in art, he introduced into his native literature a new sense of artistic freedom. His formal experiments encouraged a vigorous inventiveness in the writers who followed him, and his modernization of the diction and syntax of literary texts with infusions of living contemporary speech pointed the way to a perennial renewal of the literary language. In the area of literary subject-matter as well his influence was far-reaching: he introduced a host of suggestive themes that later writers would explore more fully, and he greatly enlarged the cast of characters in serious literature. No topic or person lay beyond the reach of his interest; his poetry and prose are filled with life's essential concerns and activities—with love, work, art, history, politics, and nature; with all the mundane trivia of everyday existence and with the more rarefied realm of dreams and thoughts. He virtually created and shaped modern Russian literature and in countless ways determined the course it would follow after him.

Those who seek labels have made numerous attempts to define and categorize this astonishing writer. He has been called variously a romantic and a realist, the poet of freedom and the bard of Russia's imperium; he has been dubbed in political terms a radical, a liberal, and a conservative, a revolutionary critic of the Czarist regime and its loyal defender. Persuasive arguments can and have been made in support of each of these characterizations, but a poet of genius always in the end evades our efforts to tame and contain him.

This brief assessment of Pushkin's place in Russian literature, although it provides a reasonably accurate recital of established critical views, ignores certain anomalies and paradoxes that are part of the Pushkin story. Rather curiously, for example, all the prolific and prodigious achievement of this 'father of Russian literature' was the work of a man whose chief public mask in his own day was that of a gadfly and wastrel. Disciplined in his art, he was often irresponsible and profligate in his social behaviour. There was about him, as the reminiscences of contemporaries observe, something of the eternal schoolboy and prankster, a bit of the renegade always at odds with the respectable adult world. For several years he played the roles of dandy or bohemian; he loved to shock with outlandish dress or outrageous behaviour, and he enjoyed flirting recklessly with the dangers of a dissolute and dissident life. Upon leaving school he put on, briefly, the mask of political rebel and quite consciously provoked, with several courageous poems of liberal sentiment, the displeasure of the emperor, for which he was punished with removal from the centres of Russian culture and power. Even then, in banishment, he courted further punitive action from the authorities by circulating verse of blasphemous, if humorous, content.

Exile seems to have been a defining experience of Pushkin's young manhood. He deeply resented his enforced absence from the social scene, yet he gained through his distance from the centre of events a clearer vision of the society he craved to rejoin. When he was permitted, eventually, to reside once again in St Petersburg and Moscow, he quickly set about to re-establish his nonconformist credentials, indulging once more in a dissipated style of life, although it now seemed less appropriate to his advancing years. Even after his marriage (at almost 32), when he had ostensibly settled down, he continued to provoke outrage, antagonism, and even ridicule with his endless literary feuds, his increasingly touchy pride in his ancient lineage, and his utter contempt for the circles of the court. Yet another cause for the contradictory impulses of his spirit was the black African strain in his ancestry, a heritage that he saw as both a source of uniqueness and a mark of his alienation from the society whose acceptance he simultaneously rejected and craved. At times he revelled in his 'African strangeness' and spoke of his 'moorish' features as the emblem of an elemental and primordial side of his identity, while on other occasions he lamented the racial characteristics that set him apart from those around him. In any case, whatever his ambivalences, it seems clear that Pushkin relished as well as resented his estrangement from society; and certainly his marginal position in it helped him to see all the triviality and hypocrisy of the *monde*. If he continued to live by its codes, he also studied it keenly as an artist and depicted it matchlessly in his work.

Even by the standards of his time and circle Pushkin's appetite for dissipation was large. He was an inveterate gambler and a famous seducer of women, behaviour that he was reluctant to relinquish, not merely out of a mindless adoption of available social roles, but because of the special powers that he attributed to chance and sensuality in his creative life. His youthful anacreontic verse with its playful eroticism, several narrative poems of refined ribaldry, and his more mature love poetry all testify to a deeply sensual nature; and his passion for gambling figures prominently in some of his finest prose works. He was always fascinated, on behalf of his art, in the play of the fortuitous, in the luck of the draw, in the creative possibilities of life's contingencies. He was willing as man and artist to trust in chance, to submit to it as the mechanism that, while it might condemn him to an outwardly undefined and precarious existence, would also assure his inner artistic freedom and his poetic destiny. Chance, in Pushkin's view, was the servant of the greater thing that he called fate, and his reverence for fate as the ultimate shaper of human destinies haunts his work at almost every stage of his career. Essentially buoyant and optimistic in his youth, perceiving fate as the artist's benign and essential guide, he would never distrust it, not even when later in his life it took on an ominous and threatening aspect. Opposition to the tyranny of human institutions was an essential element in Pushkin's conception of the free artist, but resistance to fate, he believed, was a perilous course of action for any individual; for himself he was convinced it was the surest way to destruction as a poet. These elements of Pushkin's character—his sensuality, his courting of chance, and his trust in fate—are essential clues to his artistic nature and to his conception of creativity. He is an artist for whom personality means little, for whom an ordinary human nature and a mundane existence are the very attributes and signs of the poet who is fully engaged with life and at the same time receptive to the designs of Providence.

The poet for Pushkin is a mysterious being: inspired to

exalted utterance by strange gods, yet remaining at an everyday level the most insignificant of humans, a misfit and outcast. Far from being in *propria persona* a poetic demi-urge, the poet is the instrument and voice of powers beyond the self. This is a conception of the poet that combines elements of both a romantic and an anti-romantic sensibility. It yokes together two disparate images, that of the divinely inspired seer and that of the human misfit. It is a vision, of course, with ancient roots and, in its specifically Russian variant, with links to the native tradition of the 'jurodivy', the wandering 'holy fool' of popular veneration. For Pushkin such an image of the poet provides a justification for asserting at once an enormous arrogance for his art and a fundamental humility toward his gift. And perhaps it helps to explain the peculiar instability and elusiveness of Pushkin's artistic personality, the odd sense his reader has that the author is both palpably present in his work and yet nowhere to be found. We seldom know directly what this author *thinks*, even about seemingly obvious things, and we are made uneasy by this lack of a familiar and reassuring human intelligence. The point is not that Pushkin leaves a great deal to the reader's creativity and perception, though he does, but rather that his genius is to an unusual extent of a peculiarly negative kind. He is that rare artist who possesses to an extreme degree a kind of splendid receptivity, an ability to absorb and embody the very energy of his surroundings, to take into himself with an amazing sympathy all the shapes and colours of the life that he sees and hears and responds to. He may or he may not examine intellectually the life that he describes, he may or he may not admire it or approve of it, but what he *must* do is reveal it, recreate it in its vivacity, display his sheer perception of it, refraining from an easy human judgement.

Pushkin is something of an artistic chameleon, and this is why it is so difficult to define him or to fix on a clear and consistent image of his authorial person and stance. He seems almost to lack a coherent artistic persona; like a chameleon, he seems capable of changing his colours and of adapting to almost any milieu. He is enormously alive to the ephemera of experience, fascinated by everything and everyone: the sublime and the ridiculous; the sacred and the profane; all the roles that people play and every style of behaviour; he is interested equally in the talented and the mediocre, in the articulate and the dumb; in Czars, peasants, soldiers, fops, rakes, society women, vulnerable girls, rascals, villains, and almost anyone else. He wants, if only fleetingly, to capture everything, to absorb it all in his appetite for life—even at the risk of losing himself, or perhaps out of the need to lose himself. And the vision that emerges from this fleeting race through experience is no less perceptive and suggestive than many more lengthy examinations of life. Pushkin's manner of describing phenomena is fleeting and abrupt because he is never sated, never content, never willing to stay in one place; he has to rush on to the next person or thing that catches his eye. His omnivorous curiosity lends a kind of 'lightness' as well as universality to Pushkin's work—a lightness of touch, weight, and illumination. The quality is legendary in descriptions of Pushkin's art, but it can be mistaken for superficiality. Our elusive author appears to take few things seriously (not excluding himself) and often poses as a mere 'entertainer'. Entertaining he certainly is, but if we, as readers, are taken in by his ruse and allow ourselves to become inattentive, we are in danger of missing the subtle and hidden aspect of his art.

The effect of lightness, the exceptional clarity that so famously accompanies Pushkin's breadth of interests, goes hand in hand with his vaunted terseness and simplicity, his evident and easy accessibility. But his terseness can be more apparent than real, for his art has the capacity to suggest much in a few spare and simple observations, and his simplicity can be deceptive, screening from the casual reader an art of great sophistication and delicacy. To the foreign reader, especially, Pushkin's qualities of clarity and simplicity can be an impediment to the appreciation of his work; and if the reader has first come to Russian literature through the tormented and profound explorations of

Tolstoy or Dostoevsky, Pushkin's view of the passing scene, filled with a bracing humour as well as grief, may produce a rather strange impression; he is not at all what such a reader has come to expect of a Russian writer. Unlike those two later masters, Pushkin is neither philosopher nor religious thinker, neither didactic moralist nor analytical psychologist. He is both more universal in his sympathies and more modest in his artistic person.

Perhaps, in his final years, this poet of light could not fully adjust to the passing of his youth and the waning of youth's poetic energy. If he would not become a poet of the dark, perhaps he did at the last become the seer of an 'unbearable lightness of being'. In several of his later poems some spectral beast of retribution seems to haunt the poet's mind, along with premonitions of, and even yearnings for, an early death. But the ending in human life is always the same, whereas in great art, as in the plenitude of Pushkin's work, it can at least seem otherwise. Pushkin retained to the last his humility before Providence and he went to his duel and his death completely in character. We cannot, finally, answer the question: who is Pushkin? We can only say with some degree of certainty *what* he is: Russia's most utter artist, its closest thing to the pure poet incarnate, that being who sacrifices all the other possibilities of his human existence to the expression, through language, of life's fascinating variety. The aim of poetry, Pushkin asserted, is poetry itself; the poet emerges from the creative spirit to show us the world and speak of things beyond our normal ken; he is the voice of time's fleeting and intricate fullness.

Central to any consideration of Pushkin's art is his 'novel in verse', *Eugene Onegin*, a work unique in Russian literature and one with few if any parallels outside it. Although it occupies in some respects an isolated and idiosyncratic place in Pushkin's *œuvre*, it is also his most deeply characteristic creation. It was his own favourite among his works and may well be his greatest single contribution to world literature. Despite its considerable

literary sophistication and complexity and the fact of its having
been written in verse, it may be more accessible to the
appreciation of non-Russian readers than most of Pushkin's
other work. Almost all of us, even those who are resistant to
poetry (especially in translation!), are readers of novels; and
Pushkin's long poem, with its stanzas that mimic paragraphs
and its verse that seems as natural as familiar prose, subtly
entices us by its successful masquerade as a novel. The writer
spent some eight years writing it (far longer than he devoted to
any other work), and it thus accompanied him through an
extended and crucial period of his life. It not only reflects the
vital changes that were taking place in Pushkin himself during
those years, but it also represents its author's response to a
transformation in the general literary climate. By the late 1820s
the rage was all for new works in prose rather than poetry, and
although Russian literature had as yet produced few prose
works of any lasting distinction, writers were eager to answer
the demands of the time. Pushkin was among the first of the
established authors to respond to the need for a serious prose
literature. This change in public taste and Pushkin's effort to
respond to it took place in the very years when the writer was
composing *Eugene Onegin*. Begun when Pushkin was only 24,
still ebullient in his poetic personality and still partially under
the sway of his fascination with Byron, it was completed in his
thirty-second year, when he was already the author of several
prose works of a strongly anti-romantic cast. *Onegin*, as the
work's hybrid nature suggests, belongs to a transitional phase
in Pushkin's career and constitutes a kind of bridge linking two
literary eras. It shows us its author, at the central period of his
life, in the very act of crossing that bridge, attempting to
transform himself from romantic poet into a novelist who
would paint on a large canvas an expansive picture of social
reality. Paradoxically *Eugene Onegin*, although written in verse,
is the earliest of Pushkin's works to contain a major component
of the 'prosaic' in motivation and spirit. This rather complex
set of personal and historical factors informs this first great

Russian novel (and arguably the most influential) in a number of crucial ways and provides the ground for its unique flavour and a strangeness that both delights and perplexes the reader.

The work is many things: a stylistic *tour de force*, an examination of human character and of the power in human affairs of cultural phenomena (especially social and artistic conventions), an investigation of the interconnections between literature and life, an autobiography, and an exploration of the creative process itself. It is also, of course, and above all else, incomparable poetry. Highly structured in its use of an unvarying stanzaic form and in its classically balanced design, the work nevertheless conveys an atmosphere of free-flowing spontaneity. Its verse, while observing elegantly the requirements of metre and rhyme, is able at the same time to achieve the rhythm and feel of the most natural and ordinary colloquial speech. Like a discursive prose work, the novel exhibits a wealth of genial, meandering talk and an apparently casual approach to narrative pace. The plot itself is elegantly simple. Treating of the frustrations of love, it deals, as Vladimir Nabokov puts it, 'with the emotions, meditations, acts and destinies of three men: Onegin, the bored fop; Lensky, the minor elegiast; and a stylized Pushkin, Onegin's friend'[1]—and, in a pleasing symmetry, with the affections and fates of three heroines: Tatyana, the shy and bookish provincial maiden; Olga, her beautiful but ordinary younger sister; and Pushkin's mercurial Muse. The action, set in the imperial Russia of the 1820s, begins in a glittering St Petersburg, moves for an extended stay to the bucolic country estate, sojourns for a chapter in Moscow, and then, as if closing a circle, comes to its end in the capital once more. Along its devious narrative route, the novel treats the reader to an engaging and suspenseful story; to lively scenes of city and country life; to portraits of a socially mixed cast of characters; to evocations of nature in its various seasons; and to

[1] *Eugene Onegin: A Novel in Verse by Alexander Pushkin, Translated from the Russian with a Commentary* (New York, 1964), iv. 6.

a wealth of authorial digression and commentary, à la Byron or Sterne, on the tale in the telling and on sundry literary, philosophical, and autobiographical matters—all in a shifting play of many moods and tones: lyrical, realistic, parodic, romantic, and ironic.

Much commentary on the work has focused, understandably enough, on its hero and heroine, Onegin and Tatyana, the ill-starred but non-tragic lovers who were to become the proto-types for a host of figures created by later Russian writers. Those critics who approach the text as a realistic novel and who accept its heroes as more or less psychologically plausible representatives of their society, have viewed the two main characters in quite varied and even conflicting ways. To some, Onegin is a victim of his environment, a potentially creative man whose personal fulfilment is frustrated by the limited opportunities available to him in his era. To others he is an anti-hero, an amoral hedonist and misanthropic egoist. Tatyana, though usually regarded in an almost hagiographic light (she is for many Russians the most beloved heroine in their literature), also has a few detractors, readers who see her as an immature woman in whom instinctual drives and vague intuition rather than active intelligence or innate spiritual nobility account for most of her actions. All those critics who attempt such analyses of the characters are confronted by certain puzzling inconsist-encies in their behaviour; in different parts of the novel they seem almost to be different people. A reasonable explanation, not much noted, for the antithetical interpretations the heroes have evoked is that they are dichotomous in their very natures: over the long period of the novel's composition, Pushkin's own artistic values and aims were changing, and it seems quite likely that his characters evolved as well, that his image of them ripened and deepened over that period. There is also a funda-mental, if rich, ambiguity in the author's treatment of Onegin and Tatyana as both character-studies and poetic symbols.

Other critics of the work have taken a more formalist approach, viewing the characters less as real people than as reflections of literary stereotypes. Literary art and language itself, in their view, are always self-referential, uninvolved in any realities supposed to exist outside the work. Such readings also face difficulties and complications. Pushkin's fictional heroes are themselves avid readers of fiction, they construct their identities as much from books as from available social roles. Onegin, in resisting the constrictions of social conventions, adopts the dissident poses of dandy and cynic; but these are only further conventional masks, disguises borrowed from books. Onegin's lack of a solid identity becomes clear to the reader, and to Tatyana within the novel itself, with the realization that he is mostly a congeries of literary affectations, a parody: he has modelled himself on the currently fashionable Byronic type, while at the same time he appears, in Tatyana's vivid literary imagination, as the thrilling hero of a Gothic romance. Pushkin has great satirical fun in playing with these various literary echoes and he has his hero, more empty shell than either rebel or demon, confront his fate not in a romantically primordial wilderness, but in the homely setting of a Russian country estate. Similarly, Tatyana, though less parodied by the author (because she is capable of genuine feeling), is composed of a number of literary and cultural personae. To the narrator she contains elements of the 'savage female', a being untouched by civilization's denaturing forces (a fantasy of many male romantic writers); to Onegin, when he first encounters her, she is merely a naïve provincial girl; and by the novel's end she is for both Onegin and her new aristocratic milieu the very embodiment of a successful society hostess and legislatrix. Tatyana too confronts her fate in a kind of literary parody: she discovers the true nature of her hero not by a passage into the dark recesses of a medieval castle, but by reading Onegin's books in his abandoned country house, itself a symbol of the hero's vacancy.

We may note, in order to illustrate one of Pushkin's methods for revealing the power of cultural determinants in his characters' behaviour, the various explanations the narrator gives for

Tatyana's falling in love. We are told that she does so as a 'child of nature', spontaneously and without artificial contrivance; that she falls in love in response to the neighbours' gossip, which has planted the idea in her mind; that it is due to the influence of the epistolary novels she has read; or that it was simply appropriate to her age and social expectations. Having amused his readers with this shrewd undermining of typical romantic attitudes, Pushkin then surprises them and complicates their perceptions of 'truth' by giving a beautifully poetic description of Tatyana as a girl actually in love, with all the restless pain, joy, and dreaminess of her condition. The scene occurs, furthermore, in the wonderfully effective context of Tatyana's conversation with her concerned old nurse, seen in touching and realistic counterpoint to the feverish young girl.

Lensky is yet another figure who derives from books. Creating himself out of his naïve literary readings and aspirations, he becomes a gentle parody of the sentimental romantic poet. What is particularly interesting and somewhat paradoxical, however, is that most of the characters transcend their function as parodies. They are treated by their creator with a sometimes puzzling blend of ironic detachment and sympathetic concern. It is one of the charms of the novel that the author (or at least the narrator) shares at times the viewpoint and attitudes of his most naïve reader.

The narrator constantly intrudes on his story, postponing with his various digressions its progress, speculating on where it might lead, and frequently frustrating his reader's expectations. By exposing the work's contrived 'literariness', the narrator continually threatens to subvert or deconstruct the novelistic 'truth' of his tale. But then again, on resuming his narrative, he will recapture our interest in his heroes' fates and reignite an acceptance of their 'reality'. In his frequent address to both 'readers' and 'friends' (the latter comprised apparently of more sophisticated sorts of reader), the author anticipates almost all the potential ways of approaching and interpreting his book and seems to be trying to fashion, out of an amalgam of both naïve and sophisticated sensibilities, his ideal reader. We, his actual readers, like the solvers of a Chinese puzzle, must work out for ourselves the answers to a number of riddles the work proposes. What is the true nature of art? Where do the boundaries between literature and life lie? Or are there no boundaries, only a tangled network of intersecting threads that connect the lives we lead with the books we read? Perhaps, as this thoroughly modern and timeless work suggests, we are unable, despite all our strivings for personal 'authenticity', to be anything but the roles we play, the products and the playthings of literary and social conventions.

Pushkin's intricate and playful exploration of the connections between art and life permeates the work. His own practice as a poet is a case in point, issuing not only from his own genius, but from his enormous reading and his extensive knowledge of literary tradition. The novel's verse, poetry of the highest order, is also at times a pastiche of all the many clichés of poetic imagery and diction, of the techniques and formal conventions of a vast existing literature; though the writer may violate or mix or parody these traditions, he cannot exist without them. In support of its author's sly yet revealing game, the novel is full of literary allusions and references to other writers; it mocks the easy conflation of literature and life in countless ways: by the device, for example, of mixing real with fictional personages. Most prominently, of course, Pushkin has inserted himself into his book, not only as its narrator, but as the ostensible friend of its hero, Onegin. Tatyana, to give another instance, encounters and captivates at a Moscow soirée Prince Vyazemsky, Pushkin's actual friend and fellow-poet. When the poem momentarily turns historical novel, the Emperor Napoleon briefly appears, only to be condemned as the impostor (in Russian memory) whose heroic pretensions were consumed by a Moscow conflagration and by life's intractability. Napoleon also figures in the novel as an icon of the European romantic imagination and, ironically, as the idol of the westernized Russian Onegin, who keeps a statuette of his hero in his study.

Again and again the work demonstrates that cultural myths are deeply embedded in the modern consciousness, that we cannot disentangle ourselves from our words or extricate our 'selves' from our texts. None of this, happily, seems to make human nature in Pushkin's eyes any less real or human characters any less responsible for their actions. The disguises we wear and the poses we assume or, contrastingly, the more active and creative roles that we may elect to play in life, define us as human beings.

The early-nineteenth-century critic Belinsky remarked famously that Pushkin's novel is 'an encyclopedia of Russian life'. Although it is currently fashionable to disparage Belinsky's 'crudely sociological' approach to literature, there is much to be said (especially if we remove the word 'Russian') for his observation. For all this work's literary self-consciousness (it is an encyclopedia of literature, too), what a richly woven and glittering tapestry of life it contains, much of it supplied in apparently casual passing fashion, as was Pushkin's way. He shows us the theatre, where on a public stage writers, actors, and audience all perform and where the wings become a setting for erotic adventure; he gives us dance in its many shapes and styles: the ballet, the society ball, the country shindig, the peasant stomp; other music and song: in opera, in a regimental band, in the singing of serf-girls; food and dining, in fashionable restaurants and at rustic feasts; the architectural environment in churches, palaces, city mansions, apartments, urban hovels, and country manors; the varying styles of clothing; the books; the protocols of duelling; the customs of matchmaking, courtship, and marriage; life as played out in passionate youth and in resigned middle-age; the relationships of parents and children; the ways of the contemporary city and the ancient traditions of the countryside; the horses and conveyances that people use (which are also metaphors for the Pushkinian rush to experience life's variety, or at least to observe it from the window of a moving carriage)—all the activities, codes, customs, and conventions through which we live and which determine, whether we observe or defy them, who we are. And note as well the lively capsule biographies of some of the novel's minor characters: Tatyana's parents, Onegin's father and uncle, the rake Zaretsky, and even the two alternative futures imagined for Lensky beyond the novel's time-frame. Once again, in these mini-biographies, the author's touch is light and fleeting, his method the sparing use of a few trivial and prosaic details, the more insignificant the more telling.

Let me close these brief introductory remarks on Pushkin's masterwork with a few observations on some of its autobiographical implications. It presents, among its other texts, the writer's report to himself at mid-career, recording his discoveries about life and art and his concerns for his creative future. Not only the novel's narrator, it should be noted, but also the three other major characters are quite clearly expressions of Pushkin's personality. Onegin, despite the author's disclaimer to the contrary, bears some of Pushkin's own human traits, and the two share a number of social masks; the essential and decisive difference between them, of course, is that Onegin has none of the poet in him. Lensky, on the other hand, who does possess a genuine if immature poetic sensibility, is not unlike the younger Pushkin, a persona the writer has outgrown and now regards with affectionate irony. The conflict in the novel between Onegin and Lensky, so perplexingly motivated in terms of the characters' psychology, represents much more plausibly a conflict in the soul of the author, a struggle between his 'prosaic' and 'poetic' selves (recall the description when the two characters first meet: Lensky all poetry, Onegin all prose). If it seems that Pushkin takes the cynical Onegin rather seriously and merely mocks the naïve Lensky, this is something of a subterfuge, a device to conceal his own passionate commitment, even as he questions it, to poetry. Onegin, Pushkin's 'friend', is at once his baser *alter ego* and a symbol of his new allegiance to the truths of prose. Tatyana, whom the narrator calls his 'ideal' and who by the novel's end is identified with Pushkin's Muse, seems on a symbolic plane to stand as the artist's emblem for the native sources of his poetry, or as an avatar of his art itself. She is a figure who, though unhappy and unfree (like Pushkin himself), remains steadfast in her adherence to values beyond the gratifications of the self. There is an undeniable sadness in this sparkling novel, especially at its end. If it opened to the tune of a sprightly scherzo, it closes to the strains of a somewhat mournful adagio. Pain and disappointment have a prominent place in the world of *Onegin*, but so too does the celebration of life in all its enticing minutiae; and thus the novel gives us neither a conventionally happy nor a conventionally unhappy ending. It avoids, to be sure, any overt statement of tragedy, for the hero and heroine still live, are indeed still relatively young. Their stories, abruptly abandoned in typically Pushkinian fashion, remain incomplete, their ultimate fates still unresolved. In his final chapter does Pushkin even try to rescue his hapless hero from the shallowness of his egoism? Does he seek to make him worthy through his suffering of someone's, if not Tatyana's, love? Could the tale that unwinds beyond the pages of the book be resumed, could it take unexpected turns and move in new directions, are other outcomes possible? One suspects, despite the aesthetically pleasing roundedness of the poem, that the answers are *yes*, that other roads lie ahead for the heroes, that life still beckons. In his generosity of spirit the author gives to his characters, and thereby to himself, the possibility of renewal. The concluding chapters of *Eugene Onegin* are Pushkin's farewell to his poetic youth. Henceforth, in his effort to reinvent himself, and as a sign of his commitment to become yet more fully engaged in the life of literature, he would devote his energies mainly to prose. For Pushkin, however, to cease completely to be a poet was to die, and in his 'novel in verse' he announces a continuing will to live. Life's chalice, he tells us in its final stanza, never runs dry, life's novel (which the artist both reads and writes) never comes to an end for the taker of risks.

NOTE ON THE TRANSLATION

If art holds a mirror up to nature, it frequently does so—as in this masterpiece of Pushkin's—by first directing that mirror at other works of art. The world of *Eugene Onegin* derives perhaps as much from Western European literary antecedents and traditions as it does from its author's Russia, and in doing so it provides a paradoxical picture of life mimicking art. The literary translator, in seeking to participate in this international colloquy, holds, as it were, yet another mirror up to these already doubled or tripled mirrors. It is a devilish and tricky business, this game in a house of mirrors, this effort to catch and reflect elusive reflections. There are occasions when the translator, however carefully he tries to grip his own mirror by its edges so as not to smudge the glass, will inadvertently allow his hands to enter the picture and thus obscure the view.

In attempting to reproduce poetry, the verbal art most closely tied to its native language and the most susceptible to distortion in the transfer to another, the translator faces particularly vexing difficulties. Verse, perhaps, can be translated; great poetry is something else. Russian and English poetry do not look, sound, or behave very much alike; and by choosing to work on Pushkin's poem, in which the sheer beauty of sound is so vital a part of its effect and in which all the expressive resources of the Russian language are on masterful display, the translator may find himself casting an uneasy eye at Robert Frost's cautionary definition of poetry as 'what gets lost in translation'. All he can do, having begun, is keep to his task, reassuring himself that both Russian and English, after all, assemble consonants and vowels into sounds and words, into beauty and sense.

Pushkin's long poem has had some seven English translations prior to this one (the more thorough Germans seem to have produced about twelve), and yet it has continued to be regarded by many as a classic instance of the untranslatable work. Vladimir Nabokov has argued that a literal rendering of Pushkin's sentences is about the best that can be achieved or even honestly attempted; that any translation that retains the original's metre and rhyme, since it cannot be faithful to the work's exact meaning, will necessarily result in a mere paraphrase. In his own translation of the novel, which he proudly labelled a 'pony', he shunned, accordingly, both metre and rhyme and gave us a version at once marvellously accurate and rather peculiar, most of its poetry resident in the accompanying commentary rather than in the translation itself. Pushkin, one has to say, loses where Nabokov gains. And of course a 'literal' version is, in the end, no less unfaithful to its model than a rhymed and metred one: in place of a work whose austere and harmonious shape is an essential part of its effect, it gives us something ill-proportioned and flaccid, a kind of 'formal paraphrase' that seems bland and inert where the original is expressive and alive. But the translator's dilemma doesn't lie, really, in choosing between faithfulness to form and faithfulness to meaning, for in fact neither of these goals, even separately, is attainable. In the transfer of a work from one language to another there are no exact correspondences to be found— neither in the meanings and histories of words nor in the intricacies and effects of forms. This very tendency of ours to divide a work of art into separate categories of form and content not only gives a false view of a work's complex nature but also poses the problem of literary translation in a false light.

Confronted with an evident inability to render a work faithfully in either its absolute form or its total sense, the translator, it would seem, faces an impossible task and is condemned by the very nature of his enterprise to an act of compromise and betrayal. The only solution, it seems to me, is for the translator to try to view the work not as a hopeless dichotomy but as a unified whole and to try to be faithful, in some mysterious spirit, to this vision of wholeness. In the result, perhaps we can honour, if nothing else, the poor translator's quixotic quest, a quest in some respects not unlike that of the artist he seeks to emulate.

The other translators who have put Pushkin's novel into English have chosen, unlike Nabokov, to honour in most respects the 'Onegin stanza' and to retain the original's metrical scheme and rhyme. Two of them in particular, Walter Arndt and Charles Johnston, have done so with some success and have demonstrated thereby that the task may be slightly less impossible than it seems. My own attempt to pursue the elusive Pushkin yet again has profited much by their example, following them in their virtues and avoiding, as far as possible, their defects. If the results presented here are no less provisional than their efforts or the efforts of others that have gone before, I have none the less greatly enjoyed my pursuit of Pushkin and have found the view, even from the lower altitudes, well worth the climb.

I, too, have elected, in my version, to preserve what I could of Pushkin's form, taking the Onegin stanza as one of the novel's most essential and characteristic features, the building-block with which the entire edifice is constructed. By retaining the stanza form that Pushkin uses as his poetic paragraph, the translator positions himself, in a sense, on the work's home ground and imposes upon himself a useful discipline for his journey. Furthermore, he is thereby constrained, as was the poet himself, to seek solutions without self-indulgence, to find variety within oneness, and to earn freedom within the bondage of the form. The very rigidity of the stanzaic structure can bring at times a fruitful tension to the words with which the form is made manifest, and the economy of expression it enforces upon the translator will sometimes reward him with an unexpected gift.

In working, over quite a few years, on several visions and revisions of this translation, I have found myself searching for an ever more natural and unforced flow of language, for a more fluid and straightforward syntax, a lighter and more readily comprehensible style; I have tried to avoid as much as possible the sorts of inversions and verbal contortions that have marred in my view the earlier translations—all in an effort to capture what seemed to me the poem's spontaneous and unlaboured effect in Pushkin's Russian. I have also tried to adapt the rhythms of the poem to the rhythms of English speech—a speech that in my rendition sounds somewhat more American than British in its accent and somewhat more contemporary than period in its idiom. Ultimately, I have attempted to provide the English-speaking reader of today with a more accessible version of one of the great works of the Russian literary imagination, one that would speak in a familiar, not-too-distant English voice and that would convey not only something of the novel's sense and shape, but some hints of its characteristic flavour as well: its verve and sparkle, its lyricism and wit, its succinctness and variety: the play of lights and shadows in an imperfect mirror.

A few words on the Onegin stanza. The main body of the novel consists in its final form (some stanzas having been discarded by Pushkin for a variety of reasons) of some 366 stanzas of a common design. The fourteen lines of this stanzaic form suggest, of course, the sonnet, but the rhyming pattern is unique (ababccddeffegg), as is the adherence to a fixed sequence of masculine and feminine rhymes (that is, rhymes in which the stresses fall on the final or the penultimate syllables, respectively): FMFMFFMMFMMFMM. The metre, iambic tetrameter, though it may seem somewhat terse for a long narrative poem in English, is hardly in itself alien to our tradition. Compositionally, the stanzas are organized in a variety of ways: as a single unit, as octave and sestet, or as three quatrains and a couplet. The second quatrain may function as two couplets (ccdd), and the sestet as two linked tercets (eff egg). The three quatrains, it will be noted, employ in sequence the three possible patterns for a binary rhyme scheme: alternating (abab), balanced (ccdd), and enclosed (effe). Pushkin uses his sonnet-paragraph with great virtuosity and flexibility. The opening quatrain and the closing couplet are usually the most clearly marked, while the middle sections are treated with great variety. The final masculine couplet, especially, tends to stand out as a tersely pointed and often ironic coda.

There are considerably more than 5,000 lines of verse in this work, and the sheer quantity of its rhyme, it must be admitted, sorely tests the translator's inventiveness. I am also well aware that rhyme today is somewhat less common in serious English verse than it used to be and that its pervasiveness here may seem uncongenial to the modern ear. I rely, therefore, on the reader's tolerance for traditions beyond the borders of current taste and on the hope that something archaic may have grown so unfamiliar as to offer, perhaps, the pleasure of novelty. On some of the Russian names in the text and on a few other words I have placed an accent mark on the syllable that bears the stress; in general, however, the iambic metre should be a sufficient guide to the pronunciation of unfamiliar words. The Russian text used for this translation is essentially that used by Nabokov, the so-called 'third' edition, the last to be published during Pushkin's lifetime.

Finally, let me express once again my indebtedness to the previous translators of Pushkin's poem. Vladimir Nabokov's work, in particular, was a constant challenge to strive for greater accuracy, and his extensive commentary on the novel was an endless source of both instruction and pleasure. I want also to express my gratitude to Oxford University Press for giving me, in this second edition of my translation, the opportunity to revise the text and to add to it the verse fragments on 'Onegin's Journey' that Pushkin appended to his novel. I should like also to repeat my thanks to Professor Lauren Leighton of the University of Illinois at Chicago for his considerable support and encouragement and to my colleague John Osborne for patiently reading all those early drafts and for urging me, when my energy waned, to continue with a restless ingenuity. My wife, Eve, has been a sharp but always partial critic. To all those, including those unnamed, who have helped to improve

this translation and to eliminate, at least in part, its lapses from
sense and grace, many thanks.

SELECT BIBLIOGRAPHY

BARTA, P., and GOEBEL, U. (eds.), *The Contexts of Aleksandr Sergeevich Pushkin* (Lewiston, NY, 1988).

BAYLEY, J., *Pushkin: A Comparative Commentary* (Cambridge, 1971).

BETHEA, D. (ed.), *Pushkin Today* (Bloomington, Ind., 1993).

BLOOM, H., *Alexander Pushkin* (New York, 1987).

BRIGGS, A., *Alexander Pushkin: A Critical Study* (Totowa, NJ, 1983).

—— *Alexander Pushkin: Eugene Onegin* (Cambridge, 1992).

CHIZHEVSKY, D., *Evgenij Onegin* (Cambridge, Mass., 1953).

CLAYTON, J., *Ice and Flame: A. Pushkin's Eugene Onegin* (Toronto, 1985).

DEBRECZENY, P., *The Other Pushkin: A Study of Pushkin's Prose Fiction* (Stanford, Ca., 1983).

DRIVER, S., *Pushkin: Literature and Social Ideas* (New York, 1989).

FENNELL, J., *Pushkin* (Harmondsworth, 1964).

HOISINGTON, S., *Russian Views of Pushkin's 'Eugene Onegin'* (Bloomington, Ind., 1988).

JAKOBSON, R., *Pushkin and his Sculptural Myth*, tr. J. Burbank (The Hague, 1975).

KODJAK, A., and TARANOVSKY, K. (eds.), *Alexander Pushkin: A Symposium on the 175th Anniversary of his Birth* (New York, 1976).

—— —— *Alexander Pushkin Symposium II* (Columbus, Oh. 1980).

LAVRIN, J., *Pushkin and Russian Literature* (London, 1947).

LEVITT, M., *Russian Literary Politics and the Pushkin Celebration of 1880* (Ithaca, NY, 1989).

MAGARSHACK, D., *Pushkin: A Biography* (London, 1967).

MIRSKY, D., *Pushkin* (London, 1926; repr. New York, 1963).

NABOKOV, V., *Eugene Onegin: A Novel in Verse by Alexander Pushkin, Translated from the Russian with a Commentary*, 4 vols. (New York, 1964; rev. edn. Princeton, 1975).

PROFFER, C. (ed. and tr.), *The Critical Prose of Alexander Pushkin* (Bloomington, Ind. 1969).

RICHARDS, D., and COCKRELL, C. (eds.), *Russian Views of Pushkin* (Oxford, 1976).

SANDLER, S., *Distant Pleasures: Alexander Pushkin and the Writing of Exile* (Stanford, Ca., 1989).

SHAW, J. (ed.), *The Letters of Alexander Pushkin* (Bloomington, Ind. 1963).

—— *Pushkin's Rhymes* (Madison, Wis., 1974).

SHAW, J. *Pushkin: A Concordance to the Poetry* (Columbus, Oh., 1985).

SIMMONS, E., *Pushkin* (New York, 1964).

TERTZ, A. (Sinyavsky), *Strolls with Pushkin*, tr. C. Nepomnyashchy and S. Yastremski (New Haven, Conn., 1993).

TODD, W., *Fiction and Society in the Age of Pushkin* (Cambridge, Mass., 1986).

TROYAT, H., *Pushkin*, tr. N. Amphoux (London, 1974).

VICKERY, W., *Pushkin: Death of a Poet* (Bloomington, Ind., 1968).

—— *Alexander Pushkin* (New York, 1970; rev. edn. New York, 1992).

WOLFF, T., *Pushkin on Literature* (London, 1971).

A CHRONOLOGY OF
ALEXANDER SERGEEVICH PUSHKIN

(all dates are old style)

1799   Born 26 May in Moscow. On his father's side Pushkin
was descended from a somewhat impoverished but
ancient aristocratic family. The poet's maternal great-
grandfather, Abram Hannibal, was an African princeling
(perhaps Abyssinian) who had been taken hostage as a
boy by the Turkish sultan. Brought eventually to Russia
and adopted by Peter the Great, he became a favourite
of the emperor and under subsequent rulers enjoyed a
distinguished career in the Russian military service. All
his life Pushkin retained great pride in his lineage on
both sides of the family.

1800–11 Entrusted in childhood to the care of governesses and
French tutors, Pushkin was largely ignored by his
parents. He did, however, avail himself of his father's
extensive library and read widely in French literature
of the seventeenth and eighteenth centuries. His
mastery of contemporary Russian speech owes much
to his early contact with household serfs, especially
with his nurse, Arina Rodionovna.

1811–17 Attends Lycée at Tsarskoe Selo near St Petersburg,
an academy newly established by Emperor Alexander
I for the education of young noblemen and their
preparation for government service. During these
school years he writes his earliest surviving verse.
Pushkin's poetic talent was recognized early and
admired by prominent Russian writers, including the
poets Derzhavin and Zhukovsky and the historian
Karamzin.

1817–20 Appointed to a sinecure in the Department of Foreign
Affairs, he leads a dissipated life in St Petersburg.

Writes satirical epigrams and circulates in manuscript form mildly seditious verse that incurs the displeasure of Emperor Alexander I. His first narrative poem, the mock epic *Ruslan and Lyudmila*, is published in 1820 and enjoys great success.

1820–4 Arrested for his liberal writings and exiled to service in the south of Russia (Ekaterinoslav, Kishinev, Odessa), he travels in the Caucasus, Crimea, Bessarabia. During this 'Byronic period' he composes his 'southern poems', including *The Prisoner of the Caucasus* and *The Fountain of Bakhchisarai*.

1823 Begins *Eugene Onegin* on 9 May (first chapter published in 1825).

1824 Writes narrative poem *The Gypsies*. After further conflict with the authorities he is dismissed from the service.

1824–6 Lives in exile for two more years at family estate of Mikhailovskoe.

1825 Writes verse drama *Boris Godunov*. Decembrist Revolt, in which several of the poet's friends participated, takes place while Pushkin is still absent from the capital.

1826–31 Pardoned by new Czar Nicholas I (September 1826) and allowed to return to Moscow, he resumes dissipated living. Continuing problems with censorship and growing dissatisfaction with the court and autocracy.

1827 Begins prose novel *The Moor of Peter the Great* (never completed), an account of the life and career of his ancestor Abram Hannibal.

1828 Writes narrative poem *Poltava* celebrating the victory of Peter the Great over Charles XII of Sweden.

1830 While stranded by a cholera epidemic at his country estate of Boldino he enjoys an especially productive autumn: effectively completes *Eugene Onegin*; writes *The Tales of Belkin* (prose stories); finishes 'Little

Tragedies': *The Covetous Knight, Mozart and Salieri, The Stone Guest, Feast in Time of Plague*.

1831   Marries Natalya Goncharova on 18 February; settles in St Petersburg; appointed official historiographer. Finally abandons work on *Eugene Onegin*, which has occupied him for more than eight years.

1831–7   Increasing personal and professional difficulties: financial troubles, unhappy married life, dismissal as a literary force by younger generation.

1833   Second 'Boldino autumn'. Writes short story *The Queen of Spades*, narrative poem *The Bronze Horseman*; works on *A History of the Pugachev Rebellion*

1836   Completes historical romance *The Captain's Daughter*.

1837   Incensed by the attentions paid to his wife by Baron Georges d'Antès, a French adventurer in the Russian service, Pushkin challenges him to a duel and on 27 February is mortally wounded; he dies two days later and his coffin is taken at night to Svyatogorsky Monastery near Mikhailovskoe for burial.

EUGENE ONEGIN

Pétri de vanité il avait encore plus
de cette espèce d'orgueil qui fait
avouer avec la même indifférence les
bonnes comme les mauvaises actions,
suite d'un sentiment de supériorité,
peut-être imaginaire.

        Tiré d'une lettre particulière*

Dedication*

Not thinking of the proud world's pleasure,
But cherishing your friendship's claim,
I would have wished a finer treasure
To pledge my token to your name—
One worthy of your soul's perfection,
The sacred dreams that fill your gaze,
Your verse's limpid, live complexion,
Your noble thoughts and simple ways.
But let it be. Take this collection
Of sundry chapters as my suit:
Half humorous, half pessimistic,
Blending the plain and idealistic—
Amusement's yield, the careless fruit
Of sleepless nights, light inspirations,
Born of my green and withered years . . .
The intellect's cold observations,
The heart's reflections, writ in tears.

Chapter 1

To live he hurries and to feel makes haste.
Prince Vjazemsky

1

'My uncle, man of firm convictions* . . .
By falling gravely ill, he's won
A due respect for his afflictions—
The only clever thing he's done.
May his example profit others;
But God, what deadly boredom, brothers,
To tend a sick man night and day,
Not daring once to steal away!
And, oh, how base to pamper grossly
And entertain the nearly dead,
To fluff the pillows for his head,
And pass him medicines morosely—
While thinking under every sigh:
The devil take you, Uncle. Die!'

2

Just so a youthful rake reflected,
As through the dust by post he flew,
By mighty Zeus's will elected
Sole heir to all the kin he knew.
Ludmíla's and Ruslán's adherents!*
Without a foreword's interference,
May I present, as we set sail,
The hero of my current tale:
Onégin, my good friend and brother,
Was born beside the Neva's span,
Where maybe, reader, you began,
Or sparkled in one way or other.
I too there used to saunter forth,
But found it noxious in the north.*

3

An honest man who'd served sincerely,
His father ran up debts galore;
He gave a ball some three times yearly,
Until he had no means for more.
Fate watched Eugene in his dependence;
At first *Madame* was in attendance;
And then *Monsieur* took on the child,
A charming lad, though somewhat wild.
Monsieur l'Abbé, a needy fellow,
To spare his charge excessive pain,
Kept lessons light and rather plain;
His views on morals ever mellow,
He seldom punished any lark,
And walked the boy in Letny Park.*

4

But when the age of restless turnings
Became in time our young man's fate,
The age of hopes and tender yearnings,
Monsieur l'Abbé was shown the gate.
And here's Onegin—liberated,
To fad and fashion newly mated:
A London *dandy*, hair all curled,
At last he's ready for the world!
In French he could and did acutely
Express himself and even write;
In dancing too his step was light,
And bows he'd mastered absolutely.
Who'd ask for more? The world could tell
That he had wit and charm as well.

5

We've all received an education
In something somehow, have we not?
So thank the Lord that in this nation
A little learning means a lot.
Onegin was, so some decided
(Strict judges, not to be derided),
A learned, if pedantic, sort.
He did possess the happy forte
Of free and easy conversation,
Or in a grave dispute he'd wear
The solemn expert's learned air
And keep to silent meditation;
And how the ladies' eyes he lit
With flashes of his sudden wit!

6

The Latin vogue today is waning,
And yet I'll say on his behalf,
He had sufficient Latin training
To gloss a common epigraph,
Cite Juvenal in conversation,
Put *vale* in a salutation;
And he recalled, at least in part,
A line or two of Virgil's art.
He lacked, it's true, all predilection
For rooting in the ancient dust
Of history's annals full of must,
But knew by heart a fine collection
Of anecdotes of ages past:
From Romulus to Tuesday last.

7

Lacking the fervent dedication
That sees in sounds life's highest quest,
He never knew, to our frustration,
A dactyl from an anapest.
Theocritus and Homer bored him,
But reading Adam Smith restored him,
And economics he knew well;
Which is to say that he could tell
The ways in which a state progresses—
The actual things that make it thrive,
And why for gold it need not strive,
When *basic products* it possesses.
His father never understood
And mortgaged all the land he could.

8

I have no leisure for retailing
The sum of all our hero's parts,
But where his genius proved unfailing,
The thing he'd learned above all arts,
What from his prime had been his pleasure,
His only torment, toil, and treasure,
What occupied, the livelong day,
His languid spirit's fretful play
Was love itself, the art of ardour,
Which Ovid sang in ages past,
And for which song he paid at last
By ending his proud days a martyr—
In dim Moldavia's vacant waste,
Far from the Rome his heart embraced.

(9)* 10

How early on he could dissemble,
Conceal his hopes, play jealous swain,
Compel belief, or make her tremble,
Seem cast in gloom or mute with pain,
Appear so proud or so forbearing,
At times attentive, then uncaring!
What languor when his lips were sealed,
What fiery art his speech revealed!
What casual letters he would send her!
He lived, he breathed one single dream,
How self-oblivious he could seem!
How keen his glance, how bold and tender;
And when he wished, he'd make appear
The quickly summoned, glistening tear!

11

How shrewdly he could be inventive
And playfully astound the young,
Use flattery as warm incentive,
Or frighten with despairing tongue.
And how he'd seize a moment's weakness
To conquer youthful virtue's meekness
Through force of passion and of sense,
And then await sweet recompense.
At first he'd beg a declaration,
And listen for the heart's first beat,
Then stalk love faster—and entreat
A lover's secret assignation . . .
And then in private he'd prepare
In silence to instruct the fair!

12

How early he could stir or worry
The hearts of even skilled coquettes!
And when he found it necessary
To crush a rival—oh, what nets,
What clever traps he'd set before him!
And how his wicked tongue would gore him!
But you, you men in wedded bliss,
You stayed his friends despite all this:
The crafty husband fawned and chuckled
(Faublas'* disciple and his tool),
As did the skeptical old fool,
And the majestic, antlered cuckold—
So pleased with all he had in life:
Himself, his dinner, and his wife.

(13–14) 15

Some mornings still abed he drowses,
Until his valet brings his tray.
What? Invitations? Yes, three houses
Have asked him to a grand soirée.
There'll be a ball, a children's party;
Where will he dash to, my good hearty?
Where will he make the night's first call?
Oh, never mind—he'll make them all.
But meanwhile, dressed for morning pleasure,
Bedecked in broad-brimmed *Bolivár*,*
He drives to Nevsky Boulevard,
To stroll about at total leisure,
Until Bréguet's* unsleeping chime
Reminds him that it's dinner time.

16

He calls a sleigh as daylight's dimming;
The cry resounds: 'Make way! Let's go!'
His collar with its beaver trimming
Is silver bright with frosted snow.
He's off to Talon's,* late, and racing,
Quite sure he'll find Kavérin* pacing;
He enters—cork and bottle spout!
The comet wine* comes gushing out,
A bloody roastbeef's on the table,
And truffles, youth's delight so keen,
The very flower of French cuisine,
And Strasbourg pie,* that deathless fable;
While next to Limburg's lively mould
Sits ananás in splendid gold.

17

Another round would hardly hurt them,
To wash those sizzling cutlets down;
But now the chime and watch alert them:
The brand new ballet's on in town!
He's off!—this critic most exacting
Of all that touches art or acting,
This fickel swain of every star,
And honoured patron of the *barre*—
To join the crowd, where each is ready
To greet an *entrechat* with cheers,
Or Cleopatra with his jeers,
To hiss at Phèdre—so unsteady,
Recall Moïna* . . . and rejoice
That everyone has heard his voice.

18

Enchanted land! There for a season,
That friend of freedom ruled the scene,
The daring satirist Fonvízin,
As did derivative Knyazhnín;
There Ózerov received the nation's
Unbidden tears and its ovations,
Which young Semyónova did share;
And our Katénin gave us there
Corneille's full genius resurrected;
And there the caustic Shakhovskóy
Refreshed the stage with comic joy,
Didelot his crown of fame perfected.*
There too, beneath the theatre's tent,
My fleeting, youthful days were spent.

19

My goddesses! You vanished faces!
Oh, hearken to my woeful call:
Have other maidens gained your places,
Yet not replaced you after all?
Shall once again I hear your chants?
Or see the Russian muse of dance
Perform her soaring, soulful flight?
Or shall my mournful gaze alight
On unknown faces on the stages?
And when across this world I pass
A disenchanted opera glass,
Shall I grow bored with mirth and rages,
And shall I then in silence yawn
And recollect a time that's gone?

20

The theatre's full, the boxes glitter;
The restless gallery claps and roars;
The stalls and pit are all ajitter;
The curtain rustles as it soars.
And there . . . ethereal . . . resplendent,
Poised to the magic bow attendant,
A throng of nymphs her guardian band,
Istómina* takes up her stand.
One foot upon the ground she places,
And then the other slowly twirls,
And now she leaps! And now she whirls!
Like down from Eol's lips she races;
Then spins and twists and stops to beat
Her rapid, dazzling, dancing feet.

21

As all applaud, Onegin enters—
And treads on toes to reach his seat;
His double glass he calmly centres
On ladies he has yet to meet.
He takes a single glance to measure
These clothes and faces with displeasure;
Then trading bows on every side
With men he knew or friends he spied,
He turned at last and vaguely fluttered
His eyes toward the stage and play—
Then yawned and turned his head away:
'It's time for something new,' he muttered,
'I've suffered ballets long enough,
But now Didelot is boring stuff.'

22

While all those cupids, devils, serpents
Upon the stage still romp and roar,
And while the weary band of servants
Still sleeps on furs at carriage door;
And while the people still are tapping,
Still sniffling, coughing, hissing, clapping;
And while the lamps both in and out
Still glitter grandly all about;
And while the horses, bored at tether,
Still fidget, freezing, in the snow,
And coachmen by the fire's glow
Curse masters and beat palms together;
Onegin now has left the scene
And driven home to change and preen.

23

Shall I abandon every scruple
And picture truly with my pen
The room where fashion's model pupil
Is dressed, undressed, and dressed again?
Whatever clever London offers
To those with lavish whims and coffers,
And ships to us by Baltic seas
In trade for tallow and for trees;
Whatever Paris, seeking treasure,
Devises to attract the sight,
Or manufactures for delight,
For luxury, for modish pleasure—
All this adorned his dressing room,
Our sage of eighteen summers' bloom.

24

Imported pipes of Turkish amber,
Fine china, bronzes—all displayed;
And purely to delight and pamper,
Perfumes in crystal jars arrayed;
Steel files and combs in many guises,
Straight scissors, curved ones, thirty sizes
Of brushes for the modern male—
For hair and teeth and fingernail.
Rousseau (permit me this digression)
Could not conceive how solemn Grimm*
Dared clean his nails in front of *him*,
The brilliant madcap of confession.
In this case, though, one has to say
That Freedom's Champion went astray.

25

For one may be a man of reason
And mind the beauty of his nails.
Why argue vainly with the season?—
For custom's rule o'er man prevails.
Now my Eugene, Chadáyev's* double,
From jealous critics fearing trouble,
Was quite the pedant in his dress
And what we called a fop, no less.
At least three hours he peruses
His figure in the looking-glass;
Then through his dressing room he'll pass
Like flighty Venus when she chooses
In man's attire to pay a call
At masquerade or midnight ball.

26

Your interest piqued and doubtless growing
In current fashions of *toilette*,
I might describe in terms more knowing
His clothing for the learned set.
This might well seem an indiscretion,
Description, though, is my profession;
But *pantaloons*, *gilet*, and *frock*—
These words are hardly Russian stock;
And I confess (in public sorrow)
That as it is my diction groans
With far too many foreign loans;
But if indeed I overborrow,
I have of old relied upon
Our *Academic Lexicon*.

27

But let's abandon idle chatter
And hasten rather to forestall
Our hero's headlong, dashing clatter
In hired coach towards the ball.
Before the fronts of darkened houses,
Along a street that gently drowses,
The double carriage lamps in rows
Pour forth their warm and cheerful glows
And on the snow make rainbows glitter.
One splendid house is all alight,
Its countless lampions burning bright;
While past its glassed-in windows flitter
In quick succession silhouettes
Of ladies and their modish pets.

28

But look, Onegin's at the gateway;
He's past the porter, up the stair,
Through marble entry rushes straightway,
Then runs his fingers through his hair,
And steps inside. The crush increases,
The droning music never ceases;
A bold mazurka grips the crowd,
The press intense, the hubbub loud;
The guardsman clinks his spurs and dances,
The charming ladies twirl their feet—
Enchanting creatures that entreat
A hot pursuit of flaming glances;
While muffled by the violin
The wives their jealous gossip spin.

29

In days of dreams and dissipations
On balls I madly used to dote:
No surer place for declarations,
Or for the passing of a note.
And so I offer, worthy spouses,
My services to save your houses:
I pray you, heed my sound advice,
A word of warning should suffice.
You too, you mamas, I commend you
To keep your daughters well in sight;
Don't lower your lorgnettes at night!
Or else . . . or else . . . may God defend you!
All this I now can let you know,
Since I dropped sinning long ago.

30

So much of life have I neglected
In following where pleasure calls!
Yet were not morals ill affected
I even now would worship balls.
I love youth's wanton, fevered madness,
The crush, the glitter, and the gladness,
The ladies' gowns so well designed;
I love their feet—although you'll find
That all of Russia scarcely numbers
Three pairs of shapely feet . . . And yet,
How long it took me to forget
Two special feet. And in my slumbers
They still assail a soul grown cold
And on my heart retain their hold.

31

In what grim desert, madman, banished,
Will you at last cut memory's thread?
Ah, dearest feet, where have you vanished?
What vernal flowers do you tread?
Brought up in Oriental splendour,
You left no prints, no pressings tender,
Upon our mournful northern snow.
You loved instead to come and go
On yielding rugs in rich profusion;
While I—so long ago it seems!—
For your sake smothered all my dreams
Of glory, country, proud seclusion.
All gone are youth's bright years of grace,
As from the meadow your light trace.

32

Diana's breast is charming, brothers,
And Flora's cheek, I quite agree;
But I prefer above these others
The foot of sweet Terpsichore.
It hints to probing, ardent glances
Of rich rewards and peerless trances;
Its token beauty stokes the fires,
The wilful swarm of hot desires.
My dear Elvina, I adore it—
Beneath the table barely seen,
In springtime on the meadow's green,
In winter with the hearth before it,
Upon the ballroom's mirrored floor,
Or perched on granite by the shore.

33

I recollect the ocean rumbling:
O how I envied then the waves—
Those rushing tides in tumult tumbling
To fall about her feet like slaves!
I longed to join the waves in pressing
Upon those feet these lips . . . caressing.
No, never midst the fiercest blaze
Of wildest youth's most fervent days
Was I so racked with yearning's anguish:
No maiden's lips were equal bliss,
No rosy cheek that I might kiss,
Or sultry breast on which to languish.
No, never once did passion's flood
So rend my soul, so flame my blood.

34

Another memory finds me ready:
In cherished dreams I sometimes stand
And hold the lucky stirrup steady,
Then feel her foot within my hand!
Once more imagination surges,
Once more that touch ignites and urges
The blood within this withered heart:
Once more the love . . . once more the dart!
But stop . . . Enough! My babbling lyre
Has overpraised these haughty things:
They're hardly worth the songs one sings
Or all the passions they inspire;
Their charming words and glances sweet
Are quite as faithless as their feet.

35

But what of my Eugene? Half drowsing,
He drives to bed from last night's ball,
While Petersburg, already rousing,
Answers the drumbeat's duty call.
The merchant's up, the pedlar scurries,
With jug in hand the milkmaid hurries,
Crackling the freshly fallen snow;
The cabby plods to hackney row.
In pleasant hubbub morn's awaking!
The shutters open, smoke ascends
In pale blue shafts from chimney ends.
The German baker's up and baking,
And more than once, in cotton cap,
Has opened up his window-trap.

36

But wearied by the ballroom's clamour,
He sleeps in blissful, sheer delight—
This child of comfort and of glamour,
Who turns each morning into night.
By afternoon he'll finally waken,
The day ahead all planned and taken:
The endless round, the varied game;
Tomorrow too will be the same.
But was he happy in the flower—
The very springtime of his days,
Amid his pleasures and their blaze,
Amid his conquests of the hour?
Or was he profligate and hale
Amid his feasts to no avail?

37

Yes, soon he lost all warmth of feeling:
The social buzz became a bore,
And all those beauties, once appealing,
Were objects of his thought no more.
Inconstancy grew too fatiguing;
And friends and friendship less intriguing;
For after all he couldn't drain
An endless bottle of champagne
To help those pies and beefsteaks settle,
Or go on dropping words of wit
With throbbing head about to split:
And so, for all his fiery mettle,
He did at last give up his love
Of pistol, sword, and ready glove.

38

We still, alas, cannot forestall it—
This dreadful ailment's heavy toll;
The *spleen* is what the English call it,
We call it simply *Russian soul*.
'Twas this our hero had contracted;
And though, thank God, he never acted
To put a bullet through his head,
His former love of life was dead.
Like Byron's Harold, lost in trances,
Through drawing rooms he'd pass and stare;
But neither whist, nor gossip there,
Nor wanton sighs, nor tender glances—
No, nothing touched his sombre heart,
He noticed nothing, took no part.

(39–41) 42

Capricious belles of lofty station!
You were the first that he forswore;
For nowadays in our great nation,
The manner grand can only bore.
I wouldn't say that ladies never
Discuss a Say or Bentham*—ever;
But generally, you'll have to grant,
Their talk's absurd, if harmless, cant.
On top of which, they're so unerring,
So dignified, so awfully smart,
So pious and so chaste of heart,
So circumspect, so strict in bearing,
So inaccessibly serene,
Mere sight of them brings on the spleen.*

43

You too, young mistresses of leisure,
Who late at night are whisked away
In racing droshkies bound for pleasure
Along the Petersburg *chaussée*—
He dropped you too in sudden fashion.
Apostate from the storms of passion,
He locked himself within his den
And, with a yawn, took up his pen
And tried to write. But art's exaction
Of steady labour made him ill,
And nothing issued from his quill;
So thus he failed to join the faction
Of writers—whom I won't condemn
Since, after all, I'm one of them.

44

Once more an idler, now he smothers
The emptiness that plagues his soul
By making his the thoughts of others—
A laudable and worthy goal.
He crammed his bookshelf overflowing,
Then read and read—frustration growing:
Some raved or lied, and some were dense;
Some lacked all conscience; some, all sense;
Each with a different dogma girded;
The old was dated through and through,
While nothing new was in the new;
So books, like women, he deserted,
And over all that dusty crowd
He draped a linen mourning shroud.

45

I too had parted with convention,
With vain pursuit of worldly ends;
And when Eugene drew my attention,
I liked his ways and we made friends.
I liked his natural bent for dreaming,
His strangeness that was more than seeming,
The cold sharp mind that he possessed;
I was embittered, he depressed;
With passion's game we both were sated;
The fire in both our hearts was pale;
Our lives were weary, flat, and stale;
And for us both, ahead there waited—
While life was still but in its morn—
Blind fortune's malice and men's scorn.

46

He who has lived as thinking being
Within his soul must hold men small;
He who can feel is always fleeing
The ghost of days beyond recall;
For him enchantment's deep infection
Is gone; the snake of recollection
And grim repentance gnaws his heart.
All this, of course, can help impart
Great charm to private conversation;
And though the language of my friend
At first disturbed me, in the end
I liked his caustic disputation—
His blend of banter and of bile,
His sombre wit and biting style.

47

How often in the summer quarter,
When midnight sky is limpid-light
Above the Neva's placid water—
The river gay and sparkling bright,
Yet in its mirror not reflecting
Diana's visage—recollecting
The loves and intrigues of the past,
Alive once more and free at last,
We drank in silent contemplation
The balmy fragrance of the night!
Like convicts sent in dreaming flight
To forest green and liberation,
So we in fancy then were borne
Back to our springtime's golden morn.

48

Filled with his heart's regrets, and leaning
Against the rampart's granite shelf,
Eugene stood lost in pensive dreaming
(As once some poet drew himself*).
The night grew still . . . with silence falling;
Only the sound of sentries calling,
Or suddenly from Million Street
Some distant droshky's rumbling beat;
Or floating on the drowsy river,
A lonely boat would sail along,
While far away some rousing song
Or plaintive horn would make us shiver.
But sweeter still, amid such nights,
Are Tasso's octaves' soaring flights.

49

O Adriatic! Grand Creation!
O Brenta!* I shall yet rejoice,
When, filled once more with inspiration,
I hear at last your magic voice!
It's sacred to Apollo's choir;
Through Albion's great and haughty lyre*
It speaks to me in words I know.
On soft Italian nights I'll go
In search of pleasure's sweet profusion;
A fair Venetian at my side,
Now chatting, now a silent guide,
I'll float in gondola's seclusion;
And she my willing lips will teach
Both love's and Petrarch's ardent speech.

50

Will freedom come—and cut my tether?
It's time, it's time! I bid her hail;
I roam the shore,* await fair weather,
And beckon to each passing sail.
O when, my soul, with waves contesting,
And caped in storms, shall I go questing
Upon the crossroads of the sea?
It's time to quit this dreary lee
And land of harsh, forbidding places;
And there, where southern waves break high,
Beneath my Africa's warm sky,*
To sigh for sombre Russia's spaces,
Where first I loved, where first I wept,
And where my buried heart is kept.

51

Eugene and I had both decided
To make the foreign tour we'd planned;
But all too soon our paths divided,
For fate took matters into hand.
His father died—quite unexpected,
And round Eugene there soon collected
The greedy horde demanding pay.
Each to his own, or so they say.
Eugene, detesting litigation
And quite contented with his fate,
Released to them the whole estate . . .
With no great sense of deprivation;
Perhaps he also dimly knew
His aged uncle's time was due.

52

And sure enough a note came flying;
The bailiff wrote as if on cue:
Onegin's uncle, sick and dying,
Would like to bid his heir adieu.
He gave the message one quick reading,
And then by post Eugene was speeding,
Already bored, to uncle's bed,
While thoughts of money filled his head.
He was prepared—like any craven—
To sigh, deceive, and play his part
(With which my novel took its start);
But when he reached his uncle's haven,
A laid-out corpse was what he found,
Prepared as tribute for the ground.

53

He found the manor fairly bustling
With those who'd known the now deceased;
Both friends and foes had come ahustling,
True lovers of a funeral feast.
They laid to rest the dear departed;
Then, wined and dined and heavy-hearted,
But pleased to have their duty done,
The priests and guests left one by one.
And here's Onegin—lord and master
Of woods and mills and streams and lands;
A country squire, there he stands,
That former wastrel and disaster;
And rather glad he was, it's true,
That he'd found something else to do.

54

For two full days he was enchanted
By lonely fields and burbling brook,
By sylvan shade that lay implanted
Within a cool and leafy nook.
But by the third he couldn't stick it:
The grove, the hill, the field, the thicket—
Quite ceased to tempt him any more
And, presently, induced a snore;
And then he saw that country byways—
With no great palaces, no streets,
No cards, no balls, no poets' feats—
Were just as dull as city highways;
And spleen, he saw, would dog his life,
Like shadow or a faithful wife.

55

But I was born for peaceful roaming,
For country calm and lack of strife;
My lyre sings! And in the gloaming
My fertile fancies spring to life.
I give myself to harmless pleasures
And *far niente* rules my leisures:
Each morning early I'm awake
To wander by the lonely lake
Or seek some other sweet employment:
I read a little, often sleep,
For fleeting fame I do not weep.
And was it not in past enjoyment
Of shaded, idle times like this,
I spent my days of deepest bliss?

56

The country, love, green fields and flowers,
Sweet idleness! You have my heart.
With what delight I praise those hours
That set Eugene and me apart.
For otherwise some mocking reader
Or, God forbid, some wretched breeder
Of twisted slanders might combine
My hero's features here with mine
And then maintain the shameless fiction
That, like proud Byron, I have penned
A mere self-portrait in the end;
As if today, through some restriction,
We're now no longer fit to write
On any theme but our own plight.

57

All poets, I need hardly mention,
Have drawn from love abundant themes;
I too have gazed in rapt attention
When cherished beings filled my dreams.
My soul preserved their secret features;
The Muse then made them living creatures:
Just so in carefree song I paid
My tribute to the mountain maid,
And sang the Salghir captives' praises.*
And now, my friends, I hear once more
That question you have put before:
'For whom these sighs your lyre raises?
To whom amid the jealous throng
Do you today devote your song?

58

'Whose gaze, evoking inspiration,
Rewards you with a soft caress?
Whose form, in pensive adoration,
Do you now clothe in sacred dress?'
Why no one, friends, as God's my witness,
For I have known too well the witless
And maddened pangs of love's refrain.
Oh, blest is he who joins his pain
To fevered rhyme: for thus he doubles
The sacred ecstasy of art;
Like Petrarch then, he calms the heart,
Subduing passion's host of troubles,
And captures worldly fame to boot!—
But I, in love, was dense and mute.

59

The Muse appeared as love was ending
And cleared the darkened mind she found.
Once free, I seek again the blending
Of feeling, thought, and magic sound.
I write . . . and want no more embraces;
My straying pen no longer traces,
Beneath a verse left incomplete,
The shapes of ladies' heads and feet.
Extinguished ashes won't rekindle,
And though I grieve, I weep no more;
And soon, quite soon, the tempest's core
Within my soul will fade and dwindle:
And *then* I'll write this world a song
That's five and twenty cantos long!

60

I've drawn a plan and know what's needed,
The hero's named, the plotting's done;
And meantime I've just now completed
My present novel's Chapter One.
I've looked it over most severely;
It has its contradictions, clearly,
But I've no wish to change a line;
I'll grant the censor's right to shine
And send these fruits of inspiration
To feed the critics' hungry pen.
Fly to the Neva's water then,
My spirit's own newborn creation!
And earn me tribute paid to fame:
Distorted readings, noise, and blame!

Chapter 2

O rus!
        Horace

O Rus'!*

1

The place Eugene found so confining
Was quite a lovely country nest,
Where one who favoured soft reclining
Would thank his stars to be so blest.
The manor house, in proud seclusion,
Screened by a hill from wind's intrusion,
Stood by a river. Far away
Green meads and golden cornfields lay,
Lit by the sun as it paraded;
Small hamlets too the eye could see
And cattle wand'ring o'er the lea;
While near at hand, all dense and shaded,
A vast neglected garden made
A nook where pensive dryads played.

2

The ancient manse had been erected
For placid comfort—and to last;
And all its solid form reflected
The sense and taste of ages past.
Throughout the house the ceilings towered,
From walls ancestral portraits glowered;
The drawing room had rich brocades
And stoves of tile in many shades.
All this today seems antiquated—
I don't know why; but in the end
It hardly mattered to my friend,
For he'd become so fully jaded,
He yawned alike where'er he sat,
In ancient hall or modern flat.

3

He settled where the former squire
For forty years had heaved his sighs,
Had cursed the cook in useless ire,
Stared out the window, and squashed flies.
The furnishings were plain but stable:
A couch, two cupboards, and a table,
No spot of ink on oaken floors.
Onegin opened cupboard doors
And found in one a list of wages,
Some fruit liqueurs and applejack,
And in the next an almanac
From eighteen-eight with tattered pages;
The busy master never took
A glance in any other book.

4

Alone amid his new possessions,
And merely as an idle scheme,
Eugene devised a few concessions
And introduced a new regime.
A backwoods genius, he commuted
The old *corvée* and substituted
A quitrent at a modest rate;*
His peasants thanked their lucky fate,
But thrifty neighbours waxed indignant
And in their dens bewailed as one
The dreadful harm of what he'd done.
Still others sneered or turned malignant,
And everyone who chose to speak
Called him a menace and a freak.

5

At first the neighbours' calls were steady;
But when they learned that in the rear
Onegin kept his stallion ready
So he could quickly disappear
The moment one of them was sighted
Or heard approaching uninvited,
They took offence and, one and all,
They dropped him cold and ceased to call.
'The man's a boor, he's off his rocker.'
'Must be a Mason;* drinks, they say . . .
Red wine, by tumbler, night and day!'
'Won't kiss a lady's hand, the mocker.'
'Won't call me "sir" the way he should.'
The general verdict wasn't good.

6

Another squire chose this season
To reappear at his estate
And gave the neighbours equal reason
For scrutiny no less irate.
Vladímir Lénsky, just returning
From Göttingen with soulful yearning,
Was in his prime—a handsome youth
And poet filled with Kantian truth.
From misty Germany our squire
Had carried back the fruits of art:
A freedom-loving, noble heart,
A spirit strange but full of fire,
An always bold, impassioned speech,
And raven locks of shoulder reach.

7

As yet unmarked by disillusion
Or chill corruption's deadly grasp,
His soul still knew the warm effusion
Of maiden's touch and friendship's clasp.
A charming fool at love's vocation,
He fed on hope's eternal ration;
The world's fresh glitter and its call
Still held his youthful mind in thrall;
He entertained with fond illusions
The doubts that plagued his heart and will;
The goal of life, he found, was still
A tempting riddle of confusions;
He racked his brains and rather thought
That miracles could still be wrought.

8

He knew a kindred soul was fated
To join her life to his career,
That even now she pined and waited,
Expecting he would soon appear.
And he believed that men would tender
Their freedom for his honour's splendour;
That friendly hands would surely rise
To shatter slander's cup of lies;
That there exists a holy cluster
Of chosen ones whom men should heed,
A happy and immortal breed,
Whose potent light in all its lustre
Would one day shine upon our race
And grant the world redeeming grace.*

9

Compassion, noble indignation,
A perfect love of righteous ways,
And fame's delicious agitation
Had stirred his soul since early days.
He roamed the world with singing lyre
And found the source of lyric fire
Beneath the skies of distant lands,
From Goethe's and from Schiller's hands.
He never shamed, the happy creature,
The lofty Muses of his art;
He proudly sang with open heart
Sublime emotion's every feature,
The charm of gravely simple things,
And youthful hopes on youthful wings.

10

He sang of love, by love commanded,
A simple and affecting tune,
As clear as maiden thoughts, as candid
As infant slumber, as the moon
In heaven's peaceful desert flying,
That queen of secrets and of sighing.
He sang of parting and of pain,
Of something vague, of mists and rain;
He sang the rose, romantic flower,
And distant lands where once he'd shed
His living tears upon the bed
Of silence at a lonely hour;
He sang life's bloom gone pale and sere—
He'd almost reached his eighteenth year.

11

Throughout that barren, dim dominion
Eugene alone could see his worth;
And Lensky formed a low opinion
Of neighbours' feasts and rounds of mirth;
He fled their noisy congregations
And found their solemn conversations—
Of liquor, and of hay brought in,
Of kennels, and of distant kin,
Devoid of any spark of feeling
Or hint of inner lyric grace;
Both wit and brains were out of place,
As were the arts of social dealing;
But then their charming wives he found
At talk were even less profound.

12

Well-off . . . and handsome in addition,
Young Lensky seemed the perfect catch;
And so, by countryside tradition,
They asked him round and sought to match
Their daughters with this semi-Russian.
He'd call—and right away discussion
Would touch obliquely on the point
That bachelors' lives were out of joint;
And then the guest would be invited
To take some tea while Dunya poured;
They whisper: 'Dunya, don't look bored!'—
Then bring in her guitar, excited . . .
And then, good God, she starts to bawl:
'Come to my golden chamberhall!'

13

But Lensky, having no desire
For marriage bonds or wedding bell,
Had cordial hopes that he'd acquire
The chance to know Onegin well.
And so they met—like wave with mountain,
Like verse with prose, like flame with fountain:
Their natures distant and apart.
At first their differences of heart
Made meetings dull at one another's;
But then their friendship grew, and soon
They'd meet on horse each afternoon,
And in the end were close as brothers.
Thus people—so it seems to me—
Become good friends from sheer ennui.

14

But even friendships like our heroes'
Exist no more; for we've outgrown
All sentiments and deem men zeros—
Except of course ourselves alone.
We all take on Napoleon's features,
And millions of our fellow creatures
Are nothing more to us than tools . . .
Since feelings are for freaks and fools.
Eugene, of course, had keen perceptions
And on the whole despised mankind,
Yet wasn't, like so many, blind;
And since each rule permits exceptions,
He did respect a noble few,
And, cold himself, gave warmth its due.

15

He smiled at Lensky's conversation.
Indeed the poet's fervent speech,
His gaze of constant inspiration,
His mind, still vacillant in reach—
All these were new and unexpected,
And so, for once, Eugene elected
To keep his wicked tongue in check,
And thought: What foolishness to wreck
The young man's blissful, brief infection;
Its time will pass without my knife,
So let him meanwhile live his life
Believing in the world's perfection;
Let's grant to fevered youthful days
Their youthful ravings and their blaze.

16

The two found everything a basis
For argument or food for thought:
The covenants of bygone races,
The fruits that learned science brought,
The prejudice that haunts all history,
The grave's eternal, fateful mystery,
And Good and Evil, Life and Fate—
On each in turn they'd ruminate.
The poet, lost in hot contention,
Would oft recite, his eyes ablaze,
Brief passages from Nordic lays;
Eugene, with friendly condescension,
Would listen with a look intense,
Although he seldom saw their sense.

17

More often, though, my two recluses
Would muse on passions* and their flights.
Eugene, who'd fled their wild abuses,
Regretted still his past delights
And sighed, recalling their interment.
Oh, happy he who's known the ferment
Of passions and escaped their lot;
More happy he who knew them not,
Who cooled off love with separation
And enmity with harsh contempt;
Who yawned with wife and friends, exempt
From pangs of jealous agitation;
Who never risked his sound estate
Upon a deuce, that cunning bait.

18

When we at last turn into sages
And flock to tranquil wisdom's crest;
When passion's flame no longer rages,
And all the yearnings in our breast,
The wayward fits, the final surges,
Have all become mere comic urges,
And pain has made us humble men—
We sometimes like to listen then
As others tell of passions swelling;
They stir our hearts and fan the flame.
Just so a soldier, old and lame,
Forgotten in his wretched dwelling,
Will strain to hear with bated breath
The youngbloods' yarns of courting death.

19

But flaming youth in all its madness
Keeps nothing of its heart concealed:
Its loves and hates, its joy and sadness,
Are babbled out and soon revealed.
Onegin, who was widely taken
As one whom love had left forsaken,
Would listen gravely to the end
When self-expression gripped his friend;
The poet, feasting on confession,
Naïvely poured his secrets out;
And so Eugene learned all about
The course of youthful love's progression—
A story rich in feelings too,
Although to us they're hardly new.

20

Ah yes, he loved in such a fashion
As men today no longer do;
As only poets, mad with passion,
Still love . . . because they're fated to.
He knew one constant source of dreaming,
One constant wish forever gleaming,
One ever-present cause for pain!
And neither distance, nor the chain
Of endless years of separation,
Nor pleasure's rounds, nor learning's well,
Nor foreign beauties' magic spell,
Nor yet the Muse, his true vocation,
Could alter Lensky's deep desire,
His soul aflame with virgin fire.

21

When scarce a boy and not yet knowing
The torment of a heart in flames,
He'd been entranced by Olga growing
And fondly watched her girlhood games;
Beneath a shady park's protection
He'd shared her frolics with affection.
Their fathers, who were friends, had plans
To read one day their marriage banns.
And deep within her rustic bower,
Beneath her parents' loving gaze,
She blossomed in a maiden's ways—
A valley-lily come to flower
Off where the grass grows dense and high,
Unseen by bee or butterfly.

22

She gave the poet intimations
Of youthful ecstasies unknown,
And, filling all his meditations,
Drew forth his flute's first ardent moan.
Farewell, O golden games' illusion!
He fell in love with dark seclusion,
With stillness, stars, the lonely night,
And with the moon's celestial light—
That lamp to which we've consecrated
A thousand walks in evening's calm
And countless tears—the gentle balm
Of secret torments unabated . . . .
Today, though, all we see in her
Is just another lantern's blur.

23

Forever modest, meek in bearing,
As gay as morning's rosy dress,
Like any poet—open, caring,
As sweet as love's own soft caress;
Her sky-blue eyes, devoid of guile,
Her flaxen curls, her lovely smile,
Her voice, her form, her graceful stance,
Oh, Olga's every trait . . . . But glance
In any novel—you'll discover
Her portrait there; it's charming, true;
I liked it once no less than you,
But round it boredom seems to hover;
And so, dear reader, grant me pause
To plead her elder sister's cause.

24

Her sister bore the name Tatyana.
And we now press our wilful claim
To be the first who thus shall honour
A tender novel with that name.*
Why not? I like its intonation;
It has, I know, association
With olden days beyond recall,
With humble roots and servants' hall;
But we must grant, though it offend us:
Our taste in names is less than weak
(Of verses I won't even speak);
Enlightenment has failed to mend us,
And all we've learned from its great store
Is affectation—nothing more.

25

So she was called Tatyana, reader.
She lacked that fresh and rosy tone
That made her sister's beauty sweeter
And drew all eyes to her alone.
A wild creature, sad and pensive,
Shy as a doe and apprehensive,
Tatyana seemed among her kin
A stranger who had wandered in.
She never learned to show affection,
To hug her parents—either one;
A child herself, for children's fun
She lacked the slightest predilection,
And oftentimes she'd sit all day
In silence at the window bay.

26

But pensiveness, her friend and treasure
Through all her years since cradle days,
Adorned the course of rural leisure
By bringing dreams before her gaze.
She never touched a fragile finger
To thread a needle, wouldn't linger
Above a tambour to enrich
A linen cloth with silken stitch.
Mark how the world compels submission:
The little girl with docile doll
Prepares in play for protocol,
For every social admonition;
And to her doll, without demur,
Repeats what mama taught to her.

27

But dolls were never Tanya's passion,
When she was small she didn't choose
To talk to them of clothes or fashion
Or tell them all the city news.
And she was not the sort who glories
In girlish pranks; but grisly stories
Quite charmed her heart when they were told
On winter nights all dark and cold.
Whenever nanny brought together
Young Olga's friends to spend the day,
Tatyana never joined their play
Or games of tag upon the heather;
For she was bored by all their noise,
Their laughing shouts and giddy joys.

28

Upon her balcony appearing,
She loved to greet Aurora's show,
When dancing stars are disappearing
Against the heavens' pallid glow,
When earth's horizon softly blushes,
And wind, the morning's herald, rushes,
And slowly day begins its flight.
In winter, when the shade of night
Still longer half the globe encumbers,
And 'neath the misty moon on high
An idle stillness rules the sky,
And late the lazy East still slumbers—
Awakened early none the less,
By candlelight she'd rise and dress.

29

From early youth she read romances,
And novels set her heart aglow;
She loved the fictions and the fancies
Of Richardson and of Rousseau.
Her father was a kindly fellow—
Lost in a past he found more mellow;
But still, in books he saw no harm,
And, though immune to reading's charm,
Deemed it a minor peccadillo;
Nor did he care what secret tome
His daughter read or kept at home
Asleep till morn beneath her pillow;
His wife herself, we ought to add,
For Richardson was simply mad.

30

It wasn't that she'd read him, really,
Nor was it that she much preferred
To Lovelace Grandison, but merely
That long ago she'd often heard
Her Moscow cousin, Princess Laura,
Go on about their special aura.
Her husband at the time was still
Her fiancé—against her will!
For she, in spite of family feeling,
Had someone else for whom she pined—
A man whose heart and soul and mind
She found a great deal more appealing;
This Grandison was fashion's pet,
A gambler and a guards cadet.

31

About her clothes one couldn't fault her;
Like him, she dressed as taste decreed.
But then they led her to the altar
And never asked if she agreed.
The clever husband chose correctly
To take his grieving bride directly
To his estate, where first she cried
(With God knows whom on every side),
Then tossed about and seemed demented;
And almost even left her spouse;
But then she took to keeping house
And settled down and grew contented.
Thus heaven's gift to us is this:
That habit takes the place of bliss.

32

'Twas only habit then that taught her
The way to master rampant grief;
And soon a great discovery brought her
A final and complete relief.
Betwixt her chores and idle hours
She learned to use her woman's powers
To rule the house as autocrat,
And life went smoothly after that.
She'd drive around to check the workers,
She pickled mushrooms for the fall,
She made her weekly bathhouse call,
She kept the books, she shaved the shirkers,*
She beat the maids when she was cross—
And left her husband at a loss.

33

She used to write, with blood, quotations
In maidens' albums, thought it keen
To speak in singsong intonations,
Would call Praskóvya 'chère Pauline'.
She laced her corset very tightly,
Pronounced a Russian *n* as slightly
As *n* in French . . . and through the nose;
But soon she dropped her city pose:
The corset, albums, chic relations,
The sentimental verses too,
Were quite forgot; she bid adieu
To all her foreign affectations,
And took at last to coming down
In just her cap and quilted gown.

34

And yet her husband loved her dearly;
In all her schemes he'd never probe;
He trusted all she did sincerely
And ate and drank in just his robe.
His life flowed on—quite calm and pleasant—
With kindly neighbours sometimes present
For hearty talk at evenfall,
Just casual friends who'd often call
To shake their heads, to prate and prattle,
To laugh a bit at something new;
And time would pass, till Olga'd brew
Some tea to whet their tittle-tattle;
Then supper came, then time for bed,
And off the guests would drive, well fed.

35

Amid this peaceful life they cherished,
They held all ancient customs dear;
At Shrovetide feasts their table flourished
With Russian pancakes, Russian cheer;
Twice yearly too they did their fasting;
Were fond of songs for fortune-casting,
Of choral dances, garden swings.
At Trinity, when service brings
The people, yawning, in for prayer,
They'd shed a tender tear or two
Upon their buttercups of rue.
They needed *kvas* no less than air,
And at their table guests were served
By rank in turn as each deserved.*

36

And thus they aged, as do all mortals.
Until at last the husband found
That death had opened wide its portals,
Through which he entered, newly crowned.
He died at midday's break from labour,
Lamented much by friend and neighbour,
By children and by faithful wife—
Far more than some who part this life.
He was a kind and simple *barin*,
And there where now his ashes lie
A tombstone tells the passer-by:
The humble sinner Dmitry Larin
A slave of God and Brigadier
Beneath this stone now resteth here.

37

Restored to home and its safekeeping,
Young Lensky came to cast an eye
Upon his neighbour's place of sleeping,
And mourned his ashes with a sigh.
And long he stood in sorrow aching;
'Poor Yorick!' then he murmured, shaking,
'How oft within his arms I lay,
How oft in childhood days I'd play
With his Ochákov decoration!*
He destined Olga for my wife
And used to say: "Oh grant me, life,
To see the day!" ' . . . In lamentation,
Right then and there Vladimir penned
A funeral verse for his old friend.

38

And then with verse of quickened sadness
He honoured too, in tears and pain,
His parents' dust . . . their memory's gladness . . .
Alas! Upon life's furrowed plain—
A harvest brief, each generation,
By fate's mysterious dispensation,
Arises, ripens, and must fall;
Then others too must heed the call.
For thus our giddy race gains power:
It waxes, stirs, turns seething wave,
Then crowds its forebears toward the grave.
And we as well shall face that hour
When one fine day our grandsons true
Straight out of life will crowd us too!

39

So meanwhile, friends, enjoy your blessing:
This fragile life that hurries so!
Its worthlessness needs no professing,
And I'm not loathe to let it go;
I've closed my eyes to phantoms gleaming,
Yet distant hopes within me dreaming
Still stir my heart at times to flight:
I'd grieve to quit this world's dim light
And leave no trace, however slender.
I live, I write—not seeking fame;
And yet, I think, I'd wish to claim
For my sad lot its share of splendour—
At least one note to linger long,
Recalling, like some friend, my song.

40

And it may touch some heart with fire;
And thus preserved by fate's decree,
The stanza fashioned by my lyre
May yet not drown in Lethe's sea;
Perhaps (a flattering hope's illusion!)
Some future dunce with warm effusion
Will point my portrait out and plead:
'This was a poet, yes indeed!'
Accept my thanks and admiration,
You lover of the Muse's art,
O you whose mind shall know by heart
The fleeting works of my creation,
Whose cordial hand shall then be led
To pat the old man's laurelled head!

Chapter 3

Elle était fille, elle était
amoureuse.*

Malfilâtre

1

'Ah me, these poets . . . such a hurry!'
'Goodbye, Onegin . . . time I went.'
'Well, I won't keep you, have no worry,
But where are all your evenings spent?'
'The Larin place.'—'What reckless daring!
Good God, man, don't you find it wearing
Just killing time that way each night?'
'Why not at all.'—'Well, serves you right;
I've got the scene in mind so clearly:
For starters (tell me if I'm wrong),
A simple Russian family throng;
The guests all treated so sincerely;
With lots of jam and talk to spare.
On rain and flax and cattle care. . . .'

2

'Well, where's the harm . . . the evening passes.'
'The boredom, brother, there's the harm.'
'Well, I despise your upper classes
And *like* the family circle's charm;
It's where I find . . .'—'More pastoral singing!
Enough, old boy, my ears are ringing!
And so you're off . . . forgive me then.
But tell me Lensky, how and when
I'll see this Phyllis so provoking—
Who haunts your thoughts and writer's quill,
Your tears and rhymes and what-you-will?
Present me, do.'—'You must be joking!'
'I'm not.'—'Well then, why not tonight?
They'll welcome us with great delight.'

3

'Let's go.'
          And so the friends departed—
And on arrival duly meet
That sometimes heavy, but good-hearted,
Old-fashioned Russian welcome treat.
The social ritual never changes:
The hostess artfully arranges
On little dishes her preserves,
And on her covered table serves
A drink of lingonberry flavour.
With folded arms, along the hall,
The maids have gathered, one and all,
To glimpse the Larins' brand new neighbour;
While in the yard their men reproach
Onegin's taste in horse and coach.*

4

Now home's our heroes' destination,
As down the shortest road they fly;
Let's listen to their conversation
And use a furtive ear to spy.
'Why all these yawns, Onegin? Really!'
'Mere habit, Lensky.'—'But you're clearly
More bored than usual.'—'No, the same.
The fields are dark now, what a shame.
Come on, Andryúshka, faster, matey!
These stupid woods and fields and streams!
Oh, by the way, Dame Larin seems
A simple but a nice old lady;
I fear that lingonberry brew
May do me in before it's through.'

5

'But tell me, which one was Tatyana?'
'Why, she who with a wistful air—
All sad and silent like Svetlana*—
Came in and took the window chair.'
'And really you prefer the other?'
'Why not?'—'Were I the poet, brother,
I'd choose the elder one instead—
Your Olga's look is cold and dead,
As in some dull, Van Dyck madonna;
So round and fair of face is she,
She's like that stupid moon you see,
Up in that stupid sky you honour.'
Vladimir gave a curt reply
And let the conversation die.

6

Meanwhile . . . Onegin's presentation
At Madame Larin's country seat
Produced at large a great sensation
And gave the neighbours quite a treat.
They all began to gossip slyly,
To joke and comment (rather wryly);
And soon the general verdict ran,
That Tanya'd finally found a man;
Some even knowingly conceded
That wedding plans had long been set,
And then postponed till they could get
The stylish rings the couple needed.
As far as Lensky's wedding stood,
They knew they'd settled *that* for good.

7

Tatyana listened with vexation
To all this gossip; but it's true
That with a secret exultation,
Despite herself she wondered too;
And in her heart the thought was planted . . .
Until at last her fate was granted:
She fell in love. For thus indeed
Does spring awake the buried seed.
Long since her keen imagination,
With tenderness and pain imbued,
Had hungered for the fatal food;
Long since her heart's sweet agitation
Had choked her maiden breast too much:
Her soul awaited . . . someone's touch.

8

And now at last the wait has ended;
Her eyes have opened . . . seen his face!
And now, alas! . . . she lives attended—
All day, all night, in sleep's embrace—
By dreams of him; each passing hour
The world itself with magic power
But speaks of him. She cannot bear
The way the watchful servants stare,
Or stand the sound of friendly chatter.
Immersed in gloom beyond recall,
She pays no heed to guests at all,
And damns their idle ways and patter,
Their tendency to just drop in—
And talk all day once they begin.

9

And now with what great concentration
To tender novels she retreats,
With what a vivid fascination
Takes in their ravishing deceits!
Those figures fancy has created
Her happy dreams have animated:
The lover of Julie Wolmár,*
Malék-Adhél* and de Linár,*
And Werther, that rebellious martyr,
And Grandison, the noble lord
(With whom today we're rather bored)—
All these our dreamy maiden's ardour
Has pictured with a single grace,
And seen in all . . . Onegin's face.

10

And then her warm imagination
Perceives herself as *heroine*—
Some favourite author's fond creation:
Clarissa,* Julia,* or Delphine.*
She wanders with her borrowed lovers
Through silent woods and so discovers
Within a book her heart's extremes,
Her secret passions, and her dreams.
She sighs . . . and in her soul possessing
Another's joy, another's pain,
She whispers in a soft refrain
The letter she would send caressing
Her hero . . . who was none the less
No Grandison in Russian dress.

11

Time was, with grave and measured diction,
A fervent author used to show
The hero in his work of fiction
Endowed with bright perfection's glow.
He'd furnish his beloved child—
Forever hounded and reviled—
With tender soul and manly grace,
Intelligence and handsome face.
And nursing noble passion's rages,
The ever dauntless hero stood
Prepared to die for love of good;
And in the novel's final pages,
Deceitful vice was made to pay
And honest virtue won the day.

12

But now our minds have grown inactive,
We're put to sleep by talk of 'sin';
Our novels too make vice attractive,
And even there it seems to win.
It's now the British Muse's fables
That lie on maidens' bedside tables
And haunt their dreams. They worship now
The Vampire with his pensive brow,
Or gloomy Melmoth, lost and pleading,
The Corsair, or the Wandering Jew,
And enigmatic Sbogar* too.
Lord Byron, his caprice succeeding,
Cloaked even hopeless egotism
In saturnine romanticism.

13

But what's the point? I'd like to know it.
Perhaps, my friends, by fate's decree,
I'll cease one day to be a poet—
When some new demon seizes me;
And scorning then Apollo's ire
To humble prose I'll bend my lyre:
A novel in the older vein
Will claim what happy days remain.
No secret crimes or passions gory
Shall I in grim detail portray,
But simply tell as best I may
A Russian family's age-old story,
A tale of lovers and their lot,
Of ancient customs unforgot.

14

I'll give a father's simple greetings,
An aged uncle's—in my book;
I'll show the children's secret meetings
By ancient lindens near the brook,
Their jealous torments, separation,
Their tears of reconciliation;
I'll make them quarrel yet again,
But lead them to the altar then.
I'll think up speeches tenderhearted,
Recall the words of passion's heat,
Those words with which—before the feet
Of some fair mistress long departed—
My heart and tongue once used to soar,
But which today I use no more.

15

Tatyana, O my dear Tatyana!
I shed with you sweet tears too late;
Relying on a tyrant's honour,
You've now resigned to him your fate.
My dear one, you are doomed to perish;
But first in dazzling hope you nourish
And summon forth a sombre bliss,
You learn life's sweetness . . . feel its kiss,
And drink the draught of love's temptations,
As phantom daydreams haunt your mind:
On every side you seem to find
Retreats for happy assignations;
While everywhere before your eyes
Your fateful tempter's figure lies.

16

The ache of love pursues Tatyana;
She takes a garden path and sighs,
A sudden faintness comes upon her,
She can't go on, she shuts her eyes;
Her bosom heaves, her cheeks are burning,
Scarce-breathing lips grow still with yearning,
Her ears resound with ringing cries,
And sparkles dance before her eyes.
Night falls; the moon begins parading
The distant vault of heaven's hood;
The nightingale in darkest wood
Breaks out in mournful serenading.
Tatyana tosses through the night
And wakes her nurse to share her plight.

17

'I couldn't sleep . . . O nurse, it's stifling!
Put up the window . . . sit by me.'
'What ails you, Tanya?'—'Life's so trifling,
Come tell me how it used to be.'
'Well, what about it? Lord, it's ages . . .
I must have known a thousand pages
Of ancient facts and fables too
'Bout evil ghosts and girls like you;
But nowadays I'm not so canny,
I can't remember much of late.
Oh, Tanya, it's a sorry state;
I get confused . . .' — 'But tell me, nanny,
About the olden days . . . you know,
Were you in love then, long ago?'

18

'Oh, come! Our world was quite another!
We'd never heard of love, you see.
Why, my good husband's sainted mother
Would just have been the death of me!'
'Then how'd you come to marry, nanny?'
'The will of God, I guess . . . . My Danny
Was younger still than me, my dear,
And I was just thirteen that year.
The marriage maker kept on calling
For two whole weeks to see my kin,
Till father blessed me and gave in.
I got so scared . . . my tears kept falling;
And weeping, they undid my plait,
Then sang me to the churchyard gate.

19

'And so they took me off to strangers . . .
But you're not even listening, pet.'
'Oh, nanny, life's so full of dangers,
I'm sick at heart and all upset,
I'm on the verge of tears and wailing!'
'My goodness, girl, you must be ailing;
Dear Lord have mercy. God, I plead!
Just tell me, dearest, what you need.
I'll sprinkle you with holy water,
You're burning up!'—'Oh, do be still,
I'm . . . you know, nurse . . . in love, not ill.'
'The Lord be with you now, my daughter!'
And with her wrinkled hand the nurse
Then crossed the girl and mumbled verse.

20

'Oh, I'm in love,' again she pleaded
With her old friend. 'My little dove,
You're just not well, you're overheated.'
'Oh, let me be now . . . I'm in love.'
And all the while the moon was shining
And with its murky light defining
Tatyana's charms and pallid air,
Her long, unloosened braids of hair,
And drops of tears . . . while on a hassock,
Beside the tender maiden's bed,
A kerchief on her grizzled head,
Sat nanny in her quilted cassock;
And all the world in silence lay
Beneath the moon's seductive ray.

21

Far off Tatyana ranged in dreaming,
Bewitched by moonlight's magic curse. . .
And then a sudden thought came gleaming:
'I'd be alone now . . . leave me, nurse.
But give me first a pen and paper;
I won't be long . . . just leave the taper.
Good night.' She's now alone. All's still.
The moonlight shines upon her sill.
And propped upon an elbow, writing,
Tatyana pictures her Eugene,
And in a letter, rash and green,
Pours forth a maiden's blameless plighting.
The letter's ready—all but sent. . .
For whom, Tatyana, is it meant?

22

I've known great beauties proudly distant,
As cold and chaste as winter snow;
Implacable, to all resistant,
Impossible for mind to know;
I've marvelled at their haughty manner,
Their natural virtue's flaunted banner;
And I confess, from them I fled,
As if in terror I had read
Above their brows the sign of Hades:
Abandon Hope, Who Enter Here!
Their joy is striking men with fear,
For love offends these charming ladies.
Perhaps along the Neva's shore
You too have known such belles before.

23

Why I've seen ladies so complacent
Before their loyal subjects' gaze,
That they would even grow impatient
With sighs of passion and with praise.
But what did I, amazed, discover?
On scaring off some timid lover
With stern behaviour's grim attack,
These creatures then would lure him back!—
By joining him at least in grieving,
By seeming in their words at least
More tender to the wounded beast;
And blind as ever, still believing,
The youthful lover with his yen
Would chase sweet vanity again.

24

So why is Tanya, then, more tainted?
Is it because her simple heart
Believes the chosen dream she's painted
And in deceit will take no part?
Because she heeds the call of passion
In such an honest, artless fashion?
Because she's trusting more than proud,
And by the Heavens was endowed
With such a rashness in surrender,
With such a lively mind and will,
And with a spirit never still,
And with a heart that's warm and tender?
But can't you, friends, forgive her, pray,
The giddiness of passion's sway?

25

The flirt will always reason coldly;
Tatyana's love is deep and true:
She yields without conditions, boldly—
As sweet and trusting children do.
She does not say: 'Let's wait till later
To make love's value all the greater
And bind him tighter with our rope;
Let's prick vainglory first with hope,
And then with doubt in fullest measure
We'll whip his heart, and when it's tame . . .
Revive it with a jealous flame;
For otherwise, grown bored with pleasure,
The cunning captive any day
Might break his chains and slip away.'

26

I face another complication:
My country's honour will demand
Without a doubt a full translation
Of Tanya's letter from my hand.
She knew the Russian language badly,
Ignored our journals all too gladly,
And in her native tongue, I fear,
Could barely make her meaning clear;
And so she turned for love's discussion
To French. . . . There's nothing I can do!
A lady's love, I say to you,
Has never been expressed in Russian;
Our mighty tongue, God only knows,
Has still not mastered postal prose.

27

Some would that ladies be required
To read in Russian. Dread command!
Why, I can picture them—inspired,
*The Good Samaritan** in hand!
I ask you now to tell me truly,
You poets who have sinned unduly:
Have not those creatures you adore,
Those objects of your verse . . . and more,
Been weak at Russian conversation?
And have they not, the charming fools,
Distorted sweetly all the rules
Of usage and pronunciation;
While yet a foreign language slips
With native glibness from their lips?

28

God spare me from the apparition,
On leaving some delightful ball,
Of bonneted Academician
Or scholar in a yellow shawl!
I find a faultless Russian style
Like crimson lips without a smile,
Mistakes in grammar charm the mind.
Perhaps (if fate should prove unkind!)
This generation's younger beauties,
Responding to our journals' call,
With grammar may delight us all,
And verses will be common duties.
But what care I for all they do?
To former ways I'll still be true.

29

A careless drawl, a tiny stutter,
Some imprecision of the tongue—
Can still produce a lovely flutter
Within this breast no longer young;
I lack the strength for true repentance,
And Gallicisms in a sentence
Seem sweet as youthful sins remote,
Or verse that Bogdanóvich* wrote.
But that will do. My beauty's letter
Must occupy my pen for now;
I gave my word, but, Lord, I vow,
Retracting it would suit me better.
I know that gentle Parny's* lays
Are out of fashion nowadays.

30

Bard of *The Feasts** and languid sorrow,
If you were with me still, my friend,
Immodestly I'd seek to borrow
Your genius for a worthy end:
I'd have you with your art refashion
A maiden's foreign words of passion
And make them magic songs anew.
Where are you? Come! I bow to you
And yield my rights to love's translation. . . .
But there beneath the Finnish sky,
Amid those mournful crags on high,
His heart grown deaf to commendation—
Alone upon his way he goes
And does not heed my present woes.

31

Tatyana's letter lies beside me,
And reverently I guard it still;
I read it with an ache inside me
And cannot ever read my fill.
Who taught her then this soft surrender,
This careless gift for waxing tender,
This touching whimsy free of art,
This raving discourse of the heart—
Enchanting, yet so fraught with trouble?
I'll never know. But none the less,
I give it here in feeble dress:
A living picture's pallid double,
Or *Freischütz** played with timid skill
By fingers that are learning still.

Tatyana's Letter to Onegin

I'm writing you this declaration—
What more can I in candour say?
It may be now your inclination
To scorn me and to turn away;
But if my hapless situation
Evokes some pity for my woe,
You won't abandon me, I know.
I first tried silence and evasion;
Believe me, you'd have never learned
My secret shame, had I discerned
The slightest hope that on occasion—
But once a week—I'd see your face,
Behold you at our country place,
Might hear you speak a friendly greeting,
Could say a word to you; and then,
Could dream both day and night again
Of but one thing, till our next meeting.

They say you like to be alone
And find the country unappealing;
We lack, I know, a worldly tone,
But still, we welcome you with feeling.

Why did you ever come to call?
In this forgotten country dwelling
I'd not have known you then at all,
Nor known this bitter heartache's swelling.
Perhaps, when time had helped in quelling
The girlish hopes on which I fed,
I might have found (who knows?) another
And been a faithful wife and mother,
Contented with the life I led.

Another! No! In all creation
There's no one else whom I'd adore;
The heavens chose my destination
And made me thine for evermore!
My life till now has been a token
In pledge of meeting you, my friend;
And in your coming, God has spoken,
You'll be my guardian till the end. . . .

You filled my dreams and sweetest trances;
As yet unseen, and yet so dear,
You stirred me with your wondrous glances,
Your voice within my soul rang clear. . . .
And then the dream came true for me!
When you came in, I seemed to waken,
I turned to flame, I felt all shaken,
And in my heart I cried: It's he!

And was it you I heard replying
Amid the stillness of the night,
Or when I helped the poor and dying,
Or turned to heaven, softly crying,
And said a prayer to soothe my plight?
And even now, my dearest vision,
Did I not see your apparition
Flit softly through this lucent night?
Was it not you who seemed to hover
Above my bed, a gentle lover,
To whisper hope and sweet delight?

Are you my angel of salvation
Or hell's own demon of temptation?

Be kind and send my doubts away;
For this may all be mere illusion,
The things a simple girl would say,
While Fate intends no grand conclusion. . . .

So be it then! Henceforth I place
My faith in you and your affection;
I plead with tears upon my face
And beg you for your kind protection.
You cannot know: I'm so alone,
There's no one here to whom I've spoken,
My mind and will are almost broken,
And I must die without a moan.
I wait for you . . . and your decision:
Revive my hopes with but a sign,
Or halt this heavy dream of mine—
Alas, with well-deserved derision!

I close. I dare not now reread. . . .
I shrink with shame and fear. But surely,
Your honour's all the pledge I need,
And I submit to it securely.

32

The letter trembles in her fingers;
By turns Tatyana groans and sighs.
The rosy sealing wafer lingers
Upon her fevered tongue and dries.
Her head is bowed, as if she's dozing;
Her light chemise has slipped, exposing
Her lovely shoulder to the night.
But now the moonbeams' glowing light
Begins to fade. The vale emerges
Above the mist. And now the stream
In silver curves begins to gleam.
The shepherd's pipe resounds and urges
The villager to rise. It's morn!
My Tanya, though, is so forlorn.

33

She takes no note of dawn's procession,
Just sits with lowered head, remote;
Nor does she put her seal's impression
Upon the letter that she wrote.
But now her door is softly swinging:
It's grey Filátievna, who's bringing
Her morning tea upon a tray.
'It's time, my sweet, to greet the day;
Why, pretty one, you're up already!
You're still my little early bird!
Last night you scared me, 'pon my word!
But thank the Lord, you seem more steady;
No trace at all of last night's fret,
Your cheeks are poppies now, my pet.'

34

'Oh, nurse, a favour, please . . . and hurry!'
'Why, sweetheart, anything you choose.'
'You mustn't think . . . and please don't worry . . .
But see . . . Oh, nanny, don't refuse!'
'As God's my witness, dear, I promise.'
'Then send your grandson, little Thomas,
To take this note of mine to O——,
Our neighbour, nurse, the one. . . you know!
And tell him that he's not to mention
My name, or breathe a single word. . . .'
'But who's it for, my little bird?
I'm trying hard to pay attention;
But we have lots of neighbours call,
I couldn't even count them all.'

35

'Oh nurse, your wits are all befuddled!'
'But, sweetheart, I've grown old . . . I mean . . .
I'm old; my mind . . . it does get muddled.
There was a time when I was keen,
When just the master's least suggestion. . . .'
'Oh, nanny, please, that's not the question,
It's not your mind I'm talking of,
I'm thinking of Onegin, love;
This note's to him.'—'Now don't get riled,
You know these days I'm not so clear,
I'll take the letter, never fear.
But you've gone pale again, my child!'
'It's nothing, nanny, be at ease,
Just send your grandson, will you please.'

36

The day wore on, no word came flying.
Another fruitless day went by.
All dressed since dawn, dead-pale and sighing,
Tatyana waits: will he reply?
Then Olga's suitor came a-wooing.
'But tell me, what's your friend been doing?'
Asked Tanya's mother, full of cheer;
'He's quite forgotten us, I fear.'
Tatyana blushed and trembled gently.
'He promised he would come today,'
Said Lensky in his friendly way,
'The mail has kept him evidently.'
Tatyana bowed her head in shame,
As if they all thought her to blame.

37

'Twas dusk; and on the table, gleaming,
The evening samovar grew hot;
It hissed and sent its vapour steaming
In swirls about the china pot.
And soon the fragrant tea was flowing
As Olga poured it, dark and glowing,
In all the cups; without a sound
A serving boy took cream around.
Tatyana by the window lingers
And breathes upon the chilly glass;
All lost in thought, the gentle lass
Begins to trace with lovely fingers
Across the misted panes a row
Of hallowed letters: *E* and *O*.

38

And all the while her soul was aching,
Her brimming eyes could hardly see.
Then sudden hoofbeats! . . . Now she's quaking. . . .
They're closer . . . coming here . . . it's he!
Onegin! 'Oh!'—And light as air,
She's out the backway, down the stair
From porch to yard, to garden straight;
She runs, she flies; she dare not wait
To glance behind her; on she pushes—
Past garden plots, small bridges, lawn,
The lakeway path, the wood; and on
She flies and breaks through lilac bushes,
Past seedbeds to the brook—so fast
That, panting, on a bench at last

39

She falls . . . .
        'He's here! But all those faces!
O God, what must he think of me!'
But still her anguished heart embraces
A misty dream of what might be.
She trembles, burns, and waits . . . so near him!
But will he come? . . . She doesn't hear him.
Some serf girls in the orchard there,
While picking berries, filled the air
With choral song—as they'd been bidden
(An edict that was meant, you see,
To keep sly mouths from feeling free
To eat the master's fruit when hidden,
By filling them with song instead—
For rural cunning isn't dead!):

The Girls' Song

'Lovely maidens, pretty ones,
Dearest hearts and darling friends,
Romp away, sweet lassies, now,
Have your fling, my dear ones, do!
Strike you up a rousing song,
Sing our secret ditty now,
Lure some likely lusty lad
To the circle of our dance.

When we lure the fellow on,
When we see him from afar,
Darlings, then, let's scamper off,
Pelting him with cherries then,
Cherries, yes, and raspberries,
Ripe red currants let us throw!

Never come to listen in
When we sing our secret songs,
Never come to spy on us
When we play our maiden games!'

40

Tatyana listens, scarcely hearing
The vibrant voices, sits apart,
And waits impatient in her clearing
To calm the tremor in her heart
And halt the constant surge of blushes;
But still her heart in panic rushes,
Her cheeks retain their blazing glow
And ever brighter, brighter grow.
Just so a butterfly both quivers
And beats an iridescent wing
When captured by some boy in spring;
Just so a hare in winter shivers,
When suddenly far off it sees
The hunter hiding in the trees.

41

But finally she rose, forsaken,
And, sighing, started home for bed;
But hardly had she turned and taken
The garden lane, when straight ahead,
His eyes ablaze, Eugene stood waiting—
Like some grim shade of night's creating;
And she, as if by fire seared,
Drew back and stopped when he appeared. . . .
Just now though, friends, I feel too tired
To tell you how this meeting went
And what ensued from that event;
I've talked so long that I've required
A little walk, some rest and play;
I'll finish up another day.

Chapter 4

La morale est dans la nature des choses*
Necker

(1–6) 7

The less we love her when we woo her,
The more we draw a woman in,
And thus more surely we undo her
Within the witching webs we spin.
Time was, when cold debauch was lauded
As love's high art . . . and was applauded
For trumpeting its happy lot
In taking joy while loving not.
But that pretentious game is dated,
But fit for apes, who once held sway
Amid our forbears' vaunted day;
The fame of Lovelaces has faded—
Along with fashions long since dead:
Majestic wigs and heels of red.

8

Who doesn't find dissembling dreary;
Or trying gravely to convince
(Recasting platitudes till weary)—
When all agree and have long since;
How dull to hear the same objections,
To overcome those predilections
That no young girl thirteen, I vow,
Has ever had and hasn't now!
Who wouldn't grow fatigued with rages,
Entreaties, vows, pretended fears,
Betrayals, gossip, rings, and tears,
With notes that run to seven pages,
With watchful mothers, aunts who stare,
And friendly husbands hard to bear!

9

Well, this was my Eugene's conclusion.
In early youth he'd been the prey
Of every raging mad delusion,
And uncurbed passions ruled the day.
Quite pampered by a life of leisure,
Enchanted with each passing pleasure,
But disenchanted just as quick,
Of all desire at length grown sick,
And irked by fleet success soon after,
He'd hear mid hum and hush alike
His grumbling soul the hours strike,
And smothered yawns with brittle laughter:
And so he killed eight years of youth
And lost life's very bloom, in truth.

10

He ceased to know infatuation,
Pursuing belles with little zest;
Refused, he found quick consolation;
Betrayed, was always glad to rest.
He sought them out with no elation
And left them too without vexation,
Scarce mindful of their love or spite.
Just so a casual guest at night
Drops in for whist and joins routinely;
And then upon the end of play,
Just takes his leave and drives away
To fall asleep at home serenely;
And in the morning he won't know
What evening holds or where he'll go.

11

But having read Tatyana's letter,
Onegin was profoundly stirred:
Her maiden dreams had helped unfetter
A swarm of thoughts with every word;
And he recalled Tatyana's pallor,
Her mournful air, her touching valour—
And then he soared, his soul alight
With sinless dreams of sweet delight.
Perhaps an ancient glow of passion
Possessed him for a moment's sway . . .
But never would he lead astray
A trusting soul in callous fashion.
And so let's hasten to the walk
Where he and Tanya had their talk.

12

Some moments passed in utter quiet,
And then Eugene approached and spoke:
'You wrote to me. Do not deny it.
I've read your words and they evoke
My deep respect for your emotion,
Your trusting soul . . . and sweet devotion.
Your candour has a great appeal
And stirs in me, I won't conceal,
Long dormant feelings, scarce remembered.
But I've no wish to praise you now;
Let me repay you with a vow
As artless as the one you tendered;
Hear my confession too, I plead,
And judge me both by word and deed.

13

'Had I in any way desired
To bind with family ties my life;
Or had a happy fate required
That I turn father, take a wife;
Had pictures of domestication
For but one moment held temptation—
Then, surely, none but you alone
Would be the bride I'd make my own.
I'll say without wrought-up insistence
That, finding my ideal in you,
I would have asked you—yes, it's true—
To share my baneful, sad existence,
In pledge of beauty and of good,
And been as happy . . . as I could!

14

'But I'm not made for exaltation:
My soul's a stranger to its call;
Your virtues are a vain temptation,
For I'm not worthy of them all.
Believe me (conscience be your token):
In wedlock we would both be broken.
However much I loved you, dear,
Once used to you . . . I'd cease, I fear;
You'd start to weep, but all your crying
Would fail to touch my heart at all,
Your tears in fact would only gall.
So judge yourself what we'd be buying,
What roses Hymen means to send—
Quite possibly for years on end!

15

'In all this world what's more perverted
Than homes in which the wretched wife
Bemoans her worthless mate, deserted—
Alone both day and night through life;
Or where the husband, knowing truly
Her worth (yet cursing fate unduly)
Is always angry, sullen, mute—
A coldly jealous, selfish brute!
Well, thus am I. And was it merely
For *this* your ardent spirit pined
When you, with so much strength of mind,
Unsealed your heart to me so clearly?
Can Fate indeed be so unkind?
Is this the lot you've been assigned?

16

'For dreams and youth there's no returning;
I cannot resurrect my soul.
I love you with a tender yearning,
But mine must be a brother's role.
So hear me through without vexation:
Young maidens find quick consolation—
From dream to dream a passage brief;
Just so a sapling sheds its leaf
To bud anew each vernal season.
Thus heaven wills the world to turn.
You'll fall in love again; but learn . . .
To exercise restraint and reason,
For few will understand you so,
And innocence can lead to woe.'

17

Thus spake Eugene his admonition.
Scarce breathing and bereft of speech,
Gone blind with tears, in full submission,
Tatyana listened to him preach.
He offered her his arm. Despairing,
She took it and with languid bearing
('Mechanically', as people say),
She bowed her head and moved away. . . .
They passed the garden's dark recesses,
Arriving home together thus—
Where no one raised the slightest fuss:
For country freedom too possesses
Its happy rights . . . as grand as those
That high and mighty Moscow knows.

18

I know that you'll agree, my reader,
That our good friend was only kind
And showed poor Tanya when he freed her
A noble heart and upright mind.
Again he'd done his moral duty,
But spiteful people saw no beauty
And quickly blamed him, heaven knows!
Good friends no less than ardent foes
(But aren't they one, if they offend us?)
Abused him roundly, used the knife.
Now every man has foes in life,
But from our friends, dear God, defend us!
Ah, friends, those friends! I greatly fear,
I find their friendship much too dear.

19

What's that? Just that. Mere conversation
To lull black empty thoughts awhile;
In passing, though, one observation:
There's not a calumny too vile—
That any garret babbler hatches,
And all the social rabble snatches;
There's no absurdity or worse,
Nor any vulgar gutter verse,
That your good friend won't find delightful,
Repeating it a hundred ways
To decent folk for days and days,
While never meaning to be spiteful;
He's yours, he'll say, through thick and thin:
He loves you so! . . . Why, you're like kin!

20

Hm, hm, dear reader, feeling mellow?
And are your kinfolk well today?
Perhaps you'd like, you gentle fellow,
To hear what I'm prepared to say
On 'kinfolk' and their implications?
Well, here's my view of close relations:
They're people whom we're bound to prize,
To honour, love, and idolize,
And, following the old tradition,
To visit come the Christmas feast,
Or send a wish by mail at least;
All other days they've our permission
To quite forget us, if they please—
So grant them, God, long life and ease!

21

Of course the love of tender beauties
Is surer far than friends or kin:
Your claim upon its joyous duties
Survives when even tempests spin.
Of course it's so. And yet be wary,
For fashions change, and views will vary,
And nature's made of wayward stuff—
The charming sex is light as fluff.
What's more, the husband's frank opinion
Is bound by any righteous wife
To be respected in this life;
And so your mistress (faithful minion)
May in a trice be swept away:
For Satan treats all love as play.

22

But whom to love? To trust and treasure?
Who won't betray us in the end?
And who'll be kind enough to measure
Our words and deeds as we intend?
Who won't sow slander all about us?
Who'll coddle us and never doubt us?
To whom will all our faults be few?
Who'll never bore us through and through?
You futile, searching phantom-breeder,
Why spend your efforts all in vain;
Just love yourself and ease the pain,
My most esteemed and honoured reader!
A worthy object! Never mind,
A truer love you'll never find.

23

But what ensued from Tanya's meeting?
Alas, it isn't hard to guess!
Within her heart the frenzied beating
Coursed on and never ceased to press
Her gentle soul, athirst with aching;
Nay, ever more intensely quaking,
Poor Tanya burns in joyless throes;
Sleep shuns her bed, all sweetness goes,
The glow of life has vanished starkly;
Her health, her calm, the smile she wore—
Like empty sounds exist no more,
And Tanya's youth now glimmers darkly:
Thus stormy shadows cloak with grey
The scarcely risen, newborn day.

24

Alas, Tatyana's fading quickly;
She's pale and wasted, doesn't speak!
Her soul, unmoved, grows wan and sickly;
She finds all former pleasures bleak.
The neighbours shake their heads morosely
And whisper to each other closely:
'It's time she married . . . awful waste. . . .'
But that's enough. I must make haste
To cheer the dark imagination
With pictures of a happy pair;
I can't, though, readers, help but care
And feel a deep commiseration;
Forgive me, but it's true, you know,
I love my dear Tatyana so!

25

Each passing hour more captivated
By Olga's winning, youthful charms,
Vladimir gave his heart and waited
To serve sweet bondage with his arms.
He's ever near. In gloomy weather
They sit in Olga's room together;
Or arm in arm they make their rounds
Each morning through the park and grounds.
And so? Inebriated lover,
Confused with tender shame the while
(Encouraged, though, by Olga's smile),
He sometimes even dares to cover
One loosened curl with soft caress
Or kiss the border of her dress.

26

At times he reads her works of fiction—
Some moralistic novel, say,
Whose author's powers of depiction
Make Chateaubriand's works seem grey;
But sometimes there are certain pages
(Outlandish things, mere foolish rages,
Unfit for maiden's heart or head),
Which Lensky, blushing, leaves unread. . . .
They steal away whenever able
And sit for hours seeing naught,
Above the chessboard deep in thought,
Their elbows propped upon the table;
Where Lensky with his pawn once took,
Bemused and muddled, his own rook.

27

When he drives home, she still engages
His poet's soul, his artist's mind;
He fills her album's fleeting pages
With every tribute he can find:
He draws sweet views of rustic scenery,
A Venus temple, graves and greenery;
He pens a lyre . . . and then a dove,
Adds colour lightly and with love;
And on the leaves of recollection,
Beneath the lines from other hands,
He plants a tender verse that stands—
Mute monument to fond reflection:
A moment's thought whose trace shall last
Unchanged when even years have passed.

28

I'm sure you've known provincial misses;
Their albums too you must have seen,
Where girlfriends scribble hopes and blisses—
From frontside, backside, in between.
With spellings awesome in abusage,
Unmetred lines of hallowed usage
Are entered by each would-be friend—
Diminished, lengthened, turned on end.
Upon the first page you'll discover:
Qu'écrirez-vous sur ces tablettes?
And 'neath it: *toute à vous Annette;*
While on the last one you'll uncover:
'Who loves you more than I must sign
And fill the page that follows mine.'

29

You're sure to find there decorations:
Rosettes, a torch, a pair of hearts;
You'll read, no doubt, fond protestations:
With all my love, till death us parts;
Some army scribbler will have written
A roguish rhyme to tease the smitten.
In just such albums, friends, I too
Am quite as glad to write as you,
For there, at heart, I feel persuaded
That any zealous vulgar phrase
Will earn me an indulgent gaze,
And won't then be evaluated
With wicked grin or solemn eye
To judge the wit with which I lie.

30

But you, odd tomes of haughty ladies,
You gorgeous albums stamped with gilt,
You libraries of darkest Hades
And racks where modish rhymesters wilt,
You volumes nimbly ornamented
By Tolstoy's* magic brush, and scented
By Baratynsky's pen—I vow:
Let God's own lightning strike you now!
Whenever dazzling ladies proffer
Their quartos to be signed by me,
I tremble with malicious glee;
My soul cries out and longs to offer
An epigram of cunning spite—
But madrigals they'll have you write!

31

No madrigals of mere convention
Does Olga's Lensky thus compose;
His pen breathes love, not pure invention
Or sparkling wit as cold as prose;
Whatever comes to his attention
Concerning Olga, *that* he'll mention;
And filled with truth's own vivid glows
A stream of elegies then flows.*
Thus you, Yazýkov,* with perfection,
With all the surgings of your heart,
Sing God knows whom in splendid art—
Sweet elegies, whose full collection
Will on some future day relate
The uncut story of your fate.

32

But hush! A strident critic rises
And bids us cast away the crown
Of elegy in all its guises
And to our rhyming guild calls down:
'Have done with all your lamentations,
Your endless croakings and gyrations
On "former days" and "times of yore";
Enough now! Sing of something more!'
You're right. And will you point with praises
To trumpet, mask, and dagger* too,
And bid us thuswise to renew
Our stock of dead ideas and phrases?
Is that it, friend?—'Far from it. Nay!
Write odes,* good sirs, write odes, I say . . .

33

'The way they did in former ages,
Those mighty years still rich in fame. . . .'
Just solemn odes? . . . On all our pages?!
Oh come now, friend, it's all the same.
Recall the satirist, good brother,
And his sly odist in *The Other*;*
Do you find him more pleasing, pray,
Than our glum rhymesters of today? . . . .
'Your elegy lacks all perception,
Its want of purpose is a crime;
Whereas the ode has aims sublime.'
One might to this take sharp exception,
But I'll be mute. I don't propose
To bring two centuries to blows.

34

By thoughts of fame and freedom smitten,
Vladimir's stormy soul grew wings;
What odes indeed he might have written,
But Olga didn't read the things.
How oft have tearful poets chances
To read their works before the glances
Of those they love? Good sense declares
That no reward on earth compares.
How blest, shy lover, to be granted
To read to her for whom you long:
The very object of your song,
A beauty languid and enchanted!
Ah, blest indeed . . . although it's true,
She may be dreaming not of you.

35

But I my fancy's fruits and flowers
(Those dreams and harmonies I tend)
Am quite content to read for hours
To my old nurse, my childhood's friend;
Or sometimes after dinners dreary,
When some good neighbour drops in weary—
I'll corner him and catch his coat
And stuff him with the play I wrote;
Or else (and here I'm far from jesting),
When off beside my lake I climb—
Beset with yearning and with rhyme—
I scare a flock of ducks from resting;
And hearing my sweet stanzas soar,
They flap their wings and fly from shore.

36*

And as I watch them disappearing,
A hunter hidden in the brush
Damns poetry for interfering
And, whistling, fires with a rush.
Each has his own preoccupation,
His favourite sport or avocation:
One aims a gun at ducks on high;
One is entranced by rhyme as I;
One swats at flies in mindless folly;
One dreams of ruling multitudes;
One craves the scent that war exudes;
One likes to bask in melancholy;
One occupies himself with wine:
And good and bad all intertwine.

37

But what of our Eugene this while?
Have patience, friends, I beg you, pray;
I'll tell it all in detailed style
And show you how he spent each day.
Onegin lived in his own heaven:
In summer he'd get up by seven
And, lightly clad, would take a stroll
Down to the stream below the knoll.
Gulnare's proud singer* his example,
He'd swim across this Hellespont;
Then afterwards, as was his wont,
He'd drink his coffee, sometimes sample
The pages of some dull review,
And then he'd dress. . . .

(38) 39

Long rambles, reading, slumber's blisses,
The burbling brook, the wooded shade,
At times the fresh and youthful kisses
Of white-skinned, dark-eyed country maid;
A horse of spirit fit to bridle,
A dinner fanciful and idle,
A bottle of some sparkling wine,
Seclusion, quiet—these, in fine,
Were my Onegin's saintly pleasures,
To which he yielded one by one,
Unmoved to count beneath the sun
Fair summer's days and careless treasures,
Unmindful too of town or friends
And their dull means to festive ends.

40

Our northern summers, though, are versions
Of southern winters, this is clear;
And though we're loath to cast aspersions,
They seem to go before they're here!
The sky breathed autumn, turned and darkled;
The friendly sun less often sparkled;
The days grew short and as they sped,
The wood with mournful murmur shed
Its wondrous veil to stand uncovered;
The fields all lay in misty peace;
The caravan of cackling geese
Turned south; and all around there hovered
The sombre season near at hand;
November marched across the land.

41

The dawn arises cold and cheerless;
The empty fields in silence wait;
And on the road . . . grown lean and fearless,
The wolf appears with hungry mate;
Catching the scent, the road horse quivers
And snorts in fear, the traveller shivers
And flies uphill with all his speed;
No more at dawn does shepherd need
To drive the cows outside with ringing;
Nor does his horn at midday sound
The call that brings them gathering round.
Inside her hut a girl is singing,
And by the matchwood's crackling light
She spins away the wintry night.

42

The frost already cracks and crunches;
The fields are silver where they froze . . .
(And you, good reader, with your hunches,
Expect the rhyme, so take it—Rose!)
No fine parquet could hope to muster
The ice-clad river's glassy lustre;
The joyous tribe of boys berates
And cuts the ice with ringing skates;
A waddling red-foot goose now scurries
To swim upon the water's breast;
He treads the ice with care to test . . .
And down he goes! The first snow flurries
Come flitting, flicking, swirling round
To fall like stars upon the ground.

43

But how is one, in this dull season,
To help the rural day go by?
Take walks? The views give little reason,
When only bareness greets the eye.
Go ride the steppe's harsh open spaces?
Your mount, if put to try his paces
On treacherous ice in blunted shoe,
Is sure to fall . . . and so will you.
So stay beneath your roof . . . try reading:
Here's Pradt* or, better, Walter Scott!
Or check accounts. You'd rather not?
Then rage or drink. . . . Somehow proceeding,
This night will pass (the next one too),
And grandly you'll see winter through!

44

Childe Harold-like, Onegin ponders,
Adrift in idle, slothful ways;
From bed to icy bath he wanders,
And then at home all day he stays,
Alone, and sunk in calculation,
His only form of recreation—
The game of billiards, all day through,
With just two balls and blunted cue.
But as the rural dusk encroaches,
The cue's forgot, the billiards fade;
Before the hearth the table's laid.
He waits. . . . At last his guest approaches:
It's Lensky's troika, three fine roans;
'Come on, let's dine, my stomach groans!'

45

Moët, that wine most blest and heady,
Or Veuve Cliquot, the finest class,
Is brought in bottle chilled and ready
And set beside the poet's glass.
Like Hippocrene* it sparkles brightly,
It fizzes, foams, and bubbles lightly
(A simile in many ways);
It charmed me too, in other days:
For its sake once, I squandered gladly
My last poor pence . . . remember, friend?
Its magic stream brought forth no end
Of acting foolish, raving madly,
And, oh, how many jests and rhymes,
And arguments, and happy times!

46

But all that foamy, frothy wheezing
Just plays my stomach false, I fear;
And nowadays I find more pleasing
Sedate Bordeaux's good quiet cheer.
Aï* I find is much too risky,
Aï is like a mistress—frisky,
Vivacious, brilliant . . . and too light.
But you, Bordeaux, I find just right;
You're like a comrade, ever steady,
Prepared in trials or in grief
To render service, give relief;
And when we wish it, always ready
To share a quiet evening's end.
Long live Bordeaux, our noble friend!

47

The fire goes out; the coal, still gleaming,
Takes on a film of ash and pales;
The rising vapours, faintly streaming,
Curl out of sight; the hearth exhales
A breath of warmth. The pipe smoke passes
Up chimney flue. The sparkling glasses
Stand fizzing on the table yet;
With evening's gloom, the day has set . . .
(I'm fond of friendly conversation
And of a friendly glass or two
At dusk or *entre chien et loup**—
As people say without translation,
Though why they do, I hardly know).
But listen as our friends speak low:

48

'And how are our dear neighbours faring?
Tatyana and your Olga, pray? . . . '
'Just half a glass, old boy, be sparing . . .
The family's well, I think I'd say;
They send you greetings and affection. . . .
Oh, God, my friend, what sheer perfection
In Olga's breast! What shoulders too!
And what a soul! . . . Come visit, do!
You ought to, really . . . they'll be flattered;
Or judge yourself how it must look—
You dropped in twice and closed the book;
Since then, it seems, they've hardly mattered.
In fact . . . Good Lord, my wits are bleak!
You've been invited there next week!'

49

'Tatyana's name-day celebration
Is Saturday. Her mother's sent
(And Olga too!) an invitation;
Now don't refuse, it's time you went.'
'There'll be a crush and lots of babble
And all that crowd of local rabble.'
'Why not at all, they just intend
To have the family, that's all, friend;
Come on, let's go, do *me* the favour!'
'Alright, I'll go.' 'Well done, first class!'
And with these words he drained his glass
In toast to his attractive neighbour . . .
And then waxed voluble once more
In talk of Olga. Love's a bore!

50

So Lensky soared as he awaited
His wedding day two weeks ahead;
With joy his heart anticipated
The mysteries of the marriage bed
And love's sweet crown of jubilations.
But Hymen's cares and tribulations,
The frigid, yawning days to be,
He never pictured once, not he.
While we, the foes of Hymen's banner,
Perceive full well that home life means
But one long string of dreary scenes—
In Lafontaine's* insipid manner.
But my poor Lensky, deep at heart,
Was born to play this very part.

51

Yes, he was loved . . . beyond deceiving . . .
Or so at least with joy he thought.
Oh, blest is he who lives believing,
Who takes cold intellect for naught,
Who rests within the heart's sweet places
As does a drunk in sleep's embraces,
Or as, more tenderly I'd say,
A butterfly in blooms of May;
But wretched he who's too far-sighted,
Whose head is never fancy-stirred,
Who hates all gestures, each warm word,
As sentiments to be derided,
Whose heart . . . experience has cooled
And barred from being loved . . . or fooled!

Chapter 5

Oh, never know these frightful dreams,
My dear Svetlana!

                              Zhukovsky

1

The fall that year was in no hurry,
And nature seemed to wait and wait
For winter. Then, in January,
The second night, the snow fell late.
Next day as dawn was just advancing,
Tatyana woke and, idly glancing,
Beheld outdoors a wondrous sight:
The roofs, the yard, the fence—all white;
Each pane a fragile pattern showing;
The trees in winter silver dyed,
Gay magpies on the lawn outside,
And all the hilltops soft and glowing
With winter's brilliant rug of snow—
The world all fresh and white below.

2

Ah, wintertime! . . . The peasant, cheerful,
Creates a passage with his sleigh;
Aware of snow, his nag is fearful,
But shambles somehow down the way.
A bold kibitka skips and burrows
And ploughs a trail of fluffy furrows;
The driver sits behind the dash
In sheepskin coat and scarlet sash.
And here's a household boy gone sleighing—
His *Blackie* seated on the sled,
While he plays horse and runs ahead;
The rascal froze his fingers, playing,
And laughs out loud between his howls,
While through the glass his mother scowls.

3

But you, perhaps, are not attracted
By pictures of this simple kind,
Where lowly nature is enacted
And nothing grand or more refined.
Warmed by the god of inspiration,
Another bard in exaltation
Has painted us the snow new-laid
And winter's joys in every shade.*
I'm sure you'll find him most engaging
When he, in flaming verse, portrays
Clandestine rides in dashing sleighs;
But I have no intent of waging
A contest for his crown . . . or thine,
Thou bard of Finland's maid divine!*

4

Tatyana (with a Russian duty
That held her heart, she knew not why)
Profoundly loved, in its cold beauty,
The Russian winter passing by:
Crisp days when sunlit hoarfrost glimmers,
The sleighs, and rosy snow that shimmers
In sunset's glow, the murky light
That wraps about the Yuletide night.
Those twelfthtide eves, by old tradition,
Were marked at home on their estate:
The servant maids would guess the fate
Of both young girls with superstition;
Each year they promised, as before,
Two soldier husbands and a war.

5

Tatyana heeded with conviction
All ancient folklore night and noon,
Believed in dreams and card prediction,
And read the future by the moon.
All signs and portents quite alarmed her,
All objects either scared or charmed her
With secret meanings they'd impart;
Forebodings filled and pressed her heart.
If her prim tomcat sat protected
Atop the stove to wash and purr,
Then this was certain sign to her
That guests were soon to be expected;
Or if upon her left she'd spy
A waxing crescent moon on high,

6

Her face would pale, her teeth would chatter.
Or when a shooting star flew by
To light the sombre sky and shatter
In fiery dust before her eye,
She'd hurry and, in agitation,
Before the star's disintegration,
Would whisper it her secret prayer.
Or if she happened anywhere
To meet a black-robed monk by error,
Or if amid the fields one day
A fleeing hare would cross her way,
She'd be quite overcome with terror,
As dark forebodings filled her mind
Of some misfortune ill defined.

7

Yet even in these same afflictions
She found a secret charm in part:
For nature—fond of contradictions—
Has so designed the human heart.
The holy days are here. What gladness! . . .
Bright youth divines, not knowing sadness,
With nothing that it must regret,
With all of life before it yet—
A distance luminous and boundless. . . .
Old age divines with glasses on
And sees the grave before it yawn,
All thoughts of time returning—groundless;
No matter: childish hope appears
To murmur lies in aged ears.

8

Tatyana watches, fascinated,
The molten wax submerge and turn
To wondrous shapes which designated
Some wondrous thing that she would learn.
Then from a basin filled with water
Their rings are drawn in random order;
When Tanya's ring turned up at last,
The song they sang was from the past:
'*The peasants there have hoards of treasure,*
They spade up silver from a ditch!
The one we sing to will be rich
And famous!' But the plaintive measure
Foretells a death to come ere long,
And girls prefer 'The Kitty's Song.'*

9

A frosty night, the sky resplendent
As heaven's galaxy shines down
And glides—so peaceful and transcendent. . . .
Tatyana, in her low-cut gown,
Steps out of doors and trains a mirror
Upon the moon to bring it nearer;*
But all that shows in her dark glass
Is just the trembling moon, alas. . . .
What's that . . . the crunching snow . . . who's coming?!
She flits on tiptoe with a sigh
And asks the stranger passing by,
Her voice more soft than reed pipe's humming:
'Oh, what's your name?' He hurries on,
Looks back and answers: 'Agafon.'*

10

Tatyana, as her nurse suggested,
Prepared to conjure all night through,*
And so in secret she requested
The bathhouse table laid for two.
But then sheer terror seized Tatyana . . .
And I, recalling poor Svetlana,*
Feel frightened too—so let it go,
We'll not have Tanya conjure so.
Instead, her silken sash untying,
She just undressed and went to bed.
Sweet Lel* now floats above her head,
While 'neath her downy pillow lying,
A maiden's looking-glass she keeps.
Now all is hushed. Tatyana sleeps.

11

And what an awesome dream she's dreaming:
She walks upon a snowy dale,
And all around her, dully gleaming,
Sad mist and murky gloom prevail;
Amid the drifting, snowbound spaces
A dark and seething torrent races,
A hoary frothing wave that strains
And tears asunder winter's chains;
Two slender, icebound poles lie linking
The chasm's banks atop the ridge:
A perilous and shaky bridge;
And full of doubt, her spirits sinking,
Tatyana stopped in sudden dread
Before the raging gulf ahead.

12

As at a vexing separation,
Tatyana murmured, at a loss;
She saw no friendly soul on station
To lend a hand to help her cross.
But suddenly a snowbank shifted,
And who emerged when it was lifted?
A huge and matted bear appeared!
Tatyana screamed! He growled and reared,
Then stretched a paw . . . sharp claws abhorrent,
To Tanya, who could barely stand;
She took it with a trembling hand
And worked her way across the torrent
With apprehensive step . . . then fled!
The bear just followed where she led.

13

She dare not look to see behind her,
And ever faster on she reels;
At every turn he seems to find her,
That shaggy footman at her heels! . . .
The grunting, loathesome bear still lumbers,
Before them now a forest slumbers;
The pines in all their beauty frown
And barely stir, all weighted down
By clumps of snow; and through the summits
Of naked linden, birch, and ash
The beams from heaven's lanterns flash;
There is no path; the gorge that plummets,
The shrubs, the land . . . all lie asleep,
By snowy blizzards buried deep.

14

She's reached the wood, the bear still tracking;
Soft snow, knee-deep, lies all about;
A jutting branch looms up, attacking,
And tears her golden earrings out;
And now another tries to trip her,
And from one charming foot her slipper,
All wet, comes off in crumbly snow;
And now she feels her kerchief go,
She lets it lie, she mustn't linger,
Behind her back she hears the bear,
But shy and frightened, does not dare
To lift her skirt with trembling finger;
She runs . . . but he keeps crashing on . . .
Until at last her strength is gone.

15

She sinks in snow; the bear alertly
Just picks her up and rushes on;
She lies within his arms inertly;
Her breathing stops, all sense is gone.
Along a forest road he surges,
And then, mid trees, a hut emerges;
Dense brush abounds; on every hand
Forlorn and drifting snowbanks stand;
A tiny window glitters brightly,
And from the hut come cries and din;
The bear proclaims: 'My gossip's in.'
'Come warm yourself,' he adds politely,
Then pushes straightway through the door
And lays her down upon the floor.

16

On coming to, she looks around her:
She's in a hall; no bear at least;
The clink of glasses, shouts . . . confound her,
As if it were some funeral feast;
She can't make sense of what she's hearing,
Creeps to the door and, softly peering,
Sees through a crack the strangest thing—
A horde of monsters in a ring:
Out of a dog-face horns are sprouting;
One has a rooster's head on top;
A goateed witch is on a mop;
A haughty skeleton sits pouting
Beside a short-tailed dwarf . . . and *that*
Is half a crane and half a cat.

17

More wondrous still and still more fearful:
A crab upon a spider sat;
On goose's neck a skull seemed cheerful,
While spinning round in bright red hat;
A windmill there was squat-jig dancing
And cracked and waved its sails while prancing;
Guffawing, barking, whistles, claps,
And human speech and hoofbeat taps!
But what was Tanya's stunned reaction
When mid the guests she recognized
The one she feared, the one she prized—
The hero of our novel's action!
Onegin sits amid the roar
And glances slyly through the door.

18

He gives a sign—the others hustle;
He drinks—all drink and all grow shrill;
He laughs—they all guffaw and bustle;
He frowns—and all of them grow still.
He's master here, there's no mistaking;
And Tanya, now no longer quaking,
Turns curious to see still more
And pushes slightly on the door....
The sudden gust of wind surprises
The band of goblins, putting out
The night-time lanterns all about;
His eyes aflame, Onegin rises
And strikes his chair against the floor;
All rise; he marches to the door.

19

And fear assails her; in a panic
She tries to flee . . . but feels too weak;
In anguished writhing, almost manic,
She wants to scream . . . but cannot speak;
Eugene throws wide the door, revealing
To monstrous looks and hellish squealing
Her slender form; fierce cackles sound
In savage glee; all eyes turn round,
All hooves and trunks—grotesque and curving,
And whiskers, tusks, and tufted tails,
Red bloody tongues and snouts and nails,
Huge horns and bony fingers swerving—
All point at her and all combine
To shout as one: 'She's mine! She's mine!'

20

'She's mine!' announced Eugene, commanding;
And all the monsters fled the room;
The maid alone was left there standing
With *him* amid the frosty gloom.
Onegin stares at her intently,
Then draws her to a corner gently
And lays her on a makeshift bed,
And on her shoulder rests his head. . . .
Then Olga enters in confusion,
And Lensky too; a light shines out;
Onegin lifts an arm to rout
Unbidden guests for their intrusion;
He rants at them, his eyes turn dread;
Tatyana lies there nearly dead.

21

The heated words grow louder, quicken;
Onegin snatches up a knife,
And Lensky falls; the shadows thicken;
A rending cry amid the strife
Reverberates . . . the cabin quivers;
Gone numb with terror, Tanya shivers . . .
And wakes to find her room alight,
The frozen windows sparkling bright,
Where dawn's vermilion rays are playing;
Then Olga pushes through the door,
More rosy than the dawn before
And lighter than a swallow, saying:
'Oh, tell me, do, Tatyana love,
Who was it you were dreaming of?'

22

But she ignores her sister's pleading,
Just lies in bed without a word,
Keeps leafing through some book she's reading,
So wrapt in thought she hasn't heard.
Although the book she read presented
No lines a poet had invented,
No sapient truths, no pretty scenes—
Yet neither Virgil's, nor Racine's,
Nor Seneca's, nor Byron's pages,
Nor even *Fashion Plates Displayed*
Had ever so engrossed a maid:
She read, my friends, that king of sages
Martýn Zadéck,* Chaldean seer
And analyst of dreams unclear.

23

This noble and profound creation
A roving pedlar one day brought
To show them in their isolation,
And finally left it when they bought
*Malvina** for three roubles fifty
(A broken set, but he was thrifty);
And in exchange he also took
Two Petriads,* a grammar book,
Some fables he could sell tomorrow,
Plus Marmontel*—just volume three.
Martýn Zadéck soon came to be
Tatyana's favourite. Now when sorrow
Assails her heart, he brings her light,
And sleeps beside her through the night.

24

Her dream disturbs her, and not knowing
What secret message she'd been sent,
Tatyana seeks some passage showing
Just what the dreadful vision meant.
She finds in alphabetic order
What clues the index can afford her:
There's bear and blizzard, bridge, and crow,
Fir, forest, hedgehog, night, and snow,
And many more. But her confusion
Martýn Zadéck cannot dispel;
The frightful vision must foretell
Sad times to come and disillusion.
For several days she couldn't find
A way to calm her troubled mind.

25

But lo! . . . with crimson hand Aurora
Leads forth from morning dales the sun*
And brings in merry mood before her
The name–day feast that's just begun.
Since dawn Dame Larin's near relations
Have filled the house; whole congregations
Of neighbour clans have come in drays,
Kibitkas, britzkas, coaches, sleighs.
The hall is full of crowds and bustle;
The drawing room explodes with noise,
With bark of pugs and maidens' joys,
With laughter, kisses, din and hustle;
The guests all bow and scrape their feet,
Wet nurses shout and babies bleat.

26

Fat Pustyakóv, the local charmer,
Has come and brought his portly wife;
Gvozdín as well, that model farmer,
Whose peasants lead a wretched life;
The two Skotínins, grey as sages,
With children of all shapes and ages—
From two to thirty at the top;
Here's Petushkóv, the district fop;
And my first cousin, good Buyánov,*
Lint-covered, in his visored cap
(As you, of course, well know the chap);
And former couns'lor, old man Flyánov,
A rogue and gossip night and noon,
A glutton, grafter, and buffoon.

27

The Harlikóvs were feeling mellow
And brought along Monsieur Triquet,
Late from Tambóv, a witty fellow
In russet wig and fine pince-nez.
True Gaul, Triquet in pocket carried
A verse to warn that Tanya tarried,
Set to a children's melody:
*Réveillez-vous, belle endormie.**
The printed verse had lain neglected
In some old tattered almanac
Until Triquet, who had a knack
For rhyme, saw fit to resurrect it
And boldly put for 'belle Niná'
The charming line: 'belle Tatyaná.'*

28

And now from nearby quarters, brothers,
That idol whom ripe misses cheer,
The joy and hope of district mothers—
The company commander's here!
He's brought some news to set them cheering:
The regimental band's appearing!
'The colonel's sending it tonight.'
There'll be a ball! What sheer delight!
The girls all jump and grow excited.
But dinner's served. And so by pairs,
And arm in arm, they seek their chairs:
The girls near Tanya; men delighted
To face them; and amid the din,
All cross themselves and dig right in.

29

Then for a moment chatter ceases
As mouths start chewing. All around
The clink of plates and forks increases,
The glasses jingle and resound.
But soon the guests are somewhat sated;
The hubbub grows more animated . . .
But no one hears his neighbour out;
All laugh and argue, squeal and shout.
The doors fly back; two figures enter—
It's Lensky . . . with Eugene! 'Oh dear!'
The hostess cries, 'At last you're here!'
The guests all squeeze toward the centre,
Each moves his setting, shifts his chair,
And in a trice they seat the pair.

30

Across from Tanya—there they place them;
And paler than the moon at dawn,
She cannot raise her eyes to face them
And trembles like a hunted fawn.
Inside her, stormy passion's seething;
The wretched girl is scarcely breathing;
The two friends' greetings pass unheard;
Her tears well up without a word
And almost fall; the poor thing's ready
To faint; but deep within her, will
And strength of mind were working still,
And they prevailed. Her lips more steady,
She murmured something through her pain
And managed somehow to remain.

31

All tragico-hysteric moaning,
All girlish fainting-fits and tears,
Had long since set Eugene to groaning:
He'd borne enough in former years.
Already cross and irritated
By being at this feast he hated,
And noting how poor Tanya shook,
He barely hid his angry look
And fumed in sullen indignation;
He swore that he'd make Lensky pay
And be avenged that very day.
Exulting in anticipation,
He inwardly began to draw
Caricatures of those he saw.

32

Some others too might well have noted
Poor Tanya's plight; but every eye
Was at the time in full devoted
To sizing up a lavish pie*
(Alas, too salty); now they're bringing,
In bottle with the pitch still clinging,
Between the meat and *blancmanger*,
Tsimlyánsky wine . . . a whole array
Of long-stemmed glasses . . . (quite as slender
As your dear waist, my sweet Zizí,*
Fair crystal of my soul and key
To all my youthful verses tender,
Love's luring phial, you who once
Made me a drunken, love-filled dunce!)

33

The bottle pops as cork goes flying;
The fizzing wine comes gushing fast;
And now with solemn mien, and dying
To have his couplet heard at last,
Triquet stands up; the congregation
Falls silent in anticipation.
Tatyana's scarce alive; Triquet,
With verse in hand, looks Tanya's way
And starts to sing, off-key. Loud cheering
And claps salute him. Tanya feels
Constrained to curtsey . . . almost reels.
The bard, whose modesty's endearing,
Is first to toast her where he stands,
Then puts his couplet in her hands.

34

Now greetings come, congratulations;
Tatyana thanks them for the day;
But when Eugene's felicitations
Came due in turn, the girl's dismay,
Her weariness and helpless languor,
Evoked his pity more than anger:
He bowed to her in silence, grave . . .
But somehow just the look he gave
Was wondrous tender. If asserting
Some feeling for Tatyana's lot,
Or if, unconsciously or not,
He'd only teased her with some flirting,
His look was still a tender dart:
It reawakened Tanya's heart.

35

The chairs, pushed back, give out a clatter;
The crowd moves on to drawing room:
Thus bees from luscious hive will scatter,
A noisy swarm, to meadow bloom.
Their festive dinner all too pleasing,
The squires face each other wheezing;
The ladies to the hearth repair;
The maidens whisper by the stair;
At green-baize tables players settle,
As Boston, ombre (old men's play),
And whist, which reigns supreme today,
Call out for men to try their mettle:
A family with a single creed,
All sons of boredom's endless greed.

36

Whist's heroes have by now completed
Eight rubbers; and eight times as well
They've shifted round and been reseated;
Now tea is brought. I like to tell
The time of day by teas and dinners,
By supper's call. We country sinners
Can tell the time without great fuss:
The stomach serves as clock for us;
And apropos, I might make mention
In passing that I speak as much
Of feasts and foods and corks and such
In these odd lines of my invention—
As you, great Homer, you whose song
Has lasted thirty centuries long!

(37–8) 39

But tea is brought: the girls demurely
Have scarcely taken cups in hand,
When suddenly from ballroom doorway
Bassoon and flute announce the band.
Elated by the music's bouncing,
His tea and rum at once renouncing,
That Paris of the local towns,
Good Petushkóv, to Olga bounds;
To Tanya, Lensky; Harlikóva,
A maiden somewhat ripe in glow,
My Tambov poet takes in tow;
Buyánov whirls off Pustyakóva;
Then all the crowd comes pouring in
To watch the brilliant ballroom spin.

40

At the beginning of my story
(In Chapter One, if you recall),
I wanted with Albani's glory*
To paint a Petersburg grand ball;
But then, by empty dreams deflected,
I lost my way and recollected
The feet of ladies known before.
In your slim tracks I'll stray no more,
O charming feet and mad affliction!
My youth betrayed, it's time to show
More common sense if I'm to grow,
To mend my ways in deeds and diction,
And cleanse this Chapter Five at last
Of all digressions from the past.

41

Monotonous and mad procession,
Young life's own whirlwind, full of sound,
Each pair a blur in quick succession,
The rousing waltz goes whirling round.
His moment of revenge beginning,
Eugene, with secret malice grinning,
Approaches Olga . . . idly jests,
Then spins her round before the guests;
He stays beside her when she's seated,
Proceeds to talk of this and that;
Two minutes barely has she sat . . .
And then their waltzing is repeated!
The guests all stare in mute surprise;
Poor Lensky can't believe his eyes.

42

Now the mazurka's call is sounded.
Its thunder once could even rack
The greatest hall when it resounded,
And under heels parquet would crack;
The very windows shook like Hades.
But now it's changed: we're all like ladies;
And o'er the lacquered boards we glide.
But in small town and countryside
The old mazurka hasn't faltered;
It still retains its pristine joys:
Moustaches, leaps, heel-pounding noise
Remain the same; they've not been altered
By tyrant-fashion's high decrees,
The modern Russian's new disease.

(43) 44

My bold Buyánov guides expertly
Tatyana to our hero's side,
And Olga too; Eugene alertly
Makes off with Lensky's future bride.
He steers her, gliding nonchalantly,
And bending, whispers her gallantly
Some common madrigal to please,
Then gives her hand a gentle squeeze;
She blushes in appreciation,
Her prim conceited face alight,
While Lensky rages at the sight.
Consumed with jealous indignation,
He waits till the mazurka's through,
Then asks her for the dance he's due.

45

But no, she can't. What explanation? . . .
Well, she's just promised his good friend
The next dance too. In God's creation!
What's this he hears? Could she intend? . . .
Can this be real? Scarce more than swaddler—
And turned coquette! A fickle toddler!
Already has she mastered guile,
Already learned to cheat and smile!
The blow has left poor Lensky shattered;
And cursing woman's crooked course,
He leaves abruptly, calls for horse,
And gallops off. Now nothing mattered—
A brace of pistols and a shot
Shall instantly decide his lot.

Chapter 6

La sotto i giorni nubilosi e brevi,
Nasce una gente, a cui l'morir non dole.*

                                        Petrarch

1

Though pleased with the revenge he'd taken,
Onegin, noting Lensky'd left,
Felt all his old ennui awaken,
Which made poor Olga feel bereft.
She too now yawns and, as she dances,
Seeks Lensky out with furtive glances;
The endless dance had come to seem
To Olga like some dreadful dream.
But now it's over. Supper's heeded.
Then beds are made; the guests are all
Assigned their rooms—from entrance hall
To servants' quarters. Rest is needed
By everyone. Eugene has fled
And driven home alone to bed.

2

All's quiet now. Inside the parlour,
The portly Mr. Pustyakóv
Lies snoring with his portly partner.
Gvozdín, Buyánov, Petushkóv—
And Flyánov, who'd been reeling badly—
On dining chairs have bedded gladly;
While on the floor Triquet's at rest
In tattered nightcap and his vest.
The rooms of Olga and Tatyana
Are filled with girls in sleep's embrace.
Alone, beside the windowcase,
Illumined sadly by Diana,
Poor Tanya, sleepless and in pain,
Sits gazing at the darkened plain.

3

His unexpected reappearance,
That momentary tender look,
The strangeness of his interference
With Olga—all confused and shook
Tatyana's soul. His true intention
Remained beyond her comprehension,
And jealous anguish pierced her breast—
As if a chilling hand had pressed
Her heart; as if in awful fashion
A rumbling, black abyss did yawn. . . .
'I'll die,' she whispers to the dawn,
'But death from him is sweet compassion.
Why murmur vainly? He can't give
The happiness for which I live.'

4

But forward, forward, O my story!
A new persona has arrived:
Five versts or so from Krasnogory,
Our Lensky's seat, there lived and thrived
In philosophical seclusion
(And does so still, have no illusion)
Zarétsky—once a rowdy clown,
Chief gambler and arch rake in town,
The tavern tribune and a liar—
But now a kind and simple soul
Who plays an unwed father's role,
A faithful friend, a peaceful squire,
And man of honour, nothing less:
Thus does our age its sins redress!

5

Time was, when flunkies in high places
Would praise him for his nasty grit:
He could, it's true, from twenty paces,
Shoot pistol at an ace and hit;
And once, when riding battle station,
He'd earned a certain reputation
When in a frenzied state indeed
He'd plunged in mud from Kalmuk steed,
Drunk as a pig, and suffered capture
(A prize to make the French feel proud!).
Like noble Regulus,* he bowed,
Accepting hostage bonds with rapture—
In hopes that he (on charge) might squeeze
Three bottles daily from Véry's.*

6

He used to banter rather neatly,
Could gull a fool, and had an eye
For fooling clever men completely,
For all to see, or on the sly;
Of course not all his pranks succeeded
Or passed unpunished or unheeded,
And sometimes he himself got bled
And ended up the dunce instead.
He loved good merry disputations,
Could answer keenly, be obtuse,
Put silence cunningly to use,
Or cunningly start altercations;
Could get two friends prepared to fight,
Then lead them to the duelling site;

7

Or else he'd patch things up between them
So he might lunch with them as guest,
And later secretly demean them
With nasty gossip or a jest. . . .
Sed alia tempora! Such sporting
(With other capers such as courting)
Goes out of us when youth is dead—
And my Zaretsky, as I've said,
Neath flow'ring cherries and acacias,
Secure at last from tempest's rage,
Lives out his life a proper sage,
Plants cabbages like old Horatius,
Breeds ducks and geese, and oversees
His children at their ABCs.

8

He was no fool; and consequently
(Although he thought him lacking heart),
Eugene would hear his views intently
And liked his common sense in part.
He'd spent some time with him with pleasure,
And so was not in any measure
Surprised next morning when he found,
Zaretsky had again called round;
The latter, hard upon first greeting,
And cutting off Eugene's reply,
Presented him, with gloating eye,
The poet's note about a 'meeting'.
Onegin, taking it, withdrew
And by the window read it through.

9

The note was brief in its correctness,
A proper challenge or *cartel*:
Politely, but with cold directness,
It called him out and did it well.
Onegin, with his first reaction,
Quite curtly offered satisfaction
And bade the envoy, if he cared,
To say that he was *quite prepared*.
Avoiding further explanation,
Zaretsky, pleading much to do,
Arose . . . and instantly withdrew.
Eugene, once left to contemplation
And face to face with his own soul,
Felt far from happy with his role.

10

And rightly so: in inquisition,
With conscience as his judge of right,
He found much wrong in his position:
First off, he'd been at fault last night
To mock in such a casual fashion
At tender love's still timid passion;
And why not let the poet rage!
A fool, at eighteen years of age,
Can be excused his rash intentions.
Eugene, who loved the youth at heart,
Might well have played a better part—
No plaything of the mob's conventions
Or brawling boy to take offence,
But man of honour and of sense.

11

He could have shown some spark of feeling
Instead of bristling like a beast;
He should have spoken words of healing,
Disarmed youth's heart . . . or tried at least.
'Too late,' he thought, 'the moment's wasted. . . .
What's more, that duelling fox has tasted
His chance to mix in this affair—
That wicked gossip with his flair
For jibes . . . and all his foul dominion.
He's hardly worth contempt, I know,
But fools will whisper . . . grin . . . and crow! . . .'
So there it is—the mob's opinion!
The spring with which our honour's wound!
The god that makes this world go round!

12

At home the poet, seething, paces
And waits impatiently to hear.
Then *in* his babbling neighbour races,
The answer in his solemn leer.
The jealous poet's mood turned festive!
He'd been, till now, uncertain . . . restive,
Afraid the scoundrel might refuse
Or laugh it off and, through some ruse,
Escape unscathed . . . the slippery devil!
But now at last his doubts were gone:
Next day, for sure, they'd drive at dawn
Out to the mill, where each would level
A pistol, cocked and lifted high,
To aim at temple or at thigh.

13

Convinced that Olga's heart was cruel,
Vladimir vowed he wouldn't run
To see that flirt before the duel.
He kept consulting watch and sun . . .
Then gave it up and finally ended
Outside the door of his intended.
He thought she'd blush with self-reproach,
Grow flustered when she saw his coach;
But not at all: as blithe as ever,
She bounded from the porch above
And rushed to greet her rhyming love
Like giddy hope—so gay and clever,
So frisky-carefree with her grin,
She seemed the same she'd always been.

14

'Why did you leave last night so early?'
Was all that Olga, smiling, said.
Poor Lensky's muddled mind was swirling,
And silently he hung his head.
All jealousy and rage departed
Before that gaze so openhearted,
Before that soft and simple trust,
Before that soul so bright and just!
With misty eyes he looks on sweetly
And sees the truth: *she loves him yet*!
Tormented now by deep regret,
He craves her pardon so completely,
He trembles, hunts for words in vain:
He's happy now, he's almost sane. . . .

(15–16) 17

Once more in solemn, rapt attention
Before his darling Olga's face,
Vladímir hasn't heart to mention
The night before and what took place;
'It's up to me,' he thought, 'to save her.
I'll never let that foul depraver
Corrupt her youthful heart with lies,
With fiery praise . . . and heated sighs;
Nor see that noxious worm devour
My lovely lily, stalk and blade;
Nor watch this two-day blossom fade
When it has yet to fully flower.'
All this, dear readers, meant in fine:
I'm duelling with a friend of mine.

18

Had Lensky known the deep emotion
That seared my Tanya's wounded heart!
Or had Tatyana had some notion
Of how these two had grown apart,
Or that by morn they'd be debating,
For which of them the grave lay waiting!—
Ah, then, perhaps, the love she bore
Might well have made them friends once more!
But no one knew her inclination
Or chanced upon the sad affair.
Eugene had kept his silent air;
Tatyana pined in isolation;
And only nanny might have guessed,
But her old wits were slow at best.

19

All evening Lensky was abstracted,
Remote one moment, gay the next;
But those on whom the Muse has acted
Are ever thus; with brow perplexed,
He'd sit at clavichord intently
And play but chords; or turning gently
To Olga, he would whisper low:
'I'm happy, love . . . it's true, you know.'
But now it's late and time for leaving.
His heart, so full of pain, drew tight;
And as he bid the girl goodnight,
He felt it break with desperate grieving.
'What's wrong?' She peered at him, intent.
'It's nothing.' And away he went.

20

On coming home, the youth inspected
His pistols; then he put them back.
Undressed, by candle he selected
A book of Schiller's from the rack;
But only one bright image holds him,
One thought within his heart enfolds him:
He sees before him, wondrous fair,
His incandescent Olga there.
He shuts the book and, with decision,
Takes up his pen. . . . His verses ring
With all the nonsense lovers sing;
And feverish with lyric vision,
He reads them out like one possessèd,
Like drunken Delvig* at a fest!

21

By chance those verses haven't vanished;
I have them, and I quote them here:
'Ah, whither, whither are ye banished,
My springtime's golden days so dear?
What fate will morning bring my lyre?
In vain my searching eyes enquire,
For all lies veiled in misty dust.
No matter; fate's decree is just;
And whether, pierced, I fall anointed,
Or arrow passes by—all's right:
The hours of waking and of night
Come each in turn as they're appointed;
And blest with all its cares the day,
And blest the dark that comes to stay!

22

'The morning star will gleam tomorrow,
And brilliant day begin to bloom;
While I, perhaps, descend in sorrow
The secret refuge of the tomb....
Slow Lethe, then, with grim insistence,
Will drown my memory's brief existence;
Of me the world shall soon grow dumb;
But thou, fair maiden, wilt thou come!
To shed a tear in desolation
And think at my untimely grave:
He loved me and for me he gave
His mournful life in consecration!...
Beloved friend, sweet friend, I wait,
Oh, come, Oh, come, I am thy mate!'

23

He wrote thus—*limply and obscurely*.
(We say 'romantically'—although,
That's not romanticism, surely;
And if it is, who wants to know?)
But then at last, as it was dawning,
With drooping head and frequent yawning,
Upon the modish word 'ideal'
Vladimir gently dozed for real;
But sleep had hardly come to take him
Off to be charmed by dreams and cheered,
When in that silent room appeared
His neighbour, calling out to wake him:
'It's time to rise! Past six . . . come on!
I'll bet Onegin woke at dawn.'

24

But he was wrong; that idle sinner
Was sleeping soundly even then.
But now the shades of night grow thinner,
The cock hails Vesper once again;
Yet still Onegin slumbers deeply.
But now the sun climbs heaven steeply,
And gusting snowflakes flash and spin,
But still Onegin lies within
And hasn't stirred; still slumber hovers
Above his bed and holds him fast.
But now he slowly wakes at last,
Draws back the curtains and his covers,
Looks out—and sees with some dismay,
He'd better leave without delay.

25

He rings in haste and, with a racket,
His French valet, Guillot, runs in—
With slippers and a dressing jacket,
And fresh new linen from the bin.
Onegin, dressing in a flurry,
Instructs his man as well to hurry:
They're leaving for the duelling place,
Guillot's to fetch the pistol case.
The sleigh's prepared; his pacing ceases;
He climbs aboard and off they go.
They reach the mill. He bids Guillot
To bring Lepage's deadly pieces;*
Then has the horses, on command,
Removed to where two oaklings stand.

26

Impatient, but in no great panic,
Vladimir waited near the dam;
Meanwhile Zaretsky, born mechanic,
Was carping at the millstone's cam.
Onegin, late, made explanation.
Zaretsky frowned in consternation:
'Good God, man, where's your second? Where?'
In duels a purist doctrinaire,
Zaretsky favoured stout reliance
On proper form; he'd not allow
Dispatching chaps just anyhow,
But called for strict and full compliance
With rules, traditions, ancient ways
(Which we, of course, in him should praise).

27

'My second?' said Eugene directly.
'Why here he is: Monsieur Guillot,
A friend of mine, whom you . . . *correctly*!
Will be quite pleased to greet, I know;
Though he's unknown and lives obscurely,
He's still an honest chap, most surely.'
Zaretsky bit his lip, well vexed.
Onegin turned to Lensky next:
'Shall we begin?'—'At my insistence.'
Behind the mill, without a word.
And while the 'honest chap' conferred
With our Zaretsky at a distance
And sealed the solemn compact fast,
The foes stood by with eyes downcast.

28

The foes! How long has bloodlust parted
And so estranged these former friends?
How long ago did they, warmhearted,
Share meals and pastimes, thoughts and ends?
And now, malignant in intention,
Like ancient foes in mad dissension,
As in a dreadful senseless dream,
They glower coldly as they scheme
In silence to destroy each other. . . .
Should they not laugh while yet there's time,
Before their hands are stained with crime?
Should each not part once more as brother? . . .
But enmity among their class
Holds shame in savage dread, alas.

29

The gleaming pistols wake from drowsing.
Against the ramrods mallets pound.
The balls go in each bevelled housing.
The first sharp hammer clicks resound.
Now streams of greyish powder settle
Inside the pans. Screwed fast to metal,
The jagged flints are set to go.
Behind a nearby stump Guillot
Takes up his stand in indecision.
The duellists shed their cloaks and wait.
Zaretsky paces off their fate
At thirty steps with fine precision,
Then leads each man to where he'll stand,
And each takes pistol into hand.

30

'Approach at will!' Advancing coldly,
With quiet, firm, and measured tread,
Not aiming yet, the foes took boldly
The first four steps that lay ahead—
Four fateful steps. The space decreasing,
Onegin then, while still not ceasing
His slow advance, was first to raise
His pistol with a level gaze.
Five paces more, while Lensky waited
To close one eye and, only then,
To take his aim. . . . And that was when
Onegin fired! The hour fated
Has struck at last: the poet stops
And silently his pistol drops.

31

He lays a hand, as in confusion,
On breast and falls. His misted eyes
Express not pain, but death's intrusion.
Thus, slowly, down a sloping rise,
And sparkling in the sunlight's shimmer,
A clump of snow will fall and glimmer.
Eugene, in sudden chill, despairs,
Runs to the stricken youth . . . and stares!
Calls out his name!—No earthly power
Can bring him back: the singer's gone,
Cut down by fate at break of dawn!
The storm has blown; the lovely flower
Has withered with the rising sun;
The altar fire is out and done! . . .

32

He lay quite still and past all feeling;
His languid brow looked strange at rest.
The steaming blood poured forth, revealing
The gaping wound beneath his breast.
One moment back—a breath's duration—
This heart still throbbed with inspiration;
Its hatreds, hopes, and loves still beat,
Its blood ran hot with life's own heat.
But now, as in a house deserted,
Inside it—all is hushed and stark,
Gone silent and forever dark.
The window boards have been inserted,
The panes chalked white. The owner's fled;
But where, God knows. All trace is dead.

33

With epigrams of spite and daring
It's pleasant to provoke a foe;
It's pleasant when you see him staring—
His stubborn, thrusting horns held low—
Unwillingly within the mirror,
Ashamed to see himself the clearer;
More pleasant yet, my friends, if he
Shrieks out in stupid shock: that's me!
Still pleasanter is mute insistence
On granting him his resting place
By shooting at his pallid face
From some quite gentlemanly distance.
But once you've had your fatal fun,
You won't be pleased to see it done.

34

And what would be your own reaction
If with your pistol you'd struck down
A youthful friend for some infraction:
A bold reply, too blunt a frown,
Some bagatelle when you'd been drinking;
Or what if he himself, not thinking,
Had called you out in fiery pride?
Well, tell me: what would you . . . inside
Be thinking of . . . or merely feeling,
Were your good friend before you now,
Stretched out with death upon his brow,
His blood by slow degrees congealing,
Too deaf and still to make reply
To your repeated, desperate cry?

35

In anguish, with his heart forsaken,
The pistol in his hand like lead,
Eugene stared down at Lensky, shaken.
His neighbour spoke: 'Well then, he's dead.'
The awful word, so lightly uttered,
Was like a blow. Onegin shuddered,
Then called his men and walked away.
Zaretsky, carefully, then lay
The frozen corpse on sleigh, preparing
To drive the body home once more.
Sensing the dreadful load they bore,
The horses neighed, their nostrils flaring,
And wet the metal bit with foam,
Then swift as arrows raced for home.

36

You mourn the poet, friends . . . and rightly:
Scarce out of infant clothes and killed!
Those joyous hopes that bloomed so brightly
Now doomed to wither unfulfilled!
Where now the ardent agitation,
The fine and noble aspiration
Of youthful feeling, youthful thought,
Exalted, tender, boldly wrought?
And where are stormy love's desires,
The thirst for knowledge, work, and fame,
The dread of vice, the fear of shame?
And where are you, poetic fires,
You cherished dreams of sacred worth
And pledge of life beyond this earth!

37

It may be he was born to fire
The world with good, or earn at least
A gloried name; his silenced lyre
Might well have raised, before it ceased,
A call to ring throughout the ages.
Perhaps, upon the world's great stages,
He might have scaled a lofty height.
His martyred shade, condemned to night,
Perhaps has carried off forever
Some sacred truth, a living word,
Now doomed by death to pass unheard;
And in the tomb his shade shall never
Receive our race's hymns of praise,
Nor hear the ages bless his days.

(38) 39

Or maybe he was merely fated
To live amid the common tide;
And as his years of youth abated,
The flame within him would have died.
In time he might have changed profoundly,
Have quit the Muses, married soundly;
And in the country he'd have worn
A quilted gown and cuckold's horn,
And happy, he'd have learned life truly;
At forty he'd have had the gout,
Have eaten, drunk, grown bored and stout,
And so decayed, until he duly
Passed on in bed . . . his children round,
While women wept and doctors frowned.

40

However, reader, we may wonder . . .
The youthful lover's voice is stilled,
His dreams and songs all rent asunder;
And he, alas, by friend lies killed!
Not far from where the youth once flourished
There lies a spot the poet cherished:
Two pine trees grow there, roots entwined;
Beneath them quiet streamlets wind,
Meand'ring from the nearby valley.
And there the ploughman rests at will
And women reapers come to fill
Their pitchers in the stream and dally;
There too, within a shaded nook,
A simple stone adjoins the brook.

41

Sometimes a shepherd sits there waiting
(Till on the fields, spring rains have passed)
And sings of Volga fishers, plaiting
His simple, coloured shoes of bast;
Or some young girl from town who's spending
Her summer in the country mending—
When headlong and alone on horse
She races down the meadow course,
Will draw her leather reins up tightly
To halt just there her panting steed;
And lifting up her veil, she'll read
The plain inscription, skimming lightly;
And as she reads, a tear will rise
And softly dim her gentle eyes.

42

And at a walk she'll ride, dejected,
Into the open field to gaze,
Her soul, despite herself, infected
By Lensky's brief, ill-fated days.
She'll wonder too: 'Did Olga languish?
Her heart consumed with lasting anguish?
Or did the time of tears soon pass?
And where's her sister now, poor lass?
And where that gloomy, strange betrayer,
The modish beauty's modish foe,
That recluse from the world we know—
The youthful poet's friend and slayer?'
In time, I promise, I'll not fail
To tell you all in full detail.

43

But not today. Although I cherish
My hero and of course I vow
To see how he may wane or flourish,
I'm not quite in the mood just now.
The years to solemn prose incline me;
The years chase playful rhyme behind me,
And I—alas, I must confess—
Pursue her now a good deal less.
My pen has lost its disposition
To mar the fleeting page with verse;
For other, colder dreams I nurse,
And sterner cares now seek admission;
And mid the hum and hush of life,
They haunt my soul with dreams of strife.

44

I've learned the voice of new desires
And come to know a new regret;
The first within me light no fires,
And I lament old sorrows yet.
O dreams! Where has your sweetness vanished?
And where has youth (glib rhyme) been banished?
Can it be true, its bloom has passed,
Has withered, withered now at last?
Can it be true, my heyday's ended—
All elegiac play aside—
That now indeed my spring has died
(As I in jest so oft pretended)?
And is there no return of youth?
Shall I be thirty soon, in truth?

45

And so, life's afternoon has started,
As I must now admit, I see.
But let us then as friends be parted,
My sparkling youth, before you flee!
I thank you for your host of treasures,
For pain and grief as well as pleasures,
For storms and feasts and worldly noise,
For all your gifts and all your joys;
My thanks to you. With you I've tasted,
Amid the tumult and the still,
Life's essence . . . and enjoyed my fill.
Enough! Clear-souled and far from wasted,
I start upon an untrod way
To take my rest from yesterday.

46

But one glance back. Farewell, you bowers,
Sweet wilderness in which I spent
Impassioned days and idle hours,
And filled my soul with dreams, content.
And you, my youthful inspiration,
Come stir the bleak imagination,
Enrich the slumbering heart's dull load,
More often visit my abode;
Let not the poet's soul grow bitter
Or harden and congeal alone,
To turn at last to lifeless stone
Amid this world's deceptive glitter,
This swirling swamp in which we lie
And wallow, friends, both you and I!

Chapter 7

Moscow! Russia's favourite daughter!
Where is your equal to be found!

Dmitriev

Can one not love our native Moscow?

Baratynsky

'Speak ill of Moscow! So this is what it means
to see the world! Where is it better, then?'
'Where we are not.'

Griboedov

1

Spring rays at last begin to muster
And chase from nearby hills the snow,
Whose turbid streams flow down and cluster
To inundate the fields below.
And drowsy nature, smiling lightly,
Now greets the dawning season brightly.
The heavens sparkle now with blue;
The still transparent woods renew
Their downy green and start to thicken.
The bee flies out from waxen cell
To claim its meed from field and dell.
The vales grow dry and colours quicken;
The cattle low; and by the moon
The nightingale pours forth its tune.

2

How sad I find your apparition,
O spring! . . . O time of love's unrest!
What sombre echoes of ambition
Then stir my blood and fill my breast!
What tender and oppressive yearning
Possesses me on spring's returning,
When in some quiet rural place
I feel her breath upon my face!
Or am I now inured to gladness;
And all that quickens and excites,
That sparkles, triumphs, and delights
Casts only spleen and languid sadness
On one whose heart has long been dead,
For whom but darkness lies ahead?

3

Or saddened by the re-emergence
Of leaves that perished in the fall,
We heed the rustling wood's resurgence,
As bitter losses we recall;
Or do we mark with lamentation
How nature's lively renovation
Compares with our own fading youth,
For which no spring will come, in truth?
Perhaps in thought we reassemble,
Within a dream to which we cling,
Some other and more ancient spring,
That sets the aching heart atremble
With visions of some distant place,
A magic night, the moon's embrace. . . .

4

Now is the time, you hibernators,
You epicures and sages, you;
You fortunate procrastinators,
You fledglings from our Lyóvshin's crew,*
You rustic Priams from the cities,
And you, my sentimental pretties—
Spring calls you to your country seat;
It's time for flowers, labours, heat,
Those heady walks for which you're thirsting,
And soft seductive nights as well.
Into the fields, my friends, pell-mell!
Load up your carriages to bursting,
Bring out your own or rent a horse,
And far from town now set your course!

5

You too, indulgent reader, hurry
In your imported coach, I pray,
To leave the city with its flurry,
Where you spent wintertime in play;
And with my wilful Muse let's hustle
To where the leafy woodlands rustle—
A nameless river's placid scene,
The country place where my Eugene,
That idle and reclusive schemer,
But recently this winter stayed,
Not far from our unhappy maid,
Young Tanya, my enchanted dreamer;
But where he now no longer reigns . . .
Where only his sad trace remains.

6

Where hills half circle round a valley,
Let's trace a winding brooklet's flow
Through greening fields, and watch it dally
Beside a spot where lindens grow.
And there the nightingale, spring's lover,
Sings out till dawn; a crimson cover
Of briar blooms, and freshets sound.
There too a tombstone can be found
Beneath two pine trees, old for ages.
Its legend lets the stranger know:
'Vladimir Lensky lies below.
He died too soon . . . his death courageous,
At such an age, in such a year.
Repose in peace, young poet, here!'

7

There was a time when breezes playing
Among the pines would gently turn
A secret wreath that hung there swaying
Upon a bough above that urn;
And sometimes in the evening hours
Two maidens used to come with flowers,
And by the moonlit grave they kept
Their vigil and, embracing, wept.
But now the monument stands dreary
And quite forgot. Its pathway now—
All weeds. No wreath is on the bough;
Alone the shepherd, grey and weary,
Beneath it sings as in the past
and plaits his simple shoes of bast.

(8–9) 10

My poor, poor Lensky! Yes, she mourned him;
Although her tears were all too brief!
Alas! His fiancée has scorned him
And proved unfaithful to her grief.
Another captured her affection,
Another with his love's perfection
Has lulled her wretchedness to sleep:
A lancer has enthralled her deep,
A lancer whom she loves with passion;
And at the altar by his side,
She stands beneath the crown a bride,
Her head bent down in modest fashion,
Her lowered eyes aflame the while,
And on her lips a slender smile.

11

Poor Lensky! In his place of resting,
In deaf eternity's grim shade,
Did he, sad bard, awake protesting
The fateful news, he'd been betrayed?
Or lulled by Lethe, has he slumbered,
His blissful spirit unencumbered
By feelings and perturbed no more,
His world a closed and silent door?
Just so! The tomb that lies before us
Holds but oblivion in the end.
The voice of lover, foe, and friend
Falls silent fast. Alone the chorus
Of angry heirs in hot debate
Contests obscenely our estate.

12

Soon Olga's happy voice and beauty
No longer cheered the family group.
A captive of his lot and duty,
Her lancer had to join his troop.
Dame Larin's eyes began to water
As she embraced her younger daughter
And, scarce alive, cried out goodbye.
But Tanya found she couldn't cry;
A deathly pallor merely covered
Her stricken face. When all came out
Onto the porch and fussed about
While taking leave, Tatyana hovered
Beside the couple's coach below,
Then sadly saw the lovers go.

13

And long she watched the road they'd taken,
As through a mist of stifled tears. . . .
Now Tanya is alone, forsaken!
Companion of so many years,
The darling sister whom she'd nourished,
The bosom friend she'd always cherished—
Now carried off by fate, a bride,
Forever parted from her side.
She roams in aimless desolation,
Now gazes at the vacant park. . . .
But all seems joyless, bleak and dark;
There's nothing offers consolation
Or brings her smothered tears relief;
Her heart is rent in two by grief.

14

And in the solitude her passion
Burns even stronger than before,
Her heart speaks out in urgent fashion
Of faraway Eugene the more.
She'll never see him . . . and be grateful,
She finds a brother's slayer hateful
And loathes the awful thing he's done.
The poet's gone . . . and hardly one
Remembers him; his bride's devotion
Has flown to someone else instead;
His very memory now has fled
Like smoke across an azure ocean.
Two hearts, perhaps, remain forlorn
And mourn him yet. . . . But wherefore mourn?

15

'Twas evening and the heavens darkled.
A beetle hummed. The peasant choirs
Were bound for home. Still waters sparkled.
Across the river, smoky fires
Of fishermen were dimly gleaming.
Tatyana walked, alone and dreaming,
Beneath the moonbeams' silver light
And climbed a gentle hill by night.
She walked and walked . . . till with a shiver
She spied a distant hamlet's glow,
A manor house and grove below,
A garden by the glinting river.
And as she gazed upon that place
Her pounding heart began to race.

16

Assailed by doubts, she grew dejected:
'Should I go on, turn back, or what?
He isn't here, I'm not expected. . . .
I'll glance at house and garden plot.'
And so, scarce breathing, down she hastened
And looked about, perplexed and chastened
To find herself at his estate. . . .
She entered the deserted gate.
A pack of barking dogs chased round her;
And at her frightened cry a troop
Of household urchins with a whoop
Came rushing quickly to surround her.
They made the barking hounds obey,
Then led the lady, safe, away.

17

'May I just see the house, I wonder?'
Asked Tanya . . . and the children leapt
To find Anísya and to plunder
The household keys she always kept.
Anísya came in just a second,
And soon the open doorway beckoned.
She stepped inside the empty shell
Where once our hero used to dwell.
She found a cue left unattended
Upon the table after play,
And on a rumpled sofa lay
His riding crop. And on she wended.
'And here's the hearth,' spoke up the crone,
'Where master used to sit alone.

18

'Our neighbour Lensky, lately buried,
Would dine with him in winter here.
Come this way, please . . . but don't feel hurried.
And here's the master's study, dear;
He slept, took coffee in these quarters,
Would hear the bailiff, give his orders,
And mornings read some book right through. . . .
My former master lived here too;
On Sundays at his window station,
His glasses on, he'd deign to play
Some cards with me to pass the day.
God grant his mortal soul salvation,
And may his dear old bones be blest
In Mother Earth where he's at rest.'

19

Tatyana looks in melting pleasure
At everything around the room;
She finds it all a priceless treasure,
A painful joy that lifts her gloom
And leaves her languid soul ignited:
The desk, the lamp that stands unlighted,
The heap of books, the carpet spread
Before the window on the bed,
That semi-light, so pale and solemn,
The view outdoors—the lunar pall,
Lord Byron's portrait on the wall,
The iron bust* upon its column—
With clouded brow beneath a hat,
The arms compressed and folded flat.

20

And long she stood, bewitched and glowing,
Inside that modish bachelor cell.
But now it's late. The winds are blowing,
It's cold and dark within the dell.
The grove's asleep above the river,
Behind the hill the moon's a sliver;
And now it's time, indeed long past,
That our young pilgrim leave at last.
Concealing her wrought-up condition,
Though not without a heartfelt sigh,
Tatyana turns to say goodbye,
But, taking leave, requests permission
To see the vacant house alone
And read the books he'd called his own.

21

Outside the gate Tatyana parted
From old Anísya. Next day then,
She rose at dawn and off she started
To see the empty house again;
And once inside that silent study,
Sealed off at last from everybody,
The world for just a time forgot,
Tatyana wept and mourned her lot . . .
Then turned to see the books he'd favoured.
At first she didn't wish to read,
The choice of books seemed strange indeed;
But soon her thirsting spirit savoured
The mystery that those pages told—
And watched a different world unfold.

22

Although Onegin's inclination
For books had vanished, as we know,
He did exempt from condemnation
Some works and authors even so:
The bard of Juan and the Giaour,*
And some few novels done with power,
In which our age is well displayed
And modern man himself portrayed
With something of his true complexion—
With his immoral soul disclosed,
His arid vanity exposed,
His endless bent for deep reflection,
His cold, embittered mind that seems
To waste itself in empty schemes.

23

Some pages still preserved the traces
Where fingernails had sharply pressed;
The girl's attentive eye embraces
These lines more quickly than the rest.
And Tanya sees with trepidation
The kind of thought or observation
To which Eugene paid special heed,
Or where he'd tacitly agreed.
And in the margins she inspected
His pencil marks with special care;
And on those pages everywhere
She found Onegin's soul reflected—
In crosses or a jotted note,
Or in the question mark he wrote.

24

And so, in slow but growing fashion
My Tanya starts to understand
More clearly now—thank God—her passion
And him for whom, by fate's command,
She'd been condemned to feel desire:
That dangerous and sad pariah,
That work of heaven or of hell,
That angel . . . and proud fiend as well.
What was he then? An imitation?
An empty phantom or a joke,
A Muscovite in Harold's cloak,
Compendium of affectation,
A lexicon of words in vogue . . .
Mere parody and just a rogue?

25

Can she have solved the riddle's power?
Can she have found the final clue?
She hardly notes how late the hour,
And back at home she's overdue—
Where two old friends in conversation
Speak out on Tanya's situation:
'What *can* I do? Tatyana's grown,'
Dame Larin muttered with a moan.
'Her younger sister married neatly;
It's time that she were settled too,
I swear I don't know *what* to do;
She turns all offers down completely,
Just says: "I can't", then broods away,
And wanders through those woods all day.'

26

'Is she in love?'—'With whom, I wonder?
Buyánov tried: she turned him down.
And Petushkóv as well went under.
Pykhtín the lancer came from town
To stay with us and seemed transported;
My word, that little devil courted!
I thought she might accept him then;
But no! the deal fell through again.'
'Why, my dear lady, what's the bother?
To Moscow and the marriage mart!
They've vacancies galore . . . take heart!'
'But I've so little income, father.'
'Sufficient for one winter's stay;
Or borrow then—from me, let's say.'

27

The good old lady was delighted
To hear such sensible advice;
She checked her funds and then decided,
A Moscow winter would be nice.
Tatyana heard the news morosely—
The haughty world would watch her closely
And judge her harshly from the start:
Her simple, open country heart
And country dress would find no mercy;
And antiquated turns of phrase
Were sure to bring a mocking gaze
From every Moscow fop and Circe!
O horrors! No, she'd better stay
Safe in her woods and never stray.

28

With dawn's first rays Tatyana races
Out to the open fields to sigh;
And gazing softly, she embraces
The world she loves and says goodbye:
'Farewell, my peaceful vales and fountains!
Farewell, you too, familiar mountains
And woods where once I used to roam!
Farewell, celestial beauty's home,
Farewell, fond nature, where I flourished!
I leave your world of quiet joys
For empty glitter, fuss, and noise!
Farewell, my freedom, deeply cherished!
Oh, where and why do I now flee?
And what does Fate prepare for me?'

29

And all that final summer season
Her walks were long; a brook or knoll
Would stop her now for no good reason
Except to charm her thirsting soul.
As with old friends, she keeps returning
To all her groves and meadows, yearning
To talk once more and say goodbye.
But quickly summer seems to fly,
The golden autumn now arriving.
Now nature, tremulous, turns pale—
A victim draped in lavish veil. . . .
The North now howls, the winds are driving
The clouds before them far and near:
That sorceress the winter's here!

30

She's spread herself through field and fountain,
And hung the limbs of oaks with white;
She lies atop the farthest mountain
In wavy carpets glistening bright;
She's levelled with a fluffy blanket
Both river and the shores that flank it.
The frost has gleamed, and we give thanks
For Mother Winter's happy pranks.
But Tanya's heart is far from captured:
She doesn't greet the winter's glow,
Inhale the frostdust, gather snow
From bathhouse roof to wash, enraptured,
Her shoulders, face, and breast. With dread
She views the winter path ahead.

31

Departure day was long expected;
The final hours come at last.
The covered sleigh, for years neglected,
Is checked, relined, and soon made fast.
The usual three-cart train will carry
What household goods are necessary:
The mattresses, the trunks and chairs,
Some jars of jam and kitchen wares,
The featherbeds and coops of chickens,
Some pots and basins, and the rest—
Well, almost all that they possessed.
The servants fussed and raised the dickens
About the stable, many cried;
Then eighteen nags were led outside.

32

They're harnessed to the coach and steadied;
The cooks make lunch for one and all;
The heaped-up wagons now are readied;
The wenches and the drivers brawl.
Atop a lean and shaggy trotter
The bearded postboy sits as spotter.
Retainers crowd the gate pell-mell
To bid their mistresses farewell.
They're all aboard and, slowly gliding,
The ancient coach creeps out the gate.
'Farewell, my peaceful home and fate!
Farewell, secluded place of hiding!
Shall I return?' And Tanya sighs,
As tears well up to dim her eyes.

33

When we have broadened education,
The time will come without a doubt
(By scientific computation,
Within five hundred years about),
When our old roads' decayed condition
Will change beyond all recognition.
Paved highways, linking every side,
Will cross our Russia far and wide;
Above our waters iron bridges
Will stride in broadly arching sweep;
We'll dig bold tunnels 'neath the deep
And even part whole mountain ridges;
And Christendom will institute
An inn at every stage *en route*.

34

But roads are bad now in our nation;
Neglected bridges rot and fall;
Bedbugs and fleas at every station
Won't let the traveller sleep at all.
No inns exist. At posting stages
They hang pretentious menu pages,
But just for show, as if to spite
The traveller's futile appetite;
While some rude Cyclops at his fire
Treats Europe's dainty artefacts
With mighty Russian hammer whacks,
And thanks the Lord for ruts and mire
And all the ditches that abound
Throughout our native Russian ground.

35

And yet a trip in winter season
Is often easy, even nice.
Like modish verse devoid of reason,
The winter road is smooth as ice.
Our bold Autómedons* stay cheery,
Our Russian troikas never weary;
And mileposts soothe the idle eye
As fencelike they go flashing by.
Unluckily, Dame Larin wasted
No funds on renting fresher horse,
Which meant a longer trip of course;
And so our maiden fully tasted
Her share of travel's dull delights:
They rode for seven days and nights.

36

But now they're near. Before them, gleaming,
Lies Moscow with its stones of white,
Its ancient domes and spires streaming
With golden crosses, ember-bright.
Ah, friends, I too have been delighted
When all at once far-off I've sighted
That splendid view of distant domes,
Of churches, belfries, stately homes!
How oft . . . forlorn and separated—
When wayward fate has made me stray—
I've dreamt of Moscow far away!
Ah, Moscow! How that sound is freighted
With meaning for our Russian hearts!
How many echoes it imparts!

37

And here's Petróvsky Castle,* hoary
Amid its park. In sombre dress
It wears with pride its recent glory:
Napoleon, drunk with fresh success,
Awaited here, in vain, surrender—
For kneeling Moscow's hand to tender
The ancient Kremlin's hallowed keys.
But Moscow never bent her knees,
Nor bowed her head in subjugation;
No welcome feast did she prepare
The restless hero waiting there—
But lit instead a conflagration.
From here he watched, immersed in thought,
The awesome blaze my Moscow wrought.

38

Farewell now, scene of fame unsteady,
Petróvsky Castle. Hey! Be fleet!
There gleam the city gates already!
And now along Tverskáya Street
The sleigh glides over ruts and passes
By sentry booths and peasant lasses;
By gardens, mansions, fashion shops;
Past urchins, streetlamps, strolling fops,
Bokhárins, sleighs, apothecaries,
Muzhíks and merchants, Cossack guards;
Past towers, hovels, boulevards,
Great balconies and monasteries;
Past gateway lions' lifted paws,
And crosses dense with flocks of daws.

(39) 40

This tiring trek through town extended
For two full hours; then, quite late
Nearby St Chariton's it ended
Before a mansion's double gate.
For now they'll seek accommodation
With Tanya's aunt, a kind relation—
Four years consumptive, sad to note.
In glasses and a torn old coat,
A grizzled Kalmuk came to meet them;
With sock in hand he led the way
To where the prostrate princess lay;
She called from parlour couch to greet them.
The two old ladies hugged and cried,
With shouts of joy on either side.

41

'*Princesse, mon ange!*' 'Pachette!' 'Oh, Laura!'
'Who would have thought?' 'How long it's been!'
'I hope you'll stay?' 'Dear cousin Laura!'
'Sit down. . . . How strange! . . . I can't begin . . .
I'd swear it's from some novel's pages!'
'And here's my Tanya.' 'Lord, it's ages!
Oh, Tanya sweet, come over here—
I think I must be dreaming, dear. . . .
Oh, cousin, do you still remember
Your Grandison?' 'I never knew . . .
Oh, *Grandison*! . . . of course I do!'
'He lives in Moscow. This December,
On Christmas eve, he paid a call:
He married off his son this fall.

42

'The other. . . . But we'll talk tomorrow;
And straightway too, to all her kin
We'll show your Tanya. What a sorrow
That paying visits does me in;
I drag about like some poor laggard.
But here, your trip has left you haggard;
Let's all go have a nice long rest. . . .
I've got no strength . . . this weary breast
Finds even joy at times excessive,
Not only woe. . . . It's true, my dear,
I'm good for nothing now, I fear;
When one gets old, life turns oppressive.'
And all worn out, she wept a bit,
Then broke into a coughing fit.

43

The sick old lady's kindly smile
Left Tanya moved; but she felt sad
Within this strange new domicile
And missed the room she'd always had.
In bed, beneath her silken curtain,
She lies there sleepless and uncertain;
And early church bells—when they chime,
Announcing dawn and working time—
Rouse Tanya from her bed to listen.
She sits before the windowsill.
The darkness wanes, but Tanya still
Can't see her fields and valleys glisten:
She sees an unknown yard instead:
A stable, fence, and kitchen shed.

44

And now they trundle Tanya daily
To family dinners just to share
With grandams and granduncles gaily
Her languid and abstracted air.
Those kin who've come from distant places
Are always met with warm embraces,
With shouts of joy and welcome cheer.
'How Tanya's grown! It seems, my dear,
So short a time since I baptized you!'
'And since I dried your baby tears!'
'And since I pulled you by the ears!'
'And since my gingerbread surprised you!'
And with one voice the grannies cry:
'Good gracious, how the years do fly!'

45

In *them*, though, nothing ever alters;
The same old patterns still are met:
Old Aunt Eléna never falters
And wears that same tulle bonnet yet;
Still powdered is Lukérya Lvóvna;
A liar still, Lyubóv Petróvna;
Iván Petróvich . . . no more bright;
Semyón Petróvich . . . just as tight;
And Anna Pávlovna, as ever,
Still has her friend, Monsieur Finemouch,
Her same old spouse, and same old pooch—
Her husband, clubman come whatever,
Is just as meek and deaf, it's true,
And still consumes enough for two.

46

Their daughters, after brief embraces,
Look Tanya over good and slow;
In silence Moscow's youthful graces
Examine her from head to toe.
They find her stranger than expected,
A bit provincial and affected,
And somewhat pale, too thin and small,
But on the whole, not bad at all;
Then bowing to innate compassion,
They squeeze her hand and, in the end,
Take Tanya in and call her friend;
They fluff her curls in latest fashion,
And in their singsong tones impart
Their girlish secrets of the heart—

47

Both others' and their own successes,
Their hopes, and pranks, and maiden dreams;
All innocence, their talk progresses—
Though now and then some gossip gleams.
And then they ask, in compensation
For their sweet flow of revelation,
For *her* confessions of romance.
But Tanya, in a kind of trance,
Attends their giddy conversation
Without response and takes no part;
And all the while she guards her heart
With silence and in meditation:
Her cherished trove of tears and bliss
She'll share with none, aloud like this.

48

Tatyana tries to pay attention
When in the parlour guests converse;
But all they ever seem to mention
Is incoherent rot, or worse;
They seem so pallid and so weary,
And even in their slander dreary.
In all the sterile words they use—
In arid gossip, questions, news—
Not once all day does thought but flicker,
Not even in some chance remark;
The languid mind will find no spark,
The heart no cause to beat the quicker;
And even simple-minded fun
This hollow world has learned to shun!

49

'Archival dandies'* in a cluster
Eye Tanya with a priggish frown,
And with their usual sort of bluster,
Among themselves they put her down.
One melancholy joker found her
His 'true ideal' and hovered round her—
Then, leaning by the door, prepared
An elegy, to show he cared.
Once Vyázemsky* sat down beside her
(On meeting her at some dull aunt's)
And managed to dispel her trance;
And some old man—when he espied her—
Put straight his wig and asked around
About this unknown belle he'd found.

50

But where Melpomene still stages
Her stormy scenes and wails aloud
And in her gaudy mantle rages
Before the dull and frigid crowd;
Where sweet Thalia calmly dozes,
Indifferent to admirers' roses;
Where just Terpsichore enchants
The youthful lover of the dance
(As was the case—for nothing passes—
In our day too, let's not forget),
No jealous lady trained lorgnette,
No modish connoisseur his glasses,
To spy on Tanya down below
From boxes rising row on row.

51

They take her to the Grand Assembly:*
And there the crush, the glare, the heat,
The music's roar, the ballroom trembling,
The whirling flash of pairs of feet,
The beauties in their filmy dresses,
The swarming gallery throng that presses,
The host of girls on marriage hunts—
Assault the senses all at once.
Here practised dandies bow and slither
To show their gall . . . and waistcoats too,
With negligent lorgnettes in view.
Hussars on leave come racing hither
To strut their stuff and thunder by,
To dazzle, conquer . . . and to fly.

52

The night has countless stars to light her,
And Moscow countless beauties too;
And yet the regal moon shines brighter
Than all her friends in heaven's blue;
And she, whose beauty I admire—
But dare not bother with my lyre—
Just like the moon upon her throne,
Mid wives and maidens shines alone.
With what celestial pride she grazes
The earth she walks, in splendour dressed!
What languor fills her lovely breast!
How sensuous her wondrous gazes! . . .
But there, enough; have done at last:
You've paid your due to follies past.

53

Commotion, bows . . . the glad, the solemn . . .
Galop, mazurka, waltz. . . . And there,
Between two aunts, beside a column,
Observed by none, and near despair,
Tatyana looks with eyes unseeing
And loathes this world with all her being;
She's stifled here . . . and in her mind
Calls up the life she left behind—
The countryside, poor village neighbours,
A distant and secluded nook
Beside a limpid flowing brook,
Her flowers, novels, daily labours . . .
That dusky, linden-shaded walk
Where *he* and she once had their talk.

54

And so, far off in thought she wandered:
The *monde*, the noisy ball forgot;
But all the while, as Tanya pondered,
Some general stared her way a lot.
The aunts exchanged a wink and nodded,
And with an elbow each one prodded
Tatyana, whisp'ring in her ear:
'Look quickly to your left, my dear.'
'My left? But why? It seems like gawking.'
'Just never mind . . . now look up there . . .
That group in front; you see that pair . . .
In uniform? The one not talking . . .
He just moved off. . . . He's turning round.'
'That heavy general?' Tanya frowned.

55

But here let's honour with affection
My Tanya's conquest taking wing,
And steer for now a new direction,
Lest I forget of whom I sing—
On which, herewith, these observations:
I sing strange whims and aberrations,
I sing a youthful friend of mine.
O Muse of Epics, may you shine
On my long work as I grow older!
And armed with your good staff, I pray,
May I not roam too far astray.
Enough! The burden's off my shoulder!
To classicism I've been true:
The foreword's here, if overdue.

Chapter 8

Fare thee well, and if for ever,
Still for ever, fare thee well.

                              Byron

1

In days when I still bloomed serenely
Inside our Lycée* garden wall
And read my Apuleius keenly,
But read no Cicero at all—
Those springtime days in secret valleys,
Where swans call out and beauty dallies,
Near waters sparkling in the still,
The Muse first came to make me thrill.
My student cell turned incandescent;
And there the Muse spread out for me
A feast of youthful fancies free,
And sang of childhood effervescent,
The glory of our days of old,
The trembling dreams the heart can hold.

2

And with a smile the world caressed us;
What wings our first successes gave!
The old Derzhávin* saw—and blessed us,
As he descended to the grave.

3

And I, who saw my single duty
As heeding passion's siren song—
To share with all the world her beauty,
Would take my merry Muse along
To rowdy feasts and altercations—
The bane of midnight sentry stations;
And to each mad and fevered rout
She brought her gifts . . . and danced about,
Bacchante-like, at all our revels,
And over wine she sang for guests;
And in those days when I was blest,
The young pursued my Muse like devils;
While I, mid friends, was drunk with pride—
My flighty mistress at my side.

4

But from that band I soon departed—
And fled afar . . . and she as well.
How often, on the course I charted,
My gentle Muse's magic spell
Would light the way with secret stories!
How oft, mid far Caucasia's glories,
Like fair Lenore,* on moonlit nights
She rode with me those craggy heights!
How often on the shores of Tauris,*
On misty eves, she led me down
To hear the sea's incessant sound,
The Nereids'* eternal chorus—
That endless chant the waves unfurled
In praise of him who made the world.

5

Forgetting, then, the city's splendour,
Its noisy feasts and grand events,
In sad Moldavia she turned tender
And visited the humble tents
Of wandering tribes; and like a child,
She learned their ways and soon grew wild:
The language of the gods she shed
For strange and simple tongues instead—
To sing the savage steppe,* elated;
But then her course abruptly veered,
And in my garden* she appeared—
A country miss—infatuated,
With mournful air and brooding glance,
And in her hands a French romance.

6

And now I seize the first occasion
To show my Muse a grand soirée;
I watch with jealous trepidation
Her rustic charms on full display.
And lo! my beauty calmly passes
Through ranks of men from highborn classes,
Past diplomats and soldier–fops,
And haughty dames . . . then calmly stops
To sit and watch the grand procession—
The gowns, the talk, the milling mass,
The slow parade of guests who pass
Before the hostess in succession,
The sombre men who form a frame
Around each painted belle and dame.

7

She likes the stately disposition
Of oligarchic colloquies,
Their chilly pride in high position,
The mix of years and ranks she sees.
But who is that among the chosen,
That figure standing mute and frozen,
That stranger no one seems to know?
Before him faces come and go
Like spectres in a bleak procession.
What is it—martyred pride, or spleen
That marks his face? . . . Is that Eugene?!
That figure with the strange expression?
Can that be he? It is, I say.
'But when did fate cast him our way?

8

'Is he the same, or is he learning?
Or does he play the outcast still?
In what new guise is he returning?
What role does he intend to fill?
Childe Harold? Melmoth for a while?
Cosmopolite? A Slavophile?
A Quaker? Bigot?—might one ask?
Or will he sport some other mask?
Or maybe he's just dedicated,
Like you and me, to being nice?
In any case, here's my advice:
Give up a role when it's outdated.
He's gulled the world . . . now let it go.'
'You know him then?' 'Well, yes and no.'

9

But why on earth does he inspire
So harsh and negative a view?
Is it because we never tire
Of censuring what others do?
Because an ardent spirit's daring
Appears absurd or overbearing
From where the smug and worthless sit?
Because the dull are cramped by wit?
Because we take mere talk for action,
And malice rules a petty mind?
Because in tripe the solemn find
A cause for solemn satisfaction,
And mediocrity alone
Is what we like and call our own?

10

Oh, blest who in his youth was tender;
And blest who ripened in his prime;
Who learned to bear, without surrender,
The chill of life with passing time;
Who never knew exotic visions,
Nor scorned the social mob's decisions;
Who was at twenty fop or swell,
And then at thirty, married well,
At fifty shed all obligation
For private and for other debts;
Who gained in turn, without regrets,
Great wealth and rank and reputation;
Of whom lifelong the verdict ran:
'Old X is quite a splendid man.'

11

How sad that youth, with all its power,
Was given us in vain, to burn;
That we betrayed it every hour,
And were deceived by it in turn;
That all our finest aspirations,
Our brightest dreams and inspirations,
Have withered with each passing day
Like leaves dank autumn rots away.
It's hard to face a long succession
Of dinners stretching out of sight,
To look at life as at a rite,
And trail the seemly crowd's procession—
Indifferent to the views they hold,
And to their passions ever cold.

12

When one becomes the butt of rumour,
It's hard to bear (as you well know)
When men of reason and good humour
Perceive you as a freak on show,
Or as a sad and raving creature,
A monster of Satanic feature,
Or even Demon of my pen!*
Eugene (to speak of him again),
Who'd killed his friend for satisfaction,
Who in an aimless, idle fix
Had reached the age of twenty-six,
Annoyed with leisure and inaction,
Without position, work, or wife—
Could find no purpose for his life.

13

He felt a restless, vague ambition,
A craving for a change of air
(A most unfortunate condition—
A cross not many choose to bear).
He left his home in disillusion
And fled the woods' and fields' seclusion,
Where every day before his eyes
A bloody spectre seemed to rise;
He took up travel for distraction,
A single feeling in his breast;
But journeys too, like all the rest,
Soon proved a wearisome attraction.
So he returned one day to fall,
Like Chatsky,* straight from boat to ball.

14

But look, the crowd's astir and humming;
A murmur through the ballroom steals . . .
The hostess sees a lady coming,
A stately general at her heels.
She isn't hurried or obtrusive,
Is neither cold nor too effusive;
She casts no brazen glance around
And makes no effort to astound
Or use those sorts of affectation
And artifice that ladies share—
But shows a simple, quiet air.
She seems the very illustration
Du comme il faut . . . (Shishkov,* be kind:
I can't translate this phrase, I find.)

15

The ladies flocked to stand beside her;
Old women beamed as she went by;
The men bowed lower when they spied her
And sought in vain to catch her eye;
Young maidens hushed in passing by her;
While none held head and shoulders higher
Than he who brought the lady there—
The general with the prideful air.
One couldn't label her a beauty;
But neither did her form contain,
From head to toe, the slightest strain
Of what, with fashion's sense of duty,
The London social sets decry
As *vulgar*. (I won't even try

16

To find an adequate translation
For this delicious epithet;
With us the word's an innovation,
But though it's won no favour yet,
'Twould make an epigram of style.* . . .
But where's our lady all this while?)
With carefree charm and winsome air
She took a seat beside the chair
Of brilliant Nina Voronskáya,*
That Cleopatra of the North;
But even Nina, shining forth
With all her marble beauty's fire—
However dazzling to the sight—
Could not eclipse her neighbour's light.

17

'Can it be true?' Eugene reflected.
'Can that be she? . . . It seems . . . and yet . . .
From those backwoods!' And he directed
A curious and keen lorgnette
For several minutes in succession
Upon the lady whose expression
Called up a face from long ago.
'But tell me, Prince, you wouldn't know
Who's standing there in conversation
Beside the Spanish envoy, pray . . .
That lady in the red beret?'
'You *have* been out of circulation.
But I'll present you now with joy.'
'Who is she, though?' 'My wife, old boy.'

18

'You're married! Really?'—'On my honour.'
'To whom? How long?'—'Some two years since . . .
The Larin girl.'—'You mean Tatyana!'
'She knows you?'—'We were neighbours, Prince.'
'Well then, come on . . . we'll go and meet her.'
And so the prince led up to greet her
His kinsman and his friend Eugene.
The princess looked at him—serene;
However much the situation
Disturbed her soul and caused her pain,
However great her shock or strain,
She gave no hint of agitation:
Her manner stayed the same outside,
Her bow was calm and dignified.

19

It's true! The lady didn't shiver,
Or blush, or suddenly turn white . . .
Or even let an eyebrow quiver,
Or press her lips together tight.
Although Eugene with care inspected
This placid lady, he detected
No trace of Tanya from the past.
And when he tried to speak at last,
He found he couldn't. She enquired
When he'd arrived, and if of late
he'd been back home at his estate—
Then gave her spouse a look so tired,
He took her arm. She moved away . . .
And left Eugene in mute dismay.

20

Was this the Tanya he once scolded
In that forsaken, distant place
Where first our novel's plot unfolded?
The one to whom, when face to face,
In such a burst of moral fire,
He'd lectured gravely on desire?
The girl whose letter he still kept—
In which a maiden heart had wept;
Where all was shown . . . all unprotected?
Was this that girl . . . or did he dream?
That little girl whose warm esteem
And humble lot he'd once rejected? . . .
And could she now have been so bold,
So unconcerned with him . . . so cold?

21

He left the rout in all its splendour
And drove back home, immersed in thought;
A swarm of dreams, both sad and tender,
Disturbed the slumber that he sought.
He woke to find, with some elation,
Prince N. had sent an invitation.
'Oh God! I'll see her . . . and today!
Oh yes, I'll go!'—and straightaway
He scrawled a note: *he'd be delighted.*
What's wrong with him? . . . He's in a daze.
What's stirring in that idle gaze,
What's made that frigid soul excited?
Vexation? Pride? Or youth's old yen
For all the cares of love again?

22

Once more he counts the hours, pacing;
Once more can't wait till day is past.
The clock strikes ten: and off he's racing,
And now he's at the porch at last;
He enters in some apprehension;
The princess, to his added tension,
Is quite alone. Some minutes there
They sit. Eugene can only stare,
He has no voice. Without a smile,
And ill at ease, he scarcely tries
To answer her. His mind supplies
But one persistent thought the while.
His eyes retain their stare; but she
Sits unconstrained, quite calm and free.

23

Her husband enters, thus arresting
This most unpleasant tête-à-tête;
Eugene and he recalled the jesting,
The pranks and fun when first they'd met.
They laughed. Then guests began arriving.
And on the spice of malice thriving,
The conversation sparkled bright;
The hostess kept the banter light
And quite devoid of affectations;
Good reasoned talk was also heard,
But not a trite or vulgar word,
No lasting truths or dissertations—
And no one's ears were shocked a bit
By all the flow of lively wit.

24

The social cream had gathered gaily:
The nobly born and fashion's pets;
The faces one encounters daily,
The fools one never once forgets;
The aged ladies, decked in roses,
In bonnets and malignant poses;
And several maidens, far from gay—
Unsmiling faces on display;
And here's an envoy speaking slyly
Of some most solemn state affair;
A greybeard too ... with scented hair,
Who joked both cleverly and wryly
In quite a keen, old-fashioned way,
Which seems a touch absurd today!

25

And here's a chap whose words are biting,
Who's cross with everything about:
With tea too sweet to be inviting,
With banal ladies, men who shout,
That foggy book they're all debating,
The badge on those two maids-in-waiting,*
The falsehoods in reviews, the war,
The snow, his wife, and much, much more.

26

And here's Prolázov,* celebrated
For loathesomeness of soul—a clown,
As you, Saint-Priest,* have demonstrated
In album drawings all through town.
Another ballroom king on station
(Like fashion's very illustration)
Beside the door stood tightly laced,
Immobile, mute, and cherub-faced;
A traveller home from distant faring,
A brazen chap all starched and proud,
Provoked amusement in the crowd
By his pretentious, studied bearing:
A mere exchange of looks conveyed
The sorry sight the fellow made.

27

But my Eugene all evening heeded
Tatyana . . . only her alone:
But not the timid maid who'd pleaded,
That poor enamoured girl he'd known—
But this cool princess so resplendent,
This distant goddess so transcendent,
Who ruled the queenly Néva's shore.
Alas! We humans all ignore
Our Mother Eve's disastrous history:
What's given to us ever palls,
Incessantly the serpent calls
And lures us to the tree of mystery:
We've got to have forbidden fruit,
Or Eden's joys for us are moot.

28

How changed Tatyana is! How surely
She's taken up the role she plays!
How quick she's mastered, how securely,
Her lordly rank's commanding ways!
Who'd dare to seek the tender maiden
In this serene and glory-laden
Grande Dame of lofty social spheres?
Yet once he'd moved her heart to tears!
Her virgin brooding once had cherished
Sweet thoughts of him in darkest night,
While Morpheus still roamed in flight;
And, gazing at the moon, she'd nourished
A tender dream that she someday
Might walk with him life's humble way!

29

To love all ages yield surrender;
But to the young its raptures bring
A blessing bountiful and tender—
As storms refresh the fields of spring.
Neath passion's rains they green and thicken,
Renew themselves with joy, and quicken;
And vibrant life in taking root
Sends forth rich blooms and gives sweet fruit.
But when the years have made us older,
And barren age has shown its face,
How sad is faded passion's trace! . . .
Thus storms in autumn, blowing colder,
Turn meadows into marshy ground
And strip the forest bare all round.

30

Alas! it's true: Eugene's demented,
In love with Tanya like a boy;
He spends each day and night tormented
By thoughts of love, by dreams of joy.
Ignoring reason's condemnation,
Each day he rides to take his station
Outside her glassed-in entryway,
Then follows her about all day.
He's happy just to be around her,
To help her with her shawl or furs,
To touch a torrid hand to hers,
To part the footmen who surround her
In liveried ranks where'er she calls,
Or fetch her kerchief when it falls.

31

She pays him not the least attention,
No matter what he tries to do;
At home receives him without tension;
In public speaks a word or two,
Or sometimes merely bows on meeting,
Or passes by without a greeting:
She's no coquette in any part—
The *monde* abhors a fickle heart.
Onegin, though, is fading quickly;
She doesn't see or doesn't care;
Onegin, wasting, has the air
Of one consumptive—wan and sickly.
He's urged to seek his doctors' view,
And these suggest a spa or two.

32

But he refused to go. He's ready
To join his forebears any day;
Tatyana, though, stayed calm and steady
(Their sex, alas, is hard to sway).
And yet he's stubborn . . . still resistant,
Still hopeful and indeed persistent.
Much bolder than most healthy men,
He chose with trembling hand to pen
The princess an impassioned letter.
Though on the whole he saw no sense
In missives writ in love's defence
(And with good cause!), he found it better
Than bearing all his pain unheard.
So here's his letter word for word.

Onegin's Letter to Tatyana

I know you'll feel a deep distress
At this unwanted revelation.
What bitter scorn and condemnation
Your haughty glance may well express!
What aims . . . what hopes do I envision
In opening my soul to you?
What wicked and deserved derision
Perhaps I give occasion to!

When first I met you and detected
A warmth in you quite unexpected,
I dared not trust in love again:
I didn't yield to sweet temptation
And had, it's true, no inclination
To lose my hateful freedom then.
What's more: poor guiltless Lensky perished,
And his sad fate drew us apart . . .
From all that I had ever cherished
I tore away my grieving heart;
Estranged from men and discontented,
I thought: in freedom, peace of mind,
A substitute for joy I'd find.
How wrong I've been! And how tormented!

But no! Each moment of my days
To see you and pursue you madly!
To catch your smile and search your gaze
With loving eyes that seek you gladly;
To melt with pain before your face,
To hear your voice . . . to try to capture
With all my soul your perfect grace;
To swoon and pass away . . . what rapture!

And I'm deprived of this; for you
I search on all the paths I wander;
Each day is dear, each moment too!
Yet I in futile dullness squander
These days allotted me by fate . . .
Oppressive days indeed of late.
My span on earth is all but taken,
But lest too soon I join the dead,
I need to know when I awaken,
I'll see you in the day ahead . . . .

I fear that in this meek petition
Your solemn gaze may only spy
The cunning of a base ambition—
And I can hear your stern reply.
But if you knew the anguish in it:
To thirst with love in every part,
To burn—and with the mind each minute,
To calm the tumult in one's heart;
To long to clasp in adoration
Your knees . . . and, sobbing at your feet,
Pour out confessions, lamentation,
Oh, all that I might then entreat! . . .
And meantime, feigning resignation,
To arm my gaze and speech with lies:
to look at you with cheerful eyes
And hold a placid conversation! . . .

But let it be: it's now too late
For me to struggle at this hour;
The die is cast: I'm in your power,
And I surrender to my fate.

33

No answer came. Eugene elected
to write again . . . and then once more—
With no reply. He drives, dejected,
To some soirée . . . and by the door,
Sees *her* at once! Her harshness stuns him!
Without a word the lady shuns him!
My god! How stern that haughty brow,
What wintry frost surrounds her now!
Her lips express determination
To keep her fury in control!
Onegin stares with all his soul:
But where's distress? Commiseration?
And where the tearstains? . . . Not a trace!
There's wrath alone upon that face . . .

34

And, maybe, secret apprehension
Lest *monde* or husband misconstrue
An episode too slight to mention,
The tale that my Onegin knew . . . .
But he departs, his hopes in tatters,
And damns his folly in these matters—
And plunging into deep despond,
He once again rejects the *monde*.
And he recalled with grim emotion,
Behind his silent study door,
How wicked spleen had once before
Pursued him through the world's commotion,
Had seized him by the collar then,
And locked him in a darkened den.

35

Once more he turned to books and sages.
He read his Gibbon and Rousseau;
Chamfort, Manzoni, Herder's pages;
Madame de Staël, Bichat, Tissot.
The sceptic Bayle he quite devoured,
The works of Fontenelle he scoured;*
He even read some Russians too,
Nor did he scorn the odd review—
Those journals where each modern Moses
Instructs us in a moral way—
Where I'm so much abused today,
But where such madrigals and roses
I used to meet with now and then:
E sempre bene, gentlemen.

36

And yet—although his eyes were reading,
His thoughts had wandered far apart;
Desires, dreams, and sorrows pleading—
Had crowded deep within his heart.
Between the printed lines lay hidden
Quite other lines that rose unbidden
Before his gaze. And these alone
Absorbed his soul . . . as he was shown:
The heart's dark secrets and traditions,
The mysteries of its ancient past;
Disjointed dreams—obscure and vast;
Vague threats and rumours, premonitions;
A drawn-out tale of fancies grand,
And letters in a maiden's hand.

37

But then as torpor dulled sensation,
His feelings and his thoughts went slack,
While in his mind Imagination
Dealt out her motley faro pack.
He sees a youth, quite still, reposing
On melting snow—as if he's dozing
On bivouac; then hears with dread
A voice proclaim: 'Well then, he's dead!'
He sees forgotten foes he'd bested,
Base cowards, slanderers full-blown,
Unfaithful women he had known,
Companions whom he now detested . . .
A country house . . . a windowsill . . .
Where she sits waiting . . . waiting still!

38

He got so lost in his depression,
He just about went mad, I fear,
Or else turned poet (an obsession
That I'd have been the first to cheer!)
It's true: by self-hypnotic action,
My muddled pupil, in distraction,
Came close to grasping at that time
The principles of Russian rhyme.
He looked the poet so completely
When by the hearth he'd sit alone
And *Benedetta** he'd intone
Or sometimes *Idol mio** sweetly—
While on the flames he'd drop unseen
His slipper or his magazine!

39

The days flew by. The winter season
Dissolved amid the balmy air;
He didn't die, or lose his reason,
Or turn a poet in despair.
With spring he felt rejuvenated:
The cell in which he'd hibernated
So marmot-like through winter's night—
The hearth, the double panes shut tight—
He quit one sparkling morn and sprinted
Along the Neva's bank by sleigh.
On hacked-out bluish ice that lay
Beside the road the sunlight glinted.
The rutted snow had turned to slush;
But where in such a headlong rush

40

Has my Eugene directly hastened?
You've guessed already. Yes, indeed:
The moody fellow, still unchastened,
Has flown to Tanya's in his need.
He enters like a dead man, striding
Through empty hall; then passes, gliding,
Through grand salon. And on! . . . All bare.
He opens up a door. . . . What's there
That strikes him with such awful pleading?
The princess sits alone in sight,
Quite unadorned, her face gone white
Above some letter that she's reading—
And cheek in hand as down she peers,
She softly sheds a flood of tears.

41

In that brief instant then, who couldn't
Have read her tortured heart at last!
And in the princess then, who wouldn't
Have known poor Tanya from the past!
Mad with regret and anguished feeling,
Eugene fell down before her, kneeling;
She shuddered, but she didn't speak,
Just looked at him—her visage bleak—
Without surprise or indignation.
His stricken, sick, extinguished eyes,
Imploring aspect, mute replies—
She saw it all. In desolation,
The simple girl he'd known before,
Who'd dreamt and loved, was born once more.

42

Her gaze upon his face still lingers;
She does not bid him rise or go,
Does not withdraw impassive fingers
From avid lips that press them so.
What dreams of hers were re-enacted?
The heavy silence grew protracted,
Until at last she whispered low:
'Enough; get up. To you I owe
A word of candid explanation.
Onegin, do you still retain
Some memory of that park and lane,
Where fate once willed our confrontation,
And I so meekly heard you preach?
It's my turn now to make a speech.

43

'Onegin, I was then much younger,
I daresay better-looking too,
And loved you with a girlish hunger;
But what did I then find in you?
What answer came? Just stern rejection.
A little maiden's meek affection
To you, I'm sure, was trite and old.
Oh God!—my blood can still turn cold
When I recall how you reacted:
Your frigid glance . . . that sermonette! . . .
But I can't blame you or forget
How nobly in a sense you acted,
How right toward me that awful day:
I'm grateful now in every way. . . .

44

'Back then—far off from vain commotion,
In our backwoods, as you'll allow,
You had no use for my devotion . . .
So why do you pursue me now?
Why mark me out for your attention?
Is it perhaps my new ascension
To circles that you find more swank;
Or that I now have wealth and rank;
Or that my husband, maimed in battle,
Is held in high esteem at Court?
Or would my fall perhaps be sport,
A cause for all the *monde* to tattle—
Which might in turn bring you some claim
To social scandal's kind of fame?

45

'I'm weeping. . . . Oh, at this late hour,
If you recall your Tanya still,
Then know—that were it in my power,
I'd much prefer words harsh and chill,
Stern censure in your former fashion—
To this offensive show of passion,
To all these letters and these tears.
Oh *then* at least, my tender years
Aroused in you some hint of kindness;
You pitied then my girlish dreams. . . .
But *now*! . . . What unbecoming schemes
Have brought you to my feet? What blindness!
Can you, so strong of mind and heart,
Now stoop to play so base a part?

46

'To me, Onegin, all these splendours,
This weary tinselled life of mine,
This homage that the great world tenders,
My stylish house where princes dine—
Are empty. . . . I'd as soon be trading
This tattered life of masquerading,
This world of glitter, fumes, and noise,
For just my books, the simple joys
Of our old home, its walks and flowers,
For all those haunts that I once knew . . .
Where first, Onegin, I saw you;
For that small churchyard's shaded bowers,
Where over my poor nanny now
there stands a cross beneath a bough.

47

'And happiness was ours . . . so nearly!
It came so close! . . . But now my fate
Has been decreed. I may have merely
Been foolish when I failed to wait;
But mother with her lamentation
Implored me, and in resignation
(All futures seemed alike in woe)
I married. . . . Now I beg you, go!
I've faith in you and do not tremble;
I know that in your heart reside
Both honour and a manly pride.
I love you (why should I dissemble?);
But I am now another's wife,
And I'll be faithful all my life.'

48

She left him then. Eugene, forsaken,
Stood seared, as if by heaven's fire.
How deep his stricken heart is shaken!
With what a tempest of desire!
A sudden clink of spurs rings loudly,
As Tanya's husband enters proudly—
And here . . . at this unhappy turn
For my poor hero, we'll adjourn
And leave him, reader, at his station . . .
For long . . . forever. In his train
We've roamed the world down one slim lane
For long enough. Congratulation
On reaching land at last. Hurray!
And long since time, I'm sure you'd say!

49

Whatever, reader, your reaction,
and whether you be foe or friend,
I hope we part in satisfaction . . .
As comrades now. Whatever end
You may have sought in these reflections—
Tumultuous, fond recollections,
Relief from labours for a time,
Live images, or wit in rhyme,
Or maybe merely faulty grammar—
God grant that in my careless art,
For fun, for dreaming, for the heart . . .
For raising journalistic clamour,
You've found at least a crumb or two.
And so let's part; farewell . . . adieu!

50

Farewell, you too, my moody neighbour,
And you, my true ideal, my own!
And you, small book, my constant labour,
In whose bright company I've known
All that a poet's soul might cherish:
Oblivion when tempests flourish,
Sweet talk with friends, on which I've fed.
Oh, many, many days have fled
Since young Tatyana with her lover,
As in a misty dream at night,
First floated dimly into sight—
And I as yet could not uncover
Or through the magic crystal see
My novel's shape or what would be.

51

But those to whom, as friends and brothers,
My first few stanzas I once read—
'Some are no more, and distant . . . others.'*
As Sadi* long before us said.
Without them my Onegin's fashioned.
And she from whom I drew, impassioned,
My fair Tatyana's noblest trait . . .
Oh, much, too much you've stolen, Fate!
But blest is he who rightly gauges
The time to quit the feast and fly,
Who never drained life's chalice dry,
Nor read its novel's final pages;
But all at once for good withdrew—
As I from my Onegin do.

THE END

APPENDIX

EXCERPTS FROM *ONEGIN'S JOURNEY*

PUSHKIN'S FOREWORD

The last (eighth) chapter of *Eugene Onegin* was published separately with the following foreword:

The omission of certain stanzas has given rise on more than one occasion to criticism and jesting (no doubt most just and witty). The author candidly confesses that he has removed from his novel an entire chapter, in which Onegin's journey across Russia was described. It behoved him to indicate this omitted chapter by dots or a numeral, but to avoid ambiguity he thought it preferable to label as number eight, instead of nine, the final chapter of *Eugene Onegin*, and to sacrifice one of its closing stanzas:

> It's time: my pen demands a pillow;
> Nine cantos have I duly wrought,
> And now the ninth and final billow
> To joyful shore my bark has brought.
> All praise to you, O nine Camenae,* etc.

P. A. Katenin* (whose fine poetic talent in no way prevents him from being a subtle critic as well) has observed to us that this excision, though advantageous perhaps for the reader, is none the less harmful to the work as a whole, for it makes the transition from Tatyana the provincial miss to Tatyana the exalted lady too sudden and unexplained: an observation that reveals the accomplished artist. The author himself felt the justness of this reproach but decided to omit the chapter for reasons important to him, but not to the public. Some few excerpts have been published already; we insert them here, along with several other stanzas.

ONEGIN TRAVELS FROM MOSCOW
TO NIZHNI NOVGOROD

* * *

.   .   .   .   .
.   before his eyes
Makáriev Market* stirs and bustles,
A-seethe with plenty's wares and cries.
The Hindu's here—his pearls to proffer,
All Europe—specious wines to offer;
The breeder from the steppe as well
Has brought defective steeds to sell;
The gambler's here with dice all loaded,
With decks of cards of every type,
The landed gent—with daughters ripe,
Bedraped in dresses long outmoded;
All bustle round and lie like cheats,
And commerce reigns in all the streets

* * *

Ennui! . . .

ONEGIN DRIVES TO ASTRAKHAN,
AND FROM THERE TO THE CAUCASUS

* * *

He sees the wilful Terek* roaring
Outside its banks in wayward flow;
He spies a stately eagle soaring,
A standing deer with horns held low,
By shaded cliff a camel lying,
Circassian steed on meadow flying;
All round the nomad-tented land
The sheep of Kalmuk herdsmen stand,
And far ahead—Caucasian masses.
The way lies open; war has passed
Beyond this great divide at last,
Across these once imperilled passes.
The Kúra's and Arágva's banks*
Have seen the Russians' tented ranks.

* * *

And now his gazing eye discovers
Beshtú,* the watchman of the waste;
Sharp-peaked and ringed by hills, it hovers . . .
And there's Mashúk,* all green-encased,
Mashúk, the source of healing waters;
Amid its magic brooks and quarters
In pallid swarms the patients press,
All victims: some—of war's distress,
And some of Venus, some of Piles.
Within those waves each martyred soul
Would mend life's thread and make it whole;
Coquettes would leave their ageing smiles
Beneath the waves, while older men
For just one day seek youth again.

* * *

Consumed by bitter meditation,
Onegin, mid those mournful crowds,
With gaze of keen commiseration
Regards those streams and smoky clouds,
And with a wistful sigh he muses:
Oh, why have I no bullet's bruises?
Or why am I not old and spare,
Like that poor tax collector there?
Or why not crippled with arthritis,
The fate that Tula clerk was dealt?
And why—O Lord—have I not felt
A twinge at least of some bursitis?
I'm young and still robust, you see;
So what's ahead? Ennui, ennui! . . .

ONEGIN THEN VISITS TAURIS [THE CRIMEA]

* * *

A land by which the mind is fired:
Orestes with his friend here vied,*
And here great Mithridates* died,
And here Mickiéwicz* sang inspired,
And, by these coastal cliffs enthralled,
His distant homeland he recalled.

* * *

O lovely land, you shores of Tauris,
From shipboard looming into sight,
As first I saw you rise before us,
Like Cypris* bathed in morning's light.
You came to me in nuptial splendour;
Against a sky all blue and tender
The masses of your mountains gleamed;
Your valleys, woods, and hamlets seemed
A patterned vision spread before me.
And there where Tartar tongues are spoke
What passions in my soul awoke!
What mad and magic yearnings tore me
And held my flaming bosom fast!
But now, O Muse, forget the past!

* * *

Whatever feelings then lay hidden—
Within me now they are no more:
They've passed away or changed unbidden . . .
So peace to you, you woes of yore!
Back then it seemed that I required
Those desert wastes and waves inspired,
Those massive cliffs and pounding sea,
The vision too of 'maiden free,'
And nameless pangs and sweet perdition . . .
But other days bring other dreams;
You're now subdued, you vaulting schemes
Of youthful springtime's vast ambition,
And in this poet's cup of mine
I now mix water with my wine.

* * *

Of other scenes have I grown fonder:
I like a sandy slope of late,
A cottage with two rowans yonder,
A broken fence, a wicket gate,
Grey clouds against a sky that lowers,
Great heaps of straw from threshing mowers,
And 'neath the spreading willow tree—
A pond for ducks to wallow free.
The balalaika's now my pleasure,
And by the country tavern door
The peasant dance's drunken roar.
A housewife now is what I treasure;
I long for peace, for simple fare:
Just cabbage soup and room to spare.

* * *

The other day, in rainy weather,
As I approached the farm . . . Enough!
What prosy ravings strung together,
The Flemish painter's motley stuff!
Was I like that when I was tender,
Bakhchisarái,* you fount of splendour!
Were these the thoughts that crossed my mind
When, 'neath your endless chant I pined
And then in silence meditated
And pondered my Zaréma's* fate? . . .
Within those empty halls ornate,
Upon my trail, three years belated,
While travelling near that selfsame sea,
Onegin, pausing, thought of me.

* * *

I lived back then in dry Odessa . . .
Where skies for endless days are clear,
Where commerce, bustling, crowds and presses
And sets its sails for far and near;
Where all breathes Europe to the senses,
And sparkling Southern sun dispenses
A lively, varied atmosphere.
Along the merry streets you'll hear
Italian voices ringing loudly;
You'll meet the haughty Slav, the Greek,
Armenian, Spaniard, Frenchman sleek,
The stout Moldavian prancing proudly;
And Egypt's son as well you'll see,
The one-time corsair, Moralí*

* * *

Our friend Tumánsky* sang enchanted
Odessa's charms in splendid verse,
But we must say that he was granted
A partial view—the poet's curse.
No sooner here than he went roaming,
Lorgnette in hand and senses foaming,
Above the lonely sea . . . and then
With his enraptured poet's pen
He praised Odessa's gardens greatly.
That's fine of course, but all I've found
Is barren steppeland all around,
Though here and there much labour lately
Has forced young boughs, I must admit,
To spread their grudging shade a bit.

* * *

But where's my rambling story rushing?
'In dry Odessa'—so said I.
I might have said: 'Odessa gushing'
And even so have told no lie.
For six whole weeks it happens yearly,
On stormy Zeus's orders clearly:
Odessa's flooded, drowned, and stuck,
Immersed in thickly oozing muck.
In mud waist-high the houses snuggle;
On stilts alone can feeble feet
Attempt to ford the muddy street.
The coaches and the people struggle,
And then the bent-head oxen pant
To do what helpless horses can't.

* * *

But now the hammer's smashing boulders,
And soon with ringing slabs of slate
The salvaged streets will muster shoulders,
As if encased in armoured plate.
But moist Odessa, all too sadly,
Is lacking yet one feature badly:
You'll never guess . . . it's water-short!
To find the stuff is heavy sport . . .
But why succumb to grim emotion?
Especially since the local wine
Is duty free and rather fine.
And then there's Southern sun and ocean . . .
What more, my friends, could you demand?
A blesséd and most favoured land!

* * *

No sooner would the cannon, sounding,
Proclaim from ship the dawn of day
Than, down the sloping shoreline bounding,
Towards the sea I'd make my way.
And there, my glowing pipe ignited,
By briny waves refreshed and righted,
In Muslim paradise complete,
I'd sip my Turkish coffee sweet.
I take a stroll. Inciting urges,
The great Casino's opened up;
I hear the ring of glass and cup;
The marker, half asleep, emerges
Upon the porch, with broom in hand,
Where two expectant merchants stand.

* * *

And soon the square grows gay and vital.
Life pulses full as here and there,
Preoccupied by work . . . or idle,
All race about on some affair.
That child of ventures and finances,
The merchant to the port advances,
To learn the news: has heaven brought
The long-awaited sail he sought?
Which just-delivered importations
Have gone in quarantine today?
Which wines have come without delay?
And how's the plague? What conflagrations,
What wars and famines have occurred?
He has to have the latest word.

* * *

But we, we band of callow joysters,
Unlike those merchants filled with cares,
Have been expecting only oysters . . .
From Istanbul, the seaside's wares.
What news of oysters? Here? What rapture!
And off runs glutton youth to capture
And slurp from salty shells those bites
Of plump and living anchorites,
With just a dash of lemon flavour.
What din, debates! The good Automne*
From cellar store has just now come
With sparkling wine for us to savour.
The time goes by and, as it goes,
The bill to awesome stature grows.

* * *

But now blue evening starts to darken,
And to the opera we must get,
The great Rossini there to harken,
Proud Orpheus and Europe's pet.
Before no critic will he grovel,
He's ever constant, ever novel;
He pours out tunes that effervesce,
That in their burning flow caress
The soul with endless youthful kisses,
With sweetly flaming love's refrain,
A golden, sparkling fine champagne,
A stream that bubbles, foams, and hisses.
But can one justly, friends of mine,
Compare this do-re-mi with wine?

* * *

And what of other fascinations?
And what of keen lorgnettes, I say . . . ?
And in the wings . . . the assignations?
The prima donna? The ballet?
The *loge*, where, beautiful and gleaming,
The merchant's youthful wife sits dreaming,
All vain and languorous with pride,
A crowd of slaves on every side?
She heeds and doesn't heed the roses,
The cavatina, heated sighs,
The jesting praise, the pleading eyes . . .
While in the back her husband dozes,
Cries out from sleep *Encore!*—and then
Emits a yawn and snores again.

* * *

The great finale's thunder surges.
In noisy haste the throng departs;
Upon the square the crowd emerges,
Beneath the gleam of lamps and stars.
Ausonia's * happy sons are humming
The playful tune that keeps on drumming,
Against the will, inside their brains—
While I roar out the light refrains.
But now it's late. Odessa's dreaming;
The breathless night is warm and soft,
While high above the moon's aloft,
The sky all lightly veiled and streaming.
No stir disturbs the silence round,
Except the sea's incessant sound.

* * *

And so I lived in old Odessa . . .

EXPLANATORY NOTES

2 *Pétri ... particulière*: the main epigraph to the novel, apparently written by Pushkin himself, translates roughly as follows: 'Steeped in vanity, he was possessed moreover by that particular sort of pride that makes a man acknowledge with equal indifference both his good and evil actions, a consequence of a sense of superiority, perhaps imaginary. From a private letter.'

dedication: The dedication was originally addressed to Pushkin's friend (and the first publisher of *Eugene Onegin*) P. A. Pletnyov (1792–1862). In later editions, the piece was retained as a kind of preface, but without the inscription to Pletnyov.

Chapter 1

5 *My uncle, man of firm convictions*: the novel's opening words mimic a line from the fable *The Ass and the Peasant* by Ivan Krylov (1796–1844): 'An ass of most sincere convictions.'

Ludmila's and Ruslán's adherents: the author's address to his readers and references to other of his writings are devices used throughout the novel. The allusion here is to Pushkin's first major work, the mock epic *Ruslán and Ludmíla*.

noxious in the north: 'Written in Bessarabia' (Pushkin's note). A lightly veiled allusion to the poet's troubles with the court: a few poems of liberal sentiment and some caustic epigrams had incurred the wrath of the emperor, and as a consequence, in May 1820, Pushkin was required to leave St Petersburg for an unspecified term of exile in the south of Russia. He would not return to the capital for more than six years.

6 *Letny Park*: the Summer Garden, a public park situated along the embankment of the Neva and adorned with shade trees and the statues of Greek deities.

9 (9): here and elsewhere, numbers in parentheses indicate stanzas omitted by Pushkin in the published text.

10 *Faublas*: the hero of a novel by the French writer Louvet de Couvrai (1760–97). Abetted in the seduction of other men's wives by a rakish count, Faublas, it turns out, has seduced his accomplice's bride as well.

10 *Bolivár*: 'Hat à la Bolivar' (Pushkin's note). A wide-brimmed black top hat, named after the South American liberator, which was fashionable in both Paris and St Petersburg in the 1820s.

Bréguet: an elegant pocket-watch made by the celebrated French watchmaker, Abraham Louis Bréguet (1747–1823).

11 *Talon's*: Talon was a well-known French restaurateur in St Petersburg.

Kavérin: Pyotr Kaverin (1794–1855) was a hussar, man about town, and friend of Pushkin.

comet wine: champagne from the year of the comet (1811), a year of especially good vintage.

Strasbourg pie: a rich pastry made with goose liver, for which the French city is famous.

11 *Cleopatra . . . Phèdre . . . Moïna*: the heroines of various plays, operas, or ballets performed in St Petersburg at the time. The *Cleopatra* that Pushkin had in mind is uncertain; the *Phèdre* was either Racine's tragedy or an opera based on it; Moïna is the heroine of Ozerov's tragedy, *Fingal*.

12 *Enchanted land! . . . perfected*: the stanza evokes the Russian theatre around the turn of the century, when for the most part imitations of Corneille, Racine, and Molière prevailed. D. Fonvizin (1745–92), the most noteworthy of the playwrights mentioned, was the author of two successful satires, *The Minor* and *The Brigadier*. Y. Knyazhnin (1742–91), V. Ozerov (1769–1816), and P. Katenin (1792–1852) wrote Frenchified tragedies; A. Shakhovskoy (1777–1846) wrote equally derivative comedies. E. Semyonova (1786–1849) was an accomplished Shakespearian actress who performed in Russian dramas as well. Charles-Louis Didelot (1767–1837), French ballet master and choreographer, was associated with the St Petersburg ballet.

13 *Istómina*: A. I. Istomina (1799–1848). A celebrated ballerina who was a pupil of Didelot. She danced in ballets that were based on works by Pushkin, and early in her career the poet had courted her.

15 *Grimm*: Frédéric Melchior Grimm (1723–1807). French encyclopedist. In a note to these lines Pushkin quotes from Rousseau's *Confessions* on the encounter between the two men and then comments: 'Grimm was ahead of his age: nowadays, all over enlightened Europe, people clean their nails with a special brush.'

15 *Chadáyev*: the manuscript provides evidence for the name given here. Pyotr Chadayev (1793–1856) was a friend of the poet and a brilliant personality. Both fop and philosopher, he was the author of the famous *Lettres philosophiques*, of which only one was published in Russia during his lifetime. His work helped to precipitate, through its critique of Russian history, the great debate between the Westernizer and Slavophile camps of Russian thought. For the expression of his ideas, Chadayev was officially declared insane, although he continued to take an active part in Moscow social life.

22 *Say or Bentham*: the French economist Jean Baptiste Say (1767–1832) and the English jurist and philosopher Jeremy Bentham (1748–1832) were much discussed at the time in progressive circles.

Capricious . . . spleen: in a note to the stanza Pushkin comments archly: 'The whole of this ironical stanza is nothing but a subtle compliment to our fair compatriots. Thus Boileau, under the guise of reproach, eulogizes Louis XIV. Our ladies combine enlightenment with amiability, and strict purity of morals with that Oriental charm which so captivated Mme. de Staël.' See *Dix ans d'exil*.

25 *As . . . himself*: a mocking allusion to M. Muravyov (1757–1807) and his lyric poem 'To the Goddess of the Neva'.

26 *Brenta*: the river that flows into the Adriatic near Venice.

Albion's great and haughty lyre: the reference is to Byron's poetry.

shore: 'Written in Odessa' (Pushkin's note).

my Africa's warm sky: 'The author, on his mother's side, is of African descent. His great-grandfather, Abram Petrovich Annibal, in his eighth year was abducted from the coast of Africa and taken to Constantinople. The Russian envoy, after rescuing him, sent him as a gift to Peter the Great, who had him baptized in Vilno.' Thus Pushkin begins a rather lengthy note on the life of his African ancestor. The young man was subsequently sent abroad by Peter to study fortification and military mining. After a sojourn of some seven years in France, he was recalled to the service in Russia, where he had a rather chequered career as a military engineer. He was eventually made a general by the empress Elizabeth and died in retirement, in 1781, at nearly 90 years of age, on one of the estates granted him by the crown. The third of his eleven children (by a second wife) was the poet's maternal grandfather.

30 *sang the Salghir captives' praises*: the references are to the heroines in two of Pushkin's narrative poems: the Circassian girl in *The Caucausian Captive* and the harem girls in *The Fountain of Bakhchisarai*. The Salghir is a river near Bakhchisarai, a Tartar town and former residence of the Crimean khans.

Chapter 2

33 *O rus! . . . O Rus'!*: the epigraph employs a pun. The first 'O rus!' (Horace, *Satires* 2. 6) means 'O countryside!'; the second invokes the old and lyrical name for 'Russia'.

36 *corvée . . . rate*: the *corvée* was the unpaid labour that a serf was required to provide to his master. Onegin, an enlightened squire, has decided to improve the lot of his peasants by asking instead for a small payment.

37 *Mason*: since Masonic organizations at the time were centres of liberal thought, a provincial landowner would have considered the member of such a group a revolutionary.

38 *That there exists . . . redeeming grace*: the last five lines of this stanza, which give Lensky's views on the mission of poets, were omitted by Pushkin from the final text, presumably because he anticipated the censor's objection.

43 *passions*: the dangerous emotions or 'passions' refer here not only to sensual love but also to feelings of enmity, jealousy, and avarice.

46 *that name*: 'The most euphonious Greek names, such as, for example, Agathon, Philetus, Theodora, Thecla, and so forth, are used with us only among the common people' (Pushkin's note).

50 *shaved the shirkers*: serfs who were chosen by their owners for army service had their forelocks shaved for easy recognition.

52 *At Trinity . . . deserved*: lines 5–11 were omitted in all editions during Pushkin's lifetime. On Trinity Day, the Sunday after Whitsunday, people often brought a birch-tree branch or a bouquet of field flowers to church. The tradition in some regions, according to Vladimir Nabokov, called for the worshipper to shed as many tears for his sins as there were dewdrops on the branch he carried.

53 *Ochákov decoration*: a medal that commemorated the taking of the Black Sea fortress of Ochakov in 1788, during the Turkish campaign.

Chapter 3

55 *Elle . . . amoureuse*: 'She was a girl, she was in love.'

58 *A drink . . . coach*: in most editions the final six lines of this stanza are omitted.

59 *Svetlana*: the reference is to the heroine of a ballad by Vasily Zhukovsky (1783–1852), a talented poet and Pushkin's friend.

61 *Julie Wolmár*: the heroine in a novel by Rousseau, *Julie, ou La Nouvelle Héloïse*.

Malék-Adhél: the hero of *Mathilde*, a novel by Mme Cottin (1773–1807).

de Linár: a character in the novel *Valérie* by Baroness von Krüdener (1764–1807).

Clarissa: the heroine of Richardson's *Clarissa*.

Julia: again, the character from Rousseau's *Julie*.

Delphine: the heroine in a novel of the same name by Mme de Staël.

62 *The Vampire . . . Sbogar*: the Vampire is presumably from the 1819 tale of that name by John Polidori, Byron's physician. Melmoth is the hero of *Melmoth the Wanderer*, published in 1820 by Charles Robert Maturin. *The Corsair* is the poem by Byron. The legend of the wandering Jew was widely used by writers in the Romantic era. *Jean Sbogar* is the title of a short French novel published in 1818 by Charles Nodier. These are all works of Pushkin's own time, whereas Tatyana's reading comes from an earlier generation; only in Chapter Seven will she discover Byron in Onegin's abandoned library.

70 *The Good Samaritan*: a Moscow literary journal, actually called the *Well-Intentioned* (Blagonamerennyj).

71 *Bogdanóvich*: I. F. Bogdanóvich (1743–1803): a minor poet and translator from the French. His narrative poem *Dushen'ka* (Little Psyche) exerted some influence on the young Pushkin.

Parny: Evariste-Désiré de Parny (1753–1814). French poet famed for the elegance of his love poetry. His *Poésies érotiques* influenced Russian poetry of the late eighteenth and early nineteenth centuries.

Bard of The Feasts: the reference is to Evgeny Baratynsky (1800–44), a friend of Pushkin's and a fellow poet. His elegy *The Feasts* was written in 1820, while its author was serving in the ranks in Finland, after having been expelled from military school for theft. Set in a gloomy Finland, his poem evokes a happier time with poet-friends in the Petersburg of 1819.

72 *Freischütz*: the reference is to the overture from *Der Freischütz*, an opera by Carl Maria von Weber (1786–1826).

Chapter 4

83 *La morale . . . choses*: 'Morality is in the nature of things.'

96 *Tolstoy*: Count F. P. Tolstoy (1783–1873): a well known and fashionable artist.

97 *No madrigals . . . flows:* the octave of this stanza exhibits a rare divergence from the usual pattern: like the Italian sonnet, it employs but two rhymes in the eight lines and thus provides a rather pleasing accompaniment to a discussion of poetic form.

Yazýkov: N. M. Yazýkov (1803–46): a minor poet and acquaintance of Pushkin.

trumpet, mask, and dagger: emblems of the classical drama.

odes: for Pushkin the term 'ode' suggested bombastic and heavy pieces in the eighteenth-century Russian manner; his own preference was clearly for the romantic 'elegy', by which term he would have described any short contemplative lyric. The mock debate conducted in this and the following stanza reflects an actual dispute between the 'archaists' and 'modernists' of Pushkin's day.

98 *The Other*: the allusion is to *Chuzhoi tolk* (Another's View), a satire on the writers of odes by I. Dmitriev (1760–1837).

99 *36*: this stanza appeared only in the separate edition of Chapters 4 and 5.

100 *Gulnare's proud singer*: Byron, in *The Corsair*.

102 *Pradt*: Dominique de Pradt (1759–1837): a prolific French political writer.

103 *Hippocrene*: a fountain or spring on Mount Helicon in Boeotia, sacred in Greek mythology to the Muses.

104 *Aï*: or Ay; a champagne whose name derives from a town in the Marne district of northern France.

entre chien et loup: dusk, or the time of day 'between the dog and the wolf' (i.e., when the shepherd has difficulty in distinguishing between the two).

106 *Lafontaine's*: August Lafontaine (1758–1851). A German writer, author of numerous novels on family life.

Chapter 5

110 *Another bard . . . shade*: 'See *First Snow*, a poem by Prince Vyazemsky' (Pushkin's note). Prince Pyotr Vyazemsky (1792–1878), poet, critic, and wit, was a close friend of Pushkin. He appears in the novel by name in Chapter 7, stanza 49.

bard of Finland's maid divine!: 'See the descriptions of the Finnish winter in Baratynsky's *Eda*' (Pushkin's note).

112 '*The Kitty's Song*': at Yuletide, and especially on Twelfth Night, several traditions for fortune-telling were observed by women and girls (particularly among the common people). The shapes taken by molten wax or lead when submerged in water were read as prophetic, and so-called 'dish divining songs' were sung. In the latter case, girls would place their rings in a covered bowl of water before singing carols. At the end of each song, a ring was drawn at random, and its owner would deduce some portent or meaning from the kind of song just sung. Tatyana's song on this occasion is a portent of death, whereas 'The Kitty's Song', which girls prefer, is a prophecy of marriage.

113 *trains a mirror . . . nearer*: training a mirror on the moon was another method of divination, the reflected face of the man-in-the-moon supposedly revealing to the enquiring maiden her future husband.

'*Agafon*': by asking the name of the first stranger she encountered, a girl hoped to learn the name of her future fiancé. The name that Tatyana hears, Agafon (from the Greek 'Agathon'), sounds particularly rustic and old-fashioned, and therefore comic, to a Russian ear.

conjure all night through: another device for discovering one's husband-to-be: conjuring up his spirit at an all-night vigil.

Svetlana: the heroine of Zhukovsky's ballad. In the poem, when Svetlana conjures her absent lover, he carries her off to his grave. Fortunately, Svetlana's terrors remain only a dream.

Lel: supposedly a pagan Slavic deity of love; more likely (according to Nabokov) merely derived from the chanted refrain of old songs (e.g., the *ay lyuli lyuli* of many Russian folk-songs).

119 *Martýn Zadéck*: the name, evidently a fabrication, appears as the author of several collections of prophecies and dream interpretations, published both in Russia and in Germany.

120 *Malvina*: a novel by Mme Cottin (1773–1807).

Two Petriads: heroic poems on Peter the Great, several of which were in circulation at the time.

Marmontel: Jean François Marmontel (1723–99), French encyclopedist and short-story writer.

121 *But lo!... the sun*: 'A parody of some well-known lines by Lomonosov' (Puskin's note). The crimson hand of Aurora (deriving of course from the Homeric 'rosy-fingered dawn') appears in several odes by M. V. Lomonosov (1711–65), scientist and poet and the founder of Moscow University.

Buyánov: Mr Rowdy, the hero of a popular and racy poem by Pushkin's uncle, Vasily Pushkin; thus, playfully, Pushkin's cousin. The names given to the other guests are also traditionally comic ones: Pustyakov (Trifle), Gvozdin (Bash), Skotinin (Brute), Petushkov (Rooster).

122 *Réveillez-vous, belle endormie*: Awaken, sleeping beauty.

Tatyaná: Triquet pronounces Tatyana's name in the French manner, with the stress on the last syllable.

124 *a lavish pie*: the Russian *pirog*, a meat- or cabbage-pie.

Zizí: Evpraksia Wulf (1809–83), who as a young girl lived near Pushkin's family estate at Mikhailovskoe and with whom he flirted when confined there in 1824. Pushkin became her lover briefly in 1829. Writing to a friend in 1836 from Mikhailovskoe on his last visit there, he recalls her as 'a formerly half-ethereal maiden, now a well-fed wife, big with child for the fifth time'.

127 *Albani's glory*: Francesco Albani (1578–1660): Italian painter much admired in the eighteenth and early nineteenth centuries.

Chapter 6

131 *La sotto ... dole*: 'There, where the days are cloudy and short | Is born a race that has no fear of death.'

135 *Regulus*: the Roman general Marcus Atilius Regulus, who, upon his capture by the Carthaginians, was sent to Rome to deliver harsh terms for peace; whereupon he returned to his captors as he had promised and was executed.

Véry's: Café Véry, a Parisian restaurant.

141 *Delvig*: Baron Anton Delvig (1798–1831), minor poet and one of Pushkin's closest friends, his classmate at the Lyceum in Tsarskoe Selo.

144 *Lepage's deadly pieces*: Jean Lepage (1779–1822), famous Parisian gunsmith.

Chapter 7

158 *Lyóvshin's crew*: students of works by Vasily Lyovshin (1746–1826), author of numerous tracts on gardening and agriculture.

165 *iron bust*: A statuette of Napoleon.

166 *The bard of Juan and the Giaour*: Byron.

173 *Autómedons*: Autómedon was the charioteer of Achilles in the *Iliad*.

174 *Petróvsky Castle*: the chateau not far from Moscow where Napoleon took refuge from the fires in the city.

179 *'Archival dandies'*: young men from well-connected families who held cushy jobs at the Moscow Archives of the Ministry of Foreign Affairs.

Vyázemsky: Prince Pyotr Vyazemsky (1792–1878), friend of Pushkin.

180 *Grand Assembly*: the Russian Assembly of Nobility, a Moscow club for noblemen.

Chapter 8

185 *Lycée*: the lyceum established by Alexander I at Tsarskoe Selo for young aristocrats. Pushkin attended the boarding-school there between 1811 and 1817, and to the end of his life remained deeply attached to his friends of those years. It was at the lyceum that he composed his first poems.

Derzhávin: Gavrila Derzhávin (1743–1816): the most outstanding Russian poet of the eighteenth century. In the year before he died, Derzhávin attended a school examination at which the 16-year-old Pushkin recited one of his poems, which the old man praised.

186 *Lenore*: the heroine of the romantic ballad by Gottfried Bürger (1747–94).

Tauris: an ancient name for the Crimea. Pushkin's visit to the Crimea and his earlier stay in the Caucasus (to which he refers in a line above) were commemorated in two of his so-called 'southern' poems, *The Prisoner of the Caucasus* and *The Fountain of Bakhchisarai*.

Nereids': sea-nymphs, daughters of the sea-god Nereus.

187 *sing the savage steppe*: an allusion to the narrative poem *The Gypsies*, yet another of Pushkin's southern works.

my garden: Pushkin's country place at Mikhailovskoe, to which he was confined by the government from August 1824 to September 1826 and where he resumed work on *Eugene Onegin*.

190 *Demon of my pen!*: a reference to his poem 'The Demon', in which he speaks of having been haunted in his youth by an 'evil genius', a spirit of negation and doubt who mocked the ideals of love and freedom.

191 *Chatsky*: the hero of Griboedov's comedy *Woe from Wit* (1824). Chatsky, after some three years abroad, turns up on the day of a party at the Moscow house of the girl he loves.

Shishkov: Admiral Alexander Shishkov (1754–1841), the leader of the Archaic group of writers, was a statesman and publicist who attacked both Gallicisms and liberal thought in Russian letters.

192 *epigram of style*: an allusion to some possible epigrammatic play on the word 'vulgar' and the last name of Faddei Bulgarin (1789–1859), a literary critic and notorious police informer who was hostile to Pushkin.

Nina Voronskáya: an invented name for a stylized society belle. Russian commentators on the poem have suggested various real-life prototypes.

197 *badge on those two maids-in-waiting*: a court decoration with the royal initials, given to ladies-in-waiting of the empress.

Prolázov: the name (derived from *prolaza*, roughly 'sycophant' or 'social climber') appears only in posthumous editions. According to Nabokov it was often attached to ridiculous characters in eighteenth-century Russian comedies and in popular pictures.

Saint-Priest: Count Emmanuel Sen-Pri (1806–28), the son of a French *émigré* and a noted caricaturist.

204 *Gibbon and Rousseau . . . Fontenelle he scoured*: the listing device is a favourite of Pushkin's. Besides Rousseau, this catalogue of Onegin's reading includes: Edward Gibbon (1737–94), the English historian; Sébastien Chamfort (1740–94), French writer famous for his maxims and epigrams; Alessandro Manzoni (1785–1873), Italian novelist and poet of the Romantic school; Johann Gottfried von Herder (1744–1803), the German philosopher; Mme de Staël (1766–1817), the French writer (whose novel *Delphine* was listed earlier as one of Tatyana's favourites); Marie F. X. Bichat (1771–1802), French physician and anatomist,

the author of *Recherches physiologiques sur la vie et la mort*; Simon Tissot (1728–1797), a famous Swiss doctor, author of the treatise *De la santé des gens de lettres*; Pierre Bayle (1647–1706), French philosopher, author of the famous *Dictionnaire historique et critique*; Bernard Fontenelle (1657–1757), French rationalist philosopher and man of letters, author of *Dialogues des morts*.

205 *Benedetta*: 'Benedetta sia la madre' (Blessed be the mother), a popular Venetian barcarolle.

Idol mio: 'Idol mio, piu pace non ho' (My idol, I have peace no longer), the refrain from a duet by Vincenzo Gabussi (1800–46).

212 *'Some are no more, and distant . . . others'*: though probably written in 1824, these lines were taken almost immediately as an allusion to Pushkin's friends among the executed or exiled Decembrists (participants in the ill-fated revolt of December 1825).

Sadi: the thirteenth-century Persian poet.

Appendix

215 *Camenae*: water-nymphs identified with the Greek Muses.

Katenin: Pavel Katenin (1792–1853). A minor poet and critic, whose *Recollections of Pushkin* were published in the twentieth century.

217 *Makáriev Market*: a famous market fair held in midsummer in the town of Makariev, to which it moved in 1817 from Nizhni Novgorod.

218 *Terek*: a river in the Caucasus.

Kúra's and Arágva's banks: refers to two mountain rivers in the Caucasus.

Beshtú: (or Besh Tau): a five-peaked mountain eminence in the northern Caucasus.

Mashúk: one of the peaks in the northern Caucasus.

219 *Orestes with his friend here vied*: a reference to the tale of Orestes and his friend Pylades, who argued over which of them would be sacrificed to the goddess Artemis, each wishing to die in the other's place. In the end both escaped, along with the temple priestess, who turned out to be Iphigenia, Orestes' sister.

Mithridates: King of Pontus, who in 63 BC, after being defeated by Rome, ordered one of his soldiers to kill him. Pushkin visited his alleged tomb while travelling in the Crimea in 1820.

219 *Adam Mickiéwicz*: Polish national poet (1798–1855), who spent almost five years in Russia, where he made the acquaintance of Pushkin. His visit to the Crimea in 1825 provided material for his *Crimean Sonnets*.

220 *Cypris*: Venus or Aphrodite.

221 *Bakhchisarái*: the reference is to a fountain in the garden of the Crimean Khan's palace. See Pushkin's narrative poem 'The Fountain of Bakhchisarai'.

Zaréma: the jealous wife of the Khan, one of the heroines in Pushkin's poem 'The Fountain of Bakhchisarai'.

222 *Moralí*: (or Moor Ali): apparently a Moorish seaman or pirate, whom Pushkin met during his stay in Odessa.

Tumánsky: a minor poet who served along with Pushkin as a clerk to the governor of Odessa.

225 *Automne*: César Automne, a well-known restaurateur in Odessa.

226 *Ausonia*: Italy.

*The
Oxford
World's
Classics
Website*

www.worldsclassics.co.uk

- Browse the full range of Oxford World's Classics online

- Sign up for our monthly e-alert to receive information on new titles

- Read extracts from the Introductions

- Listen to our editors and translators talk about the world's greatest literature with our Oxford World's Classics audio guides

- Join the conversation, follow us on Twitter at OWC_Oxford

- Teachers and lecturers can order inspection copies quickly and simply via our website

www.worldsclassics.co.uk

ANTON CHEKHOV	Early Stories
	Five Plays
	The Princess and Other Stories
	The Russian Master and Other Stories
	The Steppe and Other Stories
	Twelve Plays
	Ward Number Six and Other Stories
FYODOR DOSTOEVSKY	Crime and Punishment
	Devils
	A Gentle Creature and Other Stories
	The Idiot
	The Karamazov Brothers
	Memoirs from the House of the Dead
	Notes from the Underground and The Gambler
NIKOLAI GOGOL	Dead Souls
	Plays and Petersburg Tales
ALEXANDER PUSHKIN	Eugene Onegin
	The Queen of Spades and Other Stories
LEO TOLSTOY	Anna Karenina
	The Kreutzer Sonata and Other Stories
	The Raid and Other Stories
	Resurrection
	War and Peace
IVAN TURGENEV	Fathers and Sons
	First Love and Other Stories
	A Month in the Country

Eirik the Red and Other Icelandic Sagas

The German-Jewish Dialogue

The Kalevala

The Poetic Edda

LUDOVICO ARIOSTO   Orlando Furioso

GIOVANNI BOCCACCIO   The Decameron

GEORG BÜCHNER   Danton's Death, Leonce and Lena, and
                          Woyzeck

LUIS VAZ DE CAMÕES   The Lusiads

MIGUEL DE CERVANTES   Don Quixote
                          Exemplary Stories

CARLO COLLODI   The Adventures of Pinocchio

DANTE ALIGHIERI   The Divine Comedy
                          Vita Nuova

LOPE DE VEGA   Three Major Plays

J. W. VON GOETHE   Elective Affinities
                          Erotic Poems
                          Faust: Part One and Part Two
                          The Flight to Italy

E. T. A. HOFFMANN   The Golden Pot and Other Tales

HENRIK IBSEN   An Enemy of the People, The Wild Duck,
                          Rosmersholm
                          Four Major Plays
                          Peer Gynt

LEONARDO DA VINCI   Selections from the Notebooks

FEDERICO GARCIA LORCA   Four Major Plays

MICHELANGELO   Life, Letters, and Poetry
BUONARROTI

JANE AUSTEN	**Emma**
	Mansfield Park
	Persuasion
	Pride and Prejudice
	Sense and Sensibility
MRS BEETON	**Book of Household Management**
LADY ELIZABETH BRADDON	**Lady Audley's Secret**
ANNE BRONTË	**The Tenant of Wildfell Hall**
CHARLOTTE BRONTË	**Jane Eyre**
	Shirley
	Villette
EMILY BRONTË	**Wuthering Heights**
SAMUEL TAYLOR COLERIDGE	**The Major Works**
WILKIE COLLINS	**The Moonstone**
	No Name
	The Woman in White
CHARLES DARWIN	**The Origin of Species**
CHARLES DICKENS	**The Adventures of Oliver Twist**
	Bleak House
	David Copperfield
	Great Expectations
	Nicholas Nickleby
	The Old Curiosity Shop
	Our Mutual Friend
	The Pickwick Papers
	A Tale of Two Cities
GEORGE DU MAURIER	**Trilby**
MARIA EDGEWORTH	**Castle Rackrent**